# Third Workshop on Language Technology for Equality, Diversity and Inclusion (LTEDI 2023)

AA001671

Varna, Bulgaria
7 September 2023

ISBN: 978-1-7138-9056-0

**Printed from e-media with permission by:**

Curran Associates, Inc.
57 Morehouse Lane
Red Hook, NY 12571

**Some format issues inherent in the e-media version may also appear in this print version.**

Copyright© (2023) by the Association for Computational Linguistics
All rights reserved.

Printed with permission by Curran Associates, Inc. (2025)

For permission requests, please contact the Association for Computational Linguistics at the address below.

Association for Computational Linguistics
209 N. Eighth Street
Stroudsburg, Pennsylvania 18360

Phone: 1-570-476-8006
Fax: 1-570-476-0860

acl@aclweb.org

**Additional copies of this publication are available from:**

Curran Associates, Inc.
57 Morehouse Lane
Red Hook, NY 12571 USA
Phone: 845-758-0400
Fax: 845-758-2633
Email: curran@proceedings.com
Web: www.proceedings.com

LTEDI 2023

# Third Workshop on Language Technology for Equality, Diversity and Inclusion

*associated with*

**The 14th International Conference on Recent Advances in Natural Language Processing RANLP'2023**

**PROCEEDINGS**

September 7, 2023

Third Workshop on Language Technology for Equality, Diversity and Inclusion
Associated with the International Conference
Recent Advances in Natural Language Processing'2023

**PROCEEDINGS**

September 7, 2023

Designed by INCOMA Ltd.
Shoumen, BULGARIA

# Message from the General Chair

Equality, Diversity and Inclusion (EDI) is an important agenda across every field throughout the world. Language as a major part of communication should be inclusive and treat everyone with equality. Today's large internet community uses language technology (LT) and has a direct impact on people across the globe. EDI is crucial to ensure everyone is valued and included, so it is necessary to build LT that serves this purpose. Recent results have shown that big data and deep learning are entrenching existing biases and that some algorithms are even naturally biased due to problems such as 'regression to the mode'. Our focus is on creating LT that will be more inclusive of gender, racial, sexual orientation, persons with disability. The workshop will focus on creating speech and language technology to address EDI not only in English, but also in less resourced languages.

## Organizing Committee

Bharathi Raja Chakravarthi, University of Galway, Ireland
B Bharathi, SSN College of Engineering, Tamil Nadu, India
Josephine Griffith, University of Galway, Ireland
Kalika Bali, Microsoft Research, India
Paul Buitelaar, University of Galway, Ireland

## Programme Committee

Adarsh Sahu, National Institute of Technology Karnataka, India
Andrew Nedilko, Workhuman
Angel Deborah, SSN College of Engineering, India
Ankitha Reddy, SSN College of Engineering, India
Asha Hegde, Mangalore University, India
Balasubramanian Palani, National Institute of Technology, Tiruchirappalli, India
Bertille Triboulet, University of Geneva
Christina Christodoulou, Institute of Informatics and Telecommunications, National Centre for Scientific Research, Demokritos
Debora Nozza, Bocconi University
Deepalakshmi Manikandan, Kongu Engineering College, India
Eduardo Garcia, Federal University of Goias
Ilia Markov, Vrije Universiteit Amsterdam, CLTL
Ishan Sanjeev Upadhyay, IIIT Hyderabad, India
Jaya Caporusso, Jozef Stefan International Postgraduate School
Jerin Mahibha C, Meenakshi Sundararajan Engineering College, India
Jose Antonio Garcia-Diaz, Universidad de Murcia
Judith Jeyafreeda Andrew, University of Manchester
Juliana Gomes, Federal University of Goias
Jyoti Kumari, Siksha 'O' Anusandhan Deemed to be University
Kavya G, Mangalore University, India
Kayalvizhi S, SSN College of Engineering, India
Kirti Kumari, Indian Institute of Information Technology, Ranchi, India
Kogilavani S V, Kongu Engineering College, India
KV Aditya Srivatsa, International Institute of Information Technology Hyderabad, India
Malliga S, Kongu Engineering College, India
Manikandan Ravikiran, Georgia Institute of Technology, Hitachi India Pvt Ltd
Maria de Jesus Garcia Santiago, Centro de Investigacion en Matematicas
Momchil Hardalov, AWS AI Labs
Nandhini Kumaresh, Central University of TamilNadu, India
Nerses Yuzbashyan, CLiPS, University of Antwerp, Antwerp, Belgium
Nicola Fanton, University of Stuttgart
Nikolay Banar, Computational Linguistics Group (CLiPS), Antwerp Centre for Digital humanities and literary Criticism (ACDC), University of Antwerp
Nitesh Jindal, University of Galway, Ireland
Pierrette Bouillon, UNIGE FTI
Prasanna Kumar Kumaresan, Insight SFI Research Centre for Data Analytics, Data Science Institute, University of Galway, Ireland
Premjith B, Amrita School of Artificial Intelligence, Coimbatore, Amrita Vishwa Vidyapeetham, India

Priyadharshini Thandavamurthi, SSN College of Engineering, India
Rafael Valencia-Garcia, Universidad de Murcia
Rahul Ponnusamy, Insight SFI Research Centre for Data Analytics, University of Galway, Ireland
Rajalakshmi Sivanaiah, Sri Sivasubramaniya Nadar College of Engineering, India
Rajeswari Natarajan, SASTRA Deemed to be University
Ranganayaki EM, College of Engineering, Guindy, Anna University, India
Riza Batista-Navarro, Department of Computer Science, The University of Manchester
Ruba Priyadharshini, ULTRA Arts and Science College, India
Sajeetha Thavareesan, Eastern University, Sri Lanka
Salud Maria Jimenez Zafra, Universidad de Jaen
Samyuktaa Sivakumar, SSN College of Engineering, India
Sanjana Kavatagi, VTU,Belagavi
Saranya S, SSN College of Engineering, India
Senthil Kumar B, Sri Sivasubramaniya Nadar College of Engineering, India
Shankar Biradar, Indian Institute of Information Technology (IIIT), Dharwad, India
Sharal Coelho, Mangalore University, India
Shweta Soundararajan, Technological University Dublin, Ireland
Shwetha Sureshnathan, SSN College of Engineering, India
Sidney Wong, University of Canterbury
Sripriya Natarajan, SSN College of Engineering, India
SUBALALITHA CN, SRM Institute of Science and Technology, India
Suhasini S, SSN College of Engineering, India
Sulaksha B K, Meenakshi Sundararajan Engineering College , Anna University at Tamil Nadu, India
SUNIL SAUMYA, Indian Institute of Information Technology (IIIT), Dharwad , India
Thenmozhi D, SSN College of Engineering, India
Thi Hong Hanh Tran, La Rochelle University
Vajratiya Vajrobol, Delhi University South Campus, India
VASANTHARAN K, Kongu Engineering College, India

# Table of Contents

# An Exploration of Zero-Shot Natural Language Inference-Based Hate Speech Detection

**Nerses Yuzbashyan**
University of Antwerp
Belgium
nerses.yuzbashyan@uantwerpen.be

**Nikolay Banar**
University of Antwerp
Belgium
nicolae.banari@uantwerpen.be

**Ilia Markov**
Vrije Universiteit Amsterdam
The Netherlands
i.markov@vu.nl

**Walter Daelemans**
University of Antwerp
Belgium
walter.daelemans@uantwerpen.be

## Abstract

Conventional techniques for detecting online hate speech rely on the availability of a sufficient number of annotated instances, which can be costly and time consuming. For this reason, zero-shot or few-shot detection can offer an attractive alternative. In this paper, we explore a zero-shot detection approach based on natural language inference (NLI) models. The performance of the models in this approach depends heavily on the choice of a hypothesis, which represents a statement that is evaluated with a given sentence to determine the logical relationship between them. Our goal is to determine which factors affect the quality of detection. We conducted a set of experiments with three NLI models and four hate speech datasets. We demonstrate that a zero-shot NLI-based approach is competitive with approaches that require supervised learning, yet they are highly sensitive to the choice of hypothesis. In addition, our experiments indicate that the results for a set of hypotheses on different model-data pairs are positively correlated, and that the correlation is higher for different datasets when using the same model than it is for different models when using the same dataset. These results suggest that if we find a hypothesis that works well for a specific model and domain or for a specific type of hate speech, we can use that hypothesis with the same model also within a different domain. While another model might require different suitable hypotheses in order to demonstrate high performance.

## 1 Introduction

The growing use of social media platforms that allow users to remain anonymous during online discussions has led to an increase in the amount of hateful content online. This has posed a challenge in detecting hate speech for government organizations, social media platforms, and the research community. Effective hate speech detection models that are robust and reliable can provide valuable insights to moderators in their efforts to combat the prevalence of hate speech in online discussions, as well as encourage productive online discourse (Halevy et al., 2022). In this paper, we use the term *hate speech* as an umbrella term for different types of insulting content, such as offensive language, abusive language, and other types of harmful content.

Since supervised learning methods are associated with difficulties such as the need for large computing power and extensive amounts of labeled data, zero-shot learning using pre-trained language models can be an attractive alternative. Zero-shot detection is a technique that allows a model to classify texts based on their content, even if the model has not been trained for that particular task (Larochelle et al., 2008). The main advantage of the zero-shot approach is its versatility. A model pre-trained on general data can be used to detect hate speech across multiple platforms (Facebook, Twitter, etc.) and domains (different targets and types of hate speech) without having to retrain it. This reduces training costs and allows for greater flexibility in responding to changes in social media platforms, user behavior, and types of hate speech. However, since the model is not specifically trained for the task of detecting hate speech, the approach might demonstrate inferior results to the supervised models. In this paper, we investigate whether an NLI-based zero-shot approach is competitive to supervised learning



*LT-EDI 2023 – Third Workshop on Language Technology for Equality, Diversity and Inclusion*, pages 1–9, Varna, Bulgaria, Sep 7, 2023.
https://doi.org/10.26615/978-954-452-084-7_001

methods and explore its robustness for different models, datasets and targets of hate speech.

## 2 Related Work

**Hate speech detection.** Early approaches for hate speech detection were based on manual feature engineering (Burnap and Williams, 2015; Davidson et al., 2017; Waseem and Hovy, 2016). The majority of the current methods for detecting hate speech rely on one of two techniques: training machine learning models from scratch or fine-tuning pre-trained language models (Jahan and Oussalah, 2021; Markov et al., 2021; Uzan and HaCohen-Kerner, 2021; Banerjee et al., 2021; Nghiem and Morstatter, 2021; Markov et al., 2022). All of these methods require extensive amounts of labeled data, which is not consistently accessible for some languages (Poletto et al., 2021), and is extremely expensive to be annotated manually. Under these circumstances, zero-shot or few-shot detection may be an appealing option.

**Zero-shot in hate speech detection.** Ke-Li et al. (2021) used GPT-3 (Brown et al., 2020) to identify sexist and racist text passages with zero-shot, one-shot, and few-shot learning. They achieved an accuracy as high as 85% for few-shot learning and assumed that large language models with further development could eventually be used to detect hate speech. Yin et al. (2019) demonstrated that text classification tasks can be approached as natural language inference (NLI), resulting in high accuracy for zero-shot classification. Based on Yin et al. (2019), Goldzycher and Schneider (2022) developed strategies that aim at improving NLI-based zero-shot hate speech detection systems and showed that such approaches are able to outperform fine-tuned language models (acc. 79.4 for NLI zero-shot for the best performing hypothesis against acc. 76.6 for a fine-tuned model). However, NLI approaches require a *hypothesis* - a statement that is evaluated for its logical relationship with the target sentence. The performance of such approaches largely depends on the chosen hypothesis, and evaluation of the quality of each hypothesis may not be feasible. Another uncertainty lies in the formulation of supporting hypotheses. An inadequately formulated supporting hypothesis can have a detrimental impact on the model performance (Goldzycher and Schneider, 2022).

Our goal is to evaluate an NLI-based approach for various models and datasets, in order i) to find out how the choice of a hypothesis affects the quality of the model, ii) to find out how the results change for a given hypothesis when the model or domain is changed, and iii) to determine which factors affect the accuracy of NLI-based zero-shot classification.

## 3 Method and Models

In order to determine whether an input text contains hate speech, we need a hypothesis that expresses that claim. In NLI tasks, the hypothesis is a statement (e.g., "This text is racist") that needs to be either supported or contradicted by a given premise. It is typically formulated as a sentence that makes a claim or draws a conclusion based on the information presented in the premise. All experiments were conducted in a standard setup for NLI-based zero-shot classification. We feed the hypothesis with an example to a pretrained NLI model and get the probability of entailment for the target sentence and hypothesis. We ignore the logits for *neutral* and perform a softmax over the logits of *contradiction* and *entailment*. We use the coarse-grained (binary) hate speech classes: hate speech versus non-hate speech. If the probability for entailment is equal or higher than 0.5 we consider that it is hate speech. We report the results in terms of F1-score (macro-averaged).

We conduct our experiments using the following well-established models, which are available via the Huggingface transformers library (Wolf et al., 2020):

- flan-t5-large (Chung et al., 2022): T5-large model (Raffel et al., 2020) was fine-tuned on a collection of NLI datasets. The full list of datasets and fine-tuning process is described in (Chung et al., 2022).

- bart-large-mnli (Williams et al., 2017): BART-large model (Lewis et al., 2019) was fine-tuned on the Multi-Genre Natural Language Inference dataset (MNLI (Williams et al., 2017)).

- XLM-RoBERTa-large-XNLI-ANLI: RoBERTa-large model (Liu et al., 2019) is fine-tuned on the ANLI (Nie et al., 2019) and XNLI (Conneau et al., 2018) datasets.

| Dataset | Test set size | Classes | % (#) |
|---|---|---|---|
| FRENK (Ljubešić et al., 2019) | 2,095 | hate speech | 35.5 (744) |
| | | not hate speech | 64.5 (1,351) |
| HateCheck (Röttger et al., 2020) | 3,728 | hate speech | 68.8 (2,563) |
| | | not hate speech | 31.2 (1,165) |
| CAD (Vidgen et al., 2021) | 5,307 | hate speech | 16.9 (899) |
| | | not hate speech | 83.1 (4,408) |
| OLID (Zampieri et al., 2019) | 860 | hate speech | 27.9 (240) |
| | | not hate speech | 72.1 (620) |

Table 1: Statistics of the datasets used.

## 4 Datasets

We evaluated the models described in Section 3 on four datasets constructed from different online platforms, covering different topics, types and targets of hate speech. We used the binary hate speech classes: hate speech versus non-hate speech. The statistics of the datasets used are shown in Table 1.

**FRENK** (Ljubešić et al., 2019). The FRENK dataset includes comments from Facebook on LGBT and migrants topics in English. The dataset was manually annotated for fine-grained types of socially unacceptable discourse (e.g., violence, offensiveness, threat). Messages were assigned to a particular class if at least four out of eight annotators agreed on the class. The test set consists of 2,095 examples.

**HateCheck** (Röttger et al., 2020) is an English, synthetic, evaluation-only dataset annotated for binary hate speech classification. For generating the test set, templates were prepared that contained one blank space to be filled with a discriminated group: women, gay people, transgender people, black people, Muslims, immigrants, and disabled people. The templates for non-hateful content share linguistic features with hateful expressions and could be mistaken for hate speech by a classifier. In total, the dataset consists of 3,728 examples.

**CAD** (Vidgen et al., 2021). The Contextual Abuse Dataset (CAD) consists of 25,000 annotated Reddit entries. All entries were first independently annotated by two annotators. Annotators worked through entire Reddit conversations, making annotations for each entry with full knowledge of the previous content in the thread. The test set consists of 5,307 examples.

**OLID** (Zampieri et al., 2019). The Offensive Language Identification Dataset (OLID) consists of 14,100 tweets in English, annotated through crowdsourcing. During annotation, each example was initially labeled by two annotators. In the case of disagreement, a third annotation was requested, and then a majority vote was taken. The test set consists of 860 entries.

## 5 Experiments and Results

In this section, we present the key findings and analysis derived from our research. We first report performance of the models on a general set of hypotheses. Then we reduce the number of hypotheses and use only those that describe a certain type or target of hate speech.

**Evaluation of zero-shot detection.** In the first series of experiments, we tested 111 manually designed hypotheses, describing hate speech, in order to determine how classification results vary depending on the chosen hypothesis, as well as which factors affect the results. Table 2 shows the comparison of a state-of-the-art supervised learning approach with the zero-shot approach. We report the results in terms of macro-average F1-score. We compare our zero-shot results with the supervised learning results reported in Markov and Daelemans (2021) for BERT, RoBERTa, SVM and a hard majority-voting ensemble of those three models applied to the FRENK and OLID datasets. In Markov and Daelemans (2021), models were tested in in-domain and cross-domain settings (trained on FRENK, tested on OLID and vice versa). Table 2 shows that the zero-shot NLI-based approach remains inferior to the supervised mod-

| Method | Model | FRENK | | OLID | |
|---|---|---|---|---|---|
| | | In-domain | Cross-domain | In-domain | Cross-domain |
| SL | BERT | 78.30 | 69.40 | 82.20 | 72.10 |
| | RoBERTa | 78.50 | 69.20 | 80.00 | 72.40 |
| | SVM | 77.00 | 67.70 | 78.30 | 69.00 |
| | Ensemble | 79.70 | 69.70 | 83.20 | 73.60 |
| ZS | flan-t5-large | 73.43 | | 78.45 | |
| | bart-large-mnli | 72.39 | | 73.30 | |
| | xlm-roberta-large-xnli-anli | 70.37 | | 72.76 | |

Table 2: Comparison of supervised learning approach and zero-shot approach. We report macro-averaged F1-score. SL - supervised learning, ZS - zero-shot. For ZS, we report the result of the best hypothesis for each dataset-model pair. For SL, we report results from Markov and Daelemans (2021) for in-domain setting (models were trained and tested on the same dataset) and cross-domain setting (trained on FRENK, tested on OLID and vice versa).

els in the in-domain setting but surpasses it in the cross-domain setup. This indicates that a zero-shot method is more versatile and, in cases where there is not enough data for training for the current domain (e.g., in a case of "cold start"), a zero-shot approach could be preferred. However, as we can see from Table 3, even limited paraphrasing of the hypothesis can cause considerable variation in F1-score.

| Hypothesis | F1 | $\triangle$F1 |
|---|---|---|
| This text contains hateful content | 71.80 | |
| It contains hateful content | 65.76 | -6.04 |
| This text contains xenophobic content | 66.75 | |
| This text is xenophobic | 55.78 | -10.97 |
| It contains xenophobic content | 52.98 | -13.77 |
| It is racist | 69.14 | |
| This text is racist | 67.91 | -1.23 |
| This text contains racist content | 66.49 | -2.65 |
| It contains racist content | 63.12 | -6.02 |

Table 3: Examples of variations in F1-score with minor paraphrasing of hypotheses for the FRENK dataset and flan-T5 model pair.

To investigate this variability more systematically, for each model-dataset pair, we built vectors whose elements are the F1-scores for the used hypotheses (in total 12 vectors of length 111, the hypotheses were sorted alphabetically) and calculated the correlation matrix for these 12 vectors (see Appendix A). One can see that the results for all model-dataset pairs are positively correlated, except for XLM-Roberta with the CAD dataset. The matrix Table 5 shows that, on average, the correlation for a particular model and different datasets is higher than the correlation for a dataset and different models.

**Experiment with a small set of target hypotheses.** In the second set of experiments, we used only the hypotheses that described a certain type of hate speech or certain target of hate speech (e.g., "This text is racist", "This text is homophobic", "This text is sexist", etc.), hence, we excluded "general" hypotheses (e.g. "This text is hateful", "This text contains hate speech", etc.). This experiment aimed to determine whether the performance of a particular hypothesis depends on which hate speech types are represented in a test dataset. In this case we expected that the dataset-related hypotheses will perform better, while another hypotheses will show a lower F1-score, and as a consequence there will be no correlation of results for different datasets.

However, we again observe that the results for different model-dataset pairs are positively correlated. Moreover, we see that the correlation of the results for different models when using the same dataset is lower on average than the correlation of the results for different datasets when using the same model (see Appendix B). From this, we can conclude that when choosing a hypothesis, it is more important to focus on what the model understands as hate speech rather than the type of hate speech covered in a particular dataset.

**Experiment for test subsets covering a particular hate speech target.** In order to verify our conclusion from the previous set of experiments, we split the FRENK test set into two subsets, each of which covers only one target of hate speech (LGBT or migrants). We observed that the hypotheses related to the topic of the test subset are

| | FRENK LGBT | | FRENK Migrants | |
|---|---|---|---|---|
| flan-t5 | Top5 Hypothesis | F1 | Top5 Hypothesis | F1 |
| | This text is racist | 67.47 | This text is misandric | 75.11 |
| | This text is misogynistic | 66.30 | This text is racist | 66.38 |
| | This text is misandric | 64.55 | This text is hostile to migrants | 61.59 |
| | This text is hostile to lgbtq+ community | 62.21 | This text is hostile to immigrants | 61.33 |
| | This text is hostile to lgbt community | 61.12 | This text is xenophobic | 55.63 |
| bart | Top5 Hypothesis | F1 | Top5 Hypothesis | F1 |
| | This text is hostile to lgbt community | 68.54 | This text is hostile to migrants | 64.72 |
| | This text is hostile to woman | 68.12 | This text is hostile to immigrants | 62.32 |
| | This text is hostile to man | 67.77 | This text is xenophobic | 56.08 |
| | This text is hostile to lgbtq+ community | 67.29 | This text is hostile to woman | 55.57 |
| | This text is misogynistic | 66.69 | This text is misandric | 54.49 |
| roberta | Top5 Hypothesis | F1 | Top5 Hypothesis | F1 |
| | This text is xenophobic | 67.71 | This text is hostile to lgbtq+ community | 68.09 |
| | This text is sexist | 67.69 | This text is hostile to immigrants | 66.85 |
| | This text is woman-hatred | 66.67 | This text is misogynistic | 66.50 |
| | This text is racist | 64.96 | This text is xenophobic | 66.03 |
| | This text is man-hatred | 64.39 | This text is man-hatred | 65.60 |

Table 4: Top 5 hypotheses in the experiment for test subsets per target of hate speech.

on average higher, though not always in the first position (see Table 4). The results confirm that on average the scores for the same model have a positive correlation (except for xlm-roberta). A positive correlation shows that even with hypotheses not related to the type of hate speech in the dataset, the model can still perform well. Additionally, it shows that it is important what the model understands by hate speech, although the topical focus of the dataset also affects the results.

## 6 Conclusion and Future Work

The first set of experiments showed that despite the fact that an NLI-based approach can compete with supervised methods, this approach is sensitive to the choice of hypothesis and even limited paraphrasing can change F1-scores substantially. Our experiments indicate that the results using particular (sets of) hypotheses for different model-data pairs are positively correlated, and that correlation for a particular model and different datasets is higher than the correlation for a dataset and different models. This suggests that if we find a hypothesis that works well for a specific model and dataset or a specific type of hate speech, we can use the same hypothesis for the same model but a different dataset. However, if the model is changed, it is better to search for an alternative hypothesis.

In future work, we plan to experiment with automatic hypothesis engineering. We want to answer the following questions: can we automatically find a better hypothesis than the initial one and will the hypothesis optimized for one data-model pair work well for other models, other domains and other data-model pairs.

## References

Somnath Banerjee, Maulindu Sarkar, Nancy Agrawal, Punyajoy Saha, and Mithun Das. 2021. Exploring transformer based models to identify hate speech and offensive content in english and indo-aryan languages. *arXiv preprint arXiv:2111.13974*.

Tom Brown, Benjamin Mann, Nick Ryder, Melanie Subbiah, Jared D Kaplan, Prafulla Dhariwal, Arvind Neelakantan, Pranav Shyam, Girish Sastry, Amanda Askell, et al. 2020. Language models are few-shot learners. *Advances in neural information processing systems*, 33:1877–1901.

Pete Burnap and Matthew L Williams. 2015. Cyber hate speech on twitter: An application of machine classification and statistical modeling for policy and decision making. *Policy & internet*, 7(2):223–242.

Hyung Won Chung, Le Hou, Shayne Longpre, Barret Zoph, Yi Tay, William Fedus, Eric Li, Xuezhi Wang, Mostafa Dehghani, Siddhartha Brahma, et al. 2022. Scaling instruction-finetuned language models. *arXiv preprint arXiv:2210.11416*.

Alexis Conneau, Guillaume Lample, Ruty Rinott, Adina Williams, Samuel R Bowman, Holger Schwenk, and Veselin Stoyanov. 2018. Xnli: Evaluating cross-lingual sentence representations. *arXiv preprint arXiv:1809.05053*.

Thomas Davidson, Dana Warmsley, Michael Macy, and Ingmar Weber. 2017. Automated hate speech detection and the problem of offensive language. In *Proceedings of the international AAAI conference on web and social media*, volume 11, pages 512–515.

Janis Goldzycher and Gerold Schneider. 2022. Hypothesis engineering for zero-shot hate speech detection. In *Proceedings of the Third Workshop on Threat, Aggression and Cyberbullying (TRAC 2022)*, pages 75–90, Gyeongju, Republic of Korea. Association for Computational Linguistics.

Alon Halevy, Cristian Canton-Ferrer, Hao Ma, Umut Ozertem, Patrick Pantel, Marzieh Saeidi, Fabrizio Silvestri, and Ves Stoyanov. 2022. Preserving integrity in online social networks. *Communications of the ACM*, 65(2):92–98.

Md Saroar Jahan and Mourad Oussalah. 2021. A systematic review of hate speech automatic detection using natural language processing. *arXiv preprint arXiv:2106.00742*.

Chiu Ke-Li, Collins Annie, and Alexander Rohan. 2021. Detecting hate speech with gpt-3. *arXiv preprint arXiv:2103.12407*.

Hugo Larochelle, Dumitru Erhan, and Yoshua Bengio. 2008. Zero-data learning of new tasks. In *AAAI*, volume 1, page 3.

Mike Lewis, Yinhan Liu, Naman Goyal, Marjan Ghazvininejad, Abdelrahman Mohamed, Omer Levy, Ves Stoyanov, and Luke Zettlemoyer. 2019. Bart: Denoising sequence-to-sequence pre-training for natural language generation, translation, and comprehension. *arXiv preprint arXiv:1910.13461*.

Yinhan Liu, Myle Ott, Naman Goyal, Jingfei Du, Mandar Joshi, Danqi Chen, Omer Levy, Mike Lewis, Luke Zettlemoyer, and Veselin Stoyanov. 2019. Roberta: A robustly optimized bert pretraining approach. *arXiv preprint arXiv:1907.11692*.

Nikola Ljubešić, Darja Fišer, and Tomaž Erjavec. 2019. The frenk datasets of socially unacceptable discourse in slovene and english. In *Text, Speech, and Dialogue: 22nd International Conference, TSD 2019, Ljubljana, Slovenia, September 11–13, 2019, Proceedings 22*, pages 103–114. Springer.

Ilia Markov and Walter Daelemans. 2021. Improving cross-domain hate speech detection by reducing the false positive rate. In *Proceedings of the Fourth Workshop on NLP for Internet Freedom: Censorship, Disinformation, and Propaganda*, pages 17–22, Online. Association for Computational Linguistics.

Ilia Markov, Ine Gevers, and Walter Daelemans. 2022. An ensemble approach for Dutch cross-domain hate speech detection. In *Proceedings of the 27th International Conference on Natural Language & Information Systems*, pages 3–15, Valencia, Spain. Springer.

Ilia Markov, Nikola Ljubešić, Darja Fišer, and Walter Daelemans. 2021. Exploring stylometric and emotion-based features for multilingual cross-domain hate speech detection. In *Proceedings of the Eleventh Workshop on Computational Approaches to Subjectivity, Sentiment and Social Media Analysis*, pages 149–159, Online. Association for Computational Linguistics.

Huy Nghiem and Fred Morstatter. 2021. "stop asian hate!": Refining detection of anti-asian hate speech during the covid-19 pandemic. *arXiv preprint arXiv:2112.02265*.

Yixin Nie, Adina Williams, Emily Dinan, Mohit Bansal, Jason Weston, and Douwe Kiela. 2019. Adversarial nli: A new benchmark for natural language understanding. *arXiv preprint arXiv:1910.14599*.

Fabio Poletto, Valerio Basile, Manuela Sanguinetti, Cristina Bosco, and Viviana Patti. 2021. Resources and benchmark corpora for hate speech detection: a systematic review. *Language Resources and Evaluation*, 55:477–523.

Colin Raffel, Noam Shazeer, Adam Roberts, Katherine Lee, Sharan Narang, Michael Matena, Yanqi Zhou, Wei Li, and Peter J Liu. 2020. Exploring the limits of transfer learning with a unified text-to-text transformer. *The Journal of Machine Learning Research*, 21(1):5485–5551.

Paul Röttger, Bertram Vidgen, Dong Nguyen, Zeerak Waseem, Helen Margetts, and Janet B Pierrehumbert. 2020. Hatecheck: Functional tests for hate speech detection models. *arXiv preprint arXiv:2012.15606*.

Moshe Uzan and Yaakov HaCohen-Kerner. 2021. Detecting hate speech spreaders on twitter using lstm and bert in english and spanish. In *CLEF (Working Notes)*, pages 2178–2185.

Bertie Vidgen, Dong Nguyen, Helen Margetts, Patricia Rossini, and Rebekah Tromble. 2021. Introducing cad: the contextual abuse dataset. In *Proceedings of the 2021 Conference of the North American Chapter of the Association for Computational Linguistics: Human Language Technologies*, pages 2289–2303.

Zeerak Waseem and Dirk Hovy. 2016. Hateful symbols or hateful people? predictive features for hate speech detection on twitter. In *Proceedings of the NAACL student research workshop*, pages 88–93.

Adina Williams, Nikita Nangia, and Samuel R Bowman. 2017. A broad-coverage challenge corpus for sentence understanding through inference. *arXiv preprint arXiv:1704.05426*.

Thomas Wolf, Lysandre Debut, Victor Sanh, Julien Chaumond, Clement Delangue, Anthony Moi, Pierric Cistac, Tim Rault, Remi Louf, Morgan Funtowicz, Joe Davison, Sam Shleifer, Patrick von Platen, Clara Ma, Yacine Jernite, Julien Plu, Canwen Xu, Teven Le Scao, Sylvain Gugger, Mariama Drame,

Quentin Lhoest, and Alexander Rush. 2020. Transformers: State-of-the-art natural language processing. In *Proceedings of the 2020 Conference on Empirical Methods in Natural Language Processing: System Demonstrations*, pages 38–45, Online. Association for Computational Linguistics.

Wenpeng Yin, Jamaal Hay, and Dan Roth. 2019. Benchmarking zero-shot text classification: Datasets, evaluation and entailment approach. *arXiv preprint arXiv:1909.00161*.

Marcos Zampieri, Shervin Malmasi, Preslav Nakov, Sara Rosenthal, Noura Farra, and Ritesh Kumar. 2019. Predicting the type and target of offensive posts in social media. *arXiv preprint arXiv:1902.09666*.

# Appendices

## A Evaluation of Zero-Shot Detection. Correlation Matrix.

| | t5 FR | t5 HC | t5 CAD | t5 OLID | bart FR | bart HC | bart CAD | bart OLID | xlm-rb FR | xlm-rb HC | xlm-rb CAD | xlm-rb OLID |
|---|---|---|---|---|---|---|---|---|---|---|---|---|
| t5 FR | 1 | 0.76 | 0.82 | 0.83 | 0.3 | 0.43 | -0.01 | 0.24 | 0.28 | 0.39 | -0.14 | 0.21 |
| t5 HC | 0.76 | 1 | 0.84 | 0.8 | 0.19 | 0.5 | 0.13 | 0.19 | 0.33 | 0.34 | 0.01 | 0.3 |
| t5 CAD | 0.82 | 0.84 | 1 | 0.91 | 0.31 | 0.55 | 0.16 | 0.37 | 0.22 | 0.48 | -0.2 | 0.21 |
| t5 OLID | 0.83 | 0.8 | 0.91 | 1 | 0.25 | 0.47 | 0.08 | 0.36 | 0.23 | 0.48 | -0.21 | 0.27 |
| bart FR | 0.3 | 0.19 | 0.31 | 0.25 | 1 | 0.75 | 0.32 | 0.8 | 0 | 0.26 | -0.27 | -0.15 |
| bart HC | 0.43 | 0.5 | 0.55 | 0.47 | 0.75 | 1 | 0.1 | 0.72 | 0.09 | 0.38 | -0.26 | -0.04 |
| bart CAD | -0.01 | 0.13 | 0.16 | 0.08 | 0.32 | 0.1 | 1 | 0.22 | 0.25 | 0.08 | 0.17 | 0.12 |
| bart OLID | 0.24 | 0.19 | 0.37 | 0.36 | 0.8 | 0.72 | 0.22 | 1 | 0.02 | 0.35 | -0.3 | 0.02 |
| xlm-rb FR | 0.28 | 0.33 | 0.22 | 0.23 | 0 | 0.09 | 0.25 | 0.02 | 1 | 0.45 | 0.63 | 0.78 |
| xlm-rb HC | 0.39 | 0.34 | 0.48 | 0.48 | 0.26 | 0.38 | 0.08 | 0.35 | 0.45 | 1 | -0.16 | 0.47 |
| xlm-rb CAD | -0.14 | 0.01 | -0.2 | -0.21 | -0.27 | -0.26 | 0.17 | -0.3 | 0.63 | -0.16 | 1 | 0.55 |
| xlm-rb OLID | 0.21 | 0.3 | 0.21 | 0.27 | -0.15 | -0.04 | 0.12 | 0.02 | 0.78 | 0.47 | 0.55 | 1 |

Table 5: Correlation matrix for the experiment with hundred hypotheses. *FR* - FRENK, *HC* - HateCheck. We build the vectors of the results for every model-dataset combination. These vectors consist of F1-scores for the corresponding hypotheses. In total, there are 12 vectors, each of which with a length of 111. The hypotheses are sorted alphabetically, and the corresponding hypothesis vectors are used to compute the correlation matrix.

## B Experiment with a Small Set of Target Hypotheses. Correlation Matrices.

| FRENK | flan-t5 | bart-large | xlm-roberta |
|---|---|---|---|
| flan-t5 | 1 | 0.53 | 0.34 |
| bart-large | 0.53 | 1 | 0.26 |
| xlm-roberta | 0.34 | 0.26 | 1 |

| CAD | flan-t5 | bart-large | xlm-roberta |
|---|---|---|---|
| flan-t5 | 1 | 0.61 | -0.09 |
| bart-large | 0.61 | 1 | -0.2 |
| xlm-roberta | -0.09 | -0.2 | 1 |

| HateCheck | flan-t5 | bart-large | xlm-roberta |
|---|---|---|---|
| flan-t5 | 1 | 0.33 | 0.09 |
| bart-large | 0.33 | 1 | 0.53 |
| xlm-roberta | 0.09 | 0.53 | 1 |

| OLID | flan-t5 | bart-large | xlm-roberta |
|---|---|---|---|
| flan-t5 | 1 | 0.45 | 0.21 |
| bart-large | 0.45 | 1 | 0.1 |
| xlm-roberta | 0.21 | 0.1 | 1 |

Table 6: Correlation of results for each dataset for different models in the experiment with a small set of target hypotheses.

| flan-t5 | FRENK | HateCheck | CAD | OLID |
|---|---|---|---|---|
| FRENK | 1 | 0.69 | 0.6 | 0.68 |
| HateCheck | 0.69 | 1 | 0.74 | 0.73 |
| CAD | 0.6 | 0.74 | 1 | 0.87 |
| OLID | 0.68 | 0.73 | 0.87 | 1 |

| bart-large | FRENK | HateCheck | CAD | OLID |
|---|---|---|---|---|
| FRENK | 1 | 0.77 | 0.64 | 0.69 |
| HateCheck | 0.77 | 1 | 0.86 | 0.7 |
| CAD | 0.64 | 0.86 | 1 | 0.79 |
| OLID | 0.69 | 0.7 | 0.79 | 1 |

| xlm-roberta | FRENK | HateCheck | CAD | OLID |
|---|---|---|---|---|
| FRENK | 1 | 0.54 | 0.44 | 0.68 |
| HateCheck | 0.54 | 1 | -0.25 | 0.38 |
| CAD | 0.44 | -0.25 | 1 | 0.44 |
| OLID | 0.68 | 0.38 | 0.44 | 1 |

Table 7: Correlation of results for each model for different datasets in experiment with small set of target hypotheses.

# English2BSL: A Rule-Based System for Translating English into British Sign Language

**Phoebe Pinney** and **Riza Batista-Navarro**
University of Manchester, Oxford Road, Manchester, M13 9PL
phoebepinney@gmail.com, riza.batista@manchester.ac.uk

## Abstract

British Sign Language (BSL) is a complex language with its own vocabulary and grammatical structure, separate from English. Despite its long-standing and widespread use by Deaf communities within the UK, thus far, there have been no effective tools for translating written English into BSL. This overt lack of available resources made learning the language highly inaccessible for most people, exacerbating the communication barrier between hearing and Deaf individuals. This paper introduces a rule-based translation system, designed with the ambitious aim of creating the first web application that is not only able to translate sentences in written English into a BSL video output, but can also serve as a learning aid to empower the development of BSL proficiency.

## 1 Introduction

British Sign Language (BSL) is a visual-gestural language that has been widely used by Deaf[1] communities within the UK for hundreds of years. Contrary to a common misconception, BSL is not merely a visual representation of English; it developed independently of the spoken language, resulting in its distinct vocabulary and grammatical structure. This is evidenced by the fact that despite both BSL and American Sign Language (ASL) emerging in English-speaking countries, the two sign languages are mutually unintelligible, i.e., they share neither a grammar nor a lexicon (Emmorey, 2001).

The British Deaf Association (2023) states that there are more than 87,000 Deaf people in the UK whose first language is BSL. However, a significant lack of hearing people choosing to learn BSL has led to Deaf communities experiencing considerable levels of social exclusion (Berry, 2017), exacerbated by "educational segregation" and a lack of access to health services and employment opportunities (Powers, 2002). Research suggests that integrating BSL lessons and Deaf awareness education into UK schools is highly beneficial, not only for Deaf students but also for their hearing peers (Daniels, 2001). This poses the question: *how can learning BSL be made more accessible?*

Modern technology has provided access to applications that can translate between numerous spoken languages in real-time. *Google Translate*[2] can instantly convert written English into over 100 different spoken languages from any smartphone or web browser. As well as being a convenient way to quickly facilitate communication between people who speak different languages, translation applications can also be used as a learning tool. Medvedev (2016) discussed the use of Google Translate as a meaningful resource for learning English. However, there is no comparable application for translating written English into BSL. This gap forms the core motivation behind the development of the English-to-BSL translation system presented in this paper.

Our main contribution is the development of a translation pipeline that is comprised of a bespoke set of syntax-based rules created without the use of pre-existing templates. This unique rule-based translation system enables a user to input a sentence in written English and play a video showing the generated BSL translation. The translation output, which follows BSL grammar, is comprised of a series of sign videos, each representing a BSL gloss.[3] Our systematic evaluation of the system

[1]The term Deaf with a capital 'D' refers to people who identify as culturally Deaf, i.e., are part of the Deaf community and actively use sign language. The term deaf with a lowercase 'd' refers to the medical definition of having very little to no functional hearing (O'Neil, 2003).

[2]https://translate.google.com/intl/en-GB/about/languages/

[3]A *gloss* is an English-based translation that is consistently used to represent a unique sign (Cormier et al., 2017).



*LT-EDI 2023 – Third Workshop on Language Technology for Equality, Diversity and Inclusion*, pages 10–16, Varna, Bulgaria, Sep 7, 2023.
https://doi.org/10.26615/978-954-452-084-7_002

demonstrated the success of the web application from both quantitative and qualitative perspectives.

## 2 Related work

Below, we provide a summary of previously proposed methods for translating written text to sign language. This is then followed by a review of tools for English-to-BSL translation.

### 2.1 Methods for Translating to Sign Language

Statistical Machine Translation (SMT) approaches have provided significant advancements in the field of spoken language translation. However, in order to generate high-quality results, a vast amount of data is required to train statistical models. Bungeroth and Ney (2004) proposed a proof-of-concept SMT model for translating written German into German sign language (DGS). However, their model obtained low performance due to a lack of available German-to-DGS data.

In a recent survey of sign language machine translation, Núñez-Marcos et al. (2022) recognised the overt scarcity of data available for *all* sign languages, which has led to a lack of effective SMT models for translating written text into sign language. BSL is even more under-resourced than DGS in terms of data currently available, therefore developing an accurate SMT approach to English-to-BSL translation is currently not feasible. For this reason, our own English-to-BSL translation tool is underpinned by a rule-based approach that we developed (as described in Section 4).

### 2.2 English-to-BSL Translation Tools

Only very few tools for converting English to BSL exist. One of them is *WeCapable* which offers a translator that takes an English sentence specified by a user and converts it into static pictures depicting individual letter signs (Kumar, 2023). While this tool may be useful for learning how to fingerspell,[4] it cannot translate into glosses. Furthermore, as the letter signs provided are in the form of pictures rather than videos, dynamic signs may be hard to interpret, potentially generating ambiguity for the user.[5] The translation tool of WeCapable also makes no attempt to convert an input English sentence to BSL syntax. It simply takes the user input and returns a letter-by-letter translation of each word in the order that they were entered in.

*Sign Translate* (Moryossef, 2023) is a web application, similar in appearance to Google Translate, that presents the translation output using an avatar that performs dynamic signs. However, selecting "United States" as the target language (i.e., American Sign Language) produces an output that is a sequence of alphabet signs, spelling out each word in the input (similarly to WeCapable). Setting the target language to "United Kingdom" (i.e., BSL) leads to a slightly confusing output, with the avatar not spelling out the words, but instead providing a dynamic output with seemingly little or no relation to the input English sentence. As a whole, this tool also does not make any attempt to convert the input to the correct BSL grammatical structure.

*Signly* differs from the previous two translation tools in that, rather than a stand-alone web application, it is a module that can be integrated into existing websites (Signly, 2023). Organisations can register with Signly to add sign language translation to their sites. Professional sign language interpreters are hired to record the BSL translation for each section of text in a given website. Signly thus provides English-to-BSL translation as a service, one that is more accurate than can be achieved via any automated translation. However, this cannot be done in real time and the domain of translation is limited to text on registered websites. Each time a company that uses Signly updates its website, an interpreter must manually sign any new text.

Our proposed work is different from the above-described existing tools for English-to-BSL translation, in seeking to provide real-time translation for user-specified inputs, and importantly, in generating translation outputs that follow the BSL grammatical structure.

## 3 The BSL Grammatical structure

Understanding the fundamental grammatical structure of BSL is imperative when attempting to perform sign translation. This section provides a brief overview of the linguistic features of BSL.

Each individual sign can be represented by a *gloss*. Glosses are lexemes, meaning that they remain constant regardless of any modifications to the word in English. This is because BSL is agnostic to any inflectional changes. There are no tenses in BSL, thus the English words *"eat"*, *"eating"*

[4]Fingerspelling refers to signing sequences of alphabet letters comprising either full words or abbreviations (Brown and Cormier, 2017).

[5]For example, the letter $H$ is a dynamic sign where the palm of one hand is swept across the other — this would not be clear from a static image.

and *"ate"*, for example, are all encompassed by the gloss *"eat"*, and therefore share the same sign in BSL (Fenlon et al., 2015). Notably, glosses can represent phrases or emotions as well as individual words.

BSL developed independently of spoken English, so it naturally follows a different grammatical structure. Deuchar (2013) analysed the observable grammatical structure of BSL and how it differs from spoken English. However, they note that due to a significant lack of research into the linguistic structure of BSL, there is no official codified grammar. Despite this, through analysis of organic BSL communication, an overarching summation of the general structure of sentences in BSL grammar can be defined as: '**time-frame** then **topic** then **action** or a **comment**'. For example, the English sentence *"I ate a cake yesterday"* becomes [*"yesterday"* (time-frame), *"cake"* (topic), *"eat"* (action)] in BSL. As one can observe, glosses in the BSL translation follow an order that is different from that of the tokens in the English sentence.

It is also worth noting that certain English words are completely omitted in sign language; intermediary words like determiners, prepositions, and some pronouns do not have a corresponding BSL gloss. Instead, the meaning of these words is expressed via contextual signs and facial expressions. In fact, context cues are crucial in comprehending BSL as a whole. For example, a 'thumbs up' sign can mean *"good"* or *"fantastic"* depending on the level of expression. Mouthing specific words, such as nouns and verbs, whilst signing them is also useful, as lipreading is often necessary to discern between different words with similar signs. These nuances can be difficult to replicate via automated translation.

## 4 Methodology

We decided to take a Rule-Based Machine Translation (RBMT) approach to English-to-BSL translation, whereby a human expert explicitly defines a set of rules (Costa-Jussà et al., 2012). As well as not requiring large amounts of pre-existing data, RBMT systems often provide more control, as the structured design means that results are deterministic and errors are easier to identify (Okpor, 2014). Furthermore, RBMT promotes transparency and scalability, as explicit rules are more easily understood by humans and more rules can be added to improve quality and enhance system complexity.

Our proposed English-to-BSL translation approach is based on a pipeline with three stages: pre-processing of written English input, rule-based translation and post-processing of output. This pipeline was developed iteratively, leveraging continuous research into the grammatical structure of BSL and personal proficiency in the language.

### 4.1 Pre-processing

The steps outlined below were implemented and applied to a given English sentence (in the order they are presented):

(1) Contraction expansion: All tokens within a sentence that are detected as contractions (e.g., *"don't"*) were expanded to to their full form (e.g., *"do not"*).[6]

(2) Punctuation removal: A regular expression was used to match and remove all punctuation.

(3) Numeric form conversion: BSL requires that all mentions of numeric values, including those spelt out as words in the input English sentence (e.g., *"eleven"*, *"two thousand and twenty three"*), are expressed in their numeric form (e.g., *"11"*, *"2023"*). We employed a word-to-numbers conversion library[7] to carry out this transformation.

(4) Tokenisation: Tokens in the sentence (the version that is the result of the preceding steps) are identified by using whitespace as delimiter.

(5) Lowercasing: Each token is lowercased except for the pronoun *"I"* (as our rules need to be able to identify this pronoun later on, as described in Section 4.3).

The output of the above pre-processing steps (e.g., [*"next, "week"*, *"I"*, *"am"*, *"getting"*, *"a"*, *"new"*, *"dog"*] for the sentence *"Next week, I'm getting a new dog."*) is then analysed by our core translation component.

### 4.2 Rule-Based Translation

The core component of our translation pipeline is underpinned by a Part-Of-Speech (POS) tagger and a set of rules that re-order the tokens resulting from the pre-processing stage.

**POS Tagging.** The sequence of tokens obtained from the pre-processing stage is analysed by a transformation-based-learning POS tagger,[8] which was chosen for its speed (i.e., capability to tag over

[6]Using the library available at `https://www.npmjs.com/package/expand-contractions`

[7]`https://www.npmjs.com/package/words-to-numbers`

[8]`https://www.npmjs.com/package/wink-pos-tagger`

525,000 tokens per second) and accuracy (93.2% on the WSJ22-24 benchmark dataset (Marcus et al., 1999)). This POS tagger produces its output following the Penn Treebank tagset.[9]

**Handcrafted Rules.** Tokens are ordered by determining where each of them should be placed relative to the other tokens, based on the order expected in BSL. The rows of Table 1, when read from top to bottom, indicate the order in which tokens falling under different word classes (as specified by POS tags) should appear in the BSL translation of an English sentence.

In handling certain word classes, we handcrafted a number of rules, outlined below.

(1) Handling temporal expressions: Words pertaining to time frame (e.g., *"next week"*, *"yesterday"*) should come first in the BSL translation output (except in cases where the English sentence contains interjections). As POS tagging does not identify temporal expressions, we compiled a list of such expressions. Any token that matches any of the expressions in this dictionary is detected as a temporal expression, and thus considered to be the time frame of the sentence.

(2) Coordinating conjunctions: If a coordinating conjunction such as *"and"* is used to join multiple clauses (as in the sentence *"Her name is Mary and she likes to eat cake"*), the sentence is split into its individual clauses, each of which needs to be translated separately (i.e., as if each clause is a sentence). However, the sentence should not be split if the conjunction is used to join multiple items (as in the sentence *"Mary likes cats and dogs"*); this can be determined by checking if the POS tags of the tokens on both sides of the conjunction are the same.

(3) Tokens belonging to commonly used bigrams: A dictionary of commonly used token bigrams was compiled. These include phrasal verbs (e.g., *"pick up"*, *"come back"*) as well as the combination *"I am"*. If a token bigram in a given sentence matches any of the entries in our dictionary, they are kept together in the re-ordered token sequence.

(4) Handling names of months: In BSL, signs for names of months are represented by the first three letters; for example, the month *"October"* should be converted to the gloss sequence [*"O"*, *"C"* and *"T"*]. Thus, a rule was introduced so that a token corresponding to the name of a month is converted to a sequence consisting of its first three characters.

After re-ordering based on the above rules, the token sequence [*"next"*, *"week"*, *"I"*, *"am"*, *"getting"*, *"a"*, *"new"*, *"dog"*] becomes [*"next*, *"week"*, *"a"*, *"new"*, *"dog"*, *"getting"* *"I"*, *"am"*].

### 4.3 Post-processing

The sequence of tokens resulting from our rule-based re-ordering method is processed by the following post-processing steps, in order to finally generate a sequence of BSL glosses.

(1) Stopword removal: We curated a stopword list that consists of words that are not utilised in BSL, e.g., determiners (*"a"*, *"an"*, *"the"*), pronouns and a selection of verbs (such as *"am"*, *"do"*, *"did"*, *"could"*, *"should"* and *"would"*). Tokens in the sequence that match any of the stopwords are removed. It is important to note, however, that the pronoun *"I"* is handled as a special case: if it is part of the token bigram *"I am"*, the bigram is converted to the gloss *"me"*. If it, however, appears on its own (as in the sentence *"I ate a cake"*), then it is considered to be a stopword that is then removed.

(2) Lemmatisation: To convert each remaining token to its corresponding BSL gloss, we utilised a dictionary-based lemmatiser[10] to retrieve the lemmatised form (also known as lemma or baseform) of each token.

Upon post-processing the re-ordered sequence [*"next*, *"week"*, *"a"*, *"new"*, *"dog"*, *"getting"* *"I"*, *"am"*], for example, the sequence of glosses [*"next*, *"week"*, *"new"*, *"dog"*, *"get"* *"me"*] is generated as the output BSL translation.

## 5 The English2BSL Web Application

In order to facilitate user interactivity and display the English-to-BSL translation generated by our rule-based system, a novel web application, *English2BSL*,[11] was developed. The Angular framework[12] was utilised in integrating the translation pipeline into the user interface.

### 5.1 Building a Collection of Sign Videos

As discussed in Section 1, we seek to provide the final BSL translation output in the form of a series of sign videos, each representing a BSL gloss. To this end, we built a collection of sign videos. The

[9] https://www.ling.upenn.edu/courses/Fall_2003/ling001/penn_treebank_pos.html

[10] https://www.npmjs.com/package/lemmatizer

[11] https://english2bsl.vercel.app/

[12] https://angular.io/

| Word Class | POS Tags |
|---|---|
| Interjections | UH |
| Temporal expressions | - |
| Determiners | DT |
| Prepositions | IN |
| Adjectives, Numbers, Possessive pronouns | JJ, JJR, JJS, CD, PDT, PRP$ |
| Nouns | NN, NNP, NNS, NNPS |
| Foreign words | FW |
| Verbs, Adverbs | VBD, VBG, VBN, VBP, VBZ, VB, RB, RBR, RBS |
| Existential *there*, Modals | EX, MD |
| Pronouns | PRP |
| Question words | WDT, WP, WP$, WRB |

Table 1: The rows from top to bottom indicate the order in which glosses should appear in a BSL translation. The POS tags shown follow the Penn Treebank tagset. Temporal expressions are detected using a dictionary-based method.

first author of this paper recorded sign videos in one sitting (with the same background and lighting conditions) to provide consistency throughout the video collection, and ensure that transitions between videos (when put together in a sequence) are as seamless as possible. Our collection contains a total of 213 videos, spanning 273 most commonly used glosses. It is worth noting that this video collection is available in the form of a BSL sign dictionary[13] as part of the English2BSL web application.

Given a sequence of BSL glosses generated by our rule-based approach, videos depicting signs that correspond to each gloss are played in sequence by the application, as shown in Figure 1. A length limit of 45 characters is applied to the user-specified input English sentence. This is to encourage users to provide sentences that are not too complicated and are easy to understand when signed in BSL.

Figure 1: A still from an example video output displayed by English2BSL in real time, based on the sequence of BSL glosses generated by our rule-based translation approach.

Considering that our sign video collection is not complete (in that it does not include every possible sign), it is inevitable that certain glosses in the BSL translation output are out of vocabulary, i.e., sign videos for some glosses might be missing in our collection. English2BSL handles such cases by displaying a series of videos that show how to fingerspell an out-of-vocabulary word, as shown in Figure 2.

Figure 2: An example video output displayed by English2BSL where one of the glosses, *"poodle"*, is out of vocabulary and is signed by fingerspelling.

## 5.2 Spelling Correction Suggestions

To make the application more user-friendly, automatically generated spelling correction suggestions were incorporated. Firstly, a dictionary of lemmas corresponding to the 273 glosses in our video collection was compiled and then expanded so that all possible inflectional forms of each lemma are also included. Potential spelling errors in the input English sentence are then detected by checking if any of the input words do not exist in the above-mentioned dictionary. In the sentence *"I like eatin cake"*, for example, the word *"eatin"* will be detected as having a spelling error. In contrast, *"eating"* will not be flagged up as an error since it is an inflectional form of *"eat"*, one of the glosses in

[13] `https://english2bsl.vercel.app/signdictionary`

our sign video collection.

To generate a correction suggestion for a misspelt word, we employed two string similarity algorithms, Dice's coefficient (Robertson and Willett, 1993) and Levenshtein distance (Lhoussain et al., 2015), to identify the lemma or inflectional form in our dictionary that is most similar to the misspelt word. The lemma or inflectional form with the highest string similarity score (according to either of the algorithms) then becomes the correction suggestion. If matches with a similarity score above 0.50 were not found, no corrections are returned to avoid unhelpful suggestions from being generated; the misspelt word is then handled as an out-of-vocabulary word.

## 6 Evaluation

Our English-to-BSL translation system was assessed using a combination of quantitative and qualitative evaluation strategies.

### 6.1 Quantitative Evaluation

As discussed in Section 2.1, there is a significant lack of data to support the development and evaluation of English-to-BSL translation systems. To the best of our knowledge, datasets consisting of written English sentences with their corresponding BSL gloss translations were not available. For this reason, we created our own dataset.

After comparing various publicly available datasets containing natural dialogue in English, *DailyDialog*, an open-domain English-language dataset,[14] was chosen due to its varied and conversational nature. The first 150 sentences containing 45 characters or less were extracted from this dataset; then, drawing upon the first author's BSL proficiency, each of these 150 sentences was manually translated into the corresponding gloss sequence based on correct BSL syntax.

Our rule-based English-to-BSL translation approach was applied to each of the test sentences. Comparing the automatically generated translations with the manually generated ones (based on exact matching), an accuracy of 90% was obtained, with 135 of the 150 test sentences having been correctly translated.

[14] `https://paperswithcode.com/dataset/dailydialog`

### 6.2 Qualitative Evaluation

Complementing our quantitative evaluation are two User Experience (UX)-based qualitative methods, i.e., user focus groups and expert heuristic evaluation. These were chosen to explore the 'lived experiences' of users and help capture the subjective and contextual aspects of their interactions with the web application.

A focus group of six university students with varying levels of BSL proficiency was conducted alongside expert evaluation with a university-level BSL lecturer. The subjective, anecdotal data collected via these UX evaluation methods exemplifies how potential users respond to the English2BSL application. It was collected in a non-controlled manner, such that it can be generalised to real-life settings. The response to the web application was overwhelmingly positive from both potential user and expert perspectives, demonstrating the effectiveness of the rule-based translation system as well as the UX design of the user interface.

## 7 Conclusions and Future Work

This paper describes the development of English2BSL, a web application that translates written English into BSL in real time. It is underpinned by a rule-based machine translation approach that leverages the output of syntactic analysis, i.e., POS tags, and a set of handcrafted rules to determine the order in which glosses should appear in the BSL output. Quantitative evaluation of our translation approach showed that it can obtain an accuracy of up to 90%.

The English2BSL user interface displays BSL output in the form of a series of sign videos seamlessly put together, thus acting as an interactive tool for people who wish to build or improve their knowledge of BSL.

A limitation of the proposed translation system lies in its reliance on curated dictionaries (e.g., lists of temporal expressions and commonly used token bigrams) as well the finite number of signs in the video collection. Our future work will focus on expanding our dictionaries and on incorporating more signs into the video collection. Moreover, to broaden the reach of our translation tool, we will explore the development of a version of English2BSL that runs on mobile devices.

## References


Mike Berry. 2017. Being deaf in mainstream education in the United Kingdom: Some implications for their health. *Universal Journal of Psychology*, 5(3):129–139.

Matt Brown and Kearsy Cormier. 2017. Sociolinguistic variation in the nativisation of BSL fingerspelling. *Open Linguistics*, 3(1):115–144.

Jan Bungeroth and Hermann Ney. 2004. Statistical sign language translation. In *sign-lang@ LREC 2004*, pages 105–108. European Language Resources Association (ELRA).

Kearsy Cormier, Jordan Fenlon, Sannah Gulamani, and Sandra Smith. 2017. BSL corpus annotation conventions. In *Annotation Convention*, volume 3, page 19.

Marta R. Costa-Jussà, Mireia Farrús, José B. Mariño Acebal, and José A. Rodriguez Fonollosa. 2012. Study and comparison of rule-based and statistical Catalan-Spanish machine translation systems. *Computing and Informatics. 2012; 31 (2).*

Marilyn Daniels. 2001. Sign language advantage. *Sign Language Studies*, 2(1):5–19.

Margaret Deuchar. 2013. *British sign language*. Routledge.

Karen Emmorey. 2001. *Language, cognition, and the brain: Insights from sign language research*. Psychology Press.

Jordan Fenlon, Kearsy Cormier, and Adam Schembri. 2015. Building BSL SignBank: The lemma dilemma revisited. *International Journal of Lexicography*, 28(2):169–206.

Lalit Kumar. 2023. WeCapable: English to Sign Language (BSL) Translator. Available online: `https://wecapable.com/tools/text-to-british-sign-language-converter/`. Last accessed: 2023-03-24.

Aouragh Si Lhoussain, Gueddah Hicham, and Yousfi Abdellah. 2015. Adaptating the Levenshtein distance to contextual spelling correction. *International Journal of Computer Science and Applications*, 12(1):127–133.

Mitchell P Marcus, Beatrice Santorini, Mary Ann Marcinkiewicz, and Ann Taylor. 1999. Treebank-3. *Linguistic Data Consortium, Philadelphia.*

Gennady Medvedev. 2016. Google Translate in teaching English. *Journal of teaching English for specific and academic purposes*, 4(1):181–193.

Amit Moryossef. 2023. sign.mt: Effortless real-time sign language translation. Available online: `https://sign.mt/`. Last accessed: 2023-03-24.

Adrián Núñez-Marcos, Olatz Perez-de Viñaspre, and Gorka Labaka. 2022. A survey on Sign Language machine translation. *Expert Systems with Applications*, page 118993.

MD Okpor. 2014. Machine Translation Approaches: Issues and Challenges. *International Journal of Computer Science Issues (IJCSI)*, 11(5):159.

Caroline O'Neil. 2003. d or D? Who's deaf and who's Deaf? Available online: `https://www.bbc.co.uk/ouch/opinion/d_or_d_whos_deaf_and_whos_deaf.shtml`. Last accessed: 2023-02-05.

Stephen Powers. 2002. From concepts to practice in deaf education: A United Kingdom perspective on inclusion. *Journal of deaf Studies and deaf Education*, 7(3):230–243.

Alexander M Robertson and Peter Willett. 1993. A comparison of spelling-correction methods for the identification of word forms in historical text databases. *Literary and linguistic computing*, 8(3):143–152.

Signly. 2023. Signly provides synchronous in-vision sign language on websites. Available online: `https://signly.co/`. Last accessed: 2023-03-24.

The British Deaf Association. 2023. Help and resources: What is BSL? Available online: `https://bda.org.uk/help-resources/`. Last accessed: 2023-02-15.

# Multilingual Models for Sentiment and Abusive Language Detection for Dravidian Languages

**Anand Kumar M**
Department of Information Technology
National Institute of Technology Karnataka, Surathkal
India
m_anandkumar@nitk.edu.in

## Abstract

This work delves into the realm of abusive comment detection and sentiment analysis within code-mixed content, focusing specifically on Dravidian languages. The languages covered include Tulu, and Tamil. For this investigation, TFIDF-based Long Short-Term Memory (LSTM) and Hierarchical Attention Networks (HAN) are employed as the analytical tools.

Interestingly, the research highlights the prevalence of traditional TF-IDF techniques over Hierarchical Attention models in both sentiment analysis and the identification of abusive language across the diverse linguistic landscape encompassing Tulu and Tamil.

Of note is the Tulu sentiment analysis system, which demonstrates remarkable prowess in handling Positive and Neutral sentiments. In contrast, the sentiment analysis system tailored for Tamil exhibits comparatively lower performance levels. This discrepancy underscores the critical need for well-balanced datasets and intensified research endeavors to enhance the accuracy of sentiment analysis, particularly in the context of the Tamil language.

Shifting focus to abusive language detection, the TF-IDF-LSTM models consistently outperform the Hierarchical Attention models. Intriguingly, the mixed models exhibit particular strength in classifying categories like "Homophobia" and "Xenophobia." This intriguing outcome accentuates the value of incorporating both code-mixed and original script data, presenting novel avenues for advancing social media analysis research in diverse linguistic scenarios involving the Dravidian languages.

## 1 Introduction

The number of users is exponentially increasing on online social media platforms daily. More than 4.74 billion people used social media platforms [1] in the year 2022. Furthermore, the number of users will continue to grow even higher with cheaper internet and smartphones. Many online abusers use social media platforms as a venue to abuse other users through comments or posts. Nowadays, the marketing industry heavily relies on social media comments posted by users about their products. On the other hand, political parties base their political movements on the opinions expressed by citizens on social media. Government policies are revised based on the sentiments of the citizens identified through social media. Therefore, analyzing the comments posted on social media platforms is the most trending research domain in Natural Language Processing. These social media comments have opened up new and exciting research directions for NLP.

In a multilingual country like India, mixing languages while speaking is a typical behavior of the people. However, many people do not mix languages while writing for general purposes. However, this trend has changed in the era of social media, and people tend to mix languages when posting comments on online platforms. Users mainly use the Roman script to write comments, even in their native language. This phenomenon is known as code-mixing.

This paper presents a system developed for abusive language detection and sentiment analysis tasks conducted at the DravidianLangtech-2023. We have developed three different systems to identify abusive text and sentiment in social media posts. The methods used are the Hierarchical attention-based LSTM, TFIDF-based LSTM, and mixed language model. Additionally, to address the data imbalance, we have used contextualized embedding-based text generation to generate comments for the minority class.

## 2 Related Works

Recently, there has been a considerable amount of work and effort to collect resources for code-

[1]https://influencermarketinghub.com/social-media-sites/



*LT-EDI 2023 – Third Workshop on Language Technology for Equality, Diversity and Inclusion*, pages 17–24, Varna, Bulgaria, Sep 7, 2023.
https://doi.org/10.26615/978-954-452-084-7_003

switched text in various languages. However, code-switched datasets and lexicons specifically for sentiment analysis purposes are still limited in number, size, and availability (Chakravarthi et al., 2018, 2019a,b,c; Padmamala and Vijayarani, 2017; Ranjan et al., 2016; Ar et al., 2012; Devi and Kannimuthu, 2023).

For monolingual sentiment analysis, various corpora have been developed for different languages. For example, the work by (Wiebe et al., 2005) introduced an annotated corpus for sentiment analysis in English. Similarly, the Rusentiment corpus was created for sentiment analysis in Russian (Rogers et al., 2018), the Twitter Sentiment Corpus (TSC) was developed for sentiment analysis in German (Cieliebak and Diab, 2017), and the Norwegian Social Media Corpus (NoReC) was annotated for sentiment analysis in Norwegian (Mæhlum et al., 2019).

In the context of code-mixing, several datasets have been created to facilitate sentiment analysis. (Sitaram et al., 2015; Joshi et al., 2016; Patra et al., 2018) worked on building an English-Hindi corpus for sentiment analysis. (Solorio et al., 2014; Vilares et al., 2015, 2016) introduced an English-Spanish corpus for sentiment analysis. (Lee et al., 2015) collected a Chinese-English corpus from Weibo.com for sentiment analysis, and (Patra et al., 2018) released English-Bengali data for sentiment analysis.

Tamil, a Dravidian language spoken by Tamil people in India, Sri Lanka, and the Tamil diaspora, has received attention in sentiment analysis research (Padmamala and Vijayarani, 2017). The growing number of native Tamil speakers presents a potential market for commercial NLP applications (Ranjan et al., 2016). However, sentiment analysis on Tamil-English code-mixed data is relatively underdeveloped, and readily available data for research purposes is limited.

In the past, research on code-mixed corpora primarily relied on word-level annotations. However, this approach is not only time-consuming but also expensive to create. To address this limitation, researchers have explored the use of neural networks and meta-embeddings, which have shown promise in code-switched research without the need for word-level annotation (Kiela et al., 2018; Winata et al., 2019c).

(Winata et al., 2019a) demonstrated the effectiveness of utilizing information from pre-trained embeddings without explicit word-level language tags in code-switched sentiment analysis. This approach leverages the power of neural networks to learn representations that can capture sentiment in code-mixed data.

Furthermore, (Winata et al., 2019b) introduced a method to utilize subword-level information from closely related languages to enhance the performance of sentiment analysis on code-mixed text. By leveraging the linguistic similarities between languages, this approach aims to improve the accuracy of sentiment analysis in code-mixed data.

In this field, there has not been extensive Tamil language-oriented research. One important reason for this could be the scarcity of data in social media in Tamil compared to other languages, especially English, and the limited availability of linguistic resources in Tamil. Many datasets have been created in Tamil to promote more research in this language. One of them is "HopeEDI" (Equality, Diversity, and Inclusion), a dataset for hope speech in Tamil (Chakravarthi et al., 2020). Several baselines have also been created to standardize the dataset.

Research on abusive comment detection in Tamil is still in its early stages, but it has made significant progress in recent years. The earliest models on text classification used linear classifiers. This was followed by several works based on Deep Learning methods. Recurrent Neural Networks like LSTMs showed promising results. (Mandalam and Sharma, 2021) classified Dravidian Tamil and Malayalam code-mixed comments according to their polarity and used the LSTM architecture. In (Arora, 2020), a pre-trained version of ULM-FiT was used to develop a model to detect hate speech in Tamil-English social media comments.

This was followed by the use of transformer-based models after being introduced in (Vaswani et al., 2017), and further exploration was done after the release of BERT (Devlin et al., 2019). In (Mishra and Mishra, 2019), MultiLingual BERT and monolingual BERT were used for hate speech identification in Indo-European languages. In (Ziehe et al., 2021), the authors fine-tuned XLM-RoBERTa (Conneau et al., 2020) for Hope Speech Detection in English, Malayalam, and Tamil texts. Recently, in (García-Díaz et al., 2022), the authors proposed a method for detecting abusive comments in Tamil using multilingual transformer models. And in (Prasanth et al., 2022), they performed abuse detection using TF-IDF and the Random Kitchen Sink Algorithm on Tamil text.

## 3 Dataset Description

We utilized a dataset for sentiment analysis and detection of abusive language, which was sourced from the (Priyadharshini et al., 2023) and (Hegde et al., 2023) references. This dataset was employed as part of the shared task held during the third Dravidian Lang Tech workshop at RANLP-2023. The dataset provided by the organizers encompassed content in Code-Mixed Tamil, as well as Tamil and Telugu languages. The data was curated from various social media interactions, such as posts and comments.

In terms of annotation, the Code-Mixed Tamil and Tamil comments were assigned labels from a set of 8 categories: None, Misandry, Misogyny, Xenophobia, Homophobia, Transphobia, Hope Speech, and Counter Speech. Conversely, the Telugu comments were categorized into just two classes: Hate and non-Hate. The data samples with specific labels can be found in Tables 1 and 2 for your reference.

Notably, the Code-Mixed Tamil dataset contained a larger number of comments compared to the other two datasets. For evaluation purposes, approximately 20% of the data was allocated for testing in both the Tamil datasets. Within the datasets, nearly 50% of the content fell under the "None" class. It's important to highlight that the imbalanced distribution was due to the greater number of classes present in the Code-Mixed Tamil and Tamil comments. On the contrary, the Telugu dataset exhibited a balanced distribution, and no validation data was included for this dataset. The distribution of data for training, validation, and testing is presented in detail in Table 3. The prevalent class across posts was "None," followed by the "Misandry" class within the Tamil dataset. In the context of Telugu, there were 1939 posts labeled as Hate and 2061 as Non-Hate.

For the sentiment analysis task, the organizers furnished social media comments in both Tamil and Tulu languages. The Tamil dataset was annotated with four sentiment classes: positive, negative, mixed, and unknown. Similarly, the Tulu dataset encompassed four classes: positive, negative, neutral, and unknown. The training set for Tamil sentiment analysis contained around 34,000 comments, while the Tulu dataset comprised 6674 posts. In the Tamil training dataset, the positive class accounted for 20,000 posts, with the remaining classes containing between 4,000 to 5,000 posts. In the Tulu dataset, around 3,000 posts were labeled as positive and 1,800 as neutral. As a noteworthy point, since the Tamil dataset featured an unknown class and the Tulu dataset contained a neutral class, these two classes were considered equivalent within the context of language mixed models.

## 4 Methodology

### 4.1 TFIDF-LSTM

We utilized traditional and robust TF-IDF models to generate term vectors. These term vectors serve as embeddings for each word, for example the term "loose" in the example "Loose kooda interveiw panreenga kuruttu koothikku innoru .." would be represented differently based on the context for a Tamil it would be matched with the vector for crazy while in an English sentence it would retain its original vector, and TF-IDF vectors are created for each post. The learned TF-IDF vectors for each post were then inputted into a BiLSTM (Bidirectional LSTM) to further capture contextual information in both directions. The BiLSTM layer was composed of 100 units, transforming the context vector for each post. Finally, we employed a machine learning classifier to classify unseen posts. During the validation process, we discovered that the Linear SVM model provided the best results compared to other models. We employed the TweetTokenizer to tokenize the code-mixed posts and jointly learned the character and word n-gram models up to the trigram level to acquire the vectors. We determined the optimal parameters for the model using grid search.

### 4.2 Hierarchical Attention Networks

We experimented with Hierarchical attention-based LSTM models to capture the latent information from the code-mixed comments. Since the dataset is derived from social media sources, we incorporated character-level embeddings in the first layer of the Hierarchical attention network. By using the character sequence, we learned individual word vectors. This approach entails initially learning the words from the characters, followed by combining the word vectors to form the embedding for each post or comment. We employed attention mechanisms to assign importance to specific words within the post, for example in the sentence "Loose kooda **interveiw panreenga kuruttu koothikku** innoru ..", the terms that focuses on the gender and

Table 1: Language, Task, Examples and its corresponding Labels

| Language | Task | Examples | Labels |
|---|---|---|---|
| Tamil | Sentiment | Ithu yethu maathiri illama puthu maathiyaala irukku | Positive |
| | | Waste padam tharu maru flop aamai nakkis | Negative |
| Tulu | Sentiment | Irena tulu ucharane bhari likundu | Positive |
| | | Ayana pukuli n ora nadt korle... | Negative |
| Telugu | Hate Speech | Torch lite Kuda Leni rojula fake news vadu kavalane chesind | hate |
| | | Mallareddy Dookudu cenima lo bramhi character correct set aithadu | non-hate |
| Tamil Code-mixed | Misogyny | poda nee oruru punda yechakala raja | Misandry |
| | | Loose kooda interveiw panreenga kuruttu koothikku innoru .. | Misogyny |
| | | Entha Mari aravaningala seruppala adikkanum entha Mari prachanai... | Transphobic |

Table 2: Language, Task and its corresponding Labels

| Language | Task | Labels |
|---|---|---|
| Code-Mixed Tamil | Abusive Lang. Detection | None, Misandry, Misogyny, Xenophobia, |
| Tamil | Abusive Lang. Detection | Homophobia, Transphobia, Hope Speech and Counter |
| Telugu | Abusive Lang. Detection | Hate and non-Hate |
| Tamil | Sentiment Analysis | Positive, Negative, Mixed and Unknown |
| Tulu | Sentiment Analysis | Positive, Negative, Neutral and Unknown |

Table 3: Dataset distribution for Train, Test, and Validation sets

| Langauge | Task | Train Set | Validation set | Test set |
|---|---|---|---|---|
| Code-Mixed Tamil | Abusive Lang. Detection | 5948 | 1488 | 1857 |
| Tamil | Abusive Lang. Detection | 2240 | 560 | 699 |
| Telugu | Abusive Lang. Detection | 4000 | - | 500 |
| Tamil | Sentiment Analysis | 33990 | 3787 | 650 |
| Tulu | Sentiment Analysis | 6674 | 903 | 749 |

actions which relate to "Misogyny", have more attention weights than the other terms . In the case of abusive language and sentiment detection, certain words in social media comments have a significant impact on determining the type of abuse and sentiment. Hence, we utilized the hierarchical attention network to capture the underlying information. Additionally, we employed Bi-LSTM for learning the sequence vectors.

### 4.3 Multilingual Models

In the sentiment analysis model, we combined the Tulu and Tamil code-mixed datasets since both languages belong to the Dravidian language family and share common English words in their code-mixed posts. We trained a multilingual sentiment analysis model using the previously proposed TF-IDF-based Bi-LSTM models on the mixed language dataset. This model was trained once and then tested separately for Tulu and Tamil sentiment analysis. We hypothesized that the shared features between the two languages could assist each other in the sentiment analysis task.

In our pursuit of abusive language detection, we took an innovative step by merging the Tamil code-mixed dataset with the authentic Tamil dataset. The purpose behind this combination was to train a single model that could effectively identify abusive language. This approach aimed to explore how the amalgamation of code-mixed and pure script data could influence the model's performance in detecting abusive language. Additionally, English swear words are often mixed with regional social media posts. Users may post content in their regional language but incorporate English swear words to abuse someone. We believed that the mixture of both datasets would provide a unique research perspective in social media analysis. Importantly, in the future, such mixed models will become increasingly important, as opposed to relying solely on language-specific tools.

Although the Telugu abusive dataset was provided, we did not combine it with the other datasets due to the mismatch in classes. The Telugu dataset consists of only two classes: hate and not hate. These mixed language learning approaches draw inspiration from code-mixed transfer learning-based POS tagging methods (Madasamy and Padannayil, 2021).

## 5 Results and analysis

In this section, we discuss the results obtained for the proposed models, as shown in Tables 4 and 5. Generally, the Hierarchical Attention models did not outperform the traditional TF-IDF-based techniques.

In the sentiment analysis task, the accuracy and F1 score for the Tamil dataset were relatively low for all the developed methods. This could be due to the highly imbalanced nature of the dataset. Upon analyzing the class-specific performance of the Tamil sentiment analysis, we found that the recall was higher for the positive class, while the precision was higher for the negative class compared to the other precision and recall values. Although the mixed language models did not perform significantly better, they exhibited higher precision for the negative class and higher recall for the positive class compared to the TF-IDF-LSTM model. A similar trend was observed in the Tulu sentiment analysis system. Additionally, the Tulu models performed better for the Positive and Neutral classes, with an F1 score of 0.83 for positive class and 0.63 for neutral class. The macro F1 score for the mixed language model was 0.47, whereas for the TF-IDF-LSTM model, it was 0.52.

In the abusive language detection task for Telugu, the TF-IDF-LSTM models outperformed the Hierarchical Attention models. The F1 score for the hate class was 0.62 and for the non-hate class it was 0.66. For the Tamil test set, the macro F1 score for the TF-IDF-LSTM model was the same as that of the mixed model. When analyzing the class-wise performance, the mixed models performed better in the "Homophobia" and "Xenophobia" classes. The HAN model failed to detect certain classes with fewer training posts, indicating that the HAN model requires more comments to train effectively. For the Tamil code-mixed abusive language detection task, the mixed models performed better for the "Counter Speech" class and "Misandry". Overall, the recall of the mixed models was comparable to the TF-IDF model, but they exhibited lower precision.

## 6 Conclusion and Future Scope

The traditional TF-IDF-based techniques have outperformed the Hierarchical Attention models in both the sentiment analysis and abusive language detection tasks. This suggests that, for the given datasets and tasks, the TF-IDF approach provided superior results.

The sentiment analysis task for the Tamil dataset exhibited lower accuracy and F1 scores, which may be attributed to the highly imbalanced nature of the dataset. When examining the class-specific performance, it was found that the positive class had higher recall while the negative class had higher precision. This indicates the need for addressing the dataset imbalance to improve the overall performance of sentiment analysis models.

Although the mixed language models did not show significant improvements, they displayed some advantages compared to the TF-IDF-LSTM model. These models exhibited higher precision for the negative class and higher recall for the positive class in both sentiment analysis and abusive language detection tasks. This suggests that leveraging mixed language data could be beneficial, and further exploration and enhancement of these models are warranted.

In conclusion, this work provides insights into the challenges and potential improvements in sentiment analysis and abusive language detection for code-mixed data, specifically focusing on Dravidian languages. Future work should address dataset imbalance, explore enhanced mixed language models, expand datasets, improve models through advanced architectures, adopt a multilingual approach, and investigate fine-tuning and transfer learning techniques. By tackling these areas, researchers can enhance the performance and robustness of sentiment analysis and abusive language detection in code-mixed scenarios, con-

Table 4: Results for Tamil and Tulu Language Models

| Language | Models | P | R | F1 | Accuracy |
|---|---|---|---|---|---|
| Tamil | TFIDF-LSTM | 0.31 | 0.29 | 0.24 | 0.25 |
| | HNN | 0.20 | 0.20 | 0.20 | 0.20 |
| | Mixed | 0.29 | 0.25 | 0.18 | 0.18 |
| Tulu | TFIDF-LSTM | 0.55 | 0.51 | 0.51 | 0.67 |
| | HNN | 0.34 | 0.23 | 0.23 | 0.54 |
| | Mixed | 0.49 | 0.47 | 0.47 | 0.63 |

Table 5: Results for Tamil and Tulu Code-Mixed Language Models

| Language | Models | P | R | F1 | Acc |
|---|---|---|---|---|---|
| Telugu | TFIDF-LSTM | 0.65 | 0.64 | 0.64 | 0.64 |
| | HNN | 0.49 | 0.49 | 0.49 | 0.49 |
| | Mixed | - | - | - | - |
| Tamil | TFIDF-LSTM | 0.44 | 0.33 | 0.35 | 0.69 |
| | HNN | 0.23 | 0.23 | 0.23 | 0.64 |
| | Mixed | 0.43 | 0.32 | 0.35 | 0.67 |
| Code-Mixed Tamil | TFIDF-LSTM | 0.64 | 0.45 | 0.51 | 0.74 |
| | HNN | 0.34 | 0.23 | 0.23 | 0.70 |
| | Mixed | 0.60 | 0.44 | 0.49 | 0.73 |

tributing to the advancement of natural language processing in diverse linguistic contexts.


## Acknowledgements

We thank the Sentiment Analysis and Abusive language Detection Shared Task Organizers.


## References


Ortal Ar, Moshe Koppel, Dirk Börner, and Dana Soffa. 2012. Cross-lingual sentiment analysis for languages with scarce resources. In *Proceedings of the 2012 Joint Conference on Empirical Methods in Natural Language Processing and Computational Natural Language Learning (EMNLP-CoNLL)*.

Gaurav Arora. 2020. Gauravarora@hasoc-dravidian-codemix-fire2020: Pre-training ulmfit on synthetically generated code-mixed data for hate speech detection.

B. R. Chakravarthi, M. Arcan, and J. P. McCrae. 2018. Improving wordnets for under-resourced languages using machine translation. In *Proceedings of the 9th Global WordNet Conference (GWC 2018)*, page 78.

B. R. Chakravarthi, M. Arcan, and J. P. McCrae. 2019a. Comparison of different orthographies for machine translation of under-resourced dravidian languages. In *2nd Conference on Language, Data and Knowledge (LDK 2019)*.

B. R. Chakravarthi, M. Arcan, and J. P. McCrae. 2019b. Wordnet gloss translation for under-resourced languages using multilingual neural machine translation. In *Proceedings of the Second Workshop on Multilingualism at the Intersection of Knowledge Bases and Machine Translation*, pages 1–7, Dublin, Ireland. European Association for Machine Translation.

B. R. Chakravarthi, R. Priyadharshini, B. Stearns, A. S. Jayapal, M. Arcan, M. Zarrouk, and J. P. McCrae. 2019c. Multilingual multimodal machine translation for dravidian languages utilizing phonetic transcription. In *Proceedings of the 2nd Workshop on Technologies for MT of Low Resource Languages*, pages 56–63, Dublin, Ireland. European Association for Machine Translation.

Bharathi Raja Chakravarthi, Vigneshwaran Muralidaran, Ruba Priyadharshini, and John Philip McCrae. 2020. Corpus creation for sentiment analysis in code-mixed Tamil-English text. In *Proceedings of the 1st Joint Workshop on Spoken Language Technologies for Under-resourced languages (SLTU) and Collaboration and Computing for Under-Resourced Languages (CCURL)*, pages 202–210, Marseille, France. European Language Resources association.

M. Cieliebak and M. Diab. 2017. Twitter language identification of arabic-english code-switching. In *Proceedings of the Third Workshop on Computational Approaches to Linguistic Code-Switching*, pages 1–11, Vancouver, Canada. Association for Computational Linguistics.

Alexis Conneau, Kartikay Khandelwal, Naman Goyal, Vishrav Chaudhary, Guillaume Wenzek, Francisco Guzmán, Edouard Grave, Myle Ott, Luke Zettlemoyer, and Veselin Stoyanov. 2020. Unsupervised cross-lingual representation learning at scale.

Sharmila Devi and S. Kannimuthu. 2023. Author profiling in code-mixed whatsapp messages using stacked convolution networks and contextualized embedding based text augmentation. *Neural Process. Lett.*, 55(1):589–614.

Jacob Devlin, Ming-Wei Chang, Kenton Lee, and Kristina Toutanova. 2019. Bert: Pre-training of deep bidirectional transformers for language understanding.

José García-Díaz, Manuel Valencia-Garcia, and Rafael Valencia-García. 2022. UMUTeam@TamilNLP-ACL2022: Abusive detection in Tamil using linguistic features and transformers. In *Proceedings of the Second Workshop on Speech and Language Technologies for Dravidian Languages*, pages 45–50, Dublin, Ireland. Association for Computational Linguistics.

Asha Hegde, Bharathi Raja Chakravarthi, Rahul Shashirekha, Hosahalli Lakshmaiah andPonnusamy, SUBALALITHA CN, Lavanya S K, Thenmozhi D, Shreya Karunakar, Martha andShreeram, and Sarah Aymen. 2023. Findings of the shared task on sentiment analysis in tamil and tulu code-mixed text. In *Proceedings of the Third Workshop on Speech and Language Technologies for Dravidian Languages*, Varna, Bulgaria. Recent Advances in Natural Language Processing.

Aditya Joshi, Monojit Choudhury, and Mark J Carman. 2016. Towards building a code-mixed social media corpus for three indian languages. In *Proceedings of the 10th International Conference on Language Resources and Evaluation (LREC)*.

D. Kiela, C. Wang, and K. Cho. 2018. Dynamic meta-embeddings for improved sentence representations. In *Proceedings of the 2018 Conference on Empirical Methods in Natural Language Processing*, pages 1466–1477, Brussels, Belgium. Association for Computational Linguistics.

Xiaodan Lee, Yang Yao, Yaowei Zhang, Yanyan Guan, and Xiaolin Rui. 2015. Emotion classification using massive parallel data mined from social media. In *Proceedings of the 2015 Conference on Empirical Methods in Natural Language Processing (EMNLP)*.

Anand Kumar Madasamy and Soman Kutti Padannayil. 2021. Transfer learning based code-mixed part-of-speech tagging using character level representations for indian languages. *Journal of Ambient Intelligence and Humanized Computing*, pages 1–12.

Asrita Venkata Mandalam and Yashvardhan Sharma. 2021. Sentiment analysis of Dravidian code mixed data. In *Proceedings of the First Workshop on Speech and Language Technologies for Dravidian Languages*, pages 46–54, Kyiv. Association for Computational Linguistics.

Shubhanshu Mishra and Sudhanshu Mishra. 2019. 3idiots at hasoc 2019: Fine-tuning transformer neural networks for hate speech identification in indo-european languages. In *FIRE (Working Notes)*, pages 208–213.

P. Mæhlum, J. Barnes, L. Øvrelid, and E. Velldal. 2019. Annotating evaluative sentences for sentiment analysis: a dataset for norwegian. In *Proceedings of the 22nd Nordic Conference on Computational Linguistics*, pages 121–130, Turku, Finland. Linköping University Electronic Press.

Sridevi Padmamala and R Vijayarani. 2017. Sentiment analysis in tamil: A comparative study. In *Proceedings of the International Conference on Computing, Communication and Automation (ICCCA)*.

Sharmistha Patra, Monojit Choudhury, and Animesh Mukherjee. 2018. Sentiment analysis in code-mixed social media text. In *Proceedings of the 11th International Conference on Language Resources and Evaluation (LREC)*.

Prasanth, R Aswin Raj, Adhithan P, Premjith B, and Soman Kp. 2022. CEN-Tamil@DravidianLangTech-ACL2022: Abusive comment detection in Tamil using TF-IDF and random kitchen sink algorithm. In *Proceedings of the Second Workshop on Speech and Language Technologies for Dravidian Languages*, pages 70–74, Dublin, Ireland. Association for Computational Linguistics.

Ruba Priyadharshini, Bharathi Raja Chakravarthi, Malliga S, SUBALALITHA CN, Kogilavani S V, Premjith B, Abirami Murugappan, and Prasanna Kumar" Kumaresan. 2023. Overview of shared-task on abusive comment detection in tamil and telugu. In *Proceedings of the Third Workshop on Speech and Language Technologies for Dravidian Languages*, Varna, Bulgaria. Recent Advances in Natural Language Processing.

Satish Ranjan, Sandeep Kumar, Monojit Choudhury, and Shivakumar Patel. 2016. A comparative study of sentiment analysis in hindi, english, and code-mixed data. In *Proceedings of the 8th Indian Conference on Human Computer Interaction (HCI)*.

A. Rogers, A. Romanov, A. Rumshisky, S. Volkova, M. Gronas, and A. Gribov. 2018. Rusentiment: An enriched sentiment analysis dataset for social media in russian. In *Proceedings of the 27th International Conference on Computational Linguistics*, pages 755–763, Santa Fe, New Mexico, USA. Association for Computational Linguistics.

Sunayana Sitaram, AR Balamurali, and Shreekantha Rakshit. 2015. Sentiment analysis of code-mixed tweets. In *Proceedings of the International Conference on Advances in Computing, Communications and Informatics (ICACCI)*.

Thamar Solorio, Elizabeth Blair, and Suraj Maharjan. 2014. Overview for the first shared task on language identification in code-switched data. In *Proceedings of the First Workshop on Computational Approaches to Code Switching*.

Ashish Vaswani, Noam Shazeer, Niki Parmar, Jakob Uszkoreit, Llion Jones, Aidan N. Gomez, Lukasz

Kaiser, and Illia Polosukhin. 2017. Attention is all you need.

David Vilares, Miguel A Alonso, Carlos Gómez-Rodríguez, Helena Gómez-Adorno, and Thamar Solorio. 2015. Sentiment analysis on monolingual, multilingual and code-switching twitter corpora. In *Proceedings of the 16th Annual Conference of the International Speech Communication Association (INTERSPEECH)*.

David Vilares, Miguel A Alonso, Carlos Gómez-Rodríguez, Helena Gómez-Adorno, and Thamar Solorio. 2016. Semeval-2016 task 4: Sentiment analysis in twitter. In *Proceedings of the 10th International Workshop on Semantic Evaluation (SemEval)*.

J. Wiebe, T. Wilson, and C. Cardie. 2005. Annotating expressions of opinions and emotions in language. *Language Resources and Evaluation*, 39(2):165–210.

G. I. Winata, Z. Lin, and P. Fung. 2019a. Learning multilingual meta-embeddings for code-switching named entity recognition. In *Proceedings of the 4th Workshop on Representation Learning for NLP (RepL4NLP-2019)*, pages 181–186, Florence, Italy. Association for Computational Linguistics.

Genta Indra Winata, Yik-Cheung Lim, and Erik Cambria. 2019b. Code-switched sentiment analysis with pretrained contextualized embeddings. In *Proceedings of the 2019 Conference of the North American Chapter of the Association for Computational Linguistics (NAACL)*.

Genta Indra Winata, Yik-Cheung Lim, and Erik Cambria. 2019c. Hierarchical meta-embeddings for code-mixed sentiment analysis. In *Proceedings of the 57th Annual Meeting of the Association for Computational Linguistics (ACL)*.

Stefan Ziehe, Franziska Pannach, and Aravind Krishnan. 2021. GCDH@LT-EDI-EACL2021: XLM-RoBERTa for hope speech detection in English, Malayalam, and Tamil. In *Proceedings of the First Workshop on Language Technology for Equality, Diversity and Inclusion*, pages 132–135, Kyiv. Association for Computational Linguistics.

# Overview of the shared task on Detecting Signs of Depression from Social Media Text

**Kayalvizhi Sampath**
SSN College of Engineering
kayalvizhis@ssn.edu.in

**Durairaj Thenmozhi**
SSN College of Engineering
theni_d@ssn.edu.in

**Bharathi Raja Chakravarthi**
National University of Galway, Ireland
bharathi.raja@insight-centre.org

**Jerin Mahibha C**
Meenakshi Sundararajan Engineering College
jerinmahibha@gmail.com

**Kogilavani Shanmugavadivel**
Kongu Engineering College
kogilavani.sv@gmail.com

**Pratik Anil Rahood**
National University of Galway, Ireland
p.rahood1@nuigalway.ie

## Abstract

Social media has become a vital platform for personal communication. Its widespread use as a primary means of public communication offers an exciting opportunity for early detection and management of mental health issues. People often share their emotions on social media, but understanding the true depth of their feelings can be challenging. Depression, a prevalent problem among young people, is of particular concern due to its link with rising suicide rates. Identifying depression levels in social media texts is crucial for timely support and prevention of negative outcomes. However, it's a complex task because human emotions are dynamic and can change significantly over time. The DepSign-LT-EDI@RANLP 2023 shared task aims to classify social media text into three depression levels: "Not Depressed," "Moderately Depressed," and "Severely Depressed." This overview covers task details, dataset, methodologies used, and results analysis. Roberta-based models emerged as top performers, with the best result achieving an impressive macro F1-score of 0.584 among 31 participating teams.

## 1 Introduction

Depression is considered a common mental disorder that involves mood swings and a lack of interest in any activities [1]. Various aspects of life may be affected by depression. Depression may develop in people who undergo abuse, severe losses, or other stressful events. Depression has emerged as a worldwide concern for public health (Liu et al., 2022). Even though a lot many people suffer from depression, adequate treatment is received by only a fraction of them. Detecting and diagnosing depression is often delayed, imprecise, and missed. Depression is also considered an important cause of suicide. Based on the severity and impact of the symptoms, they can be categorized as mild, moderate, or severe.

Almost 72% of the population is found to be active on social media [2] which provides an opportunity for early detection of depression, particularly in young adults. Social media posts act as important information in identifying people at risk of depression or other mental disorders. There is a lot of research being carried out in the field of detecting depression from social media texts.

To analyse the massive amount of social media text, machine learning has been considered one of the most efficient approaches. The probability of the existence of depression had been predicted using different machine learning algorithms (Aleem et al., 2022). Detection of depression from social media text had also been implemented using Long-Short Term Memory (LSTM) model with Recurrent Neural Network (RNN) (Amanat et al., 2022).

With all these informations in mind, the shared task on detecting the levels of depression from social media posts has been organised which is a continuation of the shared task DepSign-LT-EDI@ACL-2022 (S et al., 2022) conducted during 2022. The shared task DepSign-LT-EDI@RANLP-2023 aims to detect levels of depression in Reddit posts.

## 2 Task description

The objective of DepSign-LT-EDI@RANLP-2023 is to identify indicators of depression in individuals based on their posts on social media platforms. By analyzing the language, feelings, and emotions expressed in these posts, the system aims to categorize individuals into three levels of depression: "Not Depressed," "Moderately Depressed," and

[1] https://www.who.int/news-room/fact-sheets/detail/depression

[2] https://www.internetlivestats.com/twitter-statistics/



*LT-EDI 2023 – Third Workshop on Language Technology for Equality, Diversity and Inclusion*, pages 25–30, Varna, Bulgaria, Sep 7, 2023.
https://doi.org/10.26615/978-954-452-084-7_004

"Severely Depressed." The system works specifically with English social media postings to detect signs of depression.

## 3 Data description

To determine the level of depression based on social media data, a dataset was created by scraping and labeling posts from Reddit. The dataset is the extension of DepSign-LT-EDI@ACL-2022 (S et al., 2022). It consists of three class labels: "Not Depressed," "Moderately Depressed," and "Severely Depressed." Detailed guidelines and annotation instructions can be found in the publication by (S and D, 2022). The dataset is provided in a "Tab Separated Value" format and is divided into three sets: the training set, evaluation set, and test set. The distribution of data across these sets is illustrated in Table 1. Examples of sample instances from the dataset are shown in Table 2.

| DepSign-LT-EDI@RANLP-2023 | Train | Dev | Test |
|---|---|---|---|
| **Not depressed** | 2755 | 848 | 136 |
| **Moderate** | 3678 | 2,169 | 275 |
| **Severe** | 768 | 228 | 88 |
| **Total instances** | **7201** | **3245** | **499** |

Table 1: Data set distribution

## 4 Methodology

A total number of 62 submissions were submitted by 31 teams.

- **DeepLearningBrasil**(Garcia et al., 2023) The submission of the team used domain-specific RoBERTa and DeBERTa models by further pre-training them on a scraped Reddit comments corpus extracted from subreddits with a mental health theme. The process was evaluated using different techniques, such as different truncation mechanisms, ordinal classification specific losses, and sample weights on the loss function, to deal with the unbalanced data. The three submissions consisted of different ensemble approaches for nine models with various techniques applied.

- **DeepBlueAI** The submission of the team had implemented the process of detecting levels of depression by fine-tuning with XLM-RoBERTa as the base model.

- **Cordyceps**(Ninalga, 2023) The team had implemented the process of self-distillation using unlabeled data from the "Reddit Mental Health Dataset". The process of prediction used a modified RoBERTa model named "MentalRoBERTa".

- **iicteam**(Vajrobol et al., 2023) The team has applied MentalRoBERTa, which is a model initialized with RoBERTa-Base (cased_L-12_H-768_A-12) and trained with mental health-related posts collected from Reddit.

- **CIMAT-NLP**(María de Jesús García Santiago and Monroy, 2023) The first two submissions used a transformer-based approach with differences in the dataset training. The dataset provided by the organizers was used but was structured differently. The third submission used an ensemble of BOW.

- **IJS**(Caporusso and Hanh Tran, 2023) The team applied language models, such as monolingual and multilingual BERT and XLNet, to predict depression levels based on given sentences. These models leverage their ability to understand contextual relationships within the text to capture nuanced linguistic features associated with depression.

- **NLP_CHRISTINE**(Christodoulou, 2023) The team had used the majority ensemble learning of three DeBERTa-V3-Large model architectures.

- **Biasbusters**(Nedilko, 2023) Three runs utilizing baseline BoW XGBoost with numeric engineered features, ChatGPT zero-shot, and the GPT-3 DaVinci model had been submitted.

- **NLP_JA**(Kumari and Kumar, 2023) The team had fine-tuned RoBERTa for detecting the depression level associated with the given text.

- **ML&AI_IIITRanchi**(Kumari et al., 2023) The submission made use of features like Tf-idf and BOW, along with sentence embeddings that were trained with deep neural networks and ensemble machine learning techniques.

- **TechSSN1**(Sivanaiah et al., 2023) The first run is based on a pre-trained BERT model

| PID | Text Data | Class label |
|---|---|---|
| train_pid_1 | My life gets worse every year : That's what it feels like anyway.... | moderate |
| train_pid_2 | Words can't describe how bad I feel right now : I just want to fall asleep forever. | severe |
| train_pid_3 | Is anybody else hoping the Coronavirus shuts everybody down? | not depressed |

Table 2: Sample instances of data set

that has been fine-tuned for depression analysis by training it on a specific dataset. To convert the target labels into numerical values, a label encoder was employed. The second run used Word2Vec to generate word embeddings that capture the contextual meaning of words in our vocabulary. The Support Vector Classifier (SVC) had been employed to train and predict based on the word vectors. The third run employed the TfidfVectorizer, which converts text into numerical feature vectors. Subsequently, the vectors were fitted to the LinearSVC model.

- **Interns**(L et al., 2023) The team had submitted three runs, of which the first run used linear SVM, the second run used textblob, and the third run was based on bi-LSTM.

- **Team-KEC** The training data had been preprocessed and balanced using SMOTE. Word embedding techniques such as N-Gram (Trigram) and Fasttext were used for feature extraction. Models like SVM, CNN, and BERT were used for prediction. Various combinations of word embedding and ML and DL models have been tried to achieve the best outcome.

- **BLP Navigator** Depression had been detected using transformer-based models.

- **Deepalaksmi** ALBERT model was used for detecting the signs of depression provided in the test dataset. Due to the large number of words in each instance of the training dataset, the text summarization method is used to extract the core words without losing the originality of the text. Also, text preprocessing methods were used to enhance the performance.

- **SENTIZEN** The team had submitted runs that implemented the process of classification using logistic regression, random forest, and the K nearest neighbors algorithm.

- **Ramya Sivakumar** Machine learning-based passive classifier was used to evaluate and predict values for the given dataset.

- **KEC_NL_DEP**(Shanmugavadivel et al., 2023) Different machine learning algorithms like logistic regression, decision tree, multinomial Naive Bayes, Gaussian Naive Bayes, and random forest have been used for detecting depression from social media text.

- **mucs**(Coelho et al., 2023) The submitted run used TF-IDF vectorizers for feature extraction and BERT models for the process of classification.

- **SIS**(B K et al., 2023) The model used bagging, which is an ensemble learning technique that helps improve the performance and accuracy of machine learning algorithms. The prediction has been done using Multi-Layer Perceptron (MLP), Recurrent Neural Network (RNN), and then Linear SVM.

- **meghaAarthi** In this system, multiple models from simple transformers have been used, and the final output is predicted on the basis of voting classification.

- **codemonkeys** Basic-bert-base-uncased had been incorporated, and the model had been fine-tuned for the specific dataset. A custom-made stopword list without using the nltk libraries has been used, and data augmentation has been done while predicting the model values.

- **the_mavericks**(Sathvika et al., 2023) The process of feature extraction from the preprocessed text data had been implemented using bag-of-words representation and count vectorization weighting. The Naive Bayes model was trained using the labeled data, learning the probabilities associated with each feature for the depressive and non-depressive classes.

- **Flamingos_python**(P S et al., 2023) An ensemble model combining three machine learning algorithms, namely Random Forest, SVM, and Naive Bayes classifier, was used to train the model for detecting the level of depression in a text.

- **KEEMS** Machine learning algorithms such as Random Forest, Support Vector Machine, and Ensembled Model with both Random Forest and Support Vector Machine were used for the three submissions. Google Translator had been used for up-sampling the dataset.

- **Tercet** The method that had been employed for the task of identifying the level of depression was Support Vector Machines. A Tf-idf vectorizer was used to extract the features based on which the SVM model had been applied.

- **Techwhiz**(M et al., 2023) Transformer-based models, namely ALBERT and RoBERTa, was used to implement the process of classification.

- **spr** Three runs were submitted by the team, which used different machine learning models. The first run was based on Logistic Regression, the second run used the Random Forest classifier, and the third run applied voting to Logistic Regression and Random Forest classifier.

- **Supernova**(Reddy et al., 2023) The team used the TF-IDF feature extraction mechanism and a Support Vector Machine to implement the process of classification.

## 5 Evaluation

The evaluation encompassed the utilization of all performance metrics available in sklearn. To account for the dataset's inherent imbalance, the submitted runs were assessed and ranked primarily based on the macro F1 score. The teams' rankings are presented in Table 3.

A notable observation from the table is that the system developed by the DeepLearningBrasil team excelled, achieving the highest macro F1 score of 0.584 and the top accuracy score of 0.565.

## 6 Analysis and discussion

Early detection of depression is crucial as it is a prevalent mental illness that profoundly affects an individual's mood and emotions. Failure to recognize and address depression at its early stages can have severe consequences. The DepSign-LT-EDI@RANLP-2023 shared task focused on utilizing Reddit postings to detect various levels of depression. The detection process involved assigning three labels to individuals: "Not Depressed," "Moderately Depressed," and "Severely Depressed." By analyzing the content of these posts, the aim was to identify and categorize individuals based on their level of depression.

## 7 Conclusion

Depression is a widespread mental health issue that profoundly affects a person's emotions and well-being. Detecting it early is crucial to prevent potential harm. The DepSign-LT-EDI@RANLP-2023 challenge aimed to identify depression levels from Reddit posts, categorizing them as "Not Depressed," "Moderately Depressed," or "Severely Depressed."

In this shared task, 31 teams participated, employing various models, with a strong focus on transformer-based methods and machine learning. The systems were assessed using the macro-averaged F1-score. Remarkably, Team DeeplearningBrasil excelled by combining Roberta in an ensemble approach, achieving an impressive F1 score of 0.584. This underscores the promise of advanced natural language processing techniques in early depression detection.

## Acknowledgments

We extend our gratitude for the financial support received from the Department of Science and Technology - Science and Engineering Research Board (DST-SERB).

One of the authors Bharathi Raja Chakravarthi was supported in part by a research grant from Science Foundation Ireland (SFI) under Grant Number SFI/12/RC/2289_P2 (Insight_2)

## References

Shumaila Aleem, Noor ul Huda, Rashid Amin, Samina Khalid, Sultan S Alshamrani, and Abdullah Alshehri. 2022. Machine learning algorithms for depression:

| Team Name | Accuracy | Weighted F1-score | Weighted Recall | Weighted Precision | Macro Recall | Macro Precision | Macro F1-score | Rank (based on Macro F1 score) |
|---|---|---|---|---|---|---|---|---|
| DeepLearningBrasil | **0.565** | 0.470 | 0.473 | 0.588 | 0.540 | 0.565 | **0.584** | 1 |
| DeepBlueAI | 0.525 | 0.446 | 0.457 | 0.554 | 0.506 | 0.525 | 0.554 | 2 |
| Cordyceps | 0.521 | 0.441 | 0.451 | 0.517 | 0.503 | 0.521 | 0.535 | 3 |
| iicteam | 0.525 | 0.439 | 0.439 | 0.513 | 0.506 | 0.525 | 0.528 | 4 |
| CIMAT-NLP | 0.505 | 0.439 | 0.447 | 0.467 | 0.493 | 0.505 | 0.503 | 4 |
| TechSSN4_English | 0.479 | 0.437 | 0.436 | 0.501 | 0.475 | 0.479 | 0.509 | 6 |
| IJS | 0.487 | 0.425 | 0.438 | 0.487 | 0.476 | 0.487 | 0.513 | 7 |
| NLP_CHRISTINE | 0.543 | 0.420 | 0.474 | 0.459 | 0.491 | 0.543 | 0.513 | 8 |
| Biasbusters | 0.499 | 0.419 | 0.442 | 0.489 | 0.481 | 0.499 | 0.518 | 9 |
| NLP_JA | 0.523 | 0.413 | 0.426 | 0.510 | 0.494 | 0.523 | 0.527 | 10 |
| ML&AI_IIITRanchi | 0.517 | 0.408 | 0.411 | 0.517 | 0.488 | 0.517 | 0.524 | 11 |
| TechSSN1 | 0.549 | 0.407 | 0.416 | 0.537 | 0.504 | 0.549 | 0.545 | 12 |
| Interns | 0.445 | 0.402 | 0.408 | 0.400 | 0.449 | 0.445 | 0.458 | 13 |
| Team-KEC | 0.451 | 0.401 | 0.414 | 0.458 | 0.445 | 0.451 | 0.486 | 14 |
| BLP Navigator | 0.453 | 0.387 | 0.415 | 0.474 | 0.439 | 0.453 | 0.500 | 15 |
| Deepalaksmi | 0.463 | 0.382 | 0.395 | 0.439 | 0.447 | 0.463 | 0.473 | 16 |
| SENTIZEN | 0.425 | 0.371 | 0.378 | 0.392 | 0.420 | 0.425 | 0.434 | 17 |
| Ramya Sivakumar | 0.451 | 0.365 | 0.385 | 0.399 | 0.436 | 0.451 | 0.455 | 18 |
| KEC_NL_DEP | 0.433 | 0.362 | 0.378 | 0.408 | 0.422 | 0.433 | 0.451 | 19 |
| mucs | 0.475 | 0.361 | 0.397 | 0.435 | 0.441 | 0.475 | 0.471 | 20 |
| testresult | 0.409 | 0.359 | 0.378 | 0.376 | 0.407 | 0.409 | 0.439 | 21 |
| SIS | 0.501 | 0.345 | 0.371 | 0.527 | 0.452 | 0.501 | 0.522 | 22 |
| meghaAarthi | 0.511 | 0.328 | 0.363 | 0.305 | 0.449 | 0.511 | 0.405 | 23 |
| codemonkeys | 0.409 | 0.323 | 0.398 | 0.432 | 0.368 | 0.409 | 0.470 | 24 |
| the_mavericks | 0.551 | 0.263 | 0.341 | 0.338 | 0.412 | 0.551 | 0.430 | 25 |
| Flamingos_python | 0.477 | 0.262 | 0.316 | 0.226 | 0.388 | 0.477 | 0.328 | 26 |
| KEEMS | 0.477 | 0.262 | 0.316 | 0.226 | 0.388 | 0.477 | 0.328 | 26 |
| Tercet | 0.533 | 0.259 | 0.331 | 0.591 | 0.403 | 0.533 | 0.541 | 28 |
| Techwhiz | 0.421 | 0.258 | 0.303 | 0.227 | 0.370 | 0.421 | 0.331 | 29 |
| spr | 0.407 | 0.245 | 0.287 | 0.216 | 0.356 | 0.407 | 0.318 | 30 |
| Supernova | 0.341 | 0.155 | 0.158 | 0.385 | 0.324 | 0.341 | 0.477 | 31 |

Table 3: Team Wise results


diagnosis, insights, and research directions. *Electronics*, 11(7):1111.

Amna Amanat, Muhammad Rizwan, Abdul Rehman Javed, Maha Abdelhaq, Raed Alsaqour, Sharnil Pandya, and Mueen Uddin. 2022. Deep learning for depression detection from textual data. *Electronics*, 11(5):676.

Sulaksha B K, Shruti Krishnaveni S, Ivana Steeve, and Monica Jenefer B. 2023. Detecting signs of depression from social media text. In *Proceedings of the Third Workshop on Speech and Language Technologies for Dravidian Languages*, Varna, Bulgaria. Recent Advances in Natural Language Processing.

Jaya Caporusso and Thi Hong Hanh Tran. 2023. Ensemble approaches to detect signs of depression from social media text. In *Proceedings of the Third Workshop on Speech and Language Technologies for Dravidian Languages*, Varna, Bulgaria. Recent Advances in Natural Language Processing.

Christina Christodoulou. 2023. Roberta deberta finetuning for detecting signs of depression from social media text. In *Proceedings of the Third Workshop on Speech and Language Technologies for Dravidian Languages*, Varna, Bulgaria. Recent Advances in Natural Language Processing.

Sharal Coelho, Asha Hegde, Kavya G, and Hosahalli Lakshmaiah Shashirekha. 2023. Detecting signs of depression in social media text. In *Proceedings of the Third Workshop on Speech and Language Technologies for Dravidian Languages*, Varna, Bulgaria. Recent Advances in Natural Language Processing.

Eduardo Garcia, Juliana Gomes, Adalberto Ferreira Barbosa Junior, Cardeque Henrique Bittes de Alvarenga Borges, and Nadia Félix Felipe da Silva. 2023. Detecting signs of depression from social media text. In *Proceedings of the Third Workshop on Speech and Language Technologies for Dravidian Languages*, Varna, Bulgaria. Recent Advances in Natural Language Processing.

Fernando Sánchez Vega María de Jesús García Santiago and Adrián Pastor López Monroy. 2023. Finegrain depression detection by multiple binary problems approach. In *Proceedings of the Third Workshop on Speech and Language Technologies for Dravidian Languages*, Varna, Bulgaria. Recent Advances in Natural Language Processing.

Jyoti Kumari and Abhinav Kumar. 2023. Empowering mental health assessment: A roberta-based approach for depression detection. In *Proceedings of the Third Workshop on Speech and Language Technologies for Dravidian Languages*, Varna, Bulgaria. Recent Advances in Natural Language Processing.

Kirti Kumari, Shirish Shekhar Jha, Zarikunte Kunal Dayanand, and Praneesh Sharma. 2023. Hybrid model for text classification for identification of various types of depression. In *Proceedings of the Third Workshop on Speech and Language Technologies for Dravidian Languages*, Varna, Bulgaria. Recent Advances in Natural Language Processing.

Koushik L, Hariharan R. L, and Anand Kumar M. 2023. Detecting signs of depression from social media text. In *Proceedings of the Third Workshop on Speech and*

*Language Technologies for Dravidian Languages*, Varna, Bulgaria. Recent Advances in Natural Language Processing.

Danxia Liu, Xing Lin Feng, Farooq Ahmed, Muhammad Shahid, Jing Guo, et al. 2022. Detecting and measuring depression on social media using a machine learning approach: systematic review. *JMIR Mental Health*, 9(3):e27244.

Madhumitha M, Jerin Mahibha C, and Thenmozhi Durairaj. 2023. Transformer models to detect levels of depression from social media text. In *Proceedings of the Third Workshop on Speech and Language Technologies for Dravidian Languages*, Varna, Bulgaria. Recent Advances in Natural Language Processing.

Andrew Nedilko. 2023. Detecting signs of depression with generative pretrained transformers. In *Proceedings of the Third Workshop on Speech and Language Technologies for Dravidian Languages*, Varna, Bulgaria. Recent Advances in Natural Language Processing.

Dean Ninalga. 2023. Depression detection with reddit and self-training. In *Proceedings of the Third Workshop on Speech and Language Technologies for Dravidian Languages*, Varna, Bulgaria. Recent Advances in Natural Language Processing.

Abirami P S, Amritha S, Pavithra Meganathan, and Jerin Mahibha C. 2023. An ensemble model to detect severity of depression. In *Proceedings of the Third Workshop on Speech and Language Technologies for Dravidian Languages*, Varna, Bulgaria. Recent Advances in Natural Language Processing.

Ankitha Reddy, Pranav Moorthi, and Ann Maria Thomas. 2023. Detecting signs of depression from social media text. In *Proceedings of the Third Workshop on Speech and Language Technologies for Dravidian Languages*, Varna, Bulgaria. Recent Advances in Natural Language Processing.

Kayalvizhi S and Thenmozhi D. 2022. Data set creation and empirical analysis for detecting signs of depression from social media postings. *CoRR*, abs/2202.03047.

Kayalvizhi S, Thenmozhi Durairaj, Bharathi Raja Chakravarthi, and Jerin Mahibha C. 2022. Findings of the shared task on detecting signs of depression from social media. In *Proceedings of the Second Workshop on Language Technology for Equality, Diversity and Inclusion*, pages 331–338, Dublin, Ireland. Association for Computational Linguistics.

V S Sathvika, S Vaishnavi, S Angel Deborah, S Rajalakshmi, and T T Mirnalinee. 2023. Detection of signs of depression from social media text quotes using navie bayse approach. In *Proceedings of the Third Workshop on Speech and Language Technologies for Dravidian Languages*, Varna, Bulgaria. Recent Advances in Natural Language Processing.

Kogilavani Shanmugavadivel, Malliga Subramanian, Vasatharan K, Prethish GA, Sankar S, and Sabari S. 2023. Detecting signs of depression from social media texts. In *Proceedings of the Third Workshop on Speech and Language Technologies for Dravidian Languages*, Varna, Bulgaria. Recent Advances in Natural Language Processing.

Rajalakshmi Sivanaiah, Venkatasai Ojus Yenumulapalli, Vijai Aravindh R, and Angel Deborah S. 2023. Depression detection and classification using bert model for social media texts. In *Proceedings of the Third Workshop on Speech and Language Technologies for Dravidian Languages*, Varna, Bulgaria. Recent Advances in Natural Language Processing.

Vajratiya Vajrobol, Nitisha Aggarwal, and Karanpreet Singh. 2023. Leveraging pre-trained transformers for fine-grained depression level detection in social media. In *Proceedings of the Third Workshop on Speech and Language Technologies for Dravidian Languages*, Varna, Bulgaria. Recent Advances in Natural Language Processing.

# Overview of the Second Shared Task on Speech Recognition for Vulnerable Individuals in Tamil

**B. Bharathi**[1], **Bharathi Raja Chakravarthi**[2],
**Subalalitha C N**[3], **N. Sripriya**[1], **Rajeswari Natarajan**[4], **S. Suhasini**[1], **Swetha Valli**[5]
[1]SSN College of Engineering
[2]National University of Ireland Galway
[3]SRM Institute Of Science And Technology
[4]Thiagarajar College of Engineering
[5]SASTRA University, India
bharathib@ssn.edu.in, bharathiraja.akr@gmail.com

## Abstract

This paper manifests the overview of the shared task on Speech Recognition for Vulnerable individuals in Tamil(LT-EDI-ACL2023). The task is provided with a Tamil dataset, which is collected from elderly people of three different genders, male, female, and transgender. The audio samples were recorded from public locations like hospitals, markets, vegetable shops, etc. The dataset is released in two phases, the training and the testing phase. The participants were asked to use different models and methods to handle audio signals and submit the result as transcription of the test samples given. The result submitted by the participants was evaluated using WER (Word Error Rate). The participants used the transformer-based model for automatic speech recognition. The results and different pre-trained transformer-based models used by the participants are discussed in this overview paper.

## 1 Introduction

The earliest Old Tamil documents are small inscriptions in Adichanallur dating from 905 BC to 696 BC. Tamil has the oldest ancient non-Sanskritic Indian literature of any Indian language. Tamil uses agglutinative grammar, which uses suffixes to indicate noun class, number, case, verb tense, and other grammatical categories. Tamil's standard metalinguistic terminology and scholarly vocabulary is itself Tamil, as opposed to the Sanskrit that is standard for most Aryan languages. Tamil has many forms, in addition to dialects: a classical literary style based on the ancient language (cankattami), a modern literary and formal style (centami), and a current colloquial form (kotuntami) (Sakuntharaj and Mahesan, 2021, 2017). These styles blend into one another, creating a stylistic continuity. It is conceivable, for example, to write centami using cankattami vocabulary, or to utilize forms connected with one of the other varieties while speaking kotuntami (Srinivasan and Subalalitha, 2019; Narasimhan et al., 2018). Tamil words are made up of a lexical root and one or more affixes. The majority of Tamil affixes are suffixes. Tamil suffixes are either derivational suffixes, which modify the part of speech or meaning of the word, or inflectional suffixes, which designate categories like as person, number, mood, tense, and so on. There is no ultimate limit to the length and scope of agglutination, which might result in large words with several suffixes, requiring many words or a sentence in English. Smart technologies have advanced significantly, and they are still developing and improving human-machine connection(Chakravarthi et al., 2020). One such modern technology is automatic speech recognition (ASR), which has made it possible for many automated systems to have voice-based user interfaces. The technology that are facilitated to assist individuals (Hämäläinen et al., 2015) in public spaces like banks, hospitals, and administrative offices are often unknown to many elderly and transgender persons. Therefore, the only media that could help them meet their demands is communication. However, the elderly, transsexual, and less educated persons rarely use these ASR systems. The majority of the automated systems in use today include voice-based interfaces that are available in English. People in rural areas and the elderly prefer to communicate in their own language. All people would benefit if the assistance systems created for use in public spaces could be equipped with speech interfaces in the local tongue. The data on spontaneous speech in Tamil is collected from elderly and transgender individuals who are deprived of the opportunity to take benefit of these services.Finding an effective ASR model to handle the elderly persons speech corpus is the goal of this task. The representation of how the audio samples are collected is shown in



*LT-EDI 2023 – Third Workshop on Language Technology for Equality, Diversity and Inclusion*, pages 31–37, Varna, Bulgaria, Sep 7, 2023.
https://doi.org/10.26615/978-954-452-084-7_005

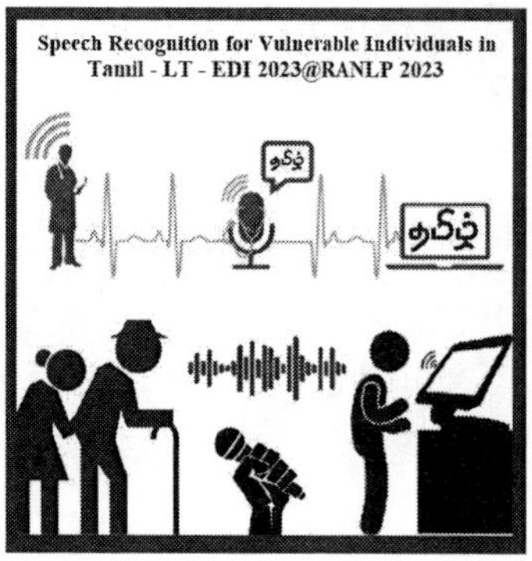


Figure 1: Speech corpus collected from vulnerable individuals in Tamil language

Fig:1

An ASR system will initially extract the relevant features from speech signal. These extracted features will also be used to generate acoustic models. Finally, the language model helps to turn these probabilities into words of coherent language. The language model, assigns probabilities to words and phrases based on statistics from training data(Das et al., 2011). Before using ASR systems in real-time applications, their performance must be assessed. An end-to-end speech recognition system has demonstrated promising performance on large-scale automatic speech recognition (ASR) tasks, placing it on par with conventional hybrid systems. The end-to-end system converts acoustic data into tag labels instantly using an acoustic model, lexicon, and language model(Zeng et al., 2021; Pérez-Espinosa et al., 2017). There are two widely used frameworks in the area of end-to-end speech recognition. Frame synchronous prediction, which assigns one target label to each input frame, distinguishes one from the other(Miao et al., 2020; Xue et al., 2021; Miao et al., 2019; Watanabe et al., 2017). With alternative test feature vectors and model settings, the effectiveness can also be evaluated in terms of phoneme recognition. The ability to recognise senior speech may be significantly influenced by the use of acoustic models for speech recognition, which are produced using the voices of younger persons(Fukuda et al., 2020; Zeng et al., 2020; Iribe et al., 2015). Few acoustic models have been developed to perform the voice recognition problem. Japanese Newspaper Article Sentences (JNAS), Japanese Newspaper Article Sentences Read Speech Corpus of the Aged (S-JNAS), and Corpus of Spontaneous Japanes (CSJ) are a few examples of the acoustic models. All of the acoustic models are compared in the literature, and it is discovered that the CSJ model only obtains the lowest WER after the adaption of the elderly voices(Fukuda et al., 2020). The same goes for dialect adaptation, which is necessary to increase recognition accuracy(Fukuda et al., 2019). Speech recognition systems are now widely used in a range of fields as a result of recent advancements in large vocabulary continuous speech recognition (LVCSR) technologies(Xue et al., 2021). One of the main reasons for the fall in speech recognition rates is assumed to be variances in the acoustics of different speakers. The acoustic differences between the speech of senior speakers and those of a typical adult should be examined and appropriately adjusted in order for older speakers to use speech recognition systems trained on normal adult speech data. Instead, as demonstrated by a document retrieval system, an acoustic model improved using utterances of senior speakers can lessen this degradation. Using cutting-edge voice recognition technology, high recognition accuracy can be achieved for speech reading a written text or anything similar; nevertheless, the accuracy declines for freely uttered spontaneous speech. The primary cause of this problem is that read speech or written language texts were predominantly used in the development of the acoustic and linguistic models used in speech recognition. However, both linguistically and acoustically, spontaneous speech and written language differ greatly(Zeng et al., 2020).

Creating ASR systems to recognise elderly people's voice data is becoming increasingly commonplace today. The need to improve voice recognition in smart devices has arisen as a result of the ageing population in contemporary society and the expansion of smart gadgets, allowing both the elderly and the younger generations to easily access information(Kwon et al., 2016; Vacher et al., 2015; Hossain et al., 2017; Teixeira et al., 2014). Speech recognition systems are frequently optimised for an average adult's voice and have a reduced accuracy rate when recognising an elderly person's voice due to the effects of speech articulation and speaking style. The cost of modifying the already existing voice recognition systems to handle the speech of older users will undoubtedly increases(Kwon et al., 2016).

## 2 Task Description

This shared task tackles a difficult problem in Automatic Speech Recognition: vulnerable elderly and transgender individuals in Tamil. People in their senior years go to primary places such as banks, hospitals, and administrative offices to meet their daily needs. Many elderly persons are unsure of how to use the devices provided to assist them. Similarly, because transgender persons are denied access to primary education as a result of societal discrimination, speech is the only channel via which they may meet their needs. The data on spontaneous speech is collected from elderly and transgender people who are unable to take advantage of these services. For the training set, a speech corpus containing 5.5 hours of transcribed speech will be released, as well as 2 hours of speech data for testing test. The participants have to submit the text transcriptions for the test utterances in a separate text file.

## 3 Related Work

When a model is fine-tuned on many languages at the same time, a single multilingual speech recognition model can be built that can compete with models that are fine-tuned on individual language speech corpus. Speech2Vec expands the text-based Word2Vec model to learn word embeddings directly from speech by combining an RNN Encoder-Decoder framework with skipgrams or cbow for training. Acoustic models are designed at phoneme/syllable level to carry out the speech recognition task. Initially, the acoustic models were created with JNAS, S-JNAS and CSJ speech corpus(Lin and Yu, 2015; Iribe et al., 2015). Later, the models were trained/fine-tuned with different speech corpus. To get a better performance and accuracy, backpropagation using the transfer learning was attempted in the literature. Similar work was performed for other languages like Bengali, Japanese, etc. Also, more speech corpus is collected from the young people for many languages(Zeng et al., 2020; Lee et al., 2021). However, speaker fluctuation, environmental noise, and transmission channel noise all degrade ASR performance. As the shared task is given with a separate training data set, an effective model has to be created during the training. Therefore, hierarchical transformer based model for large context end to end ASR can be used (Masumura et al., 2021). In the recent era, the environment is changing with smart systems and is identified that there is a need for ASR systems that are capable of handling speech of elderly people spoken in their native languages. To overcome this problem, the shared task is proposed for the research community to build an efficient model for recognizing the speech of elderly people and transgenders in Tamil language. Findings of the automatic speech recognition for vulnerable individuals are given in (S and B, 2022) (B et al., 2022), have used transformer models used for transformer based ASR for Vulnerable Individuals in Tamil.

## 4 Data-set Description

The dataset given to this shared task (Bharathi et al., 2022) is an Tamil conversational speech recorded from the elderly people whose average age is around 61 for male, 59 for female and 30 for transgender people which are tabulated in Table 1 . A total of 6 hours and 42 minutes is collected from the elderly people. 46 audio files were recorded and each audio file is split into many subsets as transformer model does not support the large audio files. The speech is recorded with a sampling rate of 16KHZ. The audio files from Audio - 1 to Audio - 36 are used for training (duration is approximately 5.5 hours) and Audio - 37 to Audio - 47 are used for testing (duration is approximately 2 hours).

## 5 Methodology

The methodology used by the participants in shared task of speech recognition for vulnerable individuals in Tamil is discussed in this section. Three teams submitted their runs for this task. Different types of pre-trained transformer models used by the participants in this shared task are as follows:

- IIT Madras transformer ASR model - It is work based on espnet.nets.pytorch backend.e2e asr transformer:E2Eself-attention mechanism[1]
- anuragshas/wav2vec2-xlsr-53-tamil [2]
- Amrrs/wav2vec2-large-xlsr-53-tamil [3]

The above mentioned second and third models are fine tuned on facebook/wav2vec-large-xlsr-53 [4] pre-trained model using multilingual common

[1] https://asr.iitm.ac.in/demo/

[2] https://huggingface.co/anuragshas/wav2vec2-xlsr-53-tamil

[3] https://huggingface.co/Amrrs/wav2vec2-large-xlsr-53-tamil

[4] https://huggingface.co/facebook/wav2vec2-large-xlsr-53

Table 1: Age, gender and duration of the utterances in speech corpus

| S.No | Filename | Gender | Age | Duration(in secs) |
|---|---|---|---|---|
| 1 | Audio - 1 | M | 72 | 10 |
| 2 | Audio - 2 | F | 61 | 9 |
| 3 | Audio - 3 | F | 71 | 11 |
| 4 | Audio - 4 | M | 68 | 8 |
| 5 | Audio - 5 | F | 59 | 14 |
| 6 | Audio - 6 | F | 67 | 9 |
| 7 | Audio - 7 | M | 54 | 8 |
| 8 | Audio - 8 | F | 65 | 16 |
| 9 | Audio - 9 | F | 55 | 3 |
| 10 | Audio - 10 | M | 60 | 13 |
| 11 | Audio - 11 | F | 55 | 17 |
| 12 | Audio - 12 | F | 52 | 6 |
| 13 | Audio - 13 | F | 53 | 11 |
| 14 | Audio - 14 | F | 61 | 9 |
| 15 | Audio - 15 | F | 54 | 1 |
| 16 | Audio - 16 | F | 56 | 6 |
| 17 | Audio - 17 | F | 52 | 12 |
| 18 | Audio - 18 | F | 54 | 6 |
| 19 | Audio - 19 | F | 52 | 8 |
| 20 | Audio - 20 | F | 52 | 9 |
| 21 | Audio - 21 | F | 62 | 13 |
| 22 | Audio - 22 | F | 52 | 12 |
| 23 | Audio - 23 | F | 62 | 13 |
| 24 | Audio - 24 | F | 53 | 4 |
| 25 | Audio - 25 | F | 65 | 3 |
| 26 | Audio - 26 | F | 64 | 8 |
| 27 | Audio - 27 | F | 54 | 6 |
| 28 | Audio - 28 | M | 62 | 8 |
| 29 | Audio - 29 | M | 54 | 16 |
| 30 | Audio - 30 | F | 76 | 9 |
| 31 | Audio - 31 | F | 55 | 9 |
| 32 | Audio - 32 | M | 50 | 6 |
| 33 | Audio - 33 | F | 63 | 6 |
| 34 | Audio - 34 | M | 84 | 6 |
| 35 | Audio - 35 | F | 70 | 6 |
| 36 | Audio - 36 | F | 50 | 6 |
| 37 | Audio - 37 | M | 53 | 6 |
| 38 | Audio - 38 | F | 55 | 6 |
| 39 | Audio - 39 | M | 62 | 6 |
| 40 | Audio - 40 | T | 24 | 6 |
| 41 | Audio - 41 | T | 22 | 7 |
| 42 | Audio - 42 | T | 40 | 8 |
| 43 | Audio - 43 | T | 25 | 11 |
| 44 | Audio - 44 | T | 29 | 10 |
| 45 | Audio - 45 | T | 35 | 9 |
| 46 | Audio - 46 | T | 33 | 16 |

| S. No | Team Name | WER (in %) |
|---|---|---|
| 1 | SANBAR_CSE_SSN ("S and B, "2023"a) | 37.7144 |
| 2 | ASR_SSN_CSE_2023 ("S and B, "2023"b) | 39.8091 |
| 3 | CSE_Speech ("Balaji et al., "2023") | 40.7562 |

Table 2: Results of the participating systems in Word Error Rate

voice dataset. To fine-tune the model, they had a classifier representing the downstreams task's output vocabulary on top of it and train it with a Connectionist Temporal Classification (CTC) loss on the labelled data. The models used are based on XLSR wav2vec model, this XLSR model is capable of learning cross-lingual speech data, where the raw speech waveform is converted to multiple languages by pre-training a single model.

## 6 Evaluation of Results

The results submitted by the participants are evaluated based on the WER computed between the ASR hypotheses submitted by the participants and the ground truth of human speech transcription.

WER ( Word Error Rate) = ( S + D + I) / N

where,
S = No. of substitutions
D = No. of deletions
I = No. of insertions
N = No. of words in the reference transcription

As discussed in the methodology, different average word error rate are measured using various pre-trained transformer based models.

Performance of the ASR submitted by the participants are tabulated in Table 2. From Table 2, IIT Madras transformer ASR model is work based on espnet.nets.pytorch backend.e2e asr transformer:E2Eself- attention mechanism model produces less WER compared to other models.

## 7 Conclusion

The shared challenge for vulnerable voice recognition in Tamil is covered in this overview paper. The speech corpus shared for this job was recorded from elderly persons. Getting older people's speech more accurately recognised is a difficult endeavour. In order to boost the accuracy and performance in recognising the elderly people's speech, the participants have been given access to the gathered speech corpus. There were two people that participated in this joint task and turned in their transcripts of the supplied data. The team estimated the WER and then compared the outcome to the human transcripts. Both participants built their recognition systems using various transformer-based models. Finally, the word error rates of the three participants are 37.7144, 39.8091 & 40.7462 respectively. Based on the observations, it is suggested that the transformer based model can be trained with given speech corpus which could give a better accuracy than the pre-trained model, as the transformer based model used are trained with common voice dataset. Also, a separate language model can also be created for this corpus.

## References


Bharathi B, Dhanya Srinivasan, Josephine Varsha, Thenmozhi Durairaj, and Senthil Kumar B. 2022. SSNCSE_NLP@LT-EDI-ACL2022:hope speech detection for equality, diversity and inclusion using sentence transformers. In *Proceedings of the Second Workshop on Language Technology for Equality, Diversity and Inclusion*, pages 218–222, Dublin, Ireland. Association for Computational Linguistics.

Varsha "Balaji, Archana J P, and Bharathi" B. "2023". "cse_speech@lt-edi-2023:automatic speech recognition: Vulnerable old-aged and transgender people in tamil". In *"Proceedings of the Third Workshop on Speech and Language Technologies for Dravidian Languages"*, "Varna, Bulgaria ". "Recent Advances in Natural Language Processing".

B Bharathi, Bharathi Raja Chakravarthi, Subalalitha Chinnaudayar Navaneethakrishnan, N Sripriya, Arunaggiri Pandian, and Swetha Valli. 2022. Findings of the shared task on Speech Recognition for Vulnerable Individuals in Tamil. In *Proceedings of the Second Workshop on Language Technology for Equality, Diversity and Inclusion*. Association for Computational Linguistics.

Bharathi Raja Chakravarthi, Ruba Priyadharshini, Vigneshwaran Muralidaran, Shardul Suryawanshi, Navya Jose, Elizabeth Sherly, and John P McCrae. 2020. Overview of the track on sentiment analysis for Dravidian languages in code-mixed text. In *Forum for Information Retrieval Evaluation*, pages 21–24.

Biswajit Das, Sandipan Mandal, and Pabitra Mitra. 2011. Bengali speech corpus for continuous auutomatic speech recognition system. In *2011 International conference on speech database and assessments (Oriental COCOSDA)*, pages 51–55. IEEE.

Meiko Fukuda, Ryota Nishimura, Hiromitsu Nishizaki, Yurie Iribe, and Norihide Kitaoka. 2019. A new corpus of elderly japanese speech for acoustic modeling, and a preliminary investigation of dialect-dependent speech recognition. In *2019 22nd Conference of the Oriental COCOSDA International Committee for the Co-ordination and Standardisation of Speech Databases and Assessment Techniques (O-COCOSDA)*, pages 1–6. IEEE.

Meiko Fukuda, Hiromitsu Nishizaki, Yurie Iribe, Ryota Nishimura, and Norihide Kitaoka. 2020. Improving speech recognition for the elderly: A new corpus of elderly japanese speech and investigation of acoustic modeling for speech recognition. In *Proceedings of the 12th Language Resources and Evaluation Conference*, pages 6578–6585.

Annika Hämäläinen, António Teixeira, Nuno Almeida, Hugo Meinedo, Tibor Fegyó, and Miguel Sales Dias. 2015. Multilingual speech recognition for the elderly: The aalfred personal life assistant. *Procedia Computer Science*, 67:283–292.

M Shamim Hossain, Md Abdur Rahman, and Ghulam Muhammad. 2017. Cyber–physical cloud-oriented multi-sensory smart home framework for elderly people: An energy efficiency perspective. *Journal of Parallel and Distributed Computing*, 103:11–21.

Yurie Iribe, Norihide Kitaoka, and Shuhei Segawa. 2015. Development of new speech corpus for elderly japanese speech recognition. In *2015 International Conference Oriental COCOSDA held jointly with 2015 Conference on Asian Spoken Language Research and Evaluation (O-COCOSDA/CASLRE)*, pages 27–31. IEEE.

Soonil Kwon, Sung-Jae Kim, and Joon Yeon Choeh. 2016. Preprocessing for elderly speech recognition of smart devices. *Computer Speech & Language*, 36:110–121.

Taewoo Lee, Min-Joong Lee, Tae Gyoon Kang, Seokyeoung Jung, Minseok Kwon, Yeona Hong, Jungin Lee, Kyoung-Gu Woo, Ho-Gyeong Kim, Jiseung Jeong, et al. 2021. Adaptable multi-domain language model for transformer asr. In *ICASSP 2021-2021 IEEE International Conference on Acoustics, Speech and Signal Processing (ICASSP)*, pages 7358–7362. IEEE.

Hui Lin and Yibiao Yu. 2015. Acoustic feature analysis and conversion of age speech. In *IET Conference Proceedings*. The Institution of Engineering & Technology.

Ryo Masumura, Naoki Makishima, Mana Ihori, Akihiko Takashima, Tomohiro Tanaka, and Shota Orihashi. 2021. Hierarchical transformer-based large-context end-to-end asr with large-context knowledge distillation. In *ICASSP 2021-2021 IEEE International Conference on Acoustics, Speech and Signal Processing (ICASSP)*, pages 5879–5883. IEEE.

Haoran Miao, Gaofeng Cheng, Changfeng Gao, Pengyuan Zhang, and Yonghong Yan. 2020. Transformer-based online ctc/attention end-to-end speech recognition architecture. In *ICASSP 2020-2020 IEEE International Conference on Acoustics, Speech and Signal Processing (ICASSP)*, pages 6084–6088. IEEE.

Haoran Miao, Gaofeng Cheng, Pengyuan Zhang, Ta Li, and Yonghong Yan. 2019. Online hybrid ctc/attention architecture for end-to-end speech recognition. In *Interspeech*, pages 2623–2627.

Anitha Narasimhan, Aarthy Anandan, Madhan Karky, and CN Subalalitha. 2018. Porul: Option generation and selection and scoring algorithms for a tamil flash card game. *International Journal of Cognitive and Language Sciences*, 12(2):225–228.

Humberto Pérez-Espinosa, Juan Martínez-Miranda, Ismael Espinosa-Curiel, Josefina Rodríguez-Jacobo, and Himer Avila-George. 2017. Using acoustic paralinguistic information to assess the interaction quality in speech-based systems for elderly users. *International Journal of Human-Computer Studies*, 98:1–13.

Saranya "S and Bharathi" B. "2023"a. "sanbar@lt-edi-2023:automatic speech recognition: vulnerable old-aged and transgender people in tamil". In *"Proceedings of the Third Workshop on Speech and Language Technologies for Dravidian Languages"*, "Varna, Bulgaria ". "Recent Advances in Natural Language Processing".

Suhasini S and Bharathi B. 2022. SUH_ASR@LT-EDI-ACL2022: Transformer based approach for speech recognition for vulnerable individuals in Tamil. In *Proceedings of the Second Workshop on Language Technology for Equality, Diversity and Inclusion*, pages 177–182, Dublin, Ireland. Association for Computational Linguistics.

Suhasini "S and Bharathi" B. "2023"b. "asr_ssn_cse 2023@lt-edi-2023: Pretrained transformer based automatic speech recognition system for elderly people". In *Proceedings of the Third Workshop on Speech and Language Technologies for Dravidian Languages*, "Varna, Bulgaria ". "Recent Advances in Natural Language Processing".

Ratnasingam Sakuntharaj and Sinnathamby Mahesan. 2017. Use of a novel hash-table for speeding-up suggestions for misspelt Tamil words. In *2017 IEEE International Conference on Industrial and Information Systems (ICIIS)*, pages 1–5.

Ratnasingam Sakuntharaj and Sinnathamby Mahesan. 2021. Missing word detection and correction based on context of Tamil sentences using n-grams. In

*2021 10th International Conference on Information and Automation for Sustainability (ICIAfS)*, pages 42–47.

R Srinivasan and CN Subalalitha. 2019. Automated named entity recognition from tamil documents. In *2019 IEEE 1st International Conference on Energy, Systems and Information Processing (ICESIP)*, pages 1–5. IEEE.

António Teixeira, Annika Hämäläinen, Jairo Avelar, Nuno Almeida, Géza Németh, Tibor Fegyó, Csaba Zainkó, Tamás Csapó, Bálint Tóth, André Oliveira, et al. 2014. Speech-centric multimodal interaction for easy-to-access online services–a personal life assistant for the elderly. *Procedia computer science*, 27:389–397.

Michel Vacher, Frédéric Aman, Solange Rossato, and François Portet. 2015. Development of automatic speech recognition techniques for elderly home support: Applications and challenges. In *International Conference on Human Aspects of IT for the Aged Population*, pages 341–353. Springer.

Shinji Watanabe, Takaaki Hori, Suyoun Kim, John R Hershey, and Tomoki Hayashi. 2017. Hybrid ctc/attention architecture for end-to-end speech recognition. *IEEE Journal of Selected Topics in Signal Processing*, 11(8):1240–1253.

Jiabin Xue, Tieran Zheng, and Jiqing Han. 2021. Exploring attention mechanisms based on summary information for end-to-end automatic speech recognition. *Neurocomputing*, 465:514–524.

Jiazhong Zeng, Jianxin Peng, and Yuezhe Zhao. 2020. Comparison of speech intelligibility of elderly aged 60–69 years and young adults in the noisy and reverberant environment. *Applied Acoustics*, 159:107096.

Zhiping Zeng, Haihua Xu, Yerbolat Khassanov, Eng Siong Chng, Chongjia Ni, Bin Ma, et al. 2021. Leveraging text data using hybrid transformer-lstm based end-to-end asr in transfer learning. In *2021 12th International Symposium on Chinese Spoken Language Processing (ISCSLP)*, pages 1–5. IEEE.

# Overview of Second Shared Task on Homophobia and Transphobia Detection in Social Media Comments

**Bharathi Raja Chakravarthi**[1], **Rahul Ponnusamy**[2], **Malliga Subramanian**[3]
**Paul Buitelaar**[2], **Miguel Ángel García-Cumbreras**[4], **Salud María Jiménez-Zafra**[4],
**José Antonio García-Díaz**[5], **Rafael Valencia-García**[5] **Nitesh Jindal**[6]
[1] School of Computer Science, University of Galway, Ireland
[2] Insight SFI Research Centre for Data Analytics, University of Galway, Ireland
[3] Kongu Engineering College, Tamil Nadu, India [4] Universidad de Jaén, Spain
[5] Universidad de Murcia, Spain [6] University of Galway, Ireland
bharathi.raja@universityofgalway.ie

## Abstract

We present an overview of the second shared task on homophobia/transphobia Detection in social media comments. Given a comment, a system must predict whether or not it contains any form of homophobia/transphobia. The shared task included five languages: English, Spanish, Tamil, Hindi, and Malayalam. The data was given for two tasks. Task A was given three labels, and Task B fine-grained seven labels. In total, 75 teams enrolled for the shared task in Codalab. For Task A, 10 teams submitted systems for English, 7 for Tamil, 4 for Spanish, 7 for Malayalam, and seven teams for Hindi. For Task B, 8 teams were submitted for English, 7 for Tamil, and 6 for Malayalam. We present and analyze all submissions in this paper.

## 1 Introduction

A victim, an aggressor, and bully-victims are all necessary components of the aggressive behavior known as bullying (Colvin et al., 1998). Students, parents, teachers, and administrators all share a considerable concern with the phenomenon of bullying that is motivated by homophobia (Horn et al., 2009; Wright et al., 1999; Basile et al., 2009). The unfavorable views, attitudes, prejudices, and behaviors that are held towards sexual minorities are what are referred to as homophobia (Hong and Garbarino, 2012). Homophobia is the underlying mentality that plays a contributing role in the practice of discrimination against LGBTQ+ vulnerable individuals (Alichie, 2022).

The fact that the most prevalent definition of homophobia is "an attitude of hostility toward male or female LGBTQI+ vulnerable individuals" implies that this idea is rather narrow and has a tendency to individualize the process of discrimination and rejection(Herek, 1988). The Internet is a tool that LGBTQI+ vulnerable young individuals in regional, remote, and rural areas use to overcome isolation and construct relationships that extend beyond the physical limitations of a geographic area by commenting on YouTube videos or reaching out via Twitter or other means in social media (Venzo and Hess, 2013; Soriano, 2014; Han et al., 2019a; Chakravarthi, 2023). Since social media is used by vulnerable individuals, it should be without homophobic/transphobic bullying or other hate speech against LGBTQ+ vulnerable individuals (Han et al., 2019b; Rokhmansyah et al., 2021; Ștefăniță and Buf, 2021). To tackle homophobia and transphobia in social media, Chakravarthi et al. (2022a) introduced a new dataset in English, Tamil, and Tamil-English. Chakravarthi et al. (2022b) conducted new shared tasks in Tamil, English, and Tamil-English (code-mixed) languages. It received 10 Tamil systems, 13 English systems, and 11 Tamil-English systems. The average macro F1-score for the top systems for Tamil, English, and Tamil-English was 0.570, 0.877, and 0.610, respectively. Chinnaudayar Navaneethakrishnan et al. (2023) conducted a shared task on Sentiment Analysis and Homophobia Detection; in that task, new language data, Malayalam, was added. In our task[1], We conducted two sub-tasks: Task A and Task B. We included English, Tamil, Spanish, Malayalam, and Hindi for Task A and English, Tamil, and Malayalam for Task B. Overall submission of eleven teams that participated in Task A and eight teams that participated in Task B. The Weighted F1 scores of top-performing models for these languages are 0.888, 0.997, 0.979, 0.969, and 0.949. For Task B, we included English, Tamil, and Malayalam; the top-performing model scored with weighted F1 scores of 0.822, 0.884, and 0.865.

[1] https://codalab.lisn.upsaclay.fr/competitions/11077



*LT-EDI 2023 – Third Workshop on Language Technology for Equality, Diversity and Inclusion*, pages 38–46, Varna, Bulgaria, Sep 7, 2023.
https://doi.org/10.26615/978-954-452-084-7_006

| set | H | T | N | Total |
|---|---|---|---|---|
| **Training** | 179 | 7 | 2,978 | 3,164 |
| **Dev** | 42 | 748 | 2 | 792 |
| **Test** | 55 | 4 | 931 | 990 |
| **Total** | 276 | 759 | 3,911 | 4,946 |

Table 1: Statistics for the Task A English Dataset (H stands for Homophobia, T for Transphobia, and N for Non-anti-LGBT+ content)

| set | H | T | N | Total |
|---|---|---|---|---|
| **Training** | 453 | 145 | 2,064 | 2,662 |
| **Dev** | 118 | 41 | 507 | 666 |
| **Test** | 152 | 47 | 634 | 833 |
| **Total** | 723 | 233 | 3,205 | 4,161 |

Table 2: Statistics for the Task A Tamil Dataset (H stands for Homophobia, T for Transphobia, and N for Non-anti-LGBT+ content)

| set | H | T | N | Total |
|---|---|---|---|---|
| **Training** | 476 | 170 | 2,468 | 3,114 |
| **Dev** | 197 | 79 | 937 | 1,213 |
| **Test** | 140 | 52 | 674 | 866 |
| **Total** | 813 | 301 | 4,079 | 5,193 |

Table 3: Statistics for the Task A Malayalam Dataset (H stands for Homophobia, T for Transphobia, and N for Non-anti-LGBT+ content)

| set | H | T | N | Total |
|---|---|---|---|---|
| **Training** | 92 | 45 | 2,423 | 2,560 |
| **Dev** | 13 | 2 | 305 | 320 |
| **Test** | 10 | 3 | 308 | 321 |
| **Total** | 115 | 50 | 3,036 | 3,201 |

Table 4: Statistics for the Task A Hindi Dataset (H stands for Homophobia, T for Transphobia, and N for Non-anti-LGBT+ content)

| set | H | T | N | Total |
|---|---|---|---|---|
| **Training** | 200 | 200 | 450 | 850 |
| **Dev** | 43 | 43 | 150 | 236 |
| **Test** | 100 | 100 | 300 | 500 |
| **Total** | 343 | 343 | 900 | 1,586 |

Table 5: Statistics for the Spanish Dataset (H stands for Homophobic, T for Transphobic, and N for None)

## 2 Task description

This is a classification task at the level of comments and posts. When presented with YouTube comments, the algorithms that the participants have developed should categorize it. Participants were given sentences in the comment section that were taken from social media. It is the responsibility of the participant's system to determine, given a comment, whether or not it contains any type of homophobia or transphobia. In order to determine whether the text contains homophobia or transphobia, the comments have been manually annotated. We divided the task into two subtasks: A and B.

### 2.1 Task A

In this task, participants were given a dataset with three labels. As a result, the participants' system must categorize the contents as homophobia, transphobia, or non-anti-LGBT+ content. The training, development, and test datasets for the following languages were given to the participants: English, Spanish, Hindi, Tamil, or Malayalam.

### 2.2 Task B

In this task, the participants were provided with the dataset with 7 labels. The participants' system needs to categorize the text into Homophobic-derogation, Homophobic-Threatening, Transphobic-derogation, Transphobic-Threatening, Hope-Speech, Counter-speech, and None-of-the-above. The participants were provided with the training, development, and test datasets for the following languages: English, Tamil, and Malayalam.

## 3 Dataset

### 3.1 Tamil, Malayalam, Hindi, and English Dataset

The comments were gathered using a tool known as the YouTube Comment Scraper[2]. These comments

[2] https://pypi.org/project/youtube-comment-scraper-python/

| set | HD | HT | TD | TT | CS | HS | N | total |
|---|---|---|---|---|---|---|---|---|
| **Training** | 167 | 12 | 6 | 1 | 302 | 436 | 2,240 | 3,164 |
| **Dev** | 41 | 1 | 2 | 0 | 84 | 111 | 553 | 792 |
| **Test** | 54 | 1 | 3 | 1 | 100 | 140 | 691 | 990 |
| **Total** | 262 | 14 | 11 | 2 | 486 | 687 | 3,484 | 4,946 |

Table 6: Statistics for the Task B English Dataset (HD stands for Homophobic-derogation, HT for Homophobic-Threatening, TD for Transphobic-derogation, TT for Transphob)

| set | HD | HT | TD | TT | CS | HS | N | total |
|---|---|---|---|---|---|---|---|---|
| **Training** | 416 | 37 | 111 | 34 | 212 | 218 | 1,634 | 2,662 |
| **Dev** | 107 | 11 | 31 | 10 | 60 | 52 | 395 | 666 |
| **Test** | 138 | 14 | 28 | 19 | 64 | 65 | 505 | 833 |
| **Total** | 661 | 62 | 170 | 63 | 336 | 335 | 2534 | 4,161 |

Table 7: Statistics for the Task B Tamil Dataset (HD stands for Homophobic-derogation, HT for Homophobic-Threatening, TD for Transphobic-derogation, TT for Transphob)

were utilized by us in the process of manually annotating our datasets. We collected Tamil, Malayalam, Hindi, and English from YouTube videos selected by us. However, we discovered that the text contained a substantial quantity of English in addition to a variety of other languages. The presence of responses written in languages other than the target language made the already challenging task of extracting pertinent text from the comment section more difficult. As part of the preparatory operations for data cleansing, we used langdetect library[3] to distinguish between distinct languages and separate them into their own categories. We separated the data into three distinct sections, including English and Tamil. The remaining code-mixed Tamil and English were maintained. For Hindi and Malayalam, we discarded all other comments, including comments in English; we only took Hindi and Malayalam comments from those videos. To comply with the regulations governing the preservation of user data, we removed all user-related information from the corpus. In order to better prepare for the exam, we eliminated any unnecessary information, including URLs. We manually annotated them into three labels and seven labels according to our guidelines with the help of trained annotators. The data statistics for Task A and B of all languages are shown in Tables 1, 2, 3, 4, 6, 7, and 8.

### 3.2 Spanish Dataset

The Spanish dataset is composed of a set of tweets collected using the UMUCorpusClassifier tool (García-Díaz et al., 2020), which allows for defining different search criteria such as keywords, accounts, and geolocation. The keywords used to collect tweets related to transphobia were: #transfobia (*#transphobia*), trans (*trans*), transexual (*transsexual*), transgénero (*transgender*), identidad de género (*gender identity*) and androginia (*androgyny*). Regarding homophobia, the words selected were: #homofobia (*#homophobia*), homosexual (*homosexual*), #AlertaHomofobia (*#HomophobiaAlert*), marica (*queer*), lesbiana (*lesbian*), maricones (*fags*), maricona (*fag*), bolleras (*dykes*), gay (*gay*), afeminado (*effeminate*), petar AND (culo OR ojete) (*butt-fucking*) and #StopLGTBIfobia *#StopLGTBIphobia*. In addition, for the latter, words related to the murder of the Samuel Luiz[4] were added: samuel luiz (*samuel luiz*), asesinato de samuel (*samuel murder*), asesinos de samuel (*samuel killers*), muerte de samuel (*samuel death*), #samuel (*#samuel*), el chico de galicia (*the boy from galicia*), #Justiciaparasamuel (*#justiceforsamuel*). In total, it was retrieved 473,191 tweets for homophobia and 451,565 for transphobia. From this collection of tweets, we discarded those tweets with short length and retweets. A subset of the collected tweets was manually labeled by organizers of the shared task to determine which were really related to homophobia, which to transphobia, and which to neither, as it is not possible to rely on keywords in the texts for the annotation. Finally, for the shared task, it was selected a total of 1,586 tweets that were distributed in development, train-

[3]https://pypi.org/project/langdetect/

[4]https://es.wikipedia.org/wiki/Asesinato_de_Samuel_Luiz

| set | HD | HT | TD | TT | CS | HS | N | total |
|---|---|---|---|---|---|---|---|---|
| **Training** | 419 | 57 | 163 | 7 | 152 | 69 | 2,247 | 3,114 |
| **Dev** | 181 | 16 | 75 | 4 | 60 | 29 | 848 | 1,213 |
| **Test** | 129 | 11 | 48 | 4 | 46 | 22 | 606 | 866 |
| **Total** | 729 | 84 | 286 | 15 | 258 | 120 | 3,701 | 5,193 |

Table 8: Statistics for the Task B Malayalam Dataset (HD stands for Homophobic-derogation, HT for Homophobic-Threatening, TD for Transphobic-derogation, TT for Transphob)

| Team Name | Run Name | weighted F1 | Rank |
|---|---|---|---|
| teamplusone | 1 | 0.9692868 | 1 |
| SuperNova (Reddy et al., 2023) | 1 | 0.9658864 | 2 |
| SsnTech2_Run1 (Sivanaiah et al., 2023) | 1 | 0.9582267 | 3 |
| Tercet_English (Sivakumar et al., 2023) | 1 | 0.9534853 | 4 |
| Cordyceps (Ninalga, 2023) | 2 | 0.9512845 | 5 |
| cantnlp (Wong et al., 2023) | 1 | 0.9425137 | 6 |
| DeepBlueAI | 1 | 0.9416178 | 7 |
| adsa_nlp_sys2 | 1 | 0.9363040 | 8 |
| MUCS_Run3 (Hegde et al., 2023) | 3 | 0.9198598 | 9 |
| JudithJeyafreeda (Andrew, 2023) | 1 | 0.8986411 | 10 |

Table 9: Task A – English

| Team Name | Run Name | weighted F1 | Rank |
|---|---|---|---|
| teamplusone | 1 | 0.9793323 | 1 |
| SuperNova (Reddy et al., 2023) | 1 | 0.9793323 | 2 |
| Cordyceps (Ninalga, 2023) | 2 | 0.9695374 | 3 |
| cantnlp (Wong et al., 2023) | 1 | 0.9653340 | 4 |
| DeepBlueAI | 1 | 0.9591820 | 5 |
| MUCS_Run3 (Hegde et al., 2023) | 3 | 0.9418278 | 6 |
| JudithJeyafreeda (Andrew, 2023) | 1 | 0.0185185 | 7 |

Table 10: Task A – Hindi

| Team Name | Run Name | weighted F1 | Rank |
|---|---|---|---|
| Cordyceps (Ninalga, 2023) | 2 | 0.9976971 | 1 |
| MUCS_Run2 (Hegde et al., 2023) | 2 | 0.9563322 | 2 |
| DeepBlueAI | 1 | 0.9493561 | 3 |
| cantnlp (Wong et al., 2023) | 1 | 0.9382083 | 4 |
| SuperNova (Reddy et al., 2023) | 1 | 0.9318975 | 5 |
| teamplusone | 1 | 0.8753247 | 6 |
| JudithJeyafreeda (Andrew, 2023) | 1 | 0.2520196 | 7 |

Table 11: Task A – Malayalam

| Team Name | Run Name | weighted F1 | Rank |
|---|---|---|---|
| Cordyceps (Ninalga, 2023) | 2 | 0.8883174 | 1 |
| MUCS_Run2 (Hegde et al., 2023) | 2 | 0.8138490 | 2 |
| SuperNova (Reddy et al., 2023) | 1 | 0.7957093 | 3 |
| VEL (Kumaresan et al., 2023) | 1 | 0.3000000 | 4 |

Table 12: Task A – Spanish

| Team Name | Run Name | weighted F1 | Rank |
|---|---|---|---|
| Cordyceps (Ninalga, 2023) | 1 | 0.9496857 | 1 |
| DeepBlueAI | 1 | 0.9424593 | 2 |
| cantnlp (Wong et al., 2023) | 1 | 0.9264145 | 3 |
| MUCS_Run2 (Hegde et al., 2023) | 2 | 0.9132474 | 4 |
| SuperNova (Reddy et al., 2023) | 1 | 0.8942428 | 5 |
| teamplusone | 1 | 0.8643490 | 6 |
| JudithJeyafreeda(Andrew, 2023) | 1 | 0.2702824 | 7 |

Table 13: Task A – Tamil

ing, and test sets, as can be seen in Table 5.

## 4 Methods of Participants

The team "teamplusone" submitted a system for Task A and B with an English dataset. They used a pre-trained model called BERT(Bidirectional Encoder Representations from Transformers). They used the default parameter setting for training. With this, they were able to achieve the weighted F1 score of 0.9692868 in Task A and 0.8221297 in Task B.

The "SuperNova" (Reddy et al., 2023) team used Term Frequency-Inverse Document Frequency (TF-IDF) for classifying both tasks. TF measures the frequency of a term within a document. Since Support Vector Machines(SVMs) are known for their ability to handle overfitting, this team used SVM to classify both tasks. This team also claimed that SVMs can perform well even with relatively small training datasets and generalize effectively from limited examples, making them suitable for sentiment analysis applications in various domains.

A team "SSNTech2" (Sivanaiah et al., 2023) classified Task A. For this task, the team first preprocessed and cleaned the dataset and assigned token values to each category. They used the nltk module for preprocessing, such as stop word removal, lemmatizing and normalizing, and removing stop words. For the first test run, the team used the SGD classifier. It produced an accuracy of 0.93, an F1 average score of 0.38, and a weighted score of 0.92. For the second test run, the team used the SVM classifier. It produced better results than the SGD classifier, with an accuracy of 0.94, an F1 average score of 0.42, and a weighted score of 0.94.

SVM is used for classifying the dataset in English under Task A by the team named "Tercet" (Sivakumar et al., 2023). Given a higher precision, F1 score, and weighted averages compared to the random forest, logistic regression, and Naive Bayes models, SVM was a good fit for classifying the test datasets. The team did preprocess the text data, such as removing punctuation, emoticons, and stop words. To convert the text data into a form that is usable by the model, the team also used the TF-IDF vectorizer algorithm. It utilized the extracted features in the SVM classifier. They used the TF-IDF vectorizer algorithm to convert the text data to the model understandable form. Then SVM classifier used the vectorized features for the classification.

The "Cordyceps" (Ninalga, 2023) team classified both tasks using a weight-space ensembling technique. First, they trained a multilingual model on a dataset that included all the languages and then created finetuned models for each language. Ultimately, for each language, they performed linear interpolation between the finetuned and multilingual models' weights. The resulting interpolated model is then used for inference. The selection of the linear interpolation parameter is based on a held-out validation set consisting of samples in the language of the finetuned model that were not encountered during training. The team also observed that weight-space ensembling enhances performance, particularly for low-resource languages. The most interesting aspect of this work is the novel application of weight-space ensembling on code-mixed data, aiming to leverage the strengths of both multilingual and finetuned models for improved performance in analyzing mixed-language text.

A custom pre-trained XLM-RoBERTa transformer-based multilingual model has been developed by the team "CantNLP" (Wong et al., 2023). This team has pre-trained the language model with a random sample of 50,000 tweets (over 50 characters) for each language condition. For the language conditions with Brahmic scripts (Hindi, Malayalam, and Tamil), the team romanized a quarter of the text samples to simulate

| Team Name | Run Name | weighted F1 | Rank |
|---|---|---|---|
| teamplusone | 1 | 0.8221297 | 1 |
| SuperNova (Reddy et al., 2023) | 1 | 0.8014732 | 2 |
| DeepBlueAI | 1 | 0.7219212 | 3 |
| KaustubhSharedTask (Lande et al., 2023) | 1 | 0.6991867 | 4 |
| cantnlp (Wong et al., 2023) | 1 | 0.5397906 | 5 |
| JudithJeyafreeda (Andrew, 2023) | 1 | 0.2255661 | 6 |
| MUCS_Run2 (Hegde et al., 2023) | 2 | 0.1462137 | 7 |
| Cordyceps (Ninalga, 2023) | 2 | 0.1113251 | 8 |

Table 14: Task B – English

| Team Name | Run Name | weighted F1 | Rank |
|---|---|---|---|
| cantnlp (Wong et al., 2023) | 1 | 0.8842916 | 1 |
| MUCS_Run2 (Hegde et al., 2023) | 2 | 0.8595397 | 2 |
| DeepBlueAI | 1 | 0.8533519 | 3 |
| teamplusone | 1 | 0.8233696 | 4 |
| JudithJeyafreeda (Andrew, 2023) | 1 | 0.0639703 | 5 |
| Cordyceps (Ninalga, 2023) | 1 | 0.0108560 | 6 |

Table 15: Task B – Malayalam

| Team Name | Run Name | weighted F1 | Rank |
|---|---|---|---|
| DeepBlueAI | 1 | 0.8651552 | 1 |
| MUCS_Run2 (Hegde et al., 2023) | 2 | 0.8219683 | 2 |
| SuperNova (Reddy et al., 2023) | 1 | 0.8162569 | 3 |
| cantnlp (Wong et al., 2023) | 1 | 0.8041158 | 4 |
| teamplusone | 1 | 0.7548580 | 5 |
| JudithJeyafreeda (Andrew, 2023) | 1 | 0.6547745 | 6 |
| Cordyceps (Ninalga, 2023) | 1 | 0.0122772 | 7 |

Table 16: Task B – Tamil

script-mixing as observed in the comments and finetuned the language model with the training data. The team also over-sampled the training data to reduce class imbalance. Each model was trained with eight epochs, with Adam as the optimizer.

The team "DeepBlueAI" finetuned XLM-RoBERTa as the base model for classifying both tasks. This team has attempted mixing multiple language datasets at different proportions and performed cross-validation.

The team "Adsa_nlp_sys" used SVM in conjunction with TF-IDF Vectorization for classifying the English comments under Task B and used the ADASYN sampling technique. In order to hypertune the model, the team has used TF-IDF Grid. The team claimed that ADASYN, with TF-IDF and Grid search, can find the best model and parameters.

The team "KaustubhSharedTask" (Lande et al., 2023) participated in Task B in the English dataset. Due to class imbalance in task B's training dataset in the English language, they used NLPAUG - a tool to augment the text data and reduce the degree of imbalance. In augmentation of the text data, they tried several parameters like synonym replacement, word insertion, and word substitution to get augmented sentences with the same meaning as the original sentence. They did text preprocessing and applied various transformers models with fine tuning and got the best results on the bilstm model trained on the word embeddings generated from word2vec.

The "MUCS" (Hegde et al., 2023) team has tried using mBERT(Multilingual BERT) and resampling with BERT to classify both tasks. For feature extraction, they used TF-IDF.

A GPT2 model has been used by the team "JudithJeyafreeda" (Andrew, 2023) to finetune the training set for classifying both tasks. For using this model, the team substituted the comments in other languages with English letters.

The team “VEL” (Kumaresan et al., 2023) utilized the ”muril-large-cased” model, which is a variant of the GPT-3.5 architecture developed by OpenAI to classify the Spanish comments under Task A. In addition to using the ”muril-large-cased” model, the team also employed machine learning techniques such as Naive Bayes (NB), Support Vector Machines (SVM), Logistic Regression (LR), Decision Trees (DT), and Random Forests (RF) with count vectorizers.

## 5 Results and Discussion

Overall, we received a total of 10,7,4,7, and 7 submissions for English, Tamil, Spanish, Malayalam, and Hindi in Task A. For Task B, we received 8,7, and 6 submissions for English, Tamil, and Malayalam in Task B. The Tables 9,13,12,10 and 11 shows the rank list of all languages of Task A, and the tables 14, 16, and 15 shows the rank list of all languages of Task B.

In Task A, the model of the team “teamplusone” achieved the top-performing model in English and Hindi language. They used BERT pretrained model with the default setting for the training and achieved the weighted F1 score of 0.96928 and 0.97933, and the “Cordyceps” model is the top-performing model in Tamil, Malayalam, and Spanish languages. They used the weight space ensembling technique, improving the performance of analyzing the mixed language text. They achieved 0.94968, 0.99769, and 0.88831.

The top-performing models in Task B are the model developed by the team “teamplusone,” ranked 1st in the English language. They used BERT model for training with a default parameter setting. They achieved a weighted F1 of 0.82212. In Tamil language, the “DeepblueAI” team’s model got the 1st rank. They used the XLM-RoBERTa base model and performed cross-validation by combining multiple language datasets in varied amounts, which gained the weighted F1 score of 0.88429. For Malayalam, the “cantnlp” team developed the custom pre-trained XLM-RoBERTa model with 50000 random tweets, and they also oversampled the training to tackle the class imbalance problem. This model achieved 0.86515.

## 6 Conclusion

We presented the second shared task findings on homophobia/transphobia detection in social media comments in this publication. We got an extensive variety of entries that fulfilled the aims of the shared task. We expect that the shared task on homophobia/transphobia detection will have a long-term impact on the NLP discipline.

## Acknowledgments

This work has been partially supported by Project CONSENSO (PID2021-122263OB-C21), Project MODERATES (TED2021-130145B-I00) and Project SocialTox (PDC2022-133146-C21) funded by MCIN/AEI/10.13039/501100011033 and by the European Union NextGenerationEU/PRTR, Project PRECOM (SUBV-00016) funded by the Ministry of Consumer Affairs of the Spanish Government, Project FedDAP (PID2020-116118GA-I00) supported by MICINN/AEI/10.13039/501100011033 and WeLee project (1380939, FEDER Andalucía 2014-2020) funded by the Andalusian Regional Government. It is also part of the research project LT-SWM (TED2021-131167B-I00) funded by MCIN/AEI/10.13039/501100011033 and by the European Union NextGenerationEU/PRTR. This work is also part of the research projects LaTe4PoliticES (PID2022-138099OB-I00) funded by MCIN/AEI/10.13039/501100011033 and the European Fund for Regional Development (FEDER)-a way to make Europe and LaTe4PSP (PID2019-107652RB-I00/AEI/ 10.13039/501100011033) funded by MCIN/AEI/10.13039/501100011033. Salud María Jiménez-Zafra has been partially supported by a grant from Fondo Social Europeo and the Administration of the Junta de Andalucía (DOC_01073). The author, Bharathi Raja Chakravarthi, was supported in part by a research grant from Science Foundation Ireland (SFI) under Grant Number SFI/12/RC/2289_P2 (Insight_2).

## References

Bridget O. Alichie. 2022. Communication at the margins: Online homophobia from the perspectives of lgbtq+social media users. *Journal of Human Rights*, 0(0):1–15.

Judith Jeyafreeda Andrew. 2023. Using gpt model for recognition of homophobia/transphobia detection from social media. In *Proceedings of the Third Workshop on Speech and Language Technologies for Dravidian Languages*, Varna, Bulgaria. Recent Advances in Natural Language Processing.

Kathleen C Basile, Dorothy L Espelage, Ian Rivers, Pamela M McMahon, and Thomas R Simon. 2009. The theoretical and empirical links between bullying behavior and male sexual violence perpetration. *Aggression and Violent Behavior*, 14(5):336–347.

Bharathi Raja Chakravarthi. 2023. Detection of homophobia and transphobia in youtube comments. *International Journal of Data Science and Analytics*.

Bharathi Raja Chakravarthi, Adeep Hande, Rahul Ponnusamy, Prasanna Kumar Kumaresan, and Ruba Priyadharshini. 2022a. How can we detect homophobia and transphobia? experiments in a multilingual code-mixed setting for social media governance. *International Journal of Information Management Data Insights*, 2(2):100119.

Bharathi Raja Chakravarthi, Ruba Priyadharshini, Thenmozhi Durairaj, John McCrae, Paul Buitelaar, Prasanna Kumaresan, and Rahul Ponnusamy. 2022b. Overview of the shared task on homophobia and transphobia detection in social media comments. In *Proceedings of the Second Workshop on Language Technology for Equality, Diversity and Inclusion*, pages 369–377, Dublin, Ireland. Association for Computational Linguistics.

Subalalitha Chinnaudayar Navaneethakrishnan, Bharathi Raja Chakravarthi, Kogilavani Shanmugavadivel, Malliga Subramanian, Prasanna Kumar Kumaresan, Bharathi, Lavanya Sambath Kumar, and Rahul Ponnusamy. 2023. Findings of shared task on sentiment analysis and homophobia detection of YouTube comments in code-mixed Dravidian languages. In *Proceedings of the 14th Annual Meeting of the Forum for Information Retrieval Evaluation*, FIRE '22, page 18–21, New York, NY, USA. Association for Computing Machinery.

Geoff Colvin, Tary Tobin, Kelli Beard, Shanna Hagan, and Jeffrey Sprague. 1998. The school bully: Assessing the problem, developing interventions, and future research directions. *Journal of behavioral education*, 8:293–319.

José Antonio García-Díaz, Ángela Almela, Gema Alcaraz-Mármol, and Rafael Valencia-García. 2020. Umucorpusclassifier: Compilation and evaluation of linguistic corpus for natural language processing tasks. *Procesamiento del Lenguaje Natural*, 65:139–142.

Xi Han, Wenting Han, Jiabin Qu, Bei Li, and Qinghua Zhu. 2019a. What happens online stays online? ——social media dependency, online support behavior and offline effects for lgbt. *Computers in Human Behavior*, 93:91–98.

Xi Han, Wenting Han, Jiabin Qu, Bei Li, and Qinghua Zhu. 2019b. What happens online stays online?——social media dependency, online support behavior and offline effects for lgbt. *Computers in Human Behavior*, 93:91–98.

Asha Hegde, Kavya G, Sharal Coelho, and Hosahalli Lakshmaiah Shashirekha. 2023. Homophobic/transphobic content detection in social media text using mbert. In *Proceedings of the Third Workshop on Speech and Language Technologies for Dravidian Languages*, Varna, Bulgaria. Recent Advances in Natural Language Processing.

Gregory M. Herek. 1988. Heterosexuals' attitudes toward lesbians and gay men: Correlates and gender differences. *The Journal of Sex Research*, 25(4):451–477.

Jun Sung Hong and James Garbarino. 2012. Risk and protective factors for homophobic bullying in schools: An application of the social–ecological framework. *Educational Psychology Review*, 24:271–285.

Stacey S Horn, Joseph G Kosciw, and Stephen T Russell. 2009. Special issue introduction: New research on lesbian, gay, bisexual, and transgender youth: Studying lives in context.

Prasanna Kumar Kumaresan, Kishore Kumar Ponnusamy, Kogilavani S V, SUBALALITHA CN, Ruba Priyadharshini, and Bharathi Raja Chakravarthi. 2023. Detecting homophobia and transphobia in code-mixed spanish social media comments. In *Proceedings of the Third Workshop on Speech and Language Technologies for Dravidian Languages*, Varna, Bulgaria. Recent Advances in Natural Language Processing.

Kaustubh Lande, Rahul Ponnusamy, Prasanna Kumar Kumaresan, and Bharathi Raja Chakravarthi. 2023. Homophobia-transphobia detection in social media comments with nlpaug-driven data augmentation. In *Proceedings of the Third Workshop on Speech and Language Technologies for Dravidian Languages*, Varna, Bulgaria. Recent Advances in Natural Language Processing.

Dean Ninalga. 2023. Patching language-specific homophobia/transphobia classifiers with a multilingual understanding. In *Proceedings of the Third Workshop on Speech and Language Technologies for Dravidian Languages*, Varna, Bulgaria. Recent Advances in Natural Language Processing.

Ankitha Reddy, Pranav Moorthi, and Ann Maria Thomas. 2023. Homophobia/transphobia detection in social media comments:-(english, tamil, hindi, spanish, malayalam). In *Proceedings of the Third Workshop on Speech and Language Technologies for Dravidian Languages*, Varna, Bulgaria. Recent Advances in Natural Language Processing.

Alfian Rokhmansyah, Widyatmike Gede Mulawarman, and Yusak Hudiyono. 2021. LGBT news on tirto. id online media: Fairclough's critical discourse analysis. In *6th International Conference on Science, Education and Technology (ISET 2020)*, pages 191–197. Atlantis Press.

Samyuktaa Sivakumar, Priyadharshini Thandavamurthi, Shwetha Sureshnathan, Thenmozhi Durairaj, Bharathi B, and G L Gayathri. 2023. Hope speech detection for equality, diversity, and inclusion. In *Proceedings of the Third Workshop on Speech and Language Technologies for Dravidian Languages*, Varna, Bulgaria. Recent Advances in Natural Language Processing.

Rajalakshmi Sivanaiah, Vaidhegi D, Priya M, Angel Deborah S, and Mirnalinee ThankaNadar. 2023. Homophobia/transphobia detection in social media comments using linear classification techniques. In *Proceedings of the Third Workshop on Speech and Language Technologies for Dravidian Languages*, Varna, Bulgaria. Recent Advances in Natural Language Processing.

Cheryll Ruth Reyes Soriano. 2014. Constructing collectivity in diversity: online political mobilization of a national lgbt political party. *Media, culture & society*, 36(1):20–36.

Paul Venzo and Kristy Hess. 2013. "honk against homophobia": Rethinking relations between media and sexual minorities. *Journal of Homosexuality*, 60(11):1539–1556. PMID: 24147586.

Sidney Wong, Matthew Durward, Benjamin Adams, and Jonathan Dunn. 2023. Homophobia/transphobia detection in social media comments using spatiotemporally retrained language models. In *Proceedings of the Third Workshop on Speech and Language Technologies for Dravidian Languages*, Varna, Bulgaria. Recent Advances in Natural Language Processing.

Lester W Wright, Henry E Adams, and Jeffery Bernat. 1999. Development and validation of the homophobia scale. *Journal of psychopathology and behavioral assessment*, 21:337–347.

Oana Ștefăniță and Diana-Maria Buf. 2021. Hate speech in social media and its effects on the lgbt community: A review of the current research. *Romanian Journal of Communication and Public Relations*, 23(1):47–55.

# Overview of the shared task on Hope Speech Detection for Equality, Diversity, and Inclusion

**Prasanna Kumar Kumaresan**[1], **Bharathi Raja Chakravarthi**[2], **Subalalitha Chinnaudayar Navaneethakrishnan** [3], **Miguel Ángel García-Cumbreras**[4], **Salud María Jiménez-Zafra**[4], **José Antonio García-Díaz**[5], **Rafael Valencia-García**[5], **Momchil Hardalov**[6], **Ivan Koychev**[7], **Preslav Nakov**[8], **Daniel García-Baena**[4], **Kishore Kumar Ponnusamy**[9], **Blake Preston**[10],

[1] Insight SFI Research Centre for Data Analytics, University of Galway, Ireland,
[2] Insight SFI Research Centre for Data Analytics, School of Computer Science, University of Galway, Ireland, [3] SRM Institute Of Science And Technology, Tamil Nadu
[4] Universidad de Jaén, Spain, [5] Universidad de Murcia, Spain, [6] Amazon, Barcelona, Spain,
[7] Sofia University St. Kliment Ohridski, Bulgaria,
[8] Mohamed bin Zayed University of Artificial Intelligence Masdar City, UAE,
[9] Guru Nanak College, Tamil Nadu, India,
[10] School of Computer Science, University of Galway, Ireland.

## Abstract

Hope serves as a potent driving force that motivates individuals to persist in the face of life's unpredictable nature. The Hope Speech poses a substantial challenge to online information credibility, mainly due to rapid content dissemination on social media. This article offers a concise overview of the "Hope Speech Detection for Equality, Diversity, and Inclusion- LT-EDI-RANLP 2023" shared task[1]. The task's objective is to classify social media posts as hopeful or not, with a specific focus on four languages: English, Hindi, Bulgarian, and Spanish. Numerous teams participated in the shared task, presenting a range of methodologies including machine learning techniques, transformer-based models, and resampling methods.

## 1 Introduction

Hope serves as a powerful driving force that encourages individuals to persevere in the face of the unpredictable nature of human existence. It instills motivation within us to remain steadfast in our pursuit of important goals, regardless of the uncertainties that lie ahead (Chakravarthi, 2020). In today's digital age, platforms such as Facebook, Twitter, Instagram, and YouTube have emerged as prominent social media outlets where people freely express their views and opinions. These platforms have also become crucial for marginalized individuals seeking online assistance and support (García-Baena et al., 2023; García-Díaz et al., 2020; Jiménez-Zafra et al., 2023a). The outbreak of the pandemic has exacerbated people's fears around the world, as they grapple with the possibility of losing loved ones and the lack of access to essential services such as schools, hospitals, and mental health facilities. As a result, people have turned to online forums as a means to fulfill their informational, emotional, and social needs. Through social networking sites, individuals can connect with others, experience a sense of social inclusion, and cultivate a feeling of belonging by actively participating in online communities (Kumaresan et al., 2022). The presence of these factors has a profound impact on both physical and psychological well-being, as well as mental health (Jiménez-Zafra et al., 2023b).

By leveraging the power of hope and utilizing online platforms, individuals are able to find solace, support, and resources during challenging times (Hande et al., 2021). These digital spaces offer an avenue for people to seek guidance, share their experiences, and foster connections with others who may be going through similar struggles. Through virtual networks, individuals can combat feelings of isolation, gain access to valuable information, and receive emotional support, all of which contribute to their overall well-being and mental resilience (Ghanghor et al., 2021). It is important to acknowledge the pivotal role that hopes and online platforms play in providing a lifeline to individuals in need. As we navigate through unpredictable circumstances, these digital resources serve as beacons of light, reminding us that we are not alone

[1]https://codalab.lisn.upsaclay.fr/competitions/11076



*LT-EDI 2023 – Third Workshop on Language Technology for Equality, Diversity and Inclusion*, pages 47–53, Varna, Bulgaria, Sep 7, 2023.
https://doi.org/10.26615/978-954-452-084-7_007

in our struggles and that there is a collective effort to support one another (Puranik et al., 2021). Through the convergence of hope, technology, and human connection, we can weather the storm and find strength in our shared experiences, ultimately emerging stronger and more resilient as a global community.

## 2 Related work

Despite the optimistic nature of Hope's speech, it has garnered relatively little attention within the research community. This lack of research interest could be attributed to the absence of available labeled datasets. In recent years, there has been a notable increase in attention towards this issue, thanks in part to the efforts of the organizers of the LT-EDI-EACL2021 workshop who shared a labeled dataset. Several frameworks were submitted during this workshop to address the challenge of detecting Hope Speech (Roy et al., 2022). While numerous research endeavors have focused on filtering out hateful and offensive comments from social media posts, the identification of hopeful comments has received comparatively less consideration (Chakravarthi, 2020).

Counter-narratives, denoting informed textual responses, have surfaced as a notable strategy, drawing recent attention from experimenters (Chung et al., 2019). This approach to counter-narratives aims to balance the preservation of freedom of speech while preventing excessive content blocking. (Mathew et al., 2019) took the initiative to construct and release a counterspeech dataset using YouTube comments. However, the central concept of directly intervening with textual responses can inadvertently escalate hostility. Although it is beneficial for content creators to comprehend why their comments or posts were removed or blocked, and subsequently adjust their discourse and attitudes favorably, this intervention can sometimes exacerbate tensions. This has directed our research focus toward the exploration of positive content, such as messages of hope, and promoting such constructive activities.

## 3 Task description

The hope speech in our context refers to comments or posts on YouTube that provide support, comfort, recommendations, motivation, and understanding. While a comment or post in the dataset could consist of multiple sentences, the average sentence length across the corpus is one. Annotations in the dataset are done at the level of individual comments or posts. Participants were provided with datasets via the CodaLab website[2] for the specific languages Bulgarian, English, Hindi, and Spanish for development, training, and testing purposes.

## 4 Dataset

The shared task's dataset comprises comments in four distinct languages: English, Spanish, Bulgarian, and Hindi, totaling 27,545, 5,859, 3,203, and 2,159 comments, respectively. These comments are sourced from social media platforms like YouTube and Twitter. For the English language subset, we utilized the HopeEDI dataset introduced (Chakravarthi, 2020). This dataset focuses on socially significant subjects, including Equality, Diversity, and Inclusion, addressing topics like LGBTIQ issues, COVID-19, women in STEM, Dravidian languages, Black Lives Matter, and more. The inter-annotator agreement was assessed using Krippendorf's alpha. These dataset details are shown in Table 1. This method is the same for all the rest of the languages and the statistics were shown int he Table 2 for Bulgarian, and Table 3 for Hindi.

Table 1: Statistics for the English Dataset (HS stands for Hope Speech, and NHS for Non-Hope Speech

| Set | HS | NHS | Total |
|---|---|---|---|
| **Train** | 1,562 | 16,630 | 18,192 |
| **Development** | 400 | 4,148 | 4,548 |
| **Test** | 21 | 4,784 | 4,805 |
| **Total** | 1,983 | 25,562 | 27,545 |

Table 2: Statistics for the Bulgarian Dataset (HS stands for Hope Speech, and NHS for Non-Hope Speech

| Set | HS | NHS | Total |
|---|---|---|---|
| **Train** | 223 | 4,448 | 4,671 |
| **Development** | 75 | 514 | 589 |
| **Test** | 150 | 449 | 599 |
| **Total** | 448 | 5,411 | 5,859 |

The Spanish dataset is an improved and extended version of the SpanishHopeEDI dataset (García-Baena et al., 2023). The SpanishHopeEDI dataset was improved by manual revision of the annotations, as some annotation errors were found in the error analysis of the baseline experiments conducted with the dataset (García-Baena et al., 2023).

[2]https://codalab.lisn.upsaclay.fr/competitions/11076

Table 3: Statistics for the Hindi Dataset (HS stands for Hope Speech, and NHS for Non-Hope Speech)

| Set | HS | NHS | Total |
|---|---|---|---|
| Train | 343 | 2,219 | 2,562 |
| Development | 45 | 275 | 320 |
| Test | 53 | 268 | 321 |
| Total | 441 | 2,762 | 3,203 |

It consists of LGTB-related tweets that were collected with the Twitter API (June 27, 2021, to July 26, 2021) and using a lexicon of LGBT-related terms, such as #OrgulloLGTBI or #LGTB, as seed for the search. This dataset was extended with a set of tweets collected using the UMUCorpus-Classifier tool (García-Díaz et al., 2020), which allows defining different search criteria such as keywords, accounts, and geolocation. The key-

Table 4: Statistics for the Spanish Dataset (HS stands for Hope Speech, and NHS for Non-Hope Speech)

| Set | HS | NHS | Total |
|---|---|---|---|
| Train | 691 | 621 | 1,312 |
| Development | 100 | 200 | 300 |
| Test | 300 | 247 | 547 |
| Total | 1,091 | 1,068 | 2,159 |

words used to collect the tweets were related to transphobia and homophobia, such as #transfobia (*#transphobia*), transexual (*transsexual*), identidad de género (*gender identity*), #homofobia (*#homophobia*), homosexual (*homosexual*), #AlertaHomofobia (*#HomophobiaAlert*), or #StopLGTBIfobia *#StopLGTBIphobia*. It should be mentioned that all the tweets of this dataset were manually labeled by the organizers of the shared task marking a tweet as HS (hope speech) if the text: i) explicitly supports the social integration of minorities; ii) is a positive inspiration for the LGTB community; iii) explicitly encourages LGTB people who might find themselves in a situation; or iv) unconditionally promotes tolerance. On the contrary, a tweet was marked as NHS (non-hope speech) if the text: i) expresses negative sentiment towards the LGTB community; ii) explicitly seeks violence; or iii) uses gender-based insults. Table 4 shows the distribution of the dataset considering the number of samples for each label and set. It should be noted that this dataset was also used, but with a different test set, in the *HOPE: Multilingual Hope Speech Detection* shared task (Jiménez-Zafra et al., 2023a) at IberLEF 2023 workshop (Jiménez-Zafra et al., 2023b).

## 5 Methodology

In this shared task, there are eight teams actively participated and implemented their models. They evaluated their model's performance on our Hope Speech Detection shared task:

**hate-alert:** (Das et al., 2023) The participants employed two types of transformer-based models, namely mBERT and XLMR-base, in their study. In the first run, they conducted fine-tuning on the mBERT model. For the second and third runs, they took the CLS embeddings from both the mBERT and XLMR models, subjected them to two Dense layers, and ultimately utilized a classification head. Notably, the utilization of cutting-edge transformer-based models for the classification task is a noteworthy aspect of their approach. The results have demonstrated the superiority of these transformer-based models over earlier deep-learning models like LSRM and CNN-GRU.

**MUCS:** (Hegde et al., 2023) The MUCS team's journey began with enhancing models for a pivotal project. Armed with determination, they fused BERT embeddings with syllable TF-IDF, promising innovative insights. Venturing further, they intertwined BERT embeddings with TF-IDF and resampling. Across three runs, they refined their approach, each iteration marking a step towards precision. This dedication culminated in a triumphant unveiling, a testament to ingenuity, poised to reshape their field.

**Team-Tamil:** (Ponnusamy et al., 2023) In our pursuit of enhancing model performance, we embarked on a journey fueled by innovation. With the creative fusion of MPNet Embeddings, we engineered a powerful and distinct form of representation. As the threads of our endeavor wove together, an H2O model emerged, infused with the essence of our collective efforts. This union of cutting-edge techniques resulted in a transformative leap forward, poised to unravel new insights and pave the way for future advancements.

**IIC_Team:** (Vajrobol et al., 2023) The method employed in this task involved utilizing Bidirectional LSTM (Long Short-Term Memory) and BiLSTM with embeddings. Additionally, XLM-ROberta models were employed for each language. Since the datasets used in this task exhibited significant class imbalances, various techniques were applied to address this issue. To balance the datasets, a combination of undersampling and other augmentation methods was implemented.

**ML_AI_IIITRanchi:** (Kumari et al., 2023) This team implemented text classification, the bag-of-words (BoW) model is used, and there are multiple steps in the procedure. The labeled dataset was first prepared by being divided into a training set and a testing set. The text data should be next preprocessed by reducing noise, standardizing the text format, and deleting stopwords. Then, they used a vectorization method, such as CountVectorizer, to construct the BoW representation. This method turns each document into a numerical vector based on word frequencies. To train the classifier, divide the BoW representation into features and labels. Then Select a classification algorithm—Random Forest and AdaBoost, for example—and train the model using the training data. Lastly, make predictions on the testing set to assess the model.

**Tercet:** (Sivakumar et al., 2023) The method that they have employed for this task is Support Vector machines (SVM). Given a higher precision, F1 score, and weighted averages as compared to models such as random forest, logistic regression, and naïve Bayes models, SVM was a good fit for classifying the given test datasets. The process starts with preprocessing of the text data such as removing punctuation, emoticons, and stop words. To convert the text data into a form that is usable by the model, they used a tf-idf vectorizer algorithm and utilized the data in the SVM model.

**Ranganayaki:** (EM et al., 2023) The data set is preprocessed to translate emojis, convert text to lowercase, username removal, and extra space removal. The vocabulary of English and Hindi data is formed to correct spelling mistakes in training and testing data using Levenshtein distance. Preprocessed data is converted into fastText embedding of dimension 100x100. The dataset is oversampled using ADASYN oversampling to handle class imbalance. The data is then fed into a capsule network, to form the model, which is used to make predictions.

**VTU_BGM:** (Sanjana M. Kavatagi and Biradar, 2023) Employing layer differential tuning, the team harnessed the ULMFiT model for advanced feature generation. ULMFiT was ingeniously designed to overcome limited labeled data challenges for specific tasks, unfolding through pretraining and fine-tuning stages. The initial pretraining phase involved training a language model on an extensive, unlabeled text corpus like Wikipedia, grasping universal language patterns and semantics. The proposed method embraced layered fine-tuning of ULMFiT, capitalizing on its core principle: first, pre-trained on general language data, then fine-tuned on task-specific datasets. This approach facilitated adaptation to task intricacies, leading to enhanced performance across a spectrum of NLP endeavors.

## 6 Result

The submissions received for the classification of English, Bulgarian, Hindi, and Spanish datasets were 6, 5, 5, and 3, respectively. Among these, the team "hate-alert" secured the top rank for both Bulgarian and Hindi languages, achieving a macro average F1 score of 0.75 and 0.68, respectively. They employed transformer-based models, specifically mBERT and XLMR-base, demonstrating the effectiveness of these models. Their approach involved fine-tuning mBERT, utilizing CLS embeddings from both mBERT and XLMR and employing Dense layers along with a classification head. This innovative use of cutting-edge transformer-based models showcased their superiority over earlier deep-learning models like LSRM and CNN-GRU, as depicted in Table 5 and Table 7.

The team "MUCS" also secured the first rank and in the Spanish languages with the macro F1 score of 0.61, which is shown in Table 8. Their journey began with enhancing models for a pivotal project, where they combined BERT embeddings with syllable TF-IDF, followed by integration with TF-IDF and resampling techniques. Through iterative refinement across three runs, their approach demonstrated a continuous progression towards precision, resulting in a notable advancement in the field.

For the English language classification, two teams, namely "Tercet-English" and "ML_AI_IIITRanchi," both achieved the top rank with a macro F1 score of 0.50. "Tercet-English" adopted Support Vector Machines (SVM) as their method of choice, benefitting from higher precision, F1 scores, and weighted averages compared to other models such as random forest, logistic regression, and naive Bayes. Their preprocessing involved text data cleaning and conversion using a TF-IDF vectorizer algorithm, subsequently utilized in the SVM model. On

Table 5: Bulgarian Rank List

| Team name | MF1 | Rank |
|---|---|---|
| hate-alert-run2 (Das et al., 2023) | 0.75 | 1 |
| MUCS_run1 (Hegde et al., 2023) | 0.75 | 1 |
| Team-Tamil (Ponnusamy et al., 2023) | 0.69 | 2 |
| IIC_Team (Vajrobol et al., 2023) | 0.65 | 3 |
| ML_AI_IIITRanchi(1) (Kumari et al., 2023) | 0.50 | 4 |

Table 6: Engilsh Rank List

| Team name | MF1 | Rank |
|---|---|---|
| Tercet_English (Sivakumar et al., 2023) | 0.50 | 1 |
| ML_AI_IIITRanchi (Kumari et al., 2023) | 0.50 | 1 |
| Ranganayaki (EM et al., 2023) | 0.49 | 2 |
| VTUBGM (Sanjana M. Kavatagi and Biradar, 2023) | 0.48 | 3 |
| IIC_Team (Vajrobol et al., 2023) | 0.47 | 4 |
| MUCS_run2 (Hegde et al., 2023) | 0.44 | 5 |

the other hand, "ML_AI_IIITRanchi" employed text classification using the bag-of-words (BoW) model. Their process included dividing the labeled dataset into training and testing sets, preprocessing text data, constructing BoW representations using vectorization methods like CountVectorizer, and training the classifier using classification algorithms such as Random Forest and AdaBoost.

These results collectively highlight the effectiveness of various techniques employed by different teams across languages, showcasing advancements in hope speech classification methodologies.

## 7 Conclusion

This paper provides an overview of the Hope Speech Detection shared task conducted during LT-EDI-RANLP 2023, with a specific focus on four languages: Bulgarian, English, Hindi, and Spanish. The task attracted participation from eight teams, each submitting predictions for evaluation. The resulting rank list, featuring macro F1 scores as outlined in the result section, is presented. In essence, this paper succinctly captures the essence of the LT-EDI-RANLP 2023 Hope Speech Detection shared task. It emphasizes the diverse range of strategies adopted by participating teams and underscores the prominence of machine learning and transformer-based methods, which have contributed to notable enhancements in performance.

## References

Bharathi Raja Chakravarthi. 2020. Hopeedi: A multilingual hope speech detection dataset for equality, diversity, and inclusion. In *Proceedings of the Third Workshop on Computational Modeling of People's Opinions, Personality, and Emotion's in Social Media*, pages 41–53.

Yi-Ling Chung, Elizaveta Kuzmenko, Serra Sinem Tekiroglu, and Marco Guerini. 2019. Conan–counter narratives through nichesourcing: a multilingual dataset of responses to fight online hate speech. *arXiv preprint arXiv:1910.03270.*

Mithun Das, Shubhankar Barman, and Subhadeep Chatterjee. 2023. Hope speech detection using transformer-based models. In *Proceedings of the Third Workshop on Speech and Language Technologies for Dravidian Languages*, Varna, Bulgaria. Recent Advances in Natural Language Processing.

Ranganayaki EM, Abirami Murugappan, Lysa Packiam R S, and Deivamani M. 2023. Hope speech detection using capsule networks. In *Proceedings of the Third Workshop on Speech and Language Technologies for Dravidian Languages*, Varna, Bulgaria. Recent Advances in Natural Language Processing.

Daniel García-Baena, Miguel García-Cumbreras, Salud María Zafra, José García-Díaz, and Rafael Valencia-García. 2023. Hope speech detection in spanish. *Language Resources and Evaluation*, pages 1–28.

José Antonio García-Díaz, Ángela Almela, Gema Alcaraz-Mármol, and Rafael Valencia-García. 2020. Umucorpusclassifier: Compilation and evaluation of linguistic corpus for natural language processing tasks. *Procesamiento del Lenguaje Natural*, 65:139–142.

Table 7: Hindi Rank List

| Team name | MF1 | Rank |
|---|---|---|
| hate-alert-run1 (Das et al., 2023) | 0.68 | 1 |
| IIC_Team (Vajrobol et al., 2023) | 0.67 | 2 |
| MUCS_run1 (Hegde et al., 2023) | 0.67 | 2 |
| Ranganayaki (EM et al., 2023) | 0.62 | 3 |
| ML_AI_IIITRanchi (Kumari et al., 2023) | 0.52 | 4 |

Table 8: Spanish Rank List

| Team Name | Macro F1 | Rank |
|---|---|---|
| MUCS (Hegde et al., 2023) | 0.61 | 1 |
| IIC_Team (Vajrobol et al., 2023) | 0.51 | 2 |
| hate-alert (Das et al., 2023) | 0.49 | 3 |


Nikhil Ghanghor, Rahul Ponnusamy, Prasanna Kumar Kumaresan, Ruba Priyadharshini, Sajeetha Thavareesan, and Bharathi Raja Chakravarthi. 2021. Iiitk@ lt-edi-eacl2021: Hope speech detection for equality, diversity, and inclusion in tamil, malayalam and english. In *Proceedings of the First Workshop on Language Technology for Equality, Diversity and Inclusion*, pages 197–203.

Adeep Hande, Ruba Priyadharshini, Anbukkarasi Sampath, Kingston Pal Thamburaj, Prabakaran Chandran, and Bharathi Raja Chakravarthi. 2021. Hope speech detection in under-resourced kannada language.

Asha Hegde, Kavya G, Sharal Coelho, and Hosahalli Lakshmaiah Shashirekha. 2023. Learning approaches for hope speech detection in social media text. In *Proceedings of the Third Workshop on Speech and Language Technologies for Dravidian Languages*, Varna, Bulgaria. Recent Advances in Natural Language Processing.

Salud María Jiménez-Zafra, Miguel Ángel García-Cumbreras, Daniel García-Baena, José Antonio García-Díaz, Bharathi Raja Chakravarthi, Rafael Valencia-García, and L. Alfonso Ureña-López. 2023a. Overview of HOPE at IberLEF 2023: Multilingual Hope Speech Detection. *Procesamiento del Lenguaje Natural*, 71.

Salud María Jiménez-Zafra, Francisco Rangel, and Manuel Montes-y Gómez. 2023b. Overview of IberLEF 2023: Natural Language Processing Challenges for Spanish and other Iberian Languages. In *Proceedings of the Iberian Languages Evaluation Forum (IberLEF 2023), co-located with the 39th Conference of the Spanish Society for Natural Language Processing (SEPLN 2023), CEUR-WS.org*.

Prasanna Kumar Kumaresan, Rahul Ponnusamy, Elizabeth Sherly, Sangeetha Sivanesan, and Bharathi Raja Chakravarthi. 2022. Transformer based hope speech comment classification in code-mixed text. In *International Conference on Speech and Language Technologies for Low-resource Languages*, pages 120–137. Springer.

Kirti Kumari, Shirish Shekhar Jha, Zarikunte Kunal Dayanand, and Praneesh Sharma. 2023. Identification of hope speech of youtube comments in mixed languages. In *Proceedings of the Third Workshop on Speech and Language Technologies for Dravidian Languages*, Varna, Bulgaria. Recent Advances in Natural Language Processing.

Binny Mathew, Punyajoy Saha, Hardik Tharad, Subham Rajgaria, Prajwal Singhania, Suman Kalyan Maity, Pawan Goyal, and Animesh Mukherjee. 2019. Thou shalt not hate: Countering online hate speech. In *Proceedings of the international AAAI conference on web and social media*, volume 13, pages 369–380.

Rahul Ponnusamy, Malliga Subramaniam, Sajeetha Thavareesan, and Ruba Priyadharshini. 2023. Teamtamil@lt-edi: Automatic detection of hope speech in bulgarian language using embedding techniques. In *Proceedings of the Third Workshop on Speech and Language Technologies for Dravidian Languages*, Varna, Bulgaria. Recent Advances in Natural Language Processing.

Karthik Puranik, Adeep Hande, Ruba Priyadharshini, Sajeetha Thavareesan, and Bharathi Raja Chakravarthi. 2021. Iiitt@ lt-edi-eacl2021-hope speech detection: there is always hope in transformers. *arXiv preprint arXiv:2104.09066*.

Pradeep Kumar Roy, Snehaan Bhawal, and Chinnaudayar Navaneethakrishnan Subalalitha. 2022. Hate speech and offensive language detection in dravidian languages using deep ensemble framework. *Computer Speech & Language*, 75:101386.

Rashmi R. Rachh Sanjana M. Kavatagi and Shankar S. Biradar. 2023. Hope speech identification using layered differential training of ulmfit. In *Proceedings of the Third Workshop on Speech and Language Technologies for Dravidian Languages*, Varna, Bulgaria. Recent Advances in Natural Language Processing.

Samyuktaa Sivakumar, Priyadharshini Thandavamurthi, Shwetha Sureshnathan, Thenmozhi Durairaj,

Bharathi B, and G L Gayathri. 2023. Hope speech detection for equality, diversity, and inclusion. In *Proceedings of the Third Workshop on Speech and Language Technologies for Dravidian Languages*, Varna, Bulgaria. Recent Advances in Natural Language Processing.

Vajratiya Vajrobol, Nitisha Aggarwal, and Karanpreet Singh. 2023. Leveraging pre-trained transformers for fine-grained depression level detection in social media. In *Proceedings of the Third Workshop on Speech and Language Technologies for Dravidian Languages*, Varna, Bulgaria. Recent Advances in Natural Language Processing.

# Computer, en*hence*: POS-tagging improvements for nonbinary pronoun use in Swedish

**Henrik Björklund***
*he/him — han/honom*
Umeå University
Umeå, Sweden
henrikb@cs.umu.se

**Hannah Devinney**†
*they/them — hen/hen*
Umeå University
Umeå, Sweden
hannahd@cs.umu.se

## Abstract

Part of Speech (POS) taggers for Swedish routinely fail for the third person gender-neutral pronoun *hen*, despite the fact that it has been a well-established part of the Swedish language since at least 2014. In addition to simply being a form of gender bias, this failure can have negative effects on other tasks relying on POS information. We demonstrate the usefulness of semi-synthetic augmented datasets in a case study, retraining a POS tagger to correctly recognize *hen* as a personal pronoun. We evaluate our retrained models for both tag accuracy and on a downstream task (dependency parsing) in a classicial NLP pipeline.

Our results show that adding such data works to correct for the disparity in performance. The accuracy rate for identifying *hen* as a pronoun can be brought up to acceptable levels with only minor adjustments to the tagger's vocabulary files. Performance parity to gendered pronouns can be reached after retraining with only a few hundred examples. This increase in POS tag accuracy also results in improvements for dependency parsing sentences containing *hen*.

## 1 Introduction

The gender-neutral third person singular pronoun *hen* (subject/object form: *hen*; possessive form: *hens*) was added to the Swedish Academy's Glossary in 2015 (SAOL, 2015), following at least occasional use since the mid-20th century (Milles, 2013). The use and acceptance of *hen* has since increased (Gustafsson Sendén et al., 2021), although it remains much less common in media than *hon* ('she') or *han* ('he') (Svensson, 2021, 2022). Berglund (2022) provides a detailed study of the use of *hen* in blog posts from the years 2001–2017.

Despite its established history, Swedish Natural Language Processing (NLP) tools struggle to handle *hen* correctly, especially when compared to other pronouns. This is problematic both from a practical perspective (*hen* is increasingly used as a generic, e.g. on official forms) and from a bias perspective, as *hen* and other neopronouns are more likely to be used by gender minorities.

Part of Speech (POS) tagging is the task of assigning the individual words in a text to classes such as *noun*, *verb*, *pronoun*, etc. It is thus a fundamental task, one which many NLP systems rely heavily upon, e.g., systems for parsing, classification, translation, etc. This means that incorrect tagging may lead to errors in later steps. As an example, if *hen* is tagged as a noun, a translation system may well translate it into a noun rather than a pronoun.[1]

Swedish is an medium-resourced language, both in terms of high-quality labeled linguistic data and available tools. The available annotated datasets are of limited size and for the most part somewhat aged. When it comes to modern data-intensive tools, there is a series of BERT models trained by the National Library of Sweden that are publicly available. In the near future, GPT-SW3, a series of GPT style LLMs is also expected to be publicly released. As a consequence, when processing Swedish, we have to rely on combinations of modern LLMs and more classical NLP pipelines.

Apart from the direct usefulness of a Swedish POS tagger that can correctly tag *hen*, we also believe that it can be of general interest to investigate how to retrain POS taggers for new words, without access to up-to-date annotated datasets, which are expensive and very rarely produced or updated.

*Supported by the Wallenberg AI, Autonomous Systems and Software Program through the NEST project *STING*.
†Supported by the Umeå Centre for Gender Studies

[1] "Hen" actually exists as a noun in Swedish; it is an archaic term for a whetstone, and extremely rare in modern Swedish.



*LT-EDI 2023 – Third Workshop on Language Technology for Equality, Diversity and Inclusion*, pages 54–61, Varna, Bulgaria, Sep 7, 2023.
https://doi.org/10.26615/978-954-452-084-7_008

### 1.1 Bias Statement

In the NLP literature, "bias" can refer to various concepts, and is often not well-defined (Blodgett et al., 2020). We consider the overarching concept of algorithmic "bias" as the concern for how power structures *manifest* in language technologies. Power structures are a way of theorizing the pattern of underlying or hidden power relations in society/ies. We draw from Patricia Hill Collins' *matrix of domination*, which "describes the overall social organization within which intersecting oppressions originate, develop, and are contained" (Collins, 2000, p. 228). This draws attention to the complex interactions of different pieces in the whole system, encompassing four domains of power specified by Collins: *structural* (organization: laws, policies, large-scale institutions), *disciplinary* (administration/implementation of those laws and policies), *hegemonic* (system and circulation of ideas, favoring dominant groups), and *interpersonal* (everyday life and individual experiences).

Language technologies can operate in and be affected by several of these domains. In the case of POS taggers, we can consider their regulation of which terms are tagged as pronouns to be part of the disciplinary domain; while the abstract concept of a "standard" language determining which words "count as" pronouns is part of the structural domain, reinforced by hegemonic beliefs about the value of standard language. When the output from POS taggers is passed into other parts of an NLP pipeline, such as dependency parsing, this disciplinary power and regulation of legitimacy is also passed on. When these tools are applied, they become part of the matrix of domination across multiple domains as part of their interactions with the world.

However, even if there are no significant or "material" downstream effects of these mistakes, they are in and of themselves harms. "Non-standardized" pronouns and neopronouns, which are often the pronouns chosen by nonbinary[2] people, are delegitimized by automatic tagging tools mislabeling them as anything-but pronouns. This contributes to erasure and feelings of invisibility, and perpetuates the idea that these pronouns are "fake" and people who use them are "incorrect" or do not belong.

[2]We use nonbinary as an umbrella term for anyone outside or between the "binary" genders of women and men.

## 2 Background

Since pronouns are a much smaller class than other parts of speech such as nouns or verbs, more-or-less perfect accuracy should be expected from taggers. Indeed, we find that for the Swedish gendered pronouns *hon* and *han*, 100% accuracy is achieved for both taggers investigated (§3.1).

**Stockholm-Umeå Corpus.** The Stockholm-Umeå Corpus[3] (SUC) is an annotated corpus of texts from the 1990s (Gustafson-Capková and Hartmann, 2006). It contains about a million annotated words and is freely available for research purposes from Språkbanken (after signing a license agreement). The latest version (V3) was released in 2012.

**efselab.** The `efselab`[4] (Efficient Sequence Labeling) package provides a sparse perceptron-based architechture for POS tagging and other NLP tasks. It aims at computational efficiency, while still delivering a high accuracy (Östling, 2018). Once trained, efselab tagging is deterministic. Apart from the software needed to train models, the GitHub distribution also contains a pre-trained pipeline for Swedish, including POS tagging, named entity recognition, and dependency parsing. This out of the box tagger was trained on SUC, and has thus never "seen" instances of *hen*.

**spaCy.** The `spaCy` package[5] has three pre-trained pipelines for Swedish, differing in their sizes: small (`sm`), medium (`md`), and large (`lg`). The models are trained on SUC, Universal Dependencies Swedish Talbanken and varying amounts of unlabeld text data collected between 2018 and 2021 (spaCy). It can thus be assumed to have had instances of *hen* in its unlabeled training data, but not in its labeled data.

**KB-BERT.** The `KB-BERT` POS tagger[6] is based on Kungliga Bibliotekets (The National Library of Sweden's) BERT model, fine-tuned using the SUC corpus. As with `spaCy`, it can thus also be assumed to have had instances of *hen* in its unlabeled, but not in its labeled, training data.

[3]`spraakbanken.gu.se/en/resources/suc3`
[4]`github.com/robertostling/efselab`
[5]`spaCy.io`
[6]`https://huggingface.co/KBLab/bert-base-swedish-cased-pos`

### 2.1 Related Work

Brandl et al. (2022) show that large language models perform worse for gender-neutral pronouns in Danish, English, and Swedish than for gendered pronouns, measured both with respect to intrinsic measures such as perplexity and on several downstream tasks.

There are a number of systems for dependency parsing for Swedish, and in principle any framework for dependency parsing can be trained on the existing Swedish treebanks, such as UD-Talbanken. The parser included in `efselab`'s Swedish pipeline, and that we use here, is a pre-trained version of MaltParser (Nivre et al., 2007).

Data augmentation strategies are well-established for mitigating (binary) gender-stereotypical associations in NLP tools such as coreference resolution (Lu et al., 2020; Zhao et al., 2018), natural language inference (Sharma et al., 2020), dialog generation (Dinan et al., 2020), and abusive language detection (Park et al., 2018). For a general overview of data augmentation in NLP, see Feng et al. (2021).

Rewriting texts for data augmentation is not always a straightforward task, as exchanging words may require updates to other parts of the sentence to maintain grammatical agreement. Sun et al. (2021) demonstrate an algorithm for replacing gendered personal pronouns with neutral singular *they* in English, and Zmigrod et al. (2019) and Jain et al. (2021) propose methods for data augmentation in languages with grammatical gender. As *hen* follows the same paradigm as its gendered counterparts (see section 3.2), we find that it is sufficient to use simple replace rules with limited manual inspection.

## 3 Method

### 3.1 Initial Evaluation

The pre-trained taggers were initially tested for overall accuracy on the SUC test set, and for pronoun-specific accuracy on the Swedish Winogender Dataset[7]. SweWinogender is a challenge set, developed for diagnosing gender bias in coreference resolution systems follows a Winograd-style schema (Hansson et al., 2021). It is useful because in our setting it has a balanced frequency of *hen*, *hon*, and *han*, and also a good mixture of objective, subjective and possessive forms. Thus we can directly compare the accuracy across the pronouns, while being able to rule out context as a cause of differences.

We test both for accuracy across all morphosyntactic feature tags and "POS accuracy" which is only concerned with the top-level POS tag. We only report POS accuracy for `KB-BERT`, as it does not provide other feature information. Table 1 shows the POS accuracy of each tagger on all forms of *hen*, *hon*, and *han* on SweWinogender.[8] Table 4 shows the overall accuracy and POS accuracy for each tagger.

`KB-BERT` shows the best performance for *hen* for SweWinoGender, identifying it as a pronoun in nearly all cases. It also has the best POS accuracy on the SUC test set. Thus, it initially seems like there is not much to improve: we do not make modifications to KB-BERT, but continue reporting its performance as a reference point throughout the paper.

Despite an initial ability to sometimes correctly tag *hen* in the Swedish Winogender set (Table 1), the overall accuracy of Swedish `spaCy` is substantially worse than `efselab` (Table 2). In fact, the `spaCy` accuracy is at a level that is nowadays unacceptable.

For these reasons, we focus on `efselab` in the rest of the paper, using it as a case study to investigate the effects of augmenting the training data of a relatively light-weight tagger with synthetic data in order to incorporate a new pronoun into its repertoire. We are interested both in how much synthetic data is needed in order for the model to perform as well for the the new pronoun as for the others and in whether the addition of synthetic data deteriorates the overall performance.

### 3.2 Augmented SUC

The SUC corpus does not contain any instances of *hen* as a pronoun. In order to have access to tagged sentences using *hen*, we extracted sentences from SUC that use binary personal pronouns and constructed copies, replacing the pronouns with *hen*. We only swap tokens when the associated gold-standard tag is PN (personal pronoun) or PS (possessive personal pronoun). This check is necessary

[7] `spraakbanken.gu.se/resurser/swewinogender` (SweWinogender v1.0)

[8] The `KB` tokenizer sometimes splits composite words into separate tokens. In these cases, we only consider the `KB-BERT` POS tagging of the stem, in order to have an equal number of tokens for each model. This holds for all tests presented in this article.

| SweWinogender | *hen* | *hon* | *han* |
|---|---|---|---|
| efselab | 0.0 | 1.0 | 1.0 |
| spaCy-sm | 0.0 | 1.0 | 1.0 |
| spaCy-md | 0.82 | 1.0 | 1.0 |
| spaCy-lg | 0.75 | 1.0 | 1.0 |
| KB-BERT | 0.99 | 1.0 | 1.0 |

Table 1: Pronoun POS accuracy for the different baseline POS taggers on the SweWinogender dataset, reported across all morphological forms of each third person personal pronoun (208 tokens considered for each pronoun).

| SUC-test | Accuracy | POS acc. |
|---|---|---|
| efselab | **0.9696** | 0.9780 |
| spaCy-sm | 0.8857 | 0.9159 |
| spaCy-md | 0.9179 | 0.9420 |
| spaCy-lg | 0.9243 | 0.9459 |
| KB-BERT | N/A | **0.9930** |

Table 2: Baseline accuracy scores for the SUC test dataset, containing 23319 tokens. Under "Accuracy" we report the accuracy for tagging with POS *and* morphological information. This does not apply to `KB-BERT`, as it does not produce morphological tags. Under "POS acc.", we report the accuracy of the POS tagging, disregarding morphological tags.

because *Hans* can be both a possessive pronoun ('His') and a proper name. The appropriate morphological form[9] of the pronoun is used, as shown in table 3. We also update the morphological tag, to indicate that *hen* may be either the subject or object form. Capitalization is always preserved.

| | *hon* | *han* | → | *hen* |
|---|---|---|---|---|
| subject | hon | han | → | hen |
| object | henne | honom | → | hen |
| possessive | hennes | hans | → | hens |

Table 3: Replacement rules for singular personal pronouns in our en*hen*ced SUC.

Sentences where the replacement resulted in either *hen eller hen* ('ze or ze') or *hen och hen* ('ey and ey') required manual checking and correction. There were less than 50 of these instances in total. In all cases of *hen eller hen*, the original sentence was expressing a generic she-or-he, meaning the whole phrase could be collapsed into *hen*. For some cases of *hen och hen* no correction was required, e.g. in cases where the conjunction connects separate clauses. For the remaining sentences, a binary-gendered pronoun was re-introduced for clarity.

This resulted in 11 370 sentences using *hen*. We performed an 80/10/10 train/dev/test split on these sentences. This left us with a training set of 9 096 available sentences. For training, we combined this with the SUC training set in different proportions. Using 227 *hen* sentences makes the ratio of *hen* about 2% of the gendered pronouns in the resulting training set. This number was picked as a reasonable estimate of actual usage in modern Swedish (see, e.g., (Svensson, 2021, 2022)). To investigate whether less common pronouns need to be "over-represented" (compared to an approximated "realistic" usage) in training data to be correctly tagged, we also used training sets augmented with 10% (1 137) and 80% (9 096) of our total *hen* sentences, taken only from the training set.

### 3.3 Retraining

An `efselab` tagger contains two parts: the actual tagger and a statistical model trained on the training data. When the tagger part is built, it is provided with data files to build a vocabulary, with corresponding POS tags and morphological information. In order for the tagger to recognize *hen* as a pronoun, it is not sufficient to just train the statistical model on data containing examples of *hen*. The files that are used to build the vocabulary must be modified.

We thus trained five `efselab` models. The **baseline** model (`baseline`) is trained on SUC, using unmodified vocabulary files. The **mod. vocab** model (`hen0`) is trained on SUC, using modified vocabulary files. The three **en*hen*ced** models (`hen2, hen10, hen80`) are trained on SUC augmented with the given percentage of *hen* sentences, using modified vocabulary files.

## 4 Evaluation and Results

### 4.1 Part of Speech Tagging

We evaluated the models for accuracy based both on the full tags which include morphological information ("Accuracy") as well as the bare part of speech tags ("POS acc."). Because *hen* can be used as both subject and object form, our replacement strategy required some adjustment before both of these scores were brought into alignment. Two test datasets of comparable size, unseen in the training of any of the models, are used. The SUC test

[9]Although the object form of *hen* may also be written *henom*, we did not include this as it is not in common usage.

dataset is provided in SUC version 3.0, and is used unchanged. The *hen* test dataset is produced from the SUC test and development sets following the modification strategy described above. The results from these datasets are reported in table 4 and 5, respectively.

We evaluated the `efselab` models by providing the tokenized test sets as input and directly comparing the output to the SUC gold standard.

### 4.2 Dependency Parsing

We use the Swedish annotation pipeline provided in `efselab` to perform dependency parsing, with the default parsing model. This pipeline makes use of MaltParser (Nivre et al., 2007) (version 1.9.0), which incorporates POS information as a feature. Thus, we expect improvement in token-level accuracy for *hen* tokens.

Because SUC is not annotated with dependency information, we use the Swedish UD-Talbanken treebank[10] and evaluate on both the provided test set (UD test) and a smaller 'UD-HEN' test set consisting of only sentences that have been augmented in the same way as SUC. We report Labeled Attachment Score (LAS), Unlabeled Attachment Score (UAS), and Label Accuracy ($L_{ACC}$) on a token level, in Tables 6 and 7.

## 5 Discussion

Our initial findings showed that two common POS taggers for Swedish either cannot identify *hen* as a pronoun at all, or identify it at notably lower rates than other pronouns. This likely has downstream consequences on performance of language technologies relying on these taggers, and on the level of the taggers themselves is a problem for gender equality. It also demonstrates a weakness of such taggers, namely their ability to be flexible in light of language shift.

In our initial tests with SweWinogender, `KB-BERT` performed nearly-perfectly for *hen*: it only missed the two instances where *hens* was the first word of a sentence (and thus capitalized). However, SweWinogender is a very regularized test set (as it is designed for challenging coreference systems, not POS taggers), and `KB-BERT`'s performance for *hen* drops to less than 95% when tested on the more complex, realistic '*hen*' SUC test dataset. This makes it plausible that having only unlabeled data might not be sufficient to learn, e.g., pronouns that have recently come into use and are underrepresented in the data. As the `KB-BERT` model was originally fine-tuned for POS tagging on SUC, it seems reasonable that fine-tuning on the en*hen*ced SUC data could mitigate this weakness. Another reason for keeping tools such as `efselab` around is that at present is that the `KB-BERT` model does not provide more complex morphological information, which is desirable in some cases.

Training existing architectures on augmented data containing even a small number of sentences containing the pronoun *hen* can effectively correct for this disparity. We reach complete parity to binary-gendered pronouns, at 100% accuracy, with a representative sample (`hen2`), and see no real improvement when adding more sentences containing *hen* (`hen10` and `hen80`). This suggests that an up to date annotated dataset, based on contemporary Swedish usage, would be enough to obtain inclusive results, without the need for synthetic data, at least for the case of *hen*.

In terms of effect on downstream tasks, this improvement carries over to label accuracy for dependency parsing on *hen* tokens, with no loss of to LAS over all tokens. As nouns and pronouns often occupy similar grammatical roles, it is somewhat unsurprising that there is not also an effect on head accuracy (as measured by UAS).

## Limitations

The current study only addresses one, relatively established, new personal pronoun in Swedish, and only pursues serious improvements to one tagger. Due to the under-resourced status of Swedish NLP, we only demonstrate the effects of this improvement on one "out of the box" downstream task. In future work, we hope to test these effects on other tasks prone to gendered biases, such as coreference resolution.

Although we find our strategy of re-training on augmented data to show good results for `efselab`, which is relatively lightweight, in general this type of constant re-training is not energy efficient, and therefore not environmentally responsible. Language, particularly inclusive language, is constantly shifting, meaning that more work of this type is inevitable to keep up with linguistic change. In future work, rule-based or other lightweight al-

[10] `https://github.com/UniversalDependencies/UD_Swedish-Talbanken`

| SUC-test | Accuracy | POS Accuracy |
|---|---|---|
| baseline | 0.9703 | 0.9786 |
| hen0 | 0.9703 | 0.9786 |
| hen2 | 0.9683 | 0.9771 |
| hen10 | 0.9687 | 0.9774 |
| hen80 | 0.9686 | 0.9774 |
| KB-BERT | N/A | 0.9929 |

Table 4: Results for the SUC test dataset, containing 23319 tokens, across different `efselab` models. `KB-BERT` is provided as a reference value for POS accuracy.

| HEN-test | Accuracy | POS acc. | Hen acc. | Hen POS acc. |
|---|---|---|---|---|
| baseline | 0.9093 | 0.9116 | 0.0000 | 0.0000 |
| hen0 | 0.9775 | 0.9798 | 0.8870 | 0.8870 |
| hen2 | 0.9941 | 0.9948 | 1.0000 | 1.0000 |
| hen10 | 0.9945 | 0.9952 | 1.0000 | 1.0000 |
| hen80 | 0.9953 | 0.9958 | 1.0000 | 1.0000 |
| KB-BERT | N/A | 0.9886 | N/A | 0.9408 |

Table 5: Results for the '*hen*' SUC test dataset, containg 20437 tokens (of which 1554 are *hen* or *hens*), across different `efselab` models. `KB-BERT` is provided as a reference value for POS accuracy.

| UD-test | LAS | UAS | $L_{ACC}$ |
|---|---|---|---|
| baseline | 0.6087 | 0.6608 | 0.7565 |
| hen0 | 0.6087 | 0.6609 | 0.7565 |
| hen2 | 0.6108 | 0.6640 | 0.7571 |
| hen10 | 0.6127 | 0.6655 | 0.7560 |
| hen80 | 0.6068 | 0.6600 | 0.7544 |

Table 6: Word-level scores on the UD test set, containing 20386 tokens, across different `efselab` models.

| UD-HEN-test | LAS | UAS | $L_{ACC}$ | Hen LAS | Hen UAS | Hen $L_{ACC}$ |
|---|---|---|---|---|---|---|
| baseline | 0.6373 | 0.6860 | 0.7802 | 0.6534 | 0.7045 | 0.8068 |
| hen0 | 0.6438 | 0.6891 | 0.7895 | 0.6932 | 0.7216 | 0.8807 |
| hen2 | 0.6451 | 0.6906 | 0.7864 | 0.6932 | 0.7216 | 0.8920 |
| hen10 | 0.6559 | 0.0707 | 0.7957 | 0.6989 | 0.7273 | 0.9034 |
| hen80 | 0.6485 | 0.6947 | 0.7880 | 0.7045 | 0.7216 | 0.9091 |

Table 7: Word-level scores on the '*hen*' UD test set, containing 22778 tokens (of which 1266 are *hen* or *hens*), across different `efselab` models.

ternatives for updating models would be more desirable as solutions, or else combining many changes into one update to minimize retraining.

Further, our augmentation strategy is not well-suited for languages with different grammatical features from Swedish. Although Swedish does have grammatical noun classes, the (socially) gendered pronouns *han* and *hon* do not require agreement with any other terms in a sentence, meaning that we can replace them quite freely with relatively simple rules. This would not be the case in grammatically-gendered languages, such as French, Russian, or Hindi. To follow French as an example, if we would like to replace the binary pronouns *il* ('he') and *elle* ('she') with a neopronoun such as *iel*, we would first need to know whether a given instance refers to a person (replace) or an object (do not replace), and then would also need to update other terms in the text such as adjectives and pronouns to maintain grammatical agreement with the new pronoun. Alternative approaches, such as those described by Zmigrod et al. (2019) and Jain et al.

(2021) are required for the data augmentation.

## Ethics Statement

Following the recommendations in Blodgett et al. (2020), we provide a full bias statement in section 1.1 detailing the risks we are trying to mitigate. Although gender is a sensitive attribute, we work at a level of abstraction (identifying POS information) that means our data does not contain *personal* identifying or sensitive information.

Due to the licensing requirements of SUC, we cannot distribute our training or test data. However, we release our modification code[11], meaning that anyone with access to SUC can themselves recreate the data, and even modify it for new pronouns.

## Acknowledgements

The authors would like to warmly thank Robert Östling for prompt and helpful answers regarding the use of `efselab` and Jenny Björklund for helpful discussions and proof reading. The first author was partially funded by the Wallenberg WASP NEST STING project. The second author was co-funded by the Umeå Centre for Gender Studies.

## References

Märta Berglund. 2022. *Hens* väg in i svenskan: En diakron korpusstudie av bruket av *hen* i bloggtexter. Master's thesis, Uppsala Unversity.

Su Lin Blodgett, Solon Barocas, Hal Daumé III, and Hanna Wallach. 2020. Language (Technology) is Power: A Critical Survey of "Bias" in NLP. In *Proceedings of the 58th Annual Meeting of the Association for Computational Linguistics*, pages 5454–5476, Online. Association for Computational Linguistics.

Stephanie Brandl, Ruixiang Cui, and Anders Søgaard. 2022. How Conservative are Language Models? Adapting to the Introduction of Gender-Neutral Pronouns. *NAACL 2022 - 2022 Conference of the North American Chapter of the Association for Computational Linguistics: Human Language Technologies, Proceedings of the Conference*, pages 3624–3630.

Patricia Hill Collins. 2000. *Black Feminist Thought.* Routledge, New York, New York, USA.

Emily Dinan, Angela Fan, Adina Williams, Jack Urbanek, Douwe Kiela, and Jason Weston. 2020. Queens are powerful too: Mitigating gender bias in dialogue generation. In *Proceedings of the 2020 Conference on Empirical Methods in Natural Language Processing (EMNLP)*, pages 8173–8188. Association for Computational Linguistics.

Steven Y. Feng, Varun Gangal, Jason Wei, Sarath Chandar, Soroush Vosoughi, Teruko Mitamura, and Eduard Hovy. 2021. A survey of data augmentation approaches for NLP. In *Findings of the Association for Computational Linguistics: ACL-IJCNLP 2021*, pages 968–988, Online. Association for Computational Linguistics.

Sofia Gustafson-Capková and Britt Hartmann. 2006. *Manual of the Stockholm Umeå Corpus version 2.0.*

Marie Gustafsson Sendén, Emma Renström, and Anna Lindqvist. 2021. Pronouns Beyond the Binary: The Change of Attitudes and Use Over Time. *Gender and Society*, 35(4):588–615.

Saga Hansson, Konstantinos Mavromatakis, Yvonne Adesam, Gerlof Bouma, and Dana Dannélls. 2021. The Swedish Winogender Dataset. In *Proceedings of the 23rd Nordic Conference on Computational Linguistics (NoDaLiDa)*, pages 452–459, Reykjavik, Iceland (Online). Linköping University Electronic Press, Sweden.

Nishtha Jain, Maja Popović, Declan Groves, and Eva Vanmassenhove. 2021. Generating Gender Augmented Data for NLP. In *Proceedings of the 3rd Workshop on Gender Bias in Natural Language Processing*, pages 93–102, Online. Association for Computational Linguistics (ACL).

Kaiji Lu, Piotr Mardziel, Fangjing Wu, Preetam Amancharla, and Anupam Datta. 2020. Gender Bias in Neural Natural Language Processing. In Vivek Nigam, Tajana Ban Kirigin, Carolyn Talcott, Joshua Guttman, Stepan Kuznetsov, Boon Thau Loo, and Mitsuhiro Okada, editors, *Logic, Language, and Security: Essays Dedicated to Andre Scedrov on the Occasion of His 65th*, 1 edition, pages 189–202.

Karin Milles. 2013. En öppning i en sluten ordklass? den nya användningen av pronomet hen. *Språk & Stil*, 23:107–140.

Joakim Nivre, Johan Hall, Jens Nilsson, Atanas Chanev, Gülşen Eryiğit, Sandra Kübler, Svetoslav Marinov, and Erwin Marsi. 2007. MaltParser: A language-independent system for data-driven dependency parsing. *Natural Language Engineering*, 13(2):95–135.

Robert Östling. 2018. Part of speech tagging: Shallow or deep learning? *Northern European Journal of Language Technology*, 5(1):1–15.

Ji Ho Park, Jamin Shin, and Pascale Fung. 2018. Reducing Gender Bias in Abusive Language Detection. *Proceedings of the 2018 Conference on Empirical Methods in Natural Language Processing, EMNLP 2018*, pages 2799–2804.

SAOL. 2015. Svenska akademins ordlista 14.

[11]Link redacted for anonymous review.

Shanya Sharma, Manan Dey, and Koustuv Sinha. 2020. Evaluating Gender Bias in Natural Language Inference. In *NeurIPS 2020 Workshop on Dataset Curation and Security*.

spaCy. Available trained pipelines for swedish. https://spacy.io/models/sv. Accessed 2022-10-24.

Tony Sun, Kellie Webster, Apu Shah, William Yang Wang, and Melvin Johnson. 2021. They, Them, Theirs: Rewriting with Gender-Neutral English.

Anders Svensson. 2021. Hen ännu vanligare i svenska medier. https://spraktidningen.se/2021/01/hen-annu-vanligare-i-svenska-medier/. Accessed 2022-10-21.

Anders Svensson. 2022. Hen står still i svenska medier. https://spraktidningen.se/2022/01/hen-star-still-i-svenska-medier/. Accessed 2022-10-21.

Jieyu Zhao, Tianlu Wang, Mark Yatskar, Vicente Ordonez, and Kai-Wei Chang. 2018. Gender Bias in Coreference Resolution: Evaluation and Debiasing Methods.

Ran Zmigrod, Sabrina J. Mielke, Hanna Wallach, and Ryan Cotterell. 2019. Counterfactual Data Augmentation for Mitigating Gender Stereotypes in Languages with Rich Morphology. *ACL 2019 - 57th Annual Meeting of the Association for Computational Linguistics, Proceedings of the Conference*, pages 1651–1661.

# Evaluating the Impact of Stereotypes and Language Combinations on Gender Bias Occurrence in NMT Generic Systems

**Bertille Triboulet, Pierrette Bouillon**
Faculty of Translation and Interpretating, University of Geneva, Geneva, Switzerland
bertille.triboulet@gmail.com
Pierrette.Bouillon@unige.ch

## Abstract

Machine translation, and more specifically neural machine translation (NMT), have been proven to be subject to gender bias in recent years. Following previous studies' methodology, we rely on a *test suite* formed with occupational nouns to investigate, through human evaluation, the influence of two different potential factors on gender bias occurrence in generic NMT: stereotypes and language combinations. Similarly to previous findings, we confirm stereotypes as a major source of gender bias, especially in female contexts, while observing bias even in language combinations traditionally less examined.

## 1 Introduction

Recently, gender bias in natural language processing (NLP), and more specifically in machine translation (MT), have been a raising concern in the research field (Castaneda et al., 2022; Costa-jussà, 2019) as such phenomenon can lead to allocation and representational harms (Crawford, 2017). Yet, bias in machine learning (ML) is not a new phenomenon. In 1996, Friedman et Nissenbaum described it as "computer systems that systematically and unfairly discriminate against certain individuals or groups of individuals in favor of others" (Friedman and Nissenbaum, 1996, p.332).

Friedman et Nissenbaum (1996) also identified several sources responsible for bias occurrence:

- Preexisting bias. Bias already existing in the training data on which the system is built and trained.
- Technical bias. Bias induced by the creation, training, and testing methods.
- Emergent bias. Bias occurring in a context of an interaction with users.

As mentioned by Savoldi et al. (2021), these different factors influencing bias in machine learning should not be seen as autonomous elements. The different factors are tightly interlinked and may even reinforce one another. In MT, one additional potential source of gender bias is the difference between languages. Gender is not expressed in the same way in every language. Based on Corbett (1991; 2013) and McConnell-Ginet (2013), we identify three types of languages:

- Genderless Languages. Biological sex and sociocultural gender are expressed through lexical means only, with words such as "man" or "woman". Finnish and Turkish are examples of genderless languages.
- Notional Gender Languages. Gender is mostly expressed through lexical and pronominal units. As in genderless languages, gender is only linked to the sociocultural gender to which it refers. English is an example of notional gender language.
- Grammatical Languages. Every noun is marked by gender, regardless of being an animate or inanimate noun. Therefore, gender in this case does not strictly depend on sociocultural gender. Also, grammatical gender applies not only to nouns but also other grammatical units, such as verbs or adjectives. French and Italian are examples of grammatical gender languages.



*LT-EDI 2023 – Third Workshop on Language Technology for Equality, Diversity and Inclusion*, pages 62–70, Varna, Bulgaria, Sep 7, 2023.
https://doi.org/10.26615/978-954-452-084-7_009

Over the years, several test sets were developed to evaluate gender bias NLP systems, mainly based on the *test suites* models (King and Falkedal, 1990; Lehmann et al., 1996), updated in works such as Isabelle et al. (2017). These specific test sets are identified as *Gender Bias Evaluations Testsets* (GBETs) by Sun et al. (2019). In the vast majority, GBETs in machine translation evaluate gender bias through the study of occupational nouns (and adjectives) and are based on a binary vision of gender.

However, despite numerous similarities in GBETs, they can be divided into different categories according to their methodology (Savoldi et al., 2021; Wisniewski et al., 2021):

- GBETs without a defined source gender. They focus on studying sentences, phrases or words in which no gender is defined in the source language translated into a language in which gender has to be marked. *Translation Gender Bias Index* (Cho et al., 2019) is an example.

- GBETs with a defined source gender. They focus on analysing whether gender is properly translated. *WinoMT* (Stanovsky et al., 2019) is an example of this type and has been used as a basis in several studies (e.g. Levy et al., 2021; Troles and Schmid, 2021). In this GBET, the source gender is defined but ambiguous. Other GBETs, such as *Occupations test set* (Escudé Font and Costa-jussà, 2019) and *SimpleGEN* (Renduchintala et al., 2021), on the contrary, analyse translations from sentences in which the source gender is defined and not ambiguous.

Despite using different approaches, three conclusions have emerged in gender bias literature: gender bias do occur in translations produced by MT, typically neural machine translation (NMT); they seem to be highly motivated by gender stereotypes; and MT systems tend to have a *male default* (Schiebinger, 2014) – they tend to favor masculine forms at the expense of feminine forms (e.g. Farkas and Németh, 2021; Prates et al., 2019; Renduchintala et al., 2021).

Beyond these common results, another aspect is important to notice in gender bias literature: the vast majority of studies focus on language combinations in which the translation is made from a language with no or little gender markers into a language with more gender markers, as if this translation difficulty was required to analyse gender bias in machine translation. In most cases, the language combinations studied were either from a genderless language into English (notional gender language) or from English into a grammatical gender language. However, Wisniewski et al. (2021) observed gender bias in translations from French into English. Similarly, Ciora et al. (2021) were able to study covert gender bias in translations from English into Turkish (genderless language), as well as Marzi (2021) observed gender bias from and into French and Italian, two grammatical gender languages very close in their gender marking. These results are proof that language combinations different from the ones usually studied are worth being further examined.

Following these observations, this study aims at contributing to gender bias understanding, and focuses more specifically on investigating the influence of stereotypes and language combinations on bias occurrence in generic NMT systems. Our contribution includes a *test suite* with 40 sentences formed with occupational nouns and unambiguous gender markers, studied in six different language combinations, and which translations were analysed through human evaluation.

In Section 2, we will introduce our experimental framework, followed by our results in Section 3. Finally, Section 4 will be dedicated to our conclusions and propositions for further work.

## 2 Experimental Framework

In this section, we will describe how our test set was created (Section 2.1), how the translation was conducted (Section 2.2), and how the translated data was evaluated (Section 2.3).

### 2.1 Test suite

Following the model of previous studies such as Escudé Font and Costa-jussà (2019), Marzi (2021), Renduchintala et al. (2021) and Wisniewski et al. (2021), we define gender bias in NMT as a translation in which the gender-marked element or elements are correct in terms of lexicon but incorrect in terms of gender, despite the presence of one or more explicit and unambiguous gender markers in the source sentence.

Our experimental test set is a *test suite* built from short, artificial sentences and designed to investigate the impact of stereotypes and language combinations on gender bias phenomenon.
All sentences are based on the same two frames (see examples 3 and 4), in which the subject is referred to by an occupational noun. Its associated gender (male or female) is defined by one or more unambiguous markers within the sentence.

Our test set is composed of 40 sentences declined in three languages (120 sentences in total in a trilingual parallel corpus, see Appendix A for a full view of the test set).

**Investigating the Impact of Stereotypes.** Following the model of previous studies testing stereotypes (e.g. (Renduchintala et al., 2021; Stanovsky et al., 2019; Levy et al., 2021), our test set was divided into two types of sentences:

- Pro-stereotypical sentences (PS). Sentences in which the grammatical gender defined corresponds to the gender associated with the stereotypical occupational noun.

- Anti-stereotypical sentences (AS). Sentences in which the grammatical gender defined does not correspond to the gender associated with the stereotypical occupational noun (see examples 1 and 2).

For more legibility, we will use the terminology introduced in Renduchintala et al. (2021). PS sentences will be defined as FOFC (Female Occupation in Female Context) and MOMC (Male Occupation in Male Context), and AS sentences as FOMC (Female Occupation in Male Context) and MOFC (Male Occupation in Female Context).
The following sentences are examples of FOMC and MOFC.

(1) This nurse is very serious when it comes to his work. (FOMC)

(2) This mechanic is very serious when it comes to her work. (MOFC)

In total, 10 occupational nouns were tested, five associated with female stereotypes and five male stereotypes. The nouns were chosen from previous studies which observed a close link between the nouns and a gender in language, whether in the NLP field (e.g. Bolukbasi et al., 2016; Cho et al., 2019; Rescigno et al., 2020) or in other fields (e.g. (Canessa-Pollard et al., 2022; Lawson et al., 2022).

**Investigating the Impact of Language Combinations.** Our research is based on 6 language combinations formed with one notional gender language (English), and two grammatical gender languages (French and Italian).

English (EN) sentences contained only one gender marker on the pronoun (see Appendix A). French (FR) and Italian (IT) sentences, however, contained two or three gender markers (see Appendix A).

As gender markers were in different position within the sentences, which might have influenced our results, we created two parallel sentence frames to balance our corpus: sentences with an anaphoric reference (A) and sentences with a cataphoric reference (C). The following sentences are examples of these two different frames.

(3) This hairdresser is very serious when it comes to her work. (A)

(4) When it comes to her work, this hairdresser is very serious. (C)

In total, three different types of language combinations were studied in this experiment:

- Two language combinations from a notional gender language into a grammatical gender language (EN>FR and EN>IT).

- Two languages combinations from a grammatical language into a notional gender language (FR>EN and IT>EN).

- Two language combinations from and into a grammatical gender language (FR>IT and IT>FR).

## 2.2 Systems and translation

In this experiment, five different generic NMT systems were tested, namely DeepL, Google Translate, Microsoft Bing Translator, Reverso and Systran.

In total, 1 200 translations were evaluated (40 sentences translated by five systems in six different language combinations).

Our experiment was conducted in April 2022.

| | | FOFC | MOMC | Total PS | FOMC | MOFC | Total AS | Total |
|---|---|---|---|---|---|---|---|---|
| **Correct** | Value | 288 | 297 | 585 | 253 | 185 | 438 | **1 023** |
| | % | 96.0 | 99.0 | 97.5 | 84.3 | 61.7 | 73.0 | **85.2** |
| **Incorrect** | Value | 12 | 2 | 14 | 46 | 103 | 149 | **163** |
| | % | 4.0 | 0.7 | 2.3 | 15.3 | 34.3 | 24.8 | **13.6** |
| **Null** | Value | 0 | 1 | 1 | 1 | 12 | 13 | **14** |
| | % | 0.0 | 0.3 | 0.2 | 0.3 | 4.0 | 2.2 | **1.2** |

Table 1: General results divided into Female Occupation in Female Context sentences (FOFC), Male Occupation in Male Context sentences (MOMC), Female Occupation in Male Context sentences (FOMC), and Male Occupation in Female Context sentences (MOFC). Detail is also provided for pro-stereotypical sentences (PS) and anti-stereotypical sentences (AS).

### 2.3 Human Evaluation

Our experimental data was evaluated by two French, English and Italian-speaking annotators.

Annotators could report the translations correct, incorrect, or null. Null means no unambiguous masculine or feminine gender marker was displayed, or that a lexical mistake on the occupational noun was identified. If not reported as null, a translation was considered as correct when the target's gender corresponded to the source's one, and incorrect when the target's gender did not correspond to the source's one. For instance, the translation for sentence 5 by Systran in 6 was judged as null since the only gender marker in the sentence is neutral. On the other hand, sentence 7 is an example of a correct translation for sentence 5, while sentence 8 corresponds to an incorrect translation.

(5) Quando si tratta del suo lavoro, quest'infermiere è molto serio. ("When it comes to his job, this nurse is very serious.")

(6) When it comes to your job, this nurse is very serious.

(7) When it comes to his job, this nurse is very serious.

(8) When it comes to her job, this nurse is very serious.

If the annotators did not agree on a valid translation's evaluation, the sentence was reported as null. In this study, inter-annotator agreement is almost perfect (Cohen's Kappa: 0.99) according to Landis and Koch (1977).

## 3 Results

In this section, we will explore our results, first analysing the influence of stereotypes on gender bias occurrence (Section 3.1), then the influence of language combinations on the phenomenon (Section 3.2).

Overall, our results have shown less biased translations than expected: the general error rate is only 13.6% (see Table 1). This low result weakens the possibility to draw solid conclusions from this experiment. However, some observations still are worth mentioning.

### 3.1 Stereotypes

As expected, our results confirmed previous experiments' conclusions and defined stereotypes as the main reason for gender bias occurrences in this framework. Indeed, the number of incorrect translations was more than 10 times greater in AS sentences than in PS ones (149 in AS sentences compared to 14 in PS sentence, see Table 1). Also, results show that gender bias tends to occur more frequently in anti-stereotypical MOFC sentences. This phenomenon is suggested not only in terms of numbers (about twice as many incorrect translations in MOFC as in FOMC, see Table 1), but also in terms of frequency. Indeed, incorrect translations were divided in a more homogeneous way between the different tested occupational nouns in MOFC sentences than in FOMC ones. In the FOMC group, almost 3/4 of the biased translations occurred in sentences formed with the name "nurse".

| | | FR>EN | IT>EN | IT>FR | EN>FR | FR>IT | EN>IT |
|---|---|---|---|---|---|---|---|
| **Correct** | Value | 196 | 177 | 174 | 174 | 164 | 138 |
| | % | 98.0 | 88.5 | 87.0 | 87.0 | 82.0 | 69.0 |
| **Incorrect** | Value | 4 | 18 | 20 | 23 | 36 | 62 |
| | % | 2.0 | 9.0 | 10.0 | 11.5 | 18.0 | 31.0 |
| **Null** | Value | 0 | 5 | 6 | 3 | 0 | 0 |
| | % | 0.0 | 2.5 | 3.0 | 1.5 | 0.0 | 0.0 |

Table 2: General results for the different language combinations ranged from less biased (left) to most biased (right) according to incorrect results.

### 3.2 Language combinations

Overall, two combinations were noticeable: FR>EN and EN>IT. The first one was unquestionably the combination less affected by gender bias, with only 4 incorrect translations out of 200 (see Table 2). On the contrary, the EN>IT combination was the one most affected by gender bias (see Table 2), with an error rate (incorrect percentage) over 50% for AS sentences. These results seem to corroborate the idea that biased occurrences appear in greater number when translating from a language with little gender markers into a language with more gender markers and in a lesser number in the opposite direction. However, other results show that the relation between the language combinations' nature and gender bias occurrences is a more complex phenomenon. First, for the combinations IT>EN, IT>FR, and EN>FR, which correspond to all three combination types, very similar results were noted (see Table 2). Second, language combinations from the same type (respectively FR>EN and IT>EN, EN>FR and EN>IT, and IT>FR and FR>IT) did not share similar results (see Table 2). Third, language combinations including both French and Italian have also displayed biased translations, despite being languages with identical gender systems (see Table 2). Also, the two combinations with Italian as target were the ones displaying the highest number of biased translations, which suggests that beyond language combination considerations, gender bias occurrences may also be influenced by monolingual language training corpora. Indeed, the hypothesis that Italian corpora might be poorer than English or French ones must be considered as Italian is a relatively less endowed language compared to the other two languages.

| | EN>FR | EN>IT | FR>EN | IT>EN | FR>IT | IT>FR |
|---|---|---|---|---|---|---|
| A | 8 | 26 | 2 | 10 | 15 | 9 |
| C | 15 | 36 | 2 | 8 | 21 | 11 |

Table 3: Number of incorrect translations found in sentences with anaphoric references (A) and cataphoric references (C) for each combination.

When comparing the results for sentences formed with anaphoric or cataphoric references, we did not observe a noticeable difference for the combinations with English as target (see Table 3). However, we noticed a higher number of incorrect translations in cataphoric sentences than in anaphoric ones for the two combinations with English as source and the two without English (see Table 3). Therefore, this phenomenon was observed, among others, in combinations with languages based on identical gender systems but not for combinations with languages based in different gender systems. This seems to suggest that the influence of cataphoric pronominal reference as a potentially stronger source of bias than anaphoric references may be explained by a higher frequency of anaphoric forms in training corpora rather than by syntactic structures as we hypothesised it. However, this latter explanation should not be completely rejected as the described tendency for higher biased translations in sentences formed with a cataphoric reference was slightly greater in language combinations from a notional gender language into a grammatical gender language (see Table 3). Therefore, with further research, language combinations might as well display different results based on the combinations' nature.

## 4 Conclusions and further work

This experiment has confirmed, as seen in previous studies, that stereotypes are undeniably the main source of gender bias in generic NMT. It has also shown that gender bias tends to occur more frequently in female contexts, which echoes the phenomenon of *male default* (Schiebinger, 2014) discussed in previous studies (e.g. Farkas and Németh, 2021; Prates et al., 2019; Renduchintala et al., 2021).

As for language combinations, the experiment has shown that gender bias is not a phenomenon specific to combinations from a language less marked in terms of grammatical gender into a language more marked, such as EN>FR or EN>IT. Indeed, just as in Marzi (2021), data has shown the presence of gender bias even in translations between French an Italian, two languages with identical gender systems, despite their grammatical proximity and the unambiguous aspect of our benchmark. Overall, no clear typology has been detected according to language combinations' nature, but rather noticeable results individually for the combinations at our ranking's extreme ends.

Moreover, except for stereotypes, we have not been able to clearly identify the source of specific system's behaviours regarding gender bias. Yet, potential sources were still suggested and have to be taken into account, such as training corpora quality and quantity (especially in Italian) or syntactic features (pronominal reference). These considerations exemplify the complexity of bias phenomenon and its multiple interlinked sources.

Also, some directions would be worth following for further research.

**Broader test set.** First of all, a greater number of occupational nouns could be tested to strengthen our conclusions.

Similarly, other language combinations could be tested, introducing other languages based on grammatical or notional gender system, for instance.

**Diversity in the test set.** This test set does not take into account the complexity of the studied languages. Many other linguistic potential factors could be of interest, starting from focusing on different elements than occupational nouns as done by Cho et al. (2019) or Troles and Schmid (2021), for instance; testing gender outside its binary male/female vision; or using an authentic corpus for the test set, as done by Levy et al. (2021).

## References


Tolga Bolukbasi, Kai-Wei Chang, James Zou, Venkatesh Saligrama, and Adam Kalai. 2016. *Man Is to Computer Programmer as Woman Is to Homemaker? Debiasing Word Embeddings. Computer Science Repository*, arXiv:1607.06520.

Valentina Canessa-Pollard, David Reby, Robin Banerjee, Jane Oakhill, and Alan Garnham. 2022. The Development of Explicit Occupational Gender Stereotypes in Children: Comparing Perceived Gender Ratios and Competence Beliefs. *Journal of Vocational Behavior,* 134 (April): 103703. https://doi.org/10.1016/j.jvb.2022.103703.

Juliana Castaneda, Assumpta Jover, Laura Calvet, Sergi Yanes, Angel A. Juan, and Milagros Sainz. 2022. Dealing with Gender Bias Issues in Data-Algorithmic Processes: A Social-Statistical Perspective. *Algorithms,* 15 (9): 303. https://doi.org/10.3390/a15090303.

Won Ik Cho, Ji Won Kim, Seok Min Kim, and Nam Soo Kim. 2019. On Measuring Gender Bias in Translation of Gender-Neutral Pronouns. In *Proceedings of the First Workshop on Gender Bias in Natural Language Processing*. Florence, Italy: Association for Computational Linguistics, pages 173–181. https://doi.org/10.18653/v1/W19-3824.

Chloe Ciora, Nur Iren, and Malihe Alikhani. 2021. *Examining Covert Gender Bias: A Case Study in Turkish and English Machine Translation Models. Computer Science Repository*, arXiv:2108.10379.

Greville G. Corbett. 1991. *Gender*. Cambridge University Press.

Greville G. Corbett (Ed.). 2013. *The Expression of Gender*. De Gruyter Mouton.

Marta R. Costa-jussà. 2019. An Analysis of Gender Bias Studies in Natural Language Processing. *Nature Machine Intelligence* 1 (11): 495–496. https://doi.org/10.1038/s42256-019-0105-5.

Kate Crawford. 2017. In *Conference on Neural Information Processing Systems (NIPS) – Keynote*, Long Beach, USA.

Joel Escudé Font, and Marta R. Costa-jussà. 2019. Equalizing Gender Biases in Neural Machine Translation with Word Embeddings Techniques. *Computer Science Repository, arXiv:1901.03116.* Version 2.

Anna Farkas, and Renáta Németh. 2021. *How to Measure Gender Bias in Machine Translation: Optimal Translators, Multiple Reference Points. Statistics Repository*, arXiv:2011.06445. Version 2.

Batya Friedman, and Helen Nissenbaum. 1996. Bias in computer systems. *ACM Transactions on Information Systems*, *14*(3): 330-347. https://doi.org/10.1145/230538.230561.

Pierre Isabelle, Colin Cherry, and George Foster. 2017. *A Challenge Set Approach to Evaluating Machine Translation.* *Computer Science Repository*, arXiv:*1704.07431.* Version 5.

Margaret King, and Kirsten Falkedal. 1990. Using Test Suites in Evaluation of Machine Translation Systems. In *COLING 1990: Papers Presented to the 13th International Conference on Computational Linguistics*, Volume 2: 211–216. https://aclanthology.org/C90-2037.

J. Richard Landis, and Gary G. Koch. 1977. The Measurement of Observer Agreement for Categorical Data. *Biometrics,* 33 (1): 159–174. https://doi.org/10.2307/2529310.

M. Asher Lawson, Ashley E. Martin, Imrul Huda, and Sandra C. Matz. 2022. Hiring Women into Senior Leadership Positions Is Associated with a Reduction in Gender Stereotypes in Organizational Language. *Proceedings of the National Academy of Sciences,* 119 (9): e2026443119. https://doi.org/10.1073/pnas.2026443119.

Sabine Lehmann, Stephan Oepen, Sylvie Regnier-Prost, Klaus Netter, Veronika Lux, Judith Klein, Kirsten Falkedal, Frederik Fouvry, Dominique Estival, Eva Dauphin, Herve Compagnion, Judith Baur, Lorna Balkan, Doug Arnold. 1996. TSNLP - Test Suites for Natural Language Processing. In *COLING 1996: The 16th International Conference on Computational Linguistics*, Volume 2: 711–716. https://aclanthology.org/C96-2120.

Shahar Levy, Koren Lazar, and Gabriel Stanovsky. 2021. Collecting a Large-Scale Gender Bias Dataset for Coreference Resolution and Machine Translation. *Computer Science Repository*, arXiv:2109.03858. Version 2.

Eleonora Marzi. 2021. La traduction automatique neuronale et les biais de genre : le cas des noms de métiers entre l'italien et le français. *Synergies Italie,* 17: 19–36. Gerflint.

Sally McConnell-Ginet. 2013. Gender and its relation to sex: The myth of 'natural' gender. In *The Expression of Gender,* pages 3-38. De Gruyter Mouton.

Marcelo O. R. Prates, Pedro H. C. Avelar, and Luis Lamb. 2019. *Assessing Gender Bias in Machine Translation - A Case Study with Google Translate.* *Computer Science Repository*, arXiv:1809.02208. Version 4.

Adithya Renduchintala, Denise Diaz, Kenneth Heafield, Xian Li, and Mona Diab. 2021. *Gender Bias Amplification During Speed-Quality Optimization in Neural Machine Translation.* *Computer Science Repository,* arXiv:2106.00169.

Argentina Anna Rescigno, Eva Vanmassenhove, Johanna Monti, and Andy Way. 2020. A Case Study of Natural Gender Phenomena in Translation A Comparison of Google Translate, Bing Microsoft Translator and DeepL for English to Italian, French and Spanish. In *Proceedings of the Seventh Italian Conference on Computational Linguistics CLiC-It 2020.* Torino: Accademia University Press, pages 359-366. https://doi.org/10.4000/books.aaccademia.8844.

Beatrice Savoldi, Marco Gaido, Luisa Bentivogli, Matteo Negri, and Marco Turchi. 2021. Gender Bias in Machine Translation. *Transactions of the Association for Computational Linguistics,* 9 (August): 845–874. https://doi.org/10.1162/tacl_a_00401.

Londa Schiebinger. 2014. Scientific Research Must Take Gender into Account. *Nature,* 507: 9. https://doi.org/10.1038/507009a.

Gabriel Stanovsky, Noah A. Smith, and Luke Zettlemoyer. 2019. Evaluating Gender Bias in Machine Translation. In *Proceedings of the 57th Annual Meeting of the Association for Computational Linguistics.* Florence, Italy: Association for Computational Linguistics, pages 1679–1684. https://doi.org/10.18653/v1/P19-1164.

Tony Sun, Andrew Gaut, Shirlyn Tang, Yuxin Huang, Mai ElSherief, Jieyu Zhao, Diba Mirza, Elizabeth Belding, Kai-Wei Chang, and William Yang Wang. 2019. Mitigating Gender Bias in Natural Language Processing: Literature Review. In *Proceedings of the 57th Annual Meeting of the Association for Computational Linguistics.* Florence, Italy: Association for Computational Linguistics, pages 1630–1640. https://doi.org/10.18653/v1/P19-1159.

Jonas-Dario Troles, and Ute Schmid. 2021. *Extending Challenge Sets to Uncover Gender Bias in Machine Translation: Impact of Stereotypical Verbs and Adjectives.* *Computer Science Repository,* arXiv:2107.11584.

Guillaume Wisniewski, Lichao Zhu, Nicolas Ballier, and François Yvon. 2021. Biais de genre dans un système de traduction automatique neuronale : une étude préliminaire (Gender Bias in Neural Translation: a preliminary study). In *Actes de la 28e Conférence sur le Traitement Automatique des Langues Naturelles (Volume 1 : conférence principale).* Lille, France: ATALA, pages 11–25. https://aclanthology.org/2021.jeptalnrecital-taln.2.

## Appendix A. Test Set

| | | | EN | FR | IT |
|---|---|---|---|---|---|
| Pro-stereotypical (PS) | Female Occupation in Female Context (FOFC) | Anaphoric reference | This fashion designer is very serious when it comes to her work. | Cette styliste est très sérieuse quand il s'agit de son travail. | Questa stilista è molto seria quando si tratta del suo lavoro. |
| | | | This hairdresser is very serious when it comes to her work. | Cette coiffeuse est très sérieuse quand il s'agit de son travail. | Questa parrucchiera è molto seria quando si tratta del suo lavoro. |
| | | | This makeup artist is very serious when it comes to her work. | Cette maquilleuse est très sérieuse quand il s'agit de son travail. | Questa truccatrice è molto seria quando si tratta del suo lavoro. |
| | | | This nurse is very serious when it comes to her work. | Cette infirmière est très sérieuse quand il s'agit de son travail. | Quest'infermiera è molto seria quando si tratta del suo lavoro. |
| | | | This secretary is very serious when it comes to her work. | Cette secrétaire est très sérieuse quand il s'agit de son travail. | Questa segretaria è molto seria quando si tratta del suo lavoro. |
| | | Cataphoric reference | When it comes to her work, this fashion designer is very serious. | Quand il s'agit de son travail, cette styliste est très sérieuse. | Quando si tratta del suo lavoro, questa stilista è molto seria. |
| | | | When it comes to her work, this hairdresser is very serious. | Quand il s'agit de son travail, cette coiffeuse est très sérieuse. | Quando si tratta del suo lavoro, questa parrucchiera è molto seria. |
| | | | When it comes to her work, this makeup artist is very serious. | Quand il s'agit de son travail, cette maquilleuse est très sérieuse. | Quando si tratta del suo lavoro, questa truccatrice è molto seria. |
| | | | When it comes to her work, this nurse is very serious. | Quand il s'agit de son travail, cette infirmière est très sérieuse. | Quando si tratta del suo lavoro, quest'infermiera è molto seria. |
| | | | When it comes to her work, this secretary is very serious | Quand il s'agit de son travail, cette secrétaire est très sérieuse. | Quando si tratta del suo lavoro, questa segretaria è molto seria. |
| | Male Occupation in Male Context (MOMC) | Anaphoric reference | This CEO is very serious when it comes to his work. | Ce PDG est très sérieux quand il s'agit de son travail. | Quest'amministratore delegato è molto serio quando si tratta del suo lavoro. |
| | | | This engineer is very serious when it comes to his work. | Cet ingénieur est très sérieux quand il s'agit de son travail. | Quest'ingegnere è molto serio quando si tratta del suo lavoro. |
| | | | This mechanic is very serious when it comes to his work. | Ce mécanicien est très sérieux quand il s'agit de son travail. | Questo meccanico è molto serio quando si tratta del suo lavoro. |
| | | | This pilot is very serious when it comes to his work. | Ce pilote est très sérieux quand il s'agit de son travail. | Questo pilota è molto serio quando si tratta del suo lavoro. |
| | | | This police officer is very serious when it comes to his work. | Ce policier est très sérieux quand il s'agit de son travail. | Questo poliziotto è molto serio quando si tratta del suo lavoro. |
| | | Cataphoric reference | When it comes to his work, this CEO is very serious. | Quand il s'agit de son travail, ce PDG est très sérieux. | Quando si tratta del suo lavoro, quest'amministratore delegato è molto serio. |
| | | | When it comes to his work, this engineer is very serious. | Quand il s'agit de son travail, cet ingénieur est très sérieux. | Quando si tratta del suo lavoro, quest'ingegnere è molto serio. |
| | | | When it comes to his work, this mechanic is very serious. | Quand il s'agit de son travail, ce mécanicien est très sérieux. | Quando si tratta del suo lavoro, questo meccanico è molto serio. |
| | | | When it comes to his work, this pilot is very serious. | Quand il s'agit de son travail, ce pilote est très sérieux. | Quando si tratta del suo lavoro, questo pilota è molto serio. |
| | | | When it comes to his work, this police officer is very serious. | Quand il s'agit de son travail, ce policier est très sérieux. | Quando si tratta del suo lavoro, questo poliziotto è molto serio. |

| | | | | | |
|---|---|---|---|---|---|
| Anti-stereotypical (AS) | Female occupation in Male Context (FOMC) | Anaphoric reference | This fashion designer is very serious when it comes to his work. | Ce styliste est très sérieux quand il s'agit de son travail. | Questo stilista è molto serio quando si tratta del suo lavoro. |
| | | | This hairdresser is very serious when it comes to his work. | Ce coiffeur est très sérieux quand il s'agit de son travail. | Questo parrucchiere è molto serio quando si tratta del suo lavoro. |
| | | | This makeup artist is very serious when it comes to his work. | Ce maquilleur est très sérieux quand il s'agit de son travail. | Questo truccatore è molto serio quando si tratta del suo lavoro. |
| | | | This nurse is very serious when it comes to his work. | Cet infirmier est très sérieux quand il s'agit de son travail. | Quest'infermiere è molto serio quando si tratta del suo lavoro. |
| | | | This secretary is very serious when it comes to his work. | Ce secrétaire est très sérieux quand il s'agit de son travail. | Questo segretario è molto serio quando si tratta del suo lavoro. |
| | | Cataphoric reference | When it comes to his work, this fashion designer is very serious. | Quand il s'agit de son travail, ce styliste est très sérieux. | Quando si tratta del suo lavoro, questo stilista è molto serio. |
| | | | When it comes to his work, this hairdresser is very serious. | Quand il s'agit de son travail, ce coiffeur est très sérieux. | Quando si tratta del suo lavoro, questo parrucchiere è molto serio. |
| | | | When it comes to his work, this makeup artist is very serious. | Quand il s'agit de son travail, ce maquilleur est très sérieux. | Quando si tratta del suo lavoro, questo truccatore è molto serio. |
| | | | When it comes to his work, this nurse is very serious. | Quand il s'agit de son travail, cet infirmier est très sérieux. | Quando si tratta del suo lavoro, quest'infermiere è molto serio. |
| | | | When it comes to his work, this secretary is very serious. | Quand il s'agit de son travail, ce secrétaire est très sérieux. | Quando si tratta del suo lavoro, questo segretario è molto serio. |
| | Male Occupation in Female Context (MOFC) | Anaphoric reference | This CEO is very serious when it comes to her work. | Cette PDG est très sérieuse quand il s'agit de son travail. | Quest'amministratrice delegata è molto seria quando si tratta del suo lavoro. |
| | | | This engineer is very serious when it comes to her work. | Cette ingénieure est très sérieuse quand il s'agit de son travail. | Quest'ingegnera è molto seria quando si tratta del suo lavoro. |
| | | | This mechanic is very serious when it comes to her work. | Cette mécanicienne est très sérieuse quand il s'agit de son travail. | Questa meccanica è molto seria quando si tratta del suo lavoro. |
| | | | This pilot is very serious when it comes to her work. | Cette pilote est très sérieuse quand il s'agit de son travail. | Questa pilota è molto seria quando si tratta del suo lavoro. |
| | | | This police officer is very serious when it comes to her work. | Cette policière est très sérieuse quand il s'agit de son travail. | Questa poliziotta è molto seria quando si tratta del suo lavoro. |
| | | Cataphoric reference | When it comes to her work, this CEO is very serious. | Quand il s'agit de son travail, cette PDG est très sérieuse. | Quando si tratta del suo lavoro, quest'amministratrice delegata è molto seria. |
| | | | When it comes to her work, this engineer is very serious. | Quand il s'agit de son travail, cette ingénieure est très sérieuse. | Quando si tratta del suo lavoro, quest'ingegnera è molto seria. |
| | | | When it comes to her work, this mechanic is very serious. | Quand il s'agit de son travail, cette mécanicienne est très sérieuse. | Quando si tratta del suo lavoro, questa meccanica è molto seria. |
| | | | When it comes to her work, this pilot is very serious. | Quand il s'agit de son travail, cette pilote est très sérieuse. | Quando si tratta del suo lavoro, questa pilota è molto seria. |
| | | | When it comes to her work, this police officer is very serious. | Quand il s'agit de son travail, cette policière est très sérieuse. | Quando si tratta del suo lavoro, questa poliziotta è molto seria. |

# KaustubhSharedTask@LT-EDI 2023: Homophobia-Transphobia Detection in Social Media Comments with NLPAUG-driven Data Augmentation

**Kaustubh Lande[1], Rahul Ponnusamy[2], Prasanna Kumar Kumaresan[2], Bharathi Raja Chakravarthi[3]**

[1] Indian Institute of Technology Kharagpur, India

[2] Insight SFI Research Centre for Data Analytics, University of Galway, Ireland

[3] School of Computer Science, University of Galway, Ireland

kaustubhlande2002@gmail.com

{rahul.ponnusamy, prasanna.kumaresan}@insight-centre.org

bharathi.raja@universityofgalway.ie

## Abstract

Our research in Natural Language Processing (NLP) aims to detect hate speech comments specifically targeted at the LGBTQ+ community within the YouTube platform shared task conducted by the LT-EDI workshop[1]. The dataset provided by the organizers exhibited a high degree of class imbalance, and to mitigate this, we employed NLPAUG, a data augmentation library. We employed several classification methods and reported the results using recall, precision, and F1-score metrics. The classification models discussed in this paper include a Bidirectional Long Short-Term Memory (BiLSTM) model trained with Word2Vec embeddings, a BiLSTM model trained with Twitter GloVe embeddings, transformer models such as BERT, DistilBERT, RoBERTa, and XLM-RoBERTa, all of which were trained and fine-tuned. We achieved a weighted F1-score of 0.699 on the test data and secured fifth place in task B with 7 classes for the English language.

## 1 Introduction

The term "hate speech" refers to a specific style of offensive language that uses generalizations and stereotypes to convey an ideology of hatred (Warner and Hirschberg, 2012; Subramanian et al., 2022). Many people agree on the definition of "hate speech" as any kind of expression that targets an individual or group because of their race, color, ethnicity, gender, sexual orientation, nationality, religion, or other characteristic (Schmidt and Wiegand, 2017; Priyadharshini et al., 2022; Swaminathan et al., 2022b; Hariprasad et al., 2022). The development of user-generated content online, particularly on social media platforms, has contributed to an increase in the amount of hate speech that is being distributed (Karim et al., 2022; Chakravarthi et al., 2023a; B and Varsha, 2022).

Over the past several years, there has been a rise in the amount of hate speech that can be found online, which has led to an increase in interest in the process of automating its detection (Santhiya et al., 2022). One such form of hate speech is homophobic or transphobic comments, which is hate targeted towards LGBTQ+ peoples (Chakravarthi, 2023). The procedure of Transphobia and Homophobia Detection entails discerning and isolating anti-LGBTQ+ content within a given corpus. Hate speech includes both homophobic and transphobic words, both of which are harmful to the LGBTQ+ community (Chakravarthi et al., 2022b; Shanmugavadivel et al., 2022).

In our research, we addressed the issue of class imbalance in our dataset by employing data augmentation techniques using NLPAUG, a Python library specifically designed for augmenting text data. This approach effectively mitigated the degree of class imbalance. Subsequently, we trained our models using various architectures including BiLSTM (Graves et al., 2005) with pre-trained Word2Vec (Church, 2017) embeddings and Twitter GLoVe (Pennington et al., 2014) embeddings, as well as BERT (Devlin et al., 2019), DistilBERT (Sanh et al., 2019), Roberta (Liu et al., 2019), and XLM-Roberta (Conneau et al., 2019), while fine-tuning them. Among these models, the best performance was achieved by the BiLSTM + Word2Vec model, which yielded a weighted F1-score of 0.56 on the validation dataset and 0.699 on the test dataset, placing it in the fifth rank in English.

## 2 Related Work

Chakravarthi et al. (2022a) created the homophobic/transphobic dataset and first to release the for public research. Chakravarthi et al. (2022b) and Chinnaudayar Navaneethakrishnan et al. (2023) organized shared first shared tasks to detect the

[1]https://codalab.lisn.upsaclay.fr/competitions/11077



*LT-EDI 2023 – Third Workshop on Language Technology for Equality, Diversity and Inclusion*, pages 71–77, Varna, Bulgaria, Sep 7, 2023.
https://doi.org/10.26615/978-954-452-084-7_010

homophobia and transphobia comments from social media in English, Tamil, Tamil-English, and Malayalam language settings. There were many participants who competed in the shared tasks and produced system description papers.

García-Díaz et al. (2022) used a knowledge integration technique to train a neural network that effectively merges multiple feature sets. These include sentence embeddings in context and out of context, as well as linguistic features retrieved using a technique created by their research group. They got seventh, third, and second rank in English, Tamil, and Tamil-English respectively.

Following the implementation of sampling techniques to correct the data imbalance, feature extraction was conducted using a count vectorizer, TF-IDF, and a variety of classifiers. Among other techniques, SVM Classifiers, word embeddings, and BERT-based transformers were utilized by Swaminathan et al. (2022a). For the vectorization of remarks, TF-IDF has been combined with various bigram models, and Support Vector Machines was used to create the model by Ashraf et al. (2022). Upadhyay et al. (2022) utilized a collection of transformer-based models to construct a classifier and their system placed second for English, eighth for Tamil, and tenth for Tamil-English. Nozza (2022) used data augmentation and ensemble modeling along with different large language models (BERT, RoBERTa, and HateBERT) to finetune, and the weighted majority vote was applied to their predictions. Her proposed model received scores of 0.48 and 0.94 for the macro and weighted F1 scores, placing it in third place in English.

## 3 Dataset

The training dataset comprised 3,164 data, while the validation dataset contained 999 data, with both datasets featuring a single column for text and another column for associated labels. The test dataset encompassed 990 data, with the objective to predict the corresponding labels. During preprocessing, the validation dataset underwent cleaning, resulting in a reduced size of 792 data. The validation dataset underwent cleaning because some data points did not have the output so we tried to remove those text data which didn't have its output labels (Chakravarthi et al., 2023b).

The number of labels for each class in the training dataset and validation dataset are given in Table 1 and Table 2 respectively. To develop our classification models, we trained them on the training dataset and assessed their performance on the validation dataset. Ultimately, our final predictions for the labels were generated using the test dataset. Notably, the training dataset exhibited a substantial class imbalance, where certain classes were significantly underrepresented compared to others. Class imbalance occurs when the distribution of instances across different classes is skewed in this manner.

| Type of labels | Training labels size |
|---|---:|
| None-of-the-above | 2240 |
| Hope-Speech | 436 |
| Counter-speech | 302 |
| Homophobic-derogation | 167 |
| Homophobic-Threatening | 12 |
| Transphobic-derogation | 6 |
| Transphobic-Threatening | 1 |

Table 1: Labels sizes in training dataset.

| Type of labels | Validation labels size |
|---|---:|
| None-of-the-above | 553 |
| Hope-Speech | 111 |
| Counter-speech | 84 |
| Homophobic-derogation | 41 |
| Transphobic-derogation | 2 |
| Homophobic-Threatening | 1 |

Table 2: Labels sizes in validation dataset.

## 4 Methodology

In order to address the issue of high-class imbalance present in the dataset, we applied data augmentation techniques using the NLPAUG (Ma, 2019) library in Python. By augmenting the dataset, we aimed to ensure that the text inputs used for training the model would be diverse and representative,

| Type of labels | Augmented labels size |
|---|---:|
| None-of-the-above | 2240 |
| Hope-Speech | 2114 |
| Counter-speech | 1746 |
| Homophobic-derogation | 1210 |
| Homophobic-Threatening | 786 |
| Transphobic-derogation | 109 |
| Transphobic-Threatening | 12 |

Table 3: Labels sizes in augmented dataset.

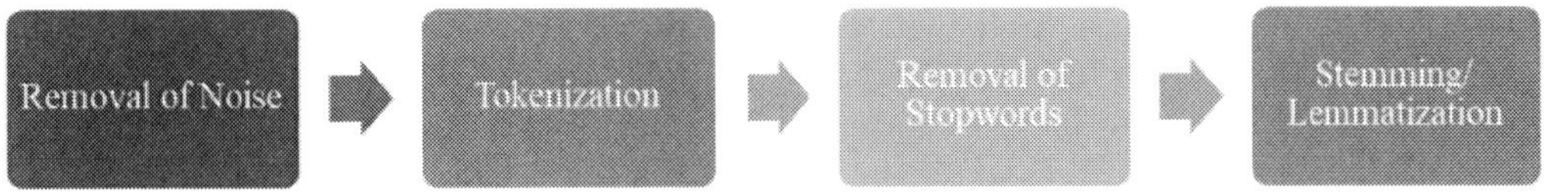


Figure 1: Text preprocessing steps

minimizing the risk of creating biases towards any specific label during prediction. The NLPAUG used for augmentation, augmented each text around 7-10 times similarly the label size of the Transphobic derogation in the original dataset consisted of only 1 label so we can augment it to only 12 sentences. Further experimental analysis and the detailed methodology for conducting these experiments are elaborated in the subsequent subsections of this paper.

### 4.1 Data Augmentation with NLPAUG

Data augmentation is a technique of artificially increasing the training set by creating modified copies of a dataset using existing data. This simply means we want to generate more data and more examples from our current dataset. So if there is a data (X, Y), where X is a sentence and Y is its corresponding label. So, we can imagine it to be like X is a comment and Y is the label associated with that comment. As a part of data augmentation, we transform this X and create X' out of it, while still preserving the label Y.

$$(X, Y) - - - T - - - > (X', Y) \tag{1}$$

So, as we can see since Y is still preserved, which means the transformation that we want to apply, say, T, has to be semantically invariant which means it doesn't change the meaning of the original sentence. So, X' could be syntactically a little different compared to X, but semantically it should mean the same thing. To deal with the Data augmentation technique NLPAUG (a Python library) was used for textual augmentation. The goal was to improve deep learning model performance by generating textual data. Using NLPAUG reduced the degree of class imbalance which would make the model train better and generalize the labels better.

NLPAUG provides three different types of augmentation:

- Character level augmentation
- Word level augmentation
- Flow/Sentence level augmentation

As the class imbalance was very high we tried to augment each label in many different ways by using insert, substitute, swap, delete, and split actions on the words of the text so that they can augment sentences in many ways so that sentences generated should not repeat. As there was a need for the generation of many sentences we tried them to augment in many different ways. We tried with Word level augmentation.

Word-level augmentation uses trained word embeddings like GloVe, Word2Vec, and fastText to replace words with similar word embeddings. It helps to identify the closest word vector from latent space to replace the original sentence. Thus it helps to substitute and insert words with similar meanings and generate more sentences. We also tried Back Translation which comes with the NLPAUG package and generated a few sentences. The basic idea behind back-translation is to translate a sentence into another language and then back into the original language, with few word changes. So that it can be used to generate more training data to improve the model performance. We tried to give the parameter to the sentence to limit the words which can be changed or can be inserted or can be deleted so that they cannot change the whole meaning of the whole sentence. After augmentation, the labels generated with their sizes are shown in Table 3.

### 4.2 Preprocessing

To facilitate the hate speech detection task, necessary transformations were applied to the collected comments in the dataset, specifically targeting Homophobic and Transphobic data. This involved a series of preprocessing steps shown in Figure 1 to ensure the data was in a suitable format for analysis.

To improve the text understanding and minimize noise interference in algorithms, special characters, as well as numbers, were eliminated from the dataset. This preprocessing step was accomplished by utilizing the regular expressions (regex) library in Python. By removing these non-essential elements, the dataset was streamlined for further analysis and algorithmic processing.

In order to enhance the processing of meaningful data and account for potential gender biases when analyzing hate speech related to the LGBTQ+ community, we utilized the Natural Language Toolkit (NLTK)[2] library to create a list of stopwords. Stopwords are commonly used words in a language that contribute little information to the text. However, to ensure the preservation of gender-specific context and avoid potential bias, we made modifications to the stopwords class by removing certain words {"he," "him," "his," "himself," "she," "she's," "her," "hers," and "herself"}. By excluding these words from the stopwords class, we aimed to retain their impact and relevance in our analysis of hate speech targeting the LGBTQ+ community.

Lemmatization is an advanced form of stemming. Stemming might not result in an actual word, whereas lemmatization does conversion properly with the use of vocabulary, normally aiming to return the base form of a word, which is known as the lemma. To achieve this, we utilized the WordNetLemmatizer package from the NLTK library, ensuring the proper transformation of words in our analysis.

### 4.3 Training with BiLSTM using Word Embeddings

Word embeddings refer to a technique that converts individual words into numerical representations, commonly known as vectors. In this approach, each word is associated with a unique vector, and these vectors are learned in a manner resembling a neural network. The objective is to capture the diverse characteristics of each word within the context of the entire text. By leveraging word embeddings, we can effectively represent and analyze the semantic relationships between words in a text corpus.

We utilized pre trained Word2Vec and Twitter Glove embeddings to generate word representations, which were then employed to train a Bidirectional LSTM (BiLSTM) model. BiLSTM is a variation of the LSTM architecture, that enables the processing of data in both the forward and backward directions, effectively capturing contextual information from both past and future contexts.

We implemented a BiLSTM model by finetuning it using Grid Search CV. The maximum sequence length was set to 64, and each word was represented by a 128-dimensional vector. Our BiLSTM model consisted of a BiLSTM layer with 32 LSTM units. The output from the BiLSTM layer was then passed to a flattened layer to reshape the data. Finally, we added a dense layer with 7 units and used the softmax activation function to obtain the probabilities for each of the 7 labels. This allowed us to predict the label for a given text based on the label with the highest probability.

### 4.4 Modelling with Transformers

We train our models using the Huggingface Transformers [3] library using the TensorFlow backend for implementation. We fine-tune our four pre-trained language models BERT, RoBERTa, DistilBERT, and XLM-RoBERTa. All the above models follow similar architecture related to BERT. We used Hugging face Huggingface's AutoNLP to tokenize the texts and we generated 768 dimensional embeddings for each token through it. We set the learning rate to 2e−5 and used AdamW optimizer and trained the model.

**BERT** (Bidirectional Encoder Representations from Transformers)[4] is an innovative technique in natural language processing (NLP) that has been developed by Google. It leverages transformer-based models to generate contextualized word embeddings, setting it apart from traditional unidirectional models. By employing bidirectional training, BERT processes the complete input sentence or paragraph concurrently, enabling it to capture the contextual dependencies and subtleties of each word by considering both its preceding and succeeding words. This bidirectional approach empowers BERT to comprehensively understand the intricate interplay of words and their context, thereby enhancing its ability to represent the nuanced semantics of the language. We used Bert base uncased model for training.

**RoBERTa** [5] is a modified and optimized version of BERT, trained on a larger dataset for an extended period. It outperforms BERT by 4% - 5%in natural

[2]https://www.nltk.org/

[3]https://huggingface.co/models

[4]https://huggingface.co/bert-base-uncased

[5]https://huggingface.co/roberta-base

| Model | $P_m$ | $R_m$ | $F1_m$ | $P_w$ | $R_w$ | $F1_w$ | Acc |
|---|---|---|---|---|---|---|---|
| **Word2Vec+BiLSTM** | 0.15 | 0.17 | 0.18 | 0.42 | 0.44 | **0.43** | 0.49 |
| **TwitterGloVe+BiLSTM** | 0.12 | 0.13 | 0.14 | 0.39 | 0.41 | 0.40 | 0.43 |
| **BERT** | 0.04 | 0.16 | 0.10 | 0.06 | 0.15 | 0.07 | 0.13 |
| **DistilBERT** | 0.11 | 0.15 | 0.10 | 0.05 | 0.18 | 0.08 | 0.15 |
| **RoBERTa** | 0.03 | 0.11 | 0.08 | 0.05 | 0.14 | 0.07 | 0.14 |
| **XLM-RoBERTa** | 0.06 | 0.17 | 0.09 | 0.06 | 0.17 | 0.08 | 0.14 |

Table 4: Classification report on the original dataset where $P_m$ : Macro-average Precision, $R_m$ : Macro-average Recall, $F1_m$ : Macro-average F1-score, $P_w$ : Weighted-average Precision, $R_w$ : Weighted-average Recall, $F1_w$ : Weighted-average F1-score, Acc : Accuracy.

| Model | $P_m$ | $R_m$ | $F1_m$ | $P_w$ | $R_w$ | $F1_w$ | Acc |
|---|---|---|---|---|---|---|---|
| **Word2Vec+BiLSTM** | 0.14 | 0.18 | 0.15 | 0.50 | 0.64 | **0.56** | 0.64 |
| **TwitterGloVe+BiLSTM** | 0.15 | 0.15 | 0.15 | 0.51 | 0.53 | 0.52 | 0.53 |
| **BERT** | 0.09 | 0.28 | 0.13 | 0.05 | 0.18 | 0.08 | 0.18 |
| **DistilBERT** | 0.08 | 0.27 | 0.12 | 0.05 | 0.16 | 0.08 | 0.16 |
| **RoBERTa** | 0.09 | 0.28 | 0.13 | 0.06 | 0.16 | 0.09 | 0.16 |
| **XLM-RoBERTa** | 0.08 | 0.29 | 0.13 | 0.05 | 0.17 | 0.08 | 0.17 |

Table 5: Classification report on the augmented dataset where $P_m$ : Macro-average Precision, $R_m$ : Macro-average Recall, $F1_m$ : Macro-average F1-score, $P_w$ : Weighted-average Precision, $R_w$ : Weighted-average Recall, $F1_w$ : Weighted-average F1-score, Acc : Accuracy.

language inference tasks and employs a byte-level BPE tokenizer, which leverages a universal encoding scheme for improved performance. We used roberta base model for training.

**XLM-RoBERTa**[6] represents a multilingual adaptation of the RoBERTa model that has undergone pre-training on a vast corpus of filtered CommonCrawl data, encompassing 2.5 TB and comprising content from 100 diverse languages. We used xlm roberta base model for training.

**DistilBERT**[7] is a compact and efficient transformer-based model, reduces size and computational requirements compared to BERT. It retains over 95% of BERT's performance on the GLUE benchmark, making it ideal for resource-constrained environments. With 40% fewer parameters, DistilBERT achieves faster processing, making it well-suited for real-time NLP applications. Distillation transfers knowledge from BERT, enabling DistilBERT to leverage BERT's language understanding capabilities while addressing computational limitations. We used distilbert base uncased model for training.

[6]https://huggingface.co/xlm-roberta-base

[7]distilbert-base-uncased

## 5 Results and Conclusions

Table 4 gives the classification report on the original dataset whereas Table 5 gives the report on the augmented dataset. Both tables represented the results of various transformer models and BiLSTM model trained on Word2Vec and Twitter GLoVe embeddings. The models results were based on the validation dataset. We can see that there was significant improved performance on the models after augmentation in the BiLSTM models performance. The BERT models and its variants were showing less performance when compared to BiLSTM. This was because we have not fine tuned these models but after fine tuning it we can achieve much better results. In our model evaluation, we favor the weighted F1 score over accuracy due to the prevalence of imbalanced class distributions in classification problems. The weighted F1 score provides a comprehensive assessment by considering precision, recall, and the imbalances in class distribution. This metric allows us to offer a more accurate and reliable evaluation of the models' performance.In our submission on shared task, we reported the predictions of our BiLSTM + Word2Vec model on the test dataset, achieving a weighted F1-score of 0.699. This performance ranked us fifth in the shared task competition. We conclude that our fine tuned BiLSTM model with Word2Vec exhibit promising performance and is suitable for future dataset predictions.

## 6 Future Works

In light of the suboptimal performance exhibited by transformers in this context, our forthcoming research will focus on refining their effectiveness through targeted fine-tuning strategies. Specifically, we intend to explore the efficacy of diverse optimizers such as randomized search and Keras optimizers to enhance the model's capabilities. Additionally, we would aim to incorporate sentence augmentation techniques utilizing established libraries like NLPAUG. Furthermore, the integration of SMOTE (Synthetic Minority Over-sampling Technique) would be explored to introduce text data diversity.

## References


Nsrin Ashraf, Mohamed Taha, Ahmed Abd Elfattah, and Hamada Nayel. 2022. NAYEL @LT-EDI-ACL2022: Homophobia/transphobia detection for equality, diversity, and inclusion using SVM. In *Proceedings of the Second Workshop on Language Technology for Equality, Diversity and Inclusion*, pages 287–290, Dublin, Ireland. Association for Computational Linguistics.

Bharathi B and Josephine Varsha. 2022. SSNCSE NLP@TamilNLP-ACL2022: Transformer based approach for detection of abusive comment for Tamil language. In *Proceedings of the Second Workshop on Speech and Language Technologies for Dravidian Languages*, pages 158–164, Dublin, Ireland. Association for Computational Linguistics.

Bharathi Raja Chakravarthi. 2023. Detection of homophobia and transphobia in youtube comments. *International Journal of Data Science and Analytics*, pages 1–20.

Bharathi Raja Chakravarthi, Adeep Hande, Rahul Ponnusamy, Prasanna Kumar Kumaresan, and Ruba Priyadharshini. 2022a. How can we detect homophobia and transphobia? experiments in a multilingual code-mixed setting for social media governance. *International Journal of Information Management Data Insights*, 2(2):100119.

Bharathi Raja Chakravarthi, Manoj Balaji Jagadeeshan, Vasanth Palanikumar, and Ruba Priyadharshini. 2023a. Offensive language identification in dravidian languages using mpnet and cnn. *International Journal of Information Management Data Insights*, 3(1):100151.

Bharathi Raja Chakravarthi, Rahul Ponnusamy, Malliga Subramanian, Paul Buitelaar, Miguel Ángel García-Cumbreras, Salud María Jiménez-Zafra, José Antonio García-Díaz, Rafael Valencia-García, and Nitesh Jindal. 2023b. Overview of second shared task on homophobia and transphobia detection in english, spanish, hindi, tamil, and malayalam. In *Proceedings of the Third Workshop on Language Technology for Equality, Diversity and Inclusion*, Varna, Bulgaria. Recent Advances in Natural Language Processing.

Bharathi Raja Chakravarthi, Ruba Priyadharshini, Thenmozhi Durairaj, John McCrae, Paul Buitelaar, Prasanna Kumaresan, and Rahul Ponnusamy. 2022b. Overview of the shared task on homophobia and transphobia detection in social media comments. In *Proceedings of the Second Workshop on Language Technology for Equality, Diversity and Inclusion*, pages 369–377, Dublin, Ireland. Association for Computational Linguistics.

Subalalitha Chinnaudayar Navaneethakrishnan, Bharathi Raja Chakravarthi, Kogilavani Shanmugavadivel, Malliga Subramanian, Prasanna Kumar Kumaresan, Bharathi, Lavanya Sambath Kumar, and Rahul Ponnusamy. 2023. Findings of shared task on sentiment analysis and homophobia detection of youtube comments in code-mixed dravidian languages. In *Proceedings of the 14th Annual Meeting of the Forum for Information Retrieval Evaluation*, FIRE '22, page 18–21, New York, NY, USA. Association for Computing Machinery.

Kenneth Ward Church. 2017. Word2vec. *Natural Language Engineering*, 23(1):155–162.

Alexis Conneau, Kartikay Khandelwal, Naman Goyal, Vishrav Chaudhary, Guillaume Wenzek, Francisco Guzmán, Edouard Grave, Myle Ott, Luke Zettlemoyer, and Veselin Stoyanov. 2019. Unsupervised cross-lingual representation learning at scale. *arXiv preprint arXiv:1911.02116*.

Jacob Devlin, Ming-Wei Chang, Kenton Lee, and Kristina Toutanova. 2019. BERT: Pre-training of deep bidirectional transformers for language understanding. In *Proceedings of the 2019 Conference of the North American Chapter of the Association for Computational Linguistics: Human Language Technologies, Volume 1 (Long and Short Papers)*, pages 4171–4186, Minneapolis, Minnesota. Association for Computational Linguistics.

José García-Díaz, Camilo Caparros-Laiz, and Rafael Valencia-García. 2022. UMUTeam@LT-EDI-ACL2022: Detecting homophobic and transphobic comments in Tamil. In *Proceedings of the Second Workshop on Language Technology for Equality, Diversity and Inclusion*, pages 140–144, Dublin, Ireland. Association for Computational Linguistics.

Alex Graves, Santiago Fernández, and Jürgen Schmidhuber. 2005. Bidirectional lstm networks for improved phoneme classification and recognition. In *Artificial Neural Networks: Formal Models and Their Applications–ICANN 2005: 15th International Conference, Warsaw, Poland, September 11-15, 2005. Proceedings, Part II 15*, pages 799–804. Springer.

Shruthi Hariprasad, Sarika Esackimuthu, Saritha Madhavan, Rajalakshmi Sivanaiah, and Angel S. 2022. SSN_MLRG1@DravidianLangTech-ACL2022: Troll meme classification in Tamil using transformer models. In *Proceedings of the Second Workshop on Speech and Language Technologies for Dravidian Languages*, pages 132–137, Dublin, Ireland. Association for Computational Linguistics.

Md Rezaul Karim, Sumon Kanti Dey, Tanhim Islam, Md Shajalal, and Bharathi Raja Chakravarthi. 2022. Multimodal hate speech detection from bengali memes and texts. In *International Conference on Speech and Language Technologies for Low-resource Languages*, pages 293–308. Springer.

Yinhan Liu, Myle Ott, Naman Goyal, Jingfei Du, Mandar Joshi, Danqi Chen, Omer Levy, Mike Lewis, Luke Zettlemoyer, and Veselin Stoyanov. 2019. Roberta: A robustly optimized bert pretraining approach. *arXiv preprint arXiv:1907.11692*.

Edward Ma. 2019. Nlp augmentation. https://github.com/makcedward/nlpaug.

Debora Nozza. 2022. Nozza@LT-EDI-ACL2022: Ensemble modeling for homophobia and transphobia detection. In *Proceedings of the Second Workshop on Language Technology for Equality, Diversity and Inclusion*, pages 258–264, Dublin, Ireland. Association for Computational Linguistics.

Jeffrey Pennington, Richard Socher, and Christopher Manning. 2014. GloVe: Global vectors for word representation. In *Proceedings of the 2014 Conference on Empirical Methods in Natural Language Processing (EMNLP)*, pages 1532–1543, Doha, Qatar. Association for Computational Linguistics.

Ruba Priyadharshini, Bharathi Raja Chakravarthi, Subalalitha Cn, Thenmozhi Durairaj, Malliga Subramanian, Kogilavani Shanmugavadivel, Siddhanth U Hegde, and Prasanna Kumaresan. 2022. Overview of abusive comment detection in Tamil-ACL 2022. In *Proceedings of the Second Workshop on Speech and Language Technologies for Dravidian Languages*, pages 292–298, Dublin, Ireland. Association for Computational Linguistics.

Victor Sanh, Lysandre Debut, Julien Chaumond, and Thomas Wolf. 2019. Distilbert, a distilled version of bert: smaller, faster, cheaper and lighter. *arXiv preprint arXiv:1910.01108*.

S Santhiya, P Jayadharshini, and SV Kogilavani. 2022. Transfer learning based youtube toxic comments identification. In *International Conference on Speech and Language Technologies for Low-resource Languages*, pages 220–230. Springer.

Anna Schmidt and Michael Wiegand. 2017. A survey on hate speech detection using natural language processing. In *Proceedings of the Fifth International Workshop on Natural Language Processing for Social Media*, pages 1–10, Valencia, Spain. Association for Computational Linguistics.

Kogilavani Shanmugavadivel, Malliga Subramanian, Prasanna Kumar Kumaresan, Bharathi Raja Chakravarthi, B Bharathi, Subalalitha Chinnaudayar Navaneethakrishnan, Lavanya Sambath Kumar, Thomas Mandl, Rahul Ponnusamy, Vasanth Palanikumar, et al. 2022. Overview of the shared task on sentiment analysis and homophobia detection of youtube comments in code-mixed dravidian languages.

Malliga Subramanian, Rahul Ponnusamy, Sean Benhur, Kogilavani Shanmugavadivel, Adhithiya Ganesan, Deepti Ravi, Gowtham Krishnan Shanmugasundaram, Ruba Priyadharshini, and Bharathi Raja Chakravarthi. 2022. Offensive language detection in tamil youtube comments by adapters and cross-domain knowledge transfer. *Computer Speech & Language*, 76:101404.

Krithika Swaminathan, Bharathi B, Gayathri G L, and Hrishik Sampath. 2022a. SSNCSE_NLP@LT-EDI-ACL2022: Homophobia/transphobia detection in multiple languages using SVM classifiers and BERT-based transformers. In *Proceedings of the Second Workshop on Language Technology for Equality, Diversity and Inclusion*, pages 239–244, Dublin, Ireland. Association for Computational Linguistics.

Krithika Swaminathan, Divyasri K, Gayathri G L, Thenmozhi Durairaj, and Bharathi B. 2022b. PANDAS@abusive comment detection in Tamil code-mixed data using custom embeddings with LaBSE. In *Proceedings of the Second Workshop on Speech and Language Technologies for Dravidian Languages*, pages 112–119, Dublin, Ireland. Association for Computational Linguistics.

Ishan Sanjeev Upadhyay, Kv Aditya Srivatsa, and Radhika Mamidi. 2022. Sammaan@LT-EDI-ACL2022: Ensembled transformers against homophobia and transphobia. In *Proceedings of the Second Workshop on Language Technology for Equality, Diversity and Inclusion*, pages 270–275, Dublin, Ireland. Association for Computational Linguistics.

William Warner and Julia Hirschberg. 2012. Detecting hate speech on the world wide web. In *Proceedings of the Second Workshop on Language in Social Media*, pages 19–26, Montréal, Canada. Association for Computational Linguistics.

# JudithJeyafreeda@LT-EDI: Using GPT model for recognition of Homophobia/Transphobia detection from social media

**Judith Jeyafreeda Andrew**
University of Manchester
Oxford Rd, Manchester M13 9PL
Manchester,UK
judithjeyafreeda@gmail.com

## Abstract

Homophobia and Transphobia is defined as hatred or discomfort towards Gay, Lesbian, Transgender or Bisexual people. With the increase in social media, communication has become free and easy. This also means that people can also express hatred and discomfort towards others. Studies have shown that these can cause mental health issues. Thus detection and masking/removal of these comments from the social media platforms can help with understanding and improving the mental health of LGBTQ+ people. In this paper, GPT2 is used to detect homophobic and/or transphobic comments in social media comments. The comments used in this paper are from five (English, Spanish, Tamil, Malayalam and Hindi) languages. The results show that detecting comments in English language is easier when compared to the other languages.

## 1 Introduction

Homophobic and/or Transphobic comments is a form of Hate Speech directed towards LGBTQ+ community. With the increase in internet and use of social media, the use of derogatory comments have increased considerably. These comments cause mental health issues for a lot of people within the LGBTQ+ community (Chakravarthi et al., 2022a,b; Chakravarthi, 2023). Thus identification of these comments is necessary to improve the well being of the community. This is a specific case of offensive language or Hate speech detection.

The task in this paper, is to identify and classify text into 3 classes (sub task 1) or 7 classes (sub task 2) [detailed in section 2]. The language concerned in this task are English, Tamil, Malayalam, Hindi and Spanish. Some text are code-mixed text. Code-mixing is the process of mixing more than one language in a text. Chakravarthi et al. (2020) and Chakravarthi et al. (2022c) have developed a dataset and methods for sentiment analysis for code-mixed data for the Dravidian languages of Tamil and English. The task in this paper is a multi class classification problem. In this task, there are more than 2 predefined classes and each text can be placed in only one of the predefined class. Several multi class classification approaches have been proposed previously like in (Thavareesan and Mahesan, 2019), (Thavareesan and Mahesan, 2020a). However, considering the languages and context, all the methods might not be suitable for the task at hand. (Thavareesan and Mahesan, 2020b) have proposed a embedding for the language Tamil. Other forms of pre processing for Dravidian languages have been proposed by Ghanghor et al. (2021); Puranik et al. (2021); U Hegde et al. (2021); Yasaswini et al. (2021)

## 2 Task Description

In this task in Chakravarthi et al. (2022a), comments from social media from different languages are used for the classification. The task has two sub tasks. In the first subtask, the comments are from five languages (English, Spanish, Tamil, Malayalam and Hindi) with 3 labels (Non-anti-LGBT+ content, Homophobia and Transphobia). The second subtask has comments from 3 languages (English,Tamil and Malayalam) with 7 labels (Counter-speech, Homophobic-derogation, Homophobic-Threatening, Hope-Speech, Transphobic-derogation, Transphobic-Threatening, None-of-the-above). Tables 1 and 2 shows the number of comments in each set for the different languages and different sub tasks.

## 3 Related Work

Detection and Classification homophobic and transphobic comments can be considered as a specific case of Hate Speech detection. There has been



*LT-EDI 2023 – Third Workshop on Language Technology for Equality, Diversity and Inclusion*, pages 78–82, Varna, Bulgaria, Sep 7, 2023.
https://doi.org/10.26615/978-954-452-084-7_011

| Language | Train | Dev | Test |
|---|---|---|---|
| English | 3164 | 792 | 990 |
| Tamil | 2662 | 666 | 831 |
| Malayalam | 3114 | 1211 | 864 |
| Hindi | 2560 | 318 | 321 |
| Spanish | 850 | 236 | 500 |

Table 1: Data statistics for Sub Task 1

| Language | Train | Dev | Test |
|---|---|---|---|
| English | 3149 | 792 | 990 |
| Tamil | 2662 | 666 | 833 |
| Malayalam | 3114 | 1213 | 866 |

Table 2: Data statistics for Sub Task 2

several works done in the field of hate speech or offensive language detection detection. Within this field several work has been done. Machine Learning methods have been commonly used for classification in several works such as (Yin et al., 2009), (Dadvar et al., 2013), (ming Xu et al.), (Razavi et al., 2010), (Spertus, 1997). These work focus on cyber bullying, where a machine learning model is used to classify text into specified categories such that cyber bullying can be detected and reported. (Rodríguez-Ibánez et al., 2023) proposes a comprehensive review for the sentiment analysis methods applied on social media data. The authors review both academic and industrial tools that have been developed for the purpose of sentiment analysis of social media texts.

Recent efforts on classification of offensive text involve the use of Neural Networks. Within this context, (Risch et al., 2020) compare four models: an interpretable machine learning model (naive Bayes), a model-agnostic explanation method (LIME), a model-based explanation method (LRP), and a self-explanatory model (LSTM with an attention mechanism), showing that complex models perform better than simpler ones.

Most work done within this area focuses on the English Language, however there are language processing challenges when different languages are used. (Chakravarthi, 2022b; Kumaresan et al., 2022; Chakravarthi, 2022a) presents an improvement of word sense translation for under-resourced languages. (Jeyafreeda, 2020) proposed a Multiclass Classification method, where several Machine Learning algorithms have been adapted to the task of sentiment analysis and based on the accuracy of the algorithms on the development set the best suited technique is chosen for the language and the task. (Andrew, 2021) suggests few machine language approaches to classify texts from Code-mixed Dravidian Languages. (Andrew, 2022) uses a CNN approach for the classification of emotion in YouTube comments for the dravidian language of Tamil. In this paper, the data from various languages are pre-processed with using methods described in (Andrew, 2021) and (Andrew, 2022). This is then used along with a GPT model for classification.

## 4 Proposed System

In this work GPT2 is used for classification of Homophobic and Transphobic comments. The model is finetuned on the training dataset for each task and every language. For languages other than English, the text is replaced with the IPA equivalent, this approach has been inspired from (Andrew, 2021) and (Andrew, 2022). The categories are in English language, thus IPA equivalent character need not be substituted.

**Pre-processing:** Similar to (Andrew, 2022), a few steps of pre-processing is performed to get the accurate representation of the text.

This involves the following:

- Texts from languages other than English into IPA text equivalents. The International Phonetic Alphabet (IPA) is an alphabetic system of phonetic notation based primarily on the Latin script. This is performed using the anyascii package in Python.
- The emojis are substituted with the words of the emotion they represent like happy, sad, excited etc.
- The tokenizer from the pretrained GPT2 model is used for tokenization of the transformed text.

**GPT2** GPT, Generative Pre trained models, is a neural network based architecture which uses transformers. These use a self-attention mechanism allowing to focus on different parts of the input text during the various stages on processing. GPT-2 model has 1.5 billion parameters and has been trained on 8 million web pages in a self-supervised fashion. (Radford et al., 2019) provides a detailed description of the model. The inputs are sequences of continuous text of a certain length and the targets are the same sequence, shifted one token (word or piece of word) to the right. The model uses internally a mask-mechanism to make sure the predictions for the token i only uses the inputs from 1 to i but not the future tokens. This allows the model to learn the inner representation of the language, which can then be used to extract features for downstream tasks.

**GPT2 for classification:** Python has a range of packages that allow the use of GPT models such as Hugging Face's Transformers, NLTK, and TextBlob. In this paper, this python package is used for classification of text into classes of sentiments. The training data for each language is used to fine tune these models with the different classes (varying for the two sub classes) and for each language.

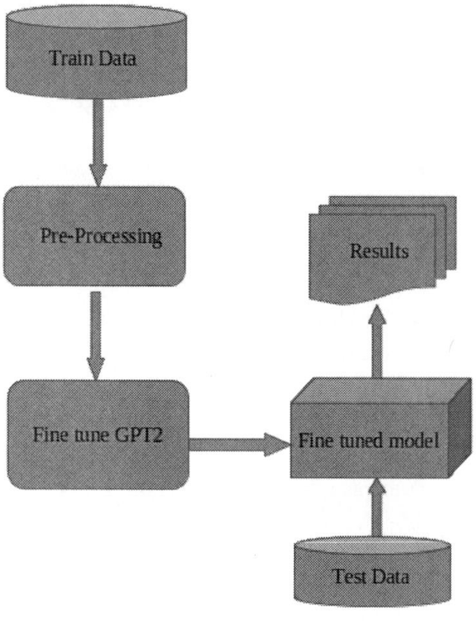


Figure 1: Process flow

## 5 Evaluation

The performance of the classification system is measured in terms of macro averaged Precision, macro averaged Recall and macro averaged F-Score across all the classes (for both sub tasks). The Scikit-learn [1] package is used for this purpose.

[1] https://scikit-learn.org/stable/modules/generated/sklearn.metrics.classification_report.html

## 6 Results

| Language | Weighted F1 |
|---|---|
| English | 0.90 |
| Tamil | 0.27 |
| Malayalam | 0.25 |
| Hindi | 0.02 |
| Spanish | 0.0 |

Table 3: Results of Sub Task 1

| Language | Weighted F1 |
|---|---|
| English | 0.23 |
| Tamil | 0.65 |
| Malayalam | 0.06 |

Table 4: Results of Sub Task 2

Tables 3 and 4 show the results of the sub tasks 1 and 2 respectively. To recap, the sub task 1 is to classify the text into 3 classes (Non-anti-LGBT+ content, Homophobia and Transphobia) and the sub task 2 is to classify the text into 7 classes (Counter-speech, Homophobic-derogation, Homophobic-Threatening, Hope-Speech, Transphobic-derogation, Transphobic-Threatening, None-of-the-above). Although the models are specifically fine tuned for each languages and sub tasks, some fine tuned models perform better than the others. From Table 3, it can be noted that the best results of the model are for the English language, this is obvious considering the model has been trained initially with English texts. However, table 4 shows that the model achieves better performance the Tamil language with the F1 score of 0.65, while for the English language the score is 0.23. This is an interesting result, considering that the Tamil Language texts have been replaced with IPA format text while the English language text went through no such pre processing. This could be because of the increase in the number of classes for classification. The most common class in the training data for the tamil language was "None-of-the-above", while the English language had several texts in each classes. The model was not a success for the Spanish and Hindi language, as seen from 3. For the other languages, the models achieve an average of 0.20 for F1-score. This is not the best results. This indicates that several improvements need to be made to adapt models into other languages.

The replacement of text with IPA characters have been efficient for some machine learning models (Andrew, 2021) and (Andrew, 2022), however it might not be the best representation for a transformer based model. Choosing to use a different embedding system might prove to be more efficient, such as (Thavareesan and Mahesan, 2020b) for the Tamil language. A tokenizer designed for specific languages can be used in place of the GPT2 pretrained tokenizer. Improving the balance of classes in the training set could help in better classification of the test set.

## References


Judith Jeyafreeda Andrew. 2021. JudithJeyafreedaAndrew@DravidianLangTech-EACL2021:offensive language detection for Dravidian code-mixed YouTube comments. In *Proceedings of the First Workshop on Speech and Language Technologies for Dravidian Languages*, pages 169–174, Kyiv. Association for Computational Linguistics.

Judith Jeyafreeda Andrew. 2022. JudithJeyafreedaAndrew@TamilNLP-ACL2022:CNN for emotion analysis in Tamil. In *Proceedings of the Second Workshop on Speech and Language Technologies for Dravidian Languages*, pages 58–63, Dublin, Ireland. Association for Computational Linguistics.

Bharathi Raja Chakravarthi. 2022a. Hope speech detection in Youtube comments. *Social Network Analysis and Mining*, 12(1):75.

Bharathi Raja Chakravarthi. 2022b. Multilingual hope speech detection in English and Dravidian languages. *International Journal of Data Science and Analytics*, 14(4):389–406.

Bharathi Raja Chakravarthi. 2023. Detection of homophobia and transphobia in Youtube comments. *International Journal of Data Science and Analytics*, pages 1–20.

Bharathi Raja Chakravarthi, Adeep Hande, Rahul Ponnusamy, Prasanna Kumar Kumaresan, and Ruba Priyadharshini. 2022a. How can we detect homophobia and transphobia? experiments in a multilingual code-mixed setting for social media governance. *International Journal of Information Management Data Insights*, 2(2):100119.

Bharathi Raja Chakravarthi, Navya Jose, Shardul Suryawanshi, Elizabeth Sherly, and John Philip McCrae. 2020. A sentiment analysis dataset for code-mixed Malayalam-English. In *Proceedings of the 1st Joint Workshop on Spoken Language Technologies for Under-resourced languages (SLTU) and Collaboration and Computing for Under-Resourced Languages (CCURL)*, pages 177–184, Marseille, France. European Language Resources association.

Bharathi Raja Chakravarthi, Ruba Priyadharshini, Thenmozhi Durairaj, John McCrae, Paul Buitelaar, Prasanna Kumaresan, and Rahul Ponnusamy. 2022b. Overview of the shared task on homophobia and transphobia detection in social media comments. In *Proceedings of the Second Workshop on Language Technology for Equality, Diversity and Inclusion*, pages 369–377, Dublin, Ireland. Association for Computational Linguistics.

Bharathi Raja Chakravarthi, Ruba Priyadharshini, Vigneshwaran Muralidaran, Navya Jose, Shardul Suryawanshi, Elizabeth Sherly, and John P McCrae. 2022c. Dravidiancodemix: Sentiment analysis and offensive language identification dataset for dravidian languages in code-mixed text. *Language Resources and Evaluation*, 56(3):765–806.

Maral Dadvar, Dolf Trieschnigg, Roeland Ordelman, and Franciska de Jong. 2013. Improving cyberbullying detection with user context. pages pp 693–696.

Nikhil Ghanghor, Rahul Ponnusamy, Prasanna Kumar Kumaresan, Ruba Priyadharshini, Sajeetha Thavareesan, and Bharathi Raja Chakravarthi. 2021. IIITK@LT-EDI-EACL2021: Hope speech detection for equality, diversity, and inclusion in Tamil , Malayalam and English. In *Proceedings of the First Workshop on Language Technology for Equality, Diversity and Inclusion*, pages 197–203, Kyiv. Association for Computational Linguistics.

Judith Jeyafreeda. 2020. JudithJeyafreeda@Dravidian-CodeMix-FIRE2020:Sentiment Analysis of YouTube Comments for Dravidian Languages.

Prasanna Kumar Kumaresan, Rahul Ponnusamy, Elizabeth Sherly, Sangeetha Sivanesan, and Bharathi Raja Chakravarthi. 2022. Transformer based hope speech comment classification in code-mixed text. In *International Conference on Speech and Language Technologies for Low-resource Languages*, pages 120–137. Springer.

Karthik Puranik, Adeep Hande, Ruba Priyadharshini, Sajeetha Thavareesan, and Bharathi Raja Chakravarthi. 2021. IIITT@LT-EDI-EACL2021-hope speech detection: There is always hope in transformers. In *Proceedings of the First Workshop on Language Technology for Equality, Diversity and Inclusion*, pages 98–106, Kyiv. Association for Computational Linguistics.

Alec Radford, Jeff Wu, Rewon Child, David Luan, Dario Amodei, and Ilya Sutskever. 2019. Language models are unsupervised multitask learners.

Amir H. Razavi, Diana Inkpen, Sasha Uritsky, and Stan Matwin. 2010. Offensive language detection using multi-level classification. In *Advances in Artificial Intelligence*, pages 16–27, Berlin, Heidelberg. Springer Berlin Heidelberg.

Julian Risch, Robin Ruff, and Ralf Krestel. 2020. Offensive language detection explained. In *Proceedings of the Second Workshop on Trolling, Aggression and Cyberbullying*, pages 137–143, Marseille, France. European Language Resources Association (ELRA).

Margarita Rodríguez-Ibánez, Antonio Casánez-Ventura, Félix Castejón-Mateos, and Pedro-Manuel Cuenca-Jiménez. 2023. A review on sentiment analysis from social media platforms. *Expert Systems with Applications*, 223:119862.

Ellen Spertus. 1997. Smokey: Automatic recognition of hostile messages. In *Aaai/iaai*, pages 1058–1065.

Sajeetha Thavareesan and Sinnathamby Mahesan. 2019. Sentiment analysis in tamil texts: A study on machine learning techniques and feature representation. In *2019 14th Conference on Industrial and Information Systems (ICIIS)*, pages 320–325.

Sajeetha Thavareesan and Sinnathamby Mahesan. 2020a. Sentiment lexicon expansion using word2vec and fasttext for sentiment prediction in tamil texts. In *2020 Moratuwa Engineering Research Conference (MERCon)*, pages 272–276.

Sajeetha Thavareesan and Sinnathamby Mahesan. 2020b. Word embedding-based part of speech tagging in tamil texts. In *2020 IEEE 15th International Conference on Industrial and Information Systems (ICIIS)*, pages 478–482.

Siddhanth U Hegde, Adeep Hande, Ruba Priyadharshini, Sajeetha Thavareesan, and Bharathi Raja Chakravarthi. 2021. UVCE-IIITT@DravidianLangTech-EACL2021: Tamil troll meme classification: You need to pay more attention. In *Proceedings of the First Workshop on Speech and Language Technologies for Dravidian Languages*, pages 180–186, Kyiv. Association for Computational Linguistics.

Jun ming Xu, Kwang sung Jun, Xiaojin Zhu, and Amy Bellmore. Learning from bullying traces in social media.

Konthala Yasaswini, Karthik Puranik, Adeep Hande, Ruba Priyadharshini, Sajeetha Thavareesan, and Bharathi Raja Chakravarthi. 2021. IIITT@DravidianLangTech-EACL2021: Transfer learning for offensive language detection in Dravidian languages. In *Proceedings of the First Workshop on Speech and Language Technologies for Dravidian Languages*, pages 187–194, Kyiv. Association for Computational Linguistics.

Dawei Yin, Zhenzhen Xue, Liangjie Hong, Brian Davison, April Edwards, and Lynne Edwards. 2009. Detection of harassment on web 2.0.

# iicteam@LT-EDI: Leveraging pre-trained Transformers for Fine-Grained Depression Level Detection in Social Media

**Vajratiya Vajrobol, Karanpreet Singh, Nitisha Aggarwal**
Institute of Informatics and Communication, University of Delhi, India.
tiya101@south.du.ac.in,
karanpreet.singh@iic.ac.in, nitisha@south.du.ac.in

## Abstract

Depression is a significant mental illness characterized by feelings of sadness and a lack of interest in daily activities. Early detection of depression is crucial to prevent severe consequences, making it essential to observe and treat the condition at its onset. At ACL-2022, the DepSign-LT-EDI project aimed to identify signs of depression in individuals based on their social media posts, where people often share their emotions and feelings. Using social media postings in English, the system categorized depression signs into three labels: "not depressed," "moderately depressed," and "severely depressed." To achieve this, our team has applied MentalRoBERTa, a model trained on big data of mental health. The test results indicated a macro F1-score of 0.439, ranking the fourth in the shared task.

## 1 Introduction

Depression is a significant mental health condition that affects individuals worldwide. It is characterized by persistent feelings of sadness, lack of interest in daily activities, and a range of emotional and physical symptoms. The World Health Organization (WHO) estimates that more than 300 million people of all ages suffer from depression, making it a significant public health concern (World Health Organization, 2017) (Organization, 2017). Early detection and intervention play a crucial role in effectively addressing depression and reducing its impact on individuals' lives (Beames et al., 2021).

Recognizing the importance of early detection, researchers have turned to artificial intelligence (AI) techniques to develop automated systems for the detection of depression. Social media platforms have emerged as a valuable source of data for understanding individuals' mental health, as people often express their thoughts, emotions, and experiences in their online posts. By leveraging the vast amount of user-generated content on social media, researchers aim to detect signs of depression in a timely manner and provide appropriate support (D'Alfonso, 2020). In this research, we focus on leveraging pre-trained learning models, specifically MentalRoBERTa transformers, for fine-grained depression detection in social media. Pre-trained transformers have shown remarkable success in various natural language processing tasks, and we seek to harness their capabilities to accurately identify and classify depression-related patterns in social media text (Vajrobol et al., 2022).

One of the challenges in depression detection is the presence of imbalanced datasets, where instances of non-depressive posts and moderate level of depression are significantly outnumbered by severe depression-related posts. To address this issue, we employ text augmentation techniques to artificially increase the number of depressive instances in the dataset, thereby enhancing the model's ability to learn from the imbalanced data distribution.

The primary contribution of our research lies in developing a robust model for fine-grained depression detection by leveraging pre-trained MentalRoBERTa transformers and employing text augmentation techniques to handle imbalanced datasets. By detecting depression at a fine-grained level, we aim to provide more nuanced insights into individuals' mental health states and facilitate targeted interventions and support.

In the following sections, we will describe the related work in the field of depression detection from social media and discuss the methodolo-



*LT-EDI 2023 – Third Workshop on Language Technology for Equality, Diversity and Inclusion*, pages 83–88, Varna, Bulgaria, Sep 7, 2023.
https://doi.org/10.26615/978-954-452-084-7_012

gies and experiments conducted in our research. The results obtained will demonstrate the effectiveness and contributions of our proposed approach for leveraging pre-trained learning in fine-grained depression detection. Ultimately the conclusion and future works will be drawn.

## 2 Literature surveys

Depression is a significant mental health issue that affects millions of people worldwide. Early detection and intervention are crucial for providing timely support to individuals suffering from depression. With the rise of social media platforms, researchers have begun exploring the potential of leveraging pre-trained learning models for fine-grained depression detection in social media posts. In a recent study, (Lam et al., 2019) employed multi-modal data and proposed a novel method that combines topic modeling using transformers and a deep 1D convolutional neural network (CNN) for acoustic feature modeling. The results demonstrated that the deep 1D CNN and transformer models achieved state-of-the-art performance for audio and text modalities, respectively. Furthermore, the multi-modal results are comparable to the state-of-the-art depression detection systems.

Furthermore, (Martnez-Castano et al., 2020) investigated early detection of signs of self-harm and measuring the severity of the signs of Depression. Their approach focused on utilizing BERT-based classifiers trained specifically for each task. The results demonstrated that this approach yielded excellent performance across various measures. The study suggested that trained BERT-based classifiers can accurately identify social media users at risk of self-harming, with a precision rate of up to 91.3 %. Recent study also performed depression detection in low-resource language like Thai, and found out XLM-RoBERTa based on Transformers has performed the best with 79.12% accuracy (Vajrobol et al., 2022).

A study by (Meng et al., 2021) focused on leveraging the application of temporal deep learning models with a transformer architecture to predict future diagnosis of depression using electronic health record (EHR) data. The model demonstrated improved precision-recall area under the curve (PRAUC) for depression prediction, achieving a PRAUC increase from 0.70 to 0.76 compared to the best baseline model.

(S et al., 2022) investigated the detection of signs of depression in social media Text using transformer models like DistilBERT, RoBERTa, and ALBERT. The prediction process involved assigning three labels to the data: Moderate, Severe, and Not Depressed. The evaluation of their models revealed Macro F1 scores of 0.337, 0.457, and 0.387 for DistilBERT, RoBERTa, and ALBERT, respectively.

One notable study by (Zhang et al., 2022) focused on utilizing a hybrid deep learning model called RoBERTa-BiLSTM to extract features from sequences of depression text. The model combines the strengths of sequence models and Transformer models while mitigating the limitations of sequence models. By utilizing the Robustly optimized BERT approach, the model maps words into a meaningful word embedding space and effectively captures long-distance contextual semantics using the Bidirectional Long Short-Term Memory model. Experimental results demonstrated that this model holds promise for improving the accuracy and robustness of depression detection, aiding in the timely identification and treatment of individuals experiencing depression.

Another relevant study by (Vetulani et al., 2023) demonstrated that transformer ensembles outperformed individual transformer-based classifiers in detecting depression. This finding underscores the significance of leveraging ensemble models to improve the accuracy and robustness of depression detection from social media posts. By harnessing the power of transfer learning, we can effectively apply knowledge gained from one dataset to enhance the performance on a different dataset, expanding the applicability of our models.

These previous studies collectively illustrated the effectiveness and versatility of leveraging pre-trained learning for fine-grained depression detection in social media. By fine-tuning pre-trained transformers, researchers have been able to capture intricate linguistic patterns and emotional expressions indicative of depression. This approach holds immense promise for developing accurate and scalable tools for early detection and intervention in individuals at risk of depression.

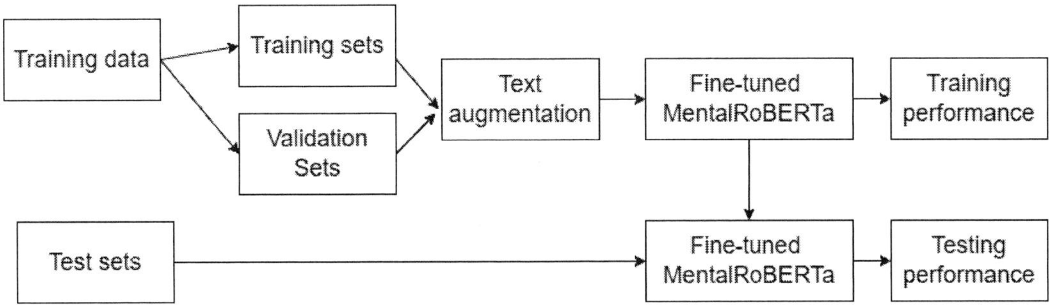


Figure 1: The process of detection level of depression

## 3 Methods

The Training data has been provided by competition organizers, further divided into training sets and validation sets 80:20 as demonstrated in Figure 1. After splitting dataset, text augmentation techniques have been applied because the shared training data is imbalanced. For the classification, MentalRoBERTa has been trained and fine-tuned on training sets. Furthermore, this fine-tuned MentalRoBERTa has been utilized to assess testing performance with test sets.

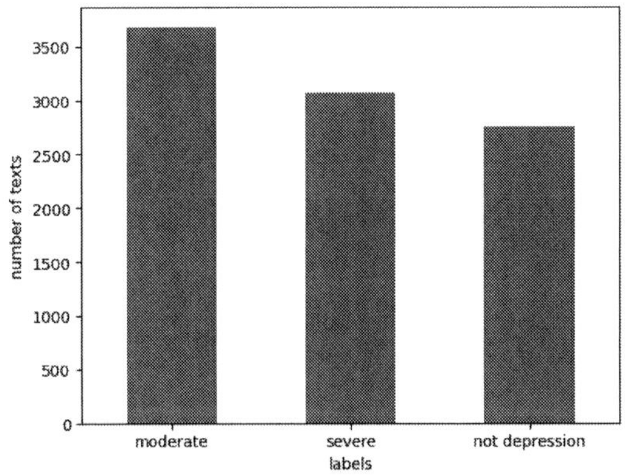


Figure 2: The distribution of the level of depression dataset after augmentation.

### 3.1 Dataset and data pre-processing

The original training dataset in the shared task (Sampath et al., 2023) has been included in 7,201 records and divided into three labels, such as moderate depression with 3,678 rows, not depression with 2,755 rows, and severe depression with 768 rows (Losada et al., 2017; DravidianLangTech, 2023). The data is hugely imbalanced. Therefore, we have applied two text augmentation techniques like synonyms (replacing words with similar meanings) and random swap (rearranging word order) enhance data variety, aiding machine learning models to better understand language and generalize effectively. Finally, the whole dataset has been added up to 9,505 rows, which include 3,678 records with moderate depression label, 2,755 records with non-depression label, and 3,072 records with severe depression label as it can be seen in Figure 2 . And an example of a dataset has been shown in Table 1. The test dataset included 499 records.

### 3.2 MentalRoBERTa

MentalRoBERTa is a pre-trained language model specifically developed for mental health-related natural language processing tasks. The training corpus for MentalRoBERTa was collected from Reddit, an network of communities where users engage in discussions on various topics of interest. For the purpose of focusing on the mental health domain, several relevant subreddits were selected to crawl users' posts. During the data collection process, user profiles were not collected, even though they are publicly available on Reddit. The aim was to ensure user privacy and adhere to ethical considerations. The selected mental health-related subreddits include "r/depression," "r/SuicideWatch," "r/Anxiety," "r/offmychest," "r/bipolar," "r/mental illness," and "r/mentalhealth." These subreddits provide a diverse range of discussions related to mental health, covering topics such as depression, anxiety, bipolar disorder, and general

| Text | Label |
|---|---|
| What to do these days?: I've struggled with Depression and anxiety for all my life now and every time I'd feel alone or down there was always something I could do. Usually when I'd want to feel better I'd go to a cafe and read or just chill to calm down or go look for cool things in stores. I could even go to the swimming pool or gym. | SEVERE |
| 2019 was my worst year with 2 depression crises. I'm happy it ended but so afraid of what 2020 will bring. : This year was rough. It started on the NYE with my puppy almost dying from the fireworks. He literally shat all over myself. In may I had my first terrible depression and anxiety crisis and had to be away from my internship for 2 weeks. Then in June I went through the first real loss of my life. My dear uncle died from a heart attack all of sudden. | MODERATE |
| Have a happy near year.... : I'm spending this new year alone and in bed. I hope you are not doing the same. I hope you can have fun today if you're reading this. Next year is gonna be lit, dont give up on yourself. You're all you got in this life. | NOT DEPRESSION |

Table 1: The example of the training dataset.

mental health issues. The resulting training corpus for MentalRoBERTa consists of a total of 13,671,785 sentences. This corpus encompasses a broad range of textual expressions, including personal narratives, experiences, questions, and support-seeking posts related to mental health. By training MentalRoBERTa on this extensive dataset, the model can effectively learn and capture the language patterns, context, and semantics specific to mental health discussions on social media. MentalRoBERTa, being pre-trained on this mental health-specific corpus, enables researchers and practitioners to leverage its knowledge and capabilities in various natural language processing tasks related to mental health. This includes sentiment analysis, mental health classification, identification of specific mental health conditions, and other text-based analyses in the field of mental healthcare (Ji et al., 2022).

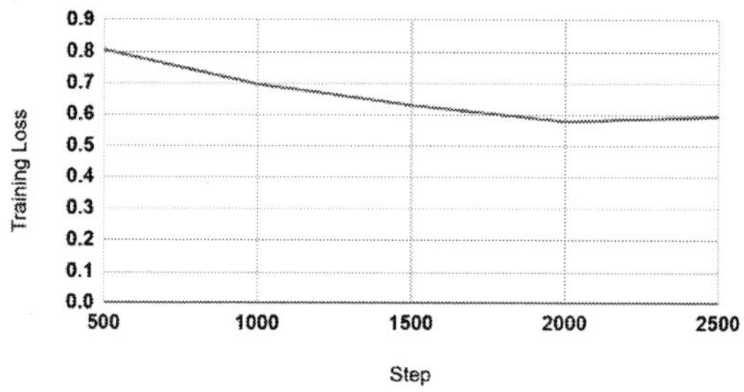


Figure 3: Training loss and steps in the training model process.

## 4 Results and Discussion

The training loss is presented at different steps of the training process in Figure 3. At step 500, the training loss is 0.8063, indicating that the model's predictions have a relatively higher deviation from the actual target values. As the training progresses, the training loss decreases, indicating that the model is improving its performance and fitting the training data better. At step 2500, the training loss is 0.5932, showing a further reduction in the loss value. Monitoring the training loss helps assess the convergence and performance of the model during training. Lower training loss values generally indicate a better fit to the training data. However, it is important to note that the training loss alone may not fully reflect the model's performance on unseen data or in real-world scenarios. Evaluation on separate validation or test datasets is necessary to assess the model's generalization ability and overall performance. The training performance results show that the model generated accuracy 69.96 %, F1-score

69.94 %. Then we evaluated the model and using the 499 samples of the test set, the results shows that a macro F1-score of 0.439, as the fourth-ranked participant in the shared task.

## 5 Conclusion

The DepSign-LT-EDI project focused on the detection of depression signs in individuals based on their social media postings. By utilizing the MentalRoBERTa model trained on mental health data, the model classified the signs of depression into three labels: "not depressed," "moderately depressed," and "severely depressed." The result obtained from the evaluation of the system showcased a macro F1-score of 0.439, positioning the system as the fourth-ranked participant.

Another area for future investigation involves incorporating multimodal analysis. By integrating textual analysis with other modalities such as images, videos, and audio, a more holistic understanding of individuals' mental health states can be achieved. This multimodal approach has the potential to improve the accuracy and reliability of depression detection systems.

Furthermore, there is room for refining the classification system to capture finer levels of depression severity. Developing models that can distinguish between different levels of depression, ranging from mild to moderate and severe, would enable a more nuanced understanding of individuals' mental well-being. This, in turn, could facilitate more targeted interventions and personalized support. It is also crucial to consider ethical considerations in future research endeavors. Addressing privacy concerns, obtaining informed consent, and mitigating potential biases in depression detection from social media are essential. Striving for transparency and interpretability in the developed models while ensuring data protection and respecting individuals' autonomy is of utmost importance. By exploring these future directions, the field of depression detection from social media can continue to advance. This progress would lead to the development of more accurate and effective tools for early intervention, support, and treatment for individuals experiencing depression.

## Acknowledgments

The authors would like to thank Project Samarth, an initiative of the Ministry of Education(MoE), Government of India, at the University of Delhi South Campus (UDSC), for their support

## References

Joanne R. Beames, Katarina Kikas, and Aliza Werner-Seidler. 2021. Prevention and early intervention of depression in young people: an integrated narrative review of affective awareness and ecological momentary assessment. *BMC Psychology*, 9:113.

DravidianLangTech. 2023. Detecting signs of depression from social media text - lt-edi@ranlp 2023.

Simon D'Alfonso. 2020. Ai in mental health. *Current Opinion in Psychology*, 36:112–117.

Shaoxiong Ji, Tianlin Zhang, Luna Ansari, Jie Fu, Prayag Tiwari, and Erik Cambria. 2022. Mentalbert: Publicly available pretrained language models for mental healthcare. In *Proceedings of the Thirteenth Language Resources and Evaluation Conference*, pages 7184–7190. European Language Resources Association.

Genevieve Lam, Huang Dongyan, and Weisi Lin. 2019. Context-aware deep learning for multimodal depression detection. In *ICASSP 2019 - 2019 IEEE International Conference on Acoustics, Speech and Signal Processing (ICASSP)*, pages 3946–3950. IEEE.

David E Losada, Fabio Crestani, and Javier Parapar. 2017. erisk 2017: Clef lab on early risk prediction on the internet: experimental foundations. In *Experimental IR Meets Multilinguality, Multimodality, and Interaction: 8th International Conference of the CLEF Association, CLEF 2017, Dublin, Ireland, September 11–14, 2017, Proceedings 8*, pages 346–360.

Rodrigo Martnez-Castano, Amal Htait, Leif Azzopardi, and Yashar Moshfeghi. 2020. Early risk detection of self-harm and depression severity using bert-based transformers. *Working Notes of CLEF*, page 16.

Yiwen Meng, William Speier, Michael K Ong, and Corey W Arnold. 2021. Bidirectional representation learning from transformers using multimodal electronic health record data to predict depression. *IEEE journal of biomedical and health informatics*, 25:3121–3129.

World Health Organization. 2017. "depression: let's talk" says who, as depression tops list of causes of ill health.

Sivamanikandan S, Santhosh V, Sanjaykumar N, Jerin Mahibha C, and Thenmozhi Durairaj. 2022. scubemsec@lt-edi-acl2022: Detection of depression using transformer models. In *Proceedings of the Second Workshop on Language Technology for Equality, Diversity and Inclusion*, pages 212–217. Association for Computational Linguistics.

Kayalvizhi Sampath, Thenmozhi Durairaj, Bharathi Raja Chakravarthi, Jerin Mahibha C, Kogilavani Shanmugavadivel, and Pratik Anil Rahood. 2023. Overview of the second shared task on detecting signs of depression from social media text. In *Proceedings of the Third Workshop on Language Technology for Equality, Diversity and Inclusion*, Varna, Bulgaria. Recent Advances in Natural Language Processing.

Vajratiya Vajrobol, Unmesh Shukla, Amit Pundir, Sanjeev Singh, and Geetika Jain Saxena. 2022. Depression detection in thai language posts based on attentive network models. *CEUR Workshop Proceedings*.

Zygmunt Vetulani, , and Patrick Paroubek and, editors. 2023. *Human Language Technologies as a Challenge for Computer Science and Linguistics – 2023*. Adam Mickiewicz University Press.

Yazhou Zhang, Yu He, Lu Rong, and Yijie Ding. 2022. A hybrid model for depression detection with transformer and bi-directional long short-term memory. In *2022 IEEE International Conference on Bioinformatics and Biomedicine (BIBM)*, pages 2727–2734. IEEE.

# JA-NLP@LT-EDI: Empowering Mental Health Assessment: A RoBERTa-Based Approach for Depression Detection

**Jyoti Kumari**
Department of CSE
Siksha 'O' Anusandhan,
Deemed to be University
Bhubaneswar, India
j2kumari@gmail.com

**Abhinav Kumar**
Department of CSE
Motilal Nehru National Institute
of Technology Allahabad,
Prayagraj, India
abhinavanand05@gmail.com

## Abstract

Depression, a widespread mental health disorder, affects a significant portion of the global population. Timely identification and intervention play a crucial role in ensuring effective treatment and support. Therefore, this research paper proposes a fine-tuned RoBERTa-based model for identifying depression in social media posts. In addition to the proposed model, Sentence-BERT is employed to encode social media posts into vector representations. These encoded vectors are then utilized in eight different popular classical machine learning models. The proposed fine-tuned RoBERTa model achieved a best macro $F_1$-score of 0.55 for the development dataset and a comparable score of 0.41 for the testing dataset. Additionally, combining Sentence-BERT with Naive Bayes (S-BERT + NB) outperformed the fine-tuned RoBERTa model, achieving a slightly higher macro $F_1$-score of 0.42. This demonstrates the effectiveness of the approach in detecting depression from social media posts.

## 1 Introduction

Depression is a prevalent mental health disorder affecting people of all ages from diverse backgrounds, irrespective of their socioeconomic status or cultural circumstances. The World Health Organization (WHO) approximates that there are over 264 million individuals globally who suffer from depression, underscoring its significant impact on public health. Depression exhibits a higher occurrence rate in women, surpassing that in men by approximately 50%. Alarmingly, suicide claims the lives of over 700,000 people each year, positioning it as the fourth leading cause of death among individuals aged 15 to 29[1] (Vioules et al., 2018).

The emergence of social media platforms has revolutionized online communication, information sharing, and self-expression. By 2021, Facebook alone had reported a staggering 2.8 billion monthly active users, while other platforms like Twitter, Instagram, and Reddit also maintained substantial user bases. This widespread adoption of social media has presented researchers with an extensive pool of user-generated content to investigate, including its application in mental health analysis and other diverse endeavors (Guntuku et al., 2017; Kumar and Kumari, 2021; Kumari and Kumar, 2021b; Gkotsis et al., 2017). There are several advantages of detecting signs of depression from social media posts. Firstly, it offers a large-scale and easily accessible data source, allowing for real-time analysis of a significant number of individuals. Secondly, social media text often reflects individuals' genuine emotions and experiences, as they express themselves freely and spontaneously on these platforms. Additionally, social media data can be collected over time, enabling the monitoring of changes in individuals' mental well-being as it evolves.

In recent years, there has been increasing interest in analyzing social media texts to detect signs of depression. Research has revealed that individuals suffering from depression often demonstrate specific language patterns in their online posts (Guntuku et al., 2019; Schwartz et al., 2013). Studies have found that depressed individuals tend to utilize more self-referential pronouns (such as "I" and "me"), expressing a higher frequency of negative emotions and words, and exhibit reduced engagement in positive social interactions (Coppersmith et al., 2014; Park et al., 2012).

However, the detection of depression signs from social media texts is not without its challenges. While specific linguistic patterns associated with depression have been identified (Coppersmith et al., 2014; Park et al., 2012; Guntuku et al., 2017), it is important to consider individual differences, personality traits, cultural variations, and context-

[1] https://www.who.int/news-room/fact-sheets/detail/depression



*LT-EDI 2023 – Third Workshop on Language Technology for Equality, Diversity and Inclusion*, pages 89–96, Varna, Bulgaria, Sep 7, 2023.
https://doi.org/10.26615/978-954-452-084-7_013

specific factors that can influence the use of language (Schwartz et al., 2013; De Choudhury et al., 2014). By exploring diverse approaches, techniques, challenges, and ethical considerations (Al-Sagri and Ykhlef, 2020; Kumari and Kumar, 2021a; He et al., 2022), our aim is to contribute to the continuous efforts of enhancing mental health outcomes through the innovative and responsible use of social media data. In accordance with existing research, this study introduces a refined RoBERTa model to detect depression in social media posts. Additionally, Sentence-BERT is employed to convert social media posts into a consistent encoded vector. These vectors are subsequently utilized as input for various well-known classical machine learning classifiers.

The remaining paper is organized as follows: Section 2 briefs the related work, Section 3 discusses the methodology adopted to perform the work, Section 4 highlights the results obtained, and finally Section 5 concludes the overall work.

## 2 Related Works

This section provides insights into the field of detecting signs of depression from social media texts. These highlights the use of linguistic analysis, sentiment analysis, machine learning, psychological frameworks, and natural language processing, providing a comprehensive understanding of the field (Park et al., 2012; Guntuku et al., 2017; Schwartz et al., 2013; Saumya et al., 2021). Machine learning algorithms play a vital role in identifying depression through text extracted from social media. Various supervised learning techniques, such as Support Vector Machines (SVM), Naïve Bayes, and Random Forests, have been utilized to classify text as depressed users or non-depressed (AlSagri and Ykhlef, 2020; Angskun et al., 2022). Moreover, deep learning approaches like Recurrent Neural Networks (RNNs) and Convolutional Neural Networks (CNNs) have demonstrated encouraging outcomes in capturing intricate linguistic patterns to detect depression (Tadesse et al., 2019).

Coppersmith et al. (2014) explores the use of Twitter data to quantify mental health signals, including depression. In this study, linguistic features including words, phrases, and linguistic structures are employed to detect mental health signals linked to depression, Post-traumatic stress disorder (PTSD), and other mental health conditions. To accomplish this, machine learning techniques are utilized to classify tweets and evaluate the models' accuracy in predicting mental health states. In addition, the paper discusses the challenges faced when quantifying mental health signals within Twitter data, such as the presence of inherent noise and bias in social media posts. Further, by incorporating various data sources, the research strives to provide a more comprehensive and robust analysis of mental health indicators.

The authors in (Park et al., 2012) with an objective of gaining insights into the expression and analysis of depressive emotions in the realm of social media, employed a large dataset of Twitter posts, and leverage natural language processing techniques to identify patterns and sentiments related to depressive language. Their study focuses on understanding how individuals express and communicate their feelings of depression through social media platforms like Twitter. The authors examine linguistic features in Twitter, such as words, emoticons, and grammatical structures, to understand the occurrence and expression of depressive moods. They discover distinct language patterns associated with depressive emotions. However, relying solely on Twitter data limits the study's representativeness and generalizability to diverse demographics.

In their study, Guntuku et al. (2017) conducts a systematic analysis of various studies utilizing social media data to detect depression and other mental health conditions. They provide a comprehensive overview of the research conducted in the field of detecting depression and mental illness through social media analysis by providing an in-depth assessment of their strengths and limitations. It examines the linguistic, behavioral, and contextual features utilized to detect signs of depression in social media posts from the application point of view of machine learning and natural language processing techniques. The challenges encompass concerns related to data privacy, the representativeness of social media users, biases arising from self-disclosure, and the requirement for more accurate ground truth labels to effectively train models.

Reece and Danforth (2017) takes a unique approach by leveraging the vast amount of user-generated data on Instagram. Their primary goal is to uncover predictive indicators of depression. To achieve this, the researchers meticulously analyzed a substantial number of Instagram photos posted by participants, along with the accompanying captions and metadata. The study revealed a significant pattern where participants diagnosed with depression exhibited a strong preference for darker, grayer, and bluer tones with less likely smiling faces in their Instagram photos, while those without depression tended to favor brighter, warmer colors. Further, the study also revealed that individuals with depression tended to engage more in frequent posting for social validation and support. Additionally, the researchers identified distinct textual markers like increased utilization of filters and more frequent references to feelings of sadness, anxiety, and loneliness. These findings provide valuable insights into the relationship between depression and online behavior, particularly in terms of text-based expression. The research primarily relies on self-reported diagnoses of depression and lacks a comprehensive clinical assessment conducted by mental health professionals. Furthermore, the study's findings are confined to data obtained solely from Instagram, which may not provide a complete representation of the broader population.

Gkotsis et al. (2017) focuses on characterizing mental health conditions by leveraging informed deep learning models to analyze user-generated content, including posts and interactions on social media platforms. The results demonstrate promising capabilities in detecting symptoms related to depression, PTSD, self-harm, and more. Additionally, the study uncovers distinct linguistic patterns and behavioral markers associated with different mental health conditions, encompassing variations in word usage, sentiment analysis, and linguistic styles employed by individuals facing diverse mental health challenges. However, the research relies on publicly available social media data, which may not fully represent the entire population. Furthermore, considerations regarding privacy, data accuracy, and generalizability need to be addressed.

Guntuku et al. (2019) adopts an innovative approach by examining the language patterns of adults with attention deficit hyperactivity disorder (ADHD) in their social media interactions. It uncovers distinct linguistic characteristics, including a higher frequency of self-referential pronouns, words related to time urgency, emotional language, and references to cognitive processes. These findings highlight the potential of language analysis to identify and understand communication patterns associated with ADHD in digital environments. However, the study relies on self-reported diagnoses and focuses on language patterns within specific social media platforms. Therefore, it may not fully encompass the experiences of all adults with ADHD or capture their interactions across a wide range of digital platforms.

Schwartz et al. (2013) explores the intriguing interplay between personality traits, gender, age, and language usage on social media platforms. Employing an open-vocabulary approach, the authors delve into an extensive analysis of large-scale social media data to uncover patterns and correlations between language use and individual characteristics. The linguistic analyses identified distinct linguistic markers associated with various personality traits, including extraversion, neuroticism, and agreeableness. Further, the study uncovers correlations between gender and linguistic choices, revealing variations in language use between male and female users. Notably, age-related disparities in language were also observed, indicating that language patterns on social media may undergo transformations as individuals grow older. The study relies on self-reported personality assessments that focus on language patterns within specific social media platforms. As a result, the study may not fully encompass the complete spectrum of personality traits, gender identities, or age groups within the broader population.

De Choudhury et al. (2014) aims to characterize and predict postpartum depression by utilizing data shared on Facebook. The authors explore different variables including language patterns, linguistic styles, social interactions, and behavioral cues exhibited by users, with the goal of identifying significant markers associated with postpartum depression. Further, they discover distinct language patterns like increased use of first-person pronouns, negatively affecting words, feelings of loneliness and isolation, etc. They also highlight the importance of social interactions and behavioral cues, such as changes in posting frequency and decreased engagement with friends, as potential indicators of postpartum depression. However, the study's reliance on Facebook data may limit the representation and understanding of individuals beyond the scope of the platform itself.

The authors in (Tadesse et al., 2019) address the prevalence of suicide and the growing influence of social media platforms in shaping public discourse. The paper emphasizes the significance of automated systems in monitoring and identifying individuals who may be at risk. Their research un-

Table 1: Data statistic used to validate proposed model

| Class | Train | Dev | Test |
|---|---|---|---|
| Moderate Depression | 3678 | 2169 | 275 |
| No Depression | 2755 | 848 | 135 |
| Severe Depression | 768 | 228 | 89 |
| Total | 7201 | 3245 | 499 |

derscores the importance of proactive measures to detect and support individuals in need within the context of social media platforms. The authors employ a comprehensive dataset consisting of posts from social media forums, which is annotated by mental health professionals. They extract textual features using pre-trained word embeddings and apply a deep learning model, specifically a CNN, for classification. However, the information reagrding the characteristics of the dataset, such as size, diversity, or representativeness is missing. Further, it does not explicitly address how the proposed deep learning model accounts for the potential challenges of adapting the model to new language patterns and emerging trends.

## 3 Methodology

The overall flow diagram of the proposed work is illustrated in Figure 1. In addition to the fine-tuned RoBERTa model, a total of eight different models were developed, namely: (i) Fine-tuned RoBERTa, (ii) Sentence-BERT + Support Vector Machine (S-BERT + SVM), (iii) Sentence-BERT + Random Forest (S-BERT + RF), (iv) Sentence-BERT + Logistic Regression (S-BERT + LR), (v) Sentence-BERT + K-Nearest Neighbors (S-BERT + KNN), (vi) Sentence-BERT + Naive Bayes (S-BERT + NB), (vii) Sentence-BERT + Gradient Boosting (S-BERT + GB), (viii) Sentence-BERT + Decision Tree (S-BERT + DT), and (ix) Sentence-BERT + AdaBoost (S-BERT + AB). The LT-EDI-2023 workshop dataset[2] was utilized to validate the proposed models. Table 1 (S et al., 2022) provides an overview of the data samples in the training, testing, and development sets (Sampath et al.), while the default pre-processing steps defined in the Ktrain library[3] were applied.

[2]https://sites.google.com/view/lt-edi-2023/home

[3]https://amaiya.github.io/ktrain/text/preprocessor.html

### 3.1 RoBERTa

RoBERTa (Robustly Optimized BERT approach) is a state-of-the-art natural language processing (NLP) model that has made significant contributions to various NLP tasks. Developed by Facebook AI in 2019, RoBERTa is built upon the architecture of BERT (Bidirectional Encoder Representations from Transformers) and leverages the power of unsupervised pretraining on large amounts of text data. Its advanced training techniques, such as using larger datasets, removing the next sentence prediction objective, and increasing the batch size, enables it to achieve superior performance on a wide range of NLP benchmarks. RoBERTa has demonstrated remarkable success in tasks like text classification, named entity recognition, sentiment analysis, question answering, and machine translation, showcasing its versatility and effectiveness. With its robustness, RoBERTa has become an invaluable tool for researchers, developers, and practitioners seeking cutting-edge solutions in the field of natural language processing.

Given the widespread use of RoBERTa in various NLP tasks, this study employed RoBERTa to detect depression from social media posts. To fine-tune RoBERTa, a maximum input size of 250 words was set for each data sample. The RoBERTa model was subsequently trained for 100 epochs, utilizing a learning rate of $2e^{-5}$ and a batch size of 32.

### 3.2 Sentence-BERT Representation

BERT is a state-of-the-art neural network architecture designed for pretraining language representations by leveraging the transformer architecture. The transformer model in BERT allows for capturing contextual information from both left and right contexts of a given word, enabling a deeper understanding of the meaning of words and sentences. The term "bert-base-nli-mean-tokens"[4] refers to a specific model architecture based on BERT (Bidirectional Encoder Representations from Transformers) that is used for natural language inference (NLI) tasks. The "bert-base-nli-mean-tokens" model specifically utilizes the "mean pooling" strategy to generate fixed-length sentence representations. In this strategy, each word in a sentence is encoded using BERT, and the resulting

[4]https://huggingface.co/sentence-transformers/bert-base-nli-mean-tokens

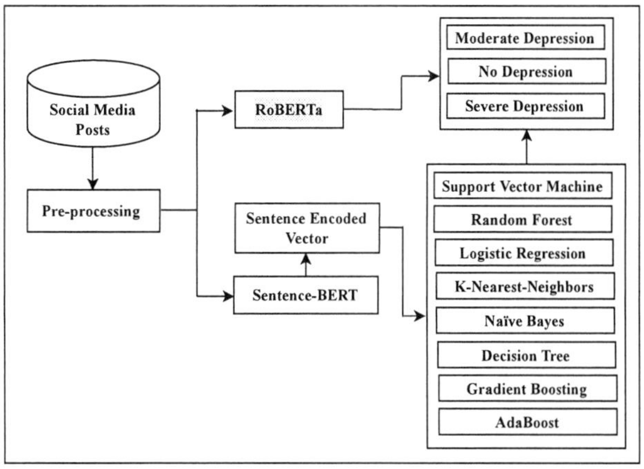


Figure 1: Flow diagram of the proposed work

contextualized word embeddings are averaged to create a single vector representation of the entire sentence. This mean pooling approach is a simple yet effective way to condense variable-length sentences into fixed-length vectors that can be fed into downstream tasks.

In this study, the text data samples underwent an initial encoding process, resulting in a 768-dimensional vector representation. Subsequently, this encoded vector, consisting of 768 dimensions, was employed in multiple well-known classical machine learning classifiers, as depicted in Figure 1.

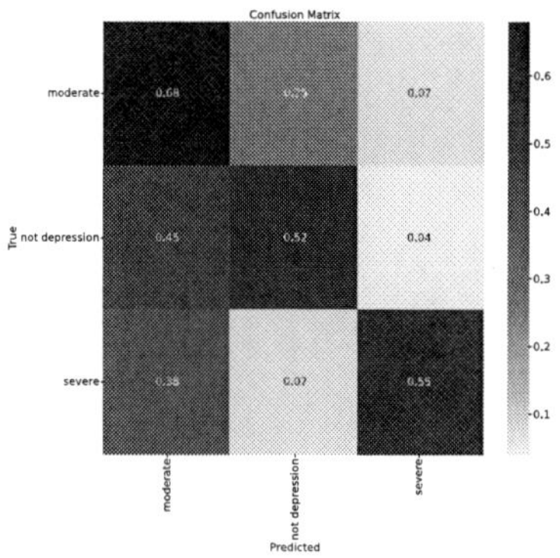


Figure 2: Confusion matrix for the proposed fine-tuned RoBERTa model (Validation dataset)

## 4 Result

The performance evaluation of the proposed model encompasses various metrics, including precision (P), recall (R), $F_1$-score ($F_1$-score), accuracy (Acc), weighted precision, weighted recall, weighted $F_1$-score, macro-precision, macro-recall, macro-$F_1$-score, confusion matrix, and AUC-ROC curve. The results of validating different deep learning models on both the testing and validation datasets are presented in Table 2. Notably, among all the implemented models, the proposed fine-tuned RoBERTa model exhibited the highest macro $F_1$-score of 0.55 for the development dataset, as shown in Table 2. The corresponding confusion matrix and AUC-ROC curve for the proposed fine-tuned RoBERTa model are depicted in Figures 2 and 3, respectively.

In the case of Sentence-BERT combined with classical machine learning models, S-BERT + LR outperformed the classical machine learning approach, achieving a macro $F_1$-score of 0.51 for the development dataset. The confusion matrix and AUC-ROC curve for the S-BERT + LR model on the development dataset can be observed in Figures 4 and 5, respectively.

Likewise, when considering the testing dataset, the proposed fine-tuned RoBERTa model again demonstrated remarkable performance, attaining a notable macro $F_1$-score of 0.41. The corresponding confusion matrix and AUC-ROC curve for the fine-tuned RoBERTa model on the testing dataset are presented in Figures 6 and 7, respectively. Regard-

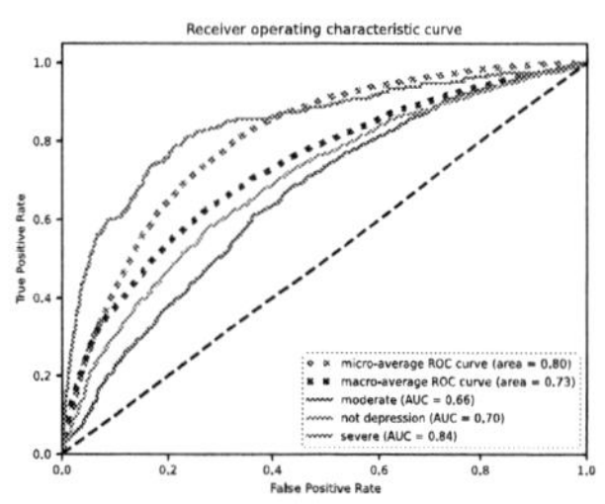


Figure 3: ROC Curve for the proposed fine-tuned RoBERTa model (Validation dataset)

Table 2: Performance of different models for the identification of depression

| Model | Class | Development data | | | | Test data | | | |
|---|---|---|---|---|---|---|---|---|---|
| | | P | R | $F_1$ | Acc | P | R | $F_1$ | Acc |
| RoBERTa | Moderate Depression | 0.76 | 0.68 | 0.72 | 0.63 | 0.58 | 0.66 | 0.62 | 0.52 |
| | No Depression | 0.44 | 0.52 | 0.48 | | 0.42 | 0.53 | 0.47 | |
| | Severe Depression | 0.40 | 0.55 | 0.47 | | 0.53 | 0.09 | 0.15 | |
| | Macro Avg. | 0.54 | 0.58 | 0.55 | | 0.51 | 0.43 | 0.41 | |
| | Weighted Avg. | 0.65 | 0.63 | 0.64 | | 0.53 | 0.52 | 0.49 | |
| S-BERT + SVM | Moderate Depression | 0.71 | 0.83 | 0.77 | 0.66 | 0.57 | 0.72 | 0.63 | 0.52 |
| | No Depression | 0.45 | 0.35 | 0.39 | | 0.41 | 0.45 | 0.43 | |
| | Severe Depression | 0.53 | 0.20 | 0.29 | | 0.67 | 0.02 | 0.04 | |
| | Macro Avg. | 0.57 | 0.46 | 0.48 | | 0.55 | 0.40 | 0.37 | |
| | Weighted Avg. | 0.63 | 0.66 | 0.63 | | 0.54 | 0.52 | 0.47 | |
| S-BERT + RF | Moderate Depression | 0.71 | 0.76 | 0.74 | 0.63 | 0.56 | 0.62 | 0.59 | 0.49 |
| | No Depression | 0.40 | 0.40 | 0.40 | | 0.38 | 0.53 | 0.45 | |
| | Severe Depression | 0.47 | 0.14 | 0.21 | | 0.40 | 0.02 | 0.04 | |
| | Macro Avg. | 0.53 | 0.43 | 0.45 | | 0.45 | 0.39 | 0.36 | |
| | Weighted Avg. | 0.61 | 0.63 | 0.61 | | 0.48 | 0.49 | 0.45 | |
| S-BERT + LR | Moderate Depression | 0.73 | 0.72 | 0.73 | 0.63 | 0.54 | 0.60 | 0.57 | 0.48 |
| | No Depression | 0.42 | 0.45 | 0.44 | | 0.37 | 0.50 | 0.43 | |
| | Severe Depression | 0.41 | 0.35 | 0.38 | | 0.50 | 0.07 | 0.12 | |
| | Macro Avg. | 0.52 | 0.51 | 0.51 | | 0.47 | 0.39 | 0.37 | |
| | Weighted Avg. | 0.63 | 0.63 | 0.63 | | 0.49 | 0.48 | 0.45 | |
| S-BERT + KNN | Moderate Depression | 0.71 | 0.79 | 0.75 | 0.63 | 0.54 | 0.72 | 0.62 | 0.48 |
| | No Depression | 0.41 | 0.31 | 0.35 | | 0.32 | 0.27 | 0.29 | |
| | Severe Depression | 0.31 | 0.25 | 0.28 | | 0.28 | 0.06 | 0.09 | |
| | Macro Avg. | 0.48 | 0.45 | 0.46 | | 0.38 | 0.35 | 0.33 | |
| | Weighted Avg. | 0.60 | 0.63 | 0.61 | | 0.43 | 0.48 | 0.43 | |
| S-BERT + NB | Moderate Depression | 0.74 | 0.47 | 0.57 | 0.47 | 0.56 | 0.41 | 0.47 | 0.44 |
| | No Depression | 0.39 | 0.40 | 0.39 | | 0.36 | 0.53 | 0.43 | |
| | Severe Depression | 0.18 | 0.77 | 0.29 | | 0.33 | 0.37 | 0.35 | |
| | Macro Avg. | 0.44 | 0.55 | 0.42 | | 0.42 | 0.44 | 0.42 | |
| | Weighted Avg. | 0.61 | 0.47 | 0.51 | | 0.47 | 0.44 | 0.44 | |
| S-BERT + GB | Moderate Depression | 0.72 | 0.76 | 0.74 | 0.63 | 0.56 | 0.64 | 0.59 | 0.49 |
| | No Depression | 0.43 | 0.40 | 0.41 | | 0.38 | 0.49 | 0.43 | |
| | Severe Depression | 0.39 | 0.27 | 0.32 | | 0.50 | 0.04 | 0.08 | |
| | Macro Avg. | 0.51 | 0.48 | 0.49 | | 0.48 | 0.39 | 0.37 | |
| | Weighted Avg. | 0.62 | 0.63 | 0.63 | | 0.50 | 0.49 | 0.46 | |
| S-BERT + DT | Moderate Depression | 0.70 | 0.54 | 0.61 | 0.50 | 0.57 | 0.51 | 0.54 | 0.43 |
| | No Depression | 0.31 | 0.44 | 0.36 | | 0.31 | 0.47 | 0.37 | |
| | Severe Depression | 0.19 | 0.31 | 0.24 | | 0.28 | 0.13 | 0.18 | |
| | Macro Avg. | 0.40 | 0.43 | 0.40 | | 0.38 | 0.37 | 0.36 | |
| | Weighted Avg. | 0.56 | 0.50 | 0.52 | | 0.44 | 0.43 | 0.43 | |
| S-BERT + AdaBoost | Moderate Depression | 0.72 | 0.72 | 0.72 | 0.61 | 0.53 | 0.58 | 0.55 | 0.45 |
| | No Depression | 0.42 | 0.42 | 0.42 | | 0.34 | 0.44 | 0.38 | |
| | Severe Depression | 0.30 | 0.30 | 0.30 | | 0.24 | 0.04 | 0.08 | |
| | Macro Avg. | 0.48 | 0.48 | 0.48 | | 0.37 | 0.36 | 0.34 | |
| | Weighted Avg. | 0.61 | 0.61 | 0.61 | | 0.42 | 0.45 | 0.42 | |

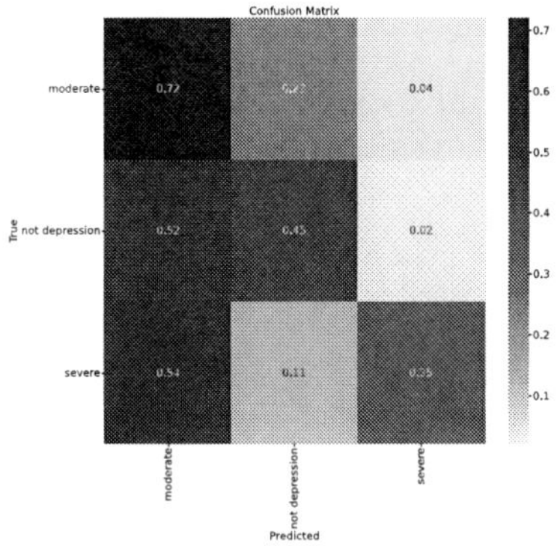


Figure 4: Confusion matrix for the proposed fine-tuned S-BERT + LR model (Validation dataset)

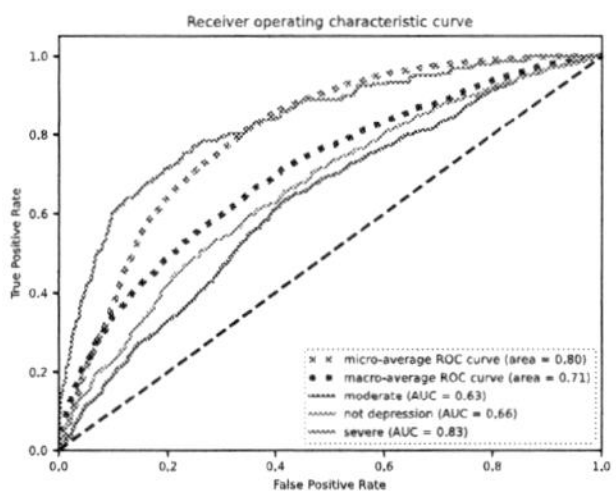


Figure 5: ROC Curve for the proposed fine-tuned S-BERT + LR model (Validation dataset)

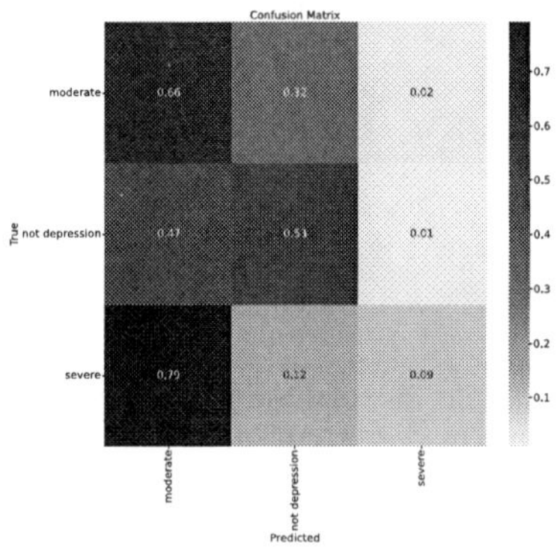


Figure 6: Confusion matrix for the proposed fine-tuned RoBERTa model (Test dataset)

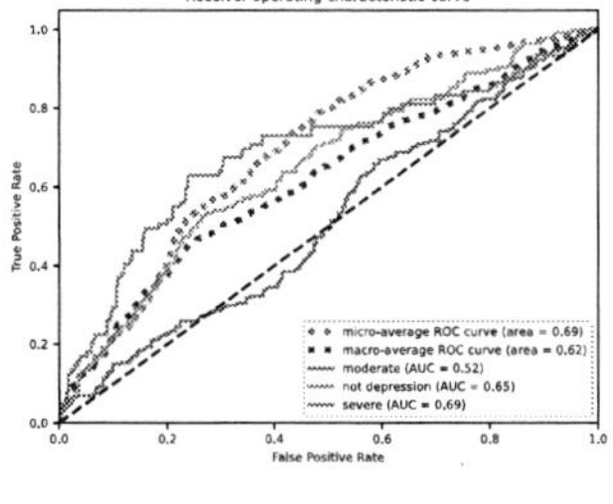


Figure 7: ROC Curve for the proposed fine-tuned RoBERTa model (Test dataset)

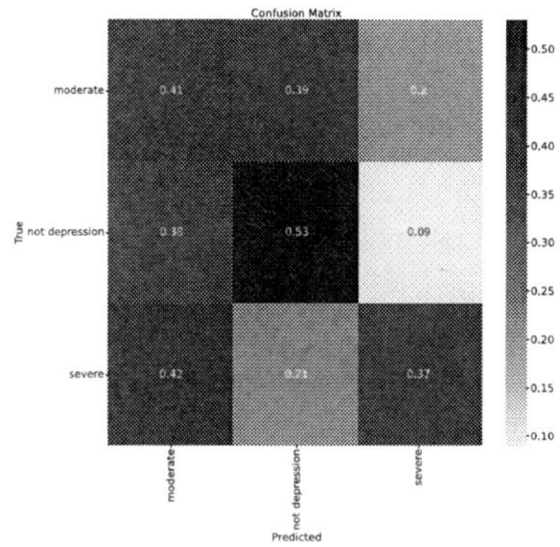


Figure 8: Confusion matrix for the proposed fine-tuned S-BERT + NB model (Test dataset)

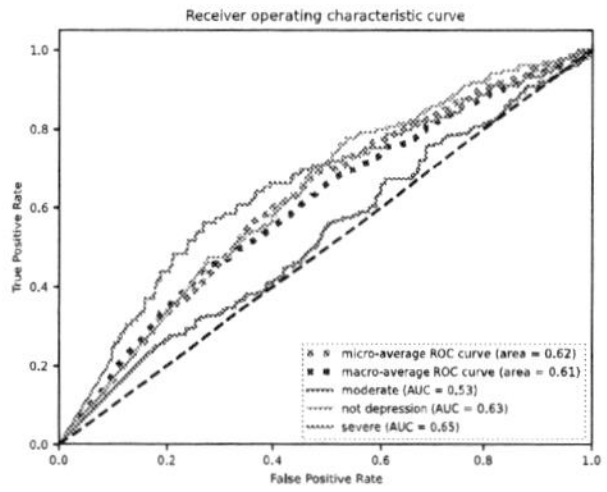


Figure 9: ROC Curve for the proposed fine-tuned S-BERT + NB model (Test dataset)

ing Sentence-BERT encoding combined with classical machine learning models, the S-BERT + NB model showcased the best performance among all implemented models for the testing dataset, achieving a macro $F_1$-score of 0.42. The confusion matrix and AUC-ROC curve for the S-BERT + NB model on the testing dataset can be observed in Figures 8 and 9, respectively.

## 5 Conclusion

Detecting depression from social media is essential for early intervention and providing timely support to those in need. Through the analysis of social media posts, we can identify indicators of depression and offer appropriate resources and assistance. Moreover, monitoring depression through social media provides valuable insights into its prevalence, distribution, and impact on different populations, aiding in public health planning, resource allocation, and targeted interventions. In this study, we explore the effectiveness of fine-tuned RoBERTa and Sentence-BERT with classical machine learning classifiers for depression identification in social media. Our findings demonstrate that RoBERTa and Sentence-BERT with Naive Bayes classifiers perform well in detecting depression. However, the overall performance of the models in this task is still limited, highlighting the need for robust systems in the future. To address this, a more comprehensive ensemble-based approach, coupled with proper pre-processing techniques to handle grammatical errors, non-standard abbreviations, and linguistic variations in social media posts, can be developed to enhance the accuracy and reliability of depression detection.

## References


Hatoon S AlSagri and Mourad Ykhlef. 2020. Machine learning-based approach for depression detection in twitter using content and activity features. *IEICE Transactions on Information and Systems*, 103(8):1825–1832.

Jitimon Angskun, Suda Tipprasert, and Thara Angskun. 2022. Big data analytics on social networks for real-time depression detection. *Journal of Big Data*, 9(1):69.

Glen Coppersmith, Mark Dredze, and Craig Harman. 2014. Quantifying mental health signals in twitter. In *Proceedings of the workshop on computational linguistics and clinical psychology: From linguistic signal to clinical reality*, pages 51–60.

Munmun De Choudhury, Scott Counts, Eric J Horvitz, and Aaron Hoff. 2014. Characterizing and predicting postpartum depression from shared facebook data. In *Proceedings of the 17th ACM conference on Computer supported cooperative work & social computing*, pages 626–638.

George Gkotsis, Anika Oellrich, Sumithra Velupillai, Maria Liakata, Tim JP Hubbard, Richard JB Dobson, and Rina Dutta. 2017. Characterisation of mental health conditions in social media using informed deep learning. *Scientific reports*, 7(1):45141.

Sharath Chandra Guntuku, J Russell Ramsay, Raina M Merchant, and Lyle H Ungar. 2019. Language of adhd in adults on social media. *Journal of attention disorders*, 23(12):1475–1485.

Sharath Chandra Guntuku, David B Yaden, Margaret L Kern, Lyle H Ungar, and Johannes C Eichstaedt. 2017. Detecting depression and mental illness on social media: an integrative review. *Current Opinion in Behavioral Sciences*, 18:43–49.

Lang He, Mingyue Niu, Prayag Tiwari, Pekka Marttinen, Rui Su, Jiewei Jiang, Chenguang Guo, Hongyu Wang, Songtao Ding, Zhongmin Wang, et al. 2022. Deep learning for depression recognition with audiovisual cues: A review. *Information Fusion*, 80:56–86.

Abhinav Kumar and Jyoti Kumari. 2021. A machine learning approach for fake news detection from urdu social media posts. In *Working Notes of FIRE 2021-Forum for Information Retrieval Evaluation (Online). CEUR*.

Jyoti Kumari and Abhinav Kumar. 2021a. A deep neural network-based model for the sentiment analysis of dravidian code-mixed social media posts. In *Working Notes of FIRE 2021-Forum for Information Retrieval Evaluation (Online). CEUR*.

Jyoti Kumari and Abhinav Kumar. 2021b. Offensive language identification on multilingual code mixing text. In *Working Notes of FIRE 2021-Forum for Information Retrieval Evaluation (Online). CEUR*.

Minsu Park, Chiyoung Cha, and Meeyoung Cha. 2012. Depressive moods of users portrayed in twitter. In *Proceedings of the 18th ACM International Conference on Knowledge Discovery and Data Mining, SIGKDD 2012*, pages 1–8.

Andrew G Reece and Christopher M Danforth. 2017. Instagram photos reveal predictive markers of depression. *EPJ Data Science*, 6(1):15.

Kayalvizhi S, Thenmozhi Durairaj, Bharathi Raja Chakravarthi, and Jerin Mahibha C. 2022. Findings of the shared task on detecting signs of depression from social media. In *Proceedings of the Second Workshop on Language Technology for Equality, Diversity and Inclusion*, pages 331–338, Dublin, Ireland. Association for Computational Linguistics.

Kayalvizhi Sampath, Thenmozhi Durairaj, Bharathi Raja Chakravarthi, Jerin Mahibha C, Kogilavani Shanmugavadivel, and Pratik Anil booktitle = Rahood. Overview of the second shared task on detecting signs of depression from social media text.

Sunil Saumya, Abhinav Kumar, and Jyoti Prakash Singh. 2021. Offensive language identification in dravidian code mixed social media text. In *Proceedings of the first workshop on speech and language technologies for Dravidian languages*, pages 36–45.

H Andrew Schwartz, Johannes C Eichstaedt, Margaret L Kern, Lukasz Dziurzynski, Stephanie M Ramones, Megha Agrawal, Achal Shah, Michal Kosinski, David Stillwell, Martin EP Seligman, et al. 2013. Personality, gender, and age in the language of social media: The open-vocabulary approach. *PloS one*, 8(9):e73791.

Michael Mesfin Tadesse, Hongfei Lin, Bo Xu, and Liang Yang. 2019. Detection of suicide ideation in social media forums using deep learning. *Algorithms*, 13(1):7.

M Johnson Vioules, Bilel Moulahi, Jérôme Azé, and Sandra Bringay. 2018. Detection of suicide-related posts in twitter data streams. *IBM Journal of Research and Development*, 62(1):7–1.

# Team-KEC@LT-EDI2023: Detecting Signs of Depression from Social Media Text

**Malliga S**
Kongu Engineering College
mallisenthil.cse@kongu.edu

**Kogilavani Shanmugavadivel**
Kongu Engineering College

**Arunaa S**
Kongu Engineering College
arunaa.20cse@kongu.edu

**Gokulkrishna R**
Kongu Engineering College
gokulkrishnar.20cse@kongu.edu

**Chandramukhii A**
Kongu Engineering College, Erode
Chandramukhiia.20cse@kongu.edu

## Abstract

The prevalence of depression has become a pressing concern in modern society, necessitating innovative approaches for early detection and intervention. This study explores the feasibility of leveraging social media text as a potential source for detecting signs of depression. This study utilized different techniques to represent the text data in a numerical format and various techniques such as CNN, BERT, and N-gram to classify social media posts into depression and non-depression categories. Text classification tasks often rely on deep learning techniques such as CNN, while the BERT model, which is pre-trained, has shown exceptional performance in a range of natural language processing tasks. To assess the effectiveness of the suggested approaches, the research employed multiple metrics, including accuracy, precision, recall, and F1-score.Our model bagged the official rank of 12 and gave an F1 score of 0.401. The outcomes of the investigation indicate that the suggested techniques can identify symptoms of depression with an average accuracy rate of 56

**Keywords** *N-gram, CNN, BERT*

## 1 Introduction

The pervasive use of social media has introduced new challenges in detecting signs of depression from text shared on these platforms(Greenberg-LS 2017). Researchers in NLP have utilized feature-based linear classifiers, CNN, and RNN architectures, as well as fine-tuning pre-trained language models like BERT and Roberta, to automatically detect signs of depression. While linear classifiers have shown competitive performance, pre-trained models have achieved state-of-the-art results. However, pre-trained models may have limitations in understanding context-specific language. This project provides an overview of existing research, describes the task and dataset, proposes machine learning and deep learning models, presents experimental results, and concludes with potential avenues for future research.Suicide is a serious public health problem; however, suicides are preventable with timely, evidence-based and often low-cost interventions[1].

The following sections of this document are structured as follows: Section 2 provides a comprehensive review of existing research on the identification of signs of depression through analysis of social media text(Wei-Yao-Wang et al. 2017). Section 3 provides a detailed explanation of the task at hand, including a description of the dataset employed in this study. Our proposed machine learning and deep learning models for detecting signs of depression are presented in Section 4. Subsequently, Section 5 outlines the conducted experiments and presents the corresponding results. A thorough discussion of these results is provided within the same section. Finally, in Section 6, we present our concluding remarks based on the findings and suggest potential avenues for future research in this field.

## 2 Literature Survey

The rapid growth of internet content and the anonymity of online platforms have made it challenging to manually identify signs of depression from social media text (Holleran 2020). However, machine learning and NLP techniques, such as Naive Bayes, Decision Trees, Random Forests, SVM, CNN, and RNN, have shown promise in automatically detecting signs of depression with high accuracy, even when tested on diverse datasets, including those associated with hate speech[2]. These

[1]https://www.who.int/news-room/fact-sheets/detail/suicide

[2]https://ojs.aaai.org/index.php/ICWSM/article/view/14432



*LT-EDI 2023 – Third Workshop on Language Technology for Equality, Diversity and Inclusion*, pages 97–102, Varna, Bulgaria, Sep 7, 2023.
https://doi.org/10.26615/978-954-452-084-7_014

advancements offer potential for efficient and automated detection and intervention in online contexts.Results obtained from the literature review stated that BiLSTM + Attention model performs well on depression related textual data. Even though the achieved result may be satisfactory, there are certain issues with the model implemented in that research(David-William 2020).For example, Guntuku S.C., Yaden D.B., Kern M.L., Ungar L.H., Eichstaedt J.C. Detecting depression and mental illness on social media(Guntuku-S.C. et al. 2017) focus on studies aimed at predicting mental illness using social media. First, they consider the methods used to predict depression, and then they consider four approaches that have been used in the literature: prediction based on survey responses, prediction based on self-declared mental health status, prediction based on forum membership, and prediction based on annotated posts.Wang Y.P., Gorenstein C. Assessment of depression in medical patients: A systematic review of the utility of the Beck Depression Inventory-II(Wang.Y.P. and Gorenstein.C 2013) examined relevant investigations with the Beck Depression Inventory-II for measuring depression in medical settings to provide guidelines for practicing clinicians. The Beck Depression Inventory-II showed high reliability and good correlation with the measures of depression and anxiety.

| DOCUMENT | TEXT | LABEL |
|---|---|---|
| Document [14] | Happy new year : Fuck 2019... 2020 will be bettexaxaxaxaxaxa why do i even have to be happy because earth did a whole circle around sun nothing will cange fuck my life hope u all have a better year that me...... | moderate |
| Document [637] | What if : What if you couldnt feel bain jelasy hate happiness sadness or anything what if you could live the life of true emotional freedom I people i had choosen the wrong choice... | |
| Document [2320] | I'm really struggling : So I don't know how to start things like this, So I'll start with basics. I'm 16yo, diagnosed depression at 14yo. Since then, my life is total mess. I've already been to two different psychologists... | severe |

Table 1: Sample Training Texts

## 3 Materials and Methods

### 3.1 Dataset Description

The dataset from the Coda Lab Competitions[3] consists of three main sections: Train data, Development data, and Test data with a sample given in Table 1. It includes train text id, train text, and labels indicating the severity of depression (No depression, Moderate, or Severely Depressed). The dataset is in English and comprises social media comments. Prior to applying machine learning and deep learning models, basic pre-processing steps like removing irrelevant characters and normalizing text were performed. The dataset is imbalanced, with varying numbers of instances across depression severity labels. The dataset includes 3678 moderate comments, 2755 not depressed comments, and 768 severely depressed comments. To address this, the SMOTE technique was used to balance class distribution by randomly increasing minority class examples by replicating them.Thus here SMOTE increases minority class (severely depressed) samples and balance the dataset(Jason-Brownlee 2020). By employing SMOTE, potential biases caused by the initial imbalance were alleviated, enhancing the reliability and robustness of the subsequent models.

[3]https://codalab.lisn.upsaclay.fr/competitions/11075

### 3.2 Preprocessing and Feature Extraction

To build an effective classifier, preprocessing or corpus cleaning is necessary. In this study, 3-grams were used to tokenize comments and extract features. 3-grams capture contextual relationships between words, allowing for a comprehensive representation of the text data and enabling better classification performance(Vairaprakash-Gurusamy 2014). By converting 3-grams into vectors based on their frequency and context, the resulting feature vectors are useful for text analysis and modeling tasks. Additionally, BERT and CNN were employed as classification models. BERT is a pre-trained language model known for its exceptional performance in various NLP tasks, while CNN is a popular deep learning technique for text classification. The combination of 3-grams, BERT, and CNN enhances the classifier's ability to identify patterns in the text data(Shizhe-Diao et al. 2020).

### 3.3 3-Gram Representation : Capturing the Contextual Relationship

3-gram representations provide a different approach to capturing the sequential nature of words in a text. Using the 3-gram technique, contiguous sequences of three words are extracted. For example, the phrase "consistent tomorrow drastically" represents one 3-gram, while "tomorrow drastically may" represents another. a few samples are given in [Table 2]. By utilizing 3-gram representations, we obtain a set of sequential word sequences that capture local word order and context information. These 3-gram sequences offer a more granular understanding of the text's structure and meaning compared to individual words or traditional n-gram representations.

In the context of text classification or language modeling, these 3-gram representations can be used as features. They provide additional contextual information that helps in capturing the nuances and dependencies within the text. These features contribute to more accurate and comprehensive analysis and inference. Overall, the utilization of 3-gram representations enhances the capability of capturing local word relationships, improving the quality of text analysis and enabling more effective processing of sequential data.

3-grams are assigned index values rather than stored as strings. These index values represent the different 3-gram units. The CountVectorizer or FastText model calculates vector representations for each 3-gram based on their frequency[4]. These vector representations capture the contextual information and co-occurrence patterns within the text. The classifiers are then trained using these vector representations to learn patterns and make predictions. Incorporating 3-grams allows the classifiers to capture both individual word features and the contextual relationships between adjacent words, improving their performance in text classification tasks.

| DOCUMENT | LABEL | 3 GRAM |
|---|---|---|
| Document [11] | moderate | ['consistent tomorrow drastically', 'tomorrow drastically may', 'drastically may view', 'may view hopeless','addictive disappointed satisfaction'.....] |
| Document[615] | no depression | ['psychologist psychiatrist physician uncomfortable', 'physician uncomfortable psychiatrist', 'uncomfortable psychiatrist medicated', 'psychologist soon based'....] |
| Document[641] | severe | ['argue bpd aspergers', 'bpd aspergers ocd', 'aspergers ocd suspected', 'ocd suspected 2018', 'suspected 2018 22', '2018 22 crap', '22 crap partner', 'crap partner seriously', 'partner seriously alcoholic'......] |

Table 2: RESULTS FROM 3 GRAM

[4]https://scikit-learn.org/stable/tutorial/basic/tutorial.html

Here's how 3-Gram is used:

1. Create an 3-Gram object and specify the desired 3-Gram range. 2. Apply the 3-Gram transformation to tokenize the text into 3-Gram. 3. Convert the 3-Gram into vector representations using techniques like Count Vectorizer or TF-IDF. 4. Use the resulting vectors for further analysis or modeling tasks. N-gram vectors capture word sequence frequency, providing contextual information for tasks like text classification and language modeling. The chosen 3-Gram range affects granularity in capturing text structure and meaning. Experimenting with different ranges optimizes performance for specific applications, ensuring originality and improving work quality.

## 4 Proposed Classifiers

The text-to-feature transformation is described, followed by the classification algorithms used for detecting signs of depression from social media text. For feature extraction, 3-gram techniques were employed, which are extensively used in NLP and text mining tasks.It capture contiguous sequences of three words, providing local word order and context information.Thus when 3-gram is used it allows machine to recognize the 3 words as one entity which makes the text classification to next level. To classify the extracted features, two classifiers are proposed: CNN and BERT. The proposed architecture is shown in [Figure 1].

Convolutional Neural Networks (CNN) are deep learning models that are effective in capturing local patterns in text data. CNNs have shown promising results in various NLP tasks. We used CNN for the 3-gram feature extraction method[5]. The architecture of CNN algorithm includes a number of convolution layers, max-pooling layers, and fully connected layers. ReLU as an activation function is used in proposed work.

This project leverages the power of BERT (Bidirectional Encoder Representations from Transformers), a highly effective pre-trained language model known for capturing contextual information from text[6].

Unlike traditional models, which looked at a text sequence only from one direction, the BERT encoder attention mechanism works bidirectional training of transformer, which learns information from both the left and right sides of a word, allowing the model to catch a deeper sense of language context.

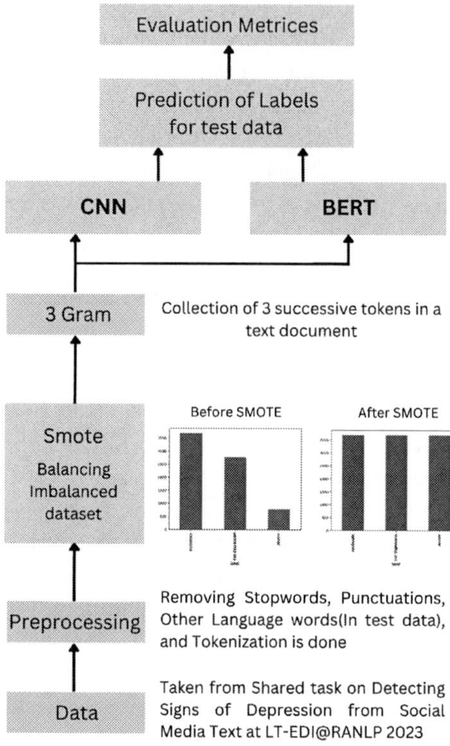


Figure 1: Proposed Model

We integrated BERT into our 3-gram feature extraction method, allowing us to benefit from its capabilities in various NLP tasks, including text classification. Each of the proposed classifiers takes the respective feature vectors as input and outputs the classification for each social media text. These classifiers have different specialties, and their performance metrics may vary.

By utilizing the 3-gram technique along with CNN and BERT classifiers, we aim to effectively detect signs of depression from social media text, providing valuable insights for mental health analysis.

## 5 Results and Discussion

The proposed classifiers have been implemented using scikit-learn(F.A.Nazira and M.F.Mridha 2021) and Python, and the training and testing processes took place on the Google Collaboratory platform. Google Collaboratory provides a cloud-based Jupyter notebook environment, eliminating the need for local setup. In our study, the coda lab

[5]https://neptune.ai/blog/vectorization-techniques-in-nlp-guide

[6]https://medium.com/analytics-vidhya/confusion-matrix-accuracy-precision-recall-f1-score-ade299cf63cd

| CLASSIFIERS | CLASS LABELS | ACCURACY | PRECISION | RECALL | F1-SCORE |
|---|---|---|---|---|---|
| CNN RESULT USING 3 GRAM | moderate | 0.55 | 0.67 | 0.65 | 0.66 |
| | not depression | 0.45 | 0.20 | 0.11 | 0.15 |
| | severe | 0.65 | 0.18 | 0.50 | 0.26 |
| | accuracy | | | 0.47 | 3246 |
| | macro avg | 0.25 | 0.31 | 0.25 | 3246 |
| | weighted avg | 0.50 | 0.47 | 0.48 | 3246 |
| BERT RESULT USING 3 GRAM | moderate | 0.52 | 0.66 | 0.64 | 0.65 |
| | not depression | 0.57 | 0.20 | 0.12 | 0.15 |
| | severe | 0.68 | 0.18 | 0.49 | 0.26 |
| | accuracy | | | 0.49 | 3246 |
| | macro avg | 0.26 | 0.32 | 0.26 | 3246 |
| | weighted avg | 0.51 | 0.49 | 0.49 | 3246 |

Table 3: PERFORMANCE OF CLASSIFIERS

LT-EDI@RANLP 2023 dataset was utilized, specifically developed for detecting signs of depression from social media text. This dataset comprises social media messages in English. We trained various classifiers, including CNN and BERT, using the extracted features from the training set. The performance of these classifiers was then evaluated on the test dataset. The combination of scikit-learn, Python, and the LT-EDI@RANLP 2023 dataset allowed us to detect signs of depression from social media text, contributing to the analysis and understanding of mental health indicators in online communication.

### 5.1 Performance Metrics

The performance evaluation of the classification models involved the calculation of several metrics, including Accuracy, Precision, Recall, and F1-Score(Qamar-un-Nisa 2021). These metrics are defined as follows:

Accuracy: It measures the proportion of texts correctly classified in a specific class, divided by the total number of texts in that class. The formula for Accuracy (Equation 1) is:

$$Accuracy = \frac{TP+TN}{TP+TN+FP+FN} \quad (1)$$

Recall (Sensitivity or True Positive Rate): It represents the number of texts correctly categorized in a certain class, divided by the total number of actual texts in that class. The formula for Recall (Equation 2) is:

$$Recall = \frac{TP}{TP+FN} \quad (2)$$

Precision (Positive Predictive Value): It measures the number of texts accurately categorized as a specific class, divided by the total number of texts categorized as that class. The formula for Precision (Equation 3) is:

$$Precision = \frac{TP}{TP+FP} \quad (3)$$

F1-Score: It is the harmonic average of Precision and Recall, providing a balanced measure of the model's performance. The F1-Score (Equation 4) is calculated as:

$$F1score = \frac{2*Precision*Recall}{Precision+Recall} \quad (4)$$

These metrics rely on the True Positive (TP), True Negative (TN), False Positive (FP), and False Negative (FN) indices. TP represents the number of texts correctly classified for a particular class, while FP represents the number of texts misclassified in other classes. FN represents the number of texts misclassified in the relevant class, and TN represents the number of texts correctly classified in other classes except the correct class[7]. The results obtained from proposed models are shown in Table 3.

## 6 Conclusion and Feature Work

In conclusion, this study successfully conducted experimental work to detect signs of depression from social media text using the provided dataset. 3-gram is employed as feature extraction technique to effectively capture textual information. Different classifiers, including CNN, and BERT, were compared and BERT with 3Gram has achieved a

[7]https://developers.google.com/machine-learning/crash-course/classification/true-false-positive-negative

goo accuracy compared to CNN and thus proving its effectiveness in this task(Vandana 2023).

For future work, there are several potential areas of improvement. Exploring alternative numerical or vectorial representations of the text, such as TF-IDF, could potentially enhance classification performance(Kapse et al. 2022). Additionally, investigating new classifiers based on neural networks, which leverage advanced linguistic features, would be valuable. These approaches can contribute to further improving the detection of signs of depression in social media texts, enabling a deeper understanding of mental health indicators in online communication.

Further, the usage of a post encoder, a sentiment-guided Transformer and a supervised severity-aware contrastive learning component may enhance the result and it can lead the classification method to a new level. Unlike the proposed model the account of sentiment and semantic information of data can lead to greater accuracy. The post encoder MentalRoBERTa and SentiLARE can be used to obtain the semantic as well as sentiment hidden features.

**Our model for bagged the official rank of 12 and gave an F1 score of 0.401.**

## References


David-William, Suhartono.D. (2020). "Text-based Depression Detection on Social Media Posts". In: *ScienceDirect*. DOI: 10.1016/j.procs.2021.01.043.

F.A.Nazira S.R.Das, S.A.Shanto and M.F.Mridha (2021). "Depression Detection Using Convolutional Neural Networks". In: *2021 IEEE International Conference on Signal Processing, Information, Communication Systems (SPICSCON), Dhaka, Bangladesh*, pp. 9–13. DOI: 10.1109/SPICSCON54707.2021.9885517..

Greenberg-LS (2017). "Emotion-focused therapy of depression. Per Centered Exp Psychother". In: 16(1), pp. 106–117.

Guntuku-S.C., Yaden-D.B., Kern-M.L., Ungar-L.H., and Eichstaedt J.C (2017). "Detecting depression and mental illness on social media: An integrative review." In: *Proceedings of the 24th International Conference on Machine Learning* 18, pp. 43–49. DOI: 10.1016/j.cobeha.2017.07.005..

Holleran (2020). "The early detection of depression from social networking sites". In.

Jason-Brownlee (2020). "smote-oversampling-for-imbalanced-classification". In: *ScienceDirect*.

Kapse, Prasanna, Garg, and Vijay Kumar (2022). "Advanced Deep Learning Techniques For Depression Detection: A Review". In: DOI: 10.2139/ssrn.4180783.

Qamar-un-Nisa, Rafi-Muhammad (2021). "Towards transfer learning using BERT for early detection of self-harm of social media users". In: *CLEF 2021 – Conference and Labs of the Evaluation Forum, September 21–24*.

Shizhe-Diao, Ruijia-Xu, Hongjin Su, Yilei-Jiang, Yan-Song, and Tong-Zhang (2020). "Taming Pretrained Language Models with N-gram Representations for Low Resource Domain Adaptation". In: *Curr. Sci.*

Vairaprakash-Gurusamy, Subbu-Kannan (2014). "Preprocessing Techniques for Text Mining". In: *Curr. Opin.*

Vandana Nikhil-Marriwala, Deepti-Chaudhary (2023). "A hybrid model for depression detection using deep learning, Measurement: Sensors". In: *ISSN* 25. DOI: 10.1016/j.measen.2022.100587.

Wang.Y.P. and Gorenstein.C (2013). "Assessment of depression in medical patients: A systematic review of the utility of the Beck Depression Inventory-II". In: *ScienceDirect*.

Wei-Yao-Wang, Yu-Chien, Tang-Wei-Wei Du, and Wen-Chih-Peng (2017). "Ensemble Models with VADER and Contrastive Learning for Detecting Signs of Depression from Social Media". In: *ScienceDirect*.

# cantnlp@LT-EDI-2023: Homophobia/Transphobia Detection in Social Media Comments using Spatio-Temporally Retrained Language Models

**Sidney G.-J. Wong, Matthew Durward, Benjamin Adams** and **Jonathan Dunn**
University of Canterbury, Christchurch, New Zealand
{sidney.wong,matthew.durward}@pg.canterbury.ac.nz
{benjamin.adams,jonathan.dunn}@canterbury.ac.nz

## Abstract

This paper describes our multiclass classification system developed as part of the LT-EDI@RANLP-2023 shared task. We used a BERT-based language model to detect homophobic and transphobic content in social media comments across five language conditions: English, Spanish, Hindi, Malayalam, and Tamil. We retrained a transformer-based cross-language pretrained language model, XLM-RoBERTa, with spatially and temporally relevant social media language data. We also retrained a subset of models with simulated script-mixed social media language data with varied performance. We developed the best performing seven-label classification system for Malayalam based on weighted macro averaged F1 score (ranked first out of six) with variable performance for other language and class-label conditions. We found the inclusion of this spatio-temporal data improved the classification performance for all language and task conditions when compared with the baseline. The results suggests that transformer-based language classification systems are sensitive to register-specific and language-specific retraining.

## 1 Introduction

The purpose of this shared task was to develop a classification system to predict whether samples of social media comments contained forms of homophobia or transphobia across different language conditions. There were no restrictions on language models or data pre-processing methods.

The five language conditions: English, Spanish, Hindi, Malayalam, and Tamil. In addition to the language conditions, participants were tasked with developing a system for a three-class and seven-class classification system defining different forms of homophobic and transphobic hate speech (Chakravarthi et al., 2021).

The main contribution of our proposed system outlined in this paper included spatio-temporal relevant social media language data to retrain a transformer-based language model to increase the sensitivity of the pretrained language model (PLM). We have also created simulated samples of script-mixed social media language data which was used as part of the retraining process.

### 1.1 Problem Description

The organisers of this shared task provided .csv files containing labelled data of pre-processed comments of users reacting to LGBT+ videos on YouTube. This was an expanded data set of the Homophobia/Transphobia Detection data set (Chakravarthi et al., 2021) with the inclusion of Hindi, Malayalam, and Spanish in addition to the pre-existing English and Tamil data.

The comments were manually annotated based on a three-class and a seven-class classification system. The participants of the shared task were not provided any further information on the annotation process or measures of inter-annotator agreement. The shared task was broken down into the following tasks:

- Task A involves developing a classification model for three classes across all five language conditions as shown in Table 1.
- Task B involves developing a classification model for seven classes across three language conditions as shown in Table 2.

The organisers of this shared task provided training and validation data to develop the system. The test data was provided once the results of the shared task were announced. The organisers evaluated the performance of each homophobia/transphobia detection system with weighted macro averaged F1 score. The performance for each language and



*LT-EDI 2023 – Third Workshop on Language Technology for Equality, Diversity and Inclusion*, pages 103–108, Varna, Bulgaria, Sep 7, 2023.
https://doi.org/10.26615/978-954-452-084-7_015

| Language Condition | H | N | T | Total |
|---|---|---|---|---|
| English | 179 | 2978 | 7 | 3164 |
| Hindi | 45 | 2423 | 92 | 2560 |
| Malayalam | 476 | 2468 | 170 | 3114 |
| Spanish | 200 | 450 | 200 | 850 |
| Tamil | 453 | 2064 | 145 | 2662 |

Table 1: The labelled training data broken down by language condition and class label for Task A. The class labels for Task A were homophobia (H), non-anti-LGBT+ content (N), and transphobia (T).

| Language Condition | CS | HT | HD | HS | NO | TT | TD | Total |
|---|---|---|---|---|---|---|---|---|
| English | 302 | 12 | 167 | 436 | 2240 | 1 | 6 | 3164 |
| Malayalam | 152 | 57 | 419 | 69 | 2247 | 7 | 163 | 3114 |
| Tamil | 212 | 37 | 416 | 218 | 1634 | 34 | 111 | 2662 |

Table 2: The labelled training data broken down by language condition and class label for Task B. The class labels for Task B were counter-speech (CS), homophobic-threatening (HT), homophobic-derogation (HD), hope-speech (HS), none-of-the-above (NO), transphobic-threatening (TT), and transphobic-derogation (TD).

class-label condition were ranked based on this score.

### 1.2 Related Work

Previous approaches in detecting homophobia and transphobia on social media comments has shown varying levels of success (Chakravarthi et al., 2022). In this shared task, participants were asked to detect homophobia and transphobia across three language conditions: English, Tamil, and an additional English-Tamil script-mixed data set.

Participants of the shared task combined various natural language processing methods such as statistical language models and machine learning to complete the task. However, the performance of transformer-based language models remained consistently high across all three language conditions.

More specifically BERT-based models with minimal fine-tuning outperformed statistical language models using TF-IDF for feature extraction. BERT, or Bidirectional Encoder Representations from Transformers, structures the complex relationship between words in a language through embeddings (Devlin et al., 2019).

The best performing BERT-based system for English yielded an average weighted macro F1 score of 0.92 compared with non-transformer-based language models (Maimaitituoheti et al., 2022). Conversely, the same BERT-based models struggled to outperform machine learning and deep learning systems approaches in Tamil and in the English-Tamil condition.

This suggests further work is needed to refine BERT-based to improve its performance outside an English-context. Based on the promising results of BERT-based language models in Chakravarthi et al. (2022), the current study extend on this transformer-based approach to develop and refine a homophobia and transphobia detection system across language conditions.

## 2 Methodology

In this section, we provide a system overview of our transformer-based language model. We also provide details on our retraining and fine-tuning procedures.

### 2.1 System Overview

Due to the number of language conditions for the current shared task, it was unfeasible to use language-specific BERT-based models. One risk for using independently developed language-specific BERT-based models was that there was no control on the source data used to train the representations. For this reason, we used a cross-lingual transformer-based language model as our baseline language model.

XLM-RoBERTa was trained on two terabytes of CommonCrawl for 100 languages (Conneau et al., 2020). Some of these languages include English, Hindi, Malayalam, Spanish, and Tamil. Furthermore, Romanised Hindi and Tamil have also been included in the pretraining of this cross-lingual transformer-based language model.

Despite these benefits, we were aware of the risk in overgeneralising the register of language

| Language | Indic | Latin | Total |
|---|---|---|---|
| English | - | 50K | 50K |
| Spanish | - | 50K | 50K |
| Hindi | 50K | - | 50K |
| Malayalam | 50K | - | 50K |
| Tamil | 50K | - | 50K |
| SM Hindi | 37.5K | 12.5K | 50K |
| SM Malayalam | 37.5K | 12.5K | 50K |
| SM Tamil | 37.5K | 12.5K | 50K |

Table 3: Corpus size of language samples for fine-tuning with simulated script-mixing (SM).

of CommonCrawl as the language used on this platform is not reflective of the language used on social media. We could retrain PLMs for a specific task to mitigate this issue without the need to train a PLM from scratch.

This retraining method has shown to improve the performance of PLMs in downstream tasks (such as label classification) for under-represented and under-resourced languages by pretraining with additional register-specific language data (Liu et al., 2019). Therefore, we have retrained the baseline XLM-RoBERTa PLM prior to fine-tuning the baseline XLM-RoBERTa PLM.

## 2.2 Retraining

We used social media language data from the Corpus of Global Language Use (CGLU) for retraining (Dunn, 2020). The CGLU is a very large digital corpora which contains over 20 billion words associated with 10,000 point locations across the globe.

Although the source of the CGLU social media language data comes from Twitter, a microblogging platform, and the training data comes from YouTube, a video sharing platform, our focus is on the written language components, and we assume some close domain alignment. We removed hashtags and hyperlinks to ensure the retraining data has a similar form to the training data. We also removed multiple punctuation and blank space characters. Short tweets with fewer than 50 characters were also systematically removed.

We controlled the spatial and temporal window of the sampled tweets by restricting the sample of tweets to those originating in India produced between 1 January 2019 and 31 December 2019. Once again, we wanted to closely match retraining data with the time and geographic source of the labelled training data (Chakravarthi et al., 2021).

We used the `langdetect`[1] library to detect the language condition for each tweet. For each of the five different language conditions, we extracted a random sample of 50,000 tweets for training. We then use the LanguageModelingModel class from the `simpletransformers` library to retrain XLM-RoBERTa on an unlabelled corpus of social media language data.

In addition to creating corpus training data for the five different language conditions, we created additional corpus training data with simulated script-mixing. A major motivation to retrain the model with the simulated script-mixed retraining data is the lack of Romanised Malayalam in XLM-RoBERTa. We used the transliteration.XlitEngine class from the `ai4bharat`[2] library to transliterate one-fifth of the sample tweets from Indic to Latin script.

The size of our retraining corpora for each language condition is shown in Table 3. We retrained the language model for 4 iterations and we evaluated the training for every 500 steps. We saved the model with the best performance determined by the loss function in our output directory.

## 2.3 Fine-tuning

Once we retrained XLM-RoBERTa with the social media language data from the CGLU, we fine-tuned the baseline and the retrained language models with the labelled training data.

As shown in Table 1 and Table 2, the class labels for both Task A and Task B are highly unbalanced. We used the RandomOverSampler class from the library to oversample the minority classes. In most cases, these minority classes related to homophobia and transphobia.

We used the classificaton class from the `simpletransformers` library to fine-tune the retrained PLMs with the labelled training data. We trained the classification model for 8 iterations and we evaluated the training for every 500 steps. We also used AdamW optimization (Loshchilov and Hutter, 2019).

We applied the same fine-tuning strategy to Task A and Task B to maintain consistency across the shared task. We saved the model with the best performance determined by the loss function in our output directory.

[1]https://pypi.org/project/langdetect/

[2]https://pypi.org/project/ai4bharat-transliteration/

| Language Condition | Baseline | Retrained | Script-Mixed | Rank |
|---|---|---|---|---|
| English | 0.93 | **0.94** | - | 7 |
| Hindi | 0.93 | 0.92 | **0.97** | 3 |
| Malayalam | 0.93 | 0.95 | **0.94** | 4 |
| Spanish | 0.83 | (0.86) | - | - |
| Tamil | 0.70 | 0.93 | **0.93** | 3 |

Table 4: Macro averaged F1 for each language condition for Task A and overall rank for the shared task. The submitted result is in **bold**. Note that the result for Spanish was invalid.

| Language Condition | Baseline | Retrained | Script-Mixed | Rank |
|---|---|---|---|---|
| English | 0.15 | **0.54** | - | 6 |
| Malayalam | 0.86 | 0.86 | **0.88** | 1 |
| Tamil | 0.77 | 0.90 | **0.80** | 4 |

Table 5: Macro averaged F1 for each language condition for Task B and overall rank for the shared task. The submitted result is in **bold**.

### 2.4 Other Settings

We completed the retraining and fine-tuning in Python3 on Google Colaboratory. We used GPU as our hardware accelerator using NVIDIA A100 Tensor Core graphics card.

## 3 Results

The results of Task A are shown in Table 4 and the results of Task B are shown in Table 5. Both tables compare the weighted macro averaged F1 metrics for the classification models derived from the baseline XLM-RoBERTa and the modified XLM-RoBERTa models produced specifically for this task. The ranking of our models are also presented in the final column of the tables.

In Task A, English, Hindi, and Malayalam performed the best of the the baseline classification models with a macro averaged F1 score of .93. Tamil performed the worst of the baseline classification models. The performance of the retrained classification models were consistently better than the baseline classification models. Malayalam performed the best with a macro averaged F1 score of 0.95 while Spanish performed the worst with a macro averaged F1 score of 0.86. The classification models fine-tuned on simulated script-mixed training data did not improve the classification performance for Tamil. Conversely, we saw a decrease in performance for Malayalam. There was a large improvement in classification performance for Hindi.

We have highlighted the performance metric in bold in terms of the optimal classification models submitted to the organisers for evaluation in Table 4. Hindi and Tamil ranked third out of seven, Malayalam ranked fourth out of seven, and English ranked seventh out of eleven. Due to issues with the labels, the submission for the Spanish condition in Task A was invalid. However, the macro averaged F1 metric is provided in brackets for reference.

In Task B, Malayalam performed the best of the baseline classification models with a macro averaged F1 score of 0.86 while English performed the worst with a macro averaged F1 score of 0.15. The performance increased once we fine-tuned the classification model with the retrained XLM-RoBERTa with the macro averaged F1 score for English improving from 0.15 to 0.54 and for Tamil improving from 0.77 to 0.90. The performance remained stable between the baseline and retrained models for Malayalam.

When we introduced the script-mixed models for Malayalam and Tamil, we saw varying levels of performance. The macro averaged F1 score for Malayalam increased from 0.86 to 0.88. This suggests an increase in performance accuracy. Counterintuitively, the macro averaged score F1 for Tamil decreased from 0.90 to 0.80 which was on par with the baseline model. This suggests a decrease in performance accuracy.

Our Malayalam classification system fine-tuned on the script-mixed social media language data ranked first out of six, while the Tamil classification system fine-tuned on the script-mixed social media language data ranked fourth out of seven despite the decrease in performance from the retrained language model. Our English classification system fine-tuned on the retrained language model ranked sixth out of nine.

## 4 Discussion

This paper addresses intrinsic issues related to hate speech detection in written social media data. This was mirrored in our training, validation, and testing data which reflects the multifaceted challenges of real-world scenarios. Hate speech is not confined to any single language or geographic region and its instances are often buried within the vast array of existing textual data, particularly in the context of social media.

The employment of the XLM-RoBERTa model has demonstrated to be an effective system in detecting homophobia and transphobia in social media comments, particularly when the PLM has been retrained with spatio-temporal data for the English and Tamil language conditions. These findings underline the potential of integrating geographic language data into models as a means of enhancing their performance not only on highly represented languages, but also on lower underrepresented languages, thus offering a robust solution.

In the preceding sections of this paper, we have outlined and highlighted in Table 1 and Table 2 an influencing challenge relating to the distribution of data across the different language conditions. The imbalance observed between language conditions as exhibited in the discrepancies in their respective training, validation, and test data sets poses an additional obstacle when it comes to drawing comparative inferences. However, there are opportunities that could help balance the data and potentially improve performance.

To alleviate this issue, the utilisation of synthetic data through data augmentation techniques could prove to be a promising approach. Data augmentation, as a broad concept, involves expanding the existing data sets to enhance their diversity, and therefore, the generalisability of the models trained on them (Hoffmann et al., 2022). The generation of synthetic data has been demonstrated to be an effective mechanism in addressing biased data sets, but it also presents a desirable practice particularly suited for hate speech detection given the prevailing concerns over text obfuscation of such instances (Aggarwal and Zesch, 2022).

To help facilitate a system that can account for these nuances, data noise injection via character, word, or even phrasal additions could be advantageous. In this sense, the application of synthetic data coupled with noise injection can help address class imbalance, while also training more robust classifiers that are less reliant on explicit instances of derogatory terms, but are more adept at discerning underlying contextual uses of hate speech.

There are real-world applications to our homophobia/transphobia detection system as we can refine our model with language-specific and region-specific information to monitor hate speech on social media directed at LGBTQ+ communities. This is particularly useful for languages that are not otherwise as well represented in large language models such as Malayalam which saw great improvement in performance with the addition of script-mixed retraining data.

## 5 Conclusion

We saw an improvement in performance in our retrained homophobia/transphobia classification model when compared with our baseline model. Our unique approach to this shared task has shown potential for retraining pretrained language models with spatio-temporal relevant language data to improve the performance of our homophobia/transphobia detection system. Counterintuitively, the inclusion of script-mixed language data gave us variable results. We will aim to refine our classification system with other attested methods such as noise injection in order to improve the performance of our system.

## References


Piush Aggarwal and Torsten Zesch. 2022. Analyzing the Real Vulnerability of Hate Speech Detection Systems against Targeted Intentional Noise. In *Proceedings of the Eighth Workshop on Noisy User-generated Text (W-NUT 2022)*, pages 230–242, Gyeongju, Republic of Korea. Association for Computational Linguistics.

Bharathi Raja Chakravarthi, Ruba Priyadharshini, Thenmozhi Durairaj, John McCrae, Paul Buitelaar, Prasanna Kumaresan, and Rahul Ponnusamy. 2022. Overview of The Shared Task on Homophobia and Transphobia Detection in Social Media Comments. In *Proceedings of the Second Workshop on Language Technology for Equality, Diversity and Inclusion*, pages 369–377, Dublin, Ireland. Association for Computational Linguistics.

Bharathi Raja Chakravarthi, Ruba Priyadharshini, Rahul Ponnusamy, Prasanna Kumar Kumaresan, Kayalvizhi Sampath, Durairaj Thenmozhi, Sathiyaraj Thangasamy, Rajendran Nallathambi, and John Phillip McCrae. 2021. Dataset for Identification of Homophobia and Transophobia in Multilingual YouTube Comments. ArXiv:2109.00227 [cs].

Alexis Conneau, Kartikay Khandelwal, Naman Goyal, Vishrav Chaudhary, Guillaume Wenzek, Francisco Guzmán, Edouard Grave, Myle Ott, Luke Zettlemoyer, and Veselin Stoyanov. 2020. Unsupervised Cross-lingual Representation Learning at Scale. ArXiv:1911.02116 [cs].

Jacob Devlin, Ming-Wei Chang, Kenton Lee, and Kristina Toutanova. 2019. BERT: Pre-training of Deep Bidirectional Transformers for Language Understanding. ArXiv:1810.04805 [cs].

Jonathan Dunn. 2020. Mapping languages: the Corpus of Global Language Use. *Language Resources and Evaluation*, 54(4):999–1018.

Jordan Hoffmann, Sebastian Borgeaud, Arthur Mensch, Elena Buchatskaya, Trevor Cai, Eliza Rutherford, Diego de Las Casas, Lisa Anne Hendricks, Johannes Welbl, Aidan Clark, Tom Hennigan, Eric Noland, Katie Millican, George van den Driessche, Bogdan Damoc, Aurelia Guy, Simon Osindero, Karen Simonyan, Erich Elsen, Jack W. Rae, Oriol Vinyals, and Laurent Sifre. 2022. Training Compute-Optimal Large Language Models. ArXiv:2203.15556 [cs].

Yinhan Liu, Myle Ott, Naman Goyal, Jingfei Du, Mandar Joshi, Danqi Chen, Omer Levy, Mike Lewis, Luke Zettlemoyer, and Veselin Stoyanov. 2019. RoBERTa: A Robustly Optimized BERT Pretraining Approach. ArXiv:1907.11692 [cs].

Ilya Loshchilov and Frank Hutter. 2019. Decoupled Weight Decay Regularization. ArXiv:1711.05101 [cs, math].

Abulimiti Maimaitituoheti, Yong Yang, and Xiaochao Fan. 2022. ABLIMET @LT-EDI-ACL2022: A Roberta based Approach for Homophobia/Transphobia Detection in Social Media. In *Proceedings of the Second Workshop on Language Technology for Equality, Diversity and Inclusion*, pages 155–160, Dublin, Ireland. Association for Computational Linguistics.

# NLP_CHRISTINE@LT-EDI: RoBERTa & DeBERTa Fine-tuning for Detecting Signs of Depression from Social Media Text

**Christina Christodoulou**
Institute of Informatics & Telecommunications,
National Centre for Scientific Research, “Demokritos“
Athens, Greece
ch.christodoulou@iit.demokritos.gr

## Abstract

The paper outlines the approach used to detect signs of depression from English social media text for the $4^{th}$ Shared Task at LT-EDI@RANLP 2023. The solution involved data cleaning and pre-processing, leveraging additional data, addressing data imbalance, and fine-tuning RoBERTa-Large and DeBERTa-V3-Large transformer-based pre-trained language models. Four different model architectures were developed using different word embedding pooling methods, including a RoBERTa-Large bidirectional GRU model using GRU pooling and three DeBERTa models using CLS pooling, mean pooling, and max pooling, respectively. Although ensemble learning of DeBERTa's pooling methods was used to improve performance, the RoBERTa bidirectional GRU model received the $8^{th}$ place out of 31 submissions with a Macro-F1 score of 0.42.

## 1 Introduction

Depression is a severe mental disorder that can significantly impact an individual's thoughts, emotions, behavior, and daily routine. (of Mental Health, 2023). This condition is classified into three levels, namely mild, moderate, and severe, based on the number of symptoms present. These symptoms may include feelings of sadness, hopelessness, irritability, guilt, insomnia, fatigue, loss of appetite, and disinterest in activities. Mild depression typically manifests with 5-6 symptoms, while moderate depression involves 7-8 symptoms, and severe depression includes 9 or more symptoms, which may include hallucinations, delusions, suicidal thoughts, or even attempts (Cherney, 2018). Depression is a widespread issue, affecting approximately 280 million individuals worldwide (WHO, 2023). As social media continues to serve as a platform for individuals to express their emotions (Alyssa, 2021), the identification of symptoms of depression through automated means holds the potential for prompt intervention, psychological aid, and the avoidance of adverse outcomes. The $4^{th}$ Shared Task on *Detecting Signs of Depression from Social Media Text* at LT-EDI@RANLP 2023 (Sampath et al., 2023) challenged participants to develop text classification systems that can classify English social media posts into three classes, namely *not depression*, *moderate* and *severe* depression. This paper presents the system developed for this competition, with the code available on the provided GitHub link.[1]

The structure of this paper is as follows: Firstly, Section 2 presents a discussion of the previous related work followed by the presentation of the data analysis in Section 3, and an overview of the developed system in Section 4. In Section 5, an outline of the experimental setup is provided, while Section 6 presents the results and error analysis. Finally, the paper concludes with Section 7, which discusses future work.

## 2 Related Work

Previous work on *Detecting Signs of Depression from Social Media Text* was conducted at LT-EDI@RANLP 2022. The majority of participating teams used transformer-based language models, such as BERT (Anantharaman et al., 2022), DistilBERT, and RoBERTa (S et al., 2022), while several teams used traditional machine learning methods like Logistic Regression (Agirrezabal and Amann, 2022), Support Vector Machines, Random Forest, and XGBoost Classifiers (Sharen and Rajalakshmi, 2022). The top-ranking team, *OPI*, experimented with BERT, RoBERTa, and XLNet,

[1] https://github.com/christinacdl/Depression_Detection_Text_Classification/blob/main/Detecting_Signs_of_Depression_from_Social_Media_Text.ipynb



*LT-EDI 2023 – Third Workshop on Language Technology for Equality, Diversity and Inclusion*, pages 109–116, Varna, Bulgaria, Sep 7, 2023.
https://doi.org/10.26615/978-954-452-084-7_016

trained RoBERTa-Large from scratch on depression corpora (*DepRoBERTa*), fine-tuned it and created an ensemble model resulting in attaining a 0.583 macro-F1 score (Poświata and Perełkiewicz, 2022). The *NYCU_TWD* team, which came in second place by achieving a 0.552 macro-F1 score, experimented with gradient boosting, pre-trained transformer language models, VADER, supervised contrastive learning, and ensemble learning (Wang et al., 2022).

## 3 Data

### 3.1 Provided Datasets

The task organizers provided both the training and development data, which included lengthy texts from social media posts along with their corresponding IDs and class labels. During the testing phase, the test data was also provided, but without labels. Thus, participants had to make predictions for the test texts and submit them without immediately knowing the results or the performance of their system. The class labels of the test data were released after the competition ended. The training data consisted of 7,201 texts, while the development data consisted of 3,245 texts. The test data comprised 499 texts. In the data cleaning process, 116 and 12 duplicate texts were removed from the training and development data, respectively. The test data did not contain any duplicates.

### 3.2 Additional Datasets

Two additional binary-class datasets were employed and combined with the train and development datasets. The first dataset was sourced from Hugging Face and contained 7,731 English posts from Reddit labeled as 0 (*not depression*) and as 1 (*depression*).[2] The second dataset was also found on Kaggle and contained 20,363 English posts from Reddit with the labels *depression* and *SuicideWatch*.[3] In this dataset, the class label *depression* was renamed as *moderate*, while the class label *SuicideWatch* was renamed as *severe*. During the data cleaning process, 81 and 8 duplicates were removed from the first and second datasets, respectively. Table 1 illustrates the class distribution of the provided train and development data as well as the class distribution of the additional data before and after data cleaning. The categorical labels were converted into the respective numerical labels denoted in brackets for training and evaluation purposes.

| Class Label | Before Data Cleaning | After Data Cleaning |
|---|---|---|
| **Provided Train Data** | | |
| not depression (0) | 2,755 | 2,697 |
| moderate (1) | 3,678 | 3,544 |
| severe (2) | 768 | 728 |
| **Provided Development Data** | | |
| not depression (0) | 848 | 841 |
| moderate (1) | 2,169 | 2,153 |
| severe (2) | 228 | 228 |
| **Additional Hugging Face Data** | | |
| not depression (0) | 3,900 | 3,879 |
| depression (1) | 3,831 | 3,718 |
| **Additional Kaggle Data** | | |
| depression (1) | 10,371 | 10,359 |
| SuicideWatch (2) | 9,992 | 9,988 |

Table 1: Class distribution of provided and additional data before and after data cleaning.

### 3.3 Data Used

The provided training and development datasets, along with additional datasets, were concatenated to form a new dataset. This was done to increase the amount of training data and improve the class distribution, particularly for the *severe* and *moderate* classes, which were essential for this task. However, only the *not depression* texts were utilized from the first additional dataset from Hugging Face. This was because there was no clarification concerning the depression level in its *depression* texts. Since there was no information regarding whether the texts were categorized as *moderate* or *severe* depression, they were not included in the new dataset. The new dataset consisted of 34,417 text entries with their respective labels. From the class distribution in Table 2, it can be demonstrated that the two classes, representing two levels of depression, constitute the majority of the dataset. This was anticipated to assist the system in detecting signs of depression. For data splitting into the train and development sets, ten-fold cross-validation with stratified sampling was implemented. This ensured that the train and development sets would have the same proportion of class values and, hence, would

[2]https://huggingface.co/datasets/hugginglearners/reddit-depression-cleaned/tree/main

[3]https://www.kaggle.com/datasets/xavrig/reddit-dataset-rdepression-and-rsuicidewatch

be equally represented. The train set consisted of 30,976 texts, and the development set consisted of 3,441 texts.

### 3.4 Tackling Data Imbalance

In addition to incorporating more depression data, the *Imbalanced Dataset Sampler* was used to create the train Dataloader. This tool balances the distribution of classes when sampling from an imbalanced dataset and automatically calculates the corresponding sampling weights.[4]

| **Final Dataset** | |
|---|---|
| **Class Label** | **Number of Texts** |
| not depression (0) | 7,417 |
| moderate (1) | 16,056 |
| severe (2) | 10,944 |
| **Train Set** | |
| **Class Label** | **Number of Texts** |
| not depression (0) | 6,675 |
| moderate (1) | 14,451 |
| severe (2) | 9,850 |
| **Development Set** | |
| **Class Label** | **Number of Texts** |
| not depression (0) | 742 |
| moderate (1) | 1,605 |
| severe (2) | 1,094 |

Table 2: Class distribution of final dataset, train and development sets used for training and evaluation.

## 4 System Overview

The presented system utilizes two robust models, RoBERTa (Liu et al., 2019) and DeBERTa (He et al., 2020), for fine-tuning purposes. RoBERTa-Large, which boasts 355M parameters, includes 24 layers with a hidden size of 1024 and a vocabulary size of 50,265. DeBERTa-V3-Large, on the other hand, contains 304M parameters, 24 layers with a hidden size of 1024, and a vocabulary size of 128,100. Both models leverage the *sentencepiece* tokenizer to ensure optimal performance. The models that were chosen for the study were selected based on their exceptional architecture and outstanding performance on various Natural Language Processing (NLP) tasks and benchmark datasets. One model architecture utilizes all output hidden states for GRU pooling, while other model architectures utilize the last hidden state for CLS pooling, mean pooling, and max pooling. Through extensive experimentation, it was determined that keeping the first 7 encoder layers frozen during fine-tuning resulted in the best performance. The flow diagram of the presented system is depicted in Figure 1.

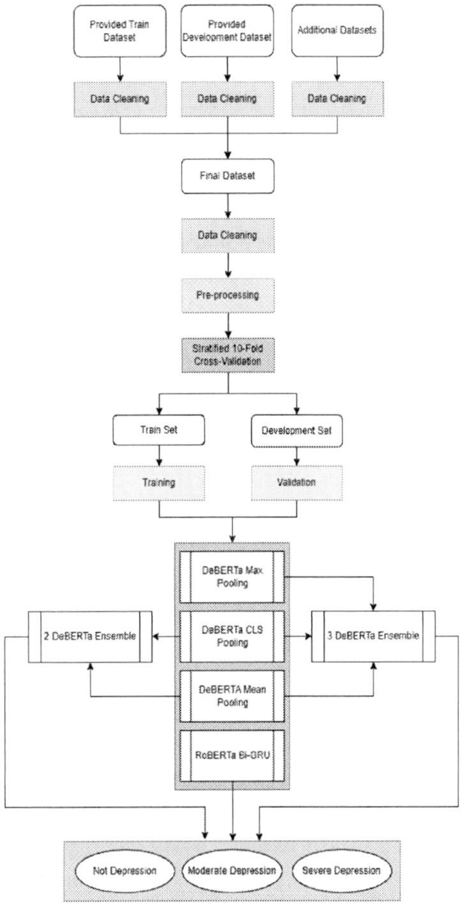


Figure 1: Flow diagram of the presented approach

### 4.1 GRU Pooling

The first model architecture was based on a BERT model using LSTM pooling for aspect-based sentiment analysis (Song et al., 2020). Unlike this BERT model, the model developed for this system is a RoBERTa-Large Bidirectional GRU network (***RoBERTa Bi-GRU***) utilizing GRU pooling. It is bidirectional, meaning that it can process the input and retain information from both directions. It takes all hidden states of RoBERTa ([initial embeddings + total number of layers, batch size, max sequence length, hidden size]) and passes them through a GRU network, which is used to connect all the [CLS] token representations. The output representation from the last GRU cell, which has

[4] `https://github.com/ufoym/imbalanced-dataset-sampler`

the size of [batch size, total number of layers, max sequence length * 2], is passed into a dropout layer. In the end, a linear layer, which has dimensions equal to the size of the maximum sequence length multiplied by two and the number of classes [max sequence length * 2, number of classes], is applied to the output from the dropout layer.

### 4.2 CLS Pooling

The second model architecture (***DeBERTa CLS Pooling***) implements the most common pooling method - the CLS pooling. During classification tasks, a special [CLS] token is added at the first position of each sequence to capture the entire context information of a sequence. The [CLS] token embeddings are aggregated in the pooling layer and are used as sentence embeddings. These embeddings pass through a dropout layer and finally, a linear layer that classifies the texts into three classes.

### 4.3 Mean Pooling

The third model architecture called (***DeBERTa Mean Pooling***), involves averaging all of the contextualized token embeddings from the last hidden state. First, the attention mask is expanded from [batch size, maximum sequence length] to [batch size, maximum sequence length, hidden size]. Then, the token embeddings are summed along the maximum sequence length axis to end up with a size of [batch size, hidden size]. The attention mask is also summed along the maximum sequence length axis so that padding tokens ([PAD]) are ignored. The mean embeddings, which are the average of the summed token embeddings and the summed attention mask, pass through a dropout layer and finally, a linear layer, which classifies the texts into the three classes.

### 4.4 Max Pooling

The fourth model architecture (***DeBERTa Max Pooling***) uses the maximum pooling method by taking the maximum value of the token embeddings from the last hidden state at each time step. The attention mask was expanded from [batch size, maximum sequence length] to [batch size, maximum sequence length, hidden size]. Then, the padding tokens were set to a large negative value (-1e9). The maximum token embeddings produce sentence embeddings that pass through a dropout layer and, finally, through the classifier linear layer.

### 4.5 Majority Vote Ensemble Learning

In this particular study, two different ensemble learning methods were utilized to predict the class labels for each given text. The ultimate label that was submitted for each text was determined by selecting the most commonly predicted label from the individual classifiers. The first ensemble method (***3 DeBERTa Ensemble***) combined predictions from all three pooling DeBERTa classifiers, while the second ensemble method (***2 DeBERTa Ensemble***) only utilized predictions from the CLS and mean pooling classifiers, since they achieved higher Macro-F1 scores compared to the max pooling classifier. This approach was taken to ensure the most accurate and reliable results possible.

## 5 Experimental Setup

### 5.1 Environment Setup

The presented approach was implemented in Python using Google Colaboratory (Colab) Pro notebook. Experiments were conducted with *Pytorch* library and NVIDIA A100-SXM4-40GB GPU.

### 5.2 Pre-processing Steps

Pre-processing steps were applied to the training, development, and test sets of text using a function that included regular expressions and other functions. The function removed URLs, usernames, and retweets. Emojis were converted to their textual representations (Taehoon et al., 2022).[5] The *&* and *&* were replaced with *and*. The ASCII encoding apostrophe was replaced with the UTF-8 encoding apostrophe. Consecutive non-ASCII characters were replaced with whitespace, and all extra whitespace was removed. Contracted words were unpacked, such as *isn't* being converted to *is not*. The *Ekphrasis* library was used to segment hashtags, correct spelling, elongate words, tokenize, and lowercase all words (Baziotis et al., 2017).[6] All punctuation marks were maintained as they contribute to the context of the text.

### 5.3 Hyperparameter Tuning

The pre-trained models required PyTorch tensors as input, including input IDs and attention masks. Sequences were padded to the fixed maximum sequence length of RoBERTa and DeBERTa (512).

[5]https://pypi.org/project/emoji/

[6]https://github.com/cbaziotis/ekphrasis

Dropout and early stopping patience were used to prevent overfitting, and gradient accumulation was employed to virtually increase batch size during training. The models utilized Cross-Entropy Loss for multi-class classification, with the *AdamW* optimizer and consistent hyperparameters across all architectures shown in Table 3. Identical hyperparameters were employed across all models to ensure easy comparison of models.

| Hyperparameters | |
|---|---|
| Number of Classes | 3 |
| Number of Epochs | 10 |
| Sequence Length | 512 |
| Train Batch Size | 10 |
| Development Batch Size | 16 |
| Learning Rate | 2e-6 |
| Weight Decay | 0.1 |
| Warm-up Steps | 0 |
| AdamW Epsilon | 1e-8 |
| AdamW Betas | 0.9, 0.999 |
| Dropout | 0.2 |
| Gradient Clipping | 1.0 |
| Gradient Accumulation | 2 |
| Early Stopping Patience | 5 |
| Random Seed | 42 |

Table 3: Hyperparameters of Models.

### 5.4 Metrics

The system's efficiency and final ranking were primarily evaluated based on the Macro-F1 score of the test set predictions. Additionally, submissions were evaluated by the organizers based on accuracy, Macro-Recall, Macro-Precision, Weighted-F1, Weighted-Recall, and Weighted-Precision scores. The evaluation also included the Macro-F1 score and Confusion Matrix for each class.

## 6 Results

### 6.1 Development Set

Table 4 shows that the DeBERTa Mean Pooling model achieved the highest Macro-F1 score among individual models (0.77), while the DeBERTa Max Pooling model scored the lowest (0.74). Notably, the RoBERTa Bi-GRU and the DeBERTa CLS Pooling both scored 0.76. Looking at the Macro-F1 score of each class, RoBERTa Bi-GRU is more successful in identifying the *not depression* class (0.82), while DeBERTa Mean Pooling is more successful in identifying the *moderate* class (0.74). All three DeBERTa pooling methods are better at detecting the *severe* class than the RoBERTa Bi-GRU, with a slightly higher Macro-F1 score (0.76). The ensemble including all three DeBERTa models achieves a slightly higher general Macro-F1 score as well as a little higher score in detecting the *severe* class.

| Development Set | |
|---|---|
| **Metric** | **RoBERTa Bi-GRU** |
| Macro-F1 | 0.76 |
| **Classes** | **Macro-F1** |
| not depression | 0.82 |
| moderate | 0.72 |
| severe | 0.75 |
| **Metric** | **DeBERTa CLS Pooling** |
| Macro-F1 | 0.76 |
| **Classes** | **Macro-F1** |
| not depression | 0.81 |
| moderate | 0.73 |
| severe | 0.76 |
| **Metric** | **DeBERTa Mean Pooling** |
| Macro-F1 | 0.77 |
| **Classes** | **Macro-F1** |
| not depression | 0.81 |
| moderate | 0.74 |
| severe | 0.76 |
| **Metric** | **DeBERTa Max Pooling** |
| Macro-F1 | 0.74 |
| **Classes** | **Macro-F1** |
| not depression | 0.80 |
| moderate | 0.68 |
| severe | 0.76 |
| **Metric** | **3 DeBERTa Ensemble** |
| Macro-F1 | 0.77 |
| **Classes** | **Macro-F1** |
| not depression | 0.81 |
| moderate | 0.73 |
| severe | 0.77 |
| **Metric** | **2 DeBERTa Ensemble** |
| Macro-F1 | 0.76 |
| **Classes** | **Macro-F1** |
| not depression | 0.81 |
| moderate | 0.73 |
| severe | 0.76 |

Table 4: Results of developed models on the development set.

### 6.2 Test Set

Table 5 shows that the RoBERTa Bi-GRU model outperformed the DeBERTa ensemble models in all metrics, securing $8^{th}$ place with a macro-F1 score of 0.42. It achieved a higher Macro-F1 score in the *not depression* class (0.11) and a slightly higher score in the *severe* class (0.46) compared to the ensemble models. Both models performed equally well in detecting *moderate* depression with a Macro-F1 score of 0.69. The ensemble models had low Macro-F1 scores across all metrics, particularly in detecting *not depression* (0.05).

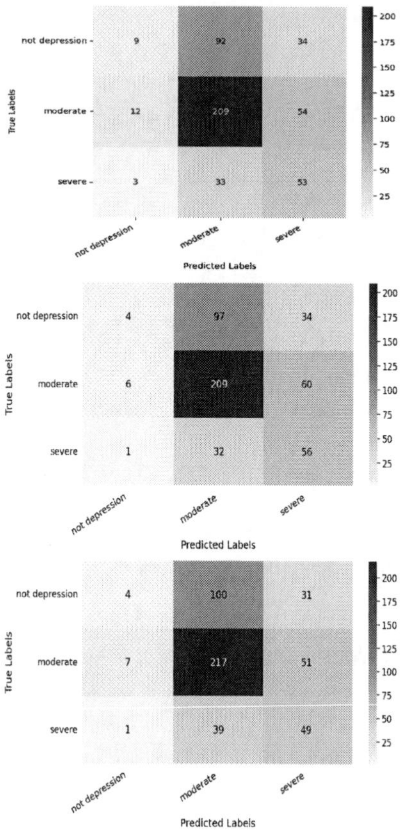


Figure 2: Test Set Confusion Matrices of RoBERTa BI-GRU, 3 DeBERTa Ensemble, 2 DeBERTa Ensemble

| Test Set | |
|---|---|
| **Metric** | **RoBERTa Bi-GRU** |
| Macro-F1 | 0.42 |
| Macro-Recall | 0.474 |
| Macro-Precision | 0.459 |
| Weighted-F1 | 0.491 |
| Weighted-Recall | 0.543 |
| Weighted-Precision | 0.513 |
| Accuracy | 0.543 |
| **Classes** | **Macro-F1** |
| not depression | 0.11 |
| moderate | 0.69 |
| severe | 0.46 |
| **Metric** | **3 DeBERTa Ensemble** |
| Macro-F1 | 0.396 |
| Macro-Recall | 0.456 |
| Macro-Precision | 0.439 |
| Weighted-F1 | 0.473 |
| Weighted-Recall | 0.541 |
| Weighted-Precision | 0.493 |
| Accuracy | 0.541 |
| **Classes** | **Macro-F1** |
| not depression | 0.05 |
| moderate | 0.69 |
| severe | 0.45 |
| **Metric** | **2 DeBERTa Ensemble** |
| Macro-F1 | 0.396 |
| Macro-Recall | 0.456 |
| Macro-Precision | 0.439 |
| Weighted-F1 | 0.473 |
| Weighted-Recall | 0.541 |
| Weighted-Precision | 0.493 |
| Accuracy | 0.541 |
| **Classes** | **Macro-F1** |
| not depression | 0.05 |
| moderate | 0.69 |
| severe | 0.45 |

Table 5: Results of submitted models on test set.

### 6.3 Error Analysis

The confusion matrices were created after the release of the test set labels so that the errors and strengths of the submitted models would be revealed. Therefore, each confusion matrix represents the performance of the RoBERTa Bi-GRU, the 3 DeBERTa Ensemble, and the 2 DeBERTa Ensemble on the test set, respectively. Considering all the confusion matrices from Figure 2, it is evident that all models tend to detect signs of depression in text with greater confidence and success, while they are not as capable of distinguishing non-depression from depression texts. They successfully detect many texts that show *moderate* signs of depression, while there seems to be confusion when it comes to identifying between the *moderate* and *severe* classes, as texts that belong to the *severe* class were assigned to the *moderate* class. A notable number of texts belonging to the *moder-*

*ate* class appear to be identified as *not depression*, while texts that should be labeled as *not depression* were labeled as *moderate* depression. This illustrates the difficulty of the models to distinguish non-depressive posts from depressive posts as well. The reason for the failure of the models in detecting non-depressive posts lies in the fact that the training data contained a significantly lower number of texts categorized as *not depression* (6,675) compared to those classified as *severe* (9,850) and *moderate* (14,451) classes. The training algorithm placed greater emphasis on boosting the depression classes, which further skewed the models' ability to accurately detect non-depressive posts.

## 7 Conclusion and Future Work

The LT-EDI@RANLP 2023 Shared Task 4 entailed the development of a system aimed at addressing data imbalance, cleaning, pre-processing, and fine-tuning pre-trained language models to accurately identify depression in English social media posts. Two pre-trained language models, RoBERTa-Large and DeBERTa-V3-Large, were employed and fine-tuned for this purpose. Among the four pooling methods tested, the RoBERTa-Large Bidirectional GRU model demonstrated the best performance. This model effectively identified posts exhibiting signs of depression, particularly at moderate levels. However, it struggled with detecting non-depressive posts and may occasionally mistake *severe* depression for *moderate* depression.

To further enhance the models' performance, future efforts should focus on incorporating more non-depressive texts into the training data and experimenting with the multi-layer structure of pre-trained Transformer models as well as various hyperparameters. Overall, this system has the potential to serve as a valuable tool for early detection of depression, enabling prompt intervention and support for individuals who may be experiencing mental health problems.

## References

Manex Agirrezabal and Janek Amann. 2022. KUCST@LT-EDI-ACL2022: Detecting signs of depression from social media text. In *Proceedings of the Second Workshop on Language Technology for Equality, Diversity and Inclusion*, pages 245–250, Dublin, Ireland. Association for Computational Linguistics.

Alyssa. 2021. Why depression is so common: Banyan mental health.

Karun Anantharaman, Angel S, Rajalakshmi Sivanaiah, Saritha Madhavan, and Sakaya Milton Rajendram. 2022. SSN_MLRG1@LT-EDI-ACL2022: Multi-class classification using BERT models for detecting depression signs from social media text. In *Proceedings of the Second Workshop on Language Technology for Equality, Diversity and Inclusion*, pages 296–300, Dublin, Ireland. Association for Computational Linguistics.

Christos Baziotis, Nikos Pelekis, and Christos Doulkeridis. 2017. Datastories at semeval-2017 task 4: Deep lstm with attention for message-level and topic-based sentiment analysis. In *Proceedings of the 11th International Workshop on Semantic Evaluation (SemEval-2017)*, pages 747–754, Vancouver, Canada. Association for Computational Linguistics.

Kristeen Cherney. 2018. Mild, moderate, or severe depression? how to tell the difference.

Pengcheng He, Xiaodong Liu, Jianfeng Gao, and Weizhu Chen. 2020. Deberta: Decoding-enhanced BERT with disentangled attention. *CoRR*, abs/2006.03654.

Yinhan Liu, Myle Ott, Naman Goyal, Jingfei Du, Mandar Joshi, Danqi Chen, Omer Levy, Mike Lewis, Luke Zettlemoyer, and Veselin Stoyanov. 2019. Roberta: A robustly optimized BERT pretraining approach. *CoRR*, abs/1907.11692.

National Institute of Mental Health. 2023. Depression.

Rafał Poświata and Michał Perełkiewicz. 2022. OPI@LT-EDI-ACL2022: Detecting signs of depression from social media text using RoBERTa pre-trained language models. In *Proceedings of the Second Workshop on Language Technology for Equality, Diversity and Inclusion*, pages 276–282, Dublin, Ireland. Association for Computational Linguistics.

Sivamanikandan S, Santhosh V, Sanjaykumar N, Jerin Mahibha C, and Thenmozhi Durairaj. 2022. scubeMSEC@LT-EDI-ACL2022: Detection of depression using transformer models. In *Proceedings of the Second Workshop on Language Technology for Equality, Diversity and Inclusion*, pages 212–217, Dublin, Ireland. Association for Computational Linguistics.

Kayalvizhi Sampath, Thenmozhi Durairaj, Bharathi Raja Chakravarthi, Jerin Mahibha C, Kogilavani Shanmugavadivel, and Pratik Anil Rahood. 2023. Overview of the second shared task on detecting signs of depression from social media text. In *Proceedings of the Third Workshop on Language Technology for Equality, Diversity and Inclusion*, Varna, Bulgaria. Recent Advances in Natural Language Processing.

Herbert Sharen and Ratnavel Rajalakshmi. 2022. DLRG@LT-EDI-ACL2022:detecting signs of depression from social media using XGBoost method. In *Proceedings of the Second Workshop on Language Technology for Equality, Diversity and Inclusion*, pages 346–

349, Dublin, Ireland. Association for Computational Linguistics.

Youwei Song, Jiahai Wang, Zhiwei Liang, Zhiyue Liu, and Tao Jiang. 2020. Utilizing BERT intermediate layers for aspect based sentiment analysis and natural language inference. *CoRR*, abs/2002.04815.

Kim Taehoon, Tahir Kevin, Wurster, and Jalilov. 2022. Emoji.

Wei-Yao Wang, Yu-Chien Tang, Wei-Wei Du, and Wen-Chih Peng. 2022. NYCU_TWD@LT-EDI-ACL2022: Ensemble models with VADER and contrastive learning for detecting signs of depression from social media. In *Proceedings of the Second Workshop on Language Technology for Equality, Diversity and Inclusion*, pages 136–139, Dublin, Ireland. Association for Computational Linguistics.

WHO. 2023. Depressive disorder (depression).

# IIITDWD@LT-EDI-2023 Unveiling Depression: Using pre-trained language models for harnessing domain-specific features and context information

**Shankar Biradar**[1] and **Sunil Saumya**[1] and **Sanjana Kavatagi**[2]
[1]Department of Computer Science and Engineering,
Indian Institute of Information Technology, Dharwad, Karnatka, India
[2]Department of Computer Science and Engineering, VTU, Belagavi
(shankar,sunil.saumya)@iiitdwd.ac.in
kawatagi.sanjana@gmail.com

## Abstract

Depression is a global health crisis affecting millions. Workplace stress and unhealthy habits have risen, leading to more people with depressive symptoms. Early detection and prediction of depression are essential for timely intervention and support. Unfortunately, social stigma prevents many from seeking help, making early detection difficult. Therefore, alternative strategies for depression prediction, such as analysing social media posts, are being explored. LT-EDI@RANLP held a shared task to promote research in this field. Our team participated in the shared task and secured 21st rank with a macro F1 score of 0.36. This article summarises the model used in the shared task.

## 1 Introduction

Depression is a common mental health illness affecting millions worldwide, causing significant suffering and even terrible outcomes such as suicide. Despite its frequency and negative impact, depression frequently remains unrecognized and untreated, particularly among young adults. It is essential to understand the wide-ranging harmful effects of this invisible killer to address the worldwide mental health crisis. Over 280 million people worldwide suffer from depression, and the number is rising, according to World Health Organisation (WHO) [1]. The effects of depression are disastrous for both mental and physical health. It limits a person's ability to succeed in life, including work, relationships, and personal fulfilment. Additionally, depression ranks as the second leading cause of teenage mortality, highlighting the urgent need for improved detection and treatment strategies[2].

Traditional diagnostic procedures, which rely on patient self-reports, remarks from family or friends, and mental state examinations, frequently encounter major problems. There are many people who are depressed who do not receive the appropriate treatment because of underdiagnosis, undertreatment, cultural stigma, and inaccurate assessments. The rise of social media platforms like Facebook, Twitter, and WhatsApp in recent years has provided new avenues for understanding mental health conditions like depression (Coppersmith et al., 2014; Lin et al., 2016; Biradar et al., 2022). More and more people are using these platforms to express their thoughts, feelings, and everyday experiences, which tells us a lot about their mental health. By leveraging user behaviours, language patterns, and social connections, researchers are exploring the potential of social media as a tool for diagnosing and forecasting depression.

The COVID-19 epidemic has underlined the necessity of technology-based interventions in mental healthcare. With the adoption of social distancing measures and lockdowns, people have resorted to social media for communication, self-expression, and support. The pandemic's impact on mental health, limited resources, and overworked healthcare systems have highlighted the need for creative and scalable methods for depression detection and treatment. Overall, depression remains a substantial global concern, demanding novel techniques for identification and treatment. The combination of social media and behavioural factors offers a promising path for forecasting depression levels. The advancement of technology, including artificial intelligence and machine learning techniques, presents an intriguing potential for leveraging the massive volumes of data available on social media networks. We can use these technologies to create strong, personalized systems that help healthcare professionals, researchers, and individuals identify and treat depression more effectively (Akbari et al., 2016; Kayalvizhi et al., 2022; Chakravarthi et al.,

[1]https://www.who.int/news-room/fact-sheets/detail/depression

[2]https://www.who.int/news-room/fact-sheets/detail/depression



*LT-EDI 2023 – Third Workshop on Language Technology for Equality, Diversity and Inclusion*, pages 117–123, Varna, Bulgaria, Sep 7, 2023.
https://doi.org/10.26615/978-954-452-084-7_017

2022).

Several methods for handling social media data to determine users' depression conditions have been presented. However, most of these approaches have relied on handcrafted features with shallow machine learning-based models (Tadesse et al., 2019; Guntuku et al., 2019; Biradar et al., 2021). These approaches often require domain expertise to identify features, resulting in biased feature values. Furthermore, the handcrafted feature extraction method is laborious and time-consuming, resulting in a longer training time. In addition, many of these models struggle to generalize successfully with new information. Researchers have recently tried to alleviate these constraints by employing pre-trained transformer models (Poerner et al., 2020; Kassner and Schütze, 2020; Puranik et al., 2021). However, to the best of our knowledge, none of these models have successfully linked domain knowledge with linguistic patterns. To overcome this gap, our proposed work performed experiments with PubMed BERT (Gu et al., 2020) trained on clinical data, to harness domain knowledge. These studies were carried out as part of the LT-EDI@RANLP joint task on Detecting Signs of Depression from social media Text. Notably, our proposed model finished in the 21st position among the participating teams.

The remaining part of paper is arranged as follows: Section 2 addresses the recent literature. Further model building details are discussed in section 3. Finally, section 4 provides insights into the model results. Furthermore, its implications on society and future research directions are provided in the last section.

## 2 Background study

Depression detection addresses the interdisciplinary topic of clinical psychology and social media data mining. Several studies have been proposed to analyze social media users' behaviour through their content. The results from these studies conclude that individuals with depression tend to use more negative verbal content when interacting with friends or posting on social media. Most of these models are conducted using either machine learning-based or deep learning-based methods. This section will provide insights into some selected works from the past.

### 2.1 Machine learning-based models

(Tadesse et al., 2019; Shankar Biradar and Chauhan, 2021) Conducted an experiment involving n-gram features representation, such as tf-idf, linguistic features, and LDA topics. The study utilized Logistic Regression (LR), Support Vector Machine (SVM), Multi-Layer Perceptron (MLP), Random Forest (RF), and AdaBoost to train the models. The experimental results indicated that SVM achieved an accuracy of 81%. However, the highest performance was achieved using the Multi-Layer Perceptron, with an accuracy of 91% for depression and non-depression classification. Several studies have also focused on syntactic and semantic features for detecting depressive comments from social media data. Liu and Shu extracted syntactic and semantic-based features to train several supervised learning models, such as Naive Bayes (NB), K-Nearest Neighbors (KNN), Logistic Regression, and Support Vector Machine, as base learners. Later, a simple logistic regression model was used to stack the outcomes of the base learners (Liu and Shi, 2022).

In a study (Tsugawa et al., 2015), semantic features were found to be integral components of depression prediction models. The researchers utilized various semantic features and word-level attributes to gauge the level of depression among Twitter users. These features included word frequency and the ratio of positive to negative words. By employing SVM classifiers, the study demonstrated that semantic features could effectively address depressive comments on social media. The findings indicate that semantic features hold promise in identifying and handling instances of depression on online platforms. In a related study (Pirina and Çöltekin, 2018; Shankar Biradar and Chauhan, 2021), the authors trained an SVM classifier using various word-level features to identify the severity of depressive comments. The study utilized features such as word n-grams and tf-idf for training LR, RF, and SVM classifiers. The study concluded that the combination of word-level features with the SVM model yielded superior results in predicting depression levels from social media comments. (Chen et al., 2018) developed a binary classifier for depression detection and achieved great accuracy by utilizing Random Forests and Support Vector Models with Radial Basis Function.

### 2.2 Deep Learning-based models

Recent studies have found that deep learning-based methods can significantly enhance model performance. In addition to this, DL models also reduce the computational overhead of ML-based models during the feature extraction stage. Traditional feature extraction in ML models requires domain expertise and is time-consuming, often leading to biased features. To address these issues, several studies have proposed the use of deep learning-based models.

For instance, (Wani et al., 2022) extracted word-level embeddings using a pre-trained word2vec neural network model. These embeddings were then passed to Convolutional Neural Networks (CNN) and Long Short-Term Memory Networks (LSTM) for classification. The results of the study concluded that using RNN-based methods improves model performance. In another study, authors attempted to build their own corpus containing binary depressive and non-depressive comments (Kim et al., 2020). They employed word2vec embeddings combined with a CNN model for depression detection. Some researchers also explored the construction of hybrid models by combining CNN and LSTM networks (Kour and Gupta, 2022; Biradar and Saumya, 2022). These hybrid networks successfully capture spatial features (CNN) and temporal features (LSTM) to address depression levels in long text. The study concluded that using hybrid networks improves model performance. Lastly, given the prevalence of COVID-19-related depressive comments on social media, researchers (Zogan et al., 2023) developed a corpus specifically related to COVID-19 depressive comments. They also presented a novel hierarchical CNN network for binary classification. These advancements in deep learning-based approaches improve model performance and alleviate the computational burden and biases associated with traditional feature extraction methods in ML models.

Both approaches significantly contribute to helping the clinical community in predicting the mental health of social media users without attaching any social stigma. However, neither of these models achieves the accuracy of a human moderator. These methods have limitations, including the fact that the majority of deep learning networks fail to capture domain knowledge because they are trained using general-purpose text data. On the other hand, machine learning-based methods struggle to generalize on unseen data.

|  | **Not depression** | **Moderate** | **Severe** |
|---|---|---|---|
| **Train** | 2,755 | 3,678 | 768 |
| **Test** | 848 | 2,169 | 228 |
| **Total** | **3,603** | **5,847** | **996** |

Table 1: Dataset distribution

The proposed model utilizes transformer-based Large Language models like PubMed BERT to generate feature vectors to address these issues. This approach allows the model to capture domain knowledge and context information from social media text, enabling it to predict depression levels more effectively. By incorporating these improvements, the proposed model aims to enhance accuracy and better understand users' mental health.

### 2.3 Task and dataset description

The current study utilizes the dataset from the LT-EDI@RANLP 2023 shared task (S et al., 2022), which focuses on detecting signs of depression in a social media text. The organizers of the shared task have provided a challenge regarding the identification of depression levels in English social media comments. The dataset consists of a text field and a label field, with the labels being "not depression," "moderate," and "severe." According to the organizers, the data was collected from YouTube comments (S et al., 2022). The detailed distribution of the dataset is presented in Table 1. However, the dataset is highly skewed, with the majority of the comments labelled as "moderate" and very few instances of "severe" comments.

## 3 Model building

In this section, we outline the model submitted for the shared task of identifying depression levels in social media data. The proposed model comprises three primary steps: data cleaning and pre-processing, feature extraction, and classification. This section will thoroughly explain each of these stages. The architecture of the model is illustrated in Fig 1.

### 3.1 Data pre-processing

According to the shared task organizers, data has been collected from YouTube comments. As social media data often contains noise, certain steps have been taken to clean the data. The text data includes punctuation, hyperlinks, URLs, stop words, and

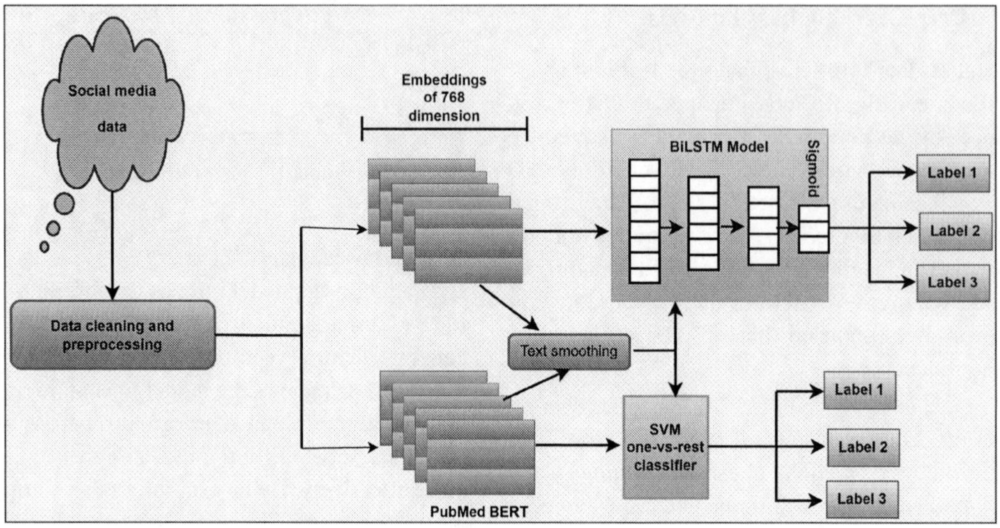


Figure 1: Experimented model architecture

| Model | Hyper-parameter |
|---|---|
| **SVM** | Kernal = 'linear'<br>C = 1 |
| **BiLSTM** | Node size = 60,30,10<br>Drop out rate = 0.5<br>Loss = 'categorical_crossentopy'<br>Optimiser = 'Adam'<br>Batch_size = 100<br>Epochs = 10 |

Table 2: Hyper-parameter

numerical data, which do not contribute to the final class prediction. To address this, we have removed these elements using simple string operations. Stop words have been eliminated using the NLTK library. Additionally, the text has been converted to lowercase to avoid token redundancy. Finally, lemmatization has been applied to convert social media slang to its root words. All of these steps have been performed using the NLTK toolkit [3].

After the pre-treatment, the data is subjected to tokenization, where we apply the BERT tokenizer to convert the text input into tokens. Subsequently, padding is performed on the tokenized data to ensure all comments possess a fixed-length sequence. Finally, masking is applied to the padded sequence to eliminate the influence of padded tokens on label prediction.

[3]https://www.nltk.org/

### 3.2 Feature Extraction

The proposed model utilizes a pre-trained language model called PubMed BERT, obtained from the Hugging Face library [4]. PubMed BERT is a variant of the original BERT model, trained on clinical data (Gu et al., 2020). Its architecture closely resembles that of the original BERT model(Kenton and Toutanova, 2019). The main objective of the feature extraction process in this model is to represent high-dimensional text data into lower-dimensional embedding vectors. To achieve this, padded and masked sequences are provided as input. The model extracts the embeddings from the [CLS] token to generate the embedding vectors. This token represents the entire sentence and provides a bidirectional representation of the input text. By utilizing the embeddings from the [CLS] token, the model captures the overall semantic meaning of the text. The advantage of employing PubMed BERT in the proposed model lies in its training on clinical data, which enables it to incorporate domain-specific information into the embeddings. This makes the model well-suited for tasks involving depression analysis. After obtaining the embeddings from PubMed BERT, they are passed as input to the data augmentation and classification stage.

To address the issue of highly skewed data towards the moderate label, the proposed method incorporates text smoothing on input embeddings to achieve a more balanced representation of the

[4]https://huggingface.co/

| Model | F1-moderate | F1-not depression | F1-severe | Macro-F1 |
|---|---|---|---|---|
| PubMed with BiLSTM (without smoothing) | 0.66 | 0.30 | 0.10 | 0.41 |
| PubMed with BiLSTM (with smoothing) | 0.20 | 0.37 | 0.64 | 0.45 |
| PubMed with SVM (without smoothing) | 0.70 | 0.40 | 0.33 | 0.48 |
| **PubMed with SVM (with smoothing)** | **0.44** | **0.55** | **0.66** | **0.54** |

Table 3: Comparative results of the proposed model

overall input text sequences. Subsequently, the balanced data is fed as input to the classification layer. The proposed method conducts experiments using both the balanced and original text data, and the results and discussion section presents the findings of these experiments.

### 3.3 Classification

The primary objective of the classification stage is to convert the input embeddings into corresponding depression levels. To achieve this, the proposed model experimented with different machine learning and deep learning-based models.

The proposed method utilized the Support Vector Machine (SVM) classifier among the machine learning-based models. Since the problem involves multiclass classification, the proposed method employed the One-Vs-Rest classifier from SVM to identify depression levels in a social media text. Further, the proposed method also experimented with a Bidirectional Long Short-Term Memory (BiLSTM) model. The BiLSTM model was constructed using two BiLSTM layers with 60 and 30 neurons, and a dense layer with ten units was added after BiLSTM layers, and a dropout rate of 0.5 was applied, indicating that 50% of the input units were randomly dropped out. Finally, the output layer consisted of a dense layer with three units representing the number of classes, and the softmax activation function was added to predict the output class. The hyperparameters used to train both models are illustrated in Table 2. These hyperparameter values were selected based on experimental trials. The input for the classification stage was taken from PubMed BERT embeddings, which have a vector dimension of 768. Implementation details of the proposed model can be found in the GitHub repository [5].

[5]https://github.com/shankarb14/RANLP-2023

| Team name | Macro-F1 | Rank |
|---|---|---|
| DeepLearningBasil | 0.47 | 1 |
| DeepBlueAI | 0.446 | 2 |
| Cordyeeps_ssl | 0.441 | 3 |
| iicteam | 0.439 | 4 |
| CIMAT-NLP | 0.439 | 5 |
| **IIITDWD** | **0.359** | **21** |

Table 4: Top performing teams

## 4 Result and Discussion

The proposed model was trained to identify class labels such as 'not depression,' 'moderate,' and 'severe.' The comparative results of the model are summarized in Table 3.

The proposed model was tested on both balanced data after smoothing and the original text to assess the impact of text smoothing on its performance. As shown in Table 3, the model exhibited significant performance in predicting the 'moderate' label before smoothing. However, its performance with the other two class labels was moderate, resulting in a reduced macro-F1 score. Text smoothing resulted in a more evenly distributed weighted F1 score across all labels.

In evaluating the model performance for the shared task LT-EDI @RANLP2023, the organizers utilized the macro-F1 score. Among the proposed methods, the combination of PubMed BERT with SVM on balanced data achieved a higher macro-F1 score and was therefore chosen for submission in the shared task. Our proposed model received the 21st rank among the participating teams, with a macro-F1 score of 0.36 on unseen data. Table 4 displays some of the top-performing teams in the competition, including our proposed model (highlighted in bold).

## 5 Conclusion and future enhancements

The study presents the model submitted to the LT-EDI@RANLP 2023 shared task, which aims to detect signs of depression in a social media text. The proposed model experimented with two approaches: SVM and BiLSTM as classifiers. The study concludes that PubMED BERT embeddings combined with SVM classifier on a balanced dataset achieve more uniformly distributed weighted F1 scores across all the labels. The proposed model secured the 21st rank in the competition. However, the model's performance could be further improved by developing a more robust algorithm capable of capturing domain-specific information and contextual details from the input text.

## References


Mohammad Akbari, Xia Hu, Nie Liqiang, and Tat-Seng Chua. 2016. From tweets to wellness: Wellness event detection from twitter streams. In *Proceedings of the AAAI Conference on Artificial Intelligence*, volume 30.

Shankar Biradar and Sunil Saumya. 2022. Iiitdwd@ tamilnlp-acl2022: Transformer-based approach to classify abusive content in dravidian code-mixed text. In *Proceedings of the Second Workshop on Speech and Language Technologies for Dravidian Languages*, pages 100–104.

Shankar Biradar, Sunil Saumya, and Arun Chauhan. 2021. Hate or non-hate: Translation based hate speech identification in code-mixed hinglish data set. In *2021 IEEE International Conference on Big Data (Big Data)*, pages 2470–2475. IEEE.

Shankar Biradar, Sunil Saumya, and Arun Chauhan. 2022. Fighting hate speech from bilingual hinglish speaker's perspective, a transformer-and translation-based approach. *Social Network Analysis and Mining*, 12(1):87.

Bharathi Raja Chakravarthi, Vigneshwaran Muralidaran, Ruba Priyadharshini, Subalalitha Cn, John Philip McCrae, Miguel Ángel García, Salud María Jiménez-Zafra, Rafael Valencia-García, Prasanna Kumaresan, Rahul Ponnusamy, et al. 2022. Overview of the shared task on hope speech detection for equality, diversity, and inclusion. In *Proceedings of the Second Workshop on Language Technology for Equality, Diversity and Inclusion*, pages 378–388.

Xuetong Chen, Martin D Sykora, Thomas W Jackson, and Suzanne Elayan. 2018. What about mood swings: Identifying depression on twitter with temporal measures of emotions. In *Companion proceedings of the the web conference 2018*, pages 1653–1660.

Glen Coppersmith, Mark Dredze, and Craig Harman. 2014. Quantifying mental health signals in twitter. In *Proceedings of the workshop on computational linguistics and clinical psychology: From linguistic signal to clinical reality*, pages 51–60.

Yu Gu, Robert Tinn, Hao Cheng, Michael Lucas, Naoto Usuyama, Xiaodong Liu, Tristan Naumann, Jianfeng Gao, and Hoifung Poon. 2020. Domain-specific language model pretraining for biomedical natural language processing.

Sharath Chandra Guntuku, Anneke Buffone, Kokil Jaidka, Johannes C Eichstaedt, and Lyle H Ungar. 2019. Understanding and measuring psychological stress using social media. In *Proceedings of the international AAAI conference on web and social media*, volume 13, pages 214–225.

Nora Kassner and Hinrich Schütze. 2020. Negated and misprimed probes for pretrained language models: Birds can talk, but cannot fly. In *Proceedings of the 58th Annual Meeting of the Association for Computational Linguistics*, pages 7811–7818.

S Kayalvizhi, Thenmozhi Durairaj, Bharathi Raja Chakravarthi, et al. 2022. Findings of the shared task on detecting signs of depression from social media. In *Proceedings of the Second Workshop on Language Technology for Equality, Diversity and Inclusion*, pages 331–338.

Jacob Devlin Ming-Wei Chang Kenton and Lee Kristina Toutanova. 2019. Bert: Pre-training of deep bidirectional transformers for language understanding. In *Proceedings of NAACL-HLT*, pages 4171–4186.

Jina Kim, Jieon Lee, Eunil Park, and Jinyoung Han. 2020. A deep learning model for detecting mental illness from user content on social media. *Scientific reports*, 10(1):1–6.

Harnain Kour and Manoj K Gupta. 2022. An hybrid deep learning approach for depression prediction from user tweets using feature-rich cnn and bi-directional lstm. *Multimedia Tools and Applications*, 81(17):23649–23685.

Huijie Lin, Jia Jia, Liqiang Nie, Guangyao Shen, and Tat-Seng Chua. 2016. What does social media say about your stress?. In *IJCAI*, pages 3775–3781.

Jingfang Liu and Mengshi Shi. 2022. A hybrid feature selection and ensemble approach to identify depressed users in online social media. *Frontiers in Psychology*, 12:6571.

Inna Pirina and Çağrı Çöltekin. 2018. Identifying depression on reddit: The effect of training data. In *Proceedings of the 2018 EMNLP Workshop SMM4H: The 3rd Social Media Mining for Health Applications Workshop & Shared Task*, pages 9–12.

Nina Poerner, Ulli Waltinger, and Hinrich Schütze. 2020. E-bert: Efficient-yet-effective entity embeddings for bert. In *Findings of the Association for Computational Linguistics: EMNLP 2020*, pages 803–818.

Karthik Puranik, Adeep Hande, Ruba Priyadharshini, Sajeetha Thavareesan, and Bharathi Raja Chakravarthi. 2021. Iiitt@ lt-edi-eacl2021-hope speech detection: there is always hope in transformers. *arXiv preprint arXiv:2104.09066*.

Kayalvizhi S, Thenmozhi Durairaj, Bharathi Raja Chakravarthi, and Jerin Mahibha C. 2022. Findings of the shared task on detecting signs of depression from social media. In *Proceedings of the Second Workshop on Language Technology for Equality, Diversity and Inclusion*, Dublin, Ireland. Association for Computational Linguistics.

Sunil Saumya Shankar Biradar and Arun Chauhan. 2021. mbert based model for identification of offensive content in south indian languages. In *Working Notes of FIRE 2021-Forum for Information Retrieval Evaluation (Online). CEUR*.

Michael M Tadesse, Hongfei Lin, Bo Xu, and Liang Yang. 2019. Detection of depression-related posts in reddit social media forum. *IEEE Access*, 7:44883–44893.

Sho Tsugawa, Yusuke Kikuchi, Fumio Kishino, Kosuke Nakajima, Yuichi Itoh, and Hiroyuki Ohsaki. 2015. Recognizing depression from twitter activity. In *Proceedings of the 33rd annual ACM conference on human factors in computing systems*, pages 3187–3196.

Mudasir Ahmad Wani, Mohammad A ELAffendi, Kashish Ara Shakil, Ali Shariq Imran, and Ahmed A Abd El-Latif. 2022. Depression screening in humans with ai and deep learning techniques. *IEEE Transactions on Computational Social Systems*.

Hamad Zogan, Imran Razzak, Shoaib Jameel, and Guandong Xu. 2023. Hierarchical convolutional attention network for depression detection on social media and its impact during pandemic. *IEEE Journal of Biomedical and Health Informatics*.

# CIMAT-NLP@LT-EDI: Finegrain Depression Detection by Multiple Binary Problems Approach

**María de J. García Santiago, Fernando Sánchez Vega, A. Pastor López-Monroy**
*Mathematics Research Center, Jalisco S/N Valenciana, 36023 Guanajuato, GTO México*
{maria.garcia, fernando.sanchez, pastor.lopez}@cimat.mx

## Abstract

This work described the work of the team CIMAT-NLP on the Shared task of Detecting Signs of Depression from Social Media Text at LT-EDI 2023 Sampath et al. (2023), which consists of depression classification on three levels: "not depression", "moderate" depression and "severe" depression on text from social media. In this work, we proposed two approaches: (1) a transformer model which can handle big text without truncation of its length, and (2) an ensemble of six binary Bag of Words. Our team placed fourth in the competition and found that models trained with our approaches could place second.

## 1 Introduction

Approximately 280 million persons suffer depression around the world, and suicide is the fourth cause of death according to World Health Organization (2022).

Other studies have highlighted the impact of social media on adolescents, introducing a phenomenon known as "Facebook depression" O'Keeffe et al. (2011). This term refers to the symptoms of depression that young people may experience when they spend significant time on social media platforms.

Additionally, a study on college students in Afghanistan revealed a correlation between social media addiction and depression Haand and Shuwang (2020). The findings suggested that individuals experience more severe symptoms of depression as their social media usage increases.

Given the increasing number of people affected by depression, developing systems to detect individuals with this mental illness is crucial. One notable effort in this direction is the Shared Task on Detecting Signs of Depression from Social Media Texts at LT-EDI Sampath et al. (2023).

Our team, CIMAT-NLP, proposed two approaches for this task. Firstly, we divided significant texts into sub-packages and utilized the RoBERTa transformer Liu et al. (2019). Secondly, we employed an ensemble of six binary Bags of Words (BOW) models with different characteristics.

The remaining sections of this paper are organized as follows: Section 2 discusses related works on detecting depression on social media. Section 3 provides an overview of the competition and data distribution. In Section 4, we describe the methods we developed for the task. Section 5 presents the results obtained by our models. Finally, in Section 6, we draw conclusions based on our work.

## 2 Related work

Detecting depression presents a challenging task due to the intricate nature of this mental disorder. The complexity of this mental illness makes screening for depression a demanding task. In this field, various workshops are dedicated to this cause, such as the Early Internet Risk Prediction workshop (CLEF eRisk) Parapar et al. (2022). This workshop focuses on developing methods for automatic systems for online risk prevention. In the context of eRisk, proposals have predominantly focused on the use of Bag of Words (BOW)-based machine learning models together with SVM classifiers or deep neural networks, due to the proven effectiveness of both approaches. Notable examples include the top three best ranks in the 2018 eRisk competition (Losada et al. (2018), Trotzek et al. (2018),Funez et al. (2018)), demonstrating the effectiveness of BOW in representing text for tasks related to detecting mental illness. Our approach follows suit, as we choose to implement BOW with several specialized classifiers, targeting different levels of depression.



*LT-EDI 2023 – Third Workshop on Language Technology for Equality, Diversity and Inclusion*, pages 124–130, Varna, Bulgaria, Sep 7, 2023.
https://doi.org/10.26615/978-954-452-084-7_018

It is evident that transformers have surpassed the state of the art in various NLP tasks. However, a drawback of transformers is their inability to process large inputs, which is a common scenario in author profiling tasks, due to the high computational resources required. In Martínez-Castaño et al. (2021), this issue was addressed by segmenting the text into subchunks per category during training and averaging the prediction probabilities of these subchunks for an overall prediction. Another limitation of transformers lies in the variability of their predictions, which stems from variations in their initialization seeds during training. To mitigate this variability and leverage the benefits of these results, multiple transformer ensemble techniques have been proposed. Poświata and Perełkiewicz (2022), Janatdoust et al. (2022), and Wang et al. (2022) have introduced such techniques, emphasizing that sets of classifiers can offer improved predictions compared to a single one. Inspired by the ensemble's design philosophy, we have extended it to methods based on Bag of Words (BOW) and SVM classifier approaches

## 3 Dataset

The DepSign-LT-EDI@RANLP-2023 dataset consists of texts collected from various social media networks. All the texts are in English and have been classified into three labels: "not depression," "moderate," and "severe."

The competition was divided into two phases. In the first phase, the organizing committee provided participants with the training and development data to work. In the second phase, participants were given the test data to make predictions and submit their results.

| | Training | Dev | Test |
|---|---|---|---|
| Total users | 7006 | 3233 | 499 |
| "not depression" label | 2667 | 844 | 135 |
| "moderate" label | 3584 | 2161 | 275 |
| "severe" label | 745 | 228 | 89 |

Table 1: Initially, the training dataset had 7201 instances where 195 were duplicated. In the case of the dev dataset, only 12 instances were duplicated.

## 4 Method

In this section, we described the approaches used for the task. In the first approach, we proposed a transformer model. Because the text is in English, we used BERT Devlin et al. (2018a), RoBERTa Liu et al. (2019), MentalBERT and MentalRoBERTa (Ji et al., 2021) for our experiments. The second approach is an ensemble of six Bags of Words, each specializing in diverse detection with different characteristics.

### 4.1 Transformer based approach

Most text in the training and dev dataset does not pass for 124 tokens. Therefore, this length was set as the maximum for tokenizing the instances.

During the training phase, if a text exceeds 124 tokens, it is truncated to 124 tokens, and the remaining text is divided into subtexts of 124 tokens each. These subtexts are then added as new instances to the training dataset. As a result, the final number of instances in the training dataset amounts to $13,238$.

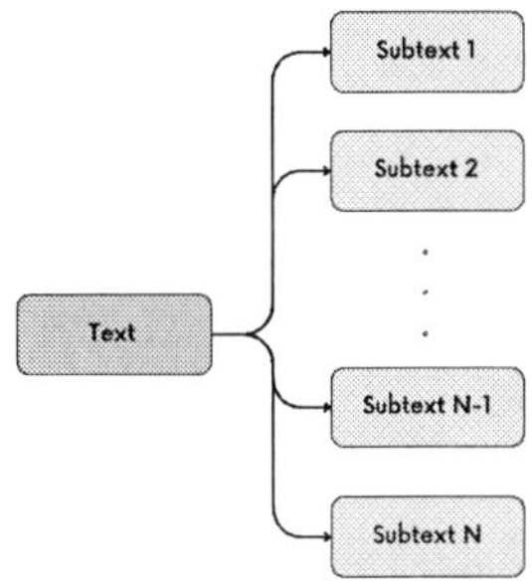


Figure 1: For example, if a text has a length of 368 tokens, the total number of subtexts is three, where the first and second have the same length and the last one has 120 tokens.

In the case of dev and test data, the datasets were not modified, however in the inference part, the process is,

- If the text to classify has a length less than 124, tokens are passed on to the model and predict its class.
- In other cases, the text is divided into sub-text with the length set before. Each sub-text class is predicted, and the final prediction is made with a voting scheme. In Fig.2, the process is illustrated.

#### 4.1.1 Voting scheme

A count of the number of subtext predicted for each subtext is made in the process.

Let be Counter Control ($CC$), the number of subtexts predicted as "not depression", Counter

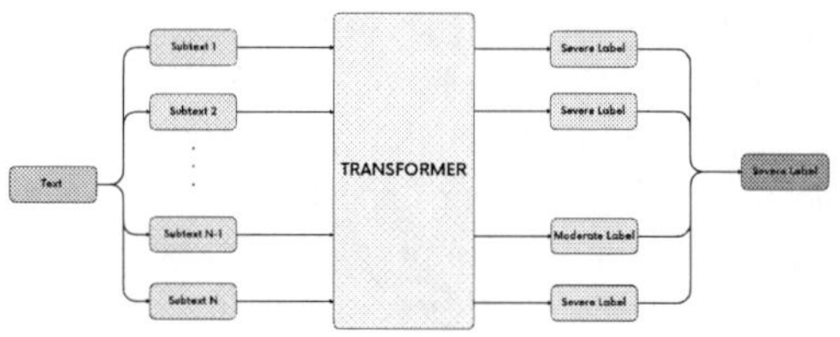


Figure 2: For each sequence of tokens representing the subtexts, the unique tokens of [CLS] and [SEP] are added.

Moderate ($CM$) for "moderate", and Counter Severe ($CS$) for "severe".

- If $CC > CM$ and $CC > CS$ then the final prediction is labeled as "not depression".
- If $CM > CS$ and $CM > CC$ then the final prediction is labeled as "moderate".
- If $CS > CM$ and $CS > CC$ then the final prediction is labeled as "severe".
- If $CC > CS$ and $CC = CM$ then the final prediction is labeled as "moderate".
- If $CS > CC$ and $CM = CS$ then the final prediction is labeled as "severe".
- If $CC > CM$ and $CC = CS$ then the final prediction is labeled as "severe".
- If $CC = CM = CS$ then the final prediction is labeled as "moderate".

Most of the subchunks from a text are from one specific label, then is correct to give that classification to the whole text. The problem arises when there is an equal quantity of subchunks from two o more classes; this happens in one of three cases: an equal number of not-depressing chunks as severe-depression classified chunks, an equal number of not-depressing chunks as moderate depression and finally if we have an equal number of severe depression chunks as moderate depression chunks. The majority of these cases are marked as severe because we prefer to make false positives instead of false negatives, as we think that if the text presented various parts of the severe-label text is because the user that wrote the original text could have symptoms of depression.

### 4.2 Multiple binary BOW approach

Instead of making a multiclass BOW, we decided to make an ensemble of binary BOWs, each of which was trained in different datasets. We decided to use binary BOWs because BOW has outstanding performance in binary classification tasks, as in the work of Ortega-Mendoza et al. (2022).

The training datasets were made from the original training data provided by the committee organizer; the strategy was the following:

- Two labels are merged into one label, and the third is left untouched. Using this strategy, we made three datasets: "moderate-severe" vs "not depression", "moderate-not depression" vs "severe", and "severe-not depression" vs "moderate".
- The second strategy only uses two labels and discards the third one from the training data. Using this strategy, we made three datasets: "moderate" vs "not depression", "moderate" vs "severe", and "severe" vs "not depression".

In total, we created six different data sets for training the BOW on the six binary decisions. The same strategy was followed for the dev data for the corresponding case. For each dataset, we construct a specific BOW using the $\chi$-square function to select the best attributes (in Section 5, we talk about the weight and number of $n$-grams used for the construction). Each BOW is passed on to its classifier and gets the prediction from all the text in the dev dataset. The fusion of the BOW is made using an ensemble; the process is now on the text level, as the decision is made for each of them. Let be the $text_j$, for this text are six predictions: $Prediction\_k_j$ with $1 \leq k \leq 6$.

Depending if the $Prediction\_k_j$ is positive or not, we add a specific weight to the three counter variables: $CS$, $CM$ and $CC$ variables for "severe", "moderate", and "not depression" respectively. The next step is to pass these variables into the voting scheme[1] for the final prediction.

## 5 Results

In this section, we present the results in the dev dataset for each approach to choosing the model and hyperparameters for the submissions in the competitions. In the second part of this section, we present the competition results for the two models.

[1]The voting scheme contains the same rules described in Subsubsection 4.1.1, except that when $CC = CM$ and $CC > CS$, the final label is "moderate".

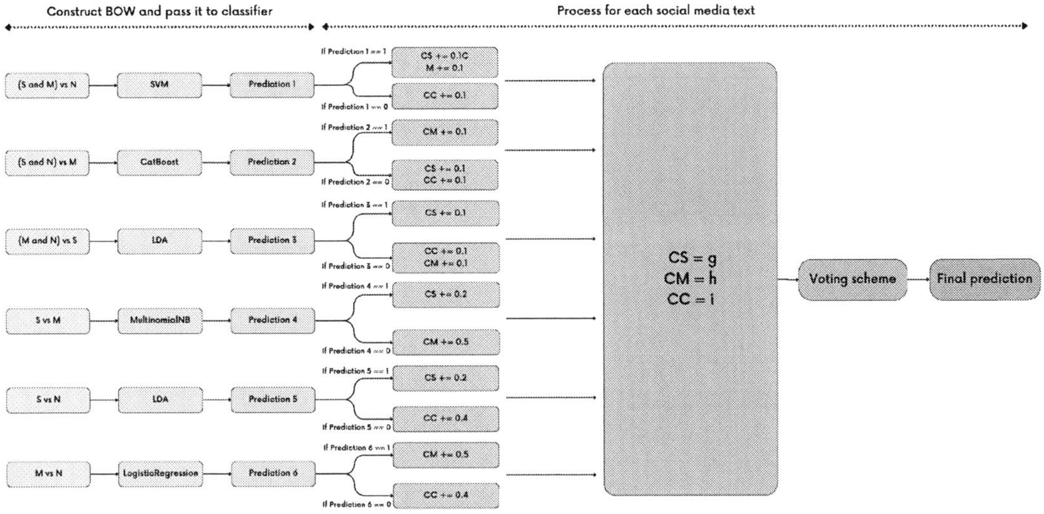


Figure 3: In this ensemble, we refer to "severe" as $S$, "moderate" as $M$, and "not depression" as $N$. The counter variables $CS$, $CM$ and $CC$ are for "severe", "moderate", and "not depression", respectively. The counter variables, voting scheme and final prediction are per user.

### 5.1 Method validations and hyperparameter selection

Because the target is multi-class the F1-score macro metric was used to select the best models for the competition. The dev data was used as test data for this part.

#### 5.1.1 Transformer based approach

For the transformer approach, we made different experiments using pre-trained base models of BERT Devlin et al. (2018b), RoBERTa Liu et al. (2019), MentalBERT and MentalRoBERTa Ji et al. (2021), using different learning rates and batch train for experimentation with fixed seed 42.

In Table 2, the best five models per transformer model are described; most of these models are ensemble models of three transformers with the same lr and train batch size. This ensemble models use majority voting for the final prediction. We decided to use RoBERTa-32, which is a single base pre-trained RoBERTa trained with learning rate $1e^{-5}$ and train batch size 32 because it was the model with the best F1-macro score.

#### 5.1.2 Multiple binary BOW approach

Considering that six different BOWs conform to the ensemble, the best hyperparameters and classificators were used; in each BOW, the best attributes were selected by $\chi^2$ function [2].

The hyperparameter and classification algorithm for each one of the six binary subproblems is:

- BOW 1 (S and M vs N): This BOW was created with unigrams and bigrams, 200 attributes, tf-idf weighting and SVM classifier.
- BOW 2 (S and N vs M): This BOW was created with unigrams and bigrams, 700 attributes, tf-idf weighting and CatBoostClassifier classifier.
- BOW 3 (M and N vs S): This BOW was created with unigrams, bigrams, tri-grams, 100 attributes, tf weighting and LinearDiscriminantAnalysis classifier.
- BOW 4 (S vs M): This BOW was created with unigrams and bigrams, 500 attributes, binary weighting and MultinomialNB classifier.

[2]All the BOWs were implemented using CountVectorizer for binary weighting and TfidfVectorizer for the other BOWs; the two functions are implemented in the sklearn library. `https://scikit-learn.org/stable/modules/generated/sklearn.feature_extraction.text.CountVectorizer.html`, `https://scikit-learn.org/stable/modules/generated/sklearn.feature_extraction.text.TfidfVectorizer.html`

| Model | lr | Train Batch Size | F1-score macro |
|---|---|---|---|
| BERT ensemble | $1e^{-5}$ | 16 | 0.5312 |
| BERT ensemble | $1e^{-5}$ | 32 | 0.5221 |
| BERT ensemble | $1e^{-5}$ | 64 | 0.5145 |
| BERT | $1e^{-5}$ | 16 | 0.5098 |
| RoBERTa | $1e^{-5}$ | 32 | **0.5475** |
| RoBERTa ensemble | $1e^{-5}$ | 32 | 0.5438 |
| RoBERTa ensemble | $1e^{-5}$ | 64 | 0.5383 |
| RoBERTa | $1e^{-5}$ | 64 | 0.5199 |
| MentalBERT ensemble | $1e^{-5}$ | 16 | 0.5358 |
| MentalBERT ensemble | $1e^{-5}$ | 128 | 0.5270 |
| MentalBERT ensemble | $1e^{-5}$ | 32 | 0.5257 |
| MentalBERT | $1e^{-5}$ | 16 | 0.5105 |
| MentalRoBERTa | $1e^{-5}$ | 64 | 0.5451 |
| MentalRoBERTa | $1e^{-5}$ | 16 | 0.5412 |
| MentalRoBERTa | $1e^{-5}$ | 128 | 0.5355 |
| MentalRoBERTa | $1e^{-5}$ | 16 | 0.5241 |

Table 2: For each experiment, three models were made with the same characteristics and then used for the ensemble models.

- BOW 5 (S vs N): This BOW was created with unigrams, bigrams, tri-grams, 100 attributes, tf weighting and LinearDiscriminantAnalysis classifier.
- BOW 6 (M vs N): This BOW was created with unigrams and bigrams, 1700 attributes, tf weighting and a LogisticRegression classifier.

In the second stage of this ensemble, we used grid search to set the best weights for the ensemble. This grid search is done into six parameters affected by the predictions of each BOW. The final values used for the submissions are described in Fig. 3. The performance of this ensemble in the dev dataset was 54.73 of F1-score macro.

### 5.2 Results in the competition

In this subsection, we present the performance obtained in the competition; the best places are shown as performance references and other strategies were added to the comparison. In Table 3, we add the BOW-multiclass, these BOWs were constructed using the sklearn implemention, with the difference that this BOW has a multiclass target because they are trained with the dataset with all the labels.

- BOW-mutliclass 1: This BOW was created with unigrams, 100 attributes, tf-idf weighting and SVM classifier.
- BOW-multiclass 2: This BOW was created with unigrams, bigrams, tri-grams, 100 attributes, tf-idf weighting and SVM classifier.
- BOW-multiclass 3: This BOW was created with unigrams, bigrams, 100 attributes, tf weighting and SVM classifier.
- BOW-multiclass 4: This BOW was created with unigrams, bigrams, tri-grams, 200 attributes, tf without stopwords weighting and SVM classifier.

| | F1-score macro |
|---|---|
| 1st place | **0.474** |
| 2nd place | 0.446 |
| 3rd place | 0.441 |
| 4th place | 0.439 |
| RoBERTa-32 (4th place) | <u>0.439</u> |
| BOW ensemble | 0.432 |
| BOW-multiclass 1 | 0.460 |
| BOW-multiclass 2 | 0.451 |
| BOW-multiclass 3 | 0.450 |
| BOW-multiclass 4 | 0.437 |
| RoBERTa ensemble 32 | 0.443 |

Table 3: Our best model is underlined. The BOW-multiclass were not proposed to submission because their performance in the dev dataset did not surpass the proposed models. BOW-multiclass 1 would be placed second at the competition.

Our model RoBERTa-32 was placed fourth on the competition. The ranking provided by the organizers take the best run from each team, so our second model could be placed on top fifteen of the models. The RoBERTa ensemble 32 refers to the ensemble of RoBERTa models with lr $1e^{-5}$ and batch size 32, this model surpass our best model with little difference, as we see only one of them have performance similar with less computational resources.

In the case of BOW-multiclass, we did not include it in our proposal submissions as in previous experiments, and they did not obtain better performances than transformers and an ensemble of BOW.

## 6 Ethical issues

The automatic detection of mental illness, such as depression, using user-generated data raises several critical ethical considerations. One key aspect is the need to prioritize and ensure the anonymity of the users whose text is recorded for training and development purposes.

Crowd-sourcing is commonly employed in the context of labelling the data, where multiple annotators assess and assign labels to the instances. However, this process introduces a level of subjectivity, and there is no guarantee of perfect accuracy or consistency in the labelling. Annotators may have different interpretations or judgments, leading to potential discrepancies in the assigned labels. Consequently, the reliability and consistency of the labelled data may be influenced by the subjective opinions of the annotators.

The data used for automatic detection should ideally be collected with explicit user consent, where individuals knowingly and willingly provide their data for such purposes. However, in some cases, the data might have been obtained without users' explicit permission or awareness. This raises concerns about privacy violations and the potential discomfort or distress users may feel upon discovering their data is being used without their knowledge.

It is essential to prioritize data anonymization and protection of user identities throughout the entire data collection and storage process. Furthermore, efforts should be made to obtain explicit user consent when collecting data, ensuring individuals are fully aware of how their data will be used and can deny the use if they wish.

## 7 Conclusion

As we see in the previous subsection, multiclass classification is a difficult task for the complexity of depression detection. Our proposed models obtained performances similar to other teams in better places in the competition. The BOW ensemble obtained an F1-macro score close to our best-proposed model using less computational resources than a transformer model, as this model does not need GPU or a large amount of storage to be used.

The BOW-multiclass surpassed too the transformer model and the ensemble, even though the dev dataset did not surpass the proposed models; this could be because the test dataset is smaller than the dev dataset, and Machine Learning models as BOW tend to function better with fewer data.

In future work, we plan to explore better strategies for the values in the weights for the ensemble models of BOW and the rules made for the final predictions.

## Acknowledgments

This research was funded by *Consejo Nacional de Humanidades Ciencia y Tecnología* (CONAHCyT) master's degree grant #1141296. The authors thank to CONACyT, CIMAT and *Instituto Nacional de Astrofísica, Óptica y Electrónica* (INAOE) for the computer resources provided through the INAOE Supercomputing Laboratory's Deep Learning Platform for Language Technologies (*Plataforma de aprendizaje profundo para tecnologías del lenguaje*) and CIMAT Bajio Supercomputing Laboratory (#300832). Sanchez-Vega acknowledges CONACyT for its support through the Program "Investigadoras e Investigadores por México" by the project "Desarrollo de Inteligencia Artificial aplicada a la prevención de violencia y salud mental." (ID.11989, No. 1311).

## References

Jacob Devlin, Ming-Wei Chang, Kenton Lee, and Kristina Toutanova. 2018a. BERT: pre-training of deep bidirectional transformers for language understanding. *CoRR*, abs/1810.04805.

Jacob Devlin, Ming-Wei Chang, Kenton Lee, and Kristina Toutanova. 2018b. BERT: pre-training of deep bidirectional transformers for language understanding. *CoRR*, abs/1810.04805.

Darío Gustavo Funez, Maria José Garciarena Ucelay, Maria Paula Villegas, Sergio Gastón Burdisso, Leticia Cecilia Cagnina, Manuel Montes y Gómez, and Marcelo Luis Errecalde. 2018. Unsl's participation at erisk 2018 lab. In *Conference and Labs of the Evaluation Forum*.

Rahmatullah Haand and Zhao Shuwang. 2020. The relationship between social media addiction and depression: a quantitative study among university students in khost, afghanistan. *International Journal of Adolescence and Youth*, 25(1):780–786.

Morteza Janatdoust, Fatemeh Ehsani-Besheli, and Hossein Zeinali. 2022. KADO@LT-EDI-ACL2022: BERT-based ensembles for detecting signs of depression from social media text. In *Proceedings of the Second Workshop on Language Technology for Equality, Diversity and Inclusion*, pages 265–269, Dublin, Ireland. Association for Computational Linguistics.

Shaoxiong Ji, Tianlin Zhang, Luna Ansari, Jie Fu, Prayag Tiwari, and Erik Cambria. 2021. Mentalbert: Publicly available pretrained language models for mental healthcare. *CoRR*, abs/2110.15621.

Yinhan Liu, Myle Ott, Naman Goyal, Jingfei Du, Mandar Joshi, Danqi Chen, Omer Levy, Mike Lewis, Luke Zettlemoyer, and Veselin Stoyanov. 2019. Roberta: A robustly optimized BERT pretraining approach. *CoRR*, abs/1907.11692.

David E. Losada, Fabio A. Crestani, and Javier Parapar. 2018. Overview of erisk: Early risk prediction on the internet (extended lab overview). In *Conference and Labs of the Evaluation Forum*.

Rodrigo Martínez-Castaño, Amal Htait, Leif Azzopardi, and Yashar Moshfeghi. 2021. Bert-based transformers for early detection of mental health illnesses. In *Experimental IR Meets Multilinguality, Multimodality, and Interaction: 12th International Conference of the CLEF Association, CLEF 2021, Virtual Event, September 21–24, 2021, Proceedings*, page 189–200, Berlin, Heidelberg. Springer-Verlag.

Gwenn Schurgin O'Keeffe, Kathleen Clarke-Pearson, Council on Communications, and Media. 2011. The Impact of Social Media on Children, Adolescents, and Families. *Pediatrics*, 127(4):800–804.

Rosa María Ortega-Mendoza, Delia Irazú Hernández-Farías, Manuel Montes y Gómez, and Luis Villaseñor-Pineda. 2022. Revealing traces of depression through personal statements analysis in social media. *Artificial Intelligence in Medicine*, 123:102202.

Javier Parapar, Patricia Martín-Rodilla, David E. Losada, and Fabio Crestani. 2022. Overview ofnbsp;erisk 2022: Early risk prediction onnbsp;thenbsp;internet. In *Experimental IR Meets Multilinguality, Multimodality, and Interaction: 13th International Conference of the CLEF Association, CLEF 2022, Bologna, Italy, September 5–8, 2022, Proceedings*, page 233–256, Berlin, Heidelberg. Springer-Verlag.

Rafał Poświata and Michał Perełkiewicz. 2022. OPI@LT-EDI-ACL2022: Detecting signs of depression from social media text using RoBERTa pretrained language models. In *Proceedings of the Second Workshop on Language Technology for Equality, Diversity and Inclusion*, pages 276–282, Dublin, Ireland. Association for Computational Linguistics.

Kayalvizhi Sampath, Thenmozhi Durairaj, Bharathi Raja Chakravarthi, Jerin Mahibha C, Kogilavani Shanmugavadivel, and Pratik Anil Rahood. 2023. Overview of the second shared task on detecting signs of depression from social media text. In *Proceedings of the Third Workshop on Language Technology for Equality, Diversity and Inclusion*, Varna, Bulgaria. Recent Advances in Natural Language Processing.

Marcel Trotzek, Sven Koitka, and C. Friedrich. 2018. Word embeddings and linguistic metadata at the clef 2018 tasks for early detection of depression and anorexia. In *Conference and Labs of the Evaluation Forum*.

Wei-Yao Wang, Yu-Chien Tang, Wei-Wei Du, and Wen-Chih Peng. 2022. NYCU_TWD@LT-EDI-ACL2022: Ensemble models with VADER and contrastive learning for detecting signs of depression from social media. In *Proceedings of the Second Workshop on Language Technology for Equality, Diversity and Inclusion*, pages 136–139, Dublin, Ireland. Association for Computational Linguistics.

World Health Organization. 2022. Depression. `https://www.who.int/news-room/fact-sheets/detail/depression`. 18 june of 2023.

# SIS@LT-EDI: Detecting Signs of Depression from Social Media Text Using Ensemble Techniques

**Sulaksha B K, Shruti Krishnaveni S, Ivana Steeve, B.Monica Jenefer**
Meenakshi Sundararajan Engineering College, Chennai
bksulaksha@gmail.com, ivanasteeve@gmail.com,
shrutiks33@gmail.com,monicamaheswaran@gmail.com

## Abstract

Various biological, genetic, psychological or social factors that feature a target oriented life with chronic stress and frequent traumatic experiences, lead to pessimism and apathy. According to WHO, about 280 million of the population have depression. The massive scale of depression should be dealt with as a disease rather than a 'phase' that is neglected by the majority. However, not a lot of people are aware of depression and its impact. Depression is a serious issue that should be treated in the right way. Many people dealing with depression do not realize that they have it due to the lack of awareness. This paper aims to address this issue with a tool built on the blocks of machine learning. This model analyzes the public social media texts and detects the signs of depression as three labels namely "not depressed", "moderately depressed", and "severely depressed" with high accuracy. The ensembled model uses three learners namely Multi-Layered Perceptron, Support Vector Machine and Multinomial Naive Bayes Classifier. The distinctive feature in this model is that it uses Artificial Neural Networks, Classifiers, Regression and Voting Classifiers to compute the final result or output.

**Index Terms**- Ensemble Modeling, Neural Networks, Naive Bayes Classifier, Multilayer Perceptron(MLP), Support Vector Machine.

## 1 Introduction

Depression is a chronic feeling of emptiness, sadness, or inability to feel pleasure that may appear to happen for no clear reason, according to 'Medical News Today'. It is distinct from grief and other emotions. It is considered to be a common mental disorder. A sense of melancholy pervades through a single word or text and to detect this the project is assigned to analyze the text with its highest accuracy rate of depression. As described in the World Health Organization's Comprehensive Mental Health Action Plan 2013-2020 [1], depression alone affects more than 300 million people worldwide and is one of the largest single causes of disability worldwide, particularly for women. Depression currently accounts for 4.3 percent of the global burden of disease, and it is expected to be the leading cause of disease burden in high-income countries by 2030 (Halfin, 2007). It is important to note that each individual's experience with depression is unique, and the causes can vary from person to person. Some of the common factors leading to Depression is said to be competitive lifestyle, need to meet high expectations and low self-esteem. People are much concerned about getting a good qualification, better career paths, social dignity etc., The spawn of internet and communication technologies, distinctly the online social networks have modernized how people interact and communicate with each other digitally. People tend to express more on Social Media compared to real life interactions and communications.It is also important to note that measuring the severity of the disorder is also a difficult task that could only be done by a highly trained professional with the use of different techniques such as text descriptions and clinical interviews, as well as their judgments (Husseini Orabi et al., 2018). This project depicts a deep architecture for explicitly predicting and classifying depression levels as 'Not Depressed', 'Moderately Depressed', or 'Severely Depressed' from their Social Media texts. Strong Learners such as Support Vector Machine (SVM), Multilayer Perceptron (MLP), Deep Neural Networks and Naive Bayes are used for classifying texts. This Project uses data from social media networks to explore various methods of early detection of Major depressive disorder (MDD) based on machine learning techniques. A thorough analysis of the dataset to characterize the subjects' behavior based on different aspects of their writings (Halfin, 2007). The main contributions of the project can be summarized as follows: Depression is a chronic feeling

[1]https://www.who.int/health-topics/depressiontab=tab$_1$



*LT-EDI 2023 – Third Workshop on Language Technology for Equality, Diversity and Inclusion*, pages 131–137, Varna, Bulgaria, Sep 7, 2023.
https://doi.org/10.26615/978-954-452-084-7_019

of emptiness, sadness, or inability to feel pleasure that may appear to happen for no clear reason, according to 'Medical News Today'. It is distinct from grief and other emotions. It is considered to be a common mental disorder. A sense of melancholy pervades through a single word or text and to detect this the project is assigned to analyze the text with its highest accuracy rate of depression. As described in the World Health Organization's Comprehensive Mental Health Action Plan 2013-2020 (?), depression alone affects more than 300 million people worldwide and is one of the largest single causes of disability worldwide, particularly for women. Depression currently accounts for 4.3 percent of the global burden of disease, and it is expected to be the leading cause of disease burden in high-income countries by 2030 (Halfin, 2007). It is important to note that each individual's experience with depression is unique, and the causes can vary from person to person. Some of the common factors leading to Depression is said to be competitive lifestyle, need to meet high expectations and low self-esteem. People are much concerned about getting a good qualification, better career paths, social dignity etc., The spawn of internet and communication technologies, distinctly the online social networks have modernized how people interact and communicate with each other digitally. People tend to express more on Social Media compared to real life interactions and communications. This project depicts a deep architecture for explicitly predicting and classifying depression levels as 'Not Depressed', 'Moderately Depressed', or 'Severely Depressed' from their Social Media texts. Strong Learners such as Support Vector Machine (SVM), Multilayer Perceptron (MLP), Deep Neural Networks and Naive Bayes are used for classifying texts. This Project uses data from social media networks to explore various methods of early detection of Major depressive disorder (MDD) based on machine learning techniquies. This paper is writtern in the format (Sampath et al.) A thorough analysis of the dataset to characterize the subjects' behavior based on different aspects of their writings (Halfin, 2007). The main contributions of the project can be summarized as follows:

• The model provides the combined outcome computed by various Learners.

• A Voting Classifier is used to get the majority outcome of the text.

• Our ensemble method achieved competitive performance in the shared task in detecting signs of depression from social media text with 72 percent f1-score accuracy. Each sample is composed of three columns: PID, Text, and Label. The below figure contains an image of the Training Dataset.

| 618 | train_pid_ | Feeling numb. : Okay this is my first post, apologies if it's | severe |
|---|---|---|---|
| 619 | train_pid_ | my mom is terribly sad and its making me anxious : Im | not depression |
| 620 | train_pid_ | 1/1/20. Iâ€™m really really hurting today. : The holidays w | not depression |
| 621 | train_pid_ | I'm tired of being a nobody. : God, I just want to fucking | moderate |
| 622 | train_pid_ | Love This Song. Itâ€™s Been Helping Me When I Feel My W | not depression |
| 623 | train_pid_ | Does anyone feel MORE depressed after they go out/leave | moderate |
| 624 | train_pid_ | I know I'm a good person but I've come to the realization t | not depression |
| 625 | train_pid_ | Getting more depressed as time goes by and its scary : Hov | not depression |
| 626 | train_pid_ | Do people just fake being excited? : Recently there was | moderate |
| 627 | train_pid_ | I'm so lonely and nobody's favorite : Last night (New Year's | not depression |
| 628 | train_pid_ | Why is it that talking to people about depression is so | not depression |

Figure 1: Samples from the Training Dataset.

## 2 Existing works

There have been many projects that have dealt with finding a tool to detect depression in social media. Most of them included the implementation of machine learning techniques such as support vector machines and naive bayes. The overall accuracy obtained from those works is 70 percent. This paper aims to increase the accuracy level of detecting depression and in a way that it doesn't affect the user's privacy. Halfin's study (Halfin, 2007) demonstrated that the early detection, intervention, and appropriate treatment can promote easing and reduce the emotional and financial burdens of depression, and (Picardi et al., 2016) observed significant improvements in depressive symptoms among subjects who had undergone early screening or diagnosis of depression. (Rost et al., 2004) found that early intervention for depression can improve employee productivity and reduce major problems and complications. The prediction of Major Depressive Disorder (MDD) at early stages is proved to improve the health and maintain peace of a subject. The Detection of MDD is so far has been predicted by one method or one weak learner.

## 3 Proposed Method

By extending the work done previously, this Machine Learning Model is based on Support Vector Machine(SVM), Multinomial Naive Bayes and Multi layer Perceptron(MLP). By combining the above algorithms, the result thus obtained will have higher accuracy as it is built on not one, but 3 highly effective ML models. The final prediction of the text is classified or computed using an ensembling technique called Bagging (Bootstrap Aggregating) and a Voting Classifier. A Voting Classifier is a

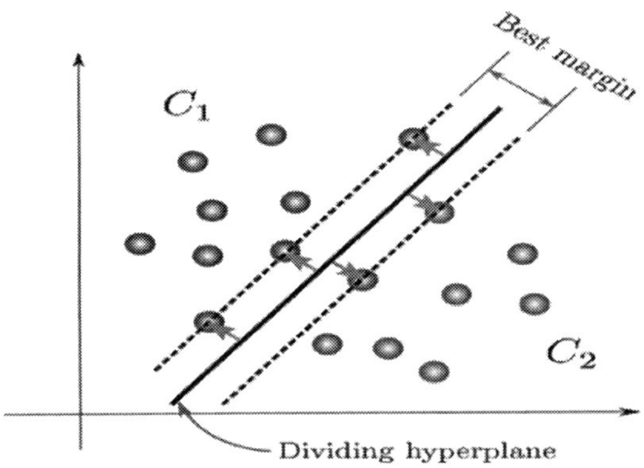

Figure 2: Illustration of Support Vector Machine.

machine learning estimator that trains various base models and predicts an outcome on the basis of aggregating and considering the majority output regarding the findings of each base estimator(Ganaie et al., 2022).

**Brief explanation about the algorithms used in the final model:**

**Support Vector Machine (SVM):** The SVM algorithm is implemented through the 'SVC' class. SVMs (Malviya et al., 2021) are powerful classifiers that aim to find an optimal hyperplane to separate different classes in the data. In this code, SVM with a linear kernel ('kernel='linear'') is used, which takes a linear decision boundary between classes. The Figure 2 is an illustration of Support Vector Machine and how it classifies different data points using regression function. Support Vector Machine (SVM) is a type of algorithm in supervised machine learning domain most used for undertaking classifications tasks(Malviya et al., 2021). While SVM algorithms can be employed for regression analysis tasks, but in practice they are most used for classification applications, such as classifying binary data into two distinct classes(Gupta et al., 2021).

**Multilayer Perceptron (MLP):** The MLP algorithm is implemented through the 'MLPClassifier' class . It's a type of neural network that consists of multiple layers of nodes. It uses a process called backpropagation to navigate through complex data. The Figure 3 is an illustration of Multilayer Perceptron and how it classifies different data points using multiple hidden layers. In this code, an MLP classifier with a single hidden layer containing 100 neurons is used. Multilayer Perceptron is used because it uses generalized delta learning rules and easily gets trained in less number of iterations(Aggarwal

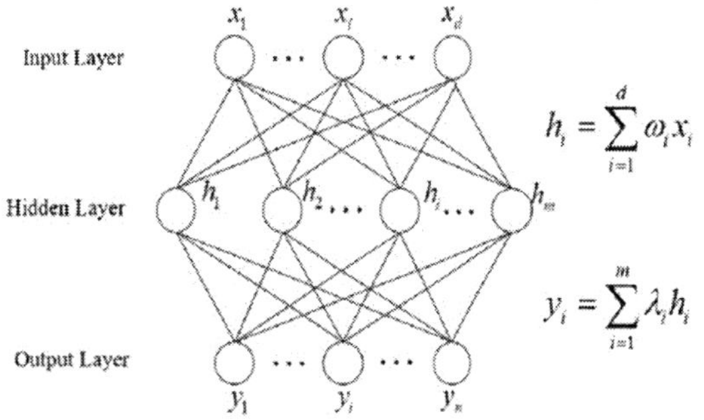

Figure 3: Illustration of Multilayer Perceptron.

and Singh, 2015). A minimal Multilayer Perceptron has 3 layers including one hidden layer, one input layer and one output layer. The increase in the number of hidden layers corresponds to more accurate results.

If it has more than 1 hidden layer, it is called a deep ANN. An MLP is a typical example of a feedforward artificial neural network.

**Multinomial Naive Bayes (NB):** Bayesian algorithms predict the class depending on the probability of belonging to that class [2]. It calculates a set of probabilities from the frequency count and the combinations of values in a given data set. This algorithm is based on Bayes' theorem, assuming that all variables are independent. Bayes' theorem follows the following formula(**?**) .

$$P(A) = P((B)(A))/(B)(1)$$

Naive Bayes algorithms assume features are independent of each other, and hence no correlation between the features tend to implement through the 'MultinomialNB' class are probabilistic classifier based on Bayes' theorem. In the code, the MultinomialNB classifier is used, which is optimal for discrete features such as word frequencies or TF-IDF values commonly encountered in text classification tasks. Including NB as a weak learner in the ensemble can improve accuracy by taking advantage of its ability to handle text data and make independent assumptions. Multinomial Naive Bayes Classifier is used to classify data that is not dependent on a time period or a scale. These algorithms are combined in the ensemble approach to leverage the strengths of each individual algorithm and create a more robust and accurate model. Hence, by combining multiple algorithms the model is gives a prediction with high accuracy. Multinomial Naïve

[2]https://towardsdatascience.com/naive-bayes-classifier-explained-50f9723571ed

Bayes Classifier is a supervised learning method that uses probability and is focused on text classification cases. This method follows the principle of multinomial distribution in conditional probability. Although using multinomial distributions, this algorithm can be applied to text cases by converting to a nominal form that can be computed with an integer value. The probability calculation is described in the below equation(Farisi et al., 2019).

$$P(c|d) \propto P(c)\Pi P(t|c)](2)$$

Where P(t) is the conditional probability of the word in the text that belongs to class c and P(c) is the prior probability.(Farisi et al., 2019)

**Ensemble Learning:** Ensemble learning is a machine learning archetype or theory where multiple learners are trained or applied to datasets to solve the same problem by extracting multiple predictions then combined into one composite prediction(Ganaie et al., 2022). Deep learning architectures are showing better performance compared to the shallow or traditional models. Deep ensemble learning models combine the advantages of both the deep learning models as well as the ensemble learning such that the final model has better generalization performance. It is a process that uses a set of models, each of them obtained by applying a learning process to a given problem. This set of models (ensemble) is integrated in some way to obtain the final prediction. Ensemble learning is a technique that combines multiple individual models (weak learners) to make predictions.(Kotsiantis and Pintelas, 2007) The model use the Voting Classifier and Bagging Classifier.The ensemble combines the predictions of the various learners to obtain the final prediction. In the first version of the code, a VotingClassifier is used with three weak learners: Multilayer Perceptron(MLP), Support Vector Machine (SVM), and Multinomial Naive Bayes. In the another model , a BaggingClassifier is used, where the ensembling model combines Multilayer Perceptron (MLP), Support Vector Machine (SVM) and Random Forest(rf). Though both models tend to compute outcomes with promising accuracy, the first model provides the highest accuracy. To prove that average voting in an ensemble is better than individual model, Marquis de Condorcet proposed a theorem wherein he proved that if the probability of each voter being correct is above 0.5 and the voters are independent, then addition of more voters increases the probability of majority vote

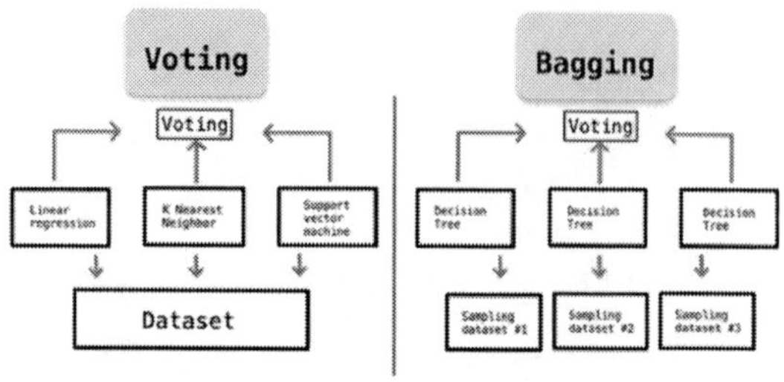


Figure 4: Illustration of ensembling techniques.

being correct until it approaches 1 (Condorcet, 1785) (Ganaie et al., 2022; Kotsiantis and Pintelas, 2007). Although Marquis de Condorcet proposed this theorem in the field of political science and had no idea of the field of Machine learning, but it is the similar mechanism that leads to better performance of the ensemble models. Assumptions of Marquis de Condorcet theorem also holds true for ensembles (Ganaie et al., 2022; Kotsiantis and Pintelas, 2007),(Hansen and Salamon, 1990). The reasons for the success of ensemble learning include: statistical, computational and representation learning, bias–variance decomposition and strength-correlation(Ganaie et al., 2022; Kotsiantis and Pintelas, 2007; Breiman, 2001).

## 4 Working of the model

The code is implemented more than once in order to obtain the optimal result, a total of 4 compilations were implemented.

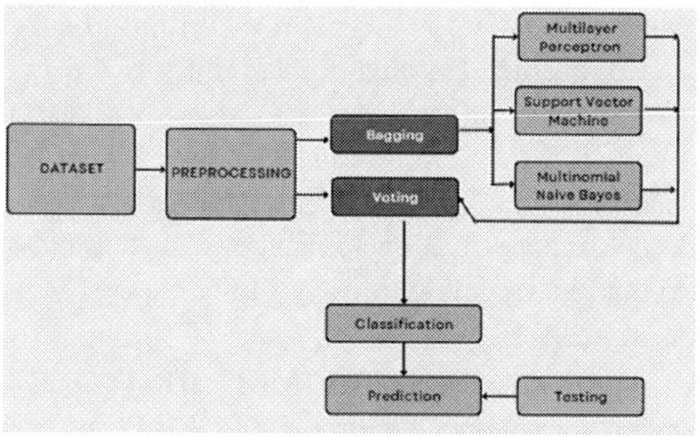


Figure 5: Working of model

Version 1: The classification report provides an evaluation of the model's performance in each class. The ensemble method - Voting Classifier is used here, which compares the prediction of multiple weak learners to make the final prediction. While using the voting ensemble technique, the predictions for the "not depression" and "severe" classes have been classified in terms of the precision , recall and F1-score. The accuracy if this model is 58 percent. This accuracy score is not appreciable for this type of text classification. So this problem needs to be addressed in the next run. The overall accuracy for detecting severe depression is 98 percent using this classifier. But the other classes remain moderately accurate. This is not the goal of this paper, hence certain changes are made to make it more accurate. The Classification Report while using the Voting Classifier is depicted below stating the model's accuracy.

| | Precision | Recall | F1-Score | Support |
|---|---|---|---|---|
| Moderate | 0.61 | 0.72 | 0.66 | 275 |
| Not Depressed | 0.37 | 0.37 | 0.37 | 135 |
| Severe | 0.98 | 0.46 | 0.63 | 89 |
| | | | | |
| Average | | | 0.58 | 499 |
| Macro Avg | 0.65 | 0.52 | 0.55 | 499 |
| Weighted Avg | 0.61 | 0.58 | 0.58 | 499 |

Table 1: The Classification Report while using the Voting Classifier

Version 2: In the updated version of the code, Bagging Classifier is implemented instead of a voting classifier. In bagging, multiple weak learners are trained on different subsets of training data and their predictions are aggregated to make the final prediction. One of the weak learners used here is Multinomial Naive Bayes, a variant of Naive Bayes instead of the random forest classifier. It's used as it provides better accuracy while handling text classification, and provides ensemble diversity. That is, adding the MNB(Multinomial Naive Bayes) alongside MLP and SVM,provides diversity to the ensemble which improves the overall accuracy. In this run, the overall accuracy obtained is 72 percent, hence the accuracy is improved compared to the previous model and this is also greater than the accuracy obtained in the existing methods. To make sure this is the maximum accuracy, the same model is run twice. It is observed that the maximum and highest accuracy of detecting depression in texts is 72 percent. The Classification Report while using Bagging Classifier is depicted below stating the model's accuracy.

| | Precision | Recall | F1-Score | Support |
|---|---|---|---|---|
| Moderate | 0.72 | 1.00 | 0.84 | 358 |
| Not Depressed | 0.00 | 0.00 | 0.00 | 138 |
| Severe | 0.00 | 0.00 | 0.00 | 3 |
| | | | | |
| Average | | | 0.72 | 499 |
| Macro Avg | 0.24 | 0.33 | 0.28 | 499 |
| Weighted Avg | 0.51 | 0.72 | 0.60 | 499 |

Table 2: The Classification Report while using the Bagging Classifier

## 5 Data

The dataset used in the paper is of public data, ensuring that the user's privacy is not invaded at any cost. But the public data might contain depressive texts in a disingenuous meaning too. This might make it hard to separate the genuine texts from them, hence public data needs to be further filtered. The dataset contains 7202 texts for training, 3,246 texts for development, and 500 texts for testing, while each sample is composed of three columns: PID(Person Identity), Text, and Label. The Test Dataset contains only PID and text for which the label is predicted using the model.

## 6 Implementation

The model can be implemented in any Python environment as long as it supports the necessary modules and libraries used in the code. Such machine learning frameworks are Jupyter Notebook, Python IDLE or Google Colab. This model is implemented in Google Colab. Libraries and modules like Pandas, Vectorizer, neural network, svm(Support Vector Machine), naive bayes are used for the implementation.

## 7 Result Analysis

As discussed previously, the updated version of the model provides the prediction with the highest accuracy of 72 percent(F1 score). This final version of the model is implemented by using the weak learners SVM, Naive Bayes, MLP, Ensemble Learning( Bagging Classifier). The model correctly predicted and classified the texts into labels namely 'Not Depressed', 'Moderately Depressed', or 'Severely Depressed'. Since preprocessing can eliminate unneeded words and make the word more structured in the created model so that it is more efficient and performance will increase. Factors like sarcastic texts, threatening, fabricated content etc.., seem to affect the accuracy and consistency of the model. Though this is a model with high accuracy to detect depression, it can be improved to give better results. The predicted results computer by the model are given in Table 3 for reference.

| Pid | Predicted label |
|---|---|
| test id 1 | moderate |
| test id 2 | moderate |
| test id 3 | not depression |
| test id 4 | severe |
| test id 5 | moderate |
| test id 6 | not depression |

Table 3: Predicted Result

## 8 Conclusion

In this era it is important to keep lead and awareness on the depression rate, some phases or events make us more vulnerable to depression. There are various factors that could trigger emotional influx, and to detect all these, different algorithms with the highest accuracy have been opted. Based on the results of testing and analysis, it can be concluded as follows: The system that was built successfully classified texts into labels namely 'Not Depressed', 'Moderately Depressed', or 'Severely Depressed'. with the most optimal result is F1-Score average of 72 percent using preprocessing based on the classification process. The optimal classification principle is to improve the model performance with standardized classification and management with the dependence of word occurrence. This change improved the performance of the dataset classification model. The ensemble technique algorithm is a fast, easy-to-implement, almost modern text classification algorithm. Proposed method and algorithm offers many possibilities for text classification. The main findings of this study is the importance of using ensemble techniques in the early detection of MDD to prevent any occurrences of tragic incidents, the comparison of the Voting Classifier and Bagging Classifier to predict the depression condition, and the improvement of state-of-the-art algorithms. It does have its own demerits that are to be figured out, yet it still provides us by attaining the goal of detecting the depression levels.

## 9 Future Enhancement

Though this model is better compared to the existing methods, it has its own shortcomings that need to be improved. It can be enhanced in several ways to improve its performance and functionality. Firstly, applying hyperparameter tuning to the individual classifiers used in the ensemble can optimize their parameters for better accuracy. Techniques like grid search or random search can be employed to find the best combination of hyperparameters. Next, considering a diverse range of classifiers or combining more models into the ensemble learning can enhance its predictive capabilities. To address imbalanced and inconsistent data, techniques like oversampling, undersampling, or generating synthetic samples can be used to balance the class distribution. Furthermore, performing thorough error analysis to identify common misclassifications or patterns where the model struggles can improve the overall performance.

## References


Ashutosh Aggarwal and Karamjeet Singh. 2015. Handwritten gurmukhi character recognition. In *2015 international conference on computer, communication and control (IC4)*, pages 1–5. IEEE.

Leo Breiman. 2001. Random forests. *Machine learning*, 45:5–32.

Arif Abdurrahman Farisi, Yuliant Sibaroni, and Said Al Faraby. 2019. Sentiment analysis on hotel reviews using multinomial naïve bayes classifier. In *Journal of Physics: Conference Series*, volume 1192, page 012024. IOP Publishing.

M.A. Ganaie, Minghui Hu, A.K. Malik, M. Tanveer, and P.N. Suganthan. 2022. Ensemble deep learning: A review. *Engineering Applications of Artificial Intelligence*, 115:105151.

Brij Mohan Gupta, Surinder M Dhawan, and Ghouse Modin N Mamdapur. 2021. Support vector machine (svm) research in india: A scientometric evaluation of india's publications output during 2002-19. *The Journal of Indian Library Association*, 57(3):12–25.

Aron Halfin. 2007. Depression: the benefits of early and appropriate treatment. *American Journal of Managed Care*, 13(4):S92.

Lars Kai Hansen and Peter Salamon. 1990. Neural network ensembles. *IEEE transactions on pattern analysis and machine intelligence*, 12(10):993–1001.

Ahmed Husseini Orabi, Prasadith Buddhitha, Mahmoud Husseini Orabi, and Diana Inkpen. 2018. Deep learning for depression detection of Twitter users. In *Proceedings of the Fifth Workshop on Computational Linguistics and Clinical Psychology: From Keyboard to Clinic*, pages 88–97, New Orleans, LA. Association for Computational Linguistics.

SB Kotsiantis and PE Pintelas. 2007. Combining bagging and boosting. *International Journal of Mathematical and Computational Sciences*, 1(8):372–381.

Keshu Malviya, Bholanath Roy, and SK Saritha. 2021. A transformers approach to detect depression in social media. In *2021 International Conference on Artificial Intelligence and Smart Systems (ICAIS)*, pages 718–723. IEEE.

A Picardi, I Lega, L Tarsitani, M Caredda, G Matteucci, MP Zerella, R Miglio, A Gigantesco, M Cerbo, A Gaddini, et al. 2016. A randomised controlled trial of the effectiveness of a program for early detection and treatment of depression in primary care. *Journal of affective disorders*, 198:96–101.

Kathryn Rost, Jeffrey L Smith, and Miriam Dickinson. 2004. The effect of improving primary care depression management on employee absenteeism and productivity a randomized trial. *Medical care*, 42(12):1202.

Kayalvizhi Sampath, Thenmozhi Durairaj, Bharathi Raja Chakravarthi, Jerin Mahibha C, Kogilavani Shanmugavadivel, and Pratik Anil booktitle = Rahood. Overview of the second shared task on detecting signs of depression from social media text.

# TEAM BIAS BUSTERS@LT-EDI: Detecting Signs of Depression with Generative Pretrained Transformers


**Andrew Nedilko**
Workhuman
agnedil@gmail.com



## Abstract

This paper describes our methodology adopted to participate in the multi-class classification task under the auspices of the Third Workshop on Language Technology for Equality, Diversity, Inclusion (LT-EDI) in the Recent Advances in Natural Language Processing (RANLP) 2023 conference. The overall objective was to employ ML algorithms to detect signs of depression in English-language social media content, classifying each post into one of three categories: no depression, moderate depression, and severe depression. To accomplish this, we utilized novel generative pretrained transformers (GPTs), leveraging the full-scale OpenAI API. Our strategy incorporated prompt engineering for zero-shot and few-shot learning scenarios with ChatGPT and fine-tuning a GPT-3 model. The latter approach yielded the best results which allowed us to outperform our benchmark XGBoost classifier based on character-level features on the dev set and score a macro F1 score of 0.419 on the final blind test set.


## 1 Introduction and Related Works

From a common-sense linguistic perspective, detecting signs of depression in text can be challenging for a number of reasons:

- Variability of language and perception: a) different people may express their feelings differently, b) the same phrase might mean different things in different contexts, c) different people might interpret the same piece of writing in very different ways, d) the way people express emotions and discuss mental health can vary widely across different cultures.
- Privacy: some people may not be eager to openly express their depressive symptoms or feelings, using vague or metaphorical language.
- Absence of non-verbal cues: a lot of nonverbal information is lost in written text, such as tone of voice, facial expression, posture, etc.
- Co-occurrence of depression with other medical conditions which can have its own impact on text.

It should be also noted that text analysis can provide only hints, but should never be used as a definitive diagnostic tool. Only trained mental health professionals can diagnose depression.

Although discovering signs of depression in a written text is challenging because such text is not a direct indicator of someone's mental state, there are certain language patterns which might indicate a higher likelihood of depression.

According to Al-Mosaiwi and Johnstone (2018) and Al-Mosaiwi (2018) the following is typical of texts written by people with depression in the order of increasing importance:

- they use more words for negative emotions - a person dealing with depression often tends to have a more negative tone in their writing;
- depressed individuals often focus heavily on themselves, possibly due to feelings of isolation or self-blame; therefore, they use significantly more first person singular pronouns and significantly fewer second and third person pronouns. For the same reason, ruminations can be also observed in their writing when they repeat the same thought over and over again;
- depressed people use significantly more absolutist words - absolute magnitude or probability (50% greater in anxiety and depression forums and 80% greater in suicidal ideation forums).




*LT-EDI 2023 – Third Workshop on Language Technology for Equality, Diversity and Inclusion*, pages 138–143, Varna, Bulgaria, Sep 7, 2023.
https://doi.org/10.26615/978-954-452-084-7_020

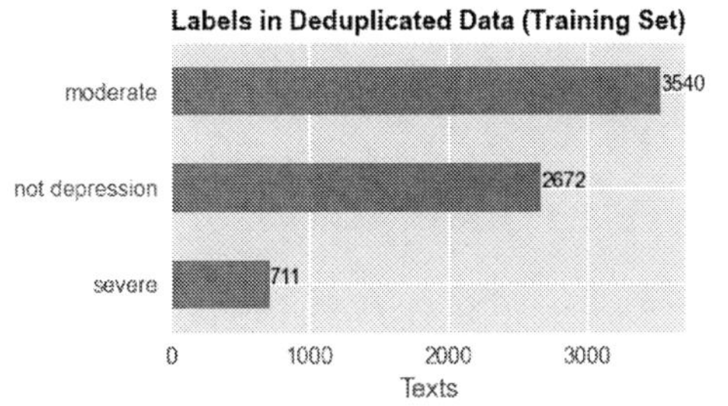


Figure 1: Distribution of Categories - Training Set

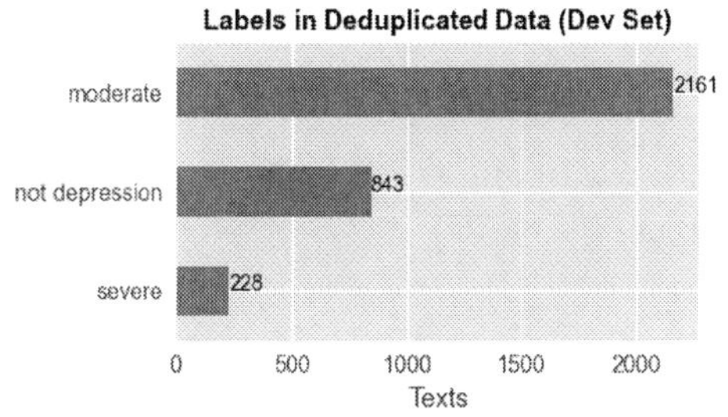


Figure 2: Distribution of Categories - Dev Set

The studies presented in Capecelatro et al. (2013) show that the depressed people prefer words related to sadness, death, avoid positive words. And the longer their depression is (5 years and more), the fewer appetitive or food-related words (eat, chew, drink, hunger) or sexual words (arousal, make out, orgasm) they use. The authors claim that this can be due to long-term changes in their brains.

Similar ideas are repeated in Newell et al. (2018) and Davis (2020). We attempted to quantify these characteristics in the form of counts of phrases that belong to each of these classes and use them as features for machine learning (ML) models. See more details in subsection 3.2 and subsection 4.2.

In addition, Havigerová et al. (2019) states the importance of early detection of the signs of depression. The goal of their research was to study automatic analysis of texts to build predictive models that can identify individuals at risk of a mental disorder. The authors came up with four regression models to predict a higher emotional state of depression using such text features as the ratio of pronouns to nouns, ratio of verbs to nouns (readiness for action), ratio of finite verbs to number of sentences, and ratio of the number of punctuation marks to the number of sentences.

## 2 Dataset and Task

The dataset consists of social media posts in which people describe their emotions and feelings. The number of examples in each subset is as follows: training set – 7201, development (dev) set – 3245, test set – 499. Given these posts, our task was to classify the signs of depression into three categories: no depression, moderate depression, severe depression. As you can see from Fig. 1 and Fig. 2, the distribution of categories is imbalanced with the majority category being "moderate depression" and the minority category – "severe depression".

Based on the common understanding that the same person cannot be both depressed and not depressed, and that two different people cannot write the same relatively long post in social media, we considered this a multi-class, but not multi-label classification i. e. each text can have only one label.

In line with this, 232 complete duplicates were removed from the training set; complete here means that all the values in these rows in all columns were identical. In addition, there were 158 cases in the training set where the text of the post was the same, but the labels were different. Since the same person cannot be depressed and not depressed at the same time, we decided to remove such cases because the true label was unknown (there were at least two different labels in each case), and we didn't feel to be qualified enough to decide which category each mislabeled text should belong to. There were only complete 23 duplicates in the dev set.

As for the data leakage – there were only three posts that occurred both in the training and dev sets. The test set didn't have any overlap with the training or dev set.

Fig. 3 and Fig. 4 demonstrate that the character length distribution across all datasets reveals a minority of abnormally lengthy texts. The majority, representing the 95th percentile, encompasses texts containing fewer than 2,500 characters. However, a substantial surge in text length is observed beyond this point, extending to and exceeding 20,000 characters. Jumping ahead, we should say that training separate classifiers for different lengths of text didn't improve the aggregate results.

A blind test set without labels was used for testing the model that had the best performance on the dev set. Unlike the training and dev sets, the test set required heavy text cleaning as certain combinations of English characters and even single characters (mostly contractions at the sub-word level)

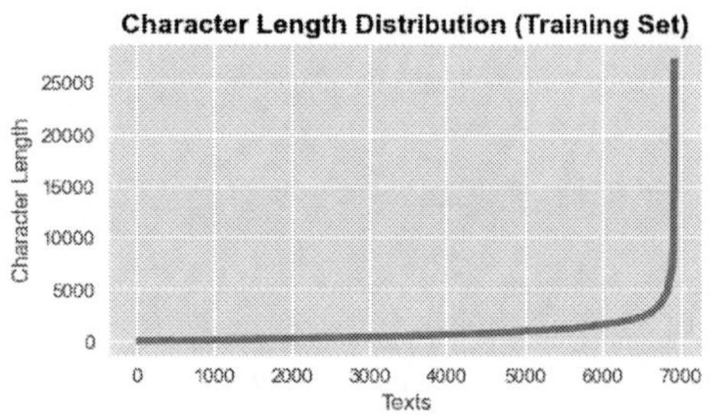


Figure 3: Character Length Distribution - Training Set

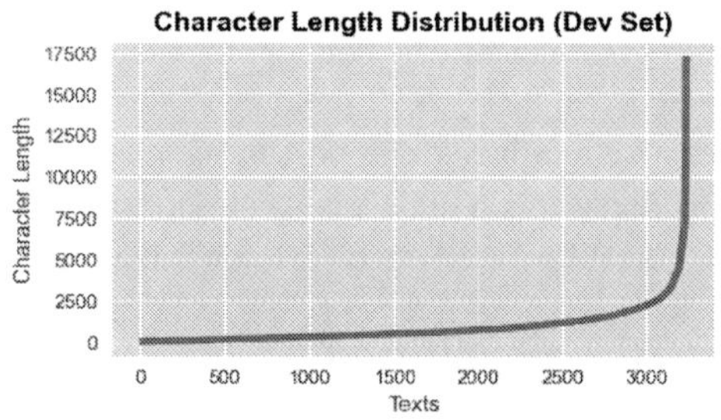


Figure 4: Character Length Distribution - Dev Set

were replaced with Chinese hieroglyphs. Examples: " 't ", " 's ", " 'm ", " 've ", " 'd " and many more.

## 3 System Description

### 3.1 Baseline Model

The baseline model, an XGBoost classifier employing word n-gram counts as features (utilizing CountVectorizer with an n-gram range of (1,3)), established the initial metrics. The initial macro F1 score was subpar, falling under 0.5. However, after implementing various enhancement techniques, including oversampling, data augmentation, and erroneous label elimination, we managed to elevate the final baseline macro F1 score to 0.54 and the micro F1 score to 0.61, as detailed in Table 1 below. See Fig. 5 for the baseline confusion matrix.

Oversampling was conducted up to the number of data points in the majority class. See subsection 4.2 below for a description of the data augmentation process.

### 3.2 Numerical Features

Using the sources of information from section 1, for each post we counted the number of occurrences of the following terms and tried to use this information as additional features to improve the classification results:

- words with a strong negative correlation in posts, e.g. self-harm, abominable, hopeless, disgraceful, etc.;
- words related to death;
- words and phrases representing absolutism, e.g. forever, never, no one, always, completely, etc.;
- first person pronouns singular: I, me, myself, mine, etc.;
- other personal pronouns: you, we, they, etc.;
- words related to the apetite and eating: bevarage, buffet, cravings, dining, etc.
- words related to sex;
- special medical terms describing specifically depression and medications for depression: delusional, exausting, mood swings, mental disorder, etc.

### 3.3 GPT: Iterative Prompt Engineering vs. Fine-Tuning

The effectiveness of transformer models and their ensembles for sequence classification has been validated by Kshirsagar et al. (2022), although with a macro F1 score remaining under 0.55. The recent rise of autoregressive models with the generative pretrained transformer (GPT) architecture and their remarkable "human-level performance on diverse professional and academic benchmarks" OpenAI (2023) have been widely recognized. Thus, we deemed it pertinent to assess if the latest, novel GPT series models could offer a more efficient solution to the task of depression detection.

For this task, we leveraged a set of OpenAI models due to their comprehensive commercial APIs that offer diverse methods of interaction with pretrained models. Primarily, we employed the ChatGPT API with prompt engineering, generating various prompts to conduct extensive experiments on the development set, with an aim to optimize the macro F1 score. Both zero-shot and few-shot learning methodologies were applied. The training set was used for the sole purpose of concatenating examples for few-shot learning.

Zero-shot prompts asked the model to select the right category from a pre-defined list of categories (no depression, moderate depression, severe depression) for each example from the dev set or test set.

Few-shot prompts followed the same schema, but several labeled examples were appended to them so that the model could learn from such examples and make more accurate classification. The labeled examples were taken randomly from the training set.

Since these APIs didn't outperform our baseline model, we sought to enhance our metrics by fine-tuning a prior GPT-series model. Presently, neither ChatGPT nor GPT-4 offer fine-tuning capabilities. Only the original GPT-3 base models, which lack instruction following training and are smaller than ChatGPT, permit fine-tuning. We chose the largest such model – DaVinci, which led to surpassing our baseline model's score. We fine-tuned the model using the standard OpenAI API, without modifying the predefined hyperparameters. This API allows users to load the training set in a special format, fine-tune the model on this dataset, and then make calls to the fine-tuned model in order to classify new examples from the dev set or test set.

## 4 Analysis of Results

### 4.1 ChatGPT

We used zero-shot learning on the basis of the idea that the labels' names are self-descriptive and could be readily understood by a pre-trained model such as ChatGPT. We opted against employing GPT-4 for this experiment due to the lengthy nature of some texts and the multitude of examples in the development set. This decision was cost-driven, as GPT-4 API calls are significantly more expensive than those of ChatGPT.

Among all models, the zero-shot ChatGPT classifier demonstrated the poorest performance. Its highest macro F1 score reached was 0.25, significantly underperforming the baseline classifier (see Table 1). As illustrated by the confusion matrix in Fig. 6 the primary cause of this outcome was the classifier's tendency to excessively classify examples into the "severe depression" category.

To enhance the zero-shot classification results, we next explored few-shot learning. Given that the ChatGPT context window is confined to 4096 tokens, we could only select a finite number of labeled examples from the training set. These examples were randomly sampled for each development set data point to be classified. An alternate strategy could involve selecting the top n most similar training set examples based on a similarity score (e.g., using embeddings), but time constraints prevented us from testing this approach.

The results of the few-shot method were better than zero-shot – the macto F1 score reached 0.39, but you can see from Fig. 7 this method had a tendency to excessively classify examples into the "moderate depression" category.

Also, there are two apparent constraints of the few-shot learning method:

- **Size constraint**: The compact context window size precludes the usage of all examples from the training set in one prompt.
- **Cost constraint**: Being a commercial API, the more examples you utilize for each data point to be classified, the higher the cost.

### 4.2 Data Augmentation

We attempted to use non-textual features described in subsection 3.2. Due to limited time for this task, our first and quick attempt at using these features alone allowed us to achieve a macro F1 score of 0.43 (micro F1 score = 0.51). Nevertheless, the non-textual features did not provide any benefits when we combined them with the text features.

Two of the three categories in our dataset are underrepresented. To augment the minority classes, we performed data augmentation, adding 2800 new examples to the "severe depression" category and 1311 to the "no depression" category. For this, we deployed GPT-4, providing it with several training set examples from a specific category with similar lengths. The model was then instructed to generate approximately 25 more examples using semantically comparable language and within the same length of text.

We varied the ranges of text length for this exercise, selecting existing examples randomly. This method enabled a slight improvement in training our baseline model, though the uplift was marginal. The semantic similarity of the newly generated examples was validated by making sure their OpenAI embeddings stayed within a certain cosine similarity range when compared with existing examples.

Other types of augmented data that we tried to use as features included a title and a meaningful summary for each text generated by ChatGPT. However, these augmented data did not improve the final results either.

### 4.3 Improving Labels

After observing consistently low results in several experiments and noting that simple oversampling

| Classifier | Macro F1 | Micro F1 |
|---|---|---|
| Baseline on text | 0.5030 | 0.5696 |
| Baseline on numeric feat. | 0.4331 | 0.5127 |
| Text + numeric features | 0.4810 | 0.5628 |
| Baseline on text, cleaned labels | 0.5352 | 0.6094 |
| Zero-shot ChatGPT, cleaned labels | 0.2484 | 0.2560 |
| Few-shot ChatGPT, cleaned labels | 0.3885 | 0.5220 |
| Fine-tuned GPT-3, cleaned labels | 0.6018 | 0.6847 |

Table 1: Performance of Various Classifiers on Development Set

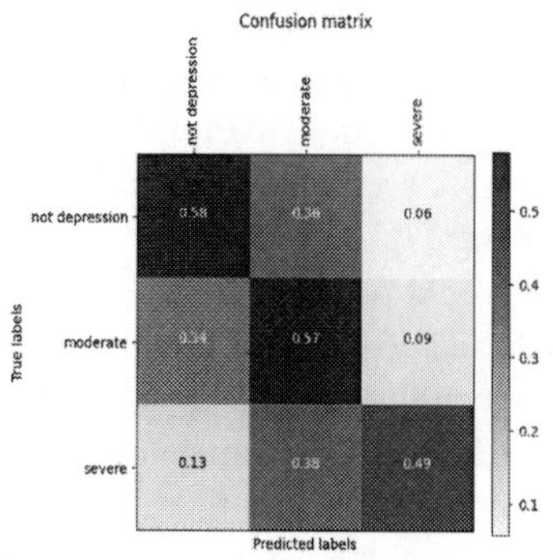


Figure 5: Confusion Matrix - Baseline Model

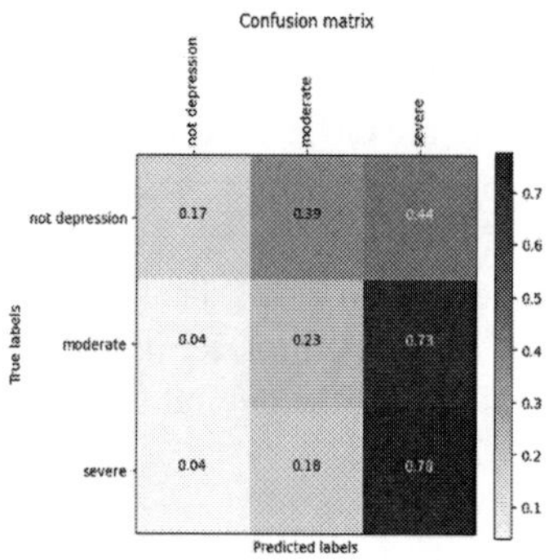


Figure 6: Confusion Matrix - Zero-Shot Learning with ChatGPT

yielded comparable low F1 scores even with data augmentation, we chose to investigate the dataset's annotation quality. As we lack expertise in clinical psychology or medicine, we refrained from verifying the "moderate depression" and "severe depression" labels. Instead, we scrutinized the "no depression" labels, searching for keywords such as "suicide" and its derivatives, "depress" and its derivatives, "harm myself", "anxiety", and so forth.

We identified approximately 450 texts in the training set and 165 texts in the development set that, to the best of our understanding and judgment, likely described some form of depression, as authors contemplated suicide or vividly discussed their depression. Several of these texts were so disheartening that we could not complete reading them. Training a baseline model without such data points, and testing it on the dev set that was pruned in a similar way, resulted in a 3% increase in the macro F1 score. Models in Table 1, trained without these data points, are designated as having "cleaned labels".

### 4.4 Model Comparison

The official competition metric for depression detection is the macro F1 score. Table 1 lists the macro and micro F1 scores for our models. All the scores in Table 1 are for the dev set. The best performing model shown in the last line of Table 1 scored 0.419 (macro F1) on the final blind test set. See Fig. 8 for the confusion matrix corresponding to the best model.

It is worth noting that the zero-shot learning method was outperformed by few-shot learning, but both of these methods scored below the baseline model. Fine-tuning a GPT-3 model demonstrated the best results on the dev set followed by the baseline model.

## 5 Conclusions

Our observations suggest that ChatGPT exhibits a degree of unpredictability, complicating the task of identifying a consistently effective configuration due to its dynamic nature. Hence, it is unsurprising that detecting depression using zero-shot and few-shot techniques proved challenging even for these cutting-edge models. In contrast, the largest fine-tunable OpenAI model, DaVinci, which is older and smaller than ChatGPT and lacks instruction following training, demonstrated superior efficiency for this task.

The fine-tuning capability addressed both few-shot learning constraints which we discussed in subsection 4.1. The model, while being fine-tuned, sees all the training set examples, and during inference, you are only charged for the tokens in the single example to be classified.

Also, if our doubts about the annotation quality

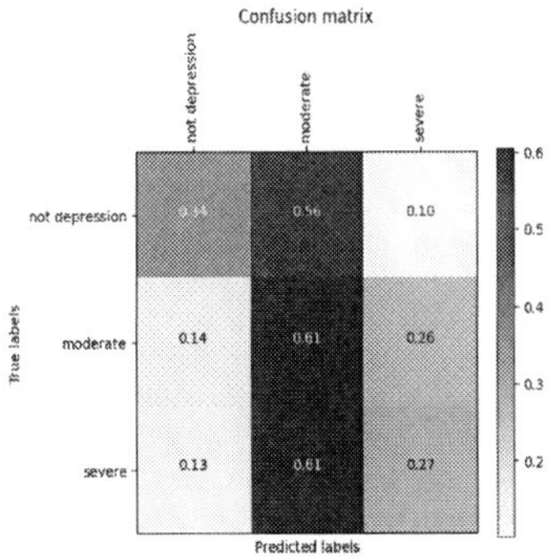


Figure 7: Confusion Matrix - Few-Shot Learning with ChatGPT

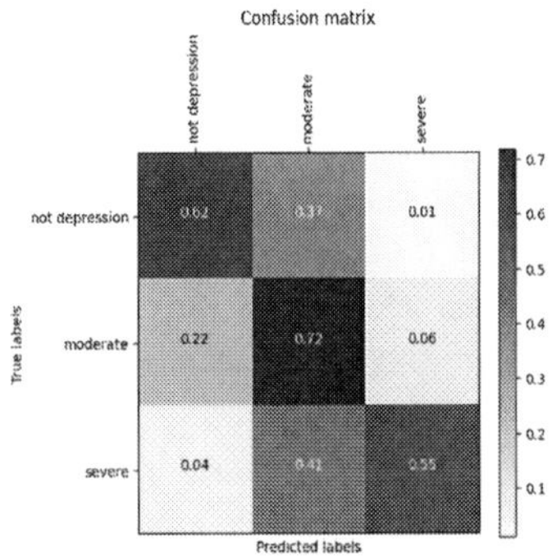


Figure 8: Confusion Matrix - GPT-3

are confirmed, then additional verification of the labels can significantly improve the classification results.

The exploration of non-textual features for depression detection warrants further study. Enhanced methods of aggregating numerical information from text could also contribute to improved classification outcomes.

## References

Mohammed Al-Mosaiwi. 2018. People with depression use language differently – here's how to spot it.

Mohammed Al-Mosaiwi and Tom Johnstone. 2018. In an absolute state: Elevated use of absolutist words is a marker specific to anxiety, depression, and suicidal ideation. *Clinical Psychological Science*, 6:529–542. PMID: 30886766.

MR Capecelatro, MD Sacchet, PF Hitchcock, SM Miller, and WB Britton. 2013. Major depression duration reduces appetitive word use: an elaborated verbal recall of emotional photographs. *Journal of psychiatric research*, 47:809–815.

Louisa Davis. 2020. How people with depression tend to speak differently. *The Mind's Journal.*

Jana M. Havigerová, Jirí Haviger, Dalibor Kucera, and Petra Hoffmannova. 2019. Text-based detection of the risk of depression. *Frontiers in Psychology*, 10.

S Kayalvizhi, Thenmozhi Durairaj, Bharathi Raja Chakravarthi, and C Jerin Mahibha. 2022. Findings of the shared task on detecting signs of depression from social media. In *Proceedings of the Second Workshop on Language Technology for Equality, Diversity and Inclusion*, pages 331–338. Association for Computational Linguistics.

Sampath Kayalvizhi, Thenmozhi Durairaj, Bharathi Raja Chakravarthi, C Jerin Mahibha, Kogilavani Shanmugavadivel, and Pratik Anil Rahood. 2023. Overview of the second shared task on detecting signs of depression from social media text. In *Proceedings of the Third Workshop on Language Technology for Equality, Diversity and Inclusion*, Varna, Bulgaria. Recent Advances in Natural Language Processing.

Atharva Kshirsagar, Shaily Desai, Aditi Sidnerlikar, Nikhil Khodake, and Manisha Marathe. 2022. Leveraging emotion-specific features to improve transformer performance for emotion classification. arXiv:2205.00283.

Ellen E. Newell, Shannon K. McCoy, Matthew L. Newman, Joseph D. Wellman, and Susan K. Gardner. 2018. You sound so down: Capturing depressed affect through depressed language. *Journal of Language and Social Psychology*, 37(4):451–474.

OpenAI. 2023. Gpt-4 technical report. arXiv:2303.08774.

# RANGANAYAKI@LT-EDI: Hope Speech Detection using Capsule Networks

**Ranganayaki E M, Abirami S, Lysa Packiam R S, Deivamani M**
Department of Information Science and Technology
College of Engineering Guindy
Anna University, Chennai, India
ranguem@gmail.com, abirami@auist.net, mailtolysa@gmail.com,
deivamani@auist.net

## Abstract

HOPE speeches convey uplifting and motivating messages that help enhance mental health and general well-being. Hope speech detection has gained popularity in the field of natural language processing as it gives people the motivation they need to face challenges in life. The momentum behind this technology has been fueled by the demand for encouraging reinforcement online. In this paper, a deep learning approach is proposed in which four different word embedding techniques are used in combination with capsule networks, and a comparative analysis is performed to obtain results. Oversampling is used to address class imbalance problem. The dataset used in this paper is a part of the LT-EDI RANLP 2023 Hope Speech Detection shared task. The approach proposed in this paper achieved a Macro Average F1 score of 0.49 and 0.62 on English and Hindi-English code mix test data, which secured 2nd and 3rd rank respectively in the above mentioned share task.

## 1 Introduction

In human life, hope plays a very vital role in healing, betterment and repairing oneself inside out. Hope speech reflects the belief that one can find ways to one's desired objectives and become motivated to utilize those ways. Social media platforms like Facebook and Instagram provide users with the opportunity to establish online communities comprising individuals who share common interests, values, or goals. These communities foster a profound sense of acceptance and belonging among their members (Sundar et al., 2022). This work aims to encourage a positive way of thinking by moving away from discrimination, loneliness, or other worst things in life to building confidence, support, and good qualities based on comments by individuals. The concept of hope typically encompasses promises, potential, support, comfort, recommendations, and inspiration, all of which are offered to individuals by their peers during challenging moments of illness, stress, loneliness, and sadness (Chakravarthi, 2020). Nevertheless, conventional approaches in natural language processing such as machine learning algorithms often fall short when it comes to accurately identifying hope speeches. Hence, there exists a critical need for innovative techniques that harness the power of deep learning, incorporating the latest advancements in the field. By leveraging these advanced techniques, we can strive to enhance the precision and effectiveness of hope speech detection, ultimately contributing to the improvement of mental health and overall well-being. This progress can be achieved through the dissemination of positive content across various online platforms, aiming to uplift individuals and promote a more optimistic outlook on life (Chakravarthi, 2022). By embracing these advancements, we can foster a society where hope thrives, enabling individuals to overcome challenges and embrace a brighter future.

## 2 Related Works

Works on Hope Speech detection have increased in recent times. Chakravarthi (2022) proposed a novel custom deep network architecture, which uses a concatenation of embedding from T5-Sentence. Eswar et al. (2022) experimented with the CNN+BiLSTM model for deep learning, with FastText, ELMo, and Keras embeddings. Demotte et al. (2021) (2021) proposed a method to use GloVe embeddings in shallow and deep capsule networks together with static and dynamic routing for sentiment analysis of tweets. Srinivasan and Subalalitha (2021) have proposed Levenshtein distance as the preprocessing technique for Tamil-English code-mixed data and also discussed the influence of using resampling techniques such as SMOTE



*LT-EDI 2023 – Third Workshop on Language Technology for Equality, Diversity and Inclusion*, pages 144–148, Varna, Bulgaria, Sep 7, 2023.
https://doi.org/10.26615/978-954-452-084-7_021

Table 1: Class Wise Distribution of Training, Validation and Test Dataset (Hindi-English Code Mix)

| Class | Train | Validation | Test |
|---|---|---|---|
| Hope-Speech | 343 | 45 | 53 |
| Non Hope-speech | 2219 | 275 | 268 |
| **Total** | 2562 | 320 | 321 |

Table 2: Class Wise Distribution of Training, Validation and Test Dataset (English)

| Class | Train | Validation | Test |
|---|---|---|---|
| Hope-speech | 1905 | 270 | 21 |
| Non Hope-speech | 20433 | 2534 | 4784 |
| **Total** | 22338 | 2804 | 4805 |

and ADASYN. Naseem et al. (2020) introduced a sentiment analysis framework known as $DICE_T$, which consists of three key components: an intelligent preprocessor, a text representation layer, and a bi-directional long- and short-term Memory (BiLSTM) integrated with attention modeling. In recent years many works are being carried out on Indian regional languages such as Hindi, and Tamil as well. Chakravarthi (2020) Chakravarthi (2022) has constructed a Hope Speech dataset that contains comments generated by YouTube users out of which 28451 comments are for English, 20198 for Tamil, and 10,705 comments for Malayalam respectively. All these comments were manually labeled as containing hope speech or not. In their study, Sundar et al. (2022) utilized a model based on stacked transformers for encoding, while also incorporating cross-lingual word embeddings.

## 3 Task and Dataset Overview

Dataset (Chakravarthi, 2020) used in this paper are provided by the Hope Speech Detection for Equality, Diversity, and Inclusion- LT-EDI-RANLP 2023 shared task. The objective of the shared task is to find hope in the text. The class labels are hope-speech and non-hope-speech. Each comment/post is assigned a class label. English and Hindi-English code mix data are considered in this work. A few weeks prior to the deadline for submitting the run, a testing dataset without labels was provided. The organizers later made available a labeled test dataset for verification purposes after the results were announced. Tables 1 and 2 present the sample counts for each class in the training, validation, and test sets.

## 4 Methodology

The overall architecture for Hope Speech Detection in English and Hindi-English code-mix is given in Figure 1.

### 4.1 Data cleaning and pre-processing

The English and Hindi-English code-mixed data is pre-processed before being converted into word embedding. The initial steps of pre-processing include lowercase conversion of the text, emoji-to-text conversion, user name removal and extra space removal. After the basic pre-processing is completed, spelling correction of misspelled words is performed on the English and Hindi-English code-mixed data. For spelling correction Levenshtein distance (Naseem et al., 2020) is used to find the distance between the correct and misspelled words. If the Levenshtein distance between the misspelled word and the correct word is 1 then the misspelled word is replaced with the correct word. A list of all possible English words is used to compare the words in training, validation, and testing data, to identify spelling mistakes using Levenshtein distance. Since there are no rules to govern the formation of Hinglish words, there cannot be any fixed vocabulary for Hinglish words. Hence the Vocabulary of Hindi and Hinglish words is created during training using all the Hindi and Hinglish words present in Hindi-English code-mix training data. These created vocabularies are used for checking and correcting spellings during testing, with respect to training data. The pre-processed text is fed into four different embedding models - FastText (Grave et al., 2018), ELMo (Peters et al., 2018), BERT (Devlin et al., 2019) and XLNet (Yang et al., 2019) respectively. Each vector representation has a different dimension and different ways of representing the input text. Since the data has high class imbalance, oversampling is performed in order to handle the class imbalance in the data. Over-sampling is done using ADASYN (He et al., 2008) oversampling method.

### 4.2 Classification model

The pre-processed and over-sampled word embedding is then fed into the capsule network (Sabour et al., 2017) to perform classification. Each of the embeddings is fed into a separate capsule network for training.

The capsule network has 5 layers, a convolution layer, a primary capsule layer, and three dense

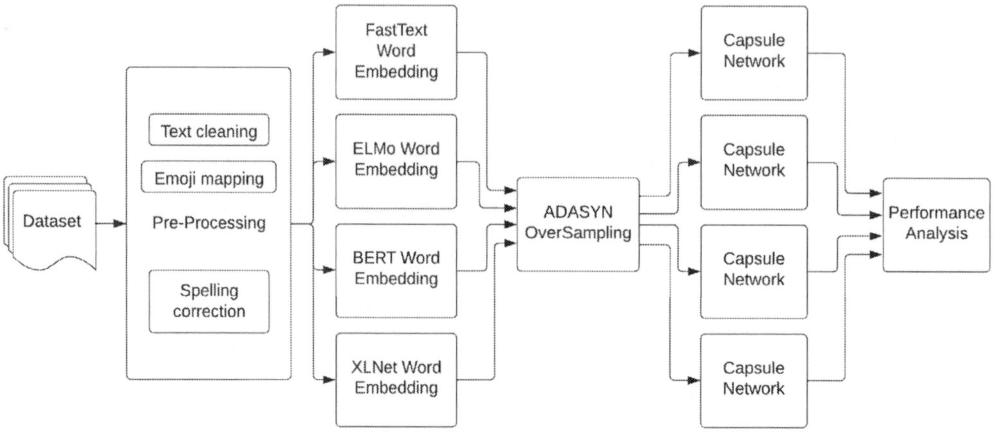


Figure 1: Hope Speech Detection Architecture

Table 3: parameters of Capsule Networks

| parameter | Value |
|---|---|
| $\epsilon$ | $1 \times 10^{-7}$ |
| $m_{plus}$ | 0.9 |
| $m_{minus}$ | 0.1 |
| $\lambda$ | 0.5 |
| $\alpha$ | 0.0005 |
| optimizer | Adam |

layers. Dynamic routing is used to determine the optimal routing of information between primary capsules and output capsules. It involves iterative communication between capsules, where the output of one capsule is weighted and passed as input to another capsule based on agreement scores. Each of the trained capsule networks is used to perform prediction to perform a comparative analysis on the embedding based on metrics such as accuracy, precision, recall, and F1 score. The parameters used are in Table 3.

## 5 Result and Analysis

After the implementation of the various modules, the results obtained detect the hope texts in the comments. The evaluation metrics taken into consideration are Accuracy, Macro-precision, Macro-recall, and Macro-F1-score. FastText word embedding combined with the capsule network produced better results than the other three embedding techniques - ELMo, BERT, and XLNet. It was also observed that over-sampling has increased the performance metrics along with preprocessing and spelling correction. Tables 4 and 5 show the performance of hope speech detection with respect to various embedding techniques used in English and Hindi-English code-mix validation data. Table 6 shows the performance of the combination of FastText and Capsule Network on test data. It has been observed that the combination outperforms the other embedding techniques in both datasets.

## 6 Conclusion

In this paper, a hope speech detection framework has been proposed by experimenting with four different embedding techniques combined with capsule networks. The preprocessing technique used to handle class imbalance and varied spelling corrections has effectively improved the performance of the proposed model. According to the analysis performed on the four word embedding techniques FastText has outperformed the other three models in terms of accuracy, macro average precision, recall, and F1 score. This is because the combination capsule network with FastText embedding preserves spatial information. The proposed model provides an accuracy and F1-score of 0.87 and 0.70 for the Hindi-English code-mix Validation data set and 0.90 and 0.65 for the English Validation data set. An accuracy and F1-score of 0.93 and 0.49 are obtained for the Hindi-English code-mix Test data set and 0.82 and 0.82 are obtained for the English Test data set respectively. In future, the work can be extended by further experimenting with different routing techniques of capsule network and other recent word embedding models.

Table 4: Performance Metrics of Hindi-English Code-Mix Validation Dataset

| Metrics | Fasttext | ELMo | BERT | XLNet |
|---|---|---|---|---|
| Accuracy | 0.87 | 0.82 | 0.81 | 0.86 |
| Precision | 0.68 | 0.61 | 0.62 | 0.50 |
| Recall | 0.72 | 0.62 | 0.61 | 0.43 |
| F1-Score | 0.70 | 0.62 | 0.62 | 0.46 |

Table 5: Performance Metrics of English Validation Dataset

| Metrics | Fasttext | ELMo | BERT | XLNet |
|---|---|---|---|---|
| Accuracy | 0.90 | 0.81 | 0.81 | 0.24 |
| Precision | 0.65 | 0.76 | 0.58 | 0.51 |
| Recall | 0.66 | 0.62 | 0.55 | 0.51 |
| F1-Score | 0.65 | 0.64 | 0.55 | 0.23 |

Table 6: Performance Metrics of Test Datasets using Fasttext and Capsule Network

| Language | Accuracy | Precision | Recall | F1-Score |
|---|---|---|---|---|
| English | 0.93 | 0.50 | 0.56 | 0.49 |
| Hindi-English Code-Mix | 0.82 | 0.64 | 0.60 | 0.82 |

## References


Bharathi Raja Chakravarthi. 2020. Hopeedi: A multilingual hope speech detection dataset for equality, diversity, and inclusion. In *Proceedings of the Third Workshop on Computational Modeling of People's Opinions, Personality, and Emotion's in Social Media*, pages 41–53.

Bharathi Raja Chakravarthi. 2022. Hope speech detection in youtube comments. *Social Network Analysis and Mining*, 12(1):75.

P Demotte, K Wijegunarathna, D Meedeniya, and I Perera. 2021. Enhanced sentiment extraction architecture for social media content analysis using capsule networks. *Multimedia tools and applications*, pages 1–26.

Jacob Devlin, Ming-Wei Chang, Kenton Lee, and Kristina Toutanova. 2019. BERT: Pre-training of deep bidirectional transformers for language understanding. In *Proceedings of the 2019 Conference of the North American Chapter of the Association for Computational Linguistics: Human Language Technologies, Volume 1 (Long and Short Papers)*, pages 4171–4186, Minneapolis, Minnesota. Association for Computational Linguistics.

Medicharla Dinesh Surya Sai Eswar, Nandhini Balaji, Vedula Sudhanva Sarma, Yarlagadda Chamanth Krishna, and S Thara. 2022. Hope speech detection in tamil and english language. In *2022 International Conference on Inventive Computation Technologies (ICICT)*, pages 51–56. IEEE.

Edouard Grave, Piotr Bojanowski, Prakhar Gupta, Armand Joulin, and Tomas Mikolov. 2018. Learning word vectors for 157 languages. In *Proceedings of the International Conference on Language Resources and Evaluation (LREC 2018)*.

Haibo He, Yang Bai, Edwardo A. Garcia, and Shutao Li. 2008. Adasyn: Adaptive synthetic sampling approach for imbalanced learning. In *2008 IEEE International Joint Conference on Neural Networks (IEEE World Congress on Computational Intelligence)*, pages 1322–1328.

Usman Naseem, Imran Razzak, Katarzyna Musial, and Muhammad Imran. 2020. Transformer based deep intelligent contextual embedding for twitter sentiment analysis. *Future Generation Computer Systems*, 113:58–69.

Matthew E. Peters, Mark Neumann, Mohit Iyyer, Matt Gardner, Christopher Clark, Kenton Lee, and Luke Zettlemoyer. 2018. Deep contextualized word representations.

Sara Sabour, Nicholas Frosst, and Geoffrey E Hinton. 2017. Dynamic routing between capsules. In *Advances in Neural Information Processing Systems*, volume 30. Curran Associates, Inc.

R Srinivasan and CN Subalalitha. 2021. Sentimental analysis from imbalanced code-mixed data using machine learning approaches. *Distributed and Parallel Databases*, pages 1–16.

Arunima Sundar, Akshay Ramakrishnan, Avantika Balaji, and Thenmozhi Durairaj. 2022. Hope speech detection for dravidian languages using cross-lingual embeddings with stacked encoder architecture. *SN Computer Science*, 3:1–15.

Zhilin Yang, Zihang Dai, Yiming Yang, Jaime Carbonell, Russ R Salakhutdinov, and Quoc V Le. 2019.

Xlnet: Generalized autoregressive pretraining for language understanding. In *Advances in Neural Information Processing Systems*, volume 32. Curran Associates, Inc.

# TechSSN1@LT-EDI: Depression Detection and Classification using BERT Model for Social Media Texts

**Venkatasai Ojus Yenumulapalli, Vijai Aravindh R, Rajalakshmi S, Angel Deborah S**
Department of Computer Science and Engineering,
Sri Sivasubramaniya Nadar College of Engineering, Chennai - 603110, Tamil Nadu, India
venkatasai2110272@ssn.edu.in, vijaiaravindh2110281@ssn.edu.in,
rajalakshmis@ssn.edu.in, angeldeborahs@ssn.edu.in

## Abstract

Depression is a severe mental health disorder characterized by persistent feelings of sadness and anxiety, a decline in cognitive functioning resulting in drastic changes in a human's psychological and physical well-being. However, depression is curable completely when treated at a suitable time and treatment resulting in the rejuvenation of an individual. The objective of this paper is to devise a technique for detecting signs of depression from English social media comments as well as classifying them based on their intensity into severe, moderate, and not depressed categories. The paper illustrates three approaches that are developed when working toward the problem. Of these approaches, the BERT model proved to be the most suitable model with an F1 macro score of 0.407, which gave us the $11^{th}$ rank overall.

## 1 Introduction

Depression has emerged as a significant mental health issue in recent years, affecting millions of individuals worldwide. Simultaneously, the use of social media platforms has skyrocketed, becoming an integral part of people's daily lives. Beck and Alford (2009) talks about the clinical causes of depression and the various treatments for it. Social media platforms provide individuals with an outlet to express their emotions and share personal experiences. Hammen (2005) examines the relationship between depression and stress over time including effects of childhood and lifetime stress exposure.

People often turn to these platforms as a means of seeking support, and validation, or simply as an avenue to connect with others who may be going through similar struggles. De Choudhury et al. (2013) conducted an analysis on various factors such as social engagement, emotion, language, and linguistic styles, as well as mentions of antidepressant medication. The purpose of this analysis was to develop a statistical classifier that can estimate the likelihood of experiencing depression.

The primary objective of the DepSign-LTEDI task (Sampath et al., 2023) is to identify indications of depression in individuals based on their social media posts, and analyze English-language social media content and classify the signs of depression into three categories, moderate, severe, and not depressed.

## 2 Related Work

Kayalvizhi and Thenmozhi (2022) developed a gold standard dataset in order to detect the various levels of depression namely moderate, severe, and not depressed using social media texts. Data augmentation techniques were applied to overcome data imbalance. Word2Vec vectorizer and Random Forest classifier model were used which provided better accuracy.

Salas-Zárate et al. (2022) employed Twitter as the primary data repository for depression sign detection. Word embeddings were used as the well-known technique for linguistic extraction. The machine-learning approach utilised was the support vector machine (SVM), and cross-validation (CV) was used to evaluate the outcomes.

Wang et al. (2022) principally used three approaches to meet the objective. The first method makes use of sentence embeddings for which VADER scores are generated following which they are passed into the gradient boosting model along with SMOTE augmentation techniques to combat data imbalance. The second technique centred on optimising pre-trained models using a multi-layer perceptron. The final technique used the multi-layer perceptron and VAD embeddings to classify the symptoms of depression.

Bucur and Dinu (2020) focused on the detection of the early onset of depression through the anal-



*LT-EDI 2023 – Third Workshop on Language Technology for Equality, Diversity and Inclusion*, pages 149–154, Varna, Bulgaria, Sep 7, 2023.
https://doi.org/10.26615/978-954-452-084-7_022

ysis of social media posts with special attention on Reddit. Topic modeling embeddings were extracted using a Latent Semantic Indexing Model and then provided as input to the neural network design. The neural network had two outputs - classifying whether the individual was depressed or not and estimating the confidence of the individual.

Trifan et al. (2020) used Reddit posts between January and October of 2016 as the source of the data. The data was pre-processed by being converted to lowercase and tokenized after any extraneous characters were eliminated. Multinomial Naive Bayes, Support Vector Machine in conjunction with Stochastic Gradient Descent, and Passive Aggressive classifiers were the final three classifiers used.

Rajalakshmi et al. (2018) developed a method to detect intensity levels of emotions with the help of rule-based feature selection using tweets as the primary data source. The input feature vectors were generated using one-hot encoding and rule-based feature selection. The model for the detection of emotional intensity classification was Multilayer Perceptron. The models for the subtasks of sentiment intensity regression and emotion intensity regression was constructed using Support Vector Regression. Anantharaman et al. (2022) and Esackimuthu et al. (2022) used transformer models to detection the depression from social media tweets and achieved F1 score of 0.412 and 0.473 respectively.

## 3 Dataset

The dataset consists of the posting id, text data, and the corresponding label (S et al., 2022). The dataset provides three labels representing the various degrees of depression namely severe, moderate, and no depression. Table 1 illustrates the distribution of the dataset.

| Label | Train | Dev | Test |
|---|---|---|---|
| Not Depressed | 2755 | 848 | 135 |
| Moderate | 3678 | 2169 | 275 |
| Severe | 768 | 228 | 89 |

Table 1: Distribution of Data

## 4 Depression Detection System

We have employed three different models in the three test runs , in this respective order:

**BERT**: We employed the 'bert-base-uncased' pre-trained model, known as BERT (Bidirectional Encoder Representations from Transformers), as the foundation for this depression analysis task. To tailor BERT to the specific given depression dataset, fine-tuning of the BERT model is done through training using the labeled train data. Additionally, to ensure compatibility with the model, a label encoder is utilized to convert the target labels into numerical values. Table 2 gives the evaluation metrics of BERT model for the development dataset.

**Word2Vec and SVC**: In this approach, Word2Vec, a technique that generates word embeddings - distributed numerical representations of word features is used for text-vector representation. These embeddings capture the contextual meaning of words within vocabulary and enable the model to identify semantic relationships among words that share similar meanings. To leverage the power of these word vectors, a classification model Support Vector Classifier (SVC) is employed to train on and predict using these word embeddings. Table 3 gives the evaluation metrics for the development dataset.

**TFIDF-LinearSVC**: LinearSVC is a machine learning algorithm implemented in Python's scikit-learn library, based on the Support Vector Machine (SVM) algorithm. LinearSVC aims to find a linear decision boundary that maximizes the margin between different classes. The model learns a set of weights for each feature and combines them linearly to make predictions. To vectorize the given texts, TfidfVectorizer is used, which converts text into numerical feature vectors. Subsequently, LinearSVC model is fitted to these vectors. Table 4 gives the evaluation metrics of this model for the development dataset.

| Metrics | Score |
|---|---|
| Accuracy | 0.67 |
| Macro Precision | 0.57 |
| Macro Recall | 0.54 |
| Macro F1-score | 0.55 |
| Weighted precision | 0.65 |
| Weighted recall | 0.67 |
| Weighted F1-score | 0.66 |

Table 2: Evaluation metrics of BERT

| Parameters | Score |
|---|---|
| Accuracy | 0.66 |
| Macro Precision | 0.58 |
| Macro Recall | 0.44 |
| Macro F1-score | 0.47 |
| Weighted precision | 0.64 |
| Weighted recall | 0.66 |
| Weighted F1-score | 0.64 |

Table 3: Evaluation metrics of Word2Vec-SVC

| Parameters | Score |
|---|---|
| Accuracy | 0.60 |
| Macro Precision | 0.51 |
| Macro Recall | 0.49 |
| Macro F1-score | 0.50 |
| Weighted precision | 0.63 |
| Weighted recall | 0.60 |
| Weighted F1-score | 0.61 |

Table 4: Evaluation Metrics of TFIDF-LinearSVC

## 5 Methodology

The codes utilized in this research paper are available within the GitHub repository GitHub Repository. This repository contains a collection of Jupyter Notebook files that correspond to the methodologies and techniques detailed in the paper.

The methodology employed in this paper consists of three approaches. The first method makes use of the Bidirectional Encoder Representations from Transformers (BERT) "bert-base-uncased" pre-trained model. The BERT model was tailored to the dataset provided. The dataset was tokenized, and converted into the input features with the assistance of the BERT tokenizer. No pre-processing steps were undertaken in this model. Following this, the input features and labels were converted to tensors, and the TensorDataset was created. The model was trained for three epochs using the optimizer AdamW, which has a learning rate of 2e-5. Finally, cross-validation was performed with the help of the development data for fine tuning the trained model and tested on the test data. Figure 1 shows the work flow of the system.

The second approach involved the usage of Word2Vec and Support Vector Classification (SVC). Word embedding is a method in which words are converted into an arithmetic representation termed a vector and each word in a sentence can be represented through this vector. These vectors capture the semantic relationships between words and can be used to assess the similarity and dissimilarity between words. The Word2Vec API trained on Google News was used to generate the word embeddings for the given data. The pre-processing step removed stop words and punctuation, lemmatized the remaining tokens, and returned the average word vector representation using spaCy's word embeddings. If no valid tokens remain, it returns a default zero vector. The Word2Vec makes use of two architectures namely bag-of-words and skip-gram. However, the word embeddings generated in this model do not strictly follow the aforementioned architectures. The Support Vector Classification is a machine learning classification algorithm that is often used to classify data with multiple labels. The generated word embedding was then fed into the Support Vector Classification model to obtain the classified results. Figure 2 shows the working of this system.

The LinearSVC and TF-IDF Vectorizer are used in the final strategy. Similar to the Word2Vec model, the Term Frequency-Inverse Document Fre-

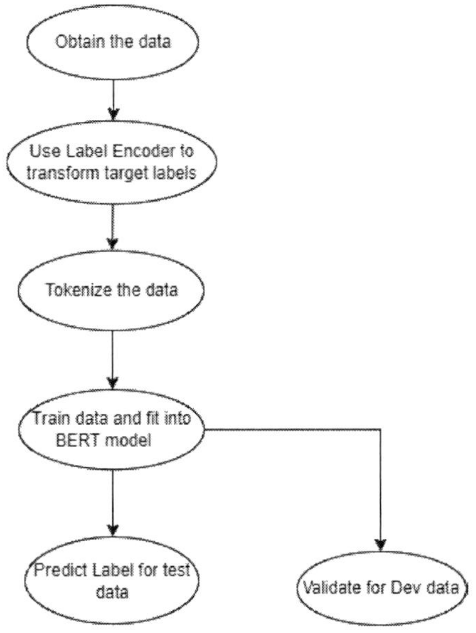


Figure 1: Flowchart for BERT

| Parameters | Score |
|---|---|
| Number of epochs | 1 |
| Batch size | 16 |
| Learning rate | 2e-5 |
| Maximum sequence length | 512 |

Table 5: Hyperparameters: BERT

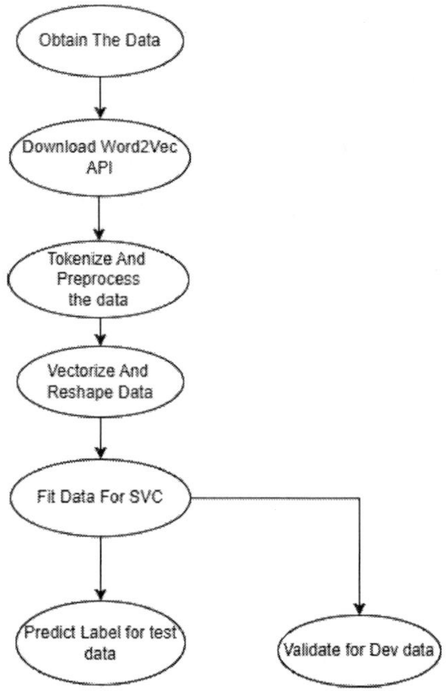


Figure 2: Flowchart for Word2Vec and SVC

quency text vectorizer combines the concepts of term frequency (TF) and document frequency (DF). No pre-processing steps were undertaken in this model. The term frequency is an indication of the frequency count of words in a document and gives an idea about the importance of a given word. The quantity of documents that use a particular term is known as the document frequency. LinearSVC is a machine learning algorithm implemented in Python's scikit-learn library, based on the Support Vector Machine (SVM) algorithm that aims to find a linear decision boundary that maximizes the margin between different classes. Figure 3 depicts the steps in developing this model.

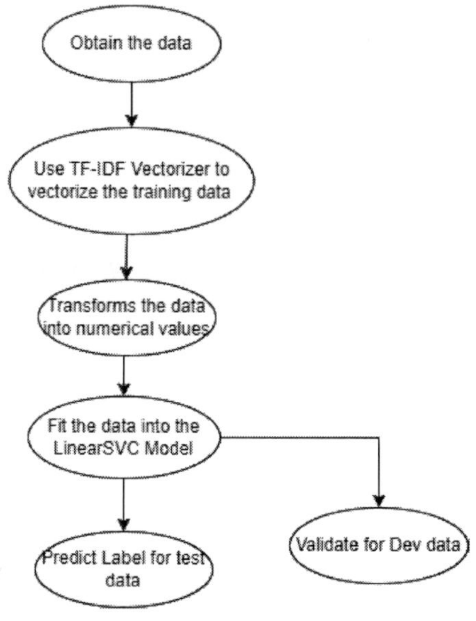


Figure 3: Flowchart for TFIDF Vectorizer and Linear SVC

## 6 Results

### 6.1 Test Data Results

Out of the three above-mentioned models, the BERT model gave the highest F1-score of 0.407 for the predicted labels on the test data the organizers gave, and an accuracy of 55 percent. On further analysis, the following metrics were obtained for the three models. Tables 6, 7 and 8 show the evaluation metrics value for accuracy, precision, recall and F1 score.

It is inferred from the results that SVC could not perform well when compared to the BERT model. This is our maiden attempt for applying the machine learning algorithms for a real life problem in the form of a challenge. We assume that the performance of the BERT model can be increased by training the model for more number of epochs.

| Parameters | Score |
|---|---|
| Accuracy | 0.55 |
| Macro Precision | 0.54 |
| Macro Recall | 0.42 |
| Macro F1-score | 0.41 |
| Weighted precision | 0.55 |
| Weighted recall | 0.55 |
| Weighted F1-score | 0.50 |

Table 6: Evaluation Metrics for Test Data: BERT

## 7 Conclusion

In conclusion, an analysis was experimented with the provided social media texts using three models: BERT, Word2Vec with SVC, and TF-IDF with LinearSVC. Among these models, BERT demonstrated the highest accuracy in predicting the target labels. It is worth noting that accurately analyzing and predicting signs of depression is challenging for any model, as it may struggle to comprehend the deeper layers of a sentence and grasp the nuanced tone of the text.

Improving the accuracy of the model can be achieved by ensuring a more balanced distribution of the dataset, where the number of cases for all three target labels is nearly equal. This would help

| Parameters | Score |
|---|---|
| Accuracy | 0.46 |
| Macro Precision | 0.47 |
| Macro Recall | 0.39 |
| Macro F1-score | 0.37 |
| Weighted precision | 0.49 |
| Weighted recall | 0.46 |
| Weighted F1-score | 0.44 |

Table 7: Evaluation Metrics for Test Data: LinearSVC and TFIDF

| Parameters | Score |
|---|---|
| Accuracy | 0.52 |
| Macro Precision | 0.65 |
| Macro Recall | 0.38 |
| Macro F1-score | 0.35 |
| Weighted precision | 0.59 |
| Weighted recall | 0.52 |
| Weighted F1-score | 0.46 |

Table 8: Evaluation Metrics for Test Data: Word2Vec and SVC

prevent biases and provide a more comprehensive understanding of different degrees of depression.

Moving forward, our aim is to advance our knowledge in the field of Natural Language Processing (NLP) by exploring various models and implementing them in different use cases to analyze signs of depression from social media texts effectively.In addition,we have planned to work on the various variants of BERT models for better understanding, such as DistilBERT. By undertaking such endeavors, we can enhance our understanding and contribute to the development of more robust and accurate NLP techniques in detecting mental health conditions.

## References


Karun Anantharaman, S Rajalakshmi, S Angel Deborah, M Saritha, and R Sakaya Milton. Ssn_mlrg1@ lt-edi-acl2022: Multi-class classification using bert models for detecting depression signs from social media text. *LTEDI 2022*, page 296, 2022.

Aaron T Beck and Brad A Alford. *Depression: Causes and treatment*. University of Pennsylvania Press, 2009.

Ana-Maria Bucur and Liviu P Dinu. Detecting early onset of depression from social media text using learned confidence scores. *arXiv preprint arXiv:2011.01695*, 2020.

Munmun De Choudhury, Michael Gamon, Scott Counts, and Eric Horvitz. Predicting depression via social media. In *Proceedings of the international AAAI conference on web and social media*, volume 7, pages 128–137, 2013.

Sarika Esackimuthu, H Shruthi, Rajalakshmi Sivanaiah, S Angel Deborah, R Sakaya Milton, and TT Mirnalinee. Ssn_mlrg3@ lt-edi-acl2022-depression detection system from social media text using transformer models. *LTEDI 2022*, page 196, 2022.

Constance Hammen. Stress and depression. *Annu. Rev. Clin. Psychol.*, 1:293–319, 2005.

S Kayalvizhi and D Thenmozhi. Data set creation and empirical analysis for detecting signs of depression from social media postings. *arXiv preprint arXiv:2202.03047*, 2022.

S Rajalakshmi, S Milton Rajendram, TT Mirnalinee, et al. Ssn mlrg1 at semeval-2018 task 1: Emotion and sentiment intensity detection using rule based feature selection. In *Proceedings of the 12th international workshop on semantic evaluation*, pages 324–328, 2018.

Kayalvizhi S, Thenmozhi Durairaj, Bharathi Raja Chakravarthi, and Jerin Mahibha C. Findings of the shared task on detecting signs of depression from social media. In *Proceedings of the Second Workshop on Language Technology for Equality, Diversity and Inclusion*, Dublin, Ireland, May 2022. Association for Computational Linguistics. doi: 10.18653/v1/2022.ltedi-1.51. URL `https://aclanthology.org/2022.ltedi-1.51`.

Rafael Salas-Zárate, Giner Alor-Hernández, María del Pilar Salas-Zárate, Mario Andrés Paredes-Valverde, Maritza Bustos-López, and José Luis Sánchez-Cervantes. Detecting depression signs on social media: a systematic literature review. In *Healthcare*, volume 10, page 291. MDPI, 2022.

Kayalvizhi Sampath, Thenmozhi Durairaj, Bharathi Raja Chakravarthi, Jerin Mahibha C, Kogilavani Shanmugavadivel, and Pratik Anil Rahood. Overview of the second shared task on detecting signs of depression from social media text. In *Proceedings of the Third Workshop on Language Technology for Equality, Diversity and Inclusion*, Varna, Bulgaria, 2023. Recent Advances in Natural Language Processing.

Alina Trifan, Rui Antunes, Sérgio Matos, and Jose Luís Oliveira. Understanding depression from psycholinguistic patterns in social media texts. In *Advances in Information Retrieval: 42nd European Conference on IR Research, ECIR 2020, Lisbon, Portugal, April 14–17, 2020, Proceedings, Part II 42*, pages 402–409. Springer, 2020.

Wei-Yao Wang, Yu-Chien Tang, Wei-Wei Du, and Wen-Chih Peng. Nycu_twd@ lt-edi-acl2022: Ensemble models with vader and contrastive learning for detecting signs of depression from social media. In *Proceedings of the Second Workshop on Language Technology for Equality, Diversity and Inclusion*, pages 136–139, 2022.

# SANBAR@LT-EDI-2023:Automatic Speech Recognition: vulnerable old-aged and transgender people in Tamil

**S Saranya & B Bharathi**
Computer Science and Engineering Department
Sri Siva Subramaniya Nadar College of Engineering
Kalavakkam - 603110
saranyascse@ssn.edu.in & bharathib@ssn.edu.in

## Abstract

An Automatic Speech Recognition systems for Tamil are designed to convert spoken language or speech signals into written Tamil text. Seniors go to banks, clinics and authoritative workplaces to address their regular necessities. A lot of older people are not aware of the use of the facilities available in public places or office. They need a person to help them. Likewise, transgender people are deprived of primary education because of social stigma, so speaking is the only way to help them meet their needs. In order to build speech enabled systems, spontaneous speech data is collected from seniors and transgender people who are deprived of using these facilities for their own benefit. The proposed system is developed with pretraind models are IIT Madras transformer ASR model and akashsivanandan/wav2vec2-large-xls-r-300m-tamil model. Both pretrained models are used to evaluate the test speech utterances, and obtained the WER as 37.7144% and 40.55% respectively.

## 1 Introduction

The earliest known Old Tamil inscriptions are found in Adichanallur and date back to the period between 905 BC and 696 BC. These inscriptions provide valuable insights into the early stages of the Tamil language.Tamil employs an agglutinative grammar system. This means that suffixes are attached to words to convey various grammatical features, such as noun class, number, case, verb tense, and other categories. Tamil's historical significance and linguistic features make it a fascinating language with a rich cultural heritage. Now a days all the people are using internet for their everyday needs. Especially old-aged and transgender who are deprived of education due to prejudice of social. So speech is only tool to do their own needs. In the present situation all people are using smartphones to do their daily needs without any direct visits to bank, hospital, etc. The integration of a voice and speech recognition system in Tamil would be highly advantageous for native Tamil users who encounter difficulties with default foreign languages on their smartphones (Kiran et al., 2017). It would elevate their user experience, facilitate accessibility, boost productivity, uphold the language's preservation, and encourage the creation of localized applications. In (Madhavaraj and Ramakrishnan, 2019), two approaches were employed to improve automatic speech recognition (ASR) for Gujarati, Tamil, and Telugu languages. The first approach involved data-pooling and phone mapping, which combined the data by mapping phones from the source languages to the target language. The second approach utilized a multi-task deep neural network (DNN) with a modified loss function to train the ASR model using the pooled data. This technique achieved relative reductions in the WERs. (Kwon et al., 2016)Because of the impact of speech articulation and speaking tendencies, older individuals tend to exhibit slower speech rates, longer pauses between syllables, and slightly reduced speech clarity. Smart devices are now not only extensively used by the younger generation but also by seniors, both indoors and outdoors throughout the day. Thus, we concluded that implementing a speech-recognition interface within a smart device could enhance its user-friendliness for the elderly and transgender. This feature would be particularly valuable for senior citizens during critical scenarios, including emergencies or situations where they might be physically restricted due to a traumatic event. Numerous seniors encounter uncertainty when attempting to utilize the provided devices meant to aid them. Similarly, transgender individuals, due to societal discrimination, are often deprived of access to primary education, leaving speech as their sole means of addressing their requirements. The information pertaining to natural speech is gathered from elderly and transgender individuals who are unable to avail themselves of



*LT-EDI 2023 – Third Workshop on Language Technology for Equality, Diversity and Inclusion*, pages 155–160, Varna, Bulgaria, Sep 7, 2023.
https://doi.org/10.26615/978-954-452-084-7_023

such assistance.

The paper is organized as follows: the following section gives a detailed description of pretrained models used for our proposed work. Section 2 discusses the related work previously done for our current work. Section 3 detailed description of the data set used for this work. Discusses on the recognition system and the various approaches used for this work. Section 4 explains in detail the pretrained models used for the proposed work. Section 6 discusses on the results. Section 7 analysis on the performance of each pretrained model. Section 8 concludes the paper and discusses the areas of further improvement.

## 2 Related Work

The ASR system, which involves fine-tuning a pretrained Wav2Vec2.0 XLSR model with CTC (Connectionist Temporal Classification), has been successfully developed. This system demonstrates the ability to recognize speech samples and provide accurate transcriptions. The average Word Error Rate (WER) achieved by the system is 0.58, indicating a relatively low rate of transcription errors. Similarly, the Character Error Rate (CER) is 0.11(Akhilesh et al., 2022). In this paper, (Rojathai and Venkatesulu, 2014), have PAC features were extracted from input speech samples,the extracted features are Energy entropy, Zero crossing rate and short time energy. The extracted PAC features were trained by ANFIS system. The process of recognition performance is validated based on test words.This proposed method gave better results with different noise levels compared to previous methods. In this work (Martin et al., 2015) Show the features extraction based on English phonemes and language-independent inferred phones (IPs). The Tamil language-independent inferred phones (IPs) are achieved better performance. But it has less number of speakers, So increasing number of speakers to the model training to avoid over-fitting. (Thamburaj et al., 2021), were presented the Deep Neural Network and Membrane Bio Reactor design for Tamil. A single vowel sound were linked with Five different mono phones. The transcription was linked with LM (Language Model). So that it will decrease the impact of domain difference in AM. The target of this work is preprocess the data in order to remove noise and improve BRNN-SOM classification method scheme gains high-accuracy. SGf method was use for removing noise present in the speech samples. We achieve highest SNR values. Preprocessing technique(Lokesh et al., 2019). (S and N, 2017), show Reduce the feature vector dimension reduction using Linear Discriminant Analysis(LDA). LDA method is perform great when compared to all other well known dimensionality reduction methods like, PCA, MDS, LLE. Deep Speech architecture is used by (Changrampadi et al., 2022) and achieves 24% WER. The accuracy depends on the training language model. Tamil dialect recognition required to be regionally based spoken Tamil data to build independent Tamil recognition system. (Nivetha S, 2020), explain the speech recognition system used Random forest algorithm to identify isolated Tamil word. Both MFCC and LPC features are extracted from speech data. This algorithm gave better result and took less time for training model building. In this work, (Radha et al., 2012) show the HMM based model used to build the speaker independent isolated Tamil words recognition. Its achieved 88% accuracy and 0.88 WER. But data set size is minimal only 2500 words are used in this recognition system. In this task, (Chakravarthi, 2020) author used 20,198 Tamil comments collected from YouTube. Its includes women in STEM, LGBTIQ issues, COVID-19, India China war and affairs of Dravidian from YouTube comments. This data has two or more languages used by a single speaker. The data set is code mixed. Naive Bayes, KNN, and SVM, logistic regression used to train the model and use held-out test set to evaluate the trained model. Evaluate the trained model. The result is shown using precision, recall, F1-score. Findings of the automatic speech recognition for vulnerable individuals are given in (Bharathi et al., 2022). (S and B, 2022) (B et al., 2022), have pretrained Rajaram1996/wav2vec-large-xlsr-53-tamil transformer model used for transformer based ASR for Vulnerable Individuals in Tamil. In this pretained model gave 39.65% WER.

## 3 Data Set Description

Tamil speech utterances are collected from the old-aged people and transgender whose mother tongue is Tamil. The recorded speech utterances of old-aged people and transgender contains how those people communicate in primary locations like bank, hospitals and administrative office.The data set contains 51 Speakers of literates, illiterates elders and transgenders. People who have their primary education till sixth grade are considered literates while collecting data. The duration of corpus is 7 hours and 30 minutes. It is ensured that no audio recorded from an individual is less than 5 minutes. No interruption or overlap of other person voices in the audio other than the speaker's audio. The speech files in the directories are in the WAV format. The sampling rate of the speech utterances are 44kHz. The speech corpus with 5.5 hours of transcribed speech will be released for the training, and 2 hours of speech data will be released for testing. Table 1. shows that detailed description about the collected speech utterances. More information about data collection is explained in (B et al., 2023).

| Speakers | Literate | Illiterate | Total |
|---|---|---|---|
| Male | 4 | 9 | 13 |
| Female | 7 | 24 | 31 |
| Transgender | 3 | 4 | 7 |

Table 1: Detailed Description of speech corpus

## 4 Proposed Work

Our proposed work, transformer model of IIT Madras and transformer model akashsivanandan/wav2vec2-large-xls-r-300m-tamil-colab-final are used. The ASR model for Indian languages described in the transformer ASR model is created by IIT Madras follows a espnet.nets.pytorch_backend.e2e_asr_transformer, E2Eself-attention mechanism architecture. The following stages are performed in ESPnet transformer architecture.

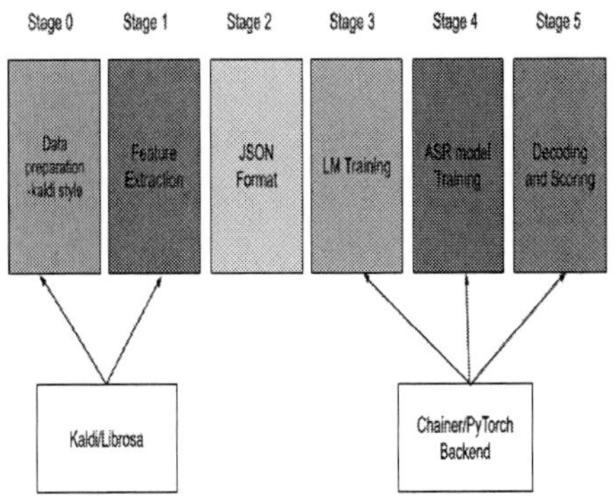


Figure 1: Architecture of ESPnet Transformer Model

- Stage 0: Preprocessing the speech data including transcription and dictionary creation.
- Stage 1: Extract the features from the speech data using Kaldi toolkit.
- Stage 2: Create a JSON configuration file to specify the details of the data preparation. This file should include paths to of the audio and transcript files, as well as other parameters like sampling rate, the language of the text, etc, are dumped.
- Stage 3: Training the language model.
- Stage 4: Train the acoustic model using the preprocessed data. Include the details such as the number of epochs, batch size, learning rate, etc.
- Stage 5: Evaluate the trained model on the test speech utterances.

The transformer model akashsivanandan/wav2vec2-large-xls-r-300m-tamil model is a variant of the Wav2Vec2 architecture that has been fine-tuned specifically for the Tamil language. The model has been trained in an unsupervised learning manner, it means the model doesn't need explicit transcriptions. The model was pre-trained using speech signal from multiple sources including Babel, Multilingual LibriSpeech (MLS), Common Voice, VoxPopuli, and VoxLingua107. The sampling rate of The original Common Voice dataset is 48kHz. However, training the XLSR model, To ensure compatibility with the XLSR model's 16kHz sampling rate, the Common Voice data was resampled and adjusted from its original 48kHz sampling rate to the desired 16kHz sampling rate. This downsampling process was implemented to align the data with the model's requirements.

## 5 Implementation

The one of the pretrained model used in our proposed work is "akashsivanandan/wav2vec2-large-xls-r-300m-tamil". This is model is fine tuned the XLSR model using the common voice Tamil speech corpus. The other model used in the proposed system is "IIT Madras transformer ASR model". The IIT Madras transformer ASR model is created using ESPnet transformer model:E2Eself-attention mechanism employs Language model

| 1 | Transformer ASR model IIT Madras | Target Speech | டாக்டர் எத்தனை மணிக்கு வருவாங்க சார்.<br>டாக்டர பாக்கலாமா, இல்ல டோக்கன்<br>போட்டு தான் வரணுமா, இல்ல கியூல<br>இருப்பாங்களா. எத்தனை மணி வரை டாக்டர்<br>இருப்பாங்க. சாந்தரத்துல இருந்தே இல்ல<br>நைட் எத்தனை மணி வரயும் ஹாஸ்பிடல்<br>இருக்கும். பீஸு எவ்ளோ பீஸ் எவ்ளோ |
|---|---|---|---|
| | | Predicted Speech | டாக்டர் எத்தனை மணிக்கு வருவாங்க சார்<br>டாக்டர் பாக்கலாமா? இல்ல டோக்கன்<br>போட்டுத்தான் வரணுமா இல்ல கூல<br>இருப்பாங்களா எத்தனை மணி வரை டாக்டர்<br>இருப்பாங்க சாந்தரத்திலிருந்து இல்ல<br>நைட்டி எத்தனை மணி வரை ஹாஸ்பிடல்<br>இருக்கும் சீஸ் எவ்ளோ பிசி எவ்வளவு |
| 2 | akashsivanandan/wav2vec2-large-xls-r-300m-tamil-colab-final | Target Speech | டாக்டர் எத்தனை மணிக்கு வருவாங்க சார்.<br>டாக்டர பாக்கலாமா, இல்ல டோக்கன்<br>போட்டு தான் வரணுமா, இல்ல கியூல<br>இருப்பாங்களா. எத்தனை மணி வரை டாக்டர்<br>இருப்பாங்க. சாந்தரத்துல இருந்தே இல்ல<br>நைட் எத்தனை மணி வரயும் ஹாஸ்பிடல்<br>இருக்கும். பீஸு எவ்ளோ பீஸ் எவ்ளோ |
| | | Predicted Speech | கு தர்று எ்ன மணிக்கி வாருவாங்க<br>தார்றறப்பார்களாவா லெட்டோகொண்<br>கொடுதா வர்கமபா ற்கூள<br>இருப்பாங்களற்றமணி வரைடர்க்க<br>இருப்பர்கதாந்தர்ககங்க இலநை<br>எத்னமணிவரைா◌ெர்ட்லருகோபீர்எவளோ<br>பீசியவல |

Figure 2: Sample recognised text using proposed system

has a 12-layer encoder and a variable decoder. Each encoder layer incorporates self-attention and 2048 units of a feed-forward neural network and ReLU activation. The decoder comprises six layers for Indian languages, each featuring self-attention and a 2048-unit feed-forward network. For Voxforge, there is a single layer with a 1024-unit feed-forwaProceedings of the Second Workshop on Language Technology for Equality, Diversity and Inclusionrd network. 104.5 hours of Tamil Speech data used for training, and unified processor was used to generate lexicon.

The model akashsivanandan/wav2vec2-large-xls-r-300m-tamil pretrained model used for testing the spoken Tamil speech data. This pretrained model is tuned by facebook/wav2vec2-large-xlsr-r-300m-tamil using common voice Tamil data. Wav2Vec2 uses a combination of convolutional neural networks (CNNs) and self-attention mechanisms to learn speech representations from raw audio waveform. By CNNs, it can extract local acoustic features, while self-attention mechanisms enable it to capture long-range dependencies in the audio data. It can cognizant and process Tamil speech data efficacious. The model take advantage of a fusion of CNN and self-attention mechanisms to learn powerful representations from raw audio waveform. It has a larger capacity, allowing it to capture complex patterns in the audio data. In this model learning rate is 0.0003, training batch size and testing batch size are 16 and 8. optimizer: Adam with betas=(0.9,0.999) and epsilon=1e-08 are used for training. The speech corpus has 239 speech files for testing. The test speech data is given as input to the both the pretrained system. Once the speech recognition is completed the output text transcription stored in a individual file. Finally WER is calculated based on what transcription got from recognition and target transcription of the speech data which is used for testing.

## 6 Results

The word error rate (WER) is calculated using the following equation,

$$WER = \left(\frac{S + I + D}{N}\right) \quad (1)$$

where as,

- S is the number of substitutions

- D is the number of deletions
- I is the number of insertions
- N is the number of words in the reference transcriptions

| S.no | Model | WER |
|---|---|---|
| 1 | Transformer model of IITM | 37.71 |
| 2 | akashsivanandan/wav2vec2-large-xls-r-300m-tamil-colab-final | 40.55 |

Table 2: Performance of the proposed system using test utterances

## 7 Discussion

From Table 2, both the pretrained model results are shown. The IIT Madras transformer ASR model WER is 37.71%. akashsivanandan/wav2vec2-large-xls-r-300m-tamil-colab-final model WER is 40.55%. IIT Madras transformer ASR model gave a better result compared to another one. akashsivanandan/wav2vec2-large-xls-r-300m-tamil-colab-final does not have language model. However IIT Madras transformer ASR has a language model (LM). LM is used to boost recognition system should help the acoustic model. For example "Enkengu" word is correctly predicted by a model which has LM, in other hand "Enkengu" word predicted as "Enkanku". It shows that LM and region-based spoken Tamil data are used to develop a better recognition ASR system.

## 8 Conclusions

An automatic speech recognition system is developed with a pretrained fine tune models which is available publicly. The speech data is collected from old-aged people and transgender whose mother tongue is Tamil. The speech data contains how the people access primary location in day to day life. Evaluate the test speech samples using pretrained models and calculated WERs. Going forward, increase speech data and create our own training model with more region-based Tamil speech data. This will enhance the performance of the proposed system.

## References


A Akhilesh, P Brinda, S Keerthana, Deepa Gupta, and Susmitha Vekkot. 2022. Tamil speech recognition using xlsr wav2vec2. 0 & ctc algorithm. In *2022 13th International Conference on Computing Communication and Networking Technologies (ICCCNT)*, pages 1–6. IEEE.

Bharathi B, Bharathi Raja Chakravarthi, Subalalitha Chinnaudayar Navaneethakrishnan, Sripirya N, Rajeswari Natarajan, Suhasini S, and Swetha Valli. 2023. Overview of the second shared task on speech recognition for vulnerable individuals in tamil. In *Proceedings of the Third Workshop on Speech and Language Technologies for Dravidian Languages*, Varna, Bulgaria. Recent Advances in Natural Language Processing.

Bharathi B, Dhanya Srinivasan, Josephine Varsha, Thenmozhi Durairaj, and Senthil Kumar B. 2022. SSNCSE_NLP@LT-EDI-ACL2022:hope speech detection for equality, diversity and inclusion using sentence transformers. In *Proceedings of the Second Workshop on Language Technology for Equality, Diversity and Inclusion*, pages 218–222, Dublin, Ireland. Association for Computational Linguistics.

B Bharathi, Bharathi Raja Chakravarthi, Subalalitha Chinnaudayar Navaneethakrishnan, N Sripriya, Arunaggiri Pandian, and Swetha Valli. 2022. Findings of the shared task on Speech Recognition for Vulnerable Individuals in Tamil. In *Proceedings of the Second Workshop on Language Technology for Equality, Diversity and Inclusion*. Association for Computational Linguistics.

Bharathi Raja Chakravarthi. 2020. HopeEDI: A multilingual hope speech detection dataset for equality, diversity, and inclusion. In *Proceedings of the Third Workshop on Computational Modeling of People's Opinions, Personality, and Emotion's in Social Media*, pages 41–53, Barcelona, Spain (Online). Association for Computational Linguistics.

Mohamed Hashim Changrampadi, A Shahina, M Badri Narayanan, and A Nayeemulla Khan. 2022. End-to-end speech recognition of tamil language. *Intelligent Automation & Soft Computing*, 32(2).

R Kiran, K Nivedha, T Subha, et al. 2017. Voice and speech recognition in tamil language. In *2017 2nd International Conference on Computing and Communications Technologies (ICCCT)*, pages 288–292. IEEE.

Soonil Kwon, Sung-Jae Kim, and Joon Yeon Choeh. 2016. Preprocessing for elderly speech recognition of smart devices. *Computer Speech Language*, 36:110–121.

S Lokesh, Priyan Malarvizhi Kumar, M Ramya Devi, P Parthasarathy, and C Gokulnath. 2019. An automatic tamil speech recognition system by using bidirectional recurrent neural network with self-organizing map. *Neural Computing and Applications*, 31:1521–1531.

A Madhavaraj and AG Ramakrishnan. 2019. Data-pooling and multi-task learning for enhanced performance of speech recognition systems in multiple low resourced languages. In *2019 National Conference on Communications (NCC)*, pages 1–5. IEEE.

Lara J Martin, Andrew Wilkinson, Sai Sumanth Miryala, Vivian Robison, and Alan W Black. 2015. Utterance classification in speech-to-speech translation for zero-resource languages in the hospital administration domain. In *2015 IEEE Workshop on Automatic Speech Recognition and Understanding (ASRU)*, pages 303–309. IEEE.

Gayathri S Nivetha S, Rathinavelu A. 2020. Speech recognition system for isolated tamil words using random forest algorithm. *International Journal of Recent Technology and Engineering (IJRTE)*, 9:2431–2435.

V Radha et al. 2012. Speaker independent isolated speech recognition system for tamil language using hmm. *Procedia Engineering*, 30:1097–1102.

S Rojathai and M Venkatesulu. 2014. Noise robust tamil speech word recognition system by means of pac features with anfis. In *2014 IEEE/ACIS 13th International Conference on Computer and Information Science (ICIS)*, pages 435–440. IEEE.

Suhasini S and Bharathi B. 2022. SUH_ASR@LT-EDI-ACL2022: Transformer based approach for speech recognition for vulnerable individuals in Tamil. In *Proceedings of the Second Workshop on Language Technology for Equality, Diversity and Inclusion*, pages 177–182, Dublin, Ireland. Association for Computational Linguistics.

Sundarapandiyan S and Shanthi N. 2017. Automatic speech recognition system of tamil language using linear discriminant analysis. *International Journal of Recent Technology and Engineering (IJRTE)*, 6:6298–6301.

Kingston Pal Thamburaj et al. 2021. A process of developing an asr system for malay and tamil languages. *Design Engineering*, pages 731–741.

# ASR_SSN_CSE@ LT-EDI-2023:Pretrained Transformer based Automatic Speech Recognition system for Elderly People

**S Suhasini**
Department of CSE
SSN College of Engineering
suhasinis@ssn.edu.in

**B Bharathi**
Department of CSE
SSN College of Engineering
bharathib@ssn.edu.in

## Abstract

This paper discusses about the result submitted in Shared Task on Speech Recognition for Vulnerable Individuals in Tamil- LT-EDI-2023(B et al., 2023). The task is to develop an automatic speech recognition system for Tamil language. The dataset provided in the task is collected from the elderly people who converse in Tamil language. The proposed ASR system is designed with pre-trained model anuragshas/wav2vec2-xlsr-53-tamil. The pre-trained model used in our system is fine-tuned with Tamil common voice dataset. The test data released from the task is given to the proposed system, now the transcriptions are generated for the test samples and the generated transcriptions is submitted to the task. The result submitted is evaluated by task, the evaluation metric used is Word Error Rate (WER). Our Proposed system attained a WER of 39.8091%.

## 1 Introduction

This shared task tackles a difficult area in Tamil automatic speech recognition system for vulnerable elderly and transgender individuals. To take care of their daily necessities, elderly people go to important places including banks, hospitals, and administrative offices. Many elderly folks are not aware of how to use the tools provided to help people. Similar to how transgender persons lack access to basic schooling due to societal discrimination, speech is the only channel that can help them meet their demands. The data on spontaneous speech is collected from elderly and transgender people who are unable to take benefit of these amenities (Fukuda et al., 2019; Hämäläinen et al., 2015). 2 hours of speech data will be made available for testing, while the speech corpus containing 5.5 hours of transcribed speech will be made available for the training set. Recently, the majority of people have begun using various electronic devices to access the internet. In this situation, the elderly people have also started using smart phones to access the internet (Vacher et al., 2015). Some elderly people attempt to acquire information from the internet using their audio message because they are not well-versed in technology. An acoustic model must be created to handle these types of audio messages from elderly individuals; the model will identify their speech and extract the output of the speech data. As a result, a text file will be the output. The speech's output will be used to determine the WER value. The WER number demonstrates how accurately the model predicted the outcome . No other corpus for elderly people is larger than the Japanese Newspaper Article Sentences (JNAS), Japanese Newspaper Article Sentences Read Speech Corpus of the Aged (S-JNAS), and Corpus of Spontaneous Japanese (CSJ) corpora (Fukuda et al., 2020). It has been determined that Automatic Speech Recognition using some standard models has not achieved a good performance (Nakajima and Aono, 2020). It is challenging to identify conversational speech in public settings since each person may have their own accent and pronunciation. Additionally, the methodology for identifying standard speech cannot be applied to the conversational speech corpus because it raises WER. A transformer model technique is utilised to treat this type of older people's conversational speech. The paper is organised as follows: Section 2 discusses the examination of related literature, Section 3 describes the data set, Section 4 discusses the methodology, Section 5 describes the implementation, Section 6 describes the observations, and Section 7 discusses the discussion. Section 8 of the essay concludes with a section on future research.



*LT-EDI 2023 – Third Workshop on Language Technology for Equality, Diversity and Inclusion*, pages 161–165, Varna, Bulgaria, Sep 7, 2023.
https://doi.org/10.26615/978-954-452-084-7_024

## 2 Related Work

There have been numerous studies on recognising the speech of elderly persons using the adaption acoustic model for CSJ corpus (Fukuda et al., 2020), which yields the lowest WER values. The performance of continuous word identification and phoneme recognition is measured from the two distinct age groups, and the corpus is collected in Bengali (Das et al., 2011). Prosodic and spectral properties are retrieved for senior people speech.The exploration of additional features (Lin and Yu, 2015), such as the speech's volume level, sampling frequency, fundamental frequency, and sentence segmentation, is also possible. Other measurements were locating the pause in the sentence and calculating how long it lasted (Nakajima and Aono, 2020). Low number of utterances is a sign of inadequate performance. If the recorded voice quality is poor (Iribe et al., 2015), the WER value rises. By integrating the transformers for a broad context (Masumura et al., 2021), the E2E ASR transformer can perform encoding and decoding in a hierarchical manner. The WER is decreased by 25.4% via transfer learning when using the hybrid-based LSTM transformer (Zeng et al., 2021). Additionally, the LSTM decoder lowers WER by 13%. Self-attention and a multi-head attention layer (Lee et al., 2021) can be used to carry out the encoding and decoding of transformer models. The transformer model is utilised for CTC/Attention based End-To-End ASR, and it produces a WER of 23.66% (Miao et al., 2020). Transformers for streaming ASR are the foundation of the end-to-end ASR system, where an output must be produced quickly after each spoken word. Time-restricted self-attention is employed for the encoder, and prompted attention is used for the encoder-decoder attention mechanism. The innovative fusion attention technique results in a WER reduction of 16.7% on the Wall Street Journal test compared to the non-fusion standard transformer and 12.1% compared to other authors' transformer-based benchmarks. Findings of the automatic speech recognition for vulnerable individuals are given in (S and B, 2022) (B et al., 2022), have used transformer models used for transformer based ASR for Vulnerable Individuals in Tamil.

## 3 Dataset Description

Tamil conversational speech data is collected from the elderly people. The speech corpus contains a total of 6 hours and 42 minutes of speech data (Bharathi et al., 2022). The recorded speech of elderly people contains how the elderly people communicate in primary locations like market, bank, shop, public transport and hospitals. It includes both male and female utterances and also this speech data is collected from the transgender people. Table 1. contains the detailed description about the collected data.

| Gender | Avg-Age | Duration(mins) |
|---|---|---|
| Male | 61 | 93 |
| Female | 59 | 242 |
| Transgender | 30 | 67 |

Table 1: Dataset Details

The below Figure 1. shows the sample prediction for the given corpus.

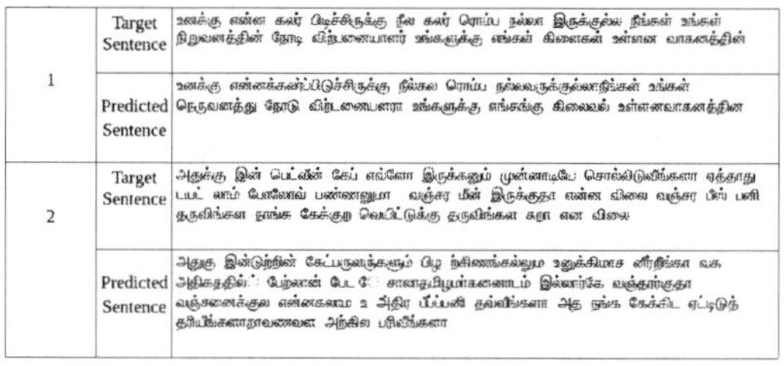

| | | |
|---|---|---|
| 1 | Target Sentence | உனக்கு என்ன கலர் பிடிச்சிருக்கு நீல கலர் ரொம்ப நல்லா இருக்குல்ல நீங்கள் உங்கள் நிறுவனத்தின் தோடி விற்பனையாளர் உங்களுக்கு எங்கள் கிளைகள் உள்ள வாகனத்தின் |
| | Predicted Sentence | உனக்கு என்னக்கலர்ப்பிடுச்சிருக்கு நீல்கல ரொம்ப நல்லைருக்குல்லாநீங்கள் உங்கள் நெருவனத்து தோடு விற்டளைபளரா உங்களுக்கு எங்கங்கு கிலைகள் உள்ளனவாகனத்தின |
| 2 | Target Sentence | அதுக்கு இன் பெட்வீன் கேப் எவ்ளோ இருக்கனும் முன்னாடியே சொல்லிடுவீங்களா ஏத்தாது டபட் லாம் போலோவ் பண்ணனுமா வஞ்சர மீன் இருக்குதா என்ன விலை வஞ்சர பீஸ் பணி தருவீங்கள நாங்க கேக்குற வெயிட்டுக்கு தருவீங்கள கறா என விலை |
| | Predicted Sentence | அதுகு இன்டுற்றின் கேட்பருனக்கலும் பிழ நசிணங்கல்லும உனுக்கிமாச வீரநீங்கா வக அதிகததில் பேற்லான் டேட சானாதுபியுமர்களைடம் இல்லார்கே வஞ்சார்குதா வஞ்சனைக்குல என்னகலம உ அதிர பீப்பனி தல்லிங்களா அத நங்க கேக்கிட ஏட்டிடுத் தரியங்களாறாவணவன அந்கில பரிவீங்களா |

Figure 1: Sample Prediction

## 4 Proposed Work

In our proposed system, the pretrained transformer model anuragshas/wav2vec2-xlsr-53-tamil[1] is used. The pretrained model "anuragshas/wav2vec2-xlsr-53-tamil" is based on the Wav2Vec2 architecture and specifically trained for the Tamil language. Wav2Vec2[2] is a state-of-the-art speech recognition model developed by Facebook AI. It utilizes a self-supervised learning approach, where it learns from large amounts of unlabeled speech data to build representations that capture meaningful information about the audio. The model is based on the transformer architecture, which has proven to be highly effective for various natural language processing tasks. Transformers enable the model to efficiently capture long-range dependencies in the audio input. The model is pretrained on a large

[1] https://huggingface.co/anuragshas/wav2vec2-xlsr-53-tamil

[2] https://huggingface.co/docs/transformers/model_doc/wav2vec2

corpus of multilingual and monolingual data containing Tamil speech. During pretraining, it learns to predict masked or distorted portions of the input audio, which helps it understand the underlying structure and features of the speech data. After pretraining, the model undergoes fine-tuning using labeled data for specific downstream tasks. Fine-tuning allows the model to adapt to a particular speech recognition task, such as transcription or keyword spotting, in this case, for Tamil language. Although the model is specifically trained for Tamil, it benefits from the multilingual nature of its pretraining data. It can understand and process speech from various languages, making it useful for multilingual applications or tasks involving code-switching. The model has been trained on a vast vocabulary, enabling it to handle a wide range of words and phrases. This makes it suitable for tasks that involve transcribing or recognizing speech with diverse vocabulary. The model's training data and fine-tuning procedure focus on capturing the unique characteristics of the Tamil language, including its phonetics, phonology, and syntax. This enhances its ability to accurately recognize and transcribe Tamil speech.

## 5 Implementation

To create an efficient acoustic model based on a pre-trained transformer model. There are many publicly accessible transformer-based pre-trained models. Here, the "anuragshas/wav2vec2-xlsr-53-tamil" pretrained model for handling Tamil speech corpus is used. This pretrained model is fine-tuned from "facebook/wav2vec2-large-xlsr-53" [3] by common voice dataset in Tamil. The model can be used directly and only accepts input if the voice data is sampled at 16 KHz. It is independent of any language model. The model for creating the wav2vec uses the XSLR (Cross-Lingual Speech Representation), which additionally tests cross-lingual speech data. The quantization of latents, which is common to all languages, can be learned by XLSR. The voice utterance is loaded into the library, saved in a variable, and tokenized using the tokenizer. This process converts the audio to text, and the results are transcripts of the audio file that is loaded into the library. The transcripts are kept in a separate folder after the voice recognition process is complete. Between the transcripts produced by the model and the actual transcripts of the audio written by humans, the WER (Word Error Rate) is determined. The degree of voice recognition can be calculated using the WER value.

[3]https://huggingface.co/facebook/wav2vec2-large-xlsr-53

## 6 Evaluation of Results

The evaluation metric used by the task to test the results submitted by us is based on the WER computed between the ASR hypotheses submitted by the participants and the ground truth of human speech transcription.

$$\text{WER ( Word Error Rate)} = ( S + D + I) / N$$

where,
S = No. of substitutions
D = No. of deletions
I = No. of insertions
N = No. of words in the reference transcription

## 7 Observation

The name of the speech data and its WER value are included in the result. Similar to this, the same procedure is used for all audio files. The number of subgroups into which each audio file is divided is also listed in the table. The test set audio files' average WER value, which comprises utterances from men, women, and transgender people, is determined in Table 2.

| S.No. | Gender | Count | Avg WER |
|---|---|---|---|
| 1 | Male | 2 | 32.29275584 |
| 2 | Female | 1 | 44.01625294 |
| 3 | Transgender | 7 | 40.33148537 |

Table 2: Average WER Value for Test Data

| S.No. | File Name | Subsets | WER Value |
|---|---|---|---|
| 1 | Audio-37 | 15 | 31.13258667 |
| 2 | Audio-38 | 17 | 44.95625294 |
| 3 | Audio-39 | 16 | 32.412925 |
| 4 | Audio-40 | 17 | 37.89848235 |
| 5 | Audio-41 | 19 | 42.65715789 |
| 6 | Audio-42 | 24 | 43.11616667 |
| 7 | Audio-43 | 30 | 37.94115667 |
| 8 | Audio-44 | 28 | 37.29702143 |
| 9 | Audio-45 | 26 | 44.35576154 |
| 10 | Audio-46 | 47 | 39.35465106 |

Table 3: WER values for Testing Set

## 8 Discussion

From the Table 2, the experimental result says that the average WER for the testing dataset. The number of test speech utterances are 239. Similarly, Table 3, says the result of total 239 audio subset files from 10 audio files which is given for testing and the WER measured is 39.80%. We ranked second position in shared task competition.

## 9 Conclusion

Conversational speech data is used to enhance the speech recognition system's ability to identify older persons. Using a trained model, an automatic speech recognition system is created. Older adults and transgender people with Tamil as their mother tongue are the subjects of a dataset collection. The dataset's utterance was captured during a conversation in a primary site in Tamil. As the system's pre-trained model was improved using a common speech dataset, in the future the model might be trained using our own dataset and utilised for testing, which could improve performance.

## References


Bharathi B, Bharathi Raja Chakravarthi, Subalalitha Chinnaudayar Navaneethakrishnan, Sripirya N, Rajeswari Natarajan, Suhasini S, and Swetha Valli. 2023. Overview of the second shared task on speech recognition for vulnerable individuals in tamil. In *Proceedings of the Third Workshop on Speech and Language Technologies for Dravidian Languages*, Varna, Bulgaria. Recent Advances in Natural Language Processing.

Bharathi B, Dhanya Srinivasan, Josephine Varsha, Thenmozhi Durairaj, and Senthil Kumar B. 2022. SSNCSE_NLP@LT-EDI-ACL2022:hope speech detection for equality, diversity and inclusion using sentence transformers. In *Proceedings of the Second Workshop on Language Technology for Equality, Diversity and Inclusion*, pages 218–222, Dublin, Ireland. Association for Computational Linguistics.

B Bharathi, Bharathi Raja Chakravarthi, Subalalitha Chinnaudayar Navaneethakrishnan, N Sripriya, Arunaggiri Pandian, and Swetha Valli. 2022. Findings of the shared task on Speech Recognition for Vulnerable Individuals in Tamil. In *Proceedings of the Second Workshop on Language Technology for Equality, Diversity and Inclusion*. Association for Computational Linguistics.

Biswajit Das, Sandipan Mandal, and Pabitra Mitra. 2011. Bengali speech corpus for continuous auutomatic speech recognition system. In *2011 International conference on speech database and assessments (Oriental COCOSDA)*, pages 51–55. IEEE.

Meiko Fukuda, Ryota Nishimura, Hiromitsu Nishizaki, Yurie Iribe, and Norihide Kitaoka. 2019. A new corpus of elderly japanese speech for acoustic modeling, and a preliminary investigation of dialect-dependent speech recognition. In *2019 22nd Conference of the Oriental COCOSDA International Committee for the Co-ordination and Standardisation of Speech Databases and Assessment Techniques (O-COCOSDA)*, pages 1–6. IEEE.

Meiko Fukuda, Hiromitsu Nishizaki, Yurie Iribe, Ryota Nishimura, and Norihide Kitaoka. 2020. Improving speech recognition for the elderly: A new corpus of elderly japanese speech and investigation of acoustic modeling for speech recognition. In *Proceedings of the 12th Language Resources and Evaluation Conference*, pages 6578–6585.

Annika Hämäläinen, António Teixeira, Nuno Almeida, Hugo Meinedo, Tibor Fegyó, and Miguel Sales Dias. 2015. Multilingual speech recognition for the elderly: The aalfred personal life assistant. *Procedia Computer Science*, 67:283–292.

Yurie Iribe, Norihide Kitaoka, and Shuhei Segawa. 2015. Development of new speech corpus for elderly japanese speech recognition. In *2015 International Conference Oriental COCOSDA held jointly with 2015 Conference on Asian Spoken Language Research and Evaluation (O-COCOSDA/CASLRE)*, pages 27–31. IEEE.

Taewoo Lee, Min-Joong Lee, Tae Gyoon Kang, Seokyeoung Jung, Minseok Kwon, Yeona Hong, Jungin Lee, Kyoung-Gu Woo, Ho-Gyeong Kim, Jiseung Jeong, et al. 2021. Adaptable multi-domain language model for transformer asr. In *ICASSP 2021-2021 IEEE International Conference on Acoustics, Speech and Signal Processing (ICASSP)*, pages 7358–7362. IEEE.

Hui Lin and Yibiao Yu. 2015. Acoustic feature analysis and conversion of age speech. In *IET Conference Proceedings*. The Institution of Engineering & Technology.

Ryo Masumura, Naoki Makishima, Mana Ihori, Akihiko Takashima, Tomohiro Tanaka, and Shota Orihashi. 2021. Hierarchical transformer-based large-context end-to-end asr with large-context knowledge distillation. In *ICASSP 2021-2021 IEEE International Conference on Acoustics, Speech and Signal Processing (ICASSP)*, pages 5879–5883. IEEE.

Haoran Miao, Gaofeng Cheng, Changfeng Gao, Pengyuan Zhang, and Yonghong Yan. 2020. Transformer-based online ctc/attention end-to-end speech recognition architecture. In *ICASSP 2020-2020 IEEE International Conference on Acoustics, Speech and Signal Processing (ICASSP)*, pages 6084–6088. IEEE.

Hideharu Nakajima and Yushi Aono. 2020. Collection and analyses of exemplary speech data to establish easy-to-understand speech synthesis for japanese elderly adults. In *2020 23rd Conference of the Oriental COCOSDA International Committee for the Co-ordination and Standardisation of Speech Databases and Assessment Techniques (O-COCOSDA)*, pages 145–150. IEEE.

Suhasini S and Bharathi B. 2022. SUH_ASR@LT-EDI-ACL2022: Transformer based approach for speech recognition for vulnerable individuals in Tamil. In *Proceedings of the Second Workshop on Language Technology for Equality, Diversity and Inclusion*, pages 177–182, Dublin, Ireland. Association for Computational Linguistics.

Michel Vacher, Frédéric Aman, Solange Rossato, and François Portet. 2015. Development of automatic speech recognition techniques for elderly home support: Applications and challenges. In *International Conference on Human Aspects of IT for the Aged Population*, pages 341–353. Springer.

Zhiping Zeng, Haihua Xu, Yerbolat Khassanov, Eng Siong Chng, Chongjia Ni, Bin Ma, et al. 2021. Leveraging text data using hybrid transformer-lstm based end-to-end asr in transfer learning. In *2021 12th International Symposium on Chinese Spoken Language Processing (ISCSLP)*, pages 1–5. IEEE.

# SSNTech2@LT-EDI-RANLP-2023: Homophobia/Transphobia Detection in Social Media Comments Using Linear Classification Techniques

**Vaidhegi D, Priya M, Rajalakshmi S, Angel Deborah S, Mirnalinee T T**
Department of Computer Science and Engineering,
Sri Sivasubramaniya Nadar College of Engineering, Chennai - 603110, Tamil Nadu, India
vaidhegi2110337@ssn.edu.in, priya2110680@ssn.edu.in,
rajalakshmis@ssn.edu.in, angeldeborahs@ssn.edu.in,
mirnalineett@ssn.edu.in

## Abstract

The abusive content on social media networks is causing destructive effects on the mental well-being of online users. Homophobia refers to the fear, negative attitudes and feeling towards homosexuality. Transphobia refers to negative attitudes, hatred and prejudice towards transsexual people. Even though, some parts of the society have started to accept homosexuality and transsexuality, there are still a large set of the population opposing it. Hate speech targeting LGBTQ+ individuals, known as homophobia/transphobia speech, has become a growing concern. This has led to a toxic and unwelcoming environment for LGBTQ+ people on online platforms. This poses a significant societal issue, hindering the progress of equality, diversity, and inclusion. The identification of homophobic and transphobic comments on social media platforms plays a crucial role in creating a safer environment for all social media users. In order to accomplish this, we built a ML model using SGD and SVM classifier. Our approach yielded promising results, with a weighted F1-score of 0.95 on the English dataset and we secured $4^{th}$ rank in this task.

## 1 Introduction

In the recent years, people have started to discover themselves and open up about homosexuality and trans-sexuality. People have the complete freedom to choose their sexuality from the different choices. The widespread use of social media platforms has revolutionized communication and provided a space for individuals to express their thoughts, opinions, and experiences. The development of social media and support by the respective communities have helped in providing the people the courage to express themselves. However, this has also led to the increase in hate speech and discriminating comments towards this set of people. Even after several laws and regulations, LGBTQIA+ communities are constantly facing violations against them in various forms.

Homophobia and transphobia, which involve negative attitudes, prejudices, and discriminatory behaviors towards LGBTQIA+ individuals, have gained prominence as pressing issues within online platforms. The proliferation of such toxic comments not only inflicts harm upon the targeted individuals but also fosters an environment of fear, intolerance, and exclusion. In response to this escalating problem, the utilization of Machine Learning (ML) techniques has garnered significant attention. ML algorithms offer the potential to automatically detect and classify homophobic and transphobic content in social media comments, enabling swift intervention and mitigating the detrimental impact on the affected individuals. This research paper aims to provide a comprehensive study of the application of ML algorithms for identifying homophobic and transphobic comments on social media platforms. The primary objective is to develop an efficient and accurate model that can autonomously identify and flag such discriminatory content, contributing to the establishment of a safer and more inclusive online environment for LGBTQIA+ individuals.

This paper involves analysing different approaches for classifying the English dataset of social media comments into three categories: Homophobic, Transphobic, and Non-anti-LGBT+ content, as part of the shared task Homophobia/Transphobia Detection @LT-EDI@RANLP-2023. Furthermore, we will discuss about the various methodologies used to process the data, implement the ML model and finally we will take a look into the outcome of the model and future developments.



*LT-EDI 2023 – Third Workshop on Language Technology for Equality, Diversity and Inclusion*, pages 166–171, Varna, Bulgaria, Sep 7, 2023.
https://doi.org/10.26615/978-954-452-084-7_025

## 2 Related Work

Research on online hate speech has predominantly centered around aggression, sexism, racism, offensive language, hatred, and harassment, with limited emphasis on identifying specific instances of homophobic and transphobic speech (11). Noteworthy studies include an examination of linguistic patterns among homosexual individuals in China using a created corpus (4). Emotion lexicons have been developed to discern acceptable and unacceptable discourse concerning LGBTQ+ topics in languages such as English, Croatian, Dutch, and Slovene (3).

A study analyzed hate speech comments related to LGBTQ+ issues on Facebook, highlighting prevalent themes like repulsion towards the LGBTQ+ community and discrediting of journalistic information (2). Furthermore, a manually annotated corpus was compiled from YouTube, encompassing homophobic and transphobic speech in multiple languages, including English, Tamil, and code-mixed Tamil-English, with the aim of categorizing speech at various levels (14). (12) used the BERT model to detect offensive language as a first level of identification of abusive content.

While psychological studies have examined aspects like homophobic bullying and the impact on mental health, there remains a requirement for empirical evidence and theoretical comprehension of online homophobia/transphobia and its association with Internet usage (5; 7).

Regarding hate speech detection in code-mixed settings, researchers have started to extract code-mixed data from social media platforms due to increased user engagement. However, countries like India, with multiple languages spoken, face a scarcity of pertinent data in low-resourced languages (8). (10) explored the significance of multi-task learning for identifying offensive language and performing sentiment analysis in closely related code-mixed languages like Kannada, Malayalam, and Tamil. Sivanaiah et al. (6) used a deep learning model to identify misogynous content against women using multimodal data.

Biradar et al. (12) (2022) utilized translational systems to convert texts to English and fine-tuned language models for hate speech classification in Hinglish (Hindi-English). However, these approaches may not fully capture contextual nuances and accurately interpret sarcasm. Additionally, pre-trained language models encounter challenges in capturing contextual relationships between code-mixed languages (9).

In summary, although research exists on identifying and addressing online hate speech, there is a need for more focused investigations into homophobic and transphobic speech. Additionally, effectively detecting hate speech in code-mixed settings requires further attention to develop precise and context-aware classification models.

## 3 Dataset used

The dataset provided in task A of the homophobia/transphobia comments detection in the LT-EDI@RANLP-2023 is used in this work. The dataset consists of 3164 entries under 3 labels namely Homophobia, Transphobia and Non-anti-LGBT+ content. The number of entries under each dataset are 179 for homophobia, 8 for transphobia and 2978 for Non-anti-LGBT+ content. Table 3 shows the data distribution of training dataset and Table 4 shows the distribution of development dataset for various classes.

| S.no | Labels | Counts |
|---|---|---|
| 1 | Non-anti-LGBT+content | 2978 |
| 2 | Homophobia | 179 |
| 3 | Transphobia | 8 |

Table 1: Number of classes in train dataset

| S.no | Labels | Counts |
|---|---|---|
| 1 | Non-anti-LGBT+content | 748 |
| 2 | Homophobia | 42 |
| 3 | Transphobia | 2 |

Table 2: Number of classes in development dataset

## 4 Methodologies

We have experimented with multi-class linear classifier ML algorithms for classifying the text into various category of the output class labels. The algorithms are explained in the following sections.

### 4.1 Stochastic Gradient Descent Classifier

The Stochastic Gradient Descent (SGD) classifier is a highly popular ML algorithm specifically designed for classification tasks. As a member of the linear classifiers family, it is widely recognized for its efficiency and effectiveness, particularly in large-scale learning scenarios. The SGD classifier leverages the optimization technique of stochastic gradient descent, a widely-used iterative approach that minimizes a loss function to find the optimal model parameters. While its primary application is binary classification, it can be extended to handle multiclass problems using techniques like one-vs-all or softmax regression. The algorithm shines when working with sparse data and high-dimensional feature spaces, demonstrating its capability to handle complex datasets.

Versatility and flexibility are among the key advantages of the SGD classifier. It finds application across a diverse range of classification tasks, including text categorization, sentiment analysis, and image classification. Furthermore, its ability to support online learning enables incremental updates to the model as new data arrives, making it suitable for real-time or streaming data scenarios. In summary, the SGD classifier stands out as a flexible and efficient algorithm for both binary and multiclass classification. With its stochastic optimization technique and adaptability to large datasets, it proves valuable in a wide array of applications.

### 4.2 Support Vector Machine classifier

The Support Vector Machine (SVM) classifier is a widely used and powerful supervised ML algorithm that excels in both classification and regression tasks. Renowned for its effectiveness in managing complex datasets and achieving high accuracy, SVM identifies an optimal hyperplane that separates distinct classes within the feature space. This hyperplane selection maximizes the margin, which denotes the distance between the hyperplane and the nearest data points from each class (known as support vectors). Consequently, SVM exhibits excellent generalization performance, even when confronted with non-linearly separable data.

An advantageous feature of SVM is its efficient handling of high-dimensional feature spaces, rendering it suitable for datasets encompassing numerous features, such as text classification and image recognition. SVM's prevalence stems from its exceptional generalization capabilities and resilience to outliers. By employing appropriate kernel functions, it can handle both linearly separable and non-linearly separable data. As a result, SVMs find application across diverse domains, including text classification, image classification, bioinformatics, and finance. In summary, the SVM classifier stands as a potent ML algorithm that determines an optimal hyperplane to distinguish between classes within the feature space. By leveraging kernel functions to transform data into higher-dimensional spaces, SVM enables effective classification. Its versatility and wide-ranging applications arise from its ability to handle intricate datasets while achieving remarkable accuracy.

## 5 Implementation

The above model implementation involves the following methodologies:

The following diagram provides a visual flowchart of the implementation steps.

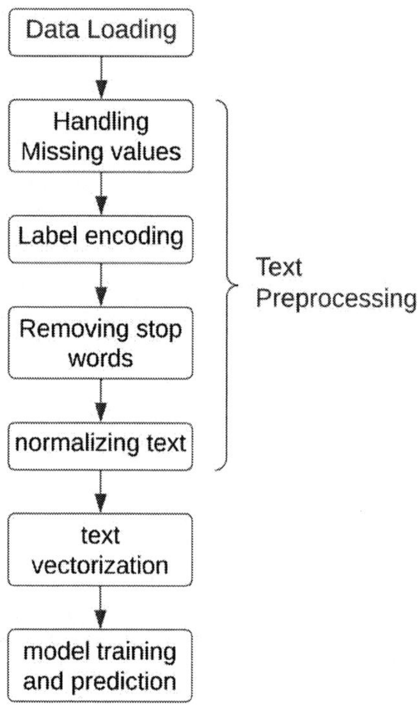


Figure 1: Flow chart of implementation

### 5.1 Data loading

First step is to import the neccessary libraries. The required libraries such as Pandas, Numpy, Matplotlib, Re, and Sklearn are imported. The dataset is loaded using the read_csv() function from the Pandas library and is converted to PANDAS dataframe. The column names of the DataFrame are renamed using the rename() function.

### 5.2 Text preprocessing

Various text preprocessing steps are performed using the NLTK library and regular expressions.

#### 5.2.1 Handling missing values

The presence of missing values in the DataFrame is checked using the isna().any() function.

#### 5.2.2 Label encoding

The categorical target variable is encoded using the LabelEncoder from sklearn.preprocessing and each label is given a numerical value.

#### 5.2.3 Removing stop words

Stopwords are words that do not add to the overall meaning of the text. The general stopwords are removed by using functions in NLTK. The NLTK corpus is used to download the required stopwords. The remove_stop_words() function is defined to remove stop words from the text column. The function tokenizes the text, filters out stop words, and joins the filtered tokens back into a string. The stop words are removed from the text column using the apply() function.

#### 5.2.4 Removing custom stop words

Additionally, some common stopwords like *you*, *your* were in short forms like *u*, *ur* as the dataset contains social media comments which can be informal. Therefore, they were not removed by standard nltk library. So, the custom stop words used as short forms which are frequently found in the given dataset are defined in the custom_stop_words set. The remove_custom_stop_words() function is defined to remove these custom stop words from the text column. Similar to the previous step, the function tokenizes the text, filters out custom stop words, and joins the filtered tokens back into a string. The custom stop words are removed from the text column using the apply() function.

#### 5.2.5 Normalizing text

The NLTK tokenizer and WordNetLemmatizer are used to normalize the text. The normalize_text_nltk() function is defined to tokenize the text, lemmatize the tokens, convert them to lowercase, and join them back into a string. The text normalization is applied to the text column using the apply() function.

#### 5.2.6 Removing numerical values

As the numerical data does not contribute to categorizing the text, they are removed. Regular expressions are used to remove numerical values from the text column. The lambda function is applied to each text value using the apply() function and RE.sub() is used to substitute numerical values with an empty string.

### 5.3 Text vectorization

The TfidfVectorizer in sklearn.feature_extraction .text is used to convert the text data into numerical vectors. The fit_transform() function is used on the training set, and transform() is used on the development and testing set.

### 5.4 Model training and prediction

Two test runs were done using two ML models, one with SGD classifier and another with SVM classifier.

#### 5.4.1 The SGD classifier

The SGDClassifier from sklearn.linear_model is instantiated and trained using the training data. The trained model is used to predict the target variable for the testing data.

#### 5.4.2 SVM classifier

The Linear SVC (SVM) classifier from sklearn.svm is instantiated and trained using the training data. The trained model is used to predict the target variable for the testing data.

### 5.5 Evaluation

The classification_report from sklearn.metrics is used to evaluate the performance of the model by comparing the predicted target values with the actual target values of development dataset. The various performance scores like accuracy, macro and weighted precision, macro and weighted recall and macro and weighted f-1 scores of both the models are tabulated in Table 5 and Table 6. Then, the model was run for test dataset and the predicted results were submitted. The evaluation of test dataset was based on weighted f-1 score.

| S.no | Labels | Counts |
|---|---|---|
| 1 | Non-anti-LGBT+content | 2978 |
| 2 | Homophobia | 179 |
| 3 | Transphobia | 8 |

Table 3: Number of classes in train dataset

## 6 Results and Discussion

This task is evaluated on the weighted averages and macro averages of three performance metrics - Precision, Recall and F1-score. The scores for these metrics and the accuracy score achieved for

| S.no | Labels | Counts |
|---|---|---|
| 1 | Non-anti-LGBT+content | 748 |
| 2 | Homophobia | 42 |
| 3 | Transphobia | 2 |

Table 4: Number of classes in development dataset

the training and development dataset of Homophobia/Transphobia Detection task under SGD classifier are tabulated in Table 5. The scores achieved for training and development dataset of this task under SVM classifier are tabulated in Table 6.

| Metrics | Train DS | Dev DS |
|---|---|---|
| Accuracy | 0.95 | 0.94 |
| Macro Precision | 0.47 | 0.57 |
| Macro Recall | 0.40 | 0.55 |
| Macro F1-score | 0.43 | 0.57 |
| Weighted precision | 0.94 | 0.94 |
| Weighted recall | 0.95 | 0.94 |
| Weighted F1-score | 0.94 | 0.91 |

Table 5: Performance of SGD classifier for training and development dataset

| Metrics | Train DS | Dev DS |
|---|---|---|
| Accuracy | 0.96 | 0.93 |
| Macro Precision | 0.56 | 0.47 |
| Macro Recall | 0.39 | 0.50 |
| Macro F1-score | 0.42 | 0.48 |
| Weighted precision | 0.95 | 0.87 |
| Weighted recall | 0.96 | 0.93 |
| Weighted F1-score | 0.95 | 0.90 |

Table 6: Performance of SVM classifier for training and development dataset

It is inferred that the transphobia and homophobia samples are much smaller than the non-anti-lgbt+ content samples. Therefore the individual accuracy and F1 scores for the categories also vary. It is inferred from the experimental results that SVM is not performing well when compared to SGD classifier as the data is highly imbalanced across the various classes. Our submission using SGD model secured the $4^{th}$ rank in Task A, i.e., Homophobia / Transphobia Detection on English dataset. Our model procured a weighted F1-score of 0.9582 while the top rank team secured 0.969 score. Thus, SGD has been an effective model for the test data also when compared to SVM.

As the given dataset was skewed, we tried for data augmentation. But this method was not effective. Since we had less number of samples in the dataset we used machine learning techniques such as SVM classifier and SGD classifier, as deep learning techniques require large amount of data to learn.

## 7 Conclusion And Future Works

In this research, we conducted a comparative analysis of various models for the shared task on homophobia/transphobia detection at LT-EDI@RANLP-2023. Our findings revealed that the SGD Classifier yielded the most favourable results for English text. The current dataset was skewed and the prediction scores were low for transphobia text. We may further train the model with enhanced datasets with more data and category labels to get more accuracy. The model was trained for monolingual text (English). Extending this, a machine model to detect multilingual text can be built. We are also aiming to investigate on the data augmentation techniques for this specific case.

## References


[1] Ashraf, N., Taha, M., Abd Elfattah, A., & Nayel, H. (2022, May). Nayel@ lt-edi-acl2022: Homophobia/transphobia detection for Equality, Diversity, and Inclusion using SVM. In Proceedings of the Second Workshop on Language Technology for Equality, Diversity and Inclusion (pp. 287-290).

[2] Silva, M. P. D., & Silva, L. S. D. (2021). Hate speech dissemination in news comments: analysis of news about LGBT universe on Facebook cybermedia from Mato Grosso do Sul. Intercom: Revista Brasileira de Ciências da Comunicação, 44, 137-155.

[3] Ljubešić, N., Markov, I., Fišer, D., & Daelemans, W. (2020). The lilah emotion lexicon of Croatian, Dutch, and Slovene. In Proceedings of the Third Workshop on Computational Modeling of People's Opinions, Personality, and Emotions in Social Media (pp. 153–157). Barcelona, Spain (Online), ACL.

[4] Wu, H. H., & Hsieh, S. K. (2017, November). Exploring Lavender Tongue from Social Media Texts [In Chinese]. In Proceedings of the 29th Conference on Computational Linguistics and Speech Processing (ROCLING 2017) (pp. 68-80).

[5] Bacchini, D., Esposito, C., Affuso, G., & Amodeo, A. L. (2021). The impact of personal values, gender stereotypes, and school climate on homophobic bullying: a multilevel analysis. Sexuality Research and Social Policy, 18, 598-611.

[6] Ventriglio, A., Castaldelli-Maia, J. M., Torales, J., De Berardis, D., & Bhugra, D. (2021). Homophobia and mental health: a scourge of the modern era. Epidemiology and Psychiatric Sciences, 30, e52.

[7] Roy, P. K., Bhawal, S., & Subalalitha, C. N. (2022). Hate speech and offensive language detection in Dravidian languages using deep ensemble framework. Computer Speech & Language, 75, 101386.

[8] Hande, A., Hegde, S. U., & Chakravarthi, B. R. (2022). Multi-task learning in under-resourced Dravidian languages. Journal of Data, Information and Management, 4(2), 137-165.

[9] Yasaswini, K., Puranik, K., Hande, A., Priyadharshini, R., Thavareesan, S., & Chakravarthi, B. R. (2021, April). IIITT@ DravidianLangTech-EACL2021: Transfer learning for offensive language detection in Dravidian languages. In Proceedings of the First Workshop on Speech and Language Technologies for Dravidian Languages (pp. 187-194).

[10] Biradar, S., Saumya, S., & Chauhan, A. (2022). Fighting hate speech from a bilingual Hinglish speaker's perspective: a transformer-and translation-based approach. Social Network Analysis and Mining, 12(1), 87.

[11] Kumar, G., Singh, J. P., & Kumar, A. (2021). A deep multi-modal neural network for the identification of hate speech from social media. In Responsible AI and Analytics for an Ethical and Inclusive Digitized Society: 20th IFIP WG 6.11 Conference on e-Business, e-Services and e-Society, I3E 2021, Galway, Ireland, September 1–3, 2021, Proceedings 20 (pp. 670-680). Springer International Publishing.

[12] Chakravarthi, B. R., Priyadharshini, R., Durairaj, T., McCrae, J. P., Buitelaar, P., Kumaresan, P., & Ponnusamy, R. (2022, May). Overview of the shared task on homophobia and transphobia detection in social media comments. In Proceedings of the Second Workshop on Language Technology for Equality, Diversity and Inclusion (pp. 369-377).

[13] Sivanaiah, R., Angel, S., Rajendram, S. M., & Mirnalinee, T. T. (2022, July). TechSSN at semeval-2022 task 5: Multimedia automatic misogyny identification using deep learning models. In Proceedings of the 16th International Workshop on Semantic Evaluation (SemEval-2022) (pp. 571-574).

[14] Sivanaiah, R., Suseelan, A., Rajendram, S. M., & Tt, M. (2020, December). TECHSSN at SemEval-2020 Task 12: Offensive language detection using BERT embeddings. In Proceedings of the Fourteenth Workshop on Semantic Evaluation (pp. 2190-2196).

[15] Chakravarthi, B. R., Hande, A., Ponnusamy, R., Kumaresan, P. K., & Priyadharshini, R. (2022). How can we detect Homophobia and Transphobia? Experiments in a multilingual code-mixed setting for social media governance. International Journal of Information Management Data Insights, 2(2), 100119.

[16] Chakravarthi, B. R., Priyadharshini, R., Durairaj, T., McCrae, J. P., Buitelaar, P., Kumaresan, P., & Ponnusamy, R. (2022, May). Overview of the shared task on homophobia and transphobia detection in social media comments. In Proceedings of the Second Workshop on Language Technology for Equality, Diversity and Inclusion (pp. 369-377).

# IJS@LT-EDI: Ensemble Approaches to Detect Signs of Depression from Social Media Texts

**Jaya Caporusso**[1,2], **Thi Hong Hanh Tran**[1,2,3] and **Senja Pollak**[2]
[1] Jožef Stefan International Postgraduate School, Jamova cesta 39, 1000 Ljubljana, Slovenia
[2] Jožef Stefan Institute, Jamova cesta 39, 1000 Ljubljana, Slovenia
[3] University of La Rochelle, L3i, La Rochelle, France
jaya.caporusso96@gmail.com
thi.tran@univ-lr.fr

## Abstract

This paper presents our ensembling solutions for detecting signs of depression in social media text, as part of the Shared Task at LT-EDI@RANLP 2023. By leveraging social media posts in English, the task involves the development of a system to accurately classify them as presenting signs of depression of one of three levels: "severe", "moderate", and "not depressed". We verify the hypothesis that combining contextual information from a language model with local domain-specific features can improve the classifier's performance. We do so by evaluating: (1) two global classifiers (support vector machine and logistic regression); (2) contextual information from language models; and (3) the ensembling results. The best results were not achieved by any of the ensembling approaches, but by employing the RoBERTa language model.

## 1 Introduction[1]

In the Diagnostic and Statistical Manual of Mental Disorders, Fifth Edition (DSM-5), depressive disorders (which include major depressive disorder) are defined by "*the presence of sad, empty, or irritable mood, accompanied by somatic and cognitive changes that significantly affect the individual's capacity to function*" (American Psychiatric Association et al., 2013). Importantly, depression differs from regular feelings and mood changes, as it has an important impact on the lives of those who suffer from it. An extreme example of this is the high comorbidity between major depressive disorder and suicidal behavior (Orsolini et al., 2020), which is the cause of death of more than 700,000 people every year (World Health Organization, 2023). Depression is worryingly common: according to the World Health Organization, around 5 percent of adults suffer from depression globally (Villarroel and Terlizzi, 2020), and a survey conducted in 2019 in the US found that 18.5 percent of the participants had experienced some sort of depressive symptoms only in the two weeks preceding the study. The situation worsened due to the Covid-19 world pandemic: only in the first year, did the presence of anxiety or depression increase by 25 percent globally (World Health Organization, 2022). Another prominent aspect of nowadays is the use of social networks: in 2022, social media users were 4.59 billion (Statista, 2023). The relationship between the use of social networks and mental health has been studied from various points of view, one of them being the correlation between using social networks and suffering from depression (Park et al., 2015; Baker and Algorta, 2016). However, social networks can also represent a place where people suffering from depression can express and share how they feel and sometimes seek help. On date $15^{th}$ of June 2023, the subreddit "*depression, because nobody should be alone in a dark place: Peer support for anyone struggling with a depressive disorder*"[2], created on the $1^{st}$ of January 2009, counted 962,000 members. Therefore, social media posts provide precious data for the investigation and the (early) detection of depression (Leiva and Freire, 2017; Trotzek et al., 2018; Chiong et al., 2021; Liu and Shi, 2022; Ortega-Mendoza et al., 2022; Poświata and Perełkiewicz, 2022; Tavchioski et al., 2022b,a; Wang et al., 2022; Tavchioski et al., 2023).

DepSign-LT-EDI@RANLP-2023 (Detecting Signs of Depression from Social Media Text) (Sampath et al., 2023) is a shared task hosted by the Language Technology for Equality, Diversity, Inclusion workshop[3]. Its aim is to detect signs

[1] Trigger warning: the paper contains mentions of suicidal behavior and ideation.

[2] www.reddit.com/r/depression/

[3] sites.google.com/view/lt-edi-2023/



*LT-EDI 2023 – Third Workshop on Language Technology for Equality, Diversity and Inclusion*, pages 172–178, Varna, Bulgaria, Sep 7, 2023.
https://doi.org/10.26615/978-954-452-084-7_026

of depression from social media posts. More specifically, the goal is to produce a system that, given social media posts in English, classifies them as presenting signs of depression belonging to one of the following classes: "severe", "moderate", or "not depression".

Our contributions are threefold. We evaluate (1) the standalone contextual information from language models; (2) the machine learning-based classifier with global information; and (3) the ensembling of the two best classifiers. Our work brings valuable insights for detecting signs of depression.

The paper is organized as follows. Section 2 provides an overview of related works. Section 3 discusses the dataset used in this research, while Section 4 explains the process of developing our solution. Section 5 shows the evaluation of the experiments, while the error analysis is presented in Section 6. Finally, Section 7 concludes the paper with our ideas for future work.

## 2 Related work

Aspects such as one's personality, emotional state, ideology, and mental health are shown to be reflected in one's language–not only in the semantics but also in the syntax used (Chung and Pennebaker, 2007; Pennebaker, 2011). Having depression as the focus opens two main paths: the analysis of which kind of language is used by individuals suffering from depression (approach a), and the detection of depression through language analysis (approach b). Furthermore, any of the two can contribute to the other (the first to the second (approach c) and the second to the first (approach d)). The first path showed, for example, that people suffering from depression use first-person singular pronouns more frequently (in spoken language: (Bucci and Freedman, 1981); in written text: (Ortega-Mendoza et al., 2022). Furthermore, as one would expect, the sentiment is more negative in individuals suffering from depression's language (Babu and Kanaga, 2022). These and other aspects have been employed as features to detect depression from text data (approach c) (Trotzek et al., 2018; Babu and Kanaga, 2022; Ortega-Mendoza et al., 2022; Kolenik et al., 2023). Depression detection is becoming a trending topic in shared tasks. An example is the Depression and PTSD on Twitter task organized in the context of the Workshop on Computational Linguistics and Clinical Psychology[4] in 2015 (Coppersmith et al., 2015). The Early Risk Detection on the Internet workshop (eRisk) has been hosting shared tasks about depression, along with shared tasks about other mental-health-related issues, since 2017[5]. The Workshop on Language Technology for Equality, Diversity, and Inclusion (LT-EDI)[6], organized by the Association for Computational Linguistics[7] since 2021, has been including the shared task "Detecting Signs of Depression from Social Media Text" since 2022 (Sampath et al., 2022).

In the occasion of the 2022 edition (LT-EDI-ACL2022) (Sampath et al., 2022), the first and second place went, respectively, to (Poświata and Perełkiewicz, 2022) and (Wang et al., 2022). The latter employed VADER and sentence embeddings from pre-trained models to generate sentiment scores. Then, the authors adopted three different methods: a) gradient boosting models, b) pre-trained models, and c) contrastive pre-trained models. They finally ensembled the three approaches, obtaining the classifier which ranked second in the competition. The winning approach (Poświata and Perełkiewicz, 2022) included three main parts. a) In the first, transformer-based language models were fine-tuned on the train set. b) In the second, a corpus based on Reddit posts on mental health, depression, and suicide was created. A transformer-based language model was pre-trained on the corpus, resulting in DepRoBERTa (Poświata and Perełkiewicz, 2022). DepRoBERTa was then fine-tuned on the train set. c) In the third step, the best between the developed models were ensembled, obtaining the best-performing classifier of last year's DepSign-LT-EDI shared task.

## 3 Dataset

We used the dataset provided by the organizers of the shared task. The dataset contains 7,201 instances for training, 3,245 instances for validation, and 499 for evaluation. Each sample is composed of three columns: *PID*, *Text*, and *Label*.

Table 1 shows the label distribution of the training, development, and test set with the overall samples per set. What is worth noting is that the dataset is imbalanced with the under-representation of the severe class, as shown in Figure 1. The sample instances (one for class) are shown in Table 2.

[4] clpsych.org

[5] erisk.irlab.org

[6] sites.google.com/view/lt-edi-2023/

[7] www.aclweb.org/portal/

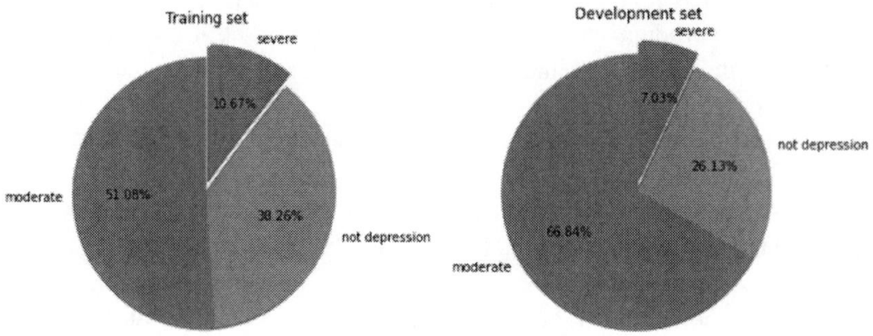


Figure 1: The distribution of sequence length for each class in the training and development sets.

| Labels | Train | Dev. | Test |
|---|---|---|---|
| **Not depression** | 2,755 | 848 | 135 |
| **Moderate** | 3,678 | 2,169 | 275 |
| **Severe** | 768 | 228 | 89 |
| **Total** | 7,201 | 3,245 | 499 |

Table 1: Data distribution by class.

| PID | Text data | Label |
|---|---|---|
| train_pid_1 | My life gets worse every year: That's what it feels like anyway.... | moderate |
| train_pid_2 | Words can't describe how bad I feel right now: I just want to fall asleep forever. | severe |
| train_pid_3 | Is anybody else hoping the Coronavirus shuts everybody down? | not depressed |

Table 2: Sample instances.

## 4 Methods

Our proposed solution involves four main steps (global classifiers, contextual classifiers, ensembling, and post-processing), as presented in the following subsections. By global classifiers, we mean classifiers that take non-contextual features into account, i.e., features that apply to the entire document, without considering the relationships between words or phrases. Contrarily, contextual classifiers do take such relationships into account.

### 4.1 Global classifiers

#### 4.1.1 Features

Based on interdisciplinary knowledge of depression (Ratcliffe, 2014), we analyzed the distribution of certain features across the three classes of text. In particular, we considered: (1) the use of first-person singular pronouns; (2) the use of first-person pronouns (both singular and plural); (3) the use of third-person pronouns (both singular and plural); (4) the use of time-related terms; and (5) the sentiment analysis scores. To select the time-related terms, we started with a set of words identified by us, such as *time*, *now*, and *today*. We then expanded the list by finding synonyms and similar words in WordNet[8], which we further filtered. We obtained the following list: *today*, *now*, *soon*, *tomorrow*, *ago*, *yesterday*, *time*, *month*, *day*, *year*, *late*, *present*, *past*, *future*, *nowadays*, *instant*, *minute*, *second*, *early*, *young*, *old*, *recent*, *nowadays*, *hereafter*, *moment*. In Table 3, we display the statistics of all the features across the three classes. The fifth feature was analyzed by using Valence Aware Dictionary and sEntiment Reasoner (VADER) (Hutto and Gilbert, 2014). All the features proved to be statistically different across groups, besides the presence of third-person pronouns (in red). Although the presence of first-person pronouns (both singular and plural) was significantly different across groups, it was less significantly different than the sole presence of first-person-singular pronouns. Therefore, we did not further take it into account in our study (and we highlighted it in yellow in Table 3). The features that we further considered are highlighted in green in Table 3.

#### 4.1.2 Models

We trained two global classifiers: support vector machine (SVM) and logistic regression (LR). In doing so, we used three attributes that we found to be different across groups as features: the presence of first-person-singular pronouns, the presence of time-related terms, and the sentiment scores. In particular, this was carried out by adapting part of the code developed by Koloski et al. (2021)[9].

[8]wordnet.princeton.edu

[9]bkolosk1/c19_rep

| Features | "Not depression" (mean) | "Moderate" (mean) | "Severe" (mean) | Difference across groups |
|---|---|---|---|---|
| **First-person singular pronouns** (e.g., *I* and *my*) | 0.0163 | 0.0275 | 0.0391 | **F-Statistic**: 6.7717<br>**p-value**: 0.0011<br>**SIGNIFICANT** |
| **First-person pronouns** (e.g., *I* and *we*) | 0.0189 | 0.0294 | 0.0417 | **F-Statistic**: 6.0417<br>**p-value**: 0.0024<br>**SIGNIFICANT** |
| **Third-person pronouns** (e.g., *they* and *she*) | 0.0374 | 0.0522 | 0.0573 | **F-Statistic**: 2.0025<br>**p-value**: 0.1351<br>**NOT SIGNIFICANT** |
| **Time-related terms** (e.g., *now* and *soon*) | 1.7877 | 2.9712 | 4.4102 | **F-Statistic**: 138.6717<br>**p-value**: 8.0705e-32<br>**SIGNIFICANT** |
| **Sentiment analysis** | -0.0800 | -0.2938 | -0.4149 | **F-Statistic**: 103.1463<br>**p-value**: 6.8241e-45<br>**SIGNIFICANT** |

Table 3: Feature analysis results.

### 4.2 Contextual classifiers

Fine-tuning pre-trained language models has proved to be a successful approach to a wide range of downstream NLP tasks, especially since it does not require the effort of training a model from scratch. In our solution, we fine-tuned several commonly used English pre-trained language models in both monolingual and multilingual settings. We did so by following a standard procedure, which involves training a pre-trained language model with a classification head on top (i.e., a linear layer on top of the pooled output).

| Parameters | Value |
|---|---|
| Max sequence length | 512 |
| Number of training epochs | 5 |
| Training batch size | 16 |
| Evaluation batch size | 32 |
| Learning rate | 5e-5 |
| Use early stopping | True |
| Early stopping patience | 3 |
| Manual seed | 42 |

Table 4: Hyper-parameters configuration.

Specifically, we employed the following models: (1) Monolingual models: RoBERTa[10] (Liu et al., 2019), ALBERT[11] (Lan et al., 2019), BERT[12] (Devlin et al., 2018), XLNET[13] (Yang et al., 2019), DistilBERT[14] (Sanh et al., 2019); (2) Multilingual models: mBERT[15], mDistilBERT[16].

[10]roberta-base

[11]albert-base-v2

[12]bert-base-cased

[13]xlnet-base-cased

[14]distilbert-base-uncased

[15]bert-base-multilingual-cased

[16]distilbert-base-multilingual-cased

We utilized multilingual models due to their ability to: capture broader linguistic patterns, facilitate the cross-lingual transfer of knowledge, enhance contextual understanding with model robustness, allow for future adaptability to other languages, and address the issue of data scarcity. Additionally, we implemented distilled versions to reduce computational time.

We used the SimpleTransformers framework[17] (Rajapakse, 2019) to capture the level of depression per sentence while fine-tuning. All experiments were run on a single GPU Tesla V100 presenting the same standard hyperparameter configuration shown in Table 4 for better comparison.

### 4.3 Ensembling approach

In the last step, we combined the best models obtained in the previous stages by using ensemble averaging. This method involves averaging the predictions (expressed as probability) from a group of models. In particular, we utilized (1) the two global, (2) the two best contextual, and (3) the best global and the best contextual classifiers.

### 4.4 Post-processing steps

Unlike the training and development sets, the test set includes several non-English characters. Thus, a post-processing step was applied to filter out them.

### 4.5 Evaluation metrics

To evaluate the performance of our classifiers, we employed the following metrics: macro-averaged F1-score across all the classes; and Precision, Recall, and F1-score (F1) for each individual class.

[17]simpletransformers

| Features | Model | Avg. Macro F1 | Not Depression | | | Moderate | | | Severe | | |
|---|---|---|---|---|---|---|---|---|---|---|---|
| | | | Precision | Recall | F1 | Precision | Recall | F1 | Precision | Recall | F1 |
| Contextual | BERT | 0.425 | 0.378 | 0.622 | 0.471 | 0.583 | 0.524 | 0.552 | 0.500 | 0.169 | 0.252 |
| | XLNET | 0.406 | 0.354 | 0.593 | 0.443 | 0.565 | 0.505 | 0.534 | 0.519 | 0.157 | 0.241 |
| | ALBERT | 0.383 | 0.386 | 0.630 | 0.479 | 0.548 | 0.524 | 0.535 | 0.438 | 0.079 | 0.133 |
| | RoBERTa | 0.447 | 0.389 | 0.622 | 0.479 | 0.592 | 0.560 | 0.576 | 0.696 | 0.180 | 0.286 |
| | DistilBERT | 0.418 | 0.368 | 0.607 | 0.458 | 0.566 | 0.513 | 0.538 | 0.556 | 0.169 | 0.259 |
| | mBERT | 0.418 | 0.332 | 0.563 | 0.418 | 0.566 | 0.498 | 0.530 | 0.643 | 0.202 | 0.308 |
| | mDistilBERT | 0.436 | 0.371 | 0.563 | 0.447 | 0.587 | 0.564 | 0.575 | 0.567 | 0.191 | 0.286 |
| Global | LR | 0.327 | 0.348 | 0.519 | 0.417 | 0.542 | 0.585 | 0.563 | 0.000 | 0.000 | 0.000 |
| | SVM | 0.331 | 0.352 | 0.570 | 0.435 | 0.554 | 0.564 | 0.559 | 0.000 | 0.000 | 0.000 |
| Ensembling | LR + SVM | 0.330 | 0.355 | 0.526 | 0.424 | 0.544 | 0.589 | 0.565 | 0.000 | 0.000 | 0.000 |
| | RoBERTa + mDistilBERT | 0.428 | 0.397 | 0.556 | 0.463 | 0.577 | 0.615 | 0.595 | 0.706 | 0.135 | 0.226 |
| | RoBERTa + SVM | 0.430 | 0.391 | 0.622 | 0.480 | 0.581 | 0.560 | 0.570 | 0.684 | 0.146 | 0.241 |

Table 5: Performance comparison.

## 5 Results

Table 5 shows the results obtained when applying our classifiers to the test set. Among the fine-tuned Transformer-based language models, the RoBERTa model presents the best Average Macro F1-score (0.447). Meanwhile, in machine learning-based approaches, SVM achieves the best Average Macro F1-score score (0.331). However, machine learning methods suffer from the lack of meaningful information to capture the "Severe" level of depression.

While testing with average ensembling, the combination of a language model with a machine learning classifier proves to perform better than combining two models of the same type. However, standalone RoBERTa still surpasses the performance of this combination. More machine learning-based features can be explored in the future.

## 6 Error Analysis

While previous studies (Poświata and Perełkiewicz, 2022; Wang et al., 2022) showed the final ensemble to be the best-performing approach, this is not the case in our study. In fact, RoBERTa shows an overall higher performance than any other contextual classifier, any global classifier, and any ensemble. One factor contributing to the fact that the best-performing ensemble, RoBERTa + SVM, has such a low performance, is that the class imbalance was not addressed properly when training the global classifiers. Besides, we noticed inconsistency among the training, development, and test sets. While the training and development sets contain only Latin alphabet characters, the test set contains special non-Latin characters (i.e., Chinese characters) as shown in Table 6. For example, the letter "'t" was decoded into 鈥檛 in the test set, which covers 24% of all the testing samples. Further data preprocessing steps would be required to solve this inconsistency.

| Non-latin patterns | Ratio |
|---|---|
| 鈥檛 | 0.240 |
| 鈥檓 | 0.214 |
| 鈥檓 | 0.214 |
| 鈥檚 | 0.196 |
| 鈥 | 0.092 |
| 鈥淳 | 0.008 |
| ... | ... |

Table 6: Examples of non-Latin characters in the test set given ratio is the frequency that the pattern appears in a sentence above all the given sentences.

## 7 Conclusion

In this paper, we presented a framework to detect signs of depression from social media text, as proposed by the LT-EDI shared task. Our procedure involved 4-steps: (1) the extraction of global information from language models, (2) the extraction of local information from SVM and LG classifiers, (3) average ensembling, and (4) post-processing. The results demonstrate the effectiveness of our framework. Our BERT-based model ranked $7^{th}$/31 while our RoBERTa model could have achieved the $2^{nd}$/31 in the LT-EDI competition. However, our ensemble approaches showed lower performance than our RoBERTa classifier.

In our future work, we intend to apply upsampling to imbalanced datasets like the one provided for DepSign-LT-EDI@RANLP-2023 and improve our feature engineering. Furthermore, depression detection could be followed by the development of interventional systems to support change in the context of mental health (Kolenik and Gams, 2021; Kolenik, 2022; Kolenik et al., 2023).

## Acknowledgements

We acknowledge the financial support from the Slovenian Research Agency for research core funding for the programme Knowledge Technologies (No. P2-0103) and from the project CANDAS (Computer-assisted multilingual news discourse analysis with contextual embeddings, No. J6-2581). We wish to thank our colleagues at the Jožef Stefan Institute, Tine Kolenik, and the anonymous reviewers for their insightful comments.

## References

D American Psychiatric Association, American Psychiatric Association, et al. 2013. *Diagnostic and statistical manual of mental disorders: DSM-5*, volume 5. American psychiatric association Washington, DC.

Nirmal Varghese Babu and E Grace Mary Kanaga. 2022. Sentiment analysis in social media data for depression detection using artificial intelligence: a review. *SN Computer Science*, 3:1–20.

David A Baker and Guillermo Perez Algorta. 2016. The relationship between online social networking and depression: A systematic review of quantitative studies. *Cyberpsychology, Behavior, and Social Networking*, 19(11):638–648.

Wilma Bucci and Norbert Freedman. 1981. The language of depression. *Bulletin of the Menninger Clinic*, 45(4):334.

Raymond Chiong, Gregorius Satia Budhi, Sandeep Dhakal, and Fabian Chiong. 2021. A textual-based featuring approach for depression detection using machine learning classifiers and social media texts. *Computers in Biology and Medicine*, 135:104499.

Cindy Chung and James W Pennebaker. 2007. The psychological functions of function words. *Social communication*, 1:343–359.

Glen Coppersmith, Mark Dredze, Craig Harman, Kristy Hollingshead, and Margaret Mitchell. 2015. Clpsych 2015 shared task: Depression and ptsd on twitter. In *Proceedings of the 2nd workshop on computational linguistics and clinical psychology: from linguistic signal to clinical reality*, pages 31–39.

Jacob Devlin, Ming-Wei Chang, Kenton Lee, and Kristina Toutanova. 2018. Bert: Pre-training of deep bidirectional transformers for language understanding. *arXiv preprint arXiv:1810.04805*.

Clayton Hutto and Eric Gilbert. 2014. Vader: A parsimonious rule-based model for sentiment analysis of social media text. In *Proceedings of the international AAAI conference on web and social media*, volume 8, pages 216–225.

Tine Kolenik. 2022. Methods in digital mental health: smartphone-based assessment and intervention for stress, anxiety, and depression. In *Integrating Artificial Intelligence and IoT for Advanced Health Informatics: AI in the Healthcare Sector*, pages 105–128. Springer.

Tine Kolenik and Matjaž Gams. 2021. Intelligent cognitive assistants for attitude and behavior change support in mental health: state-of-the-art technical review. *Electronics*, 10(11):1250.

Tine Kolenik, Günter Schiepek, and Matjaž Gams. 2023. Computational psychotherapy system for mental health prediction and behavior change with a conversational agent. Manuscript submitted for publication.

Boshko Koloski, Timen Stepišnik-Perdih, Senja Pollak, and Blaž Škrlj. 2021. Identification of covid-19 related fake news via neural stacking. In *Combating Online Hostile Posts in Regional Languages during Emergency Situation: First International Workshop, CONSTRAINT 2021, Collocated with AAAI 2021, Virtual Event, February 8, 2021, Revised Selected Papers 1*, pages 177–188. Springer.

Zhenzhong Lan, Mingda Chen, Sebastian Goodman, Kevin Gimpel, Piyush Sharma, and Radu Soricut. 2019. Albert: A lite bert for self-supervised learning of language representations. *arXiv preprint arXiv:1909.11942*.

Victor Leiva and Ana Freire. 2017. Towards suicide prevention: early detection of depression on social media. In *Internet Science: 4th International Conference, INSCI 2017, Thessaloniki, Greece, November 22-24, 2017, Proceedings 4*, pages 428–436. Springer.

Jingfang Liu and Mengshi Shi. 2022. A hybrid feature selection and ensemble approach to identify depressed users in online social media. *Frontiers in Psychology*, 12:6571.

Yinhan Liu, Myle Ott, Naman Goyal, Jingfei Du, Mandar Joshi, Danqi Chen, Omer Levy, Mike Lewis, Luke Zettlemoyer, and Veselin Stoyanov. 2019. Roberta: A robustly optimized bert pretraining approach. *arXiv preprint arXiv:1907.11692*.

Laura Orsolini, Roberto Latini, Maurizio Pompili, Gianluca Serafini, Umberto Volpe, Federica Vellante, Michele Fornaro, Alessandro Valchera, Carmine Tomasetti, Silvia Fraticelli, et al. 2020. Understanding the complex of suicide in depression: from research to clinics. *Psychiatry investigation*, 17(3):207.

Rosa María Ortega-Mendoza, Delia Irazú Hernández-Farías, Manuel Montes-y Gómez, and Luis Villaseñor-Pineda. 2022. Revealing traces of depression through personal statements analysis in social media. *Artificial Intelligence in Medicine*, 123:102202.

Sungkyu Park, Inyeop Kim, Sang Won Lee, Jaehyun Yoo, Bumseok Jeong, and Meeyoung Cha. 2015. Manifestation of depression and loneliness on social networks: a case study of young adults on facebook. In *Proceedings of the 18th ACM conference on computer supported cooperative work & social computing*, pages 557–570.

James W Pennebaker. 2011. The secret life of pronouns. *New Scientist*, 211(2828):42–45.

Rafał Poświata and Michał Perełkiewicz. 2022. Opi@ lt-edi-acl2022: Detecting signs of depression from social media text using roberta pre-trained language models. In *Proceedings of the Second Workshop on Language Technology for Equality, Diversity and Inclusion*, pages 276–282.

TC Rajapakse. 2019. Simple transformers. *URL: https://simpletransformers. ai/[accessed 2022-08-25]*.

Matthew Ratcliffe. 2014. *Experiences of depression: A study in phenomenology*. OUP Oxford.

Kayalvizhi Sampath, Thenmozhi Durairaj, Bharathi Raja Chakravarthi, and Jerin Mahibha C. 2022. Findings of the shared task on detecting signs of depression from social media. In *Proceedings of the Second Workshop on Language Technology for Equality, Diversity and Inclusion*, pages 331–338, Dublin, Ireland. Association for Computational Linguistics.

Kayalvizhi Sampath, Thenmozhi Durairaj, Bharathi Raja Chakravarthi, Jerin Mahibha C, Kogilavani Shanmugavadivel, and Pratik Anil Rahood. 2023. Overview of the second shared task on detecting signs of depression from social media text. In *Proceedings of the Third Workshop on Language Technology for Equality, Diversity and Inclusion*, Varna, Bulgaria. Recent Advances in Natural Language Processing.

Victor Sanh, Lysandre Debut, Julien Chaumond, and Thomas Wolf. 2019. Distilbert, a distilled version of bert: smaller, faster, cheaper and lighter. *arXiv preprint arXiv:1910.01108*.

Statista. 2023. Number of social media users worldwide from 2017 to 2027. `https://www.statista.com/statistics/278414/number-of-worldwide-social-network//-users/`. Accessed on 2023-06-22.

Ilija Tavchioski, Boshko Koloski, Blaž Škrlj, and Senja Pollak. 2022a. E8-ijs@ lt-edi-acl2022-bert, automl and knowledge-graph backed detection of depression. In *Proceedings of the second workshop on language technology for equality, diversity and inclusion*, pages 251–257.

Ilija Tavchioski, Marko Robnik-Šikonja, and Senja Pollak. 2023. Detection of depression on social networks using transformers and ensembles. *arXiv preprint arXiv:2305.05325*.

Ilija Tavchioski, Blaž Škrlj, Senja Pollak, and Boshko Koloski. 2022b. Early detection of depression with linear models using hand-crafted and contextual features. *Working Notes of CLEF*, pages 5–8.

Marcel Trotzek, Sven Koitka, and Christoph M Friedrich. 2018. Utilizing neural networks and linguistic metadata for early detection of depression indications in text sequences. *IEEE Transactions on Knowledge and Data Engineering*, 32(3):588–601.

Maria A Villarroel and Emily P Terlizzi. 2020. *Symptoms of depression among adults: United States, 2019*. US Department of Health and Human Services, Centers for Disease Control and ....

Wei-Yao Wang, Yu-Chien Tang, Wei-Wei Du, and Wen-Chih Peng. 2022. Nycu_twd@ lt-edi-acl2022: Ensemble models with vader and contrastive learning for detecting signs of depression from social media. In *Proceedings of the Second Workshop on Language Technology for Equality, Diversity and Inclusion*, pages 136–139.

World Health Organization. 2022. Covid-19 pandemic triggers 25% increase in prevalence of anxiety and depression worldwide. `https://www.who.int/news/item/02-03-2022-covid-19-pandemic-\triggers-25-increase-in-\prevalence-of-anxiety-and-\depression-worldwide`. Accessed on 2023-06-22.

World Health Organization. 2023. Depressive disorder (depression). `https://www.who.int/news-room/fact-sheets/detail/depression`. Accessed on 2023-06-22.

Zhilin Yang, Zihang Dai, Yiming Yang, Jaime Carbonell, Russ R Salakhutdinov, and Quoc V Le. 2019. Xlnet: Generalized autoregressive pretraining for language understanding. *Advances in neural information processing systems*, 32.

# Team-Tamil@LT-EDI-RANLP2023: Automatic Detection of Hope Speech in Bulgarian Language using Embedding Techniques

**Rahul Ponnusamy** [1], **Malliga Subramaniam**[2], **Sajeetha Thavareesan**[3], **Ruba Priyadharshini**[4]
[1] Insight SFI Research Centre for Data Analytics, University of Galway, Ireland, India
[2] Kongu Engineering College, Tamil Nadu, India [3] Eastern University, Sri Lanka
[4] Department of Mathematics, Gandhigram Rural Institute-Deemed to be University, Tamil Nadu, India
rahulponnusamy160032@gmail.com
mallinishanth72@gmail.com
sajeethas@esn.ac.lk, rubapriyadharshini.a@gmail.com

## Abstract

Many people may find motivation in their lives by spreading content on social media that is encouraging or hopeful. Creating an effective model which helps in accurately predicting the target class is a challenging task. The problem of Hope speech identification is dealt with in this work using machine learning and deep learning methods. In this paper, we present the description of the system submitted by our team(Team-Tamil) to the Hope Speech Detection for Equality, Diversity, and Inclusion(HSD-EDI) LT-EDI-RANLP 2023 shared task for the Bulgarian language. The main goal of this shared task is to identify the given text into the Hope speech or Non-Hope speech category. The proposed method using H2O deep learning model with MPNet embeddings and achieved the second rank for the Bulgarian language with the Macro F1 score of 0.69.

## 1 Introduction

One of the remarkable human characteristics is hope, which enables a person to envision future events and the diversity of outcomes that may be anticipated (Snyder, 1994). These visions have a significant effect on a person's emotions, behaviors, and mental state, despite the fact that the desired outcome has a much-reduced likelihood of occurring. Hope is essential to the well-being, recuperation, and restoration of human existence. Greater optimism is consistently associated with improved academic, athletic, and physical health, psychological adjustment, and psychotherapeutic outcomes. Hope theory is similar to learned optimism, optimism, self-efficacy, and self-esteem theories (Snyder, 2002; Chakravarthi, 2022a,b; García-Baena et al., 2023).

People are able to freely express their opinions on numerous social networks today, which has a significant impact on human existence (B and Varsha, 2022; Subramanian et al., 2022). The significant characteristics of social media, including rapid dissemination, low cost, accessibility, and anonymity, have increased the popularity of social media platforms such as Instagram and Twitter (B and A, 2021; Chakravarthi et al., 2023a). Despite the numerous advantages of using OSNs, a growing body of evidence suggests that an increasing number of malicious actors are exploiting these networks to disseminate hate speech and cause harm to others (Chakravarthi et al., 2023b; Santhiya et al., 2023). In addition, social media platforms provide a profound comprehension of people's behaviors and are important sources for Natural Language Processing(NLP)-related scientific research (Chakravarthi et al., 2022a; Shanmugavadivel et al., 2022; Chakravarthi, 2023).

Examining people's expressed levels of hope on social media is therefore believed to be an essential factor in determining their overall happiness (Kumaresan et al., 2023; Subramanian et al., 2023). This type of research can shed light on the progression of goal-directed activities, resilience in the face of adversity, and the mechanisms underlying acclimation to both positive and negative life changes.

In this paper, we present the work carried out on HSD-EDI - LT-EDI-RANLP 2023 in Bulgarian language. The main goal of the shared task is to categorize the comments into Hope speech or Non-Hope speech class. To solve this problem, our team(Team-Tamil) presents the approach based on an embedding technique using MPNet(Song et al., 2020) sentence transformer and deep learning technique with H2O(Candel et al., 2016) deep learning model. Our approach achieved the second rank with a macro F1 score of 0.69 in the Bulgarian language.

The rest of the paper is structured as follows:



*LT-EDI 2023 – Third Workshop on Language Technology for Equality, Diversity and Inclusion*, pages 179–184, Varna, Bulgaria, Sep 7, 2023.
https://doi.org/10.26615/978-954-452-084-7_027

Table 1: Data statistics

| Dataset | Hope speech | Non-Hope speech | Total |
|---|---|---|---|
| Train | 223 | 4448 | 4671 |
| Development | 75 | 514 | 589 |
| Test | 150 | 449 | 599 |

Section 2 provides a brief overview of the studies related to the Hope speech detection problem, Section 3 provides a full explanation of the dataset, Section 4 shows the proposed approach, and Section 5 provides the findings of the experiments that were conducted and followed by the conclusion in Section 6.

## 2 Related Work

Two shared task was released by Chakravarthi and Muralidaran (2021) and Chakravarthi et al. (2022b). Mahajan et al. (2021) used RoBERTa for Hope Speech detection in English and XLM-RoBERTa for Hope Speech detection in Tamil and Malayalam, two low-resourced Dravidian languages. Their performance in classifying text into hope-speech, non-hope, and not-language is demonstrated. Their methodology was rated first in English(F1 = 0.93), first in Tamil(F1 = 0.61), and third in Malayalam(F1 = 0.83). Junaida and Ajees (2021) used Deep learning-based context-aware string embeddings for word representations and Recurrent Neural Network(RNN) and aggregated document embeddings for text representation. The authors examined and contrasted each language's three models using diverse methodologies. Their approach outperforms baselines, and English, Tamil, and Malayalam models beat baselines by 3%, 2%, and 11%, respectively. Pre-processing and transfer-learning models enable the trials.

Dowlagar and Mamidi (2021) used pre-trained multilingual-BERT with convolution neural networks for English, Malayalam-English, and Tamil-English code-mixed datasets, and they ranked first, third, and fourth. S et al. (2021) used transformer models, mBERT for Tamil and Malayalam and BERT for English, yielded weighted average F1-scores of 0.46, 0.81, and 0.92 for Tamil, Malayalam, and English, respectively. Vijayakumar et al. (2022) used BERT to do this work, and their model ranked first in Kannada, second in Malayalam, third in Tamil, and sixth in English for the hope speech 2022 shared task. B et al. (2022) used m-BERT, MLNet, BERT, XLMRoberta, and XLM_MLM to identify and classify them. BERT and m-BERT had the highest weighted F1-scores of 0.92, 0.71, 0.76, 0.87, and 0.83 for English, Tamil, Spanish, Kannada, and Malayalam, respectively.

Our study varies from the previous research in which we used MPNet and doc2vec(Le and Mikolov, 2014) for creating the embedding of the comments. For detecting the Hope speech, we employed H2O deep learning model.

## 3 Dataset and Task Description

We participated in the HSD-EDI task in LT-EDI-RANLP 2023. The main challenge of this task is to create a model that automatically detects whether the comment is a Hope speech or a Non-Hope speech. For this task, the organizers provided the dataset with annotated labels for Bulgarian, English, Hindi, and Spanish languages. Out of these four languages, we worked only on the Bulgarian language. The comments are annotated with two labels: True and False for the Hope speech and Non-Hope speech. The in-depth details of the dataset are provided in (Chakravarthi, 2020). In the first phase, a training and development set was released for creating the model. In the second phase, test sets were released only with the comments to make the prediction with the model that was created with the training set in the first phase. We need to submit the prediction that took from the test set to the organizers. In the last phase, the test set with the labels will be released test set with labels to know the performance of the model. The statistics of the datasets are shown in Table 1.

## 4 Methodology

We conducted an in-depth analysis of the Bulgarian Hope speech dataset utilizing a range of classifiers, from basic machine learning methods to powerful deep learning algorithms. The manner we carried out our research is outlined below. We utilized the scikit-learn[1] library for building machine learning algorithms. We used the h2o library to implement

[1] https://scikit-learn.org

Table 2: List of parameters that are used for creating embedding using doc2vec

| Parameters | Values |
|---|---|
| dm | 0 |
| vector_size | 300 |
| negative | 5 |
| min_count | 1 |
| alpha | 0.065 |
| min_alpha | 0.065 |

Table 3: The table shows the model results on the Development set using doc2vec(ACC: Accuracy, MAC_P: Macro Precision, MAC_R: Macro Recall, MAC_F1: Macro F1, WEI_P: Weighted Precision, WEI_R: Weighted Recall, WEI_F1: Weighted F1)

| MODELS | ACC | MAC_P | MAC_R | MAC_F1 | WEI_P | WEI_R | WEI_F1 |
|---|---|---|---|---|---|---|---|
| **H2O** | 0.84 | 0.63 | 0.62 | **0.62** | 0.83 | 0.84 | 0.84 |
| **DT** | 0.83 | 0.58 | 0.56 | 0.57 | 0.81 | 0.83 | 0.82 |
| **LR** | 0.87 | 0.72 | 0.53 | 0.53 | 0.84 | 0.87 | 0.83 |
| **RF** | 0.87 | 0.44 | 0.50 | 0.47 | 0.76 | 0.87 | 0.81 |
| **SVM** | 0.87 | 0.44 | 0.50 | 0.47 | 0.76 | 0.87 | 0.81 |

Table 4: The table shows the model results on the Development set using MPNet(ACC: Accuracy, MAC_P: Macro Precision, MAC_R: Macro Recall, MAC_F1: Macro F1, WEI_P: Weighted Precision, WEI_R: Weighted Recall, WEI_F1: Weighted F1)

| MODELS | ACC | MAC_P | MAC_R | MAC_F1 | WEI_P | WEI_R | WEI_F1 |
|---|---|---|---|---|---|---|---|
| **H2O** | 0.83 | 0.65 | 0.68 | **0.66** | 0.85 | 0.83 | 0.84 |
| **DT** | 0.83 | 0.56 | 0.53 | 0.54 | 0.80 | 0.83 | 0.81 |
| **RF** | 0.87 | 0.44 | 0.50 | 0.47 | 0.76 | 0.87 | 0.81 |
| **SVM** | 0.87 | 0.44 | 0.50 | 0.47 | 0.76 | 0.87 | 0.81 |
| **LR** | 0.87 | 0.44 | 0.50 | 0.47 | 0.76 | 0.87 | 0.81 |

the deep neural network. We used Google Colaboratory[2] to train the models because of its user interface and quicker access to GPU resources.

For detecting the hope speech from the text, Firstly, we remove noise from data in order to improve data quality for improved performance and remove URLs and Unhelpful expressions(terms that start with @). Secondly, we converted the cleaned text to feature vectors using doc2vec and MPNet. The doc2vec[3] is also known as paragraph vectors, an unsupervised method for learning fixed-length feature representations from texts with varying lengths, such as paragraphs, sentences, and documents. Each sentence is represented by a dense vector. We set up parameters with dm=0(training algorithm with a distributed bag of words),vector_size=300(dimensionality of the feature vectors), negative=5 for negative sampling, and the remaining parameters are listed in Table 2. MPNet is a cutting-edge pre-training technique that inherits the benefits of BERT and XLNet while avoiding their drawbacks. We get embedding from the text using the pretrained model('all-mpnet-base-v2' from sentence transformer[4]). Thirdly, we experimented with the traditional machine learning techniques, namely, Logistic Regression(LR), Random Forest(RF), Decision Tree(DT), and Support Vector Machine(SVM) Classifier using the scikit-learn library and the Deep learning technique using H2O framework[5] with rectifier as activation function and [100,100] of hidden layer size. The model is trained for ten epochs.

In the next section, we explained the performance of the models.

[2] https://colab.research.google.com

[3] https://radimrehurek.com/gensim/models/doc2vec.html

[4] https://huggingface.co/sentence-transformers/all-mpnet-base-v2

[5] https://github.com/h2oai/h2o-3/tree/master

Table 5: This table shows the result on the Test set with the H2O model using MPNet embeddings

| H2O_MPNet | Scores |
|---|---|
| Accuracy | 0.80 |
| Macro Precision | 0.74 |
| Macro Recall | 0.67 |
| Macro F1 | **0.69** |
| Weighted Precision | 0.78 |
| Weighted Recall | 0.80 |
| Weighted F1 | 0.78 |

Figure 1: Confusion matrix of the H2O deep learning model with MPNet on the test set. Support value for False(Non-Hope speech) is 449 and True(Hope speech) is 150.

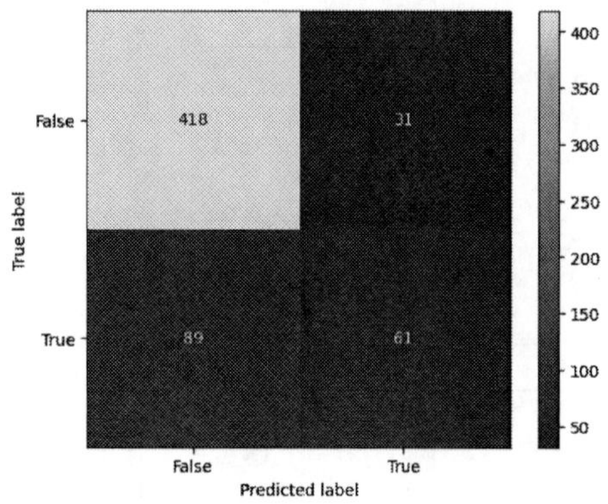


## 5 Results and discussion

In this section, we discussed the outcomes of the experiments of the model that we used. The performance of the models is evaluated with Accuracy, Macro Precision, Macro Recall, Macro F1, Weighted Precision, Weighted Recall, and Weighted F1 score. There are 449 samples of Non-Hope speech and 150 samples of Hope speech. We used four machine learning models and one deep learning model with two embedding techniques: doc2vec and MPNet. Among all other models, H2O deep learning model performed well with both doc2vec and MPNet embeddings on the development set with macro F1 scores of 0.62 and 0.66, respectively. The results of the models with doc2vec and MPNet are shown in Table 3 and Table 4. We selected the top-performing model on the development set, that is H2O deep learning model with MPNet embeddings, to make predictions on the test set. The final leaderboard results revealed that the proposed methodology ranked in second place in the Bulgarian language with a Macro F1-score of 0.69. The results of the test set are shown in Table 5. The confusion matrix in Figure 1 displays the right prediction as 418 out of 449 is false and 61 out of 150 is true.

## 6 Conclusion

Social media platforms have evolved into a forum for people to discuss their thoughts, successes, achievements, and errors. Social networking members leave comments on various types of content. Positive words can assist in increasing confidence and sometimes push you to be strong in difficult situations. This article describes our model that was submitted to the HSD-EDI - LT-EDI-RANLP 2023 competition. We used the H2O framework to build a deep neural network for categorization. We utilized MPNet from the sentence transformer for creating embeddings. Our proposed method comes in second place with a weighted F1 score of 0.69 which is above the baselines. To improve performance further, the model can be fine-tuned with model architecture as well as by doing hyper-parameter tuning.

## References


Bharathi B and Agnusimmaculate Silvia A. 2021. SSNCSE_NLP@DravidianLangTech-EACL2021: Offensive language identification on multilingual code mixing text. In *Proceedings of the First Workshop on Speech and Language Technologies for Dravidian Languages*, pages 313–318, Kyiv. Association for Computational Linguistics.

Bharathi B, Dhanya Srinivasan, Josephine Varsha, Thenmozhi Durairaj, and Senthil Kumar B. 2022. SSNCSE_NLP@LT-EDI-ACL2022:hope speech detection for equality, diversity and inclusion using sentence transformers. In *Proceedings of the Second Workshop on Language Technology for Equality, Diversity and Inclusion*, pages 218–222, Dublin, Ireland. Association for Computational Linguistics.

Bharathi B and Josephine Varsha. 2022. SSNCSE NLP@TamilNLP-ACL2022: Transformer based approach for detection of abusive comment for Tamil language. In *Proceedings of the Second Workshop on Speech and Language Technologies for Dravidian Languages*, pages 158–164, Dublin, Ireland. Association for Computational Linguistics.

Arno Candel, Viraj Parmar, Erin LeDell, and Anisha Arora. 2016. Deep learning with h2o. *H2O. ai Inc*, pages 1–21.

Bharathi Raja Chakravarthi. 2020. Hopeedi: A multilingual hope speech detection dataset for equality, diversity, and inclusion. In *Proceedings of the Third Workshop on Computational Modeling of People's Opinions, Personality, and Emotion's in Social Media*, pages 41–53.

Bharathi Raja Chakravarthi. 2022a. Hope speech detection in youtube comments. *Social Network Analysis and Mining*, 12(1):75.

Bharathi Raja Chakravarthi. 2022b. Multilingual hope speech detection in english and dravidian languages. *International Journal of Data Science and Analytics*, 14(4):389–406.

Bharathi Raja Chakravarthi. 2023. Detection of homophobia and transphobia in youtube comments. *International Journal of Data Science and Analytics*, pages 1–20.

Bharathi Raja Chakravarthi, Adeep Hande, Rahul Ponnusamy, Prasanna Kumar Kumaresan, and Ruba Priyadharshini. 2022a. How can we detect homophobia and transphobia? experiments in a multilingual code-mixed setting for social media governance. *International Journal of Information Management Data Insights*, 2(2):100119.

Bharathi Raja Chakravarthi, Manoj Balaji Jagadeeshan, Vasanth Palanikumar, and Ruba Priyadharshini. 2023a. Offensive language identification in dravidian languages using mpnet and cnn. *International Journal of Information Management Data Insights*, 3(1):100151.

Bharathi Raja Chakravarthi and Vigneshwaran Muralidaran. 2021. Findings of the shared task on hope speech detection for equality, diversity, and inclusion. In *Proceedings of the First Workshop on Language Technology for Equality, Diversity and Inclusion*, pages 61–72, Kyiv. Association for Computational Linguistics.

Bharathi Raja Chakravarthi, Vigneshwaran Muralidaran, Ruba Priyadharshini, Subalalitha Cn, John McCrae, Miguel Ángel García, Salud María Jiménez-Zafra, Rafael Valencia-García, Prasanna Kumaresan, Rahul Ponnusamy, Daniel García-Baena, and José García-Díaz. 2022b. Overview of the shared task on hope speech detection for equality, diversity, and inclusion. In *Proceedings of the Second Workshop on Language Technology for Equality, Diversity and Inclusion*, pages 378–388, Dublin, Ireland. Association for Computational Linguistics.

Bharathi Raja Chakravarthi, Ruba Priyadharshini, Shubanker Banerjee, Manoj Balaji Jagadeeshan, Prasanna Kumar Kumaresan, Rahul Ponnusamy, Sean Benhur, and John Philip McCrae. 2023b. Detecting abusive comments at a fine-grained level in a low-resource language. *Natural Language Processing Journal*, 3:100006.

Suman Dowlagar and Radhika Mamidi. 2021. EDIOne@LT-EDI-EACL2021: Pre-trained transformers with convolutional neural networks for hope speech detection. In *Proceedings of the First Workshop on Language Technology for Equality, Diversity and Inclusion*, pages 86–91, Kyiv. Association for Computational Linguistics.

Daniel García-Baena, Miguel Ángel García-Cumbreras, Salud María Jiménez-Zafra, José Antonio García-Díaz, and Rafael Valencia-García. 2023. Hope speech detection in spanish: The lgbt case. *Language Resources and Evaluation*, pages 1–28.

MK Junaida and AP Ajees. 2021. Ku_nlp@ lt-edi-eacl2021: a multilingual hope speech detection for equality, diversity, and inclusion using context aware embeddings. In *Proceedings of the first workshop on language technology for equality, diversity and inclusion*, pages 79–85.

Prasanna Kumar Kumaresan, Rahul Ponnusamy, Elizabeth Sherly, Sangeetha Sivanesan, and Bharathi Raja Chakravarthi. 2023. Transformer based hope speech comment classification in code-mixed text. In *Speech and Language Technologies for Low-Resource Languages*, pages 120–137, Cham. Springer International Publishing.

Quoc Le and Tomas Mikolov. 2014. Distributed representations of sentences and documents. In *International conference on machine learning*, pages 1188–1196. PMLR.

Khyati Mahajan, Erfan Al-Hossami, and Samira Shaikh. 2021. TeamUNCC@LT-EDI-EACL2021: Hope speech detection using transfer learning with transformers. In *Proceedings of the First Workshop on Language Technology for Equality, Diversity and Inclusion*, pages 136–142, Kyiv. Association for Computational Linguistics.

Arunima S, Akshay Ramakrishnan, Avantika Balaji, Thenmozhi D., and Senthil Kumar B. 2021. ssn_diBERTsity@LT-EDI-EACL2021:hope speech detection on multilingual YouTube comments via transformer based approach. In *Proceedings of the First Workshop on Language Technology for Equality, Diversity and Inclusion*, pages 92–97, Kyiv. Association for Computational Linguistics.

S. Santhiya, P. Jayadharshini, and S. V. Kogilavani. 2023. Transfer learning based Youtube toxic comments identification. In *Speech and Language Technologies for Low-Resource Languages*, pages 220–230, Cham. Springer International Publishing.

Kogilavani Shanmugavadivel, Sai Haritha Sampath, Pramod Nandhakumar, Prasath Mahalingam, Malliga Subramanian, Prasanna Kumar Kumaresan, and Ruba Priyadharshini. 2022. An analysis of machine learning models for sentiment analysis of Tamil code-mixed data. *Computer Speech Language*, 76:101407.

C Richard Snyder. 2002. Hope theory: Rainbows in the mind. *Psychological inquiry*, 13(4):249–275.

Charles Richard Snyder. 1994. *The psychology of hope: You can get there from here*. Simon and Schuster.

Kaitao Song, Xu Tan, Tao Qin, Jianfeng Lu, and Tie-Yan Liu. 2020. Mpnet: Masked and permuted pre-training for language understanding. *Advances in Neural Information Processing Systems*, 33:16857–16867.

Malliga Subramanian, Ramya Chinnasamy, Prasanna Kumar Kumaresan, Vasanth Palanikumar, Madhoora Mohan, and Kogilavani Shanmugavadivel. 2023. Development of multi-lingual models for detecting hope speech texts from social media comments. In *Speech and Language Technologies for Low-Resource Languages*, pages 209–219, Cham. Springer International Publishing.

Malliga Subramanian, Rahul Ponnusamy, Sean Benhur, Kogilavani Shanmugavadivel, Adhithiya Ganesan, Deepti Ravi, Gowtham Krishnan Shanmugasundaram, Ruba Priyadharshini, and Bharathi Raja Chakravarthi. 2022. Offensive language detection in Tamil Youtube comments by adapters and cross-domain knowledge transfer. *Computer Speech Language*, 76:101404.

Praveenkumar Vijayakumar, Prathyush S, Aravind P, Angel S, Rajalakshmi Sivanaiah, Sakaya Milton Rajendram, and Mirnalinee T T. 2022. SSN_ARMM@ LT-EDI -ACL2022: Hope speech detection for equality, diversity, and inclusion using ALBERT model. In *Proceedings of the Second Workshop on Language Technology for Equality, Diversity and Inclusion*, pages 172–176, Dublin, Ireland. Association for Computational Linguistics.

# Cordyceps@LT-EDI: Patching Language-Specific Homophobia/Transphobia Classifiers with a Multilingual Understanding

**Dean Ninalga**
justin.ninalga@mail.utoronto.ca

## Abstract

Detecting transphobia, homophobia, and various other forms of hate speech is difficult. Signals can vary depending on factors such as language, culture, geographical region, and the particular online platform. Here, we present a joint multilingual (M-L) and language-specific (L-S) approach to homophobia and transphobic hate speech detection (HSD). M-L models are needed to catch words, phrases, and concepts that are less common or missing in a particular language and subsequently overlooked by L-S models. Nonetheless, L-S models are better situated to understand the cultural and linguistic context of the users who typically write in a particular language. Here we construct a simple and successful way to merge the M-L and L-S approaches through simple weight interpolation in such a way that is interpretable and data-driven. We demonstrate our system on task A of the *Shared Task on Homophobia/Transphobia Detection in social media comments* dataset for homophobia and transphobic HSD. Our system achieves the best results in three of five languages and achieves a 0.997 macro average F1-score on Malayalam texts.

## 1 Introduction

In general, the US is seeing an increase in institutionalized transphobia in the form of banning gender-affirming care and the banning of transgender youth from several sports (Kline et al., 2023). However, studies on individuals who experience institutionalized transphobia in the US experience more psychological distress and instances of suicidal ideation (Price et al., 2023). The codifying of anti-trans laws then certainly must give confidence to those with transphobic beliefs and desires to spread anti-trans rhetoric in online spaces. Berger et al. (2022) recently presented results showing that LGBTQ youth often rely on social media for improved mental health outcomes and as a source of social connection that helps close mental health disparities. Therefore, appropriate content moderation on social media platforms stands to benefit from accurate NLP systems that can identify homophobia, transphobia, and other forms of hate speech.

Good knowledge of hate speech in a particular language may not always be useful for other languages, yet many common phrases and sayings are often expressed across languages. Namely, purveyors of hate speech often do not openly say hateful comments but instead rely on equally vicious code phrases, or *dogwhistles*, to avoid existing content moderation systems (Henderson and McCready, 2017; Magu et al., 2017). Knowledge of the hidden meanings of these encoded sayings can create powerful tools for improving online moderation (Mendelsohn et al., 2023). These phrases can easily transcend the regions of their origin, spreading across online communities without detection in vulnerable communities. Hence,



*LT-EDI 2023 – Third Workshop on Language Technology for Equality, Diversity and Inclusion*, pages 185–191, Varna, Bulgaria, Sep 7, 2023.
https://doi.org/10.26615/978-954-452-084-7_028

knowledge of dogwhistles in their current form will make content moderation systems more robust to these signals as they appear in different languages in new online spaces.

Textual databases built for hate speech analysis are predominantly in English, which creates language-based performance disparities (Jahan and Oussalah, 2021; Poletto et al., 2020; Aluru et al., 2020). As Wang et al. (2020) suggested, in M-L models languages are in competing for model resources, potentially resulting in worse performance for low-resources languages. This performance bias is possibly due to that many M-L datasets used for pretraining popular language models often are majority English samples, often by a wide margin (Barbieri et al., 2021; Xue et al., 2020; Ri et al., 2021)). Consequently, there is a general disparity in performance when comparing English-only and M-L HSD models (Röttger et al., 2022).

Nozza et al. (2020) push for more pre-trained models in non-English languages as they will (naturally) be best for downstream tasks in the same language domain they are trained in. However, pre-training techniques typically require large datasets to guarantee good downstream performance. Given a relative lack of language-specific data for HSP, more indirect and creative approaches are required to alleviate the performance gap between English and non-English tasks.

For our present purposes, we are presented with multiple target languages and tasked to detect levels of homophobia and transphobia for each specified language using an automated system. We introduce Language-PAINT to jointly model M-L and L-S knowledge that incorporates recent work on weight interpolation.

In summary, our main contributions are the following:

- We publicize a language-based weight interpolation approach as the next step in advancing HSD research.
- We provide a demonstration of our framework on task A of the *Shared Task on Homophobia/Transphobia Detection in social media comments* (Chakravarthi et al., 2022).
- We provide preliminary evidence suggesting that our framework is robust to label distribution shifts.

## 2 Related Work

### 2.1 Language Transfer in Hate Speech Detection

Several techniques from recent years have worked on closing the performance disparity between majority and minority languages in HSD. Namely, several attempts directly translate low-resource languages into high-resource ones (Pamungkas and Patti, 2019; Ibrohim and Budi, 2019). Pelicon et al. (2021) presents a data-based approach that first trains a M-L model for HSD, similar to our training scheme's initial step. Pelicon et al. (2021) use a percentage of L-S data to finetune their model where the percentage is chosen empirically. Choudhury et al. (2017) delay training with code-mixed data, opting to first train with mono-lingual samples using the two languages used in the code-mixed data. The popular IndicNLP (Kunchukuttan et al., 2020) uses bilingual word embeddings for translation and transliteration, typically between English and a target low-resource language. Biradar et al. (2021) subsequently attempt to incorporate IndicNLP's (Kunchukuttan et al., 2020) embeddings for code-mixed HSD.

### 2.2 Weight Interpolation

In this paper, we adopt the interpolation strategy of *Weight-space ensembles for fine-tuning*

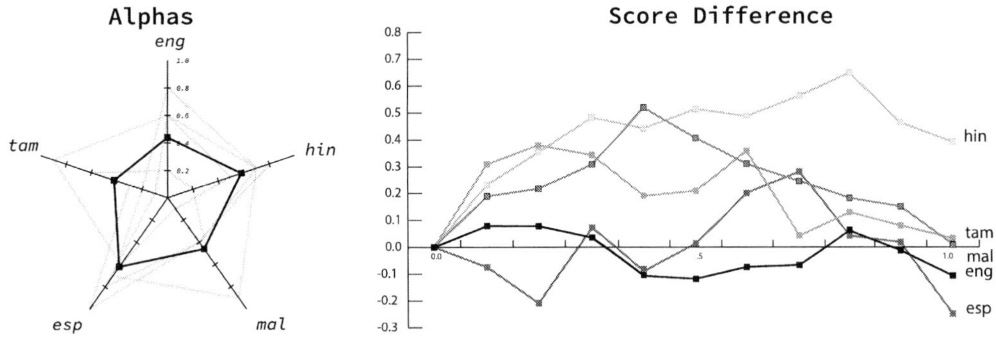


Figure 1: Left: Average selected value for $\alpha$ (thick black line) averaged over five runs for each language. Right: Average validation F1 score as a function of $\alpha$ reported for each language, averaged over five runs.

(WiSE-FT) (Wortsman et al., 2021). In particular, we base our framework on a subsequent variation called PAINT (Ilharco et al., 2022) constructed to incorporate the input robustness of a zero-shot model into finetuned models across diverse tasks. Formally, given a single task $t$ takes the weights of the *zero-shot* model $\theta_z$ and a finetuned model $\theta_f$, the weight interpolation of PAINT performs the interpolation:

$$\theta^t = \alpha\theta_z + (1-\alpha)\theta_f$$

with $\alpha \in [0, 1]$. In addition to the specific experiments performed by (Ilharco et al., 2022), recent work shows that averaging two (or more) language models has the potential to leverage knowledge contained in each (Gueta et al., 2023; Don-Yehiya et al., 2022; Choshen et al., 2022). However, no prior work has studied weight space ensembling based on language to the best of our knowledge.

## 3 Methodology

Here, we use Bernice (DeLucia et al., 2022), a language model exclusively on Twitter[1] data and is known to be performant on HSD across multiple languages. Indeed, many studies rely on Twitter, to construct datasets of code-mixed samples for various HSD approaches (Bhat et al., 2018; Bansal et al., 2020; Farooqi et al., 2021; Choudhury et al., 2017), which in aggregate, motivates our choice of language model.

[1]https://twitter.com

### 3.1 Language-PAINT

Given $k$ distinct groups of (possibly code-mixed) languages, we first train a M-L model on a dataset that includes all the languages. We continue training until saturation on a validation set, where we take the average F1 score across languages. Next, we create an additional $k$ L-S models, - one for each language - where each is initialized with the weights of the M-L model. Finally, we perform linear interpolation between the weights of the M-L and each of the $k$ L-S models. The resulting $k$ models are used for inference on each language.

In mathematical terms, Language-PAINT takes the weights of the trained L-S model $\theta^i_{ls}$ and the weights of the M-L model $\theta_{ml}$ and performs the following interpolation:

$$\theta^i = \alpha\theta^i_{ls} + (1-\alpha)\theta_{ml}.$$

Where $\theta^i$ is used to create predictions for the respective language $i = 1, .., k$ in the test set. In practice, we select alpha from a discrete set

| Paramter | Value |
|---|---|
| Batch Size | 16 |
| Learning Rate | 1e-5 |
| Optimizer | Adam |
| Loss | cross-entropy |

Table 1: Training Hyper-parameters

$\alpha \in \{0, 0.1, 0.2, ..., 1\}$ and select based on the resulting model's F1 performance on a held-out validation set.

### 3.2 Ensembling

Our final prediction on the test sets is an ensembled output of five models trained on five stratified folds. To create these folds, we first conjoined the original training and development sets. Next, we divided the conjoined dataset into five folds using 80-20 train-validation splits, ensuring we maintain the label distribution across each fold. We then trained a fresh model on each training and validation fold using the methodology that is described above. For final inference, we sum the output probabilities of the five models selecting the maximum probability as the final prediction.

### 3.3 Data Cleaning

To preserve as much textual information as possible, we apply minimal additional cleaning steps. Namely, we only remove a sample if it is found to be overlapping in both the train and development data. In total, we removed 1695 duplicate samples, where 54% of the dropped samples are in Tamil and 41% are in Malayalam.

## 4 Experiments and Results

### 4.1 Experimental Setup

Here, we will perform experiments comparing the L-S, M-L, and, LangPAINT approaches. For our first experiment, we combine the training and development set into a single case study. We train five models re-sampling a random 80-20 train-validation split for each run and report the average results on the test set. For our second experiment, we combine the training, development, and, test sets into a single dataset. Where we train ten models re-sampling a random 80-10-10 train-validation-test split for each run, reporting the average of the results on each test set. For each of our two experiments, we use the *weighted* F1 score to evaluate performance. All experiments were run on a single Tesla V4 GPU and we provide the training hyperparameters in Table 1.

## 5 Results

The results of our experiments are given in Table 2. We can see for most languages, the L-S approach tends to perform best, with the exception of the Malayalam language. This is reflective of our final leaderboard results where we used an ensemble method (see Section 3.2) that achieves a 0.997 macro average F1-score on Malayalam texts. Additionally, we report the selected values for $\alpha$ and validation score as a function of $\alpha$ in Figure 1 for this first experiment.

For our second experiment, our results (see Table 2) are much more in favor of our method. Perhaps the considerably worse performance of the L-S and M-S models is due to the high label-distribution shift between the re-sampled train and test splits. Nonetheless, LangPAINT appears to be robust to this shift and is still able to maintain good performance, with the only exception being the Spanish language.

## 6 Conclusion

In this paper, we introduce LangPAINT. LangPAINT is a weight space ensembling strategy (Wortsman et al., 2021) repurposed to jointly model the multi-lingual and language-specific

| Language | Test set L-S | Test set M-L | Test set LangPAINT (ours) | 10 Fold L-S | 10 Fold M-L | 10 Fold LangPAINT (ours) |
|---|---|---|---|---|---|---|
| eng | **0.93** | 0.928 | **0.93** | 0.565 | 0.584 | **0.94** |
| hin | **0.943** | 0.939 | 0.939 | 0.478 | 0.541 | **0.932** |
| mal | 0.965 | 0.97 | **0.971** | 0.834 | 0.827 | **0.930** |
| esp | **0.878** | 0.874 | 0.877 | 0.91 | **0.932** | 0.877 |
| tam | **0.927** | 0.923 | **0.927** | 0.87 | 0.878 | **0.895** |

Table 2: Results of our experiments comparing the language-specific (L-S), multi-lingual (M-L) and, LangPAINT approaches across languages. We report the *weighted* F1 score for each, where the results are the average of five runs.

signals of homophobia and transphobia. Our experiments suggest that our method is competitive with the language expert models and has the potential to be very robust to label distribution shifts. On task A of the *Shared Task on Homophobia/Transphobia Detection in social media comments* (Chakravarthi et al., 2022) achieving the best results in three of five languages and achieves a 0.997 macro average F1-score on Malayalam, a low-resource language.

## References


Sai Saket Aluru, Binny Mathew, Punyajoy Saha, and Animesh Mukherjee. 2020. Deep learning models for multilingual hate speech detection. *ArXiv*, abs/2004.06465.

Srijan Bansal, Vishal Garimella, Ayush Suhane, Jasabanta Patro, and Animesh Mukherjee. 2020. Code-switching patterns can be an effective route to improve performance of downstream nlp applications: A case study of humour, sarcasm and hate speech detection. In *Annual Meeting of the Association for Computational Linguistics*.

Francesco Barbieri, Luis Espinosa Anke, and José Camacho-Collados. 2021. Xlm-t: Multilingual language models in twitter for sentiment analysis and beyond. In *International Conference on Language Resources and Evaluation*.

Matthew N Berger, Melody Taba, Jennifer L. Marino, Megan S. C. Lim, and S. Rachel Skinner. 2022. Social media use and health and well-being of lesbian, gay, bisexual, transgender, and queer youth: Systematic review. *Journal of Medical Internet Research*, 24.

Irshad Ahmad Bhat, Riyaz Ahmad Bhat, Manish Shrivastava, and Dipti Misra Sharma. 2018. Universal dependency parsing for hindi-english code-switching. In *North American Chapter of the Association for Computational Linguistics*.

Shankar Biradar, Sunil Saumya, and Arun Chauhan. 2021. Hate or non-hate: Translation based hate speech identification in code-mixed hinglish data set. *2021 IEEE International Conference on Big Data (Big Data)*, pages 2470–2475.

Bharathi Raja Chakravarthi, Adeep Hande, Rahul Ponnusamy, Prasanna Kumar Kumaresan, and Ruba Priyadharshini. 2022. How can we detect homophobia and transphobia? experiments in a multilingual code-mixed setting for social media governance. *International Journal of Information Management Data Insights*, 2(2):100119.

Leshem Choshen, Elad Venezian, Noam Slonim, and Yoav Katz. 2022. Fusing finetuned models for better pretraining. *ArXiv*, abs/2204.03044.

Monojit Choudhury, Kalika Bali, Sunayana Sitaram, and Ashutosh Baheti. 2017. Curriculum design for code-switching: Experiments with language identification and language modeling with deep neural networks. In *ICON*.

Alexandra DeLucia, Shijie Wu, Aaron Mueller, Carlos Aguirre, Philip Resnik, and Mark

Dredze. 2022. Bernice: A multilingual pre-trained encoder for Twitter. In *Proceedings of the 2022 Conference on Empirical Methods in Natural Language Processing*, pages 6191–6205, Abu Dhabi, United Arab Emirates. Association for Computational Linguistics.

Shachar Don-Yehiya, Elad Venezian, Colin Raffel, Noam Slonim, Yoav Katz, and Leshem Choshen. 2022. Cold fusion: Collaborative descent for distributed multitask finetuning. *ArXiv*, abs/2212.01378.

Zaki Mustafa Farooqi, Sreyan Ghosh, and Rajiv Ratn Shah. 2021. Leveraging transformers for hate speech detection in conversational code-mixed tweets. In *Fire*.

Almog Gueta, Elad Venezian, Colin Raffel, Noam Slonim, Yoav Katz, and Leshem Choshen. 2023. Knowledge is a region in weight space for fine-tuned language models. *ArXiv*, abs/2302.04863.

Robert Henderson and Eric McCready. 2017. How dogwhistles work. In *JSAI-isAI Workshops*.

Muhammad Okky Ibrohim and Indra Budi. 2019. Translated vs non-translated method for multilingual hate speech identification in twitter. *International Journal on Advanced Science, Engineering and Information Technology*.

Gabriel Ilharco, Mitchell Wortsman, Samir Yitzhak Gadre, Shuran Song, Hannaneh Hajishirzi, Simon Kornblith, Ali Farhadi, and Ludwig Schmidt. 2022. Patching open-vocabulary models by interpolating weights. *ArXiv*, abs/2208.05592.

Md Saroar Jahan and Mourad Oussalah. 2021. A systematic review of hate speech automatic detection using natural language processing. *ArXiv*, abs/2106.00742.

Nolan S. Kline, Nathaniel J. Webb, Kaeli C. M. Johnson, Hayley D. Yording, Stacey B. Griner, and David J. Brunell. 2023. Mapping transgender policies in the us 2017-2021: The role of geography and implications for health equity. *Health & place*, 80:102985.

Anoop Kunchukuttan, Divyanshu Kakwani, Satish Golla, C. GokulN., Avik Bhattacharyya, Mitesh M. Khapra, and Pratyush Kumar. 2020. Ai4bharat-indicnlp corpus: Monolingual corpora and word embeddings for indic languages. *ArXiv*, abs/2005.00085.

Rijul Magu, Kshitija Joshi, and Jiebo Luo. 2017. Detecting the hate code on social media. In *International Conference on Web and Social Media*.

Julia Mendelsohn, Ronan Le Bras, Yejin Choi, and Maarten Sap. 2023. From dogwhistles to bullhorns: Unveiling coded rhetoric with language models. *ArXiv*, abs/2305.17174.

Debora Nozza, Federico Bianchi, and Dirk Hovy. 2020. What the [mask]? making sense of language-specific bert models. *ArXiv*, abs/2003.02912.

Endang Wahyu Pamungkas and Viviana Patti. 2019. Cross-domain and cross-lingual abusive language detection: A hybrid approach with deep learning and a multilingual lexicon. In *Annual Meeting of the Association for Computational Linguistics*.

Andraz Pelicon, Ravi Shekhar, Bla krlj, Matthew Purver, and Senja Pollak. 2021. Investigating cross-lingual training for offensive language detection. *PeerJ Computer Science*, 7.

Fabio Poletto, Valerio Basile, Manuela Sanguinetti, Cristina Bosco, and Viviana Patti. 2020. Resources and benchmark corpora for hate speech detection: a systematic review. *Language Resources and Evaluation*, 55:477 – 523.

Maggi A. Price, Nathan L. Hollinsaid, Sarah C. McKetta, Emily J Mellen, and Marina Rakhilin. 2023. Structural transphobia is associated with psychological distress and suicidality in a large national sample of transgender adults. *Social Psychiatry and Psychiatric Epidemiology*, pages 1 – 10.

Ryokan Ri, Ikuya Yamada, and Yoshimasa Tsuruoka. 2021. mluke: The power of entity representations in multilingual pretrained language models. In *Annual Meeting of the Association for Computational Linguistics*.

Paul Röttger, Haitham Seelawi, Debora Nozza, Zeerak Talat, and Bertie Vidgen. 2022. Multilingual hatecheck: Functional tests for multilingual hate speech detection models. *ArXiv*, abs/2206.09917.

Zirui Wang, Zachary Chase Lipton, and Yulia Tsvetkov. 2020. On negative interference in multilingual models: Findings and a meta-learning treatment. In *Conference on Empirical Methods in Natural Language Processing*.

Mitchell Wortsman, Gabriel Ilharco, Mike Li, Jong Wook Kim, Hannaneh Hajishirzi, Ali Farhadi, Hongseok Namkoong, and Ludwig Schmidt. 2021. Robust fine-tuning of zero-shot models. *2022 IEEE/CVF Conference on Computer Vision and Pattern Recognition (CVPR)*, pages 7949–7961.

Linting Xue, Noah Constant, Adam Roberts, Mihir Kale, Rami Al-Rfou, Aditya Siddhant, Aditya Barua, and Colin Raffel. 2020. mt5: A massively multilingual pre-trained text-to-text transformer. In *North American Chapter of the Association for Computational Linguistics*.

# Cordyceps@LT-EDI : Depression Detection with Reddit and Self-training

**Dean Ninalga**
justin.ninalga@mail.utoronto.ca

## Abstract

Depression is debilitating, and not uncommon. Indeed, studies of excessive social media users show correlations with depression, ADHD, and other mental health concerns. Given that there is a large number of people with excessive social media usage, then there is a significant population of potentially undiagnosed users and posts that they create. In this paper, we propose a depression severity detection system using a semi-supervised learning technique to predict if a post is from a user who is experiencing severe, moderate, or low (non-diagnostic) levels of depression. Namely, we use a trained model to classify a large number of unlabelled social media posts from Reddit[1], then use these generated labels to train a more powerful classifier. We demonstrate our framework on *Detecting Signs of Depression from Social Media Text - LT-EDI@RANLP 2023* (Sampath et al., 2023) shared task, where our framework ranks 3rd overall.

## 1 Introduction

### 1.1 Depression and Social Media

A unique feature of depression is its effect on cognitive and verbal patterns. For example, depression diagnosis is correlated to the frequency of personal pronoun usage and the usage of positive-negative words (Edwards and Holtzman, 2017; Tølbøll, 2019). Additionally, persons suffering from depression often connect vicious yet potentially fictional narratives to benign experiences, generally increasing the number of overwhelming situations they may experience (Kanter et al., 2008). People may then go to social media and online forums like Reddit to discuss and post about traumatizing experiences and may publicly reflect on their thoughts and behavior. It is unsurprising, therefore, to find a wealth of attempts (as surveyed by Hasib et al. (2023)) to use social media posts to create a potential diagnostic screening tool through language modeling. Recently, language models can accurately predict symptoms before practitioners record them (Eichstaedt et al., 2018; Reece et al., 2016).

There are significant challenges to data collection in the depression detection setting despite a potential abundance of data that likely exists on social media. Indeed, excessive social media usage itself correlates with depression, ADHD, and other serious mental health diagnoses (Hussain and Griffiths, 2019). However, Guntuku et al. (2017) observe that most attempts at data collection rely on a self-declaration or a past diagnosis of depression, allowing for the possibility of non-actively depressed individuals creating depression-positive data. In this paper, we will attempt to apply an automatic data collection process from social media through a semi-supervised approach.

[1] https://www.reddit.com/



*LT-EDI 2023 – Third Workshop on Language Technology for Equality, Diversity and Inclusion*, pages 192–197, Varna, Bulgaria, Sep 7, 2023.
https://doi.org/10.26615/978-954-452-084-7_029

### 1.2 Background on Self-training

Self-training techniques (Scudder, 1965) are a type of semi-supervised learning and are well known in various areas of research (e.g. Zoph et al. (2020); Xie et al. (2019); Sahito et al. (2021)). These techniques in broad terms, take a trained model, generate labels for a large set of unlabeled data, then train a new model incorporating the clean labels, generated labels, and unlabeled data. Where the new model is typically of the same size, or bigger, as the original trained model. Surprisingly, however, little work has been done exploring how to apply this process in the specific case of depression detection across many social media.

To summarize, our main contributions are the following:

- We describe our framework based on self-training.
- We demonstrate our framework on *Detecting Signs of Depression from Social Media Text - LT-EDI@RANLP 2023* (Sampath et al., 2023) shared task, comparing to recent work.
- We describe areas where pseudo-labeling can advance depression detection modeling.

## 2 Related Work

Recent work has demonstrated semi-supervised learning techniques using unlabeled Twitter data for depression detection as surveyed by (Zhang et al., 2022). However, these studies tend to solely rely on Twitter[2] data as their source of unlabeled texts (Zhang et al., 2022; Yazdavar et al., 2017). Here, we will use Reddit for our semi-supervised approach.

Poswiata and Perelkiewicz (2022) also uses the *Reddit Mental Health Dataset* (Low et al., 2020) in their depression detection system for last year's iteration of the shared task. However, Poswiata and Perelkiewicz (2022) do not generate pseudo-labels but instead use the data for a pre-training task that is specifically designed for depression detection. Pirina and Çagri Çöltekin (2018) suggested that the selection of Reddit forums (or *subreddits*) in the training data may influence the quality of classifiers. Here, our goal is to automate this selection process without having to rely on *subreddit* specific information and rely solely on the posts themselves.

[2]https://twitter.com/

## 3 Methodology

Here we will provide the major implementation details of our solution in this section. See Table 2 for further information on training hyper-parameter details used throughout.

### 3.1 Data Cleaning

We perform a few basic data-cleaning steps for any samples fed to the classifier. That is, we remove any newline and tab characters, strip leading and trailing white spaces, and replace all links with an identical string. Additionally, we remove duplicated texts and drop samples in the shared-task training set if it is also contained in the shared-task development set. In total, we dropped 128 duplicated samples.

### 3.2 Pre-Trained Models

Leveraging pre-trained language representations is a proven way to boost performance on essentially any given NLP task. Downstream task performance gains are even more prominent if the pre-training task is identical to the downstream tasks and uses large amounts of data. To that end, we use MentalRoBERTa (Ji et al., 2022) as our model of choice for training and inference. MentalRoBERTa (Ji et al., 2022) is a RoBERTa (Liu et al., 2019b) model

| Name | Dev | Test |
|---|---|---|
| MentalRoBERTa (Ji et al., 2022) + *pl+ft* (ours) | **0.7407** | 0.4309 |
| MentalRoBERTa (Ji et al., 2022) + *pl* | 0.5359 | 0.3975 |
| MentalRoBERTa (Ji et al., 2022) | 0.578 | 0.44 |
| MentalXLNet (Ji et al., 2023) | 0.5714 | **0.4443** |
| MentalBERT (Ji et al., 2022) | 0.5648 | 0.3901 |
| RoBERTa (Liu et al., 2019a) | 0.5627 | 0.3953 |
| BERT (Devlin et al., 2018) | 0.5512 | 0.3981 |

Table 1: *Macro*-averaged F1-Score results on the development and test set of the shared task. The best score on each set is highlighted. The top two rows highlight a single run of our approach: training on only pseudo-labels (*pl*) and then finetuning (*ft*). The next three rows detail the finetuning results of recently release pre-trained models for mental health. In the last two rows, we present a baseline using well-known models.

| Hyper-Parameter | Value |
|---|---|
| Optimizer | Adam |
| Learning Rate | 1e-5 |
| Max Input Length | 256 |
| Batch Size | 8 |

Table 2: Training Hyper-parameter Details

that is further pre-trained on Reddit mental-health-related data.

### 3.3 Self-Training

The details of our self-training and pseudo-labeling procedure are as follows. Firstly, we train a teacher model using the annotated training data. Next, we use the trained teacher model to generate predictions on the unlabeled data: *Reddit Mental Health Dataset* (Low et al., 2020). Here, we want to keep the highest-ranked 30,000 samples with the highest-valued predicted logit for any of the three label categories. For example, we only include a post in the severe depression category if the teacher model is very confident that a sample belongs in the depression category relative to all other posts. Subsequently, the resulting 90,000 posts are then assigned pseudo-labels based on the previously assigned groupings, where we assume that each sample belongs to its respective category. Here, we do not consider the categorical probability distribution (as predicted by the teacher) since we are only keeping samples with high confidence. In practice, the predicted output probabilities of the 90,000 posts are very close to 1 for their respective category, hence, using the predicted probabilities adds very little information. Next, we use the 90,000 posts alongside the pseudo-labels to construct a new dataset which is used to train a new student model. Note, here we use the same model architecture for both the teacher and student. Finally, the student model is finetuned with the clean training data and then used for inference on the test set.

## 4 Experiments

### 4.1 Experimental Setup

We compare our setup to several other state-of-the-art pre-trained models we finetuned for the shared task. We report the macro-averaged F1-Score on the test and development sets. Where report the average score over five runs, unless otherwise stated. We perform all experiments on a single T4 GPU.

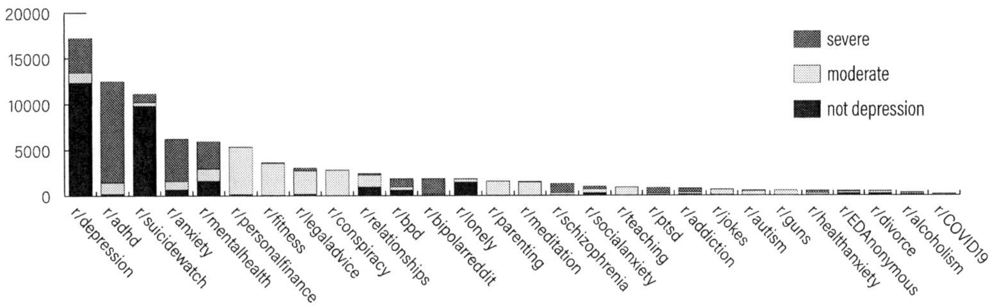


Figure 1: Breakdown of the pseudo-labels on each subreddit in the *Reddit Mental Health Dataset* (Low et al., 2020)

### 4.2 Results

We present our full results in Table 1. Indeed, our complete approach of self-training with MentalRoBERTa (Ji et al., 2022) performs the best on the development set by a wide margin. However, our approach performs narrowly worse than MentalXLNet (Ji et al., 2023) on the test set. Given this disparity in development and test set performance, future work should explore regulation techniques (e.g. augmentation and ensembling methods) to accompany the self-training approach. Nonetheless, our approach still places 3rd overall in the shared task.

## 5 Exploratory analysis

We present an analysis of our generated pseudo-labels on the *Reddit Mental Health Dataset* (Low et al., 2020). Recall, that we assign a pseudo-label to a post only if the post is ranked in the top 30,000 in any of the three depression severity labels. In Figure 1 we break down the distribution of the labels across the sources of these labels. Notably, we find about 60% of our generated labels are contained in five subreddits: *'r/depression'*, *'r/adhd'* *'r/suicidewatch'*, *'r/anxiety'*, *'r/mentalhealth'*. In particular, the subreddit *'r/adhd'* hosts the most pseudo-labels in the *severe* category out of any subreddit by a wide margin, accounting for about 37% of all pseudo-labels in the category.

There are multiple explanations for the above findings. Indeed, ADHD can co-occur with depression and can be seen as an early indication of a future depression diagnosis (Meinzer and Chronis-Tuscano, 2017). Additionally, ADHD and depression have overlapping symptoms (Riglin et al., 2020). Thus, it is possible that there is some level of overlapping language or similar verbal processes shared between the two disorders. We encourage future work to explore alternative explanations and leverage this connection between ADHD and depression in the depression-detection setting.

## 6 Conclusion

In this paper, we present our framework based on self-training and demonstrate its performance on the *Detecting Signs of Depression from Social Media Text - LT-EDI@RANLP 2023* (Sampath et al., 2023) shared task. Given the disparities observed in the development set and test set F1-score performance, future work should explore regulation techniques (e.g. augmentation and ensembling methods) to accompany the self-training approach. Nonetheless, our approach still places 3rd overall in the shared task.

With our use of pseudo-labeling on Reddit,

we highlighted ADHD-focused forums as a major source of (non-diagnostic) severe depression classifications and discussed some explanations. We hope our work serves as a starting point for further investigation of the linguistic patterns of depression overlapping with other mental disorders.

## References


Jacob Devlin, Ming-Wei Chang, Kenton Lee, and Kristina Toutanova. 2018. BERT: pre-training of deep bidirectional transformers for language understanding. *CoRR*, abs/1810.04805.

T. Edwards and Nicholas S. Holtzman. 2017. A meta-analysis of correlations between depression and first person singular pronoun use. *Journal of Research in Personality*, 68:63–68.

Johannes C. Eichstaedt, Robert J. Smith, Raina M. Merchant, Lyle H. Ungar, Patrick Crutchley, Daniel Preotiuc-Pietro, David A. Asch, and H. A. Schwartz. 2018. Facebook language predicts depression in medical records. *Proceedings of the National Academy of Sciences of the United States of America*, 115:11203 – 11208.

Sharath Chandra Guntuku, David Bryce Yaden, Margaret L. Kern, Lyle H. Ungar, and Johannes C. Eichstaedt. 2017. Detecting depression and mental illness on social media: an integrative review. *Current Opinion in Behavioral Sciences*, 18:43–49.

Khan Md Hasib, Md Rafiqul Islam, Shadman Sakib, Md. Ali Akbar, Imran Razzak, and Mohammad Shafiul Alam. 2023. Depression detection from social networks data based on machine learning and deep learning techniques: An interrogative survey. *IEEE Transactions on Computational Social Systems*.

Zaheer Hussain and Mark D. Griffiths. 2019. The associations between problematic social networking site use and sleep quality, attention-deficit hyperactivity disorder, depression, anxiety and stress. *International Journal of Mental Health and Addiction*, 19:686 – 700.

Shaoxiong Ji, Tianlin Zhang, Luna Ansari, Jie Fu, Prayag Tiwari, and Erik Cambria. 2022. MentalBERT: Publicly Available Pretrained Language Models for Mental Healthcare. In *Proceedings of LREC*.

Shaoxiong Ji, Tianlin Zhang, Kailai Yang, Sophia Ananiadou, Erik Cambria, and Jörg Tiedemann. 2023. Domain-specific continued pretraining of language models for capturing long context in mental health. *arXiv preprint arXiv:2304.10447*.

Jonathan W. Kanter, Andrew M. Busch, Cristal E. Weeks, and Sara J. Landes. 2008. The nature of clinical depression: Symptoms, syndromes, and behavior analysis. *The Behavior Analyst*, 31:1–21.

Yinhan Liu, Myle Ott, Naman Goyal, Jingfei Du, Mandar Joshi, Danqi Chen, Omer Levy, Mike Lewis, Luke Zettlemoyer, and Veselin Stoyanov. 2019a. Roberta: A robustly optimized BERT pretraining approach. *CoRR*, abs/1907.11692.

Yinhan Liu, Myle Ott, Naman Goyal, Jingfei Du, Mandar Joshi, Danqi Chen, Omer Levy, Mike Lewis, Luke Zettlemoyer, and Veselin Stoyanov. 2019b. Roberta: A robustly optimized bert pretraining approach. *ArXiv*, abs/1907.11692.

Daniel M Low, Laurie Rumker, John Torous, Guillermo Cecchi, Satrajit S Ghosh, and Tanya Talkar. 2020. Natural language processing reveals vulnerable mental health support groups and heightened health anxiety on reddit during covid-19: Observational study. *Journal of medical Internet research*, 22(10):e22635.

Michael C. Meinzer and Andrea Chronis-Tuscano. 2017. Adhd and the development of depression: Commentary on the prevalence, proposed mechanisms, and promising interventions. *Current Developmental Disorders Reports*, 4:1–4.

Inna Loginovna Pirina and Çagri Çöltekin. 2018. Identifying depression on reddit: The effect of training data. In *Conference on Empirical Methods in Natural Language Processing*.

Rafal Poswiata and Michal Perelkiewicz. 2022. Opi@lt-edi-acl2022: Detecting signs of depression from social media text using roberta pretrained language models. In *LTEDI*.

Andrew G. Reece, Andrew J. Reagan, Katharina L. M. Lix, Peter Sheridan Dodds, Christopher M.

Danforth, and Ellen J. Langer. 2016. Forecasting the onset and course of mental illness with twitter data. *Scientific Reports*, 7.

Lucy Riglin, Beate Leppert, Christina Dardani, Ajay K Thapar, Frances Rice, Michael C. O'Donovan, George Davey Smith, Evie Stergiakouli, Kate Tilling, and Anita Thapar. 2020. Adhd and depression: investigating a causal explanation. *Psychological Medicine*, 51:1890 – 1897.

Attaullah Sahito, Eibe Frank, and Bernhard Pfahringer. 2021. Better self-training for image classification through self-supervision. *ArXiv*, abs/2109.00778.

Kayalvizhi Sampath, Thenmozhi Durairaj, Bharathi Raja Chakravarthi, Jerin Mahibha C, Kogilavani Shanmugavadivel, and Pratik Anil Rahood. 2023. Overview of the second shared task on detecting signs of depression from social media text. In *Proceedings of the Third Workshop on Language Technology for Equality, Diversity and Inclusion*, Varna, Bulgaria. Recent Advances in Natural Language Processing.

H. J. Scudder. 1965. Probability of error of some adaptive pattern-recognition machines. *IEEE Trans. Inf. Theory*, 11:363–371.

Katrine Bønneland Tølbøll. 2019. Linguistic features in depression: a meta-analysis.

Qizhe Xie, Eduard H. Hovy, Minh-Thang Luong, and Quoc V. Le. 2019. Self-training with noisy student improves imagenet classification. *2020 IEEE/CVF Conference on Computer Vision and Pattern Recognition (CVPR)*, pages 10684–10695.

Amir Hossein Yazdavar, Hussein S. Al-Olimat, Monireh Ebrahimi, Goonmeet Bajaj, Tanvi Banerjee, Krishnaprasad Thirunarayan, Jyotishman Pathak, and A. Sheth. 2017. Semi-supervised approach to monitoring clinical depressive symptoms in social media. *Proceedings of the 2017 IEEE/ACM International Conference on Advances in Social Networks Analysis and Mining 2017.*

Tianlin Zhang, Annika Marie Schoene, Shaoxiong Ji, and Sophia Ananiadou. 2022. Natural language processing applied to mental illness detection: a narrative review. *NPJ Digital Medicine*, 5.

Barret Zoph, Golnaz Ghiasi, Tsung-Yi Lin, Yin Cui, Hanxiao Liu, Ekin Dogus Cubuk, and Quoc V. Le. 2020. Rethinking pre-training and self-training. *ArXiv*, abs/2006.06882.

# TechWhiz@LT-EDI : Transformer Models to Detect Levels of Depression from Social Media Text

**Madhumitha M, C.Jerin Mahibha**
Meenakshi Sundararajan Engineering College, Chennai
madhumithamurthy2002@gmail.com
jerinmahibha@gmail.com

**Durairaj Thenmozhi**
Sri Sivasubramaniya Nadar College of Engineering, Chennai
theni_d@ssn.edu.in

## Abstract

Depression is a mental fitness disorder characterised by persistent reactions of unhappiness, voiding, and a deficit of interest in activities. It can influence differing facets of one's life, containing their hopes, sympathy, and nature. Depression can stem from a sort of determinant, in the way that ancestral willingness, life occurrences, and social circumstances In recent years, the influence of social media on mental fitness has become an increasing concern. Excessive use of social media and the negative facets that guide it can exacerbate or cause impressions of distress. Nonstop exposure to cautiously curated lives, social comparison, cyberbullying, and the pressure to meet unreal standards can impact an individual's pride, social connections, and overall well-being. We participated in the shared task at DepSign-LT-EDI@RANLP 2023 and have proposed a model that identifies the levels of depression in social media text using the data set shared for the task. Different transformer models, like ALBERT and RoBERTa, are used by the proposed model for implementing the task. The macro F1 scores obtained by the ALBERT model and the RoBERTa model are 0.258 and 0.143, respectively.

## 1 Introduction

Social media has transformed the way we combine, correspond, and share facts. While it has led to numerous benefits, there is an increasing concern regarding its negative effect on mental health, specifically when it comes to depression (Jones et al., 2022). The loyal uncovering of carefully curated lives, social comparison, and cyberbullying are just instances of how social media can cause feelings of depression. One of the negative effects of social media is the phenomenon of social comparison. Platforms like Instagram and Facebook frequently present idealized interpretations of crowd's lives, stressing their realizations, travels, and happy moments. This never ending risk to seemingly perfect lives can lead human beings to compare themselves negatively, developing feelings of failure, envy, and depression (Winstone et al., 2023). Cyberbullying is another important concern on social media podiums. The obscurity and distance given by these platforms can encourage human beings to undertake harmful behaviors, like spreading rumors, making cruel comments, or posting offensive content (Roy et al., 2022). Such experiences can lead to increased social isolation, reduced pride, and depression. To address the negative impact of social media on mental health, it is owned by adopting healthy habits and practices. Firstly, limiting social media use can help humble exposure and counter excessive comparison or rumination. Engaging in offline activities, spending time accompanying loved ones, and the following amusement can determine a much-needed break from the in-essence globe. Cultivating a healthful online atmosphere is important. This includes being aware of the content we consume and share, encouraging positiveness and support, and vigorously combating cyberbullying. Building a forceful support network online and offline can supply more emotional support and neutralize the negative effects of social media. While social media has transformed communication, it is crucially expected to be aware of its potential negative effects on mental health, particularly depression. Depression is considered as one of the most severe mental health diseases, as it often leads to suicide. Hence identifying and summarizing existing evidence concerning depression from data provided by users on social media has become important (Salas-Zárate et al., 2022). The shared task on Detecting Signs of Depression from Social Media Text (Sampath et al., 2023) was a part of RANLP 2023 which is based on English comments.

The task of detecting signs of depression from Social Media Text is a multi-class classification problem, in which the model has to predict the la-



*LT-EDI 2023 - Third Workshop on Language Technology for Equality, Diversity and Inclusion*, pages 198–203, Varna, Bulgaria, Sep 7, 2023.
https://doi.org/10.26615/978-954-452-084-7_030

bel associated with the text as severe, moderate, or not depression. For example, the text "I didn't deserve all of this: I have been suffering from depression for 5 years following personal traumas, I am surviving, in certain situations, I put on an infinite sadness, the panic disorder truncates all my attempts at recourse" represents severe depression. The text, "Any advice? : So... I don't know where to start and even if I should post this here is moderate and insecurities, fuck em. : I constantly feel like anyone I talk to at all, or act like myself around is just trying to get me to shut up." represents a not depressed case

## 2 Related Works

A gold standard data set had been developed by Kayalvizhi and Thenmozhi (2022) to classify the text based on the levels of depression. An empirical analysis using different traditional machine learning algorithms had been presented. The problem of data imbalance had been overcome using data augmentation. The model with Word2Vec victories and Random Forest classifier on augmented data had outperformed the other models.

Salas-Zárate et al. (2022) summarized different works on detecting depression from social media posts. It had been identified that Twitter was the most studied social media for depression sign detection, and Word embedding was the most prominent linguistic feature extraction method. Support vector machine (SVM) was the most used machine-learning algorithm.

Long-Short Term Memory (LSTM) model with two hidden layers and large bias together with Recurrent Neural Network (RNN) with two dense layers had been used by Amanat et al. (2022) to predict depression from text and had provided better results.

Different transformer models like DistilBERT, RoBERTa and ALBERT had been used by Sivamanikandan et al. (2022) to classify social media posts based on the severity of depression associated with them.

The detection of mental illness including depression had been implemented as a multi-class classification problem by Ameer et al. (2022). The use of traditional machine learning, deep learning, and transfer learning-based methods had been explored and the pre-trained RoBERTa transfer learning model resulted in better outcomes.

The strengths of the sequence model and Transformer model had been consolidated by Zhang et al. (2022). The model used a robustly optimized BERT approach to map words into word embedding space and a bidirectional Long Short-Term Memory model to capture the long-distance contextual semantics.

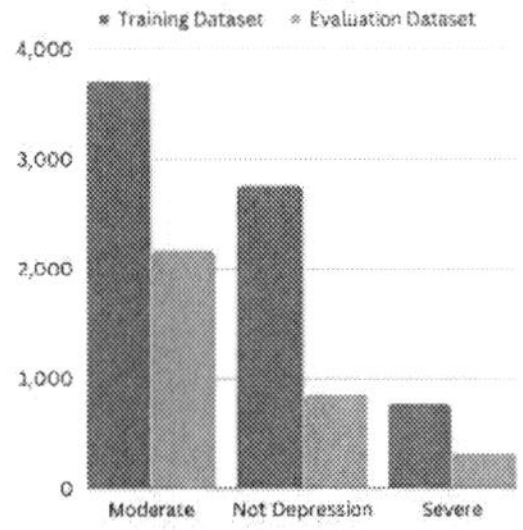


Figure 1: Data Distribution

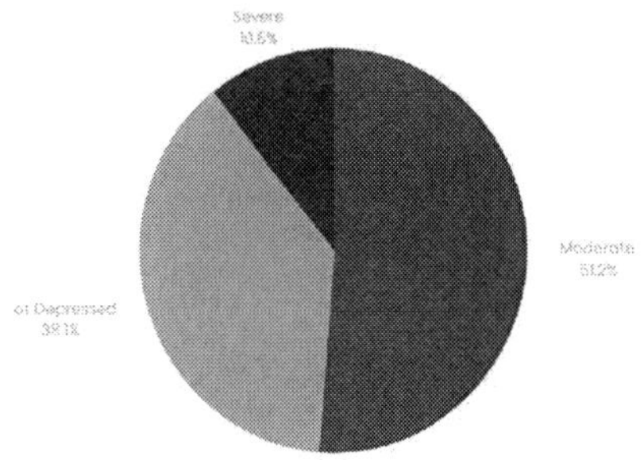


Figure 2: Training Dataset Statistics

## 3 Dataset Description

The data set that is used to implement the depression detection was the training, evaluation and test dataset that was provided by the organizers of the shared task. Each instance of the training dataset had a label specifying whether the text is moderate, severe, or not depression. The previous version of the task (S et al., 2022) had used a dataset in which the social media text were classified as one of the same three categories.

The data distribution of the training and development dataset for the task is shown in Table 1. The training dataset of the Task had 7201 instances of which 3700 instances were under the moderate category and 2755 instances were under the not depression category and 768 instances were under the severe category. The development dataset of the same task had 2169, 848, and 316 instances under the moderate, not depression, and severe categories respectively. This is also represented by Figure 1. This shows the unbalanced nature of the data set.

| Category | Training dataset | Evaluation dataset |
|---|---|---|
| Moderate | 3700 | 2169 |
| Not depression | 2755 | 848 |
| Severe | 768 | 316 |

Table 1: Dataset Statics

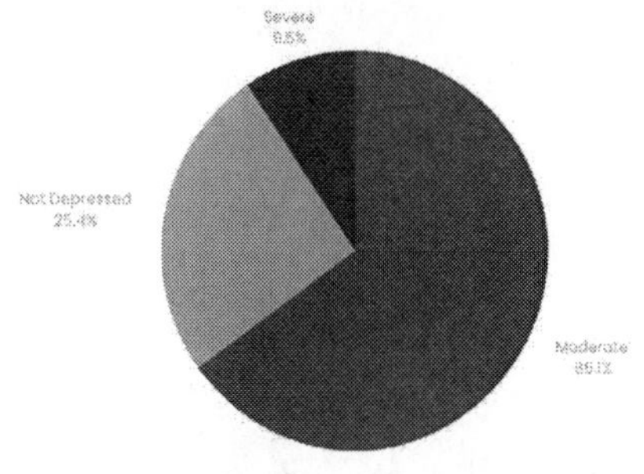


Figure 3: Evaluation Dataset Statistics

The test data had 499 instances for which the predictions had to be done using the proposed model. The data distribution of different classes of data in the training data is represented in Figure 2 and the development dataset is represented in Figure 3.

## 4 System Description

Initially, the three datasets provided by the task organizers, namely the training dataset, development dataset, and testing dataset were collected. The training dataset is preprocessed where unnecessary digits, characters, and white spaces are removed using tokenization and it is followed by an encoding process. Then the model is created. In this system, two pre-trained transformer models were used namely ALBERT and RoBERTa. The preprocessed dataset along with the model created is used for the training phase. Each model is then evaluated using the development dataset. The ALBERT model that provided the highest accuracy is taken as the final run for submission and was used to find the predictions for the testing dataset.

The proposed architecture is represented in Figure 4. The removal of unnecessary information is taken care of by the preprocessing phase. All three datasets namely the training, evaluation, and test dataset are preprocessed. This is followed by the process of model building, where trained models namely ALBERT and RoBERTa were used. In the training phase, the pre-trained models are trained using the preprocessed training dataset. The evaluation of the trained model is carried out in the evaluation phase using the evaluation dataset which makes use of the accuracy as the parameter of evaluation. Fine-tuning of hyper-parameters is performed to improve the accuracy of the proposed system. The labels for the text in the dataset are predicted during the testing phase. Contextual embeddings are generated and are used during the training of the model.

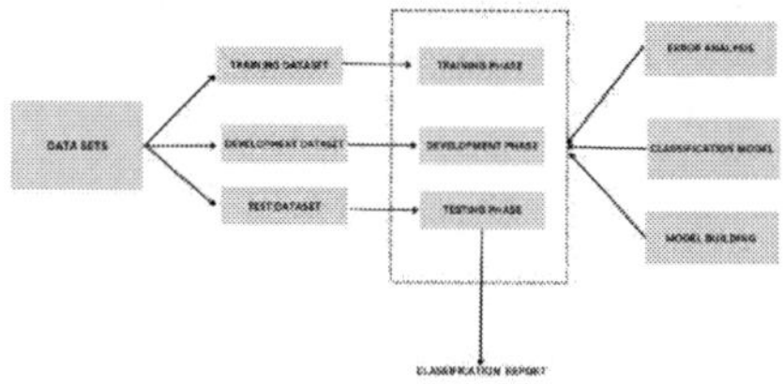


Figure 4: Proposed Architecture

### 4.1 ALBERT

ALBERT (Lan et al., 2019) is a powerful transformer-based language model introduced by Lan et al. as a more efficient and scalable alternative to BERT. ALBERT follows a similar pre-training approach as BERT but introduces parameter-sharing techniques to reduce the model's size and computational requirements. ALBERT has the ability to achieve impressive performance while significantly reducing the number of parameters. By employing parameter sharing and factorization techniques, ALBERT achieves parameter reduction of up to 89%, making it more lightweight and computationally efficient compared to BERT.

The "Albert-base-v2" model consists of 12 transformer layers, 768 hidden units, and 12 attention heads. This model retains the expressive power and linguistic understanding of larger models like BERT while being more efficient to train and deploy. ALBERT's reduced parameter size not only makes it more computation friendly but also enables faster training and inference times.

### 4.2 RoBERTa

RoBERTa (Liu et al., 2019) is a transformer model pre-trained on a large corpus of English data and is

| Model | F1-Score | Accuracy |
|---|---|---|
| ALBERT | 0.258 | 0.421 |
| ROBERTA | 0.143 | 0.263 |

Table 2: Performance Score

based on the BERT model and modifies key hyperparameters and training is implemented with larger mini-batches and learning rates. RoBERTa is a Robust BERT method that has been trained on a far extra large data set and for a whole lot of large quantities of iterations with a bigger batch length of 8k.

The "RoBERTa–base" model was also used for the task which is a pre-trained model on the English language using a masked language modeling (MLM) objective. This model is case-sensitive and it comprises 12 layers, 768-hidden layers, 12-heads, and 125M parameters.

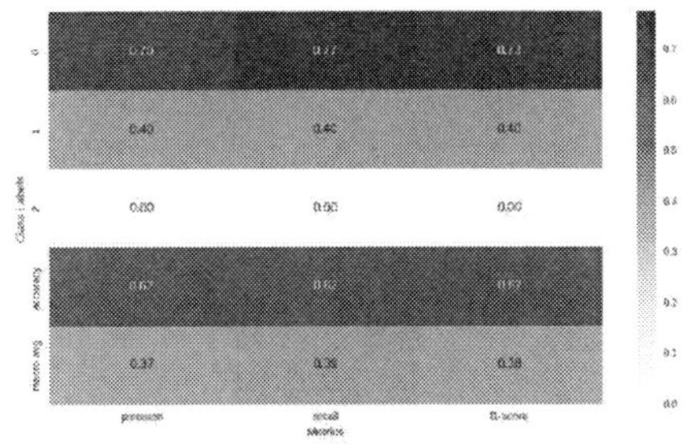

Figure 5: Classification Report - RoBERTa Model

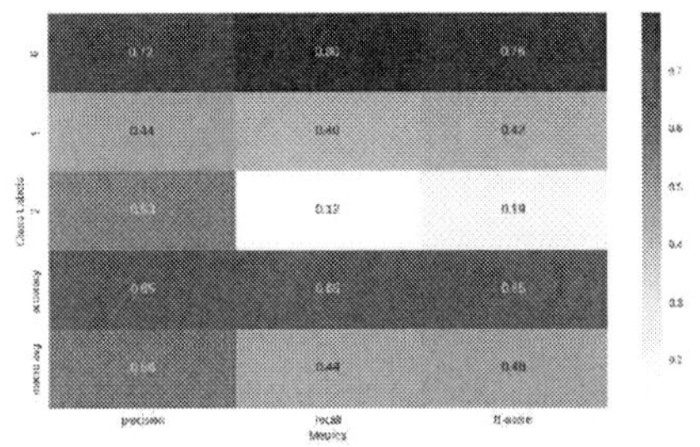

Figure 6: Classification Report - ALBERT Model

## 5 Results

The metrics that were considered for the evaluation of the task was the macro-F1 score and Accuracy. The F1 score is an overall measure of a model's accuracy that merges precision and recall. An extreme F1 score represents that the classification has happened accompanying the reduced number of false positives and low false negatives. The values of the performance metrics particularly the F1 score and accuracy acquired for various models are shown in Table 2. It could be found that the ALBERT model outperformed the other model. The tasks were evaluated based on the macro F1 score acquired by the proposed model. The proposed model resulted in a macro F1 score of 0.258 based on which the task was evaluated. The accuracy acquired was 0.421 and have obtained the 29th rank on the leaderboard. The values for different metrics associated with the ALBERT and ROBERTA models are represented by Figure 6 and Figure 5 respectively.

## 6 Error Analysis

The F1 score obtained for the Task using the proposed ALBERT model shows that more false positive and false negative classification has occurred. One reason for this could be considered as the data imbalance nature of the dataset. Considering the number of instances for the class labeled severe is higher, and the F1 score, precision, and recall associated with this class are high when compared to the class, not depression. This represents that the number of misclassifications increases when the number of instances for training is lower, which is associated with data imbalance. Data augmentation could be considered to improve the model's performance. Examples of texts that are misclassified are shown in Table 3. Considering the first text of the table, it has a specific depression marker "kill myself" and is classified as moderate instead of the correct label of severe. The second text of the table, does not have any specific depression marker and is classified as severe instead of the correct label of moderate. The table also shows texts that are sarcastic which are misclassified. All the example texts show that depression markers and sarcasm play a major role in the process of classification and identifying whether the text is associated with depression.

## 7 Conclusions

Depression detection has become an important area of research as it is interlinked with different application areas. Having this in mind RANLP 2023 had come up with the task of depression detection where the text is classified into moderate, severe, and not depression. The exploration of detecting signs of depression from social media text using the ALBERT and RoBERTa models at LT-EDI@RANLP 2023 demonstrates the significance of leveraging advanced natural language process-

| S.No. | Text | Predicted Label | Actual Label |
|---|---|---|---|
| 1 | I hate that people don't understand that i don't want to kill myself, I just don't want to be alive anymore | Moderate | Severe |
| 2 | But here I am, 24 years old man and doing exactly that | Severe | Moderate |
| 3 | I'm trapped inside. Does anyone else get that feeling? My memories from the past few years are shoddy at best. I think I'm losing it | Severe | Moderate |

Table 3: Examples of Wrong Predictions

ing techniques for mental health analysis. Through the utilization of these models, we were able to classify social media text into three categories: severe, moderate, and not depression. This multi-class classification approach provides a more comprehensive understanding of individuals' mental states and allows for targeted interventions and support. The results obtained from the ALBERT and RoBERTa models contribute to the growing body of research in depression detection from social media. The successful application of these models highlights their effectiveness in capturing subtle linguistic cues and contextual information that indicate depressive symptoms.

Future enhancement to this work can be associated with handling contextual information which can help in effectively detecting depression. The usage of hybrid approaches where different deep learning models are combined can also facilitate the efficient detection of depression from the text.

## References


Amna Amanat, Muhammad Rizwan, Abdul Rehman Javed, Maha Abdelhaq, Raed Alsaqour, Sharnil Pandya, and Mueen Uddin. 2022. Deep learning for depression detection from textual data. *Electronics*, 11(5):676.

Iqra Ameer, Muhammad Arif, Grigori Sidorov, Helena Gòmez-Adorno, and Alexander Gelbukh. 2022. Mental illness classification on social media texts using deep learning and transfer learning. *arXiv preprint arXiv:2207.01012*.

Amelia Jones, Megan Hook, Purnaja Podduturi, Haley McKeen, Emily Beitzell, and Miriam Liss. 2022. Mindfulness as a mediator in the relationship between social media engagement and depression in young adults. *Personality and individual differences*, 185:111284.

S Kayalvizhi and D Thenmozhi. 2022. Data set creation and empirical analysis for detecting signs of depression from social media postings. *arXiv preprint arXiv:2202.03047*.

Zhenzhong Lan, Mingda Chen, Sebastian Goodman, Kevin Gimpel, Piyush Sharma, and Radu Soricut. 2019. Albert: A lite bert for self-supervised learning of language representations. *arXiv preprint arXiv:1909.11942*.

Yinhan Liu, Myle Ott, Naman Goyal, Jingfei Du, Mandar Joshi, Danqi Chen, Omer Levy, Mike Lewis, Luke Zettlemoyer, and Veselin Stoyanov. 2019. Roberta: A robustly optimized bert pretraining approach. *arXiv preprint arXiv:1907.11692*.

Pradeep Kumar Roy, Snehaan Bhawal, and Chinnaudayar Navaneethakrishnan Subalalitha. 2022. Hate speech and offensive language detection in dravidian languages using deep ensemble framework. *Computer Speech & Language*, 75:101386.

Kayalvizhi S, Thenmozhi Durairaj, Bharathi Raja Chakravarthi, and Jerin Mahibha C. 2022. Findings of the shared task on detecting signs of depression from social media. In *Proceedings of the Second Workshop on Language Technology for Equality, Diversity and Inclusion*, pages 331–338, Dublin, Ireland. Association for Computational Linguistics.

Rafael Salas-Zárate, Giner Alor-Hernández, María del Pilar Salas-Zárate, Mario Andrés Paredes-Valverde, Maritza Bustos-López, and José Luis Sánchez-Cervantes. 2022. Detecting depression signs on social media: a systematic literature review. In *Healthcare*, volume 10, page 291. MDPI.

Kayalvizhi Sampath, Thenmozhi Durairaj, Bharathi Raja Chakravarthi, Jerin Mahibha C, Kogilavani Shanmugavadivel, and Pratik Anil Rahood. 2023. Overview of the second shared task on detecting signs of depression from social media text. In *Proceedings of the Third Workshop on Language Technology for Equality, Diversity and Inclusion*, Varna, Bulgaria. Recent Advances in Natural Language Processing.

S Sivamanikandan, V Santhosh, N Sanjaykumar, Thenmozhi Durairaj, et al. 2022. scubemsec@ lt-edi-acl2022: detection of depression using transformer models. In *Proceedings of the second workshop on language technology for equality, diversity and inclusion*, pages 212–217.

Lizzy Winstone, Becky Mars, Claire MA Haworth, and Judi Kidger. 2023. Types of social media use and digital stress in early adolescence. *The Journal of Early Adolescence*, 43(3):294–319.

Yazhou Zhang, Yu He, Lu Rong, and Yijie Ding. 2022. A hybrid model for depression detection with transformer and bi-directional long short-term memory. In *2022 IEEE International Conference on Bioinformatics and Biomedicine (BIBM)*, pages 2727–2734. IEEE.

# CSE_SPEECH@LT-EDI-2023:Automatic Speech Recognition: vulnerable old-aged and transgender people in Tamil

**Varsha Balaji , Archana JP & B. Bharathi**
Department of CSE
Sri Sivasubramaniya Nadar College of Engineering,
Tamil Nadu, India
varsha2010399@ssn.edu.in
archana2120056@ssn.edu.in
bharathib@ssn.edu.in

## Abstract

The crucial technology known as automatic speech recognition (ASR) transforms spoken language into written text and has a variety of uses, including voice commands and customer support. The lives of the elderly and the disabled are considerably improved by ASR, which is essential to the digitization of daily life. The Tamil voice recognition model presented in this paper was created by CSE_SPEECH using three pre-trained models that were improved from the XLSR Wav2Vec2 model from Facebook. The Common Voice Dataset was used to train the models, and the word error rate (WER) on the data was used to assess which model performed the best. This work explains the submission made by the team CSE_SPEECH in the shared task organized by LT-EDI at ACL 2023. The proposed system achieves a word error rate of 40%.

## 1 Introduction

Speech recognition, commonly referred to as speech-to-text or automatic speech recognition, is a method for turning spoken language into written text. It is a crucial tool with numerous uses, including voice search and call routing on mobile phones, customer service, emotion recognition, and, most crucially, aiding the disabled. In addition to helping deaf individuals translate words into text, it can also allow physically disabled people use voice commands to conduct tasks like typing and surfing rather than needing to manually operate a computer.

Singapore, Sri Lanka, Tamil Nadu, and Puducherry all have Tamil as their official language. Out of the more than 22 scheduled languages in India, Tamil was the first language to be categorized as a classical language. It is also of the oldest languages in the world, with an apparent origin dating back more than 2000 years.

Speech recognition is accomplished by taking Tamil's linguistic characteristics into account. The speech recognition problem is handled using the natural language processing methodology. In the Speech Recognition for Vulnerable Individuals in Tamil shared challenge, the team SANBAR_CSE_SSN came in first place with a word error rate of 37%.

Older folks and those who are physically or cognitively challenged have a tendency to speak with minor dysarthria, or slurred speech, which causes inaccurate transcription of the data. The transcription of the data varies from person to person since, in Tamil-speaking areas, people from different locations talk with non-identical dialects, accents, and speeds. The ability to effectively guess what someone from another location is saying when trained with audio from that region is not present.

The authors (Bharathi et al., 2022b) offer an overview of a collaborative project centered on Tamil automated speech recognition (ASR). Using data on spontaneous Tamil speech recorded from elderly and transgender people was the joint task. This dataset was given to the participants, who were then charged with identifying and rating the speech utterances. The information was acquired from open sources like marketplaces, hospitals, and vegetable shops. The speech corpus was split into training and testing data and included utterances from men, women, and transgender people. The Word Error Rate (WER) served as the basis for the task's evaluation. Participants used transformer-based models for ASR, and this overview paper summarises the diverse outcomes obtained utilizing several transformer models that have already been trained.

This paper serves as a submission to a conference, offering insights into the field of automatic speech recognition (B et al., 2023). It provides an overview of the conference's focus on ASR, high-



*LT-EDI 2023 – Third Workshop on Language Technology for Equality, Diversity and Inclusion*, pages 204–208, Varna, Bulgaria, Sep 7, 2023.
https://doi.org/10.26615/978-954-452-084-7_031

lighting relevant references such as (Bharathi et al., 2022a).

In our study, spoken audio were converted into tokens using pre-trained models created specifically for the Tamil language, which were then converted back into text. We used the Amrrs/wav2vec2-large-xlsr-53-tamil1 pre-trained model.

## 2 Related Works

Recently, researchers have tested a few methods to cope with speech recognition in minority languages like Tamil. The usage of a Hidden Markov Model, often known as an HMM, is suggested by the authors of Voice and speech recognition in the Tamil language (Fournier-Viger et al., 2017). This method of statistical pattern matching can produce speech using a variety of states for each model. The HMM model scales effectively and decreases the length and complexity of the recognition process because it only needs positive data.

Convolutional neural networks (CNNs) are used by the authors of Speech Rate Control for Improving Elderly Speech Recognition of Smart Devices (Thamburaj et al., 2021) to produce feature vectors that are then fed into fully connected networks (FCs) for the classification of syllable transition boundaries frame by frame. In order to segment the syllables, the syllable transition probability is determined. They use a Synchronised Overlap-Add (SOLA) Algorithm to help them change the speech rate in accordance with the time-scale ratio that is being measured.

By utilizing transformer networks in the neural transducer, the authors of TransformerTransducer: End-to-End Speech Recognition with Self-Attention (Yeh et al., 2019) aim to create a model for end-to-end speech recognition. They suggest two approaches: shortened self-attention to enable streaming for transformer and minimize computational complexity, and VGGNet with causal convolution to add positional information and lower frame rate for efficient inference.

The authors (Madhavaraj and Ramakrishnan, 2017) construct two distinct recognition systems for phone recognition (PR) and for continuous speech recognition (CSR) using deep neural networks (DNN) in the Design and Development of a big vocabulary, continuous voice recognition system for Tamil. It has been demonstrated that the DNN-based triphone acoustic model produces noticeably improved outcomes in CSR and PR.

In (Lin et al., 2020), the research discusses the rising concern over cybersecurity and software industry security issues. It is necessary to make more improvements because the current methods for vulnerability detection are deemed insufficient. Machine learning and data mining techniques can be used to find patterns in the vast amount of open-source software code that is now available.(Madhavaraj and Ramakrishnan, 2017) Deep learning has the capacity to comprehend natural languages, as seen by the success of its applications in speech recognition and machine translation. Researchers in software engineering and cybersecurity have been encouraged by this to investigate deep learning and neural network-based methods for finding software vulnerabilities. The survey examines the use of neural approaches to comprehend code semantics and spot vulnerable patterns in the literature that is currently available in this field. The authors of (S and B, 2022) uses transformer model Rajaram1996/wav2vec-large-xlsr-53-tamil transformer model for recognizing the Tamil speech utterances of vulnerable individuals. In (Srinivasan et al., 2022) uses akashsivanandan/wav2vec-large-xlsr-53-tamil pre-trained model for recognizing the vulnerable individual's Tamil speech utterances. In this paper, however, we use a pre-trained XLSR model to transcript the audio.

## 3 Dataset Analysis

Tamil speech utterances are collected from old-aged people and transgender whose mother tongue is Tamil. The recorded speech utterances of old-aged people and transgender contain how those people communicate in primary locations like banks, hospitals, and administrative offices. The data set contains 51 Speakers of literates and illiterates. The duration of the corpus is 7 hours and 30 minutes. The speech files in the directories are in the WAV format. The sampling rate of the speech utterances is 44kHz. The speech corpus with 5.5 hours of transcribed speech will be released for the training, and 2 hours of speech data will be released for testing. Table 1. shows that detailed description of the collected speech utterances.

## 4 Methodology and data

The strategy for the discourse acknowledgment errand includes a few steps. At first, a different agent dataset of discourse recordings in Tamil

| Speakers | Literate | Illiterate | Total |
|---|---|---|---|
| Male | 4 | 9 | 13 |
| Female | 7 | 24 | 31 |
| Transgender | 3 | 4 | 7 |

Table 1: Detailed Description of speech corpus

(Chakravarthi and Muralidaran, 2021) is collected. The particular demonstration utilized for this errand is the Amrrs/wav2vec2-large-xlsr-53-tamil show, known for its adequacy in discourse acknowledgment. The collected dataset is at that point subject to information preprocessing strategies, counting sound cleaning, portioning and labeling, highlight extraction, normalization, and language-specific preprocessing, to improve the quality and appropriateness of the information.

Following this, the preprocessed dataset is separated into preparing, approval, and testing subsets. The Amrrs/wav2vec2-large-xlsr-53-Tamil demonstration is prepared utilizing the preparing dataset, with parameters optimized to play down misfortune and make strides in precision. The execution of the prepared demonstration is assessed utilizing the approval dataset, and the Word Error Rate (WER) is calculated to the degree of its precision.

The ultimate step includes testing the demonstration utilizing the isolated testing dataset to survey its generalization and real-world execution. Execution examination is conducted to distinguish qualities, shortcomings, and ranges for enhancement. The demonstration and preprocessing methods are iteratively refined based on the examination and input gotten

## 5 Model Description

The advanced voice recognition model "Amrrs/wav2vec2-large-xlsr-53-tamil" was developed especially for the Tamil language. It makes use of the powerful "wav2vec2" architecture, which is renowned for enabling the self-supervised learning of voice representation. The large scale allows the model to record complex acoustic patterns, which leads to greater performance.

The model name "xlsr-53" implies that it was pre-trained on a varied dataset that included 53 languages. By utilizing shared representations between languages, this multilingual pretraining improves the model's capability to comprehend and accurately transcribe Tamil speech.

This model (Yeo et al., 2022) stands out due to its focus on voice recognition for vulnerable people. The model has been improved to handle issues experienced by people with speech problems, non-native speakers, and other disadvantaged populations, despite the fact that the task's specific requirements are unknown. Because of its flexibility, it is especially useful for supporting accurate and accessible speech recognition for users who would have trouble with more traditional systems.

The "Amrrs/wav2vec2-large-xlsr-53-tamil" model, created by "Amrrs," provides a potent remedy for Tamil speech recognition. It offers a powerful tool for accurately transcribing speech in Tamil and enhancing communication by fusing cutting-edge architecture, multilingual pretraining, and customized training for vulnerable individuals. Due to its emphasis on inclusivity and accessibility, this model is a priceless tool for resolving speech recognition issues that vulnerable populations encounter.

(Yeo et al., 2022)The difficulty of low data availability for dysarthria severity categorization, which impedes research advancement in this area, is addressed in this work. The importance of language-specific traits has been disregarded, despite the fact that the cross-lingual approach has been utilized to overcome this problem. In response, the research suggests a multilingual classification system for the degree of dysarthria in Tamil, Korean, and English. The approach makes use of both language-specific and language-independent features. From different speech dimensions, such as voice quality, pronunciation, and prosody, 39 features are derived. The best feature set for each language is then determined using feature selection techniques. Shared features and distinctive features can be distinguished by comparing the results of feature selection across the three languages.The suggested method uses these two feature sets to automatically classify severity, taking into account the elimination of language-specific features to prevent adverse impacts on other languages. For classification, the eXtreme Gradient Boosting (XGBoost) technique is used since it can deal with missing data. For validation, two baseline experiments are carried out using the intersection and union sets of monolingual feature sets. With a 67.14 F1 score as opposed to 64.52 for the Intersection trial and 66.74 for the Union experiment, the data show that the proposed technique performs better. Furthermore, for all three languages, English, Korean, and Tamil, the suggested method performs better than monolingual classifications, with relative percentage improvements of 17.67, 2.28, and 7.79 for each language. These results highlight the significance of classifying the severity of cross-language dysarthria independently by taking into account common and language-specific traits.

## 6 Observation and Results

Upon initial analysis of the translations created by the Amrrs demonstrate, certain challenges are apparent. They demonstrate battles to precisely separate between the boundaries of words, regularly blending adjoining words or erroneously sectioning them. This issue postures troubles in accurately translating the expected meaning of talked sentences.

Moreover, the demonstration experiences challenges in precisely capturing pushed consonants, driving to mistakes in translation. Focused consonants play a noteworthy part in Tamil dialect articulation, and their error can result in mistakes and mistaken assumptions.

Moreover, the show faces confinements in recognizing and accurately translating certain vowel sounds, especially those that are overwhelmingly utilized as pushed consonants in Tamil. This error emerges due to the nearness of a going before vowel sound that's often undefined within the translations.

Whereas the Amrrs show illustrates an, by and large, translation precision of 40% Word Error Rate (WER), it is critical to encourage investigation of the particular effect of these mistakes on powerless people. Assessing client criticism and conducting focused appraisals with the aiming client bunch would give profitable bits of knowledge into the ease of use and adequacy of the demonstration for people with discourse impedances, hearing impedances, or cognitive inabilities.

It is basic to proceed with refining the Amrrs show, tending to the recognized challenges, and endeavoring for progressed accuracy in discourse acknowledgment for defenseless people within the Tamil dialect.

## 7 Conclusion

In conclusion, the assessment of the Amrrs/wav2vec2-large-xlsr-53-tamil show for discourse acknowledgment among helpless people within the Tamil dialect gives profitable bits of knowledge. The ponder uncovers challenges in word division, focused consonant acknowledgment, and separation of certain vowel sounds, coming about in translation mistakes. In spite of these confinements, the demonstrate accomplishes a Word Error Rate (WER) of 40%, demonstrating its potential in discourse acknowledgment. In any case, encourage investigate is essential to investigate the particular affect on defenseless people, counting those with discourse impedances or cognitive inabilities. This consider emphasizes the significance of tending to the one of a kind needs of powerless populaces to create comprehensive and available discourse acknowledgment frameworks. Client input and engagement with the target bunch will be instrumental in moving forward convenience and viability. By progressing discourse acknowledgment innovation in Tamil for powerless people, this investigate contributes to making more comprehensive arrangements and cultivating availability in dialect handling applications.

## References


Bharathi B, Bharathi Raja Chakravarthi, Subalalitha Chinnaudayar Navaneethakrishnan, Sripirya N, Rajeswari Natarajan, Suhasini S, and Swetha Valli. 2023. Overview of the second shared task on speech recognition for vulnerable individuals in tamil. In *Proceedings of the Third Workshop on Speech and Language Technologies for Dravidian Languages*, Varna, Bulgaria. Recent Advances in Natural Language Processing.

B Bharathi, Bharathi Raja Chakravarthi, Subalalitha Chinnaudayar Navaneethakrishnan, N Sripriya, Arunaggiri Pandian, and Swetha Valli. 2022a. Findings of the shared task on Speech Recognition for Vulnerable Individuals in Tamil. In *Proceedings of the Second Workshop on Language Technology for Equality, Diversity and Inclusion*. Association for Computational Linguistics.

B Bharathi, Bharathi Raja Chakravarthi, Subalalitha Cn, N Sripriya, Arunaggiri Pandian, and Swetha Valli. 2022b. Findings of the shared task on speech recognition for vulnerable individuals in tamil. In *Proceedings of the Second Workshop on Language Technology for Equality, Diversity and Inclusion*, pages 339–345.

Bharathi Raja Chakravarthi and Vigneshwaran Muralidaran. 2021. Findings of the shared task on hope speech detection for equality, diversity, and inclusion. In *Proceedings of the first workshop on language technology for equality, diversity and inclusion*, pages 61–72.

Philippe Fournier-Viger, Jerry Chun-Wei Lin, Rage Uday Kiran, Yun Sing Koh, and Rincy Thomas. 2017. A survey of sequential pattern mining. *Data Science and Pattern Recognition*, 1(1):54–77.

Guanjun Lin, Sheng Wen, Qing-Long Han, Jun Zhang, and Yang Xiang. 2020. Software vulnerability detection using deep neural networks: a survey. *Proceedings of the IEEE*, 108(10):1825–1848.

A Madhavaraj and AG Ramakrishnan. 2017. Design and development of a large vocabulary, continuous speech recognition system for tamil. In *2017 14th IEEE India Council International Conference (INDICON)*, pages 1–5. IEEE.

Suhasini S and Bharathi B. 2022. SUH_ASR@LT-EDI-ACL2022: Transformer based approach for speech recognition for vulnerable individuals in Tamil. In *Proceedings of the Second Workshop on Language Technology for Equality, Diversity and Inclusion*, pages 177–182, Dublin, Ireland. Association for Computational Linguistics.

Dhanya Srinivasan, Bharathi B, Thenmozhi Durairaj, and Senthil Kumar B. 2022. SSNCSE_NLP@LT-EDI-ACL2022: Speech recognition for vulnerable individuals in Tamil using pre-trained XLSR models. In *Proceedings of the Second Workshop on Language Technology for Equality, Diversity and Inclusion*, pages 317–320, Dublin, Ireland. Association for Computational Linguistics.

Kingston Pal Thamburaj, Kartheges Ponniah, Ilangkumaran Sivanathan, and Muniisvaran Kumar. 2021. An critical analysis of speech recognition of tamil and malay language through artificial neural network.

Charles D Yeh, Christopher D Richardson, and Jacob E Corn. 2019. Advances in genome editing through control of dna repair pathways. *Nature cell biology*, 21(12):1468–1478.

Eun Jung Yeo, Kwanghee Choi, Sunhee Kim, and Minhwa Chung. 2022. Cross-lingual dysarthria severity classification for english, korean, and tamil. In *2022 Asia-Pacific Signal and Information Processing Association Annual Summit and Conference (APSIPA ASC)*, pages 566–574. IEEE.

# VTUBGM@LT-EDI-2023: Hope Speech Identification using Layered Differential Training of ULMFit

**Sanjana Kavatagi**[1] and **Rashmi Rachh**[1] and **Shankar Biradar**[2]
[1]Department of Computer Science and Engineering,
VTU,Belagvi, Karnatka, India
[2]Department of Computer Science and Engineering,
IIIT, Dharwad, Karnataka, India
kawatagi.sanjana@gmail.com
rashmirachh@gmail.com

## Abstract

Hope speech embodies optimistic and uplifting sentiments, aiming to inspire individuals to maintain faith in positive progress and actively contribute to a better future. In this article, we outline the model presented by our team, VTUBGM, for the shared task "Hope Speech Detection for Equality, Diversity, and Inclusion" at LT-EDI-RANLP 2023. This task entails classifying YouTube comments, which is a classification problem at the comment level. The task was conducted in four different languages: Bulgarian, English, Hindi, and Spanish, with our team participating in the English subtask. The suggested model was developed using layered differential training of the ULMFit and received a macro F1 score of 0.48, placing third in the competition.

## 1 Introduction

The exponential growth of internet usage has led to a significant rise in the prominence of social media platforms. In recent times, these platforms have evolved to become the primary means of communication for millions of individuals worldwide(Biradar and Saumya, 2022; Shankar Biradar and Chauhan, 2021). As the popularity of social media continues to soar, people are increasingly sharing their thoughts, opinions, and experiences on various issues. This widespread adoption of social media has revolutionized the way individuals communicate and express themselves. Platforms like Facebook, Twitter, Instagram, and YouTube have become integral components of our daily lives. These platforms allow users to express their thoughts, ideas, and feelings to a global audience. In recent times, social media has emerged as a powerful tool for social and political activism, as users leverage these platforms to raise awareness about various social issues and rally support for causes.

Social media has also become a thriving environment for the dissemination of hate speech and fake news, which can spread rapidly across the globe. This harmful content can be targeted toward individuals, groups, religions, or political parties (Biradar et al., 2021; Chakravarthi et al., 2022). Extensive research has been conducted to address this issue and develop strategies to identify and prevent such material's publication and rapid spread on the internet.

While numerous individuals are involved in promoting fake news and hate speech, several groups and individuals are actively working to create and spread positivity and hope. These efforts have surfaced in various social media campaigns to counteract online platforms' negativity and polarisation. Hope is a multifaceted and complex emotion that holds immense importance for human well-being. It encompasses an optimistic outlook on life, enabling us to endure challenging circumstances, nurture the belief that things can get better, and have faith in ourselves and others. Hope has been linked to numerous positive outcomes, such as enhanced physical and mental health, heightened resilience, and increased motivation.

To promote research in the identification of hope speech on social media platforms, the organizers of the "Hope Speech Detection for Equality, Diversity, and Inclusion" shared task at LT-EDI-RANLP 2023 offer an opportunity for researchers to develop machine learning and deep learning models capable of effectively classifying hope speech and non-hope speech within the provided dataset. This initiative encourages the exploration of innovative approaches to accurately distinguish between hopeful and non-hopeful content, thus contributing to the advancement of understanding and harnessing the power of hope in online discourse. In order to construct a model for classifying hope speech and non-hope speech, our team employed the ULMFit



*LT-EDI 2023 – Third Workshop on Language Technology for Equality, Diversity and Inclusion*, pages 209–213, Varna, Bulgaria, Sep 7, 2023.
https://doi.org/10.26615/978-954-452-084-7_032

model, an LSTM-based model that was fine-tuned specifically for the task of hope speech detection. Our model achieved third place among the participating teams with a macro F1 score of 0.48.

The remainder of the paper is structured as follows: Section 2 presents a comprehensive literature review, highlighting key studies and research related to the topic. Section 3 explains our proposed model, outlining its architecture and training methodology. The results obtained from our model are discussed in Section 4. Finally, Section 6 concludes the paper by summarizing the key findings and contributions and outlines potential trajectories for future research in this field.

## 2 Literature Review

While numerous researchers have recently focused on identifying offensive and fraudulent content in social media (Biradar et al., 2022), only a limited number of studies have been conducted on identifying hope within individuals' opinions expressed on social media. In an environment permeated by toxicity, violence, and discrimination, hope speech is a powerful tool that assists and encourages countless needy individuals. It serves as a beacon of hope for those grappling with personal or professional challenges, including issues related to health, finances, relationships, and more (Chakravarthi, 2022). Identifying and automatically detecting such statements can play a crucial role in facilitating their widespread dissemination. By detecting and recognizing these statements, we can amplify their reach and impact, inspiring and motivating the individuals who create them for the betterment of others. This, in turn, fosters a positive and supportive environment where hope speech can serve as a catalyst for positive change, resilience, and empowerment (Palakodety et al., 2019). In the realm of hope speech detection, data is collected by performing web crawling techniques. Researchers have extensively investigated and conducted studies focused on extracting comments and posts from popular social media platforms, including Twitter, Facebook, and YouTube. These platforms serve as rich sources of valuable data for analyzing and understanding hope speech in online discourse (Marrese-Taylor et al., 2017; Muralidhar et al., 2018).

In a pioneering effort, (Chakravarthi, 2020) developed a comprehensive dataset for hope speech encompassing multiple languages such as English, Malayalam, and Tamil. This dataset served as the foundation for the shared task called HopeEDI, designed to promote research and exploration in the field of detecting hopeful and encouraging content within social media. HopeEDI aimed to encourage advancements in understanding and leveraging the power of hope speech in online environments by providing a platform for studying and analyzing such content.

(Dave et al., 2021) directed their attention towards harnessing classic machine learning classifiers, specifically logistic regression (LR) and support vector machine (SVM), for the purpose of categorizing text into hope speech and non-hope speech categories. They utilized TF-IDF and character n-gram techniques for feature extraction to achieve this. By leveraging these advanced classifiers and feature extraction methods, their approach demonstrated promising results in accurately identifying and distinguishing between hope speech and non-hope speech texts. This study exemplifies the effectiveness of employing machine learning techniques for the task of hope speech detection. A novel method that employed an ensemble approach for the classification of hope and non-hope speech was introduced by (Kumar et al., 2022). Their approach involved utilizing both character-level and word-level TF-IDF embedding techniques to extract meaningful features from the text data. By combining these two levels of embeddings in an ensemble model, the authors demonstrated an effective approach for accurately categorizing text into hope and non-hope speech categories. This methodology showcased the potential of leveraging multiple embedding techniques in tandem to improve classification performance in the context of hope speech detection. (Balouchzahi et al., 2021) introduced a strategy that involved extracting features from the given dataset using TF-IDF and syntactic n-grams. They further trained a neural network model and a voting classifier using LR, eXtreme Gradient Boosting (XGB), and MLP algorithms. Additionally, in the context of the HopeEDI shared task, a BERT model was trained specifically to identify hope speech in English. This BERT model showcased remarkable performance, achieving an average F1 score of 0.92. This approach highlights the effectiveness of utilizing advanced language models for hope speech detection, yielding impressive accuracy and classification performance results.

In some of the studies, researchers have utilized transformer models for the identification of the hope speech. The embeddings for the text data were extracted using the BERT (Bidirectional Encoder Representations from Transformers) model, as introduced by (Dowlagar and Mamidi, 2021). The BERT model was utilized with an embedding length of 768, and a sub-word level tokenizer was employed to tokenize each sentence. Specifically, the bert-base-multilingual-cased model was chosen for this method. A Convolutional Neural Network (CNN) was developed to classify the sentences into their respective categories. The rectified linear unit (ReLU) activation function was used in the CNN design, which is a popular choice for nonlinear transformations. Using BERT embeddings and the CNN architecture, this method is intended to effectively identify texts as hopeful or non-hopeful. In the domain of hope speech detection, this combination of BERT embeddings with CNN architecture shows the possibility for accurate classification results.

(Gowda et al., 2022) proposed an innovative method for effectively categorising minority groups by combining resampling approaches with 1D-Convolutional Neural Networks (CNN) combined with Long Short-term Memory (LSTM). This model seeks to solve the widespread issue of imbalanced datasets, in which minority groups are frequently underrepresented. To address this issue, the researchers used resampling techniques to improve minority class representation in the training data, resulting in a more balanced distribution. The model design includes a 1D-CNN with LSTM layers, which allows the network to detect local and temporal relationships in the input data. This combination enables the model to learn patterns and features from resampled minority class data successfully.

### 2.1 Task and dataset description

The dataset used in this study was obtained from the shared task 'Hope Speech Detection for Equality, Diversity, and Inclusion - LT-EDI-RANLP 2023'(Chakravarthi, 2020). The organizers of the task shared a dataset compiled from YouTube comments. The objective of the task was to classify the provided YouTube comments into two categories: 'Hope Speech' and 'Non-Hope Speech.' The task encompassed four different languages: Bulgarian, English, Hindi, and Spanish. However, our proposed model focuses exclusively on the English language.

| Label | Training set | Validation set |
|---|---|---|
| Hope_speech | 1562 | 400 |
| Non_hope_speech | 16630 | 4148 |
| Total | 18192 | 4548 |

Table 1: Distribution of data

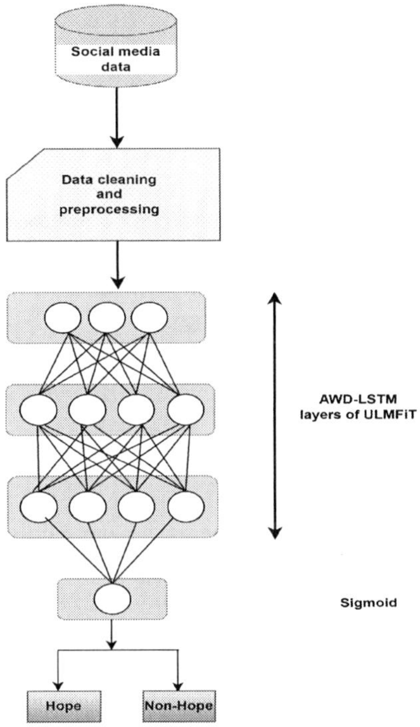


Figure 1: Proposed model

The English dataset, outlined in Table 1, comprises two primary columns: 'Text' and 'Labels.' The 'Text' column contains comments scraped from YouTube, while the 'Labels' column consists of two labels: 'Hope_Speech' and 'Non_Hope_Speech.' The dataset provided by the organizers exhibits an imbalance towards the 'Non_Hope_Speech' class.

## 3 Methodology

This section presents a comprehensive description of the proposed model, which is outlined in two subsections: Data Preprocessing and Model Description.

### 3.1 Data pre-treatment

The data provided by the organizers of the task is obtained from YouTube comments. In order to im-

| Hyperparameters | Values |
|---|---|
| Batch size | 64 |
| Dropoutvrate | 0.3 |
| Learning rate | Best LR is selected by applying grid search between start_LR=slice(10e-7, 10e-5) end_ LR=slice(0.1, 10) |
| No of epochs | 2 for first two layers, 3 for last layer |

Table 2: Hyper-parameter tuning

prove the accuracy of the classification, it is crucial to remove the noise present in the data. YouTube comments often contain numerical data, punctuation, emoticons, hyperlinks, and URLs, which are not necessary for classification. Therefore, these elements are removed from the text. Stop words, which do not contribute significantly to the classification, are also eliminated. The entire text is converted to lowercase to avoid redundancy and ensure consistency. Word lemmatization is done to convert all forms of the word into their root word.

### 3.2 Model description

This section describes the model and training strategy submitted for the shared task "Hope Speech Detection for Equality, Diversity, and Inclusion- LT-EDI-RANLP 2023." Our proposed model utilizes the pre-trained language model ULMFiT from the fast.ai [1] library for classifying hope speech and non-hope speech. ULMFiT is a Long Short-Term Memory (LSTM) based model consisting of multiple layers of Average Weight Dropped (AWD) LSTM (Average Stochastic Gradient Descent weight dropped LSTM) stacked on top of each other. This model has shown promising results in various natural language processing tasks (Howard and Ruder, 2018; Azhan and Ahmad, 2021).

A layered differential training approach was employed to adapt the ULMFiT model for hope speech identification. This approach, which has been successful in computer vision problems, is applied to solve the hope speech problem. In layered differential training, the last three layers of the ULMFiT model are sequentially freezed and unfreezed. This process allows us to fine-tune the model's weights specifically for hope speech data. The last layer is trained slightly longer compared to the previous layers to prevent overfitting and retain valuable information. Finally, the features extracted from the ULMFiT model are passed through a sigmoid layer for classification. Table 2 provides the hyperparameters used in model training. These hyperparameters have been selected based on extensive experimentation and trial runs to optimize the model's performance. The proposed model demonstrates promising capabilities in identifying hope speech by leveraging the ULMFiT language model and employing layered differential training. The architecture of the proposed model is illustrated in Fig 1.

[1] https://www.fast.ai/

## 4 Result and Discussion

The organizers of the shared task "Hope Speech Detection for Equality, Diversity, and Inclusion-LT-EDI-RANLP 2023" evaluated the performance of the models using the macro-F1 score. Our team submitted a single run with the ULMFit model. Table 3 presents the top-performing models along with their macro-F1 scores. Notably, our proposed model achieved a macro-F1 score of 0.48, which is highlighted in bold in the table. This result showcases the effectiveness and competitiveness of our approach in accurately identifying hope speech in the English language.

| Team Name | MF1 | Rank |
|---|---|---|
| Tercet_English | 0.50 | 1 |
| ML_AI_IIITRanchi | 0.50 | 1 |
| Ranganayaki | 0.49 | 2 |
| **VTUBGM** | **0.48** | **3** |
| IIC_Team | 0.47 | 4 |
| MUCS_run2 | 0.44 | 5 |

Table 3: Top performing models

## 5 Conclusion and future enhancements

In the shared task "Hope Speech Detection for Equality, Diversity, and Inclusion" at LT-EDI-RANLP 2023, our team, VTUBGM, proposed a model built upon the ULMFit framework. We employed a layered differential approach to fine-tune the model specifically for classifying Hope and

Non_Hope speech. The proposed model achieved a macro-F1 score of 0.48 on the dataset provided by the organizers. As a result, our team secured 3rd rank in the competition. In this work the language considered is English, further, the proposed approach can be used to identify hope speech in other low-resource and code-mixed texts.

## References


Mohammed Azhan and Mohammad Ahmad. 2021. Ladiff ulmfit: a layer differentiated training approach for ulmfit. In *Combating Online Hostile Posts in Regional Languages during Emergency Situation: First International Workshop, CONSTRAINT 2021, Collocated with AAAI 2021, Virtual Event, February 8, 2021, Revised Selected Papers 1*, pages 54–61. Springer.

Fazlourrahman Balouchzahi, BK Aparna, and HL Shashirekha. 2021. Mucs@ dravidianlangtech-eacl2021: Cooli-code-mixing offensive language identification. In *Proceedings of the First Workshop on Speech and Language Technologies for Dravidian Languages*, pages 323–329.

Shankar Biradar and Sunil Saumya. 2022. Iiitdwd@ tamilnlp-acl2022: Transformer-based approach to classify abusive content in dravidian code-mixed text. In *Proceedings of the Second Workshop on Speech and Language Technologies for Dravidian Languages*, pages 100–104.

Shankar Biradar, Sunil Saumya, and Arun Chauhan. 2021. Hate or non-hate: Translation based hate speech identification in code-mixed hinglish data set. In *2021 IEEE International Conference on Big Data (Big Data)*, pages 2470–2475. IEEE.

Shankar Biradar, Sunil Saumya, and Arun Chauhan. 2022. Fighting hate speech from bilingual hinglish speaker's perspective, a transformer-and translation-based approach. *Social Network Analysis and Mining*, 12(1):87.

Bharathi Raja Chakravarthi. 2020. HopeEDI: A multilingual hope speech detection dataset for equality, diversity, and inclusion. In *Proceedings of the Third Workshop on Computational Modeling of People's Opinions, Personality, and Emotion's in Social Media*, pages 41–53, Barcelona, Spain (Online). Association for Computational Linguistics.

Bharathi Raja Chakravarthi. 2022. Hope speech detection in youtube comments. *Social Network Analysis and Mining*, 12(1):75.

Bharathi Raja Chakravarthi, Vigneshwaran Muralidaran, Ruba Priyadharshini, Subalalitha Cn, John McCrae, Miguel Ángel García, Salud María Jiménez-Zafra, Rafael Valencia-García, Prasanna Kumaresan, Rahul Ponnusamy, Daniel García-Baena, and José García-Díaz. 2022. Overview of the shared task on hope speech detection for equality, diversity, and inclusion. In *Proceedings of the Second Workshop on Language Technology for Equality, Diversity and Inclusion*, pages 378–388, Dublin, Ireland. Association for Computational Linguistics.

Bhargav Dave, Shripad Bhat, and Prasenjit Majumder. 2021. Irnlp_daiict@ lt-edi-eacl2021: hope speech detection in code mixed text using tf-idf char n-grams and muril. In *Proceedings of the First Workshop on Language Technology for Equality, Diversity and Inclusion*, pages 114–117.

Suman Dowlagar and Radhika Mamidi. 2021. Edione@ lt-edi-eacl2021: Pre-trained transformers with convolutional neural networks for hope speech detection. In *Proceedings of the First Workshop on Language Technology for Equality, Diversity and Inclusion*, pages 86–91.

Anusha Gowda, Fazlourrahman Balouchzahi, Hosahalli Shashirekha, and Grigori Sidorov. 2022. Mucic@ lt-edi-acl2022: Hope speech detection using data re-sampling and 1d conv-lstm. In *Proceedings of the Second Workshop on Language Technology for Equality, Diversity and Inclusion*, pages 161–166.

Jeremy Howard and Sebastian Ruder. 2018. Universal language model fine-tuning for text classification. *arXiv preprint arXiv:1801.06146*.

Abhinav Kumar, Sunil Saumya, and Pradeep Roy. 2022. Soa_nlp@ lt-edi-acl2022: an ensemble model for hope speech detection from youtube comments. In *Proceedings of the Second Workshop on Language Technology for Equality, Diversity and Inclusion*, pages 223–228.

Edison Marrese-Taylor, Jorge A Balazs, and Yutaka Matsuo. 2017. Mining fine-grained opinions on closed captions of youtube videos with an attention-rnn. *arXiv preprint arXiv:1708.02420*.

Skanda Muralidhar, Laurent Nguyen, and Daniel Gatica-Perez. 2018. Words worth: Verbal content and hirability impressions in youtube video resumes. In *Proceedings of the 9th workshop on computational approaches to subjectivity, sentiment and social media analysis*, pages 322–327.

Shriphani Palakodety, Ashiqur R KhudaBukhsh, and Jaime G Carbonell. 2019. Hope speech detection: A computational analysis of the voice of peace. *arXiv preprint arXiv:1909.12940*.

Sunil Saumya Shankar Biradar and Arun Chauhan. 2021. mbert based model for identification of offensive content in south indian languages. In *Working Notes of FIRE 2021-Forum for Information Retrieval Evaluation (Online). CEUR*.

# ML&AI_IIIT Ranchi@LT-EDI-2023: Identification of Hope Speech of YouTube comments in Mixed Languages

**Kirti Kumari**
IIIT Ranchi, India
kirti@iiitranchi.ac.in

**Shirish Shekhar Jha**
IISER Bhopal, India
shirish20@iiserb.ac.in

**Zarikunte Kunal Dayanand**
IISER Bhopal, India
zarikunte20@iiserb.ac.in

**Praneesh Sharma**
KIIT, Bhubaneswar, India
praneeshsharma30@gmail.com

## Abstract

Hope speech analysis refers to the examination and evaluation of speeches or messages that aim to instill hope, inspire optimism, and motivate individuals or communities. It involves analyzing the content, language, rhetorical devices, and delivery techniques used in a speech to understand how it conveys hope and its potential impact on the audience. The objective of this study is to classify the given text comments as Hope Speech or Not Hope Speech. The provided dataset consists of YouTube comments in four languages: English, Hindi, Spanish, Bulgarian; with pre-defined classifications. Our approach involved pre-processing the dataset and using TF-IDF (Term Frequency-Inverse Document Frequency) as well as BOW(Bag Of Words) feature vectors on various machine learning algorithms. Our approach also involved fine-tuning of DistilROBERTa, a pre-trained model by hugging face.

## 1 Introduction

In a world full with problems, uncertainties, and moments of despair, the power of hope becomes an urgent appeal for resilience and transformation. Hope speeches, a distinct mode of communication, have evolved as a powerful tool for instilling optimism, inspiring action, and fostering a renewed feeling of possibilities in individuals and communities. These speeches capture the spirit of optimism by combining words, emotions, and ideas of a brighter future.

Hope talks overcome linguistic boundaries, reaching audiences of all cultures and languages. They have an extraordinary power to touch hearts, ignite emotions, and motivate people for positive change. This study work tries to uncover the universal characteristics that underlying these messages through the analysis of hope speeches in four different languages; English, Hindi, Spanish, and Bulgarian.

This study examines the tremendous impact of hope speeches on individuals and societies, drawing on studies undertaken by several research institutes. The Institute of Hope Studies at the University of Oklahoma has conducted research that demonstrates the transforming power of hope in improving mental well-being, increasing resilience, and improving outcomes in a variety of circumstances. Furthermore, the University of Oklahoma's Centre for Hope Studies provides unique insights into the psychological and social implications of hope speeches in various cultural contexts.

We faced some difficulties while analysing hope speech text snippets. The subjective nature of hope was one such obstacle. The distinctive emotional and psychological responses of individuals within a certain cultural and linguistic framework has to be considered when determining the effectiveness of a hope speech. Another difficulty was translating and interpreting hope speeches across languages, as variations, cultural allusions, and rhetorical strategies may differ, potentially changing the impact on varied audiences.

In this study we have attempted to provide a greater knowledge of hope speech analysis by looking into these difficulties. We aimed to develop a viable system that could detect and categorise hope speech in this language by leveraging several machine learning and deep learning approaches. Our experiments involved training and fine-tuning models applying cutting-edge methodologies. By fine-tuning DistilRoBERTa, a language model trained on numerous languages, we hoped to improve the accuracy and effectiveness of our categorization system.

Our experiment produced encouraging results, with a Precision-Score of 0.66. This performance displayed the effectiveness of our strategy as well as the efforts put in in tackling the obstacles unique to the English language. We improved our system's



*LT-EDI 2023 – Third Workshop on Language Technology for Equality, Diversity and Inclusion*, pages 214–222, Varna, Bulgaria, Sep 7, 2023.
https://doi.org/10.26615/978-954-452-084-7_033

capabilities and got commendable results in detecting and categorising hope speech by leveraging the power of transfer learning and combining it with domain-specific fine-tuning.

In conclusion, hope speech analysis, particularly text analysis, provides vital insights regarding their universal significance. We can learn how these speeches inspire optimism and resonate with varied audiences by evaluating linguistic and rhetorical aspects such as metaphors, imagery, and narrative frameworks. Text analysis allows us to delve into the complexities of language, revealing the tactics used by speakers to provoke emotions and transmit positive messages. However, difficulties arise in the subjective interpretation and translation of hope speeches, highlighting the importance of taking cultural settings and language variations into account. By negotiating these intricacies, we gain a better grasp of hope speech analysis, allowing us to use words to inspire good change in individuals and communities alike.

Our Work has been organized in a step–by–step to represent our work in a much efficient way. Section 2 describes work done in the related field, Section 3 & 4 identifies the outlines of the task and dataset description, Section 5 mentions the various methodologies adapted and their results on validation dataset. Lastly, we have discussed the result and concluded in Section 6 and 7 respectively.

## 2 Related Works

For the purpose of fostering hope and uplifting individuals, researchers and organizations involved in hope speech analysis have recognized the importance of exploring and developing effective methodologies and models. In order to inspire and empower individuals, studies have been conducted to examine various approaches to hope speech analysis across different fields. Just as social media companies have been obligated to support sentiment analysis research for the protection of users from cyberbullying, researchers in hope speech analysis strive to enhance their understanding of the key components that instill hope and promote optimism. Through the examination of different methodologies and models, researchers of (Kumaresan et al., 2023) seek to uncover the most impactful elements that contribute to the effectiveness of hope speeches. By investing in hope speech analysis research, scholars and organizations aim to unlock the potential for positive change, resilience, and motivation in individuals and communities.

The authors of (Kumar et al., 2022) used YouTube comments to do opinion mining and trend analysis. The researchers examined attitudes to determine trends, seasonality, and projections; user sentiments were discovered to be highly associated with the impact of real-world events. The research (Severyn et al., 2014) conducted a thorough study of opinion mining using YouTube comments. The authors created a comment corpus with 35K hand labelled data in order to predict the opinion polarity of the comments using tree kernel models.

The works (Chakravarthi, 2022; Chakravarthi et al., 2022; Chakravarthi, 2020) used a social network analysis and mining approach to find hope speech in YouTube comments. Their study emphasises the role of hope within online networks and its potential impact on human well-being. They create a framework specifically designed to identify instances of hope speech using sentiment analysis and natural language processing techniques. They successfully extract relevant patterns and features for accurate detection by employing data mining techniques and taking into account linguistic, visual, and social elements. Their study contributes to a better understanding of the role of hope in digital communities by providing significant insights into the detection of hope speech in online platforms. The researchers of (Palakodety et al., 2019) investigate the application of computational approaches to analyse peace discourse in the context of Kashmir in their research. Through computer analysis, their research provides unique insights into the dynamics of peace-related communication. They use powerful computational approaches to shed light on the voices advocating for peace in the region.

The work (Maas et al., 2011) explored using deep learning, specifically Convolutional Neural Networks (CNNs), for sentiment analysis. They investigate various word vector representations' effectiveness and advances understanding of using neural networks for discerning sentiment in text data. The works (Aurpa et al., 2022; Lucky et al., 2021) employed deep neural network models based on transformers to detect offensive remarks in Bangla social media. BERT (Bidirectional Encoder Representations from Transformers) and ELECTRA (Efficiency Learning an Encoder that Classifies Token Replacements Accurately) pretraining language architectures are used in tandem.

The authors constructed a one-of-a-kind dataset that includes 44,001 comments from a wide range of Bangla-language Facebook postings.

Hence, the existing literature on hope speech analysis includes a diverse set of ideas and methodologies. The evaluated works in this subject stress the importance of experimenting with various data mining techniques, using benchmark datasets, leveraging deep learning models, and conducting comparative studies. These findings highlight the necessity of building thorough frameworks, using credible datasets, and using lessons from prior research in order to progress the area of hope speech analysis. The proposed approaches, benchmark datasets, and findings from these studies are useful tools for scholars and practitioners interested in developing successful computational strategies for instilling hope and optimism. Building on these references, our work in hope speech analysis intends to be inspired by proven methodology and to perform a comparative research of our dataset in order to uncover and develop effective ways. We intend to contribute to the development of strong approaches in hope speech analysis that can empower individuals and communities, create resilience, and inspire positive change by incorporating insights from prior studies and utilising our own comparative analysis.

## 3 Task Description

The primary objective of this task is to perform Hope Speech analysis on YouTube comments in four different languages, which are English, Hindi, Spanish and Bulgarian. Health professionals believe that hope is important for human well-being, healing, and repair. Hope speech represents the notion that one may uncover and get motivated to employ pathways to one's desired goals. Our approach strives to shift popular thinking away from preoccupations with prejudice, loneliness, or the negative aspects of life and towards fostering confidence, support, and positive traits based on individual comments.

Hope speech analysis refers to the examination and evaluation of speeches or messages that aim to instill hope, inspire optimism, and motivate individuals or communities.It entails analysing a speech's content, language, rhetorical devices, and delivery tactics to determine how it transmits hope and its potential impact on the listener.

Participants are presented with training, development, and test datasets in four languages (Hindi, English, Spanish, Bulgarian), some of them being code-mixed. The datasets are annotated at the comment/post level. A comment or post may contain more than one sentence, although the corpus's average sentence length is one. Participants can opt to classify one or more code-mixed languages. Each language's leaderboard results were released.

We address this problem using a variety of machine learning approaches and methodologies. These include typical machine learning algorithms, deep learning models, or a combination of the two. By training and fine-tuning such models on the available information, we hope to develop a robust classifier capable of accurately predicting the level of depression displayed in unseen social media posts.

## 4 Dataset Description

The dataset utilized for the Hope Speech Analysis task in multiple languages comprises a diverse collection of YouTube comments. It is segmented into three distinct subsets: a training dataset, a development dataset, and a test dataset. The dataset consists of 2 labels, which differ for the languages. For English, "Hope speech" is used for Hope Speech and "Non hope speech" for Not Hope Speech. For Hindi, "Hope" is used for Hope Speech and "Not-Hope" for Not Hope Speech. For Spanish, "HS" is used for Hope Speech and "NHS" for Not Hope Speech. For Bulgarian, "TRUE" is used for Hope Speech and "FALSE" for Not Hope Speech.

Table 1 shows samples of text excerpts together with their corresponding labels to help the reader understand the dataset. These examples from the dataset demonstrate the wide range of postings to which each label can be applied.

The dataset was separated into three parts for the competition: the training set, the development set, and the test set. The labels for the test set were hidden by the competition's administrators because this section was exclusively utilised to evaluate the competitors' solutions.

The training dataset provided to us contains a large number of YouTube comments composed in many languages and code-mixed format. Each post in the training dataset is labelled with a label indicating whether it is a hope or non-hope comment. These labelled annotations served as the basis for training classification models, helping the construction and refining of machine learning

Table 1: Text Excerpts from Dataset

| Text | Label | Dataset | Language |
|---|---|---|---|
| Totally agree! All Lives matter! | Hope_Speech | Train | English |
| Uggghhhhh so vile and ego out of control he | Non_Hope_Speech | Dev | English |
| LGBTQ+ means Lets Get Biden To Quit plus Kamal.. | Non_Hope_Speech | Test | English |
| Syndrome bolte kya | Not_Hope | Train | Hindi |
| Bahut kam nahi hote he sir.....bas log open ho.. | Hope | Dev | Hindi |
| Sir I have always watched your videos and I appre.. | Hope | Test | Hindi |
| Todas ellas coinciden, además, en que la p.. | HS | Train | Spanish |
| ¿Quien me puede explicar que tiene que.. | NHS | Dev | Spanish |
| Si no apoyas el avance de ley trans, eres transfobicx y punto | NHS | Test | Spanish |
| Velik si.. s takiva klipove :D | TRUE | Train | Bulgarian |
| Tova ne sa drekhi za makhane i slagane.. | FALSE | Dev | Bulgarian |
| che se pravyat na tezhkari i biyat vsichki | FALSE | Test | Bulgarian |

Table 2: Dataset Distribution

| Language | Train | Dev | Test | Total |
|---|---|---|---|---|
| English | 18192 | 4548 | 4805 | 27545 |
| Hindi | 2563 | 320 | 321 | 3204 |
| Spanish | 1312 | 300 | 547 | 2159 |
| Bulgarian | 4671 | 589 | 599 | 5859 |

or deep learning models. The dev dataset, also known as the validation dataset, supplements the labelled data provided. It enabled us to analyse model performance and fine-tune hyperparameters during the development period. The labelled information in the development dataset aids in determining whether the algorithms are accurate in categorising social media text as original or fake news.

Table 2 provides an overview of the distribution in the dataset and lists the number of instances for each language. The training set has a greater number of instances than the development set. This size disparity allows for more effective fine-tuning of hyperparameters in both machine learning algorithms and deep learning neural networks. A bigger training set allows for more robust model optimisation, which leads to enhanced performance and generalisation capabilities.

## 5 Methodology

In our study, we used a variety of approaches on the development dataset to determine the most successful approach for making predictions on the test dataset. numerous methodologies were used in the experiments carried out during the inquiry. These included data preprocessing, TF-IDF based classification and bag of words classification.

The raw English social media postings were processed through a range of text cleansing processes during the initial data pre-processing step. To standardise the textual data, these include the removal of punctuation, stop words, and special characters, as well as tokenization and stemming procedures. This stage of pre-processing ensures that the text is properly prepared for further analysis.

Following that, TF-IDF-based classification is implemented. Each document, i.e., YouTube comment, is represented as a numerical feature vector using the TF-IDF (Term Frequency-Inverse Document Frequency) approach. The methodology involves bag of words classification after TF-IDF-based classification. The text data is represented using a bag of words model, which creates a vocabulary comprised of unique words extracted from the corpus.

Following this methodology, which includes data pre-processing, TF-IDF and bag of words classification, a comprehensive and effective approach for accurately categorising code-mixed YouTube comments was developed.

### 5.1 Data Pre-processing

We began our task preparations by performing data pre-processing and visualisation. We began by inspecting the data for any occurrences of null or missing values. We performed a text statistical study after establishing the lack of such values. This entailed assessing the word count, character count, and word density per phrase.

$$\textbf{WordCount(T)} = |\textbf{words(T)}|$$
$$\textbf{CharacterCount(T)} = |\textbf{characters(T)}|$$
$$\textbf{WordDensity(T)} = \frac{\textbf{WordCount}(T)}{\textbf{SentenceCount}(T)}$$

The initial step entailed removing punctuation marks, Emojis, and alphanumeric characters to reduce noise and assure a better depiction of the textual information. Following that, we removed stopwords, which are frequently occurring words that do not contribute significantly to the overall meaning of the text. Furthermore, we concentrated on expanding any contracted terms to their full forms, allowing for a more comprehensive study of the text.

The next step in the data pre-processing pipeline was tokenization, which involves breaking down the text into discrete units such as words or subwords. By providing a structured representation of the text data, this method makes subsequent analysis and modelling activities easier. Furthermore, we used lemmatization to reduce inflected or variant words to their base or dictionary form, increasing consistency and coherence within the dataset.

We obtained a cleaner and more refined version of the text suitable for additional feature representation through these systematic and formalised data pre-processing methods. These activities set the groundwork for our task's later stages of feature extraction, categorization, and analysis.

We hoped to improve the quality and dependability of the text data by meticulously implementing these data pretreatment techniques, preparing it for subsequent analysis and classification jobs. Following the extraction of features step, we performed the classification job using a variety of machine learning models and deep learning techniques. The specific methodologies used are addressed in the following subsections of this study, emphasising the complexities and nuances connected with each methodology.

### 5.2 Classification using TF-IDF

In this research study, we began experimenting with the TF-IDF (Term Frequency-Inverse Document Frequency) technique for machine learning-based classification problems. The primary goal of our study was to evaluate the performance of TF-IDF-based techniques for text classification.

TF-IDF is a popular natural language processing method that assigns weights to individual terms based on their frequency of occurrence within a given text and their rarity over the entire corpus. TF-IDF identifies discriminative features important for classification by taking into account the particular significance inside a document and its wider distinctiveness across the corpus.

$$\textbf{TF-IDF}: \textbf{TF-IDF}(t, d, D) = \textbf{tf}(t, d) \times \textbf{idf}(t, D)$$
$$\textbf{Max Document Frequency (max\_df)} = 0.9$$
$$\textbf{Min Document Frequency (min\_df)} = 5$$

where
t is the term (word)
d is the document
D is the entire corpus or collection

To perform the TF-IDF-based classification, we applied a variety of machine learning methods, including the random forest classifier and the gradient boosting classifier. These algorithms are well-known for their ability to handle text categorization jobs. In addition, we investigated other similar algorithms to assess their effectiveness and compare the findings acquired.

For the TF-IDF method, we used a value of 0.9 for max_df, indicating that we ignored terms appearing in more than 90% of the texts. Furthermore, min_df was set to 5, suggesting that terms appearing in fewer than five documents would be excluded. This parameter selection attempted to achieve a balance between capturing rich vocabulary and avoiding computational complexity. We sought to ensure robust classification performance while managing the dimensionality of the feature space by limiting the dictionary to the most common and informative terms. Tables 4, 6, 8 and 10 summarise the results of utilising several machine learning methods on the training and development datasets.

Table 3: Hyperparameters

| Hyperparameters | Values |
|---|---|
| **Number of Layers** | 4 |
| **Activation Function(s)** | ReLU, Swish, Sigmoid |
| **Dropout Rate** | 0.4 |
| **Optimizer** | Adam |
| **Number of Epochs** | 13 |

Table 4: TF-IDF Features based Results on Training and Validation Datasets for English Language

| Classifier | Macro F1 | Macro Pre-ci-sion | Macro Re-call |
|---|---|---|---|
| Ridge-Classifier | 0.427 | **0.681** | 0.391 |
| Perceptron-Classifier | 0.467 | 0.533 | 0.43 |
| SGD-classifier | 0.499 | 0.641 | 0.449 |
| Passive-Aggressive-Classifier | 0.51 | 0.536 | 0.489 |
| Decision-Tree-Classifier | 0.458 | 0.457 | 0.46 |
| Random-Forest-Classifier | 0.519 | 0.548 | **0.494** |
| AdaBoost-Classifier | 0.519 | 0.548 | **0.494** |
| Gradient Boosting-Classifier | 0.479 | 0.617 | 0.432 |
| SVM Classifier | **0.521** | 0.614 | 0.473 |

Table 5: BOW Features based Results on Training and Validation Datasets for English Language

| Classifier | Macro F1 | Macro Preci-sion | Macro Re-call |
|---|---|---|---|
| Ridge-Classifier | 0.48 | 0.5 | 0.463 |
| Perceptron-Classifier | 0.398 | 0.507 | 0.359 |
| SGD-classifier | 0.492 | 0.507 | 0.49 |
| Passive-Aggressive-Classifier | 0.482 | 0.46 | **0.508** |
| Decision-Tree-Classifier | 0.471 | 0.465 | 0.478 |
| Random-Forest-Classifier | 0.425 | 0.664 | 0.403 |
| AdaBoost-Classifier | **0.51** | 0.559 | 0.478 |
| Gradient Boosting-Classifier | **0.51** | 0.559 | 0.478 |
| SVM Classifier | 0.478 | **0.612** | 0.434 |

Table 6: TF-IDF Features based Results on Training and Validation Datasets for Hindi Language

| Classifier | Macro F1 | Macro Preci-sion | Macro Re-call |
|---|---|---|---|
| Ridge-Classifier | 0.489 | **0.699** | 0.507 |
| Perceptron-Classifier | 0.616 | 0.59 | **0.654** |
| SGD-classifier | 0.585 | 0.617 | 0.571 |
| Passive-Aggressive-Classifier | 0.557 | 0.558 | 0.557 |
| Decision-Tree-Classifier | 0.576 | 0.571 | 0.583 |
| Random-Forest-Classifier | 0.549 | 0.629 | 0.541 |
| AdaBoost-Classifier | **0.632** | 0.653 | 0.617 |
| Gradient Boosting-Classifier | 0.565 | 0.622 | 0.552 |
| SVM Classifier | 0.589 | 0.655 | 0.57 |

### 5.3 Bag-Of-Words Feature Classification

In the field of natural language processing, Bag-of-Words (BOW) text classification has developed as a popular method for representing text documents as numerical feature vectors. In this research project, we also used BOW-based text classification in conjunction with machine learning algorithms to effectively analyse and classify textual data.

The first step in the BagOfWords-based text classification method was to create a list or glossary of unique words or phrases. This vocabulary was used to lay the groundwork for presenting the documents. To achieve complete coverage, we developed a vocabulary of 10,000 terms that included the most frequent and informative terms from the training dataset.

After forming the dictionary, each document was converted into a sparse vector representation. Using techniques such as term frequency-inverse document frequency (TF-IDF), this representation recorded the presence or absence of dictionary words inside the document, as well as their corresponding frequencies or weighted values.

We used a variety of machine learning algorithms to help with the training and classification of the BOW representations, including well-known models like logistic regression, support vector machines, random forests, and decision trees. These algorithms were trained using a labelled dataset of documents and their associated class labels.

The machine learning algorithms discovered the underlying patterns and correlations between the BOW characteristics and their related classes during the training phase. Following that, we assessed the trained models' effectiveness and generalization capabilities using performance metrics including Macro Precision, Macro Recall, and Macro

F1-score on a separate development dataset.

## 6 Results

Table 7: BOW Features based Results on Training and Validation Datasets for Hindi Language

| Classifier | Macro F1 | Macro Precision | Macro Recall |
|---|---|---|---|
| Ridge-Classifier | 0.606 | 0.695 | 0.581 |
| Perceptron-Classifier | 0.634 | 0.587 | **0.721** |
| SGD-classifier | 0.624 | 0.634 | 0.617 |
| Passive-Aggressive-Classifier | 0.611 | 0.647 | 0.591 |
| Decision-Tree-Classifier | 0.608 | 0.615 | 0.601 |
| Random-Forest-Classifier | 0.547 | **0.762** | 0.54 |
| AdaBoost-Classifier | **0.636** | 0.663 | 0.619 |
| Gradient Boosting-Classifier | 0.619 | 0.718 | 0.591 |
| SVM Classifier | 0.598 | 0.623 | 0.585 |

Table 8: TF-IDF Features based Results on Training and Validation Datasets for Spanish Language

| Classifier | Macro F1 | Macro Precision | Macro Recall |
|---|---|---|---|
| Ridge-Classifier | **0.794** | **0.797** | **0.794** |
| Perceptron-Classifier | 0.696 | 0.762 | 0.644 |
| SGD-classifier | 0.761 | 0.761 | 0.761 |
| Passive-AggressiveClassifier | 0.737 | 0.74 | 0.733 |
| Decision-Tree-Classifier | 0.67 | 0.672 | 0.671 |
| Random-Forest-Classifier | 0.787 | 0.789 | 0.773 |
| AdaBoost-Classifier | 0.705 | 0.705 | 0.705 |
| Gradient Boosting-Classifier | 0.749 | 0.754 | 0.748 |
| SVM Classifier | 0.789 | 0.789 | 0.789 |

Table 9: BOW Features based Results on Training and Validation Datasets for Spanish Language

| Classifier | Macro F1 | Macro Precision | Macro Recall |
|---|---|---|---|
| Ridge-Classifier | 0.782 | 0.784 | 0.782 |
| Perceptron-Classifier | 0.601 | 0.842 | 0.472 |
| SGD-classifier | 0.776 | 0.758 | 0.795 |
| Passive-AggressiveClassifier | **0.804** | 0.8 | **0.807** |
| Decision-Tree-Classifier | 0.686 | 0.687 | 0.686 |
| Random-Forest-Classifier | 0.775 | 0.787 | 0.769 |
| AdaBoost-Classifier | 0.761 | 0.762 | 0.761 |
| Gradient Boosting-Classifier | 0.780 | 0.787 | 0.779 |
| SVM Classifier | 0.801 | **0.803** | 0.801 |

Table 10: TF-IDF Features based Results on Training and Validation Datasets for Bulgarian Language

| Classifier | Macro F1 | Macro Precision | Macro Recall |
|---|---|---|---|
| Ridge-Classifier | 0.523 | **0.967** | 0.521 |
| Perceptron-Classifier | **0.663** | 0.638 | **0.629** |
| SGD-classifier | 0.575 | 0.656 | 0.555 |
| Passive-AggressiveClassifier | 0.609 | 0.63 | 0.61 |
| Decision-Tree-Classifier | 0.576 | 0.586 | 0.568 |
| Random-Forest-Classifier | 0.519 | 0.634 | 0.518 |
| AdaBoost-Classifier | 0.627 | 0.706 | 0.596 |
| Gradient Boosting-Classifier | 0.564 | 0.642 | 0.547 |
| SVM Classifier | 0.587 | 0.674 | 0.556 |

Table 11: BOW Features based Results on Training and Validation Datasets for Bulgarian Language

| Classifier | Macro F1 | Macro Precision | Macro Recall |
|---|---|---|---|
| Ridge-Classifier | 0.597 | 0.699 | 0.57 |
| Perceptron-Classifier | 0.584 | 0.671 | 0.56 |
| SGD-classifier | 0.642 | 0.654 | **0.633** |
| Passive-Aggressive-Classifier | 0.639 | 0.69 | 0.61 |
| Decision-Tree-Classifier | 0.619 | 0.646 | 0.603 |
| Random-Forest-Classifier | 0.546 | 0.78 | 0.533 |
| AdaBoost-Classifier | 0.649 | 0.7 | 0.622 |
| Gradient Boosting-Classifier | 0.607 | **0.71** | 0.578 |
| SVM Classifier | **0.65** | 0.676 | 0.632 |

In this section, we show the results of the task we submitted. We used the TF-IDF model setup for prediction since it generated a considerably better overall result. The F1-Score, precision, and recall macros were used to evaluate us. The confusion matrices are displayed below, and they display the classification of classes as well as classes that were mistakenly classified. It is a critical instrument for evaluating the efficacy and performance of our model. The Table 12 displays our positions in each subtask. The rankings were not obtained for the Spanish language.

Table 12: DistilROBERTa results on the test dataset

| Task | Macro F1-Score | Rank |
|---|---|---|
| **English** | 0.50 | 1 |
| **Hindi** | 0.52 | 4 |
| **Bulgarian** | 0.50 | 4 |

## 7 Conclusion

To summarise, this study looked into a variety of text classification techniques, including Bag-of-

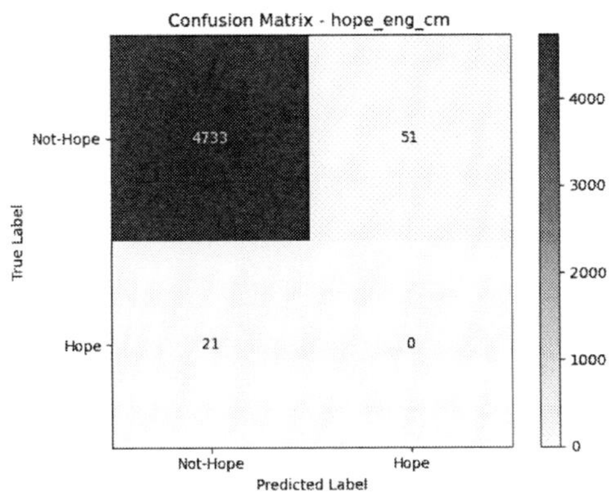


Figure 1: Confusion Matrix of English Predictions

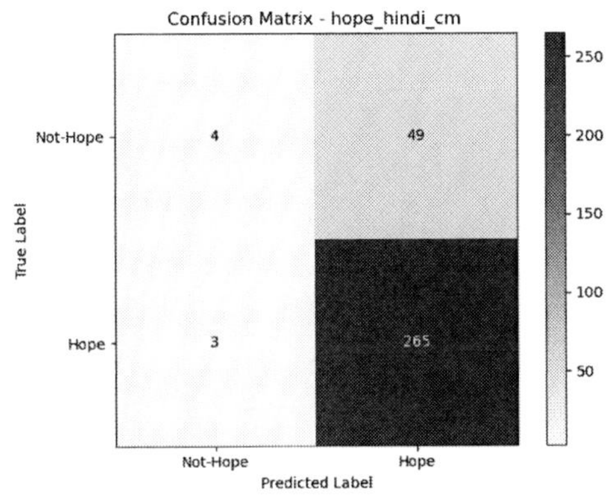


Figure 2: Confusion Matrix of Hindi Predictions

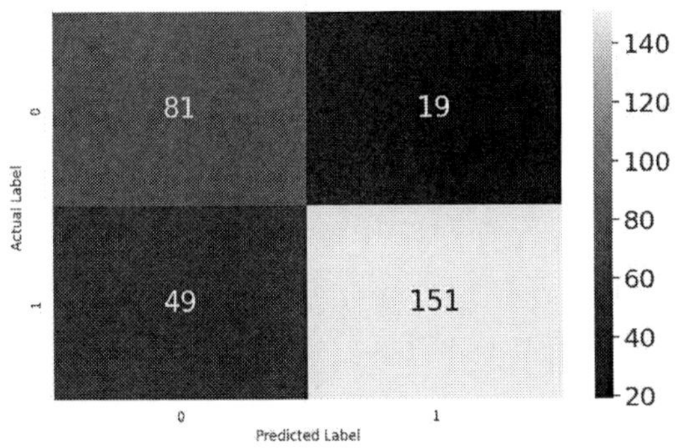


Figure 3: Confusion Matrix of Spanish Predictions

Words (BOW) features based classification, TF-IDF features based classification, and fine-tuning of the pre-trained DistilRoBERTa model. Each method has various advantages and shown its ability to effectively categorise textual data. Our model and experiments completed the task successfully. We can improve performance by fine-tuning the pre-trained model for additional similar data and through data augmentation.

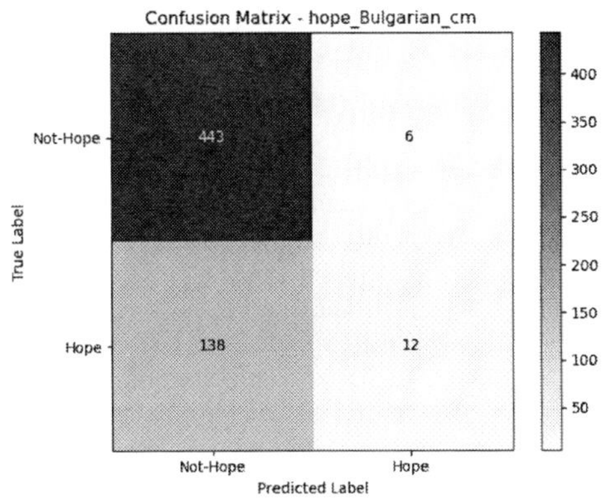


Figure 4: Confusion Matrix of Bulgarian Predictions

## Acknowledgements

We are thankful to Indian Institute of Information Technology Ranchi for all the support during our research.

## References

Tanjim Taharat Aurpa, Rifat Sadik, and Md Shoaib Ahmed. 2022. Abusive bangla comments detection on facebook using transformer-based deep learning models. *Social Network Analysis and Mining*, 12(1):24.

Bharathi Raja Chakravarthi. 2020. HopeEDI: A multilingual hope speech detection dataset for equality, diversity, and inclusion. In *Proceedings of the Third Workshop on Computational Modeling of People's Opinions, Personality, and Emotion's in Social Media*, pages 41–53, Barcelona, Spain (Online). Association for Computational Linguistics.

Bharathi Raja Chakravarthi. 2022. Hope speech detection in youtube comments. *Social Network Analysis and Mining*, 12(1):75.

Bharathi Raja Chakravarthi, Vigneshwaran Muralidaran, Ruba Priyadharshini, Subalalitha Cn, John McCrae, Miguel Ángel García, Salud María Jiménez-Zafra, Rafael Valencia-García, Prasanna Kumaresan, Rahul Ponnusamy, Daniel García-Baena, and José García-Díaz. 2022. Overview of the shared task on hope speech detection for equality, diversity, and inclusion. In *Proceedings of the Second Workshop on Language Technology for Equality, Diversity and Inclusion*, pages 378–388, Dublin, Ireland. Association for Computational Linguistics.

Abhinav Kumar, Sunil Saumya, and Pradeep Roy. 2022. Soa_nlp@ lt-edi-acl2022: an ensemble model for hope speech detection from youtube comments. In *Proceedings of the second workshop on language technology for equality, diversity and inclusion*, pages 223–228.

Prasanna Kumar Kumaresan, Bharathi Raja Chakravarthi, Subalalitha Chinnaudayar Navaneethakrishnan, Miguel Ángel García-Cumbreras, Salud María Jiménez-Zafra, José Antonio García-Díaz, Rafael Valencia-García, Momchil Hardalov, Ivan Koychev, Preslav Nakov, Daniel García-Baena, and Kishore Kumar Ponnusamy. 2023. Overview of the third shared task on hope speech detection for equality, diversity, and inclusion. In *Proceedings of the Third Workshop on Speech and Language Technologies for Dravidian Languages*, Varna, Bulgaria. Recent Advances in Natural Language Processing.

Effat Ara Easmin Lucky, Md Mahadi Hasan Sany, Mumenunnessa Keya, Sharun Akter Khushbu, and Sheak Rashed Haider Noori. 2021. An attention on sentiment analysis of child abusive public comments towards bangla text and ml. In *2021 12th international conference on computing communication and networking technologies (ICCCNT)*, pages 1–6. IEEE.

Andrew Maas, Raymond E Daly, Peter T Pham, Dan Huang, Andrew Y Ng, and Christopher Potts. 2011. Learning word vectors for sentiment analysis. In *Proceedings of the 49th annual meeting of the association for computational linguistics: Human language technologies*, pages 142–150.

Shriphani Palakodety, Ashiqur R KhudaBukhsh, and Jaime G Carbonell. 2019. Kashmir: A computational analysis of the voice of peace. *CoRR, abs/1909.12940*.

Aliaksei Severyn, Olga Uryupina, Barbara Plank, Alessandro Moschitti, and Katja Filippova. 2014. Opinion mining on youtube.

# ML&AI_IIIT Ranchi@LT-EDI-2023: Hybrid Model for Text Classification aimed at Identifying Different Forms of Depression

**Kirti Kumari**
IIIT Ranchi, India
kirti@iiitranchi.ac.in

**Shirish Shekhar Jha**
IISER Bhopal, India
shirish20@iiserb.ac.in

**Zarikunte Kunal Dayanand**
IISER Bhopal, India
zarikunte20@iiserb.ac.in

**Praneesh Sharma**
KIIT, Bhubaneswar, India
praneeshsharma30@gmail.com

## Abstract

DepSign–LT–EDI@RANLP–2023 is a dedicated task that addresses the crucial issue of identifying indications of depression in individuals through their social media posts, which serve as a platform for expressing their emotions and sentiments. The primary objective revolves around accurately classifying the signs of depression into three distinct categories: "not depressed", "moderately depressed", and "severely depressed". Our study entailed the utilization of machine learning algorithms, coupled with features such as sentence embeddings and feature representations like TF-IDF, and Bag-of-Words. Remarkably, the adoption of hybrid models yielded promising outcomes, culminating in a $10^{th}$ rank achievement out of 31 participants, supported by a macro F1-Score of 0.408. This research underscores the effectiveness and potential of employing advanced text classification methodologies to discern and identify signs of depression within social media data. The findings hold implications for the development of mental health monitoring systems and support mechanisms, contributing to the well-being of individuals in need.

## 1 Introduction

Depression is a widespread mental health condition that affects a significant number of individuals worldwide. The identification of depression symptoms in individuals is a crucial step in providing timely support and intervention. Given the growing use of social media platforms as channels for emotional expression and experience sharing, there is an increasing interest in leveraging these platforms to detect indications of mental health issues, including depression. Accordingly, the DepSign-LT-EDI@RANLP-2023 task focuses on the detection of depression signs in individuals based on their social media posts.

Past works in this field offer valuable insights into the importance of monitoring mental health and the challenges associated with identifying and addressing mental health problems. The Global Health Data Exchange (GHDx) by the Institute of Health Metrics and Evaluation (Glo) serves as a valuable resource for accessing global health data and understanding the prevalence of mental health disorders. Additionally, the study conducted by (Evans-Lacko et al., 2018) highlights socioeconomic disparities in the treatment gap for individuals with anxiety, mood, and substance use disorders, underscoring the need for targeted interventions and support. The eRISK 2017 study (Losada et al., 2017) carried out further emphasizes the importance of early risk prediction and underscores the experimental foundations in the field.

This research aims to employ machine learning algorithms and text classification techniques to identify signs of depression in social media posts. By leveraging features such as sentence embeddings and utilizing feature representations like the TF-IDF, and Bag-oF-Words, we aim to develop an effective classification model capable of categorizing signs of depression into three distinct labels: **"not depressed", "moderately depressed",** and **"severely depressed"**. The hybrid models utilized in our study incorporate a combination of these features, enabling enhanced classification performance.

The ultimate objective of this research is to contribute to the field of mental health monitoring and support systems by providing a reliable and efficient method for detecting signs of depression through social media analysis. By harnessing the abundant data available on social media platforms, we aim to facilitate timely intervention and support for individuals experiencing depressive symptoms.

Through the DepSign-LT-EDI@RANLP-2023 task, we aim to address the urgent need for inno-



*LT-EDI 2023 – Third Workshop on Language Technology for Equality, Diversity and Inclusion*, pages 223–232, Varna, Bulgaria, Sep 7, 2023.
https://doi.org/10.26615/978-954-452-084-7_034

vative approaches to mental health detection and intervention. By utilizing advanced machine learning algorithms and integrating diverse features, our goal is to offer an easy to use but effective solution for identifying signs of depression in social media data. Although BERTs and other Large Language Models (LLMs) are available for the classification task a major drawback that holds them back is their massive size and training time. Not every individual or organization possesses the capability to leverage the LLM power and supremacy for text classification. Also, there is not much data present to perform the fine-tuning task and get great results. To overcome this and still utilize the abilities of the LLM, we were motivated to get a way around by making use of sentence embeddings that are generated from the LLM but are of smaller size and can be computed in a limited amount of time. The results obtained from our study, as evidenced by our 10th rank and an F1 score of 0.408, demonstrate the potential and promise of our proposed approach.

This paper presents the related work Section 2, dataset description Section 3, task description Section 4, methodology and validation results Section 5, result Section 6, and conclusions Section 7 of our research, shedding light on the effectiveness of text classification techniques in detecting signs of depression. Furthermore, the findings contribute to the broader field of mental health research and pave the way for the development of scalable and efficient solutions for mental health monitoring and support systems.

## 2 Related Work

In the past many efforts have been made in the field of depression identification from social media texts. The authors of (De Choudhury et al., 2013) were among the pioneers in researching the detection of depression through social media posts. Their study focused on Twitter users who had been diagnosed with depression, and they collected one year's worth of posts from this group. Using this dataset, they developed a statistical classifier that aimed to estimate the risk of depression. The classifier utilized various linguistic and behavioral features extracted from the users' posts to predict the likelihood of depression. This research marked an important milestone in the field, providing insights into the potential of social media data for identifying mental health conditions. By employing a rigorous statistical approach, it also laid the groundwork for subsequent studies on detecting depression through social media, contributing to the advancement of research in this domain.

The authors of (William and Suhartono, 2021) conducted a study that explores the use of machine learning techniques to detect depression from social media posts. By employing linguistic features and classifiers, the authors achieve promising results, demonstrating the potential of utilizing social media data for identifying signs of depression. They compare various machine learning algorithms and feature selection methods to determine the most effective combination. The study highlights the importance of pre-processing techniques and feature engineering in improving classification performance. The findings contribute to the development of reliable and efficient methods for detecting signs of depression through social media analysis, supporting timely intervention and support for individuals experiencing depressive symptoms. The authors of (Dessai and Usgaonkar, 2022) carried research that focuses on the scientific aspect of detecting depression from social media data using machine learning techniques and text mining. The authors propose a novel approach that combines text and image information for improved depression detection accuracy. They extract textual features from posts and visual features from associated images, and then employ a multi-modal fusion model to integrate these features. The study evaluates the proposed approach on a large-scale dataset and compares it with existing methods, demonstrating its superior performance. The findings highlight the importance of considering both textual and visual cues for accurate depression detection, offering valuable insights for developing effective mental health monitoring systems. Observing the multi modality of the task, advancements have been made to make the text based identification more robust. Work presented by The authors of (Wolohan et al., 2018) have led emphasis on detecting the linguistic features from the text corpora generated from Reddit, so as to classify them into the categories of depression based on lexical and predictive analysis. The introduction of deep learning architectures like transformer models have also significantly improvised the results (Devlin et al., 2018) presents work that leverages the power of transfer learning to classify text into depression.

The authors of (Salas-Zárate et al., 2022) pre-

sented a thorough search of the literature, the authors found 34 primary papers that satisfied their inclusion requirements. The studies employed several techniques, such as language feature extraction, machine learning, and statistical analysis, to find symptoms of depression on social media. The research findings were conflicting, but taken together, they imply that social media can be used to identify depression symptoms with some degree of accuracy.
Our work has been inspired by past related works and motivated us to develop a simple system to test and identify depression. Past methods have inculcated various experimentation's like statistical analysis, pre-trained model-based research, and employing classical machine learning algorithms on various features; considering them, we have devised a solution that involves sentence embeddings as features and further classified them using multiple machine learning classifiers.

## 3 Dataset

The English-language postings in the dataset for the competition were taken from the Reddit platform. "Not depression", "moderate", or "severe" are the three labels that have been manually added to each post in the dataset (Kayalvizhi et al., 2022; Sampath and Durairaj, 2022; S et al., 2022; Sampath et al., 2023). When there were no signs of depression found in the post, the label "not depression" is used to denote those cases. Alternatively, the terms "moderate" and "severe" denote increasing degrees of depression symptoms in the text.

Table 1 displays examples of text excerpts together with their matching labels to help the reader comprehend the dataset. These illustrations from the dataset highlight the variety of postings that each label can be applied to.

The training set, the development set, and the test set were the three separate parts of the dataset that were divided up for the competition. It is important to note that the labels for the test set were withheld by the competition's administrators because this section was only used to assess the competitors' solutions. Table 2 provides an overview of the label distribution in the dataset and lists the number of instances for each label category.

Notably, the training set contains a larger number of instances compared to the development set. This discrepancy in size enables more effective fine-tuning of hyperparameters for both machine learning algorithms and deep learning neural networks. The availability of a larger training set facilitates more robust model optimization, ultimately leading to improved performance and generalization capabilities.

## 4 Task Description

The objective of this task is to develop a system that can effectively classify signs of depression within social media postings written in English. The system should be able to categorize these signs into one of three distinct labels: "not depressed", "moderately depressed", and "severely depressed". By automating this classification process, the system can provide valuable insights into individuals' mental well-being and potentially facilitate timely intervention and support.

The dataset provided for this task consists of a collection of social media posts expressed in the English language. Each post has been carefully annotated with one of the three aforementioned labels, indicating the level of depression detected within the content. This labeling scheme enables the development of a comprehensive classification system that can effectively gauge the severity of depression symptoms expressed in social media postings.

The authors of (Lin et al., 2020), have shown depression identification with the use of deep visual-textual multimodal learning approach which embarks a great development in this field and simultaneously introduces the domain where machine learning approaches can be applied where the features can be multimodal, meaning it can be in the form of text, video or both. The authors of (Poświata and Perełkiewicz, 2022; AlSagri and Ykhlef, 2020) have performed on a similar task where they have used large pre-trained models to make accurate predictions. They finally used the features and greatly performed using an average ensemble approach. The text cited acted as our motivation for this task, and we leveraged various machine-learning techniques and methodologies. These include traditional machine learning algorithms, deep learning models, or a combination of both. By training and fine-tuning such models on the provided dataset, we aim to create a robust classifier capable of accurately predicting the level of depression exhibited in unseen social media posts.

Table 1: Text Excerpt From Dataset

| S.No. | Text | Label | Dataset |
|---|---|---|---|
| train_pid_7197 | arent tired ive depressed month lost trust peo... | severe | Train |
| dev_pid_1 | im scared lie every day say ill make think mig... | moderate | Dev |
| test_id_3 | But here I am, 24 years old man and doing exac... | moderate | Test |

Table 2: Dataset Distribution

| Class | Training | Development | Test | Total |
|---|---|---|---|---|
| moderate | 3678 | 2169 | 275 | 6122 |
| severe | 768 | 228 | 89 | 1085 |
| Not depression | 2755 | 848 | 135 | 3738 |
| Total | 7201 | 3245 | 499 | 10945 |

## 5 Methodology and Validation Results

The methodology employed in the classification task comprises several sequential steps: data pre-processing, TF-IDF features based classification, bag of words features based classification, and the utilization of sentence embeddings for classification.

In the initial data pre-processing step, the raw English social media postings underwent a series of text cleansing procedures. These include the removal of punctuation, stop words, and special characters, as well as tokenization and stemming operations to standardize the textual data. This pre-processing stage ensures the text is appropriately formatted for subsequent analysis.

Subsequently, TF-IDF based classification is implemented. The TF-IDF (Term Frequency-Inverse Document Frequency) technique is employed to represent each document, i.e., social media post, as a numerical feature vector. Following TF-IDF based classification, the methodology incorporates bag of words classification. In this approach, the text data is represented using a bag of words model, which establishes a vocabulary consisting of unique words derived from the corpus. Finally, sentence embeddings are leveraged for classification. Sentence embeddings aim to capture the semantic meaning of a sentence through a compact vector representation.

By adhering to this methodology, which encompasses data pre-processing, TF-IDF and bag of words classification, and the utilization of sentence embeddings, a classical and effective approach was formulated for accurately categorizing signs of depression within English social media postings.

### 5.1 Data Pre Processing

To commence our preparations for the task, we initiated the process by conducting data pre-processing and visualization. Initially, we conducted an inspection of the data to identify any instances of null or missing values. Upon confirming the absence of such values, we proceeded to perform an analysis of the text statistics. This involved examining the word count, character count, and word density per sentence. The statistical insights derived from this analysis proved instrumental in the subsequent generation of sentence embeddings.

$$\text{WordCount(T)} = |\text{words(T)}|$$
$$\text{CharacterCount(T)} = |\text{characters(T)}|$$
$$\text{WordDensity(T)} = \frac{WordCount(T)}{SentenceCount(T)}$$

Given the nature of the data sourced from social media platforms, we made the assumption that certain text elements required cleaning. Consequently, we focused on the removal of character encodings deemed improper, contractions, and special characters. Furthermore, we undertook the task of eliminating hyperlinks and social media hashtags, as well as alphanumeric characters. In order to enhance the cleanliness and quality of the text, we also implemented the removal of stop words. Additionally, we performed tokenization to segment the text into individual units and applied lemmatization to obtain a refined version of the text suitable for subsequent feature representation.

Through these systematic and formalized data pre-processing steps, we obtained a cleaner and more refined version of the text suitable for further feature representation. These operations laid the foundation for subsequent stages of feature extraction, classification, and analysis in our task.

### 5.2 Classification using TF-IDF Features

In this research study, we started experimentation with the application of the TF-IDF (Term Frequency-Inverse Document Frequency) technique for machine learning-based classification tasks. The primary aim of our investigation was to assess the efficacy of TF-IDF-based approaches for text classification.

TF-IDF is a widely employed method in the field of natural language processing, which assigns weights to individual terms based on their occurrence frequency within a specific document and their rarity across the entire corpus. By considering both the local significance within a document and the global distinctiveness across the corpus, TF-IDF enables the identification of discriminative features crucial for classification purposes.

$$\text{TF-IDF: TF-IDF}(t, d) = \text{TF}(t, d) \times \text{IDF}(t)$$

Max Document Frequency (max_df) = 0.9

Min Document Frequency (min_df) = 5

To implement the TF-IDF-based classification, we utilized a range of machine learning algorithms, such as the random forest classifier and logistic regression wrapped in OneVsRest Classifier to perform the task. These algorithms are renowned for their effectiveness in handling text classification tasks. Additionally, we explored other similar algorithms to evaluate their performance and compare the obtained results.

For the configuration of the TF-IDF approach, we selected a value of 0.9 for max_df, indicating that we disregarded terms appearing in more than 90% of the documents. Furthermore, min_df was set to 5, implying the exclusion of words appearing in fewer than five documents. This parameter selection aimed to strike a balance between capturing diverse vocabulary while avoiding computational complexity. By limiting the dictionary to the most prevalent and informative terms, we sought to ensure robust classification performance while managing the dimensionality of the feature space. Table 3 provides a summary of the outcomes obtained from employing various machine learning algorithms using the training and development datasets.

### 5.3 Bag-Of-Words Features based Classification

In the domain of natural language processing, Bag-of-Words (BoW) features based text classification has emerged as a prevalent methodology for representing text documents as numerical feature vectors. Within the context of this research study, we also employed BoW-based text classification in conjunction with machine learning algorithms to effectively analyze and classify textual data.

The initial step in the BoW-based text classification process involved constructing a dictionary or vocabulary comprising unique words or terms. This dictionary served as the foundation for representing the documents. To ensure comprehensive coverage, we curated a dictionary consisting of 10,000 terms, encompassing the most frequent and informative terms derived from the training dataset.

Once the dictionary was established, each document was transformed into a sparse vector representation. This representation captured the presence or absence of terms from the dictionary within the document, along with their respective frequencies or weighted values, using techniques such as term frequency-inverse document frequency (TF-IDF).

To facilitate the training and classification of the BoW representations, we employed a diverse range of machine learning algorithms, including established models such as logistic regression, support vector machines, random forests, and decision trees, among others. These algorithms underwent training using a labeled dataset comprising documents and their respective class labels.

During the training phase, the machine learning algorithms learned the underlying patterns and relationships between the BoW features and their associated classes. Subsequently, we evaluated the trained models on a separate development dataset, employing performance metrics such as macro precision, macro recall, and macro F1-score, to assess their effectiveness and generalization capabilities.

In selecting the size of the dictionary, we consci-

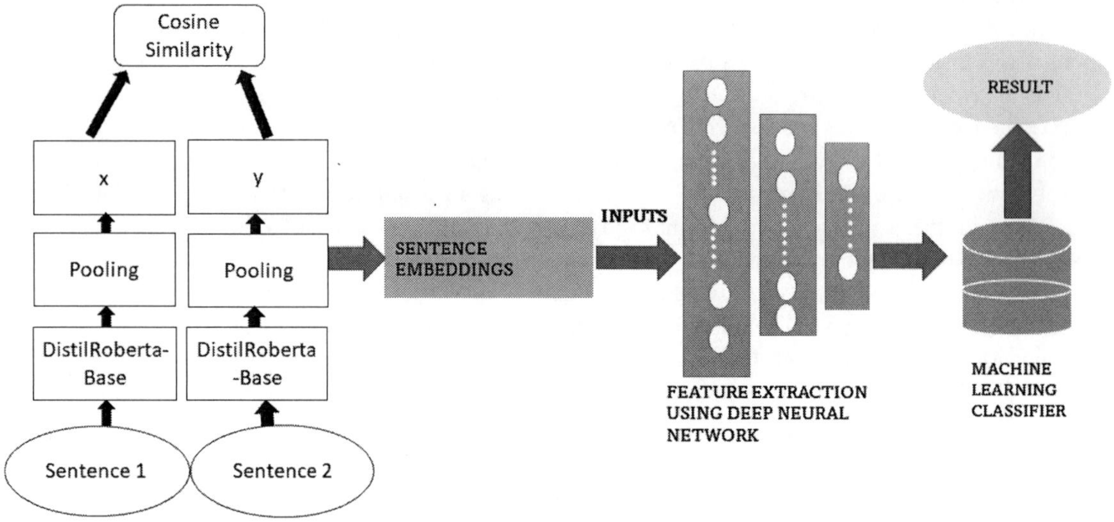


Figure 1: Overview of Proposed System

Table 3: TF-IDF features based Classification Results Summary on Training and Validation Datasets

| Classifier | Macro Precision | Macro Recall | Macro F1 |
|---|---|---|---|
| Ridge-Classifier | 0.653 | 0.465 | 0.488 |
| Perceptron-Classifier | 0.482 | 0.471 | 0.474 |
| SGD-classifier | 0.583 | 0.487 | 0.511 |
| Passive-AggressiveClassifier | 0.498 | 0.465 | 0.477 |
| Decision-Tree-Classifier | 0.417 | 0.455 | 0.393 |
| Random-Forest-Classifier | 0.625 | 0.430 | 0.432 |
| AdaBoost-Classifier | 0.536 | 0.496 | 0.511 |
| Gradient Boosting -Classifier | 0.601 | 0.477 | 0.499 |
| SVM Classifier | 0.560 | 0.489 | 0.510 |

entiously considered the trade-off between capturing an adequate diversity of vocabulary and managing computational complexity. By opting for a dictionary size of 10,000, we aimed to strike an optimal balance between these considerations. Table 4 provides a summary of the experimental results obtained from training and evaluating the models using the training and validation datasets. Notably, it was observed that the Bag-of-Words features exhibited enhanced efficacy in classifying the text data.

### 5.4 Embeddings based Classification

In our research experiment, we employed classical Deep Learning algorithms, specifically the Multilayer Perceptron (MLP), to classify the sentence embeddings generated. To generate these embeddings, we utilized the widely used SBERT all-distilroberta-v1 model (Reimers and Gurevych, 2019). For this a pre-trained model distilroberta-base was used and then it has been trained on an extensive dataset consisting of 1 billion training pairs. It maps input sentences to a 768-dimensional vector space, enabling a comprehensive representation of the semantic information.To create embeddings(x,y) (Reimers and Gurevych, 2020) with a high level of semantic similarity, the all-distilroberta-v1 model uses a contrastive learning strategy. It measures language similarity using the

Table 4: BOW features based Classification Summary on Training and Validation Datasets

| Classifier | Macro Precision | Macro Recall | Macro F1 |
|---|---|---|---|
| Ridge-Classifier | 0.505 | 0.473 | 0.484 |
| Perceptron-Classifier | 0.429 | 0.422 | 0.425 |
| SGD-classifier | 0.493 | 0.478 | 0.482 |
| Passive-AggressiveClassifier | 0.445 | 0.459 | 0.450 |
| Decision-Tree-Classifier | 0.401 | 0.447 | 0.384 |
| Random-Forest-Classifier | 0.609 | 0.426 | 0.430 |
| AdaBoost-Classifier | 0.53 | 0.48 | 0.50 |
| Gradient Boosting -Classifier | 0.593 | 0.472 | 0.493 |
| SVM Classifier | 0.476 | 0.476 | 0.475 |

Table 5: Embedding Based Classification Summary on Training and Validation Datasets

| Classifier | Macro Precision | Macro Recall | Macro F1 |
|---|---|---|---|
| SBERT + Decision Tree Classifier | 0.449 | 0.452 | 0.450 |
| SBERT + Random Forest Classifier | 0.717 | 0.376 | 0.428 |
| SBERT + DNN | 0.635 | 0.511 | 0.540 |
| SBERT+DNN+Random Forest | 0.626 | 0.510 | 0.552 |
| SBERT+DNN+AdaBoost | 0.578 | 0.547 | 0.560 |
| SBERT+DNN+Gaussian NB | 0.498 | 0.598 | 0.505 |
| SBERT+DNN+Decision Tree Classifier | 0.506 | 0.515 | 0.510 |
| SBERT+DNN+Ensemble | 0.601 | 0.558 | 0.573 |

cosine similarity, dot product, and Euclidean distance. The model is appropriate for our classification assignment because it was created primarily as a sentence and brief paragraph encoder.

To generate the sentence embedding we set the maximum sequence length of the embedding model as 512. Following the generation of the sentence embeddings using SBERT all-distilroberta-v1, we proceeded to deploy various machine learning classifiers to make predictions based on these embeddings. Additionally, we constructed a Deep Neural Network (DNN) tailored for the classification of these embeddings. For training and evaluation purposes, we utilized the complete set of training and development embeddings, with a validation split of 0.1 to ensure reliable performance assessment.

To enhance the classification performance further, we extracted the last layer features of the DNN, which served as input for the machine learning classifiers. These last layer features encapsulated the learned representation of the embeddings and captured their discriminative properties. To exploit the complementary strengths of classical machine learning algorithms, we constructed a custom ensemble model that employed these extracted features for classification. This ensemble model combined the predictions from multiple classifiers, aiming to leverage their collective intelligence and improve overall classification performance.

The incorporation of the DNN in our methodology played a crucial role in learning the generalized distribution of the data. By employing deep neural networks, we enabled the model to capture complex patterns and relationships within the embeddings, enhancing its ability to generalize to unseen instances. The DNN's architecture, consisting of multiple layers with interconnected nodes, facilitated the extraction of hierarchical representations, enabling the model to uncover intricate features and capture underlying dependencies. To complement the textual description (Reimers and Gurevych, 2019), we have included Figure 1 showcasing the architecture of the proposed model. This visual representation provides a comprehensive overview of the connections and flow of information within the current model, enhancing the clarity and understanding of the methodology employed.
To provide comprehensive insights about this experimentation, we have documented all the obtained results in Table 5. This table presents a detailed overview of the performance achieved by the dif-

ferent classification models utilized in our study. Furthermore, we have submitted the architecture of the DNN in Table 6, illustrating the configuration and arrangement of the model's layers and nodes. This architectural representation facilitates a clear understanding of the underlying structure and organization of the DNN. The comprehensive results and model details provided offer valuable insights into the effectiveness and performance of our approach.

Table 6: Deep Neural Network Architecture and Hyperparameters

| **Hyperparameters** | **Values** |
|---|---|
| **Number of Layers** | 4 |
| **Activation Function(s)** | Tanh and ReLU |
| **Dropout Rate** | 0.2 |
| **Optimizer** | Adam |
| **Number of Epochs** | 2 |

## 6 Results

Table 7: Final Model results on the test dataset

| **Method** | **Macro F1-Score** |
|---|---|
| **SBERT+DNN+Ensemble** | 0.408 |

We demonstrate the outcomes of the task we submitted in this part. We utilised the configuration SBERT+DNN+Ensemble Model for prediction because we could see that it produced a significantly superior overall result. We were assessed using the Macro F1-Score, Macro Precision, and Macro Recall. On the test dataset shown in Table 7, we received an macro F1-Score of 0.408. The confusion matrix, which details the classification of numerous classes as well as classes that were incorrectly classified, is shown below as Figure 2. It is an essential tool for assessing the effectiveness and performance of our model. From the confusion matrix it is made clear that the classifier is more biased towards the label *Not depression*; as for the training data, it was more in number as compared to other labels, which are less in number Table 2. The Figure 3 shows that the classifier is biased and has not very well adapted towards the minority class. The problem can be overcome in future if the minority class is assigned a class weight and utilization of data augmentation methods for addressing class balance issues.

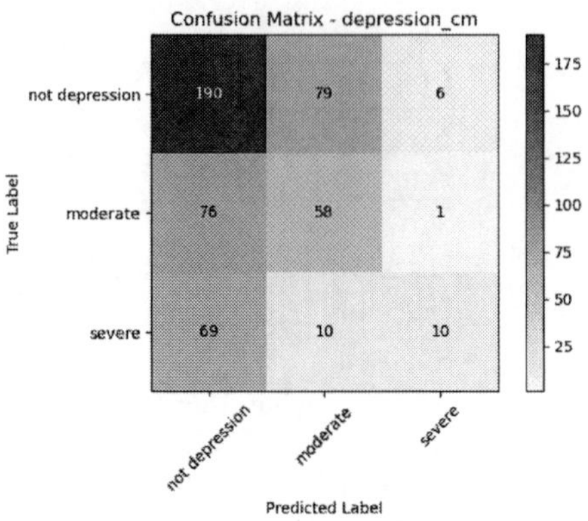


Figure 2: Confusion Matrix of Test Predictions

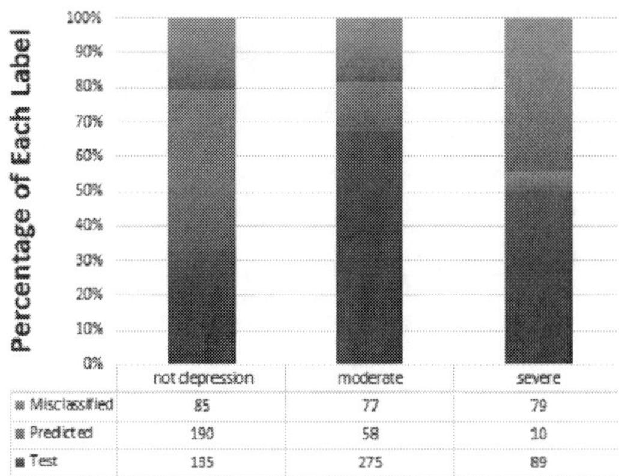


Figure 3: Comparison Results on Different Depression Classes

## 7 Conclusion

The successful completion of this task holds great potential for various applications and benefits. By accurately classifying the signs of depression within social media postings, the developed system can aid in the identification of individuals who may be at risk or in need of mental health support. This classification system could be integrated into social media platforms or utilized as a standalone tool to provide real-time insights into users' mental well-being. Early identification and intervention can play a crucial role in promoting mental health and well-being, and the system developed through this task has the potential to contribute significantly in this regard.

## 8 Future Work

The study can be further expanded for the related domains. One can empower one's studies with newer techniques like active learning. Semi-supervised learning can also propose some findings as we might be able to generate synthetic data that act as an element for our training process.

## Acknowledgements

We are thankful to Indian Institute of Information Technology Ranchi for all the support during our research.

## References

Hatoon S AlSagri and Mourad Ykhlef. 2020. Machine learning-based approach for depression detection in twitter using content and activity features. *IEICE Transactions on Information and Systems*, 103(8):1825–1832.

Munmun De Choudhury, Michael Gamon, Scott Counts, and Eric Horvitz. 2013. Predicting depression via social media. In *Proceedings of the international AAAI conference on web and social media*, volume 7, pages 128–137.

Sukanya Dessai and Soniya Shakil Usgaonkar. 2022. Depression detection on social media using text mining. In *2022 3rd International Conference for Emerging Technology (INCET)*, pages 1–4.

Jacob Devlin, Ming-Wei Chang, Kenton Lee, and Kristina Toutanova. 2018. Bert: Pre-training of deep bidirectional transformers for language understanding. *arXiv preprint arXiv:1810.04805*.

SAGS Evans-Lacko, Sergio Aguilar-Gaxiola, Ali Al-Hamzawi, Jordi Alonso, Corina Benjet, Ronny Bruffaerts, WT Chiu, Silvia Florescu, Giovanni de Girolamo, Oye Gureje, et al. 2018. Socio-economic variations in the mental health treatment gap for people with anxiety, mood, and substance use disorders: results from the who world mental health (wmh) surveys. *Psychological medicine*, 48(9):1560–1571.

S Kayalvizhi, Thenmozhi Durairaj, Bharathi Raja Chakravarthi, et al. 2022. Findings of the shared task on detecting signs of depression from social media. In *Proceedings of the Second Workshop on Language Technology for Equality, Diversity and Inclusion*, pages 331–338.

Chenhao Lin, Pengwei Hu, Hui Su, Shaochun Li, Jing Mei, Jie Zhou, and Henry Leung. 2020. Sensemood: depression detection on social media. In *Proceedings of the 2020 international conference on multimedia retrieval*, pages 407–411.

David E Losada, Fabio Crestani, and Javier Parapar. 2017. erisk 2017: Clef lab on early risk prediction on the internet: experimental foundations. In *Experimental IR Meets Multilinguality, Multimodality, and Interaction: 8th International Conference of the CLEF Association, CLEF 2017, Dublin, Ireland, September 11–14, 2017, Proceedings 8*, pages 346–360. Springer.

Rafał Poświata and Michał Perełkiewicz. 2022. Opi@lt-edi-acl2022: Detecting signs of depression from social media text using roberta pre-trained language models. In *Proceedings of the Second Workshop on Language Technology for Equality, Diversity and Inclusion*, pages 276–282.

Nils Reimers and Iryna Gurevych. 2019. Sentence-bert: Sentence embeddings using siamese bert-networks. In *Proceedings of the 2019 Conference on Empirical Methods in Natural Language Processing*. Association for Computational Linguistics.

Nils Reimers and Iryna Gurevych. 2020. Making monolingual sentence embeddings multilingual using knowledge distillation. In *Proceedings of the 2020 Conference on Empirical Methods in Natural Language Processing*. Association for Computational Linguistics.

Kayalvizhi S, Thenmozhi Durairaj, Bharathi Raja Chakravarthi, and Jerin Mahibha C. 2022. Findings of the shared task on detecting signs of depression from social media. In *Proceedings of the Second Workshop on Language Technology for Equality, Diversity and Inclusion*, pages 331–338, Dublin, Ireland. Association for Computational Linguistics.

Rafael Salas-Zárate, Giner Alor-Hernández, María del Pilar Salas-Zárate, Mario Andrés Paredes-Valverde, Maritza Bustos-López, and José Luis Sánchez-Cervantes. 2022. Detecting depression signs on social media: a systematic literature review. In *Healthcare*, volume 10, page 291. MDPI.

Kayalvizhi Sampath and Thenmozhi Durairaj. 2022. Data set creation and empirical analysis for detecting signs of depression from social media postings. In *Computational Intelligence in Data Science: 5th IFIP TC 12 International Conference, ICCIDS 2022, Virtual Event, March 24–26, 2022, Revised Selected Papers*, pages 136–151. Springer.

Kayalvizhi Sampath, Thenmozhi Durairaj, Bharathi Raja Chakravarthi, Jerin Mahibha C, Kogilavani Shanmugavadivel, and Pratik Anil Rahood. 2023. Overview of the Second Shared Task on Detecting Signs of Depression from Social Media Text. In *Proceedings of the Third Workshop on Language Technology for Equality, Diversity and Inclusion*, Varna, Bulgaria. Recent Advances in Natural Language Processing.

David William and Derwin Suhartono. 2021. Text-based depression detection on social media posts: A systematic literature review. *Procedia Computer Science*, 179:582–589.

JT Wolohan, Misato Hiraga, Atreyee Mukherjee, Zeeshan Ali Sayyed, and Matthew Millard. 2018. Detecting linguistic traces of depression in topic-restricted text: Attending to self-stigmatized depression with nlp. In *Proceedings of the first international workshop on language cognition and computational models*, pages 11–21.

# VEL@LT-EDI-2023: Detecting Homophobia and Transphobia in Code-Mixed Spanish Social Media Comments

**Prasanna Kumar Kumaresan**[1], **Kishore Kumar Ponnusamy**[2], **Kogilavani Shanmugavadivel**[3], **Subalalitha Chinnaudayar Navaneethakrishnan**[4] **Ruba Priyadharshini**[5], **Bharathi Raja Chakravarthi**[6]

[1]Insight SFI Research Centre for Data Analytics, University of Galway, Ireland
[2]Guru Nanak College, Chennai, Tamil Nadu, India. [3]Kongu Engineering College, Tamil Nadu, India
[4]Department Of Computer Science & Engineering, SRM Institute Of Science And Technology, Tamil Nadu, India
[5] Gandhigram Rural Institute-Deemed to be University, Tamil Nadu, India
[6] Insight SFI Research Centre for Data Analytics, School of Computer Science, University of Galway, Ireland.

prasanna.kumaresan@insight-centre.org
{kishorep16002, kogilavani.sv}@gmail.com
{subalalitha, rubapriyadharshini.a}@gmail.com
bharathi.raja@universityofgalway.ie

## Abstract

Our research aims to address the task of detecting homophobia and transphobia in social media code-mixed comments written in Spanish. Code-mixed text in social media often violates strict grammar rules and incorporates non-native scripts, posing challenges for identification. To tackle this problem, we perform pre-processing by removing unnecessary content and establishing a baseline for detecting homophobia and transphobia. Furthermore, we explore the effectiveness of various traditional machine-learning models with feature extraction and pre-trained transformer model techniques. Our best configurations achieve weighted F1 scores of 0.86 on the test set and 0.86 on the development set for Spanish, demonstrating promising results in detecting instances of homophobia and transphobia in code-mixed comments.

## 1 Introduction

Hate speech is speech that is directly or indirectly against a person or group and contains animosity because of something inherent to that person or group (Schmidt and Wiegand, 2017; Chetty and Alathur, 2018; Fortuna and Nunes, 2018). Locating hate speech on the Internet is a difficult task that even the most advanced models struggle to complete (Govers et al., 2023; Chakravarthi et al., 2023a). As a result of the rapid development in user-generated online content, which has not only resulted in a vast increase in the accessibility of information but has also delivered a vast increase in the accessibility of information (Subramanian et al., 2022a), individuals have been provided with a simple platform on which to express their opinions and communicate with others in a public forum (Jahan and Oussalah, 2023; Chakravarthi, 2022a). This has resulted in some undesirable uses of online spaces, such as the dissemination of hate speech, which is regrettable. The use of abusive language frequently accompanies the dissemination of hate speech in everyday life, especially on social media (Chakravarthi et al., 2023c; Subramanian et al., 2022b; Chakravarthi, 2022b).

In studies conducted under the headings of hate speech, offensive language, and aggressive language, the examination of homophobic language is typically grouped with analyses of other forms of hostility (Waseem and Hovy, 2016; Espinosa Anke et al., 2019; Priyadharshini et al., 2022). "Emotional disgust towards individuals who do not conform to society's gender expectations" is one definition of transphobia (Nagoshi et al., 2008). Homophobia is the unreasonable fear, loathing, and intolerance of homosexual men and women in close proximity (Chakravarthi, 2023). Typically, hate speech detection models are evaluated by measuring how well they perform on data set aside for testing. Most of the evaluation, accuracy, and F1 score are used as metrics (Chakravarthi et al., 2021; Santhiya et al., 2022; Priyadharshini et al., 2022). The overview paper (Chakravarthi et al., 2023b), described the overall descriptions of the participants participated and the dataset of the shared task on Homophobia and Transphobia Detection in so-



*LT-EDI 2023 – Third Workshop on Language Technology for Equality, Diversity and Inclusion*, pages 233–238, Varna, Bulgaria, Sep 7, 2023.
https://doi.org/10.26615/978-954-452-084-7_035

cial media comments.

We participated in Task A for Spanish, which focused on the detection of Homophobia and Transphobia in social media comments. The task was organized by LT-EDI@RANLP-2023. With the provided dataset, we developed machine learning models using feature extraction as baselines, as well as the MuRIL transformer model. Among our models, the MuRIL model yielded the best results, achieving a weighted F1 score of 0.86. These scores indicate the effectiveness of our approach in accurately identifying instances of Homophobia and Transphobia in Spanish social media comments. Our participation in this shared task has provided valuable insights into the detection and understanding of discriminatory behavior in online platforms.

## 2 Related Work

Researchers examined the linguistic behaviors of homosexual individuals in China by compiling a corpus of their texts (Espinosa Anke et al., 2019). (Chakravarthi et al., 2022a) created fine-grained taxonomy for homophobia and transphobia for English and Tamil languages. (Chakravarthi et al., 2022b) conducted a shared task to the identification of homophobia, transphobia, and non-anti-LGBT+ content from the given corpus. This task was centered on three subtasks for the Tamil, English, and Tamil-English (code-mixed) languages. It received 10 Tamil systems, 13 English systems, and 11 Tamil-English systems. The average macro F1-score for the top systems for Tamil, English, and Tamil-English was 0.570, 0.877, and 0.610, respectively.

(Chinnaudayar Navaneethakrishnan et al., 2022) conducted sentiment analysis and homophobia detection shared task in code-mixed Dravidian language YouTube comments for Tamil, Malayalam and English. At FIRE 2022 the DravidianCodeMix organized task A for detecting sentiment analysis and task B for detecting homophobia. 95 individuals signed up for the shared task, 13 teams submitted their results for task-A a, and 10 teams submitted their results for task B. Traditional machine learning and deep learning models were used to investigate tasks A and B.

Transphobic and homophobic insults directed at LGBTQI+ persons for the shared task have been identified using transformer-based model methodologies such as BERT and XLMROBERTa models by (Manikandan et al., 2022). BERT offers 91%, while XLM-RoBERTa offers 93%. The content was predicted using the IndicBERT and LaBSE machine learning models. The following were the results: IndicBERT was utilized to train Tamil, Malayalam, and Tamil-English, whereas LaBSE was utilized to predict the English content. The weighted average F1 scores for English, Malayalam, Tamil-English, and Tamil were 0.46, 0.54, 0.39, and 0.28, respectively by (Pranith et al., 2022). (Varsha et al., 2022) participated in both sentiment analysis and homophobia detection tasks. Under the feature extraction techniques of Count Vectorizer and TF-IDF, pre-trained models such as BERT, XLM, and MPNet were used alongside classifiers such as SVM, MLP, and Random Forest. The rankings for sentiment analysis assignment are rank 1 in the Tamil dataset, rank 6 in the Malayalam dataset, and rank 7 in the Kannada dataset. The sentiment analysis task in the Malayalam dataset yielded the highest F1 score of 0.63, while the homophobia detection task yielded 0.95. Various machine learning algorithms are contrasted with the proposed system's performance (Shanmugavadivel et al., 2022; Kumaresan et al., 2022).

We discuss the existing research in the field of text classification, particularly focusing on the specific context of Indian languages. We implemented the MuRIL (Multilingual Representations for Indian Languages)(Khanuja et al., 2021) pre-trained transformer model, which we utilize in our study. MuRIL, available through the Hugging Face model repository, is specifically designed to handle the linguistic complexities and nuances of Indian languages, enabling effective text classification tasks. While previous works have explored various approaches for text classification in Indian languages, our paper distinguishes itself by leveraging the MuRIL model and fine-tuning it on a diverse range of downstream tasks. By highlighting the advantages of MuRIL and showcasing the results of our fine-tuning experiments, we contribute to the growing body of research focused on enhancing the performance of text classification in Indian languages.

## 3 Task and Dataset Description

This research paper discusses our participation in the shared task Homophobia/Transphobia Detection in social media comments[1], which was or-

[1] https://codalab.lisn.upsaclay.fr/competitions/11077

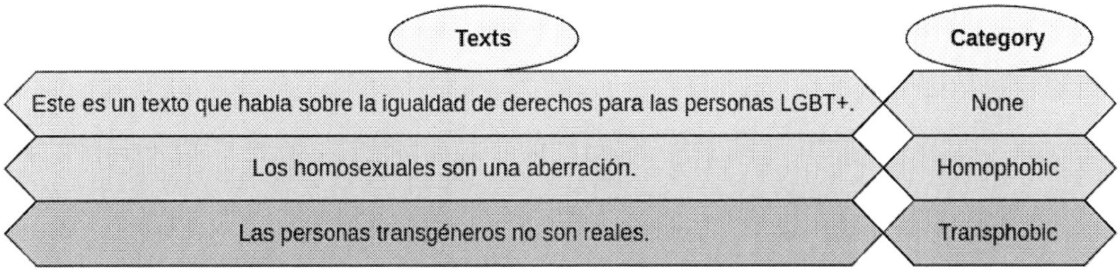


Figure 1: Examples comments from the datasets in Spanish

ganized by LT-EDI@RANLP-2023. The objective of this task was to identify instances of homophobia and transphobia in social media comments across multiple languages, including English, Hindi, Tamil, Spanish, and Malayalam. Our focus was specifically on Task A, which involved detecting these forms of discrimination in Spanish comments using a 3-class classification approach. The dataset provided for this task consisted of 1586 social media comments, each annotated as Homophobic, Transphobic, or None. We divided this dataset into a training set of 850 comments, a development set of 236 comments, and a test set of 500 comments. The class distribution for each set is presented in Table 1. Further details about the dataset can be found in the study by (Chakravarthi et al., 2022a). The shared task consisted of three phases: in the first phase, a training and development set was provided to train our model; in the second phase, only the test set comments were released, and we were required to make predictions using the model trained in the first phase; finally, in the last phase, the test set with labels was released to assess the performance of our model. We will submit our predictions based on the test set comments to the organizers for evaluation.

Table 1: Data statistics for Spanish in Task A

| Category | Train | Test | Dev |
|---|---|---|---|
| None | 450 | 300 | 150 |
| Homophobic | 200 | 100 | 43 |
| Transphobic | 200 | 100 | 43 |
| **Total** | **850** | **500** | **236** |

## 4 Methodology

The methodology section outlines the step-by-step process we employed to identify instances of homophobia and transphobia in code-mixed text in the Spanish language. This involved utilizing feature extraction with machine learning and transformer-based approaches for text classification.

### 4.1 Machine learning

In this task, we employed traditional machine learning models as our baseline, along with CountVectorizer[2] feature extraction. Before proceeding with the models, we executed essential preprocessing steps, which involved removing tags, punctuation, URLs, and other unwanted elements. Additionally, we converted the labels into numerical values using a LabelEncoder[3]. To facilitate effective machine learning, we utilized the CountVectorizer technique to transform the text data into vectorized representations, which would be conducive to the performance of our models. Consequently, we implemented several popular algorithms including Naive Bayes (NB), Support Vector Machines (SVM), Logistic Regression (LR), Decision Trees (DT), and Random Forests (RF), by leveraging the sci-kit-learn library[4]. By combining these steps, we were able to establish a strong foundation for our machine-learning approach using traditional models and CountVectorizer extraction.

### 4.2 Transformers

We utilized the MuRIL (Multilingual Representations for Indian Languages) pre-trained transformer model[5], trained on BERT Large (24L) with 17 Indian languages. Categorical labels were encoded using LabelEncoder from sci-kit-learn. The Hugging Face library trained a transformer model,

[2]https://scikit-learn.org/stable/modules/generated/sklearn.feature_extraction.text.CountVectorizer.html

[3]https://scikit-learn.org/stable/modules/generated/sklearn.preprocessing.LabelEncoder.html

[4]https://scikit-learn.org/stable/index.html

[5]https://huggingface.co/google/muril-large-cased

"google/muril-large-cased"[6]. Tokenizer encoded train and test texts into tensors. A TensorDataset organized encoded data, and a data loader batched the data. The model was trained on a preferred device, optimized using AdamW, and adjusted learning rate with a scheduler. After training, the model was evaluated in the test mode. Predictions were generated using test data, and the highest probability class was chosen. Classification report printed with precision, recall, F1-score, and support. Confusion matrix computed using sci-kit-learn's confusion_matrix function. Visualization was created using Matplotlib and seaborn, representing correctly and incorrectly classified samples. This approach provided insights into the performance of the MuRIL transformer model for the task.

## 5 Results and Discussion

In this section, we evaluated the results of various models used to detect homophobia and transphobia in the Spanish language. The performance of these models was assessed using metrics such as Accuracy (ACC), Macro Precision (MP), Macro Recall (MR), Macro F1 (MF1), Weighted Precision (WP), Weighted Recall (WR), and Weighted F1 (WF1) scores. We experimented with five machine learning models, including NB, SVM, LR, DT, and RF utilizing CountVectorizer feature extraction. The weighted F1 scores obtained for these models were 0.60, 0.78, 0.82, 0.79, and 0.77, respectively.

Next, we explored the performance of a large language model, specifically the MuRIL large cased model, which was originally pre-trained on Indian languages. However, we adapted it for detecting homophobia and transphobia in the Spanish language. Comparing the results in Table 3, it was evident that the pre-trained transformer model outperformed the other models, achieving a weighted F1 score of 0.84 on the test set and 0.82 on the development set shown int he Table 2. This higher score indicates its superior performance in classifying instances of homophobia and transphobia. To gain further insights, we visualized the model's predictions using a confusion matrix, which is shown in Figure 2. This visualization provides a clear representation of how well the best model performed for each class, demonstrating its ability to correctly identify instances of homophobia and transphobia. Overall, based on the evaluation metrics and the clear performance superiority of the pre-trained transformer model, we selected it as the best model for detecting homophobia and transphobia in the Spanish language.

[6]https://huggingface.co/google/muril-large-cased

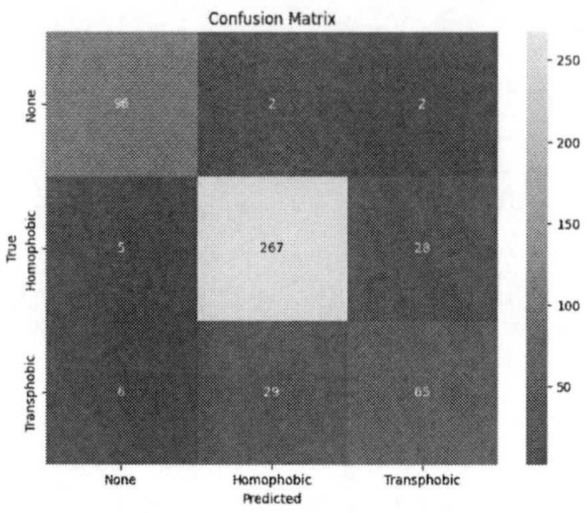


Figure 2: Confusion matrix for MuRIL transformer model

## 6 Conclusion

In this study, we examined the detection of homophobia and transphobia in the Spanish language using machine learning models and a pre-trained transformer model. Among the traditional models with CountVectorizer feature extraction, the MuRIL pre-trained transformer model outperformed them with a weighted F1 score of 0.84 on the test set. The transformer model's superior performance demonstrates its effectiveness in classifying instances of homophobia and transphobia. The confusion matrix visualization further supported the model's ability to correctly identify such instances. Consequently, we conclude that the pre-trained transformer model is a suitable choice for this task, offering the potential for addressing social issues and promoting inclusivity in online spaces. Future research can explore fine-tuning techniques and larger datasets to enhance the model's performance.

## References

Bharathi Raja Chakravarthi. 2022a. Hope speech detection in youtube comments. *Social Network Analysis and Mining*, 12(1):75.

Bharathi Raja Chakravarthi. 2022b. Multilingual hope speech detection in english and dravidian languages. *International Journal of Data Science and Analytics*, 14(4):389–406.

Table 2: Develpment set results for Homophobia and Transphobia in Spanish

| Models | ACC | MP | MR | MF1 | WP | WR | WF1 |
|---|---|---|---|---|---|---|---|
| NB | 0.78 | 0.79 | 0.65 | 0.69 | 0.78 | 0.78 | 0.76 |
| SVM | 0.82 | 0.80 | 0.77 | 0.78 | 0.82 | 0.82 | 0.82 |
| LR | 0.82 | 0.78 | 0.80 | 0.79 | 0.83 | 0.82 | 0.82 |
| DT | 0.81 | 0.76 | 0.79 | 0.78 | 0.83 | 0.81 | 0.82 |
| RF | 0.85 | 0.81 | 0.81 | 0.81 | 0.84 | 0.85 | 0.85 |
| **MuRIL** | **0.86** | **0.81** | **0.84** | **0.82** | **0.86** | **0.86** | **0.86** |

Table 3: Test set results for Homophobia and Transphobia in Spanish

| Models | ACC | MP | MR | MF1 | WP | WR | WF1 |
|---|---|---|---|---|---|---|---|
| NB | 0.74 | 0.77 | 0.60 | 0.62 | 0.75 | 0.74 | 0.70 |
| SVM | 0.82 | 0.80 | 0.77 | 0.78 | 0.82 | 0.82 | 0.81 |
| LR | 0.84 | 0.81 | 0.83 | 0.82 | 0.84 | 0.84 | 0.84 |
| DT | 0.82 | 0.79 | 0.80 | 0.79 | 0.82 | 0.82 | 0.82 |
| RF | 0.82 | 0.81 | 0.76 | 0.77 | 0.82 | 0.82 | 0.81 |
| **MuRIL** | **0.86** | **0.83** | **0.85** | **0.84** | **0.86** | **0.86** | **0.86** |


Bharathi Raja Chakravarthi. 2023. Detection of homophobia and transphobia in YouTube comments. *International Journal of Data Science and Analytics*.

Bharathi Raja Chakravarthi, Adeep Hande, Rahul Ponnusamy, Prasanna Kumar Kumaresan, and Ruba Priyadharshini. 2022a. How can we detect homophobia and transphobia? experiments in a multilingual code-mixed setting for social media governance. *International Journal of Information Management Data Insights*, 2(2):100119.

Bharathi Raja Chakravarthi, Manoj Balaji Jagadeeshan, Vasanth Palanikumar, and Ruba Priyadharshini. 2023a. Offensive language identification in dravidian languages using mpnet and cnn. *International Journal of Information Management Data Insights*, 3(1):100151.

Bharathi Raja Chakravarthi, Rahul Ponnusamy, Malliga Subramanian, Paul Buitelaar, Miguel Ángel García-Cumbreras, Salud María Jiménez-Zafra, José Antonio García-Díaz, Rafael Valencia-García, and Nitesh Jindal. 2023b. Overview of second shared task on homophobia and transphobia detection in english, spanish, hindi, tamil, and malayalam. In *Proceedings of the Third Workshop on Language Technology for Equality, Diversity and Inclusion*, Varna, Bulgaria. Recent Advances in Natural Language Processing.

Bharathi Raja Chakravarthi, Ruba Priyadharshini, Shubanker Banerjee, Manoj Balaji Jagadeeshan, Prasanna Kumar Kumaresan, Rahul Ponnusamy, Sean Benhur, and John Philip McCrae. 2023c. Detecting abusive comments at a fine-grained level in a low-resource language. *Natural Language Processing Journal*, 3:100006.

Bharathi Raja Chakravarthi, Ruba Priyadharshini, Thenmozhi Durairaj, John McCrae, Paul Buitelaar, Prasanna Kumaresan, and Rahul Ponnusamy. 2022b. Overview of the shared task on homophobia and transphobia detection in social media comments. In *Proceedings of the Second Workshop on Language Technology for Equality, Diversity and Inclusion*, pages 369–377, Dublin, Ireland. Association for Computational Linguistics.

Bharathi Raja Chakravarthi, Ruba Priyadharshini, Navya Jose, Anand Kumar M, Thomas Mandl, Prasanna Kumar Kumaresan, Rahul Ponnusamy, Hariharan R L, John P. McCrae, and Elizabeth Sherly. 2021. Findings of the shared task on offensive language identification in Tamil, Malayalam, and Kannada. In *Proceedings of the First Workshop on Speech and Language Technologies for Dravidian Languages*, pages 133–145, Kyiv. Association for Computational Linguistics.

Naganna Chetty and Sreejith Alathur. 2018. Hate speech review in the context of online social networks. *Aggression and violent behavior*, 40:108–118.

Subalalitha Chinnaudayar Navaneethakrishnan, Bharathi Raja Chakravarthi, Kogilavani Shanmugavadivel, Malliga Subramanian, Prasanna Kumar Kumaresan, Bharathi, Lavanya Sambath Kumar, and Rahul Ponnusamy. 2022. Findings of shared task on sentiment analysis and homophobia detection of youtube comments in code-mixed dravidian languages. In *Proceedings of the 14th Annual Meeting of the Forum for Information Retrieval Evaluation*, pages 18–21.

Luis Espinosa Anke, Thierry Declerck, Dagmar Gromann, Ziqi Zhang, Lei Luo, Dagmar Gromann, Luis Espinosa Anke, and Thierry Declerck. 2019. Hate speech detection: A solved problem? the challenging case of long tail on twitter. *Semant. Web*, 10(5):925–945.

Paula Fortuna and Sérgio Nunes. 2018. A survey on automatic detection of hate speech in text. *ACM Comput. Surv.*, 51(4).

Jarod Govers, Philip Feldman, Aaron Dant, and Panos Patros. 2023. Down the rabbit hole: Detecting online extremism, radicalisation, and politicised hate speech. *ACM Computing Surveys*.

Md Saroar Jahan and Mourad Oussalah. 2023. A systematic review of hate speech automatic detection using natural language processing. *Neurocomputing*, page 126232.

Simran Khanuja, Diksha Bansal, Sarvesh Mehtani, Savya Khosla, Atreyee Dey, Balaji Gopalan, Dilip Kumar Margam, Pooja Aggarwal, Rajiv Teja Nagipogu, Shachi Dave, Shruti Gupta, Subhash Chandra Bose Gali, Vish Subramanian, and Partha Talukdar. 2021. Muril: Multilingual representations for indian languages.

Prasanna Kumar Kumaresan, Rahul Ponnusamy, Elizabeth Sherly, Sangeetha Sivanesan, and Bharathi Raja Chakravarthi. 2022. Transformer based hope speech comment classification in code-mixed text. In *International Conference on Speech and Language Technologies for Low-resource Languages*, pages 120–137. Springer.

Deepalakshmi Manikandan, Malliga Subramanian, and Kogilavani Shanmugavadivel. 2022. A system for detecting abusive contents against lgbt community using deep learning based transformer models. In *Working Notes of FIRE 2022-Forum for Information Retrieval Evaluation (Hybrid). CEUR.*

Julie L Nagoshi, Katherine A Adams, Heather K Terrell, Eric D Hill, Stephanie Brzuzy, and Craig T Nagoshi. 2008. Gender differences in correlates of homophobia and transphobia. *Sex roles*, 59:521–531.

P Pranith, V Samhita, D Sarath, and Durairaj Thenmozhi. 2022. Homophobia and transphobia detection of youtube comments in code-mixed dravidian languages using deep learning.

Ruba Priyadharshini, Bharathi Raja Chakravarthi, Subalalitha Cn, Thenmozhi Durairaj, Malliga Subramanian, Kogilavani Shanmugavadivel, Siddhanth U Hegde, and Prasanna Kumaresan. 2022. Overview of abusive comment detection in Tamil-ACL 2022. In *Proceedings of the Second Workshop on Speech and Language Technologies for Dravidian Languages*, pages 292–298, Dublin, Ireland. Association for Computational Linguistics.

S Santhiya, P Jayadharshini, and SV Kogilavani. 2022. Transfer learning based youtube toxic comments identification. In *International Conference on Speech and Language Technologies for Low-resource Languages*, pages 220–230. Springer.

Anna Schmidt and Michael Wiegand. 2017. A survey on hate speech detection using natural language processing. In *Proceedings of the Fifth International Workshop on Natural Language Processing for Social Media*, pages 1–10, Valencia, Spain. Association for Computational Linguistics.

Kogilavani Shanmugavadivel, Sai Haritha Sampath, Pramod Nandhakumar, Prasath Mahalingam, Malliga Subramanian, Prasanna Kumar Kumaresan, and Ruba Priyadharshini. 2022. An analysis of machine learning models for sentiment analysis of tamil code-mixed data. *Computer Speech & Language*, 76:101407.

Malliga Subramanian, Ramya Chinnasamy, Prasanna Kumar Kumaresan, Vasanth Palanikumar, Madhoora Mohan, and Kogilavani Shanmugavadivel. 2022a. Development of multi-lingual models for detecting hope speech texts from social media comments. In *International Conference on Speech and Language Technologies for Low-resource Languages*, pages 209–219. Springer.

Malliga Subramanian, Rahul Ponnusamy, Sean Benhur, Kogilavani Shanmugavadivel, Adhithiya Ganesan, Deepti Ravi, Gowtham Krishnan Shanmugasundaram, Ruba Priyadharshini, and Bharathi Raja Chakravarthi. 2022b. Offensive language detection in tamil youtube comments by adapters and cross-domain knowledge transfer. *Computer Speech & Language*, 76:101404.

Josephine Varsha, B Bharathi, and A Meenakshi. 2022. Sentiment analysis and homophobia detection of youtube comments in code-mixed dravidian languages using machine learning and transformer models. In *Working Notes of FIRE 2022-Forum for Information Retrieval Evaluation (Hybrid). CEUR.*

Zeerak Waseem and Dirk Hovy. 2016. Hateful symbols or hateful people? predictive features for hate speech detection on Twitter. In *Proceedings of the NAACL Student Research Workshop*, pages 88–93, San Diego, California. Association for Computational Linguistics.

# TechSSN4@LT-EDI-RANLP2023: Depression Sign Detection in Social Media Postings using DistilBERT Model

**Krupa Elizabeth Thannickal, Sanmati P, Rajalakshmi S, Angel Deborah S**
Department of Computer Science and Engineering,
Sri Sivasubramaniya Nadar College of Engineering, Chennai - 603110, Tamil Nadu, India
krupa19054@cse.ssn.edu.in, sanmati19098@cse.ssn.edu.in,
rajalakshmis@ssn.edu.in, angeldeborahs@ssn.edu.in

## Abstract

As world population increases, more people are living to the age when depression or Major Depressive Disorder (MDD) commonly occurs. Consequently, the number of those who suffer from such disorders is rising. There is a pressing need for faster and reliable diagnosis methods. This paper proposes a method to analyse text input from social media posts of subjects to determine the severity class of depression. We have used the DistilBERT transformer to process these texts and classify the posts across three severity labels - 'not depression', 'moderate' and 'severe'. The results showed the macro F1-score of 0.437 when the model was trained for 5 epochs with a comparative performance across the labels.The team acquired $6^{th}$ rank while the top team scored macro F1-score as 0.470. We hope that this system will support further research into the early identification of depression in individuals to promote effective medical research and related treatments.

## 1 Introduction

The role of deep learning (DL) is growing in importance when it comes to automating the diagnosis and treatment of diseases, particularly in the field of mental health. Mental health disorders are a major cause of disability globally, as reported by the World Health Organization (WHO).

Depression, or Major Depressive Disorder (MDD), is denoted by symptoms such as low mood, loss of interest in activities, and negative effects on thoughts, behavior, motivation, and emotions, which can even lead to suicide. The causes of depression can be attributed to various factors, including biological, social, and psychological influences. According to WHO's 2022 report (Freeman, 2022), approximately 970 million people worldwide are living with mental disorders, of which 28.9% are depressive disorders.

While there are different treatment options available including psychological therapies like behavioral activation and problem-solving therapy, self-care plays a significant role in addressing depression. Accurate identification of mental health conditions is vital for effective care, especially considering the shortage of psychiatrists in many areas. Depression, as a prevalent mental health disorder, requires early identification and a comprehensive approach combining various treatment options to tackle its significant impact on individuals and society.

The following paper proposes a method to analyse text input from social media posts of subjects to determine the severity class of depression. Our work covers the research question of how the application of a developed typology for social media texts, which aims to detect depression severity, contribute to effectively identifying subtle signs of depressive disorders in tweets. We have used the DistilBERT transformer to process these texts and classify the posts across three severity labels - 'not depression', 'moderate' and 'severe'.

## 2 Related Work

Studies have been carried out to detect the presence or absence of depression in individuals by analysing any one or a combination of text, audio and video inputs.

Islam et al. (2018) present their efforts to analyze depression based on Facebook data obtained from an online public source utilizing machine learning (ML) techniques. Their findings resulted in a substantially enhanced accuracy and reduced classification error rates, demonstrating that Decision Tree (DT) models outperform other simpler ML methods.

(Sadeque et al., 2018) attempt to overcome the shortcomings in accurately assessing model latency during depression detection. They have identified concerns regarding the widely used ERDE metric and put forth an alternative measure called latency-weighted F1, which effectively addresses these is-



*LT-EDI 2023 – Third Workshop on Language Technology for Equality, Diversity and Inclusion*, pages 239–243, Varna, Bulgaria, Sep 7, 2023.
https://doi.org/10.26615/978-954-452-084-7_036

sues. Subsequently, this evaluation approach is used to assess multiple models as part of the eRisk 2017 shared task on depression detection. Their results showed more effective distinctions captured between systems by using this metric.

Another study merges posts of users from two platforms, Twitter and Facebook, in order to detect the level of depression (Asad et al., 2019). This research employs ML techniques to classify data using Support Vector Machine (SVM) and Naïve Bayes algorithms and potentially identify depression.

A survey-based study carried out by Zafar and Chitnis (2020) indicated the increasing interest in data-mining and analysis of information from social networking sites for recognizing depression in users. Yasaswini et al. (2021) use tweets from Twitter to examine users' expressions and gain insights into their emotional states. Their use of the DistilBERT model for a binary classification of depressed or non-depressed subjects resulted in an enhanced accuracy.

With respect to DL models, a comparison study was carried out by Senn et al. (2022). They considered three variants of BERT and four ensemble models of these variants in classifying depression using transcripts of responses to 12 clinical interview questions. Their findings reveal that the utilization of ensembles leads to improved mean F1 scores.

As part of DepSign-LT-EDI@ACL-2022, Janatdoust et al. (2022) present a predictive ensemble model that leverages the fine-tuned contextualized word embeddings from DistilBERT, BERT, RoBERTa and ALBERT base models. Their findings demonstrated a performance surpassing the baseline models across all evaluated metrics, achieving an impressive 61% accuracy and F1 score of 54%.

A predictive model from text has also been developed using Long-Short Term Memory (LSTM) and Recurrent Neural Network (RNN) models (Amanat et al., 2022). The RNN is trained on text-based data to recognize depression using semantics and written content. With a 99.0% accuracy rate, this framework performed better than frequency-based DL models for textual detection, and has a lower false positive rate.

Zavorina and Makarov (2021) use a transformer encoder model for their research on voice-base depression detection. In order to address the limited size of the available dataset, the researchers extracted low-level features from audio recordings and applied augmentation techniques. By leveraging these approaches, their network achieved a recognition accuracy of 73.51% on the E-DAIC database. Anantharaman et al. (2022) uses BERT model for detecting depression from text while Esackimuthu et al. (2022) uses AlBERT model for depression detection.

## 3 Proposed System

Our depression detection system involves data preprocessing, encoding, model building and predicting the unseen test samples. Various experiments were conducted and it was concluded that the DistilBERT model outperformed other models in terms of accuracy, leading to its selection for text processing. The model is implemented using Python's torch library based on the transformer architecture. It takes the encoded input text and utilizes a pretrained "distilbert-base-uncased" model to generate contextualized embeddings for each token. In order to mitigate the risk of overfitting, a dropout layer is included, employing a dropout rate of 0.1. Additionally, a linear classification layer is employed to map the hidden state size of the DistilBERT model to the desired number of output classes. As a result, logits are obtained, representing raw scores that indicate the likelihood of the input belonging to each output class.

Our system comprises of the DistilBERT model trained using the train and dev sets provided, over 5 epochs. The trained model was subsequently evaluated on the test dataset, yielding an accuracy of 47.9%.

## 4 Dataset and Methodologies Used

### 4.1 Dataset Used

The dataset used is provided as part of the DepSign-LT-EDI@RANLP-2023 challenge (Kayalvizhi et al., 2022; Evans-Lacko et al., 2017; Losada et al., 2017). It comprises labelled training and development sets of 7201 and 3245 texts respectively. Testing is carried out over a set of 499 social media posts. The distribution of training and development set data across the three severity labels is seen in Table 1.

Dataset balancing has not been carried out as can be seen in Table 1 where the number of samples for the Severe class is much lesser than those for the Not Depression and Moderate classes. Since

| Classes | Train | Dev | Test |
|---|---|---|---|
| Not Depression | 2755 | 848 | 135 |
| Moderate | 3678 | 2169 | 275 |
| Severe | 768 | 228 | 89 |
| Total samples | 7201 | 3245 | 499 |

Table 1: Class distribution over train, dev and test sets

the dataset focuses on social media texts, this may limit its generalizability to other forms of communication or contexts. It also may not capture the impact of external factors, such as cultural differences, language variations, or contextual elements, which can influence the interpretation of social media texts and the detection of depression.

### 4.2 DistilBERT

DistilBERT is a transformer-based text model used in tasks involving Natural Language Processing (NLP) like translation and text classification (Sanh et al., 2019). Although based on the BERT network, it relies on the idea of knowledge distillation during the pre-training phase itself to reduce the size of the model and make it faster. The DistilBERT architecture comprises several transformer layers that are each fed a sequence of contextualized embeddings generated by encoding the input text. The transformer layers learn to grasp connections among the tokens within the sequence, resulting in the production of more significant representations of the input text.

### 4.3 Implementation Modules

The system comprises of two modules corresponding to the stages of training and testing. The training module is where the DistilBERT model is defined. The model takes the train and development set as input and performs training for 5 epochs. On completion of training, the model is evaluated with the development dataset and the parameters are tweaked. The final model is saved for later use.

The testing module loads the previously trained model and then feeds the test set as input to it. The model is used to classify the test inputs as one of the three depression severity classes.

The results of testing are evaluated against the expected outcomes in terms of accuracy for the whole set and class-wise. The confusion matrix is also plotted in order to better analyse the performance of the model for individual classes and check for scope of improvements.

## 5 Results and Discussion

The performance of DistilBert model trained on depression dataset is evaluated on test dataset to predict the output depression class labels. The overall performance of the system was determined across several metrics including accuracy and weighted and macro averaged values of precision, recall and F1-Score and is tabulated in Table 2. The system achieved the macro F1 score of 0.437 and secured $6^{th}$ rank while the first rank team achieved 0.470 macro F1 score.

| Metric | Value |
|---|---|
| Accuracy | 0.479 |
| Macro Precision | 0.501 |
| Macro Recall | 0.436 |
| Macro F1-Score | 0.437 |
| Weighted Precision | 0.509 |
| Weighted Recall | 0.479 |
| Weighted F1-Score | 0.475 |

Table 2: Performance metrics for test dataset

Accuracy measures the effectiveness of classification models by determining the proportion of accurate predictions out of the total predictions made, represented as a percentage while F1 score gives the blend of precision and recall. The class-wise accuracy and F1-scores of the model are depicted in Table 3. We can infer that the classes 'not depression' and 'moderate' have a better accuracy compared to the 'severe' class. Similarly, these classes have a higher F1-score as well, compared to the 'severe' class label.

| Classes | Accuracy | F1-Score |
|---|---|---|
| Not Depression | 54.81 | 0.54 |
| Moderate | 52.36 | 0.44 |
| Severe | 23.59 | 0.34 |

Table 3: Individual class accuracy for test data

The confusion matrix was also visualized over the results for a better class-wise comparison as seen in Table 4. This matrix also presents the scope of improvement of model performance for individual classes.

| **Labels** | **Not Depression** | **Moderate** | **Severe** |
|---|---|---|---|
| **Not Depression** | 74 | 59 | 2 |
| **Moderate** | 118 | 144 | 13 |
| **Severe** | 12 | 56 | 21 |

Table 4: Confusion matrix for test dataset

It is noticed from Table 3 that the accuracy for severe class is half of the other classes. It is inferred that the reason for this low score is because the total number of samples in severe class is very less for learning when compared to the moderate and non depression classes. Also from the confusion matrix in Table 4, the severe cases are classified as moderate, since most of the severe class sentences more or less give the meaning of moderate depression class. There is a thin line dividing the moderate and severe class.

It is also noticed that 59 non-depression cases are considered as moderate and 2 as severe, which leads to a major problem. These non-depression classes need to be given more importance as we are mainly concentrating on the depression classes alone. We have to investigate more on the methods to differentiate these classes in a fine-grained manner in future.

## 6 Conclusion and Future Work

Our DistilBERT model was trained by combining both the train and dev sets of data, but other approaches could consider these separately and improve the model through a validation phase post training. Another technique that can improve training is running the model for a larger number of epochs, allowing for more iterations and potentially better learning. Prior to training and testing, it is also crucial to ensure the cleanliness of the text data, as incorrect encoding and decoding can lead to the loss of important information.

While this study focuses on detecting depression through social media postings it can be extended for analysis of longer texts that could also be speech transcripts. However, analyzing longer sequences of text poses a challenge as prevalent models in NLP typically have limited input lengths.

While mental health awareness has increased, there is still a stigma associated with depression. The implications for society with the availability of a rapid and reliable depression detection system are immense. Early identification of such conditions can result in enhanced treatment results and a higher standard of living for individuals impacted by them.

## References


Amna Amanat, Muhammad Rizwan, Abdul Rehman Javed, Maha Abdelhaq, Raed Alsaqour, Sharnil Pandya, and Mueen Uddin. 2022. Deep learning for depression detection from textual data. *Electronics*, 11(5):676.

Karun Anantharaman, S Rajalakshmi, S Angel Deborah, M Saritha, and R Sakaya Milton. 2022. Ssn_mlrg1@ lt-edi-acl2022: Multi-class classification using bert models for detecting depression signs from social media text. *LTEDI 2022*.

Nafiz Al Asad, Md. Appel Mahmud Pranto, Sadia Afreen, and Md. Maynul Islam. 2019. Depression detection by analyzing social media posts of user. In *2019 IEEE International Conference on Signal Processing, Information, Communication Systems (SPICSCON)*, pages 13–17.

Sarika Esackimuthu, H Shruthi, Rajalakshmi Sivanaiah, S Angel Deborah, R Sakaya Milton, and TT Mirnalinee. 2022. Ssn_mlrg3@ lt-edi-acl2022-depression detection system from social media text using transformer models. *LTEDI 2022*, page 196.

Sara Evans-Lacko, Sergio Aguilar-Gaxiola, Ali Al-Hamzawi, Jordi Alonso, Corina Benjet, Ronny Bruffaerts, W. Chiu, Silvia Florescu, Giovanni de Girolamo, Oye Gureje, Josep Maria Haro, Y. He, Chenchung Hu, Elie Karam, Norito Kawakami, Sing Lee, Crick Lund, Viviane Kovess, Daphna Levinson, and G. Thornicroft. 2017. Socio-economic variations in the mental health treatment gap for people with anxiety, mood, and substance use disorders: Results from the who world mental health (wmh) surveys. *Psychological Medicine*, 48:1–12.

Melvyn Freeman. 2022. The world mental health report: transforming mental health for all. *World psychiatry: official journal of the World Psychiatric Association (WPA)*, 21(3):391–392.

Md Rafiqul Islam, Muhammad Ashad Kabir, Ashir Ahmed, Abu Raihan M. Kamal, Hua Wang, and Anwaar Ulhaq. 2018. Depression detection from social network data using machine learning techniques. *Health information science and systems*, 6(1).

Morteza Janatdoust, Fatemeh Ehsani-Besheli, and Hossein Zeinali. 2022. KADO@LT-EDI-ACL2022: BERT-based ensembles for detecting signs of depression from social media text. In *Proceedings of the Second Workshop on Language Technology for Equality, Diversity and Inclusion*, pages 265–269, Dublin, Ireland. Association for Computational Linguistics.

S Kayalvizhi, Thenmozhi Durairaj, Bharathi Raja Chakravarthi, and Jerin Mahibha C. 2022. Findings of the shared task on detecting signs of depression from social media. In *Proceedings of the Second Workshop on Language Technology for Equality, Diversity and Inclusion*, pages 331–338. Association for Computational Linguistics.

David E. Losada, Fabio Crestani, and Javier Parapar. 2017. erisk 2017: Clef lab on early risk prediction on the internet: Experimental foundations. In *Experimental IR Meets Multilinguality, Multimodality, and Interaction*, pages 346–360, Cham. Springer International Publishing.

Farig Sadeque, Dongfang Xu, and Steven Bethard. 2018. Measuring the latency of depression detection in social media. page 495–503, New York, NY, USA. Association for Computing Machinery.

Victor Sanh, Lysandre Debut, Julien Chaumond, and Thomas Wolf. 2019. Distilbert, a distilled version of BERT: smaller, faster, cheaper and lighter. *CoRR*, abs/1910.01108.

Saskia Senn, ML Tlachac, Ricardo Flores, and Elke Rundensteiner. 2022. Ensembles of bert for depression classification. In *2022 44th Annual International Conference of the IEEE Engineering in Medicine Biology Society (EMBC)*, pages 4691–4694.

U. Yasaswini, Y. Sasidhar, P. Siva Sai, P. Eswar, and V. Swathi. 2021. Detecting depression in tweets using distilbert. *SSRN Electronic Journal*.

Aqsa Zafar and Sanjay Chitnis. 2020. Survey of depression detection using social networking sites via data mining. In *2020 10th International Conference on Cloud Computing, Data Science Engineering (Confluence)*, pages 88–93.

Evgeniya Zavorina and Ilya Makarov. 2021. Depression detection by person's voice. In *Analysis of Images, Social Networks and Texts: 10th International Conference, AIST 2021, Tbilisi, Georgia, December 16–18, 2021, Revised Selected Papers*, page 250–262.

# The Mavericks@LT-EDI: Detection of Signs of Depression from Social Media Text Quotes using Naive Bayes Approach

Sathvika V S, Vaishnavi S, Angel Deborah S ,Rajalakshmi S, Mirnalinee T T
Department of Computer Science and Engineering,
Sri Sivasubramaniya Nadar College of Engineering, Chennai - 603110, Tamil Nadu, India
sathvika2110166@ssn.edu.in, vaishnavi2110562@ssn.edu.in,
angeldeborahs@ssn.edu.in,rajalakshmis@ssn.edu.in,
mirnalineett@ssn.edu.in

## Abstract

Social media platforms have revolutionized the landscape of communication, providing individuals with an outlet to express their thoughts, emotions, and experiences openly. This paper focuses on the development of a model to determine whether individuals exhibit signs of depression based on their social media texts. With the aim of optimizing performance and accuracy, a Naive Bayes approach was chosen for the detection task.The Naive Bayes algorithm, a probabilistic classifier, was applied to extract features and classify the texts. The model leveraged linguistic patterns, sentiment analysis, and other relevant features to capture indicators of depression within the texts. Preprocessing techniques, including tokenization, stemming, and stop-word removal, were employed to enhance the quality of the input data. The performance of the Naive Bayes model was evaluated using standard metrics such as accuracy, precision, recall, and F1-score.it acheived a macro- avergaed F1 score of 0.263.

## 1 Introduction

Depression, Brown and Harris [1989] a widespread and serious medical illness, poses a significant burden on individuals globally. The timely detection of depression signs plays a crucial role in providing appropriate interventions and improving treatment outcomes. Social media platforms have emerged as a valuable resource for identifying mental health issues, including depression. By analyzing social media text, researchers can gain valuable insights into an individual's emotional state and detect potential signs of depression.

This paper presents our solution for the Shared Task on Detecting Signs of Depression from Social Media Text. Our main objective is to classify the level of depression in English social media posts, categorizing them as 'not depressed,' 'moderately depressed,' or 'severely depressed.' We aim to contribute to the improvement of individuals' lives by effectively detecting and addressing depression through the analysis of social media text.

For this task, we utilize a carefully curated dataset specifically designed for the LT-EDI@RANLP Shared Task. This dataset is composed of social media posts in English, annotated with the corresponding depression levels. We describe the dataset in detail, including its composition, annotation process, and any necessary modifications made for the task. Additionally, we discuss the preprocessing steps employed to ensure the quality and suitability of the data for training our depression detection model.

In conclusion, our solution for the LT-EDI@RANLP Shared Task on Detecting Signs of Depression from Social Media Text demonstrates the potential of utilizing social media platforms to detect and address depression. By leveraging social media text, we aim to facilitate the timely identification of depression and contribute to improved intervention and treatment outcomes. In our study, we employed five distinct models - K-Nearest Neighbors (KNN), Naive Bayes, Random Forest, Decision Tree, and Support Vector Machine (SVM). The evaluation process encompassed various metrics, including accuracy, macro-averaged precision, macro-averaged recall, and macro-averaged F1-score across all classes. Notably, the macro-averaged F1-score emerged as the primary measure for assessing solutions. Among these models, our solution harnessed Naive Bayes, as it yielded a commendable F1-score, solidifying its effectiveness in addressing the problem at hand.

## 2 Related Works

The study by Reece and Danforth [2017] demonstrated the effectiveness of ML algorithms in analyzing Twitter data for depression detection. By



*LT-EDI 2023 – Third Workshop on Language Technology for Equality, Diversity and Inclusion*, pages 244–249, Varna, Bulgaria, Sep 7, 2023.
https://doi.org/10.26615/978-954-452-084-7_037

incorporating lexical, syntactic, and social network features, the model achieved promising results, revealing strong correlations between linguistic patterns and depression.

Tsugawa et al. [2015]conducted a comprehensive study using ML techniques to detect depressive symptoms from social media data. Their classification model integrated linguistic,Varsini et al. [2022] sentiment, and behavioral features, showcasing the potential of ML in accurately identifying individuals with depression.

MacAvaney et al. [2018] focused on detecting depression and PTSD(Post-traumatic stress disorder) from Reddit posts using an ML approach. Their model incorporated linguistic, psycholinguistic, and social contextual features, achieving high accuracy in identifying individuals with depression.

Kim et al. [2020] developed a deep learning-based approach for depression detection from social media text. Their hierarchical attention network effectively captured textual information and demonstrated the power of deep learning in accurately detecting depression symptoms.

Coppersmith et al. [2018] conducted a large-scale study involving various social media platforms for depression detection. Their ML algorithms analyzed linguistic, sentiment, and contextual features, showcasing the scalability of depression detection from social media data.

Research was conducted by a large-scale study utilizing the BERT model on multiple social media platforms to detect depression. The machine learning algorithms analyzed linguistic, sentiment, and contextual features, demonstrating the BERT model's effectiveness and scalability in identifying depression from social media data Anantharaman et al. [2022].similary another variant of BERT ALBERT model was used for detecting the signs of depression Esackimuthu et al. [2022].
A chat bot was created using the Bayesian modeling and it was used to detect single emotion only.Employing multiple kernels may be used to predict several labels with higher performance Angel Deborah et al. [2021].

These notable works collectively emphasize the potential of ML models in detecting signs of depression from social media text. By incorporating diverse features and utilizing advanced techniques such as deep learning, researchers have achieved significant advancements in accurately identifying individuals with depression. These studies contribute to the growing understanding of the role of social media analysis in mental health monitoring and highlight the importance of continued research in this critical field.

## 3 Data Set

The dataset used in the competition for detecting signs of depression from social media text comprises English posts. Each post was annotated with one of three labels: "not depression," "moderate," or "severe" . The "not depression" label indicates posts without any signs of depression, while the other labels indicate varying levels of depression severity.

The dataset was divided into train, dev, and test sets. The test set, used for evaluating solutions, had undisclosed labels. The datset had a large number of duplicate records this was the reason for the lower efficiency.The data was biased containing a large number of moderately depressed samples.

It is worth noting that the dataset is unbalanced, with the "severe" class being underrepresented.

we used a similar dataset as a reference that was created by Kayalvizhi, S and Thenmozhi, D Sampath et al..

In summary, the dataset used for detecting signs of depression from social media text exhibited class imbalance .The sample data is shown in Table 1

## 4 Experimental Results using various models

The data was examined on multiple models after the preparation processes, and the results are reported below.

### 4.1 Experimental Setup

1. Tokenization: The text data is split into individual words or tokens.
2. Vocabulary Building: A vocabulary is created by collecting all unique words from the corpus.
3. Counting: Each document is represented as a vector, where each element represents the frequency of a word from the vocabulary within that dataset.

### 4.2 Navie Bayes Algorithm

For training a model for detecting signs of depression using the Naive Bayes algorithm Peng et al. [2019].we Extracted numerical features using techniques like Bag-of-Words or count vectorization. we Split the dataset into training and testing sets

Table 1: Samples from the dataset

| PID | Text | Label |
|---|---|---|
| train_pid_1550 | New year : New year and it feels like I am already behind. Is this ever going to end? | Not Depressed |
| train_pid_5 | Sat in the dark and cried myself going into the new year. Great start to 2020 : | Moderate |
| train_pid_617 | Feeling numb. : Okay this is my first post, apologies if it's long or anything. I'm just venting about stuff so if it's boring or anything you don't have to read it, that's fine. | Severe |

Table 2: Dataset Description

| Dataset Information | |
|---|---|
| Labels | "not depression", "moderate", "severe" |
| Train set size | 7201 |
| Dev set size | 3245 |
| Test set size | 499 |

and train the Naive Bayes model by estimating probability distributions. we then Evaluated the model's performance using metrics like accuracy, precision, recall, F1 score. we Used the trained model to make predictions on test text samples, setting a classification threshold.The accuracy was about 59.62

### 4.3 KNN

The k-Nearest Neighbors (kNN) algorithm is a non-parametric and instance-based learning method used for classification and regression tasks.It classifies data points based on the majority class among their k nearest neighbors in the feature space.We tried using the k-Nearest Neighbors (kNN) algorithm,Islam et al. [2018] we Determined the value of k, the number of neighbors to consider.we then trained the kNN model by storing feature vectors and labels.we then Evaluated the model using metrics like accuracy and F1 score.The accuracy was about 43.74.

### 4.4 Random Forest

we used random forest to train our model because of its use in robustness and to handle high dimensional data.Narayanrao and Kumari [2020] The Random Forest model is an ensemble learning method that combines multiple decision trees to make predictions.Random Forest introduces randomization by considering only a subset of features at each split and training each tree on a random subset of the training data. The predictions of individual trees are combined through voting or averaging to obtain the final prediction. Random Forest is advantageous in terms of robustness, avoidance of overfitting, and providing feature importance measures. It is trained using labeled data, evaluated using appropriate metrics,and the accuracy obtained was

### 4.5 Decision Tree

Decision Trees are supervised machine learning algorithms that construct tree-like structures to make predictions based on feature values. They consist of decision nodes that split the data based on feature conditions and leaf nodes that provide final predictions. Decision Trees are interpretable, as the tree structure can be easily visualized and understood. They handle missing values and are susceptible to overfitting, we then Evaluated the model using metrics like accuracy and F1 score.The accuracy was about

### 4.6 support vector machine

Support Vector Machines (SVM)is a supervised machine learning algorithm that aims to find an optimal hyperplane to separate classes by maximizing the margin between them.Tadesse et al. [2019] It can handle linearly separable data and nonlinearly separable data using the kernel trick. SVM focuses on support vectors, which are crucial data points near the decision boundary. It introduces a regularization parameter to balance the margin size and misclassifications. SVM can be used for multi-class classification and regression tasks. It is evaluated using metrics like accuracy and mean squared error and the accuracy obtained is

### 4.7 Metrics

The metrics used during the experiments are accuracy, macro-averaged precision, macro-averaged recall and macro-averaged F1-score across all the classes. The macro-averaged F1-score was the main measure when evaluating solutions.

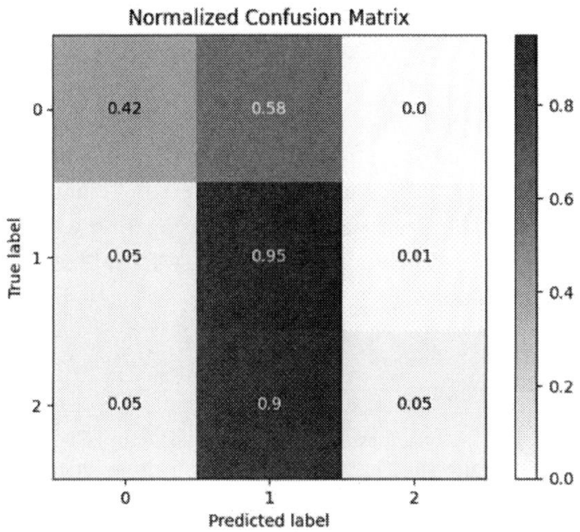


Figure 1: Navie Bayse

### 4.8 Model Evaluation

The results obtained different models are shown in the Table 3.

## 5 Our Solution

When comparing the results of several machine learning algorithms like random forest, support vector machine (SVM), k-nearest neighbors (KNN), decision tree, and naive Bayes algorithms, each has its strengths and weaknesses that make them suitable for different scenarios. Random forest is

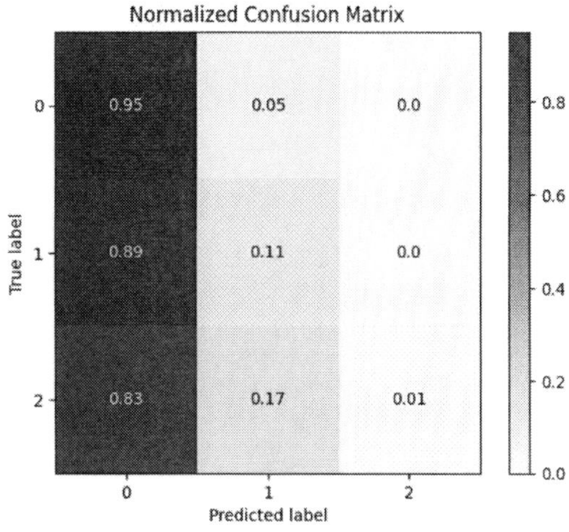


Figure 2: KNN

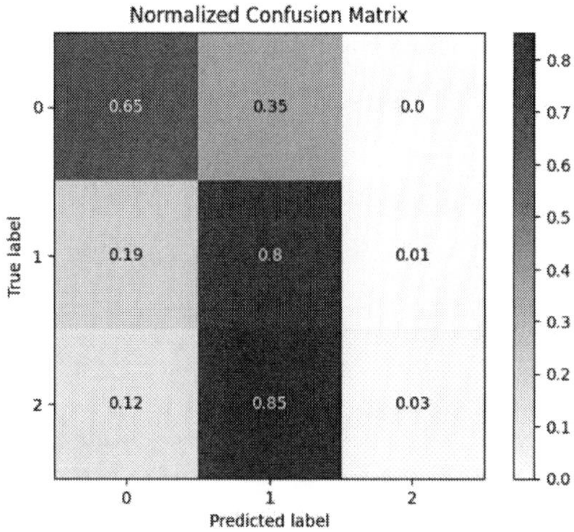


Figure 3: Random Forest

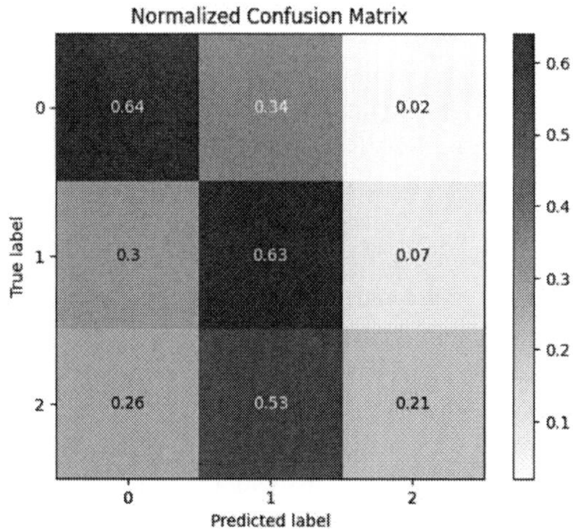


Figure 4: Decission Tree

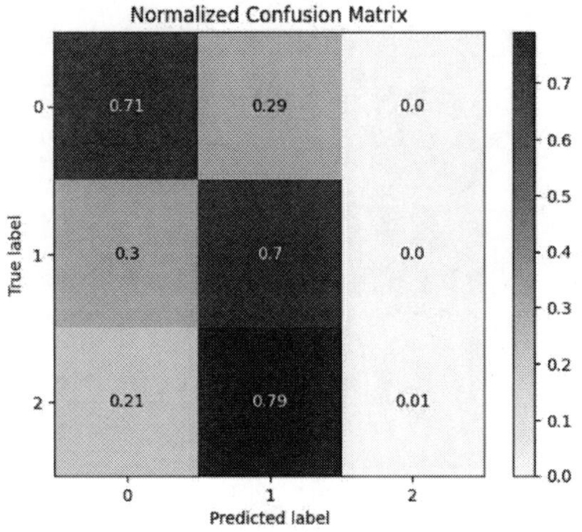


Figure 5: Support Vector Machine

Table 3: Comparison of Metrics

| Model | Precision | Recall | F1 Score | Accuracy |
|---|---|---|---|---|
| Naive Bayes | 0.66 | 0.47 | 0.47 | 65.82 |
| KNN | 0.68 | 0.36 | 0.26 | 43.73 |
| Random Forest | 0.60 | 0.49 | 0.48 | 63.28 |
| Decision Tree | 0.51 | 0.49 | 0.50 | 59.76 |
| SVM | 0.48 | 0.47 | 0.45 | 64.27 |

an ensemble method that effectively handles non-linearity and noisy data, making it useful for large datasets. However, it is less interpretable due to its ensemble nature.

SVM is a powerful algorithm that can handle non-linearity through kernel functions. However, it can be sensitive to noisy data and might not scale well with larger datasets.

KNN is an instance-based algorithm that is relatively interpretable but can struggle with high-dimensional data. It is also sensitive to noisy data and can be influenced by outliers.

Naive Bayes is a probabilistic algorithm that assumes feature independence, making it efficient and scalable for large datasets. It provides interpretable results but may not capture complex non-linear relationships well.

In the context of text processing, naive Bayes is often favored due to its computational efficiency, handling of high-dimensional data, interpretability, and ability to work with limited training data.

However, the choice of algorithm ultimately depends on the specific problem, dataset characteristics, and desired performance metrics. So we implemented all the above mentioned algorithms and we found that naïve bayes is good for this problem. The implementation results are given below

## 6 Future Work

As a future work, the efficiency of the model can be further enhanced by addressing two key aspects: removing duplicates from the given dataset and fine-tuning the model to achieve a balanced representation of the data. Currently, the dataset exhibits an underrepresented distribution, which can impact the model's performance. By implementing duplicate removal techniques and leveraging the robustness of models like RoBERTa, it is possible to optimize the model's efficiency and enhance its overall performance.

## 7 Conclusion

In conclusion, the application of the naive Bayes algorithm in detecting signs of depression from social media text LT-EDI@RANLPhas shown promising results. Naive Bayes offers several advantages in this context, making it a suitable choice for such tasks. The computational efficiency of naive Bayes enables the processing of large volumes of social media text data efficiently. Its ability to handle high-dimensional feature spaces, often encountered in text data, is advantageous when dealing with the diverse and extensive vocabulary found in social media posts.

## References

Karun Anantharaman, S Angel, Rajalakshmi Sivanaiah, Saritha Madhavan, and Sakaya Milton Rajendram. Ssn_mlrg1@ lt-edi-acl2022: Multi-class classification using bert models for detecting depression signs from social media text. In *Proceedings of the Second Workshop on Language Technology for Equality, Diversity and Inclusion*, pages 296–300, 2022.

S Angel Deborah, TT Mirnalinee, and S Milton Rajendram. Emotion analysis on text using multiple kernel gaussian... *Neural Processing Letters*, 53: 1187–1203, 2021.

George W Brown and Tirril O Harris. Depression. *New York: Guilford*, 1989.

Glen Coppersmith, Ryan Leary, Patrick Crutchley, and Alex Fine. Natural language processing of social media as screening for suicide risk. *Biomedical informatics insights*, 10:1178222618792860, 2018.

Sarika Esackimuthu, Shruthi Hariprasad, Rajalakshmi Sivanaiah, S Angel, Sakaya Milton Rajendram, and TT Mirnalinee. Ssn_mlrg3@ lt-edi-acl2022-depression detection system from social media text using transformer models. In *Proceedings of the Second Workshop on Language Technology for Equality, Diversity and Inclusion*, pages 196–199, 2022.

Md Rafiqul Islam, Abu Raihan M Kamal, Naznin Sultana, Robiul Islam, Mohammad Ali Moni, et al. Detecting depression using k-nearest neighbors (knn) classification technique. In *2018 International Conference on Computer, Communication, Chemical, Material and Electronic Engineering (IC4ME2)*, pages 1–4. IEEE, 2018.

Jina Kim, Jieon Lee, Eunil Park, and Jinyoung Han. A deep learning model for detecting mental illness from user content on social media. *Scientific reports*, 10 (1):1–6, 2020.

Sean MacAvaney, Bart Desmet, Arman Cohan, Luca Soldaini, Andrew Yates, Ayah Zirikly, and Nazli Goharian. Rsdd-time: Temporal annotation of self-reported mental health diagnoses. *arXiv preprint arXiv:1806.07916*, 2018.

Purude Vaishali Narayanrao and P Lalitha Surya Kumari. Analysis of machine learning algorithms for predicting depression. In *2020 international conference on computer science, engineering and applications (iccsea)*, pages 1–4. IEEE, 2020.

Zhichao Peng, Qinghua Hu, and Jianwu Dang. Multi-kernel svm based depression recognition using social media data. *International Journal of Machine Learning and Cybernetics*, 10:43–57, 2019.

Andrew G. Reece and Christopher M. Danforth. Instagram photos reveal predictive markers of depression. *EPJ Data Science*, 6(1):15, 2017.

Kayalvizhi Sampath, Thenmozhi Durairaj, Bharathi Raja Chakravarthi, Jerin Mahibha C, Kogilavani Shanmugavadivel, and Pratik Anil booktitle = Rahood. Overview of the second shared task on detecting signs of depression from social media text.

Michael M Tadesse, Hongfei Lin, Bo Xu, and Liang Yang. Detection of depression-related posts in reddit social media forum. *IEEE Access*, 7:44883–44893, 2019.

Sho Tsugawa, Yusuke Kikuchi, Fumio Kishino, Kosuke Nakajima, Yuichi Itoh, and Hiroyuki Ohsaki. Recognizing depression from twitter activity. In *Proceedings of the 33rd annual ACM conference on human factors in computing systems*, pages 3187–3196, 2015.

S Varsini, Kirthanna Rajan, S Angel, Rajalakshmi Sivanaiah, Sakaya Milton Rajendram, and TT Mirnalinee. Varsini_and_kirthanna@ dravidianlangtech-acl2022-emotional analysis in tamil. In *Proceedings of the Second Workshop on Speech and Language Technologies for Dravidian Languages*, pages 165–169, 2022.

# hate-alert@LT-EDI-2023: Hope Speech Detection Using Transformer-Based Models

**Mithun Das**
IIT Kharagpur
mithundas@iitkgp.ac.in

**Shubhankar Barman**
BITS Pilani, India
contact.shubhankarbarman@gmail

**Subhadeep Chatterjee**
Siemens EDA, India
subhadeep.ju@gmail.com

## Abstract

Social media platforms have become integral to our daily lives, facilitating instant sharing of thoughts and ideas. While these platforms often host inspiring, motivational, and positive content, the research community has recognized the significance of such messages by labeling them as "hope speech". In light of this, we delve into the detection of hope speech on social media platforms. Specifically, we explore various transformer-based model setups for the LT-EDI shared task at RANLP 2023. We observe that the performance of the models varies across languages. Overall, the finetuned m-BERT model showcases the best performance among all the models across languages. Our models secured the **first** position in Bulgarian and Hindi languages and achieved the **third** position for the Spanish language in the respective task.

## 1 Introduction

Social media enables people to instantly share their thoughts and connect with billions of other users. However, it has been observed that malicious users sometimes exploit social media to spread harmful speech. Consequently, significant efforts have been made to detect and mitigate hate speech. Nevertheless, social media is not solely characterized by hateful messages (Das et al., 2020). People also express their feelings and the mental stress they experience in their lives, which may arise from online harassment or workplace discrimination. Analyzing people's posting patterns can provide insights into their mental health (Tortoreto et al., 2019; Chakravarthi, 2022).

In contrast, social media posts can also be inspiring, motivational, or offer positive suggestions. For instance, individuals may share stories about overcoming life's stresses, furnishing hope and encouragement to others facing similar challenges. Such posts can particularly benefit individuals feeling down or experiencing mental stress. Recognizing the significance of these positive messages, researchers have started investigating this field, labeling such posts as "hope speech" (Chakravarthi, 2020).

Hope is commonly associated with *offering promises, support, reassurance, suggestions, or inspiration to individuals during periods of illness, stress, loneliness, and depression* (Chakravarthi, 2020). Psychologists, sociologists, and social workers affiliated with the Association of Hope have concluded that hope can serve as a valuable tool in preventing suicide or self-harm (Herrestad and Biong, 2010).

By studying the dynamics of hope speech on social media, researchers aim to understand better its impact and potential in promoting well-being and mental health. This research has the potential to contribute to the development of strategies and interventions that utilize hope speech to support individuals in difficult times, ultimately fostering a more positive and supportive social media environment Chakravarthi (2020, 2022).

Although English is the most commonly used language on social media platforms, people from various linguistic backgrounds participate and share their thoughts in local languages or dialects. As a result, there is a need for a comprehensive understanding across multiple languages. To promote research on hope speech detection, the organizers of the Hope Speech Detection for Equality, Diversity, and Inclusion (LT-EDI - RANLP 2023) (Kumaresan et al., 2023)[1] shared task has introduced the task of detecting hope speech in four languages: Bulgarian, English, Hindi, and Spanish. Since our team, hate-alert, is particularly interested in low-resource languages, we participated in the Bulgarian, Hindi, and Spanish languages.

This paper presents the methodologies we employed to identify hope speech detection, which led

[1] `https://sites.google.com/view/lt-edi-2023/`



*LT-EDI 2023 – Third Workshop on Language Technology for Equality, Diversity and Inclusion*, pages 250–256, Varna, Bulgaria, Sep 7, 2023.
https://doi.org/10.26615/978-954-452-084-7_038

to our team achieving first place for the Bulgarian and Hindi languages and third place for the Spanish language in the overall leaderboard standings of the shared tasks.

## 2 Related Work

This section explores some of the related topics around hope speech detection.

### 2.1 Sentiment Analysis

The task of sentiment analysis is a well-studied topic in the research community (Medhat et al., 2014). Its primary objective is to identify the sentiment or opinion expressed in the text. Sentiments are categorized into positive, negative, or neutral based on the emotions conveyed in a post. Early approaches to sentiment analysis relied on lexicon-based methods (Taboada et al., 2011), where sentiment polarity was assigned to words using predefined sentiment lexicons or dictionaries. With the advancement of deep learning techniques, models like recurrent neural networks (RNNs) (Baktha and Tripathy, 2017), convolutional neural networks (CNNs) (Ouyang et al., 2015), and Long Short-Term Memory (LSTM) (Miedema and Bhulai, 2018) networks are also being utilized for sentiment analysis. These models have shown promising results in capturing sentiment patterns within text. Furthermore, Transformer-based language models such as BERT are gaining popularity in various tasks, including sentiment analysis, due to their effectiveness and performance (Pipalia et al., 2020). Sentiment analysis has also expanded to incorporate other modalities, such as images, audio, and video (Soleymani et al., 2017). This extension has given rise to multimodal sentiment analysis, which combines information from multiple modalities to gain a deeper understanding of sentiment expressed in various media formats. By leveraging multiple modalities, more comprehensive sentiment analysis can be achieved.

### 2.2 Harmful Speech Detection

Harmful language detection, plays a crucial role in natural language processing (NLP) and computational linguistics. Numerous studies have examined the dissemination of hateful content on social media platforms (Das et al., 2021b, 2022c). A significant line of research focuses on detecting harmful speech by developing datasets and machine learning models similar to sentiment analysis (Pramanick et al., 2021; Chandra et al., 2021; Das et al., 2022b, 2023; Das and Mukherjee, 2023). Davidson et al. (2017) conducted a notable study where they publicly released a Twitter dataset containing thousands of labeled tweets categorized as offensive, hate speech, or neither. Earlier attempts to build classifiers for harmful speech detection utilized simple methods such as linguistic features, word n-grams, bag-of-words, and so on. Das et al. (2022a) contributed to the field by developing models specifically designed to detect abusive speech in Indic languages, showcasing the effectiveness of Transformer-based models (Vaswani et al., 2017). The utilization of Transformer-based models has proven to be highly effective in detecting harmful speech(Das et al., 2021a; Banerjee et al., 2021),. Inspired by the exceptional performance of these Transformer-based models, we also employ such models, namely mBERT (Devlin et al., 2019) and XLMR (Conneau et al., 2019), for our research.

### 2.3 Research on Hope Speech

Only a limited amount of work has been conducted so far on hope speech detection. Chakravarthi (2020, 2022) significantly contributed by creating the HopeEDI dataset, which consists of user-generated comments from the social media platform YouTube. The dataset comprises 28,451 comments in English, 20,198 comments in Tamil, and 10,705 comments in Malayalam. The authors also implemented several baseline approaches by utilizing the developed datasets and exploring various traditional machine-learning models. In addition, several shared tasks (Chakravarthi et al., 2021, 2022) have been organized using these datasets to encourage and facilitate research on hope speech detection within the research community.

## 3 Dataset Description

The Language Technology for Equality, Diversity, and Inclusion (LT-EDI-2023) shared task at RANLP 2023 focuses on the detection of hope speech in social media through a classification problem. The main objective of this shared task is to develop methodologies for detecting hope speech in multiple languages. Table 2 presents the class distribution of the dataset, showcasing the proportions of different categories. Although our team did not participate in the English language category, we provide the dataset distribution for all languages for the sake of completeness. For the Bulgarian

| Text | Label | Lang |
|---|---|---|
| Is topic pe aap bimar lagte hai, it's natural mr.khan ,Soch badlo | *HS* | HI |
| सच मे सर आपकी पढ़ाने का तरीका देख के मन करता है हमेशा हम पढ़ते ही रहे | *NHS* | HI |
| Наистина се забавлявах докато го гледах! Евала за това което правиш! | *HS* | BG |
| Estoy de acuerdo. 4 tipos de humores distintos, viva la diversidad #lgtb 🏁 | *HS* | ES |

Table 1: Example of Hope Speech. *HS*: Hope Speech, *NHS*: Not Hope Speech. Lang: Langauges

| | Bulgarian | | English | | Hindi | | Spanish | |
|---|---|---|---|---|---|---|---|---|
| | *HS* | *NHS* | *HS* | *NHS* | *HS* | *NHS* | *HS* | *NHS* |
| **Train** | 223 | 4,448 | 1,562 | 16,630 | 343 | 2,219 | 691 | 621 |
| **Val** | 75 | 514 | 400 | 4,148 | 45 | 275 | 100 | 200 |
| **Test** | 150 | 449 | 21 | 4,784 | 53 | 268 | 300 | 247 |
| **Total** | 448 | 5,411 | 1,983 | 25,562 | 441 | 2,762 | 1,091 | 1,068 |
| | 5,859 | | 27,545 | | 3,203 | | 2,159 | |

Table 2: Dataset statistics. *HS*: Hope Speech, *NHS*: Not Hope Speech

language, the dataset consists of a total of 5,859 data points, with 448 labeled as 'hope speech' and the remaining 5,411 as 'non-hope speech'. In the case of English, a total of 27,545 data points were shared, with 1,983 falling under the 'hope speech' category. There are 3,203 instances for Hindi, out of which 441 are labeled as 'hope speech'. Lastly, the Spanish language dataset includes 2,159 instances, with 1,091 instances categorized as 'hope speech'. One notable observation is that, except for Spanish, the other languages exhibit a significantly lower proportion of hope speech compared to non-hope speech, indicating a high-class imbalance within the datasets. We show some examples of data points in Table 1.

## 4 Methodology

This section discusses the preprocessing steps and various models that we implement for the detection of hope speech.

### 4.1 Problem formulation

We formulate the hope speech detection task in this paper as follows. Given a dataset **D** consisting of pairs (***X***, **Y**), where $\boldsymbol{X} = \{w_1, w_2, ..., w_m\}$, represents a text sample, consisting of a sequence of words and $Y$ represents its corresponding label, the goal is to learn a classifier $F : F(\boldsymbol{X}) \rightarrow \mathbf{Y}$, that can accurately predict the presence or absence of hope speech in unseen text samples, where $\mathbf{Y} \in \{0, 1\}$ is the ground-truth label.

### 4.2 Preprocessing

Before applying the models, we perform several preprocessing steps to prepare the data for hope speech detection. We utilize a combination of custom functions and helpful libraries such as "emoji" and "nltk" for baseline preprocessing tasks. The following pre-processing steps are performed –

- *Replacing Tagged User Names*: We replace all tagged user names with the "@user" token to remove personal identifiers from the text.
- *Removing Non-Alphanumeric Characters*: Non-alphanumeric characters, except for full stops and punctuation marks like "।" and ",", are removed. This step ensures that the machine can identify the sequence of characters accurately.
- *Removing Emojis, Flags, and Emotions*: We also remove emojis, flags, and emotional symbols from the text as they do not contribute to the semantic content of hope speech.
- *Removing URLs*: All URLs are eliminated from the text to exclude any web links that may not be relevant to hope speech detection.
- *Keeping Hashtags*: We retain hashtags in the text as they often contain contextual information that can be valuable for identifying hope speech.

By performing these preprocessing steps, we ensure that the text data is clean and optimized for the classification task.

| | Bulgarian | | | Hindi | | | Spanish | | |
|---|---|---|---|---|---|---|---|---|---|
| **Model** | Acc | MF1 | F1(H) | Acc | MF1 | F1(H) | Acc | MF1 | F1(H) |
| **mBERT FT.** | **0.836** | 0.743 | 0.588 | **0.791** | **0.678** | **0.488** | **0.610** | **0.586** | **0.486** |
| **mBERT+ANN** | 0.799 | **0.747** | **0.631** | 0.785 | 0.629 | 0.389 | 0.515 | 0.458 | 0.281 |
| **XLMR+ANN** | 0.756 | 0.661 | 0.482 | 0.735 | 0.561 | 0.285 | 0.537 | 0.485 | 0.321 |

Table 3: Performance Comparisons of Each Model. FT.: fine-tuned, H: hope speech. MF1: Macro F1 Score. The best performance in each column is marked in **bold** and the second best is underlined

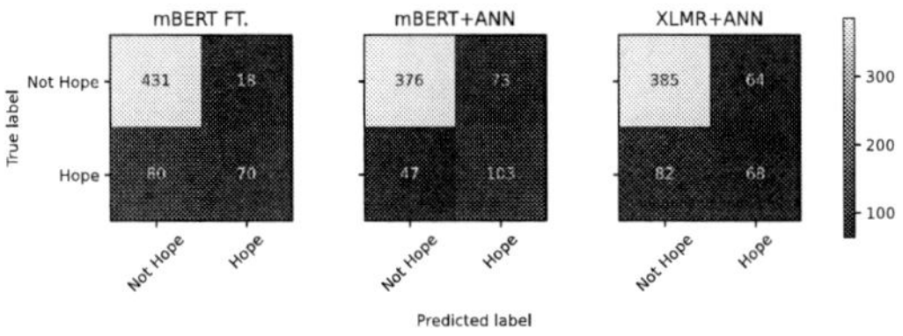


(a) Bulgarian

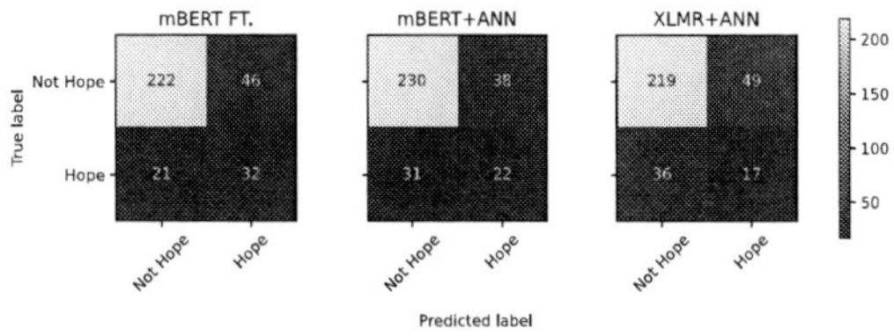


(b) Hindi

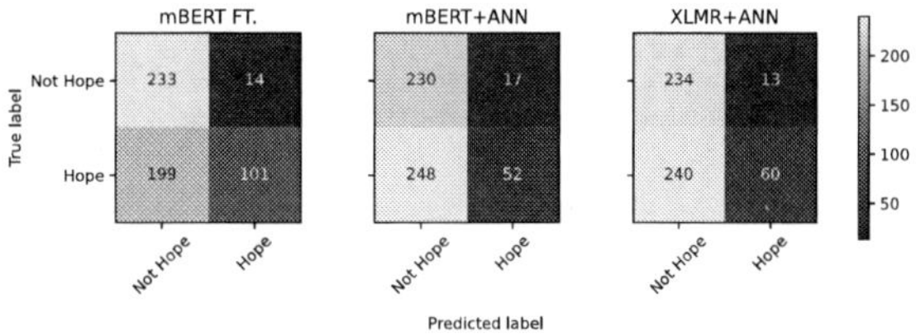


(C) Spanish

Figure 1: Confusion-matrix for all the models across languages

### 4.3 Models

**mBERT** (Devlin et al., 2019) (Multilingual BERT) represents a widely-used multilingual language model developed by Google. It utilizes the BERT (Bidirectional Encoder Representations from Transformers) architecture and has been trained on a vast corpus of text encompassing multiple languages. With its ability to comprehend texts in various languages. In our work, we employ two different approaches with the mBERT model: 1) *finetuning* and 2) *pre-trained embedding + ANN.*

For the *finetuning* process, we augment the mBERT model by adding an additional classification head and then finetune the model for the classification task. This allows us to adapt the mBERT model to capture the nuances of hope speech better. We use the `bert-base-multilingual-uncased` model[2] for our experiment.

In the case of *pre-trained embedding + ANN* setting, we pass the texts through the pre-trained mBERT model and obtain 768-dimensional feature vectors. These vectors serve as representations of the texts' semantic properties. Finally, we feed these feature vectors into an Artificial Neural Network (ANN) model to perform the classification task. This combination of pre-trained embeddings from mBERT and an ANN classifier enables us to leverage both the contextual information from mBERT and the discriminative power of the ANN for hope speech detection.

**XLMR** (Conneau et al., 2020) (Cross-lingual Language Model Representation) is a state-of-the-art multilingual language model developed by Facebook AI. It is built upon the Transformer architecture and trained on a vast amount of multilingual data from different languages. For the case of XLMR, we only explore the *pre-trained embedding + ANN* setting. Here again, we extract the 768-dimensional feature vectors from the `xlm-roberta-base` model[3] and feed these feature vectors into an Artificial Neural Network (ANN) model to perform the classification task.

[2]`https://huggingface.co/bert-base-multilingual-uncased`

[3]`https://huggingface.co/xlm-roberta-base`

### 4.4 Experimenal Setup

We finetune the mBERT model using a maximum token length of 128 and a batch size of 16. The model is trained for five epochs without utilizing early stopping. The ANN model consists of two hidden layers with 256 and 128 nodes respectively, which are then connected to an output layer with two nodes. As in this scenario, we are using pre-trained embedding, we used the maximum token length of 512 to extract features. The ANN models are trained with a batch size of 32. We run the ANN-based models for 20 epochs. For all the models, we employ the Adam optimizer with binary cross-entropy with an initial learning rate of 2e-5 and epsilon set to 1e-8. We train the models for each language separately and saved the model checkpoint for the best validation performance in terms of macro-F1 score.

## 5 Results

Table 3 presents the performance of each model. In the case of the Bulgarian language, we observe that although the fine-tuned mBERT model achieves the highest accuracy (0.836), the mBERT+ANN setting outperforms other models in terms of macro F1 score, achieving the highest score (0.747). For the Hindi language, mBERT demonstrates the best performance across all metrics, while mBERT+ANN achieves the second-best performance. Regarding the Spanish language, fine-tuned mBERT again attains the highest score, whereas the XLMR+ANN model becomes the second-highest scorer. Overall, we observe that fine-tuning the mBERT model end-to-end yields better scores compared to using extracted pre-trained embeddings and passing them through an ANN model. We further show the confusion matrix of each model for all the languages in Figure 1.

## 6 Conclusion

In this shared task, we deal with a novel challenge of detecting hope speech across multiple languages. To evaluate the performance, we employed transformer-based models such as m-BERT and XLMR. Our observations revealed that for the Bulgarian language, the **mBERT+ANN** model configuration achieved the best results. Conversely, for Hindi and Spanish, **fine-tuned mBERT** models exhibited superior performance. In the future, we plan to explore additional transformer-based models, as well as the recent LLM (Large Language Model) models, to enhance our approach in this domain further.

## References


Kiran Baktha and BK Tripathy. 2017. Investigation of recurrent neural networks in the field of sentiment analysis. In *2017 International Conference on Communication and Signal Processing (ICCSP)*, pages 2047–2050. IEEE.

Somnath Banerjee, Maulindu Sarkar, Nancy Agrawal, Punyajoy Saha, and Mithun Das. 2021. Exploring transformer based models to identify hate speech and offensive content in english and indo-aryan languages. *arXiv preprint arXiv:2111.13974*.

Bharathi Raja Chakravarthi. 2020. HopeEDI: A multilingual hope speech detection dataset for equality, diversity, and inclusion. In *Proceedings of the Third Workshop on Computational Modeling of People's Opinions, Personality, and Emotion's in Social Media*, pages 41–53, Barcelona, Spain (Online). Association for Computational Linguistics.

Bharathi Raja Chakravarthi. 2022. Hope speech detection in youtube comments. *Social Network Analysis and Mining*, 12(1):75.

Bharathi Raja Chakravarthi, Vigneshwaran Muralidaran, Ruba Priyadharshini, Subalalitha Cn, John Philip McCrae, Miguel Ángel García, Salud María Jiménez-Zafra, Rafael Valencia-García, Prasanna Kumaresan, Rahul Ponnusamy, et al. 2022. Overview of the shared task on hope speech detection for equality, diversity, and inclusion. In *Proceedings of the Second Workshop on Language Technology for Equality, Diversity and Inclusion*, pages 378–388.

Bharathi Raja Chakravarthi, Ruba Priyadharshini, Navya Jose, Thomas Mandl, Prasanna Kumar Kumaresan, Rahul Ponnusamy, RL Hariharan, John Philip McCrae, Elizabeth Sherly, et al. 2021. Findings of the shared task on offensive language identification in tamil, malayalam, and kannada. In *Proceedings of the first workshop on speech and language technologies for Dravidian languages*, pages 133–145.

Mohit Chandra, Dheeraj Pailla, Himanshu Bhatia, Aadilmehdi Sanchawala, Manish Gupta, Manish Shrivastava, and Ponnurangam Kumaraguru. 2021. "subverting the jewtocracy": Online antisemitism detection using multimodal deep learning. In *13th ACM Web Science Conference 2021*, pages 148–157.

Alexis Conneau, Kartikay Khandelwal, Naman Goyal, Vishrav Chaudhary, Guillaume Wenzek, Francisco Guzmán, Edouard Grave, Myle Ott, Luke Zettlemoyer, and Veselin Stoyanov. 2019. Unsupervised cross-lingual representation learning at scale. *arXiv preprint arXiv:1911.02116*.

Alexis Conneau, Kartikay Khandelwal, Naman Goyal, Vishrav Chaudhary, Guillaume Wenzek, Francisco Guzmán, Édouard Grave, Myle Ott, Luke Zettlemoyer, and Veselin Stoyanov. 2020. Unsupervised cross-lingual representation learning at scale. In *Proceedings of the 58th Annual Meeting of the Association for Computational Linguistics*, pages 8440–8451.

Mithun Das, Somnath Banerjee, and Animesh Mukherjee. 2022a. Data bootstrapping approaches to improve low resource abusive language detection for indic languages. In *Proceedings of the 33rd ACM Conference on Hypertext and Social Media*, pages 32–42.

Mithun Das, Somnath Banerjee, and Punyajoy Saha. 2021a. Abusive and threatening language detection in urdu using boosting based and bert based models: A comparative approach. *arXiv preprint arXiv:2111.14830*.

Mithun Das, Somnath Banerjee, Punyajoy Saha, and Animesh Mukherjee. 2022b. Hate speech and offensive language detection in bengali. In *Proceedings of the 2nd Conference of the Asia-Pacific Chapter of the Association for Computational Linguistics and the 12th International Joint Conference on Natural Language Processing*, pages 286–296.

Mithun Das, Binny Mathew, Punyajoy Saha, Pawan Goyal, and Animesh Mukherjee. 2020. Hate speech in online social media. *ACM SIGWEB Newsletter*, (Autumn):1–8.

Mithun Das and Animesh Mukherjee. 2023. Transfer learning for multilingual abusive meme detection. In *Proceedings of the 15th ACM Web Science Conference 2023*, pages 245–250.

Mithun Das, Rohit Raj, Punyajoy Saha, Binny Mathew, Manish Gupta, and Animesh Mukherjee. 2023. Hatemm: A multi-modal dataset for hate video classification. In *Proceedings of the International AAAI Conference on Web and Social Media*, volume 17, pages 1014–1023.

Mithun Das, Punyajoy Saha, Ritam Dutt, Pawan Goyal, Animesh Mukherjee, and Binny Mathew. 2021b. You too brutus! trapping hateful users in social media: Challenges, solutions & insights. In *Proceedings of the 32nd ACM Conference on Hypertext and Social Media*, pages 79–89.

Mithun Das, Punyajoy Saha, Binny Mathew, and Animesh Mukherjee. 2022c. Hatecheckhin: Evaluating hindi hate speech detection models. In *Proceedings of the Thirteenth Language Resources and Evaluation Conference*, pages 5378–5387.

Thomas Davidson, Dana Warmsley, M. Macy, and Ingmar Weber. 2017. Automated hate speech detection and the problem of offensive language. In *ICWSM*.

J. Devlin, Ming-Wei Chang, Kenton Lee, and Kristina Toutanova. 2019. Bert: Pre-training of deep bidirectional transformers for language understanding. In *NAACL*.

Henning Herrestad and Stian Biong. 2010. Relational hopes: A study of the lived experience of hope in some patients hospitalized for intentional self-harm. *International journal of qualitative studies on health and well-being*, 5(1):4651.

Prasanna Kumar Kumaresan, Bharathi Raja Chakravarthi, Subalalitha Chinnaudayar Navaneethakrishnan, Miguel Ángel García-Cumbreras, Salud María Jiménez-Zafra, José Antonio García-Díaz, Rafael Valencia-García, Momchil Hardalov, Ivan Koychev, Preslav Nakov, Daniel García-Baena, and Kishore Kumar Ponnusamy. 2023. Overview of the third shared task on hope speech detection for equality, diversity, and inclusion. In *Proceedings of the Third Workshop on Speech and Language Technologies for Dravidian Languages*, Varna, Bulgaria. Recent Advances in Natural Language Processing.

Walaa Medhat, Ahmed Hassan, and Hoda Korashy. 2014. Sentiment analysis algorithms and applications: A survey. *Ain Shams engineering journal*, 5(4):1093–1113.

Fenna Miedema and Sandjai Bhulai. 2018. Sentiment analysis with long short-term memory networks. *Vrije Universiteit Amsterdam*, 1:1–17.

Xi Ouyang, Pan Zhou, Cheng Hua Li, and Lijun Liu. 2015. Sentiment analysis using convolutional neural network. In *2015 IEEE international conference on computer and information technology; ubiquitous computing and communications; dependable, autonomic and secure computing; pervasive intelligence and computing*, pages 2359–2364. IEEE.

Keval Pipalia, Rahul Bhadja, and Madhu Shukla. 2020. Comparative analysis of different transformer based architectures used in sentiment analysis. In *2020 9th international conference system modeling and advancement in research trends (SMART)*, pages 411–415. IEEE.

Shraman Pramanick, Shivam Sharma, Dimitar Dimitrov, Md Shad Akhtar, Preslav Nakov, and Tanmoy Chakraborty. 2021. Momenta: A multimodal framework for detecting harmful memes and their targets. In *Findings of the Association for Computational Linguistics: EMNLP 2021*, pages 4439–4455.

Mohammad Soleymani, David Garcia, Brendan Jou, Björn Schuller, Shih-Fu Chang, and Maja Pantic. 2017. A survey of multimodal sentiment analysis. *Image and Vision Computing*, 65:3–14.

Maite Taboada, Julian Brooke, Milan Tofiloski, Kimberly Voll, and Manfred Stede. 2011. Lexicon-based methods for sentiment analysis. *Computational linguistics*, 37(2):267–307.

Giuliano Tortoreto, Evgeny Stepanov, Alessandra Cervone, Mateusz Dubiel, and Giuseppe Riccardi. 2019. Affective behaviour analysis of on-line user interactions: Are on-line support groups more therapeutic than twitter? In *Proceedings of the Fourth Social Media Mining for Health Applications (# SMM4H) Workshop & Shared Task*, pages 79–88.

Ashish Vaswani, Noam M. Shazeer, Niki Parmar, Jakob Uszkoreit, Llion Jones, Aidan N. Gomez, Lukasz Kaiser, and Illia Polosukhin. 2017. Attention is all you need. *ArXiv*, abs/1706.03762.

# TERCET@LT-EDI-RANLP2023: Hope Speech Detection for Equality, Diversity, and Inclusion


**Priyadharshini T**
SSN College of Engineering
priyadharshini2210228@ssn.edu.in

**Samyuktaa Sivakumar**
SSN College of Engineering
samyuktaa2210189@ssn.edu.in

**S Shwetha**
SSN College of Engineering
shwetha2210210@ssn.edu.in

**Durairaj Thenmozhi**
SSN College of Engineering
thenid@ssn.edu.in

**B. Bharathi**
SSN College of Engineering
bharathib@ssn.edu.in

**Gayathri G L**
SSN College of Engineering
gayathri2010090@ssn.edu.in



## Abstract

Hope is a cheerful and optimistic state of mind which has its basis in the expectation of positive outcomes. Hope speech reflects the same as they are positive words that can motivate and encourage a person to do better. Non-hope speech reflects the exact opposite. They are meant to ridicule or put down someone and affect the person negatively. The shared Task on Hope Speech Detection for Equality, Diversity, and Inclusion at LT-EDI - RANLP 2023 was created with data sets in English, Spanish, Bulgarian and Hindi. The purpose of this task is to classify human-generated comments on the platform, YouTube, as Hope speech or non-Hope speech. We employed multiple traditional models such as SVM (support vector machine), Random Forest classifier, Naïve Bayes and Logistic Regression. Support Vector Machine gave the highest macro average F1 score of 0.49 for the training data set and a macro average F1 score of 0.50 for the test data set. We ranked 1st for this task in the English language.


## 1 Introduction

With the world around us developing at an incomprehensible speed and the advent of the 'Digital Age,' the way we communicate has fundamentally evolved. Technology has become a pivotal role in ensuring connectivity among humans in the form of calls, messages and most importantly, social media. Social media is a platform for people to create, share and collaborate their ideas, information and opinions with each other virtually. The number of users only keeps increasing and these platforms show no signs of slowing down. (Drus and Khalid, 2019) Social media is a platform of the masses, for the masses.

While social media is a great tool to enable, entertain and equip people, it has its own drawbacks. Not every user has positive intentions while using popular platforms like Facebook and Twitter. This may lead to presence of unwanted content and comments that can range from discouragement to targeted hate speech. Detrimental speech on such platforms have an extended psychological impact on the victim of such comments (Gongane et al., 2022). To ensure the cleanliness and positive environment of such platforms, it is quintessential to identify such texts and moderate them.

Applying sentiment analysis using data from social media platforms is a great tool to analyse and understand the feelings of the general population (Chauhan et al., 2021). Sentiment analysis is a process where multiple people's opinions, views, feelings and emotions are analysed based on different projects, topics and general discourse. It is also known as opinion mining (Wankhade et al., 2022). Sentiment analysis is an incredibly useful tool to automate the detection of negative comments on social media by analysing the sentiments from the user-generated text. Both supervised and unsupervised learning can be applied to perform sentiment analysis. The only drawback of performing supervised learning is that high-quality training data with proper labels are required for the model to predict accurately. Due to the non-requirement of a labelled training data, unsupervised learning is more robust and can be used more widely to perform sentiment analysis (Neri et al., 2012).

The given task is related to detecting Hope speech and non-Hope speech from user-generated text on the popular video-sharing platform, YouTube. Hope being a positive sentiment, caters to increasing the general positivity of the social me-



*LT-EDI 2023 – Third Workshop on Language Technology for Equality, Diversity and Inclusion*, pages 257–261, Varna, Bulgaria, Sep 7, 2023.
https://doi.org/10.26615/978-954-452-084-7_039

dia platform and thus improving the mood of users alike.(Chakravarthi, 2020) Hope speech therefore contributes the same and helps motivate, encourage and inspire individuals on the platform. Non-hope speech being a negative sentiment has an adverse impact on the social media environment by propagating negative feelings through the users. Detecting and moderating these comments is imperative to create an inclusive and safe space for millions of users to share a part of themselves.(Chakravarthi et al., 2022)

The text in the given text is in the form of code-mixed data. Usually, on social media, most data is not grammatical in nature and has some words and phrases from the native language but in non-native scripts. (Chakravarthi et al., 2020) In our data set, the text is code-mixed in English-Tamil. This can be attributed to the ease of typing in the Roman script on social media while conveying the same intended sentiment. (Patra et al., 2018)Being able to write code-mixed text on social media provides users with a wider choice to express themselves freely and more accurately.

The paper is organized as follows: section 2 pertains to related works as per the literature survey; section 3 is related to the task and data description; section 4 pertains to the methodology used to perform this task; section 5 shows the results and analysis of the results and section 6 entails the conclusion.

## 2 Related Works

Opinion mining or sentiment analysis is a growing field with increasing applications on social media and e-commerce platforms. To cater to the same, extensive research is going on in this field to build the most efficient and robust models which range from Multi-Layer Models (MLMs) to Natural Language Processing(NLP) models. Research conducted by (Vijayakumar et al., 2022) used the transformer model, ALBERT for doing hope speech detection in the English, Tamil, Malayalam and Kannada language.

A new Convolutional Neural Network(CNN) based model was proposed by (Chakravarthi, 2022) that outperformed other traditional models for detecting hope-speech. Both binary hope speech classification as well as multi-class hope speech classification was performed by (Balouchzahi et al., 2022). The binary task involved only two labels whereas the multi-class task involved three labels. Multiple traditional, transformer and deep learning models were applied on the dataset.

A logistic regression classifier was applied by (Palakodety et al., 2019) with a L2 regularization whose results indicated that a hope-speech classifier with good precision and recall can be constructed.

Models based on Long Short Term Memory (LSTM) network, deep learning and hybrid learning on the Tamil and Malayalam language dataset were used by (Saumya and Mishra, 2021). The best performing model on the English dataset was the 2-parallel CNN-LSTM that used GloVe and Word2Vec embeddings. The best performing model on the Malayalam dataset was the 3-parallel Bi-LSTM.

Multiple transformer models for hope speech detection in the English, Tamil and Malayalam languages were applied by (Ghanghor et al., 2021) . The models applied were the multilingual m-BERT-cased, XLM-Roberta(XLMR), and IndicBERT. Among these models, the m-BERT-cased model gave the best F1-score.

Hope detection was done by (Chinnappa, 2021) for three language data sets in Tamil, English and Malayalam. They applied language models that include Compact Language Detector 2, Compact Language Detector 3, langid, textblob language detector, and langdetect. The experimental results from the same showed that detecting hope detection from text is a difficult task especially with code-mixed data.

These papers exhibit the versatility of the models that can be applied to perform sentiment analysis on comments from social media. Based on literature survey, we decided to apply traditional models with the application of a simple transformer model for a more accurate classification of text.

## 3 Task and Data Description

The shared Task on Hope Speech Detection for Equality, Diversity, and Inclusion at LT-EDI - RANLP 2023(Kumaresan et al., 2023) is intended to determine whether the text was Hope speech or non-Hope speech. The data set was available for four languages, English, Hindi, Bulgarian and Spanish, but we submitted the English data set only. The data set consisted of two fields: Text and Labels which were gathered from YouTube comments. The training data set consisted of around 18191 texts out of which 16630 were labelled as non-Hope speech and 1561 were labelled as Hope speech. The development data set for English consisted of 4547 comments out of which 4148 were labelled as non-Hope speech and 399 were labelled as Hope speech. The test data had 4805 texts out of which 4783 were classified as non-Hope speech and 22 were classified as Hope speech.

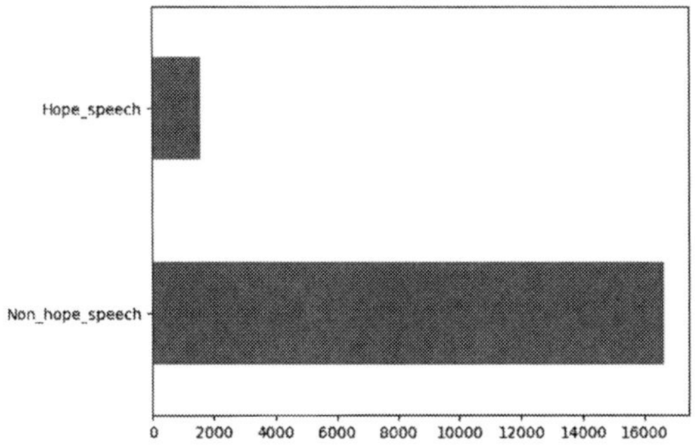


Figure 1: Distribution of data

| Label | Example | Instances in Train | Instances in Dev |
|---|---|---|---|
| Hope-Speech | Totally agree! All Lives matter! | 1561 | 399 |
| non-Hope Speech | Sadly, slaves were hunted by rival tribes in Africa | 16630 | 4148 |

Data Description

Figure 2: Description of Data

# 4 Methodology

Multiple traditional models were employed to identify which texts were hope speech from the YouTube comments given in the data set.

## 4.1 Data Preprocessing and Cleaning

To convert the raw data into readable data for the model, we performed various data cleaning processes.

1)Firstly, all punctuation and emoticons were removed from the text. All the text data was then converted to lower case to create uniformity in the data set. It is important to remove signs and emoticons as the model solely focuses on the words themselves and has no requirement for punctuation and emoticons.

2)It is important to remove stop words as they are redundant words that do not have any significant contributions to the sentiments of the analysed texts. Using the nltk library, we removed the English stop words as well as extended the list to include stop words in Tamil. This was done as the text consisted of words in Tamil(code-mixed) in addition to English.

3)Machine learning models generally take mathematical inputs in the form of numbers or 2D-arrays. Considering that the existing data is in the form of raw text, it is necessary to transform them into a vector. The vectorizer we employed is the Term frequency-inverse document frequency (TF-IDF) vectorizer to transform the given texts into its vector form. Here, term frequency refers to how important a specific term is in a document whereas inverse document frequency refers to the weight of the term. The weight is reduced if the term is scattered all over the document.

## 4.2 Feature Extraction

The Language Agnostic BERT Sentence Embedding model(Feng et al., 2022) is a model released by Google which is based on the BERT model. It focuses on Bi-text mining and sentence embedding tasks. The tokenization algorithm that is used by LaBSE is WordPiece which was developed by Google to pretrain the BERT model. LaBSE's architecture is a dual-encoder model with two encoders that encode source and target sentences independently. The encodings are then passed to a scoring function where it is ranked based on similarity. (Miłkowski et al., 2022) used LaBSE to aid in classification of sentiment polarization. It was proved that language-agnostic representations are quite efficient. The best results were obtained for the LaBSE embeddings and the same was implemented in their online service. We applied the LaBSE model for embedding the preprocessed text. These embeddings were fed to the classifier model for classifying the text based on the labels of emotions associated with them.

## 4.3 Classification model

To classify the text data, we experimented with multiple traditional models that include SVM, Random Forest, Naïve Bayes and Logistic regression as well as the simple transformer model, LaBSE. After evaluating the metrics of multiple models, we focused on combining the LaBSE feature extraction model along with the SVM classifier. Support Vector Machine is a popular supervised learning algorithm used mainly in classification problems. It operates by creating a decision boundary that separates n-dimensional spaces into classes so that a new data point can be assigned to its relevant category.

## 5 Results and Analysis

### 5.1 Performance Metrics:

The sklearn metrics library provides the classification report for evaluation of the performance of the model. It consists of the following metrics:

1) Precision: Precision is defined as the ratio of true positives to sum of true and false positives.

$$Precision = \frac{TP}{TP+FP}$$

2) Recall: Recall is defined as the ratio of true positives to sum of true positives and false negatives.

$$Recall = \frac{TP}{TP+FN}$$

3) F1-Score: The F1 is the weighted harmonic mean of precision and recall. The closer the value of F1 is to 1, better is the performance of the model.

$$F1\text{-}score = 2 * \frac{Precision * Recall}{Precision + Recall}$$

4) Support: Support is the number of actual occurrences of the class in the data set.

### 5.2 Results

The classification report was applied on the development data after training the model using the training data.

It is observed that the overall accuracy on the development data is 0.90 which is higher compared to the 0.68 accuracy of the Naïve Bayes model and 0.68 accuracy of the Logistic Regression model.

Upon testing the accuracy of the data on the unlabelled test data against the labelled test data (released after evaluation), the accuracy score was found to be 0.99105. The rank list released by the organizers of the task ranked our model at 1st position with a macro F1 score of 0.50.

| | precision | recall | f1-score | support |
|---|---|---|---|---|
| 0 | 0.91 | 0.98 | 0.95 | 4152 |
| 1 | 0.08 | 0.02 | 0.03 | 396 |
| accuracy | | | 0.90 | 4548 |
| macro avg | 0.50 | 0.50 | 0.49 | 4548 |
| weighted avg | 0.84 | 0.90 | 0.87 | 4548 |

Figure 3: Classification Report for SVM on Dev Data

| | precision | recall | f1-score | support |
|---|---|---|---|---|
| 0 | 1.00 | 1.00 | 1.00 | 4784 |
| 1 | 0.00 | 0.00 | 0.00 | 21 |
| accuracy | | | 0.99 | 4805 |
| macro avg | 0.50 | 0.50 | 0.50 | 4805 |
| weighted avg | 0.99 | 0.99 | 0.99 | 4805 |

Figure 4: Classification Report for SVM on Test Data

## 6 Conclusion

Through the scope of this paper, we have explored and presented a traditional model coupled with a simple sentence transformer model (LaBSE) to perform classification of Hope-speech and non-Hope speech on the given data by DravidianLangTech in the English language. It was noted that SVM gave the best performance metrics against other traditional models with a macro F1 score of 0.50. It is our belief that the classification can be improved by applying deep learning models on the given data set to obtain a higher accuracy.

## References


Fazlourrahman Balouchzahi, Grigori Sidorov, and Alexander Gelbukh. 2022. Polyhope: Dataset creation for a two-level hope speech detection task from tweets. *arXiv preprint arXiv:2210.14136*.

Bharathi Raja Chakravarthi. 2020. HopeEDI: A multilingual hope speech detection dataset for equality, diversity, and inclusion. In *Proceedings of the Third Workshop on Computational Modeling of People's Opinions, Personality, and Emotion's in Social Media*, pages 41–53, Barcelona, Spain (Online). Association for Computational Linguistics.

Bharathi Raja Chakravarthi. 2022. Hope speech detection in youtube comments. *Social Network Analysis and Mining*, 12(1):75.

Bharathi Raja Chakravarthi, Vigneshwaran Muralidaran, Ruba Priyadharshini, Subalalitha Cn, John McCrae, Miguel Ángel García, Salud María Jiménez-Zafra, Rafael Valencia-García, Prasanna Kumaresan, Rahul Ponnusamy, Daniel García-Baena, and José García-Díaz. 2022. Overview of the shared task on hope speech detection for equality, diversity, and inclusion. In *Proceedings of the Second Workshop on*

*Language Technology for Equality, Diversity and Inclusion*, pages 378–388, Dublin, Ireland. Association for Computational Linguistics.

Bharathi Raja Chakravarthi, Vigneshwaran Muralidaran, Ruba Priyadharshini, and John P McCrae. 2020. Corpus creation for sentiment analysis in code-mixed tamil-english text. *arXiv preprint arXiv:2006.00206*.

Priyavrat Chauhan, Nonita Sharma, and Geeta Sikka. 2021. The emergence of social media data and sentiment analysis in election prediction. *Journal of Ambient Intelligence and Humanized Computing*, 12:2601–2627.

Dhivya Chinnappa. 2021. dhivya-hope-detection@LT-EDI-EACL2021: Multilingual hope speech detection for code-mixed and transliterated texts. In *Proceedings of the First Workshop on Language Technology for Equality, Diversity and Inclusion*, pages 73–78, Kyiv. Association for Computational Linguistics.

Zulfadzli Drus and Haliyana Khalid. 2019. Sentiment analysis in social media and its application: Systematic literature review. *Procedia Computer Science*, 161:707–714.

Fangxiaoyu Feng, Yinfei Yang, Daniel Cer, Naveen Arivazhagan, and Wei Wang. 2022. Language-agnostic bert sentence embedding.

Nikhil Ghanghor, Rahul Ponnusamy, Prasanna Kumar Kumaresan, Ruba Priyadharshini, Sajeetha Thavareesan, and Bharathi Raja Chakravarthi. 2021. Iiitk@ lt-edi-eacl2021: Hope speech detection for equality, diversity, and inclusion in tamil, malayalam and english. In *Proceedings of the First Workshop on Language Technology for Equality, Diversity and Inclusion*, pages 197–203.

Vaishali U Gongane, Mousami V Munot, and Alwin D Anuse. 2022. Detection and moderation of detrimental content on social media platforms: current status and future directions. *Social Network Analysis and Mining*, 12(1):129.

Prasanna Kumar Kumaresan, Bharathi Raja Chakravarthi, Subalalitha Chinnaudayar Navaneethakrishnan, Miguel Ángel García-Cumbreras, Salud María Jiménez-Zafra, José Antonio García-Díaz, Rafael Valencia-García, Momchil Hardalov, Ivan Koychev, Preslav Nakov, Daniel García-Baena, and Kishore Kumar Ponnusamy. 2023. Overview of the third shared task on hope speech detection for equality, diversity, and inclusion. In *Proceedings of the Third Workshop on Speech and Language Technologies for Dravidian Languages*, Varna, Bulgaria. Recent Advances in Natural Language Processing.

Piotr Miłkowski, Marcin Gruza, Przemysław Kazienko, Joanna Szołomicka, Stanisław Woźniak, and Jan Kocoń. 2022. Multi-model analysis of language-agnostic sentiment classification on multiemo data. In *International Conference on Computational Collective Intelligence*, pages 163–175. Springer.

Federico Neri, Carlo Aliprandi, Federico Capeci, and Montserrat Cuadros. 2012. Sentiment analysis on social media. In *2012 IEEE/ACM international conference on advances in social networks analysis and mining*, pages 919–926. IEEE.

Shriphani Palakodety, Ashiqur R KhudaBukhsh, and Jaime G Carbonell. 2019. Hope speech detection: A computational analysis of the voice of peace. *arXiv preprint arXiv:1909.12940*.

Braja Gopal Patra, Dipankar Das, and Amitava Das. 2018. Sentiment analysis of code-mixed indian languages: An overview of sail_code-mixed shared task@ icon-2017. *arXiv preprint arXiv:1803.06745*.

Sunil Saumya and Ankit Kumar Mishra. 2021. Iiit_dwd@ lt-edi-eacl2021: hope speech detection in youtube multilingual comments. In *Proceedings of the First Workshop on Language Technology for Equality, Diversity and Inclusion*, pages 107–113.

Praveenkumar Vijayakumar, S Prathyush, P Aravind, S Angel, Rajalakshmi Sivanaiah, Sakaya Milton Rajendram, and TT Mirnalinee. 2022. Ssn_armm@ lt-edi-acl2022: hope speech detection for equality, diversity, and inclusion using albert model. In *Proceedings of the Second Workshop on Language Technology for Equality, Diversity and Inclusion*, pages 172–176.

Mayur Wankhade, Annavarapu Chandra Sekhara Rao, and Chaitanya Kulkarni. 2022. A survey on sentiment analysis methods, applications, and challenges. *Artificial Intelligence Review*, 55(7):5731–5780.

# Interns@LT-EDI : Detecting Signs of Depression from Social Media Text

**L. Koushik[1], Anand Kumar M[2], Hariharan R L[3]**
Department of Information Technology,
National Institute of Technology Karnataka, Surathkal
koushik.201it131@nitk.edu.in[1],
m_anandkumar@nitk.edu.in[2],
hariharanrl.197it003@nitk.edu.in[3]

## Abstract

In this paper we show our approach to solve the Shared Task on Detecting Signs of Depression from Social Media Text at LT-EDI@RANLP 2023. The given task is to classify the Reddit posts present in the dataset provided, into 3 levels of depression: 'not depression', 'moderate' and 'severe'. We have attempted classifying the posts using two models. We have explored multiple models for this task. Three of which will be included in this paper. The first model uses sentiment labels automatically extracted using TextBlob with TF-IDF for feature extraction and support vector machines (SVMs) for classification. For the second model, we leverage a convolutional neural network architecture for feature extraction and classification. Lastly, the third model incorporates a Bi-LSTM architecture with GloVe embeddings for feature extraction and classification. All the above models also used SMOTE for oversampling the dataset. Through our experimentation, we aim to evaluate the effectiveness of these models in accurately identifying signs of depression in social media text.

## 1 Introduction

Depression is one of the most severe mental-health diseases right now and it is important to detect the signs early on and take actions to stop troubled individuals from taking their own life and provide them with the help they need. Most methods we rely on today are medical procedures in clinics or actual human interaction which is highly ineffective leading to the high rates of suicide and a significant percentage of individuals affected by depression. According to the World Health Organization(WHO) almost 280 million people in the world suffer from depression and on an average about 703,000 people take their lives around the world as on 2022. However with the huge online presence in various social media platforms and individuals giving daily updates through social media posts it would make detecting depression very easy if we had a model that uses the social media texts and classifies it into multiple levels of depression. By using natural language processing, machine learning, and data mining techniques, researchers have made significant strides in automating the detection of depression in social media data. These include traditional machine learning algorithms like SVMs, Random Forest or Naive Bayes algorithms in the past and advanced Deep Learning algorithms in the recent times like Recurrent Neural Networks(RNN), Convolutional Neural Networks(CNN), Long Short-Term Memory (LSTM) and Generative Adversarial Networks (GAN) to name a few (William and Suhartono, 2021). In this paper we present our model for detecting depression for the competition **Shared Task on Detecting Signs of Depression from Social Media Text** at **LT-EDI@RANLP 2023**. This paper has 6 sections. Section 2 contains a short summary of the related works on depression detection using social media text referred to by the authors. Section 3 contains the details of the datasets used and any pre-processing done on them. Section 4 is on the methodology of our model. Section 5 shows the experiments done and the results obtained. Section 6 gives the conclusion of the paper and future work.

## 2 Related Works

Most of the work right now is focused on detecting depression from social media texts. One of the very first papers on depression detection in social media texts was written by De Choudhury et al.(2013), where the authors used a statistical classifier to estimate the level of depression. Chatterjee et al.(2019) used Long Short-Term Memory (LSTM) and Convolutional Neural Networks (CNN). Kim et al.(2020) used Convolutional Neural Networks (CNN) and XGBoost in their model of text classifier in an attempt to use ensemble learning. Amanat et al.(2022) created a hybrid model using Long Short-Term Memory (LSTM) and Re-



*LT-EDI 2023 – Third Workshop on Language Technology for Equality, Diversity and Inclusion*, pages 262–265, Varna, Bulgaria, Sep 7, 2023.
https://doi.org/10.26615/978-954-452-084-7_040

| PID | Text data | Label |
|---|---|---|
| $train\_pid_1$ | My life gets worse every year : That's what it feels like anyway.... | moderate |
| $train\_pid_2$ | Words can't describe how bad I feel right now : I just want to fall asleep forever. | severe |
| $train\_pid_3$ | Is anybody else hoping the Coronavirus shuts everybody down? | not depression |

Table 1: The data files are in Comma Separated Values (csv) format with three columns namely PID, Text data and Label. The above table shows a sample for each of the labels.

current Neural Networks (RNN). (Poświata and Perełkiewicz, 2022) presented the winning solution for Shared Task on Detecting Signs of Depression from Social Media Text at LT-EDI@ACL 2022. In their paper they have prepared a new pre-trained language model, DepRoBERTa. They have presented three models for the competition: RoBERTa-large, DepRoBERTa and ensemble model. They achieved a macro-averaged F1-score of 0.583. For feature extraction many works have made use of the Linguistic Inquiry and Word Count (LIWC) and models based on contextual word embeddings (Tadesse et al., 2019). In recent times more emphasis has been on deep learning and large pre-trained transformer-based language models. Deep learning techniques, such as convolutional neural networks (CNNs) and recurrent neural networks (RNNs), have shown more promise in detecting depression from social media text (Aswathy et al., 2019). These techniques are able to learn complex patterns in language, which can help them to distinguish between genuine expressions of depression and other types of emotional expression. However it is important to note that this depends on the quality and the quantity of the data we have with us. The quality of datasets impact the accuracy of the models a lot which makes the balancing of datasets crucial. Chawla et al.(2002) introduces SMOTE, a method for oversampling the minority class in imbalanced datasets. The paper evaluated SMOTE on a variety of imbalanced datasets and found that it was able to improve the performance of classifiers on these datasets.

## 3 Dataset

The datasets provided for the competition includes Train data, Development data and Test data (Sampath et al.). Train data and Development data contain reddit posts in English language and each post is annotated with one of the labels: 'not depression', 'moderate' and 'severe'. The first label indicates absence of any sign of depression in the post. The second label indicates the presence of some signs of depression and the third one indicates severe depression. The distribution indicates an imbalance among the classes, with the 'moderate' label being the most prevalent, followed by 'not depression', and 'severe' being the least represented category. Class imbalance can pose challenges during model training, as the minority class (in this case, 'severe') may have fewer samples to learn from, potentially resulting in biased predictions. To address this class imbalance we used SMOTE oversampling for Training dataset on the class 'severe'. SMOTE works by creating synthetic minority class examples that are located between existing minority class examples. This is done by randomly selecting a minority class example and then selecting one of its k nearest neighbors. A new synthetic example is then created at a point along the line connecting the two selected examples. To understand the datasets better and prepare the data for analysis, several preprocessing steps were undertaken. Firstly, duplicates were removed from both the Training and Development datasets to ensure the uniqueness of the samples. Additionally, the word '[removed]' was eliminated from the datasets as it indicated that certain posts were removed by Reddit moderators for various reasons, such as containing inappropriate or banned content. We will be using the Development dataset as Test dataset for the sake of the paper to compare the models on the basis of F1-score which won't be possible for test data as the posts are not labelled.

Table 2: Label Distribution in the Dataset

| Labels | Number | Percentage |
|---|---|---|
| Not Depression | 2755 | 38 |
| Moderate | 3678 | 51 |
| Severe | 768 | 11 |

## 4 Methodology

For depression detection from text a few steps are involved. This includes data preprocessing which involves cleaning and preprocessing the collected data, feature extraction which involves identifying the most informative features that are likely to be associated with depression and model development which involves choosing an appropriate algorithm to develop a predictive model. For data preprocessing we are cleaning the data and using SMOTE to balance the dataset.

### 4.1 SVM model with TextBlob(TF-IDF)

In this model we are using a LinearSVM model for classification, TextBlob for sentiment analysis and TfidfVectorizer is used to convert the preprocessed text data into a numerical representation using TF-IDF (Term Frequency-Inverse Document Frequency). The sentiment scores are calculated using the polarity and subjectivity scores of the text. The sentiment scores and the TF-IDF representations are combined by concatenating them together to form a single feature vector for each text data point. This combined feature vector is then used as input to the model. All the models were downloaded from the Python Package Index. The results of the model will be discussed in section 5.

### 4.2 CNN model with TextBlob(TF-IDF)

In this model, we will utilize a convolutional neural network (CNN) for classification. TextBlob will be used for sentiment analysis, and TF-IDF (Term Frequency-Inverse Document Frequency) will be employed to convert the pre-processed text data into a numerical representation. The sentiment scores are calculated using the polarity and subjectivity scores of the text. The sentiment scores and the TF-IDF representations are combined by concatenating them together to form a single feature vector for each text data point. This combined feature vector is then used as input to the model. The Python Package Index will be used to download the necessary models. The results of this model will be discussed in section 5.

### 4.3 Bi-LSTM model with TextBlob and GloVe embeddings

In this model, we utilize a bidirectional long short-term memory (Bi-LSTM) model for classification, TextBlob for sentiment analysis, and GloVe embeddings for word representation. The input text data is tokenized using TextBlob, and GloVe embeddings are employed to convert the tokens into numerical representations. This model uses two input layers: an embedding layer uses the pre-trained GloVe embeddings as initial weights and a Bi-LSTM layer. The Bi-LSTM architecture is capable of capturing contextual information from the text data by processing it in both forward and backward directions. The results of this model will also be discussed in section 5.

### 4.4 Experimentation

In addition to the models mentioned above, we conducted further experimentation to explore different approaches and techniques for detecting signs of depression from social media text. We recognized the importance of considering alternative methods and evaluating their performance to find out the best model for the given dataset.

During our experimentation, we explored the utilization of Word2Vec embeddings in combination with other machine learning algorithms. We observed that the SVM model with TextBlob (TF-IDF) outperformed the other variations. This finding indicates that the combination of SVM, TextBlob sentiment analysis, and TF-IDF representation effectively captures the necessary information from social media text to detect signs of depression.

## 5 Results and Dicussion

Table-3 shows the results of the three models. The SVM model with TextBlob (TF-IDF) was the best in terms of accuracy (0.603) and F1-score (0.479). Following that was the CNN model with TextBlob (TF-IDF) with an accuracy of 0.584 and F1-score of 0.442. Finally the model based on Bi-LSTM model with TextBlob and GloVe embeddings had an accuracy of 0.47 and F1-score of 0.34. The macro F1-score for each of them were 0.48, 0.44 and 0.34 respectively. The main challenge faced in this shared task was the imbalanced dataset. The reason for the better performance of the SVM model could be because of the simplicity of the problem. To compare the models the metrics used during the experiments are accuracy, precision, recall and macro F1-score and weighted F1-score for all the classes. The macro F1-score is the main metric to evaluate the models.

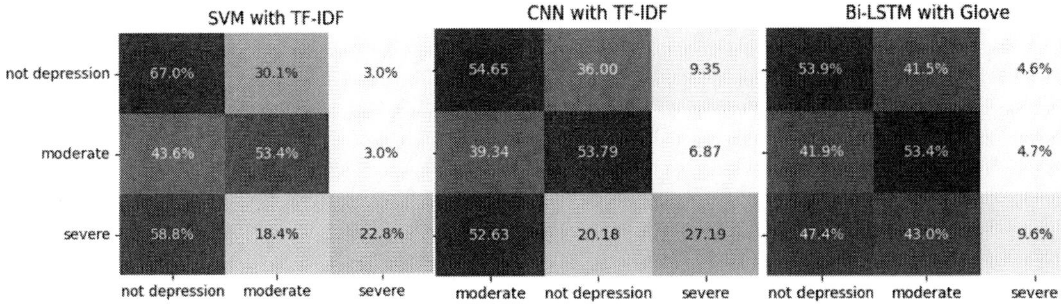


Figure 1: Confusion matrices for the the three models

| Model | Accuracy | F1 score |
|---|---|---|
| SVM model with TextBlob(TF-IDF) | 0.603 | 0.479 |
| CNN model with TextBlob(TF-IDF) | 0.584 | 0.442 |
| Bi-LSTM model with TextBlob and GloVe embeddings | 0.47 | 0.34 |

Table 3: Results of each model on the development set.

## 6 Conclusion and Future Works

In this paper, we presented three solutions to the Shared Task on Detecting Signs of Depression from Social Media Text at LT-EDI@RANLP 2023. The SVM model with TextBlob for feature extraction proved to be the best one among the three and the CNN model with a close second. For future works we plan to implement models better suited for both feature extraction and classification and use a better split training data and testing data. Also the accuracy could be improved by balancing the dataset better by using other methods.

## References

Amna Amanat, Muhammad Rizwan, Abdul Rehman Javed, Maha Abdelhaq, Raed Alsaqour, Sharnil Pandya, and Mueen Uddin. Deep learning for depression detection from textual data. *Electronics*, 11 (5):676, 2022.

KS Aswathy, PC Rafeeque, and Reena Murali. Deep learning approach for the detection of depression in twitter. In *Proceedings of the International Conference on Systems, Energy Environment (ICSEE)*, 2019.

Ankush Chatterjee, Umang Gupta, Manoj Kumar Chinnakotla, Radhakrishnan Srikanth, Michel Galley, and Puneet Agrawal. Understanding emotions in text using deep learning and big data. *Computers in Human Behavior*, 93:309–317, 2019.

Nitesh V Chawla, Kevin W Bowyer, Lawrence O Hall, and W Philip Kegelmeyer. Smote: synthetic minority over-sampling technique. *Journal of artificial intelligence research*, 16:321–357, 2002.

Munmun De Choudhury, Michael Gamon, Scott Counts, and Eric Horvitz. Predicting depression via social media. In *Proceedings of the international AAAI conference on web and social media*, volume 7, pages 128–137, 2013.

Jina Kim, Jieon Lee, Eunil Park, and Jinyoung Han. A deep learning model for detecting mental illness from user content on social media. *Scientific reports*, 10 (1):1–6, 2020.

Rafał Poświata and Michał Perełkiewicz. Opi@ lt-edi-acl2022: Detecting signs of depression from social media text using roberta pre-trained language models. In *Proceedings of the Second Workshop on Language Technology for Equality, Diversity and Inclusion*, pages 276–282, 2022.

Kayalvizhi Sampath, Thenmozhi Durairaj, Bharathi Raja Chakravarthi, and booktitle = "Proceedings of the Second Workshop on Language Technology for Equality, Diversity and Inclusion" month = may year = Mahibha C, Jerin ". Findings of the shared task on Detecting Signs of Depression from Social Media.

Michael M Tadesse, Hongfei Lin, Bo Xu, and Liang Yang. Detection of depression-related posts in reddit social media forum. *IEEE Access*, 7:44883–44893, 2019.

David William and Derwin Suhartono. Text-based depression detection on social media posts: A systematic literature review. *Procedia Computer Science*, 179:582–589, 2021.

# Tercet@LT-EDI: Homophobia/Transphobia Detection in social media comment

**S Shwetha**
SSN College of Engineering
shwetha2210210@ssn.edu.in

**Samyuktaa Sivakumar**
SSN College of Engineering
samyuktaa2210189@ssn.edu.in

**Priyadharshini T**
SSN College of Engineering
priyadharshini2210228@ssn.edu.in

**Durairaj Thenmozhi**
SSN College of Engineering
thenid@ssn.edu.in

**B. Bharathi**
SSN College of Engineering
bharathib@ssn.edu.in

**Krithika S**
SSN College of Engineering
krithika2010039@ssn.edu.in

## Abstract

The advent of social media platforms has revolutionized the way we interact, share, learn, express, and build our views and ideas. One major challenge of social media is hate speech. Homophobia and transphobia encompass a range of negative attitudes and feelings towards people based on their sexual orientation or gender identity. Homophobia refers to the fear, hatred, or prejudice against homosexuality, while transphobia involves discrimination against transgender individuals. Natural Language Processing can be used to identify homophobic and transphobic texts and help make social media a safer place. In this paper, we explore the use of Support Vector Machine, Random Forest Classifier, and Bert Model for homophobia and transphobia detection. The best model was a combination of LaBSE and SVM, achieving a weighted F1 score of 0.95.

## 1 Introduction

The advent of social media platforms has revolutionized the way we interact, share, learn, express, and build our views and ideas. As these platforms have made communication with a large audience incredibly easy and available to everyone, free speech has become a governing concept of the virtual social realm. However, this newfound freedom has also posed its own threats. One major challenge of social media is hate speech. Hateful comments directed at minorities and vulnerable groups pose a significant threat because they can perpetuate existing prejudices and stereotypes, normalize or incite discrimination, and alienate these groups.

Homophobia and transphobia encompass a range of negative attitudes and feelings towards people based on their sexual orientation or gender identity. Homophobia refers to the fear, hatred, or prejudice against homosexuality, while transphobia involves discrimination against transgender individuals.

Research (Huebner et al., 2021) shows that sustained exposure to homophobic attitudes and behaviors can increase a person's stress levels. Studies (Wang et al., 2018) have demonstrated that adolescent victims of cyberbullying are more likely to experience depression and anxiety than adolescent non-victims. Disparities in mental health among LGBTQ youths persist into adulthood and adversely affect their development in social relationships, academic achievements, and self-concepts.

Sexual minorities also often make greater use of the internet as a result of seeking specific socialization environments in which they can meet other people with the same sexual orientation or avoid face-to-face social rejection and homophobic bullying (Gamez et al., 2021). This makes it even more necessary to address the problem of anti-LGBT hate speech.

The task given to us is detection of homophobia and transphobia in social media comments (Chakravarthi et al., 2023). In this paper, we have used the Language-Agnostic Sentence Embedder (LaBSE), along with Support Vector Machine (SVM). LaBSE encodes sentences in a way that captures their semantic meanings across multiple languages, enabling it to capture nuances and context more accurately than models that do not consider cross-lingual semantics. Along with this, SVM is used, known for its ability to handle high-dimensional data and effectively separate different classes. The combination of LaBSE and SVM constitutes an ensemble approach, where the strengths of both components are leveraged. Ensemble methods often result in better performance than individual models.

The paper is organized as follows: In Section 2, related works identified through a literature survey are presented. Section 3 offers an overview of the dataset, while Section 4 elaborates on the methodology employed for the task. The results are discussed in Section 5, and finally, Section 6 presents the concluding remarks.



*LT-EDI 2023 – Third Workshop on Language Technology for Equality, Diversity and Inclusion*, pages 266–271, Varna, Bulgaria, Sep 7, 2023.
https://doi.org/10.26615/978-954-452-084-7_041

## 2 Related Work

Debora Nozza (Nozza et al., 2022) proposed a solution for homophobia and transphobia detection based on data augmentation and ensemble modeling for high class imbalance dataset This task used large language models (BERT, RoBERTa, and HateBERT) and used the weighted majority vote on their prediction. This obtained 0.48 and 0.94 for macro and weighted F1-score, respectively.

Sushil Ugursandi and Anand Kumar M (Ugursandi and Anand Kumar, 2022) analyzed social media texts such as comments from YouTube to detect homophobic sentiments using deep learning or machine learning models. In this work, a 6-layer classification model was used and and an F1-Score of 0.5 on multi-class classification and 0.97 on homophobic/transphobic classification was achieved.

Konstantinos Perifanos and Dionysis Goutsos (Perifanos and Goutsos, 2021) employed transfer learning and fine-tuning of Bidirectional Encoder Representations from Transformers (BERT) and Residual Neural Networks (Resnet) for hate speech classification. They produced a high accuracy score of 0.970 and f1-score of 0.947 in racist and xenophobic speech detection.

Sunil Saumya and Ankit Kumar Mishra (Saumya and Mishra, 2021) analyzed social media texts, including comments from YouTube, to detect homophobic sentiments using deep learning and machine learning models. They employed a 6-layer classification model, achieving an F1-score of 0.5 for multi-class classification and 0.97 for homophobic/transphobic classification.

Shanita Biere (Biere et al., 2018) used a Convolutional Neural Network classifier to assign tweets to the categories : hate, offensive language, and neither. The model gave an accuracy of 0.91, precision of 0.91, recall of 0.90 and a F-measure of 0.90.

In another paper,(Lu et al., 2023) J. Lu and H. Lin utilized Dual Contrastive Learning to address the challenges posed by complex semantic information in hate speech and the imbalanced distribution between hate speech and non-hate speech data. The experimental results outperformed state-of-the-art models.

Orestes Appel (Appel et al., 2016) conducted sentiment analysis using a sentiment lexicon enhanced with the assistance of SentiWordNet, and fuzzy sets to estimate the semantic orientation polarity and its intensity for sentences. The results of the hybrid method was compared with Naïve Bayes and Maximum Entropy techniques. The hybrid method emerged to be the better performer. In addition, it is shown that when applied to datasets containing snippets, this method performs similarly to state of the art techniques.

Bharathi Raja Chakravarthi (Chakravarthi et al., 2022) addresses the challenge of limited resources for studying homophobia and transphobia detection. They propose a solution involving data augmentation through Pseudolabeling. This approach involves transliterating code-mixed text into the parent language, enhancing model performance on a newly generated dataset.

## 3 Dataset

The datasets provided were to us in Task A of Homophobia/Transphobia Detection in social media comments:-LT-EDI-2023 [1]. It consisted of social media comments in English where each comment had a label corresponding to it. The labels given were 'Non-anti LGBT+ content', 'Homophobia' and 'Transphobia'. The data was divided into three parts: training, development and testing, consisting of the columns 'text' and 'category'. The testing dataset was not provided with labels. The task was to predict the labels on our own. The training dataset consisted of 3164 entries with 2978 for Non-anti-LGBT+ content, 179 for Homophobia and 7 for Transphobia. The development dataset consisted of 792 entries with 748 for Non-anti-LGBT+ content, 42 for Homophobia and 2 for Transphobia. The train and dev datasets were used to train the model which was then tested on the test dataset. The test dataset had 991 entries. The development and training datasets given were severely imbalanced.

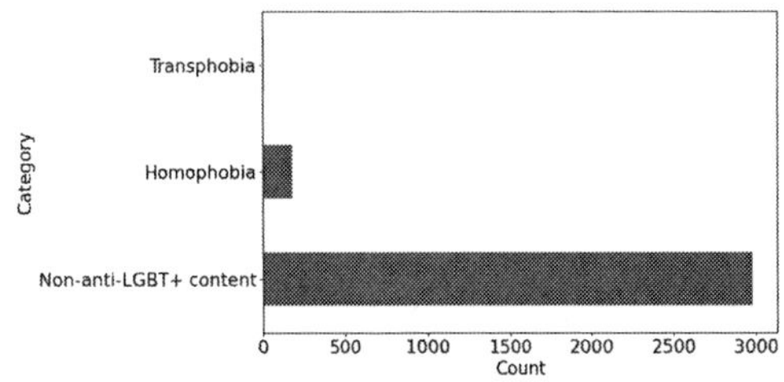


Figure 1: Train Dataset

[1] https://codalab.lisn.upsaclay.fr/competitions/11077

| Label | Example | Instances in Train | Instances in Development |
|---|---|---|---|
| Non anti-LGBT+ content | Archana Shree what | 2978 | 748 |
| Homophobia | Shoot him all Dust bin | 179 | 42 |
| Transphobia | Hey seriously I thought She was a Transgender | 7 | 2 |

Table 1: Dataset Description

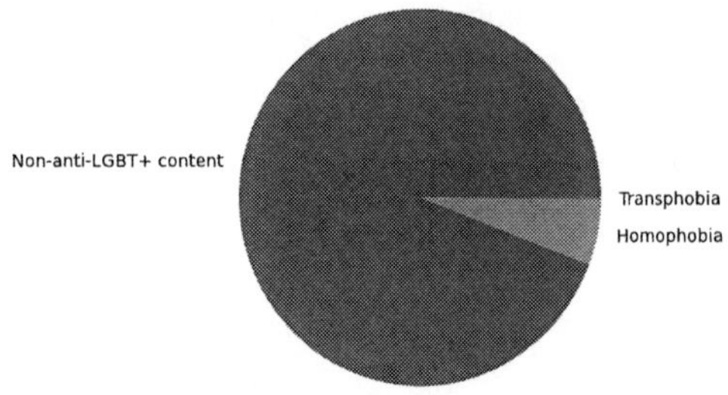


Figure 2: Dev Dataset

## 4 Methodology

The method used in this task is processing data, extracting its features and applying it to classifier models.

### 4.1 Data preprocessing

Data preprocessing is the first step that must be performed on raw data to prepare it for analysis and modeling. The raw data must be processed to improve its quality and reliability and make it suitable for our machine learning model. First the data must be cleansed. Data cleaning is the process of fixing or removing incorrect, corrupted, incorrectly formatted, duplicate, or incomplete data within a dataset. These errors are called as noise and can diminish the performance of our machine learning models. Any data must be cleansed before we begin our work with it. The models used in this task are based on finding common words that occur in the texts corresponding to each label. So the next step is manipulating the data to be suitable for the models. The following procedure was adopted in the task:

1) Checking for null values: First the data is checked for missing values. Most machine or deep learning models require you to clean up the data of null values before it is used. If missing values are present, they are dropped.

2) Removing punctuation and special characters: Since the models used focus on finding common words, punctuations and special characters are meaningless and are considered as noise in the data. A list of punctuations from the string library are used to remove the punctuations and special characters from the text.

3) Converting to lowercase: The text is converted to lowercase to standardize the text data so that different forms of the same words are considered the same( For example, "Eating", "EATING", "eating ). By converting to lowercase, the analysis becomes case sensitive and enables an accurate frequency counts of words.

4)Removing stop words: Stop words are filler words that are insignificant and do not carry any meaning in the context of the task (for example: the, a, are, in). Stop words occur so frequently that they can skew the result of the models. A list of predefined stop words is used to remove the stop words from the text.

### 4.2 Embeddings and Feature Extraction

Word embeddings are representations of words as vectors in vector space such that words with similar meanings are closer together. These embeddings can be used for a wide range of NLP tasks, such as text classification, semantic similarity, clustering, and information retrieval.

Features are the individual measurable properties of the data that are used as input variables for a model. Features provide information or attributes that help the model understand and make predictions or classifications based on the patterns and relationships present in the data. The selection and quality of features play a crucial role in the performance and accuracy of the machine learning model.

Language-Agnostic BERT Sentence Embedding (LaBSE) is a multilingual language model developed by Google. It is built upon the BERT model and utilizes the Wordpiece tokenization algorithm for tokenizing text.

LaBSE follows a dual encoder architecture, meaning it has two separate encoders. These en-

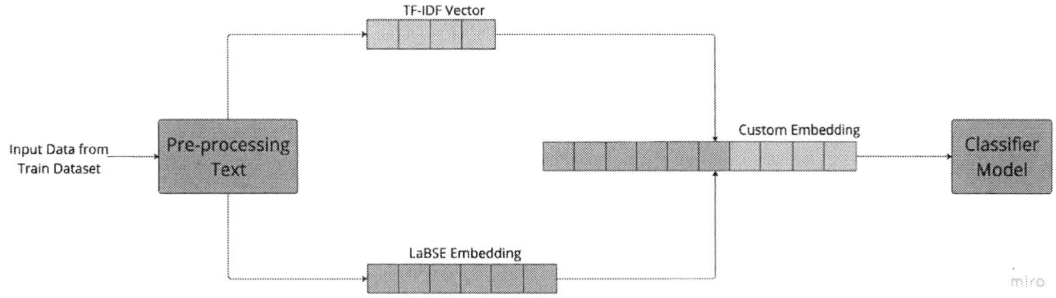


Figure 3: Methodology

coders independently process source and target sentences. The encoded representations of the sentences are then passed through a scoring function that ranks them based on their similarity. This technique enables LaBSE to store similar sentences close to each other in a shared embedding space.

LaBSE learns to capture universal semantic patterns across different languages. This enables the model to generate meaningful sentence embeddings for sentences in multiple languages, even for languages that were not included in the training data.

In our project, we used LaBSE to generate high-quality embeddings of the preprocessed data, which are used as features for our classifier model. The classifier model classifies the given text into its corresponding labels.

### 4.3 Models Used

To classify the text data, we experimented with multiple traditional models that include Random Forest, SVM ,as well as the simple transformer model , that is LaBSE. After evaluating the metrics of multiple models, we focused on combining the LaBSE feature extraction model along with the SVM classifier.

#### 4.3.1 Random Forest

Random forest is a supervised machine learning algorithm used for classification that is based on the concept of ensemble learning. Ensemble learning is the process of combining multiple classifiers to solve a complex problem and improve the performance of the model. RF contains a number of decision trees on various subsets of the dataset. Instead of relying on one decision tree, the random forest takes the prediction from each tree. based on the majority votes of predictions, it predicts the final output.

#### 4.3.2 Support Vector Machine

Support vector machine or SVM is a supervised machine learning model that is popularly used for classification. SVM algorithm finds an optimal hyperplane in an N-dimensional space that can separate the data points in different classes in the feature space, such that the margin between points of different classes is maximized. The accuracy of an SVM classifier model can be increased by increasing the number of dimensions.

## 5 Result and Analysis

After evaluating the metrics of multiple models, we focused on combining the LaBSE feature extraction model along with the SVM classifier as this gave us the best results.

### 5.1 Performance Metrics

Three performance metrics were used for evaluating the task, namely Recall, Precision and F1 score. The macro average and the weighted average of these metrics were also calculated.

Precision: It is the ratio of correctly classified data points to the total number of data points that have been predicted to be of that class. High precision indicates that the model makes fewer false positive predictions.

$$Precision = \frac{TP}{TP + FP} \tag{1}$$

Recall: It is the ratio of correctly predicted positive instances out of all actual positive instances. High recall indicates that the model successfully identifies a larger portion of the actual positive instances.

$$Recall = \frac{TP}{TP + FN} \tag{2}$$

F1 Score: The F1 score is the harmonic mean of precision and recall. It provides a balanced evaluation of the model by considering both precision and recall. It balances precision and recall, making it useful when both measures are important, such as in imbalanced datasets, or when avoiding false positives and false negatives is crucial.

$$F1 - score = \frac{2 \cdot precision \cdot recall}{precision + recall} \quad (3)$$

The models were evaluated on development dataset. Random Forest yielded a weighted F1 score of 0.92. Support Vector Machine yielded a weighted F1 score of 0.93. However, the best results were shown when LaBSE feature extraction was combined with SVM Classifier, yielding an F1 score of 0.95. This could be attributed to the advantage of using ensemble techniques.

| | Precision | Recall | F1-Score | Support |
|---|---|---|---|---|
| 0 | 0.95 | 1.00 | 0.97 | 748 |
| 1 | 0.67 | 0.05 | 0.09 | 42 |
| 2 | 0.00 | 0.00 | 0.00 | 2 |
| Accuracy | | | 0.95 | 792 |
| Macro Avg | 0.54 | 0.35 | 0.35 | 792 |
| Weighted Avg | 0.93 | 0.95 | 0.92 | 792 |

Table 2: RF Classification Report

| | Precision | Recall | F1-Score | Support |
|---|---|---|---|---|
| 0 | 0.95 | 0.99 | 0.97 | 748 |
| 1 | 0.44 | 0.10 | 0.16 | 42 |
| 2 | 0.00 | 0.00 | 0.00 | 2 |
| Accuracy | | | 0.94 | 792 |
| Macro Avg | 0.46 | 0.36 | 0.38 | 792 |
| Weighted Avg | 0.92 | 0.94 | 0.93 | 792 |

Table 3: SVM Classification Report

| | Precision | Recall | F1-Score | Support |
|---|---|---|---|---|
| 0 | 0.96 | 0.98 | 0.97 | 748 |
| 1 | 0.70 | 0.45 | 0.55 | 42 |
| 2 | 0.00 | 0.00 | 0.00 | 2 |
| Accuracy | | | 0.96 | 792 |
| Macro Avg | 0.55 | 0.48 | 0.51 | 792 |
| Weighted Avg | 0.94 | 0.96 | 0.95 | 792 |

Table 4: SVM with LaBSE Classification Report

In the classified test data submitted for Task A of Homophobia/Transphobia Detection in social media comments:-LT-EDI@RANLP-2023 on English Dataset, SVM with LaBSE yielded an F1 score of 0.95.

Our submission was ranked the 5th place in Task A of Homophobia/Transphobia Detection in social media comments:-LT-EDI@RANLP-2023 on English Dataset.

## 6 Conclusion

In this paper, we have presented traditional classification models coupled with LaBSE, a pre-trained language agnostic BERT model, for the classification of Non-Anti LGBT, Homophobia and Transphobia comments on the data given by DravidianLangTech in the English language. The traditional models explored were Random Forest and Support Vector Machine and it was found that SVM yields a higher F1 score of 0.95. We believe that we can improve the accuracy of our results using more sophisticated models such as deep learning architectures (e.g., convolutional neural networks, recurrent neural networks, transformers) and combining predictions from multiple models or model variations through techniques like ensemble learning.

## References


Orestes Appel, Francisco Chiclana, Jenny Carter, and Hamido Fujita. 2016. A hybrid approach to the sentiment analysis problem at the sentence level. *Knowledge-Based Systems*, 108:110–124.

Shanita Biere, Sandjai Bhulai, and Master Business Analytics. 2018. Hate speech detection using natural language processing techniques. *Master Business AnalyticsDepartment of Mathematics Faculty of Science*.

Bharathi Raja Chakravarthi, Adeep Hande, Rahul Ponnusamy, Prasanna Kumar Kumaresan, and Ruba Priyadharshini. 2022. How can we detect homophobia and transphobia? experiments in a multilingual code-mixed setting for social media governance. *International Journal of Information Management Data Insights*, 2(2):100119.

Bharathi Raja Chakravarthi, Rahul Ponnusamy, Malliga Subramanian, Paul Buitelaar, Miguel Ángel García-Cumbreras, Salud María Jiménez-Zafra, José Antonio García-Díaz, Rafael Valencia-García, and Nitesh Jindal. 2023. Overview of second shared task on homophobia and transphobia detection in english, spanish, hindi, tamil, and malayalam. In *Proceedings of the Third Workshop on Language Technology for Equality, Diversity and Inclusion*, Varna, Bulgaria. Recent Advances in Natural Language Processing.

Junyu Lu, Hongfei Lin, Xiaokun Zhang, Zhaoqing Li, Tongyue Zhang, Linlin Zong, Fenglong Ma, and

Bo Xu. 2023. Hate speech detection via dual contrastive learning. *IEEE/ACM Transactions on Audio, Speech, and Language Processing*, 31:2787–2795.

Debora Nozza et al. 2022. Nozza@ lt-edi-acl2022: Ensemble modeling for homophobia and transphobia detection. In *Proceedings of the Second Workshop on Language Technology for Equality, Diversity and Inclusion*. Association for Computational Linguistics.

Konstantinos Perifanos and Dionysis Goutsos. 2021. Multimodal hate speech detection in greek social media. *Multimodal Technologies and Interaction*, 5(7):34.

Sunil Saumya and Ankit Kumar Mishra. 2021. Iiit_dwd@ lt-edi-eacl2021: hope speech detection in youtube multilingual comments. In *Proceedings of the First Workshop on Language Technology for Equality, Diversity and Inclusion*, pages 107–113.

Sushil Ugursandi and M Anand Kumar. 2022. Sentiment analysis and homophobia detection of youtube comments. In *Working Notes of FIRE 2022-Forum for Information Retrieval Evaluation (Hybrid). CEUR.*

# DeepLearningBrasil@LT-EDI-2023: Exploring Deep Learning Techniques for Detecting Depression in Social Media Text

**Eduardo Garcia[1], Juliana Gomes[1], Adalberto Barbosa Junior[2], Cardeque Borges[1], Nádia da Silva[3]**
Institute of Informatics
Federal University of Goiás, Brazil
[1]{edusantosgarcia, julianarsg13, cardequeh}@gmail.com,
[2]{adalbertojunior}@discente.ufg.br, [3]{nadia}@inf.ufg.br

## Abstract

In this paper, we delineate the strategy employed by our team, DeepLearningBrasil, which secured us the first place in the shared task DepSign-LT-EDI@RANLP-2023, achieving a 47.0% Macro F1-Score and a notable 2.4% advantage. The task was to classify social media texts into three distinct levels of depression - "not depressed," "moderately depressed," and "severely depressed." Leveraging the power of the RoBERTa and DeBERTa models, we further pre-trained them on a collected Reddit dataset, specifically curated from mental health-related Reddit's communities (Subreddits), leading to an enhanced understanding of nuanced mental health discourse. To address lengthy textual data, we used truncation techniques that retained the essence of the content by focusing on its beginnings and endings. Our model was robust against unbalanced data by incorporating sample weights into the loss. Cross-validation and ensemble techniques were then employed to combine our k-fold trained models, delivering an optimal solution. The accompanying code is made available for transparency and further development.

## 1 Introduction

Depression, a prevalent mental disorder, profoundly affects individuals' mood and emotions, impacting approximately 300 million people worldwide, representing 4.4% of the global population (Organization et al., 2017). Early detection of depression plays a vital role in preventing serious consequences and providing timely support. With the rise of social media platforms, people often express their thoughts and experiences, making these platforms potential sources for detecting mental health issues.

In light of this, the DepSign-LT-EDI@RANLP-2023 shared task (Sampath et al., 2023) was organized to identify signs of depression by analyzing social media posts. Building on the success of the previous task in 2022 (S et al., 2022), where Transformer-based models were used to detect different levels of depression, this paper presents the winning approach developed by DeepLearningBrasil for the DepSign-LT-EDI@RANLP-2023 shared task.

Our solution combines state-of-the-art transformer models, namely RoBERTa and DeBERTa v3 (Liu et al., 2019; He et al., 2023), trained on a comprehensive Reddit dataset collected from mental health-related Subreddits. To address the challenge of lengthy texts, we employed truncation techniques that capture the essential information by focusing on the beginnings and endings of the posts. Additionally, we address the issue of imbalanced data distribution by incorporating sample weights into the loss function. Through cross-validation and ensemble techniques, we combined multiple models trained on different folds, resulting in an optimized solution. For transparency and further development, the code for our solution is available on our GitHub repository [1].

The remaining sections of this paper are organized as follows: Section 2 provides an overview of previous research on detecting depression through social media analysis and on employed techniques; Section 3 details the task, including its dataset composition and distribution among the different classes; Section 4 explains the methodology and techniques employed in our approach; Section 5 presents the results of our experiments; Section 6 shows the results of our final submission, comparing between different approaches. In Section 7, we discuss the results obtained from comparing RoBERTa and DeBERTa models, as well as the effectiveness of ensemble methods and ordinal classification losses.

[1] https://github.com/eduagarcia/depsign-2023-ranlp



*LT-EDI 2023 – Third Workshop on Language Technology for Equality, Diversity and Inclusion*, pages 272–278, Varna, Bulgaria, Sep 7, 2023.
https://doi.org/10.26615/978-954-452-084-7_042

## 2 Related Work

Zhang et al., 2022 conducted reviews on mental illness detection, they concluded that depression is the topic most researched between 2012 and 2020. According to the study, Twitter and Reddit have been increasingly used as a data source, comprising up to 55% of the distribution.

DepSign-LT-EDI@RANLP-2023 shared task, and the previous edition followed this trend, whose aim is to detect different levels of depression using Reddit posts (S et al., 2022). The DepSign competitions were created based on the eRisk - early detection of depression tasks hosted in 2017 and 2018 (Sampath and Durairaj, 2022). Given depressed and non-depressed users, the dataset was composed of a collection of posts for each user (in chronological order); the objective was to detect risk signals as soon as possible (Parapar et al., 2022).

In text classification benchmarks, Transformer models are the current state-of-art, such as BERT, RoBERTa, and DeBERTa v3 (Devlin et al., 2018; Liu et al., 2019; He et al., 2023). Transformer models leverage contextual linguistic knowledge from massive corpora training in a masked-language task. This initial step called pre-training. Then, the pre-trained architecture can be finetuned for a specific task, transferring the initial knowledge acquired in the pre-training step.

The winner's of DepSign-LT-EDI@ACL-2022 shared task employed various classification techniques, mostly around Language Models with the Transformer architecture. Poświata and Perełkiewicz, 2022 achieved first place by using techniques such as further pretraining a RoBERTa model on depression corpora and used ensemble techniques by taking the average of the probabilities outputs of multiple models. Wang et al., 2022 achieved second place by employing a weighted ensemble of gradient boosting model, LightGBM and XGBoost, and fine-tuned RoBERTa, ELECTRA, and DeBERTa v3 models. Singh and Motlicek, 2022 employed voting ensembles from XLNET, BERT, and RoBERTa.

Another strategy used to deal with unbalanced data used by Haque et al., 2021, which aims to detect child depression from the cross-sectional survey, was to use sample class weight on the classification loss.

For dealing with long texts, previous work by Sun et al., 2019 explored truncation methods on BERT models for classifying long articles from IMDb and Chinese Sogou News datasets. They hypothesized that the key information in an article is typically found at the beginning and end. We explore this technique as explained in 5.3.

## 3 Task

DepSign-LT-EDI@RANLP-2023 shared task was organized to identify signs of depression by analyzing posts on social networks. Task follows the previous edition (DepSign-LT-EDI@ACL-2022). Given a posting in English on social media, the task is to detect the signs of depression in that posting, classifying it into three levels of depression: 'Not Depressed', 'Moderately Depressed', and 'Severely Depressed'. The main evaluation metric is macro-F1 (S et al., 2022).

Data was gathered from Reddit post archives from Subreddits where the people discuss mental health, such as r/Mental Health and r/depression. After the post collection, the data was cleaned, removing non-ASCII characters and emoticons and annotated from two domain experts following guidelines (Sampath and Durairaj, 2022; S et al., 2022).

Annotators were oriented to label "Not depressed", examples that reflect momentary feelings, ask for medications or ask for help for other people's conditions. Secondly, examples labelled as "Moderate" reflect change in feelings or shows hope for life or do not indicate the feeling completely immersed in any situations. Thirdly, examples considered as "Severe depression" were the ones containing more than one disorder conditions or explained about history of suicide attempts (Sampath and Durairaj, 2022).

From the annotation guidelines and the training data examples, they notice that simply expressing as sad does not indicate depression. Therefore, the task domain is challenging, since depression is a clinical condition that is not as easy to detect as negative feelings such as sadness, which could easily contribute to false positive examples. The task data also contains internet slang, whereas traditional models are not trained on these terms. We pretrain the models as mentioned in Section 5.2 in other to leverage these domain problems.

The task data are composed of all the examples from 2022 tasks plus newly annotated samples, summing up to 10,446 examples in training and development sets. Following the 2022 task, the label distribution is unbalanced, the most representative class being 'moderate', followed by 'not depression' and the least representative, severe. The imbalance is similar in the training and development splits, as shown in Table 1. To treat data unbalance, as detailed in Section 5.1, we apply loss sample weights.

| Label | Train | Dev |
|---|---|---|
| Not depression | 2755 (38.3%) | 848 (26.1%) |
| Moderately | 3678 (51.1%) | 2169 (66.8%) |
| Severe | 768 (10.7%) | 228 (7.03%) |

Table 1: Number of examples and percentages per label in training and development splits in DepSign-LT-EDI@RANLP-2023.

The task data also contains 210 duplicated examples, representing 2.0% of the training and development sets. Initial deduplications of the examples from the training set were used, but the results deteriorated, as in Section 5.1, similar to undersampling. We suggest in future work to explore further the usage of data augmentation methods.

When tokenizing with RoBERTa large, 798 examples (7.6%) from the training and development data splits contained over the maximum sequence length supported by the Transformer model, which is 512 tokens. In these long sequence examples, truncation methods are applied and further investigated in Section 5.3.

## 4 Methodology

During the development of our solution, we employ various techniques to address different challenges associated with the task, including unbalanced data, domain-specific characteristics, and lengthy sentences in the datasets. Due to time constraints during the competition, we approach each aspect sequentially and evaluate the performance of different techniques using our evaluation methodology. We adopt an iterative process, where techniques that demonstrated superior performance were retained and carried forward to subsequent experiments.

For our solution, we adopt the fine-tuning approach proposed by Devlin et al., 2018 to train a bidirectional transformer model for text classification. In line with this approach, we pass the final features of the *[CLS]* token through a pooling layer, and subsequently through a classifier output layer, the default loss function used in our implementation is Cross Entropy.

We opt for a two-step validation methodology. First, to fine-tune our models' hyperparameters, we perform a grid search operation by training on the training set and evaluating with the Macro-F1 metric on the development set of the task data. The hyperparameters we tuned included the learning rate, the dropout rate of the task layer, the number of warm-up steps, and weight decay. Table 2 presents the grid of hyperparameters that were explored during the grid search process, along with the constants we maintained.

| **Hyperparameter** | **Tested Values** |
|---|---|
| Learning Rate | {2e-6, 4e-6, 6e-6, 8e-6} |
| Dropout of task layer | {0, 0.2, 0.4} |
| Warmup steps | {200, 500} |
| Weight Decay | {0, 0.01} |
| Batch Size | 8 |
| Maximun Training Epochs | 100 |
| Learning Rate Scheduler | Constant |
| Optimizer | Adam |
| Adam $\epsilon$ | 1e-8 |
| Adam $\beta_1$ | 0.9 |
| Adam $\beta_2$ | 0.999 |
| Early Stopping Patience | 2 (Epochs) |
| Early Stopping Threshold | 0.0025 (Macro F1-score) |

Table 2: Grid search space for the hyperparameter tuning process.

After identifying the best performing hyperparameters, we conduct a final evaluation using the k-fold cross-validation technique. This involved dividing the combined training and development sets into four different folds, training and evaluating the model on each fold. This process was repeated four times, each time one fold was used for validation. The performance of our models was then assessed based on the mean Macro-F1 score across all folds.

The selection of the grid search and k-fold cross-validation methodologies ensured that our models were robust and not overly biased towards the training set, and hence are expected to perform well on unseen data. The results reported in the follows this methodology.

## 5 Experiments

The experiments were performed on a machine using 2 Nvidia Tesla V100 GPUs. We experiment different strategies on Transformers in sequentially in order to save time. The base model for our experiments is the RoBERTa Large (Liu et al., 2019), unless cited otherwise.

### 5.1 Dealing with unbalanced data

Addressing the challenge of unbalanced data is crucial in classification tasks, and we explored some techniques to mitigate the impact of imbalanced class distributions. One common approach is undersampling, which involves randomly selecting a subset of samples from the majority class to match the number of samples in the minority class. Although this technique helps balance the class distribution, it may result in the loss of valuable information. In contrast, oversampling involves replicating or generating synthetic samples from the minority class to equalize the representation of the class, thereby mitigating the class imbalance issue.

In addition to sampling techniques, we employed loss sample weights to assign higher weights to the loss computed for samples belonging to minority classes. This approach allows the model to prioritize the correct classification of minority class samples during training, improving their representation in the learned model.

To evaluate the effectiveness of these techniques, we conducted experiments and compared their performance on the test set. The results are presented in Table 3. Using sample weights was the best resulting technique in this experiment, undersampling models did not converge well due to the resulted low quantity of data.

| Unbalanced Technique | Metric |
|---|---|
| Do-Nothing | 0.608 |
| Undersampling | – |
| Oversampling | 0.610 |
| Loss Sample Weights | **0.613** |

Table 3: Experiment 1 - Performance comparison of techniques for dealing with unbalanced data, with Sample Weights outperforming sampling data techniques. Undersampling models did not converge well due to the resulted low quantity of data. The Metric represents the mean Macro F1-Score on the cross-validation data.

### 5.2 Domain adaptation

Domain adaptation is a technique used to optimize pre-trained Transformer models for specific domains of data. In this study, we explore the effectiveness of domain adaptation through further pre-training on a domain-specific corpus of unlabeled data. This approach enhances the models' ability to learn domain-related words and relations, thereby improving their performance in mental-health related tasks. Successful implementations of domain adaptation using this technique have been reported by Poświata and Perełkiewicz, 2022, who achieved first place in the 2022 edition of the shared task by applying further pre-training on Transformer models.

To perform domain adaptation, we leveraged the vast collection of user-generated content available on the Reddit platform. Using the Python Reddit API Wrapper (PRAW) library, we collected pre-training data from a total of 117 subreddits, including 82 subreddits related to depression and 35 non-depression subreddits. The data collection process aimed to capture the top $n$ posts from each subreddit, where $n$ was determined as 2% of the follower count of the respective subreddit. This approach ensured a representative sample of posts from each subreddit, taking into account the size of their respective communities. The resulting dataset consisted of approximately 7.3 million comments. To respect the privacy of Reddit users, all data was preprocessed to anonymize user information.

For further pre-training, we performed a text deduplication process on the corpus, resulting in a balanced dataset of 6.6 million comments. This dataset comprised 3.4 million comments from mental health-related subreddits and 3.2 million comments from other subreddits. The pre-training data occupied approximately 1.4 GB of raw text on disk.

For the further pre-training of our models, we employed two popular architectures: RoBERTa (Liu et al., 2019), used by the previous winner, and DeBERTa v3 (He et al., 2023), which has shown promising results in various benchmarks. Using the public English checkpoints of each model as the starting point, we further pre-train the RoBERTa Large model using Masked Language Modeling (MLM) on the collected Reddit Mental Health dataset; similarly, we further pre-trained the DeBERTa v3 Large model using Replaced Token Detection (RTD) on the same dataset.

Table 4 provides a comparison of different pre-trained models and their performance after domain adaptation. The results demonstrate that further pre-training on the Reddit mental health dataset resulted in performance improvements for both RoBERTa and DeBERTa v3 models. However, the RoBERTa models consistently outperformed the DeBERTa v3 models in this task, as indicated by higher Macro F1-Scores. We label the new model **"MentalBERTa"** and we will use it as a base model

| Model | Futher Pre-train Dataset | Pre-Training Task | Metric |
|---|---|---|---|
| RoBERTa Large (Liu et al., 2019) | - | - | 0.613 |
| RoBERTa Large | Reddit Mental Health | MLM | **0.616** |
| DeBERTa V3 Large (He et al., 2023) | - | - | 0.605 |
| DeBERTa V3 Large | Reddit Mental Health | RTD | 0.607 |

Table 4: Experiment 2 - Comparison of different pre-trained models used and domain adaptations results. There was a gain in performance by realizing a further pre-training on domain data, but overall the DeBERTa models did not perform well in comparison with the RoBERTa models in this task. The Metric represents the mean Macro F1-Score on the cross-validation data.

in our next experiments.

### 5.3 Truncation methods

In the DepSign-LT-EDI@RANLP-2023 competition, approximately 7.6% of the training and development data splits exceeded 512 tokens when tokenized with the RoBERTa vocabulary. To address this limitation imposed by the maximum sequence length of the RoBERTa model, we experimented with different truncation methods.

Sun et al., 2019 tested three truncation methods: *head-only*, which retains the first 512 tokens; *tail-only*, which keeps the last 512 tokens; and *head+tail*, which selects the first 128 (25%) tokens and the last 384 (75%) tokens. Their experiments revealed that the *head+tail* truncation method yielded the best results.

In our study, we evaluated additional truncation regimens, including:

1. **100% head (head-only):** keep the first 512 tokens;
2. **75% head + 25% tail**: select the first 128 tokens and the last 384 tokens;
3. **50% head + 50% tail**: select the first 256 tokens and the last 256 tokens;
4. **25% head + 75% tail**: select the first 384 tokens and the last 128 tokens;
5. **100% tail (tail-only)**: keep the last 512 tokens.

Table 5 presents the results of our experiments using different truncation methods. Our findings indicate that the *50% head + 50% tail* regimen achieved the best performance, closely followed by the *25% head + 75% tail* regimen, which aligns with the findings of Sun et al., 2019. These results suggest that the optimal truncation distribution may depend on the characteristics of the dataset.

| Truncation method | Metric |
|---|---|
| 100% head | 0.616 |
| 75% head + 25% tail | 0.613 |
| **50% head + 50% tail** | **0.618** |
| 25% head + 75% tail | 0.617 |
| 100% tail | 0.606 |

Table 5: Experiment 3 - Results of different truncation methods. *50% head + 50% tail* achieves the bests results. The Metric represents the mean Macro F1-Score on the cross-validation data.

### 5.4 Ensemble Techniques

Ensembling is a powerful technique that combines multiple models to achieve improved prediction performance compared to individual models. In the 2022 edition of the shared task, each of the top three winners applied a different ensemble technique: the 1st place winner (Poświata and Perełkiewicz, 2022) used the mean of the raw output vectors (Logits Mean), the 2nd place winner (Wang et al., 2022) used a weighted sum of the probabilities (Weighted Softmax Mean), and the 3rd place winner (Singh and Motlicek, 2022) employed a majority voting system (Voting).

In our internal tests on the development set, we experimented with various ensemble techniques. Interestingly, the best results came from treating the task as a regression problem. We assigned values from 0 to 2 for each label of the shared task and took the mean of the models' predictions, then the result is rounded to the nearest valid integer for the final classification (referred to as Regression Mean). However, these results were inconsistent when evaluated on the cross-validation data, with the performance of the Voting or Softmax Mean systems sometimes outperform the Regression Mean.

For the final submission, we decided to use the Regression Mean and Voting ensembles. However, upon evaluating the test data after the competition ended, we found that a Softmax Mean ensemble would have significantly improved the results, while Voting and Regression degraded the results in relation to the predictions of a single model. Table 6 presents the results of the test set for different ensemble techniques using the cross-validation results of our best model.

| Model | Macro F1 (Test set) |
|---|---|
| Single Model (best fold) | 0.4683 |

| Ensemble method | Macro F1 (Test set) |
|---|---|
| Logits Mean | 0.4878 |
| Softmax Mean | **0.4915** |
| Voting | 0.4635 |
| Regression Mean | 0.4678 |

Table 6: Results of different ensemble methods using the outputs of each fold of our Best Model on the Test Set. The model was trained using the cross-validation dataset, comprising 4 folds.

## 6 Final submission and Results

Our best performing model, MentalBERTa, trained with Loss Sample Weights and *50% head + 50% tail* truncation, achieved a Macro F1 score of 0.618 on the cross-validation data. The models resulting from the experiments were also included in the final submission ensemble. We selected the top 9 models and used each model's 4 folds to compose part of the final ensemble submissions.

Our three final submissions were:

1. **KFoldMean9Mode:** A hierarchical ensemble approach involving Regression Mean on each k-fold (4), followed by a Voting ensemble of the 9 models.
2. **BestModel4Mean:** The Regression Mean ensemble of the best model.
3. **All36Mode:** A simple Voting ensemble of all 36 outputs (9 models x 4 folds).

The best results were obtained from the BestModel4Mean submission, with a score of 0.470. This secured us the 1st place in the DepSign-LT-EDI@RANLP2023 shared task. It is worth noting that ensembling more than 4 models resulted in a degradation of the final score.

## 7 Conclusion

In this paper, we have described our approach and techniques that led our team, DeepLearningBrasil, to secure the 1st place in the DepSign-LT-EDI@RANLP2023 shared task. Our objective was to classify social media texts into three levels of depression. Leveraging the power of RoBERTa and DeBERTa models, we pre-trained them on a curated Reddit dataset from mental health-related communities. To address the challenge of lengthy texts, we employed truncation methods that focused on the beginnings and endings of the content. In dealing with unbalanced data, we used techniques such as undersampling, oversampling, loss of sample weights, and data augmentation to mitigate the impact of imbalanced class distributions.

Ensemble techniques were employed to combine the strengths of multiple models. Our experiments showed that the choice of ensemble method varied depending on the fold and dataset characteristics. Overall, our winning approach highlights the importance of effective pre-training, addressing unbalanced data, domain adaptation, and strategic ensemble techniques. We will make available pretraining data [2] and our MentalBERTa model [3].

## Acknowledgments

This work has been supported by the AI Center of Excellence (Centro de Excelência em Inteligência Artificial – CEIA) of the Institute of Informatics at the Federal University of Goiás (INF-UFG).

## References

Jacob Devlin, Ming-Wei Chang, Kenton Lee, and Kristina Toutanova. 2018. BERT: pre-training of deep bidirectional transformers for language understanding. *CoRR*, abs/1810.04805.

Umme Marzia Haque, Enamul Kabir, and Rasheda Khanam. 2021. Detection of child depression using machine learning methods. *PLOS ONE*, 16(12):1–13.

Pengcheng He, Jianfeng Gao, and Weizhu Chen. 2023. Debertav3: Improving deberta using electra-style pretraining with gradient-disentangled embedding sharing.

Yinhan Liu, Myle Ott, Naman Goyal, Jingfei Du, Mandar Joshi, Danqi Chen, Omer Levy, Mike Lewis,

[2] https://huggingface.co/datasets/dlb/mentalreddit

[3] https://huggingface.co/dlb/MentalBERTa

Luke Zettlemoyer, and Veselin Stoyanov. 2019. Roberta: A robustly optimized BERT pretraining approach. *CoRR*, abs/1907.11692.

World Health Organization et al. 2017. Depression and other common mental disorders: global health estimates. Technical report, World Health Organization.

Javier Parapar, Patricia Martín-Rodilla, David E. Losada, and Fabio Crestani. 2022. erisk 2022: Pathological gambling, depression, and eating disorder challenges. In *Advances in Information Retrieval*, pages 436–442, Cham. Springer International Publishing.

Rafał Poświata and Michał Perełkiewicz. 2022. OPI@LT-EDI-ACL2022: Detecting signs of depression from social media text using RoBERTa pretrained language models. In *Proceedings of the Second Workshop on Language Technology for Equality, Diversity and Inclusion*, pages 276–282, Dublin, Ireland. Association for Computational Linguistics.

Kayalvizhi S, Thenmozhi Durairaj, Bharathi Raja Chakravarthi, and Jerin Mahibha C. 2022. Findings of the shared task on detecting signs of depression from social media. In *Proceedings of the Second Workshop on Language Technology for Equality, Diversity and Inclusion*, pages 331–338, Dublin, Ireland. Association for Computational Linguistics.

Kayalvizhi Sampath and Thenmozhi Durairaj. 2022. Data set creation and empirical analysis for detecting signs of depression from social media postings. In *Computational Intelligence in Data Science*, pages 136–151, Cham. Springer International Publishing.

Kayalvizhi Sampath, Thenmozhi Durairaj, Bharathi Raja Chakravarthi, Jerin Mahibha C, Kogilavani Shanmugavadivel, and Pratik Anil Rahood. 2023. Overview of the second shared task on detecting signs of depression from social media text. In *Proceedings of the Third Workshop on Language Technology for Equality, Diversity and Inclusion*, Varna, Bulgaria. Recent Advances in Natural Language Processing.

Muskaan Singh and Petr Motlicek. 2022. IDIAP submission@LT-EDI-ACL2022: Detecting signs of depression from social media text. In *Proceedings of the Second Workshop on Language Technology for Equality, Diversity and Inclusion*, pages 362–368, Dublin, Ireland. Association for Computational Linguistics.

Chi Sun, Xipeng Qiu, Yige Xu, and Xuanjing Huang. 2019. How to fine-tune bert for text classification? In *Chinese Computational Linguistics*, pages 194–206, Cham. Springer International Publishing.

Wei-Yao Wang, Yu-Chien Tang, Wei-Wei Du, and Wen-Chih Peng. 2022. NYCU_TWD@LT-EDI-ACL2022: Ensemble models with VADER and contrastive learning for detecting signs of depression from social media. In *Proceedings of the Second Workshop on Language Technology for Equality, Diversity and Inclusion*, pages 136–139, Dublin, Ireland. Association for Computational Linguistics.

Tianlin Zhang, Annika M Schoene, Shaoxiong Ji, and Sophia Ananiadou. 2022. Natural language processing applied to mental illness detection: a narrative review. *npj Digital Medicine*, 5(1):46.

# MUCS@LT-EDI2023: Learning Approaches for Hope Speech Detection in Social Media Text

**Asha Hegde[a], Kavya G[b], Sharal Coelho[c],**
**Hosahalli Lakshmaiah Shashirekha[d]**
Department of Computer Science, Mangalore University, Mangalore, India
{[a]hegdekasha, [b]kavyamujk, [c]sharalmucs}@gmail.com
[d]hlsrekha@mangaloreuniversity.ac.in

## Abstract

Hope exerts a substantial influence on human cognition and behavior, yet hope related content remains under explored in the realm of social media data analysis. Investigating this content unveils valuable insights into users' emotions, aspirations, and anticipations, offering researchers and analysts a richer comprehension of hope's impact on digital-era individuals' well-being, choices, and actions. Further, this area is rarely explored even for high-resource languages. To address the identification of hope text in social media platforms, this paper describes the models submitted by the team MUCS to "Hope Speech Detection for Equality, Diversity, and Inclusion (LT-EDI)" shared task organized at Recent Advances in Natural Language Processing (RANLP) - 2023. This shared task aims to classify a comment/post in English and code-mixed texts in three languages (Bulgarian, Spanish, and Hindi) into one of the two predefined categories: "Hope" or "Non Hope". Two models: i) Hope_BERT - Linear Support Vector Classifier (LinearSVC) model trained by concatenating Bidirectional Encoder Representations from Transformers (BERT) embeddings and Term Frequency-Inverse Document Frequency (TF-IDF) of character n-grams with word boundary (char_wb) for English and ii) Hope_mBERT - LinearSVC model trained by concatenating Multilingual BERT (mBERT) embeddings and TF-IDF of char_wb for Bulgarian, Spanish, and Hindi code-mixed texts, are proposed for the shared task to classify the given text into Hope or Non-Hope categories. The proposed models obtained 1st, 1st, 2nd, and 5th ranks by exhibiting macro F1 scores of 0.61, 0.75, 0.67, and 0.44 for Spanish, Bulgarian, Hindi, and English texts respectively.

## 1 Introduction

Social media has a profound impact on society, providing a platform for individuals to express their opinions and communicate with others effectively at a much faster rate. It also enables access to diverse opinions, facilitates connection with different individuals, promotes art and culture, and provides a platform for marginalized voices. Social media platforms are also being used effectively to spread awareness and support various causes, for instance: inequality, human rights violations, discrimination, health and wellness, environmental concerns, etc. (Chakravarthi and Muralidaran, 2021; Balouchzahi et al., 2021b). While constructive criticism have fostered healthy discussions, the misuse of freedom of speech on social media has become a prevalent issue (Hegde et al., 2021b). Trolling and online bullying have become unfortunate consequences of this freedom, causing significant harm to individuals' mental well-being. Numerous studies have consistently highlighted the detrimental effects of heavy social media usage, including increased risk of depression, anxiety, loneliness, self-harm, and even suicidal thoughts (Hegde et al., 2022c). Efforts can be made to reduce these negative thoughts by promoting more positive and supportive hope content on social media. Hence, analyzing hope content/speech in social media is considered as an essential determinant for the well-being of users which can also motivate users in a positive way and provide valuable insights into the trajectory of goal-directed behaviors, persistence in the face of misfortunes, and adjusting to positive or negative changes in life (Balouchzahi et al., 2023; Ghanghor et al., 2021).

Hope speech detection refers to the analysis of social media content for the detection of inspirational text/posts with positive vibes. However, hope speech detection has rarely been experimented even for high-resource languages (Chakravarthi et al., 2022). Social media text is often code-mixed and the analysis of code-mixed texts in low-resource languages has been the focus of several studies



*LT-EDI 2023 – Third Workshop on Language Technology for Equality, Diversity and Inclusion*, pages 279–286, Varna, Bulgaria, Sep 7, 2023.
https://doi.org/10.26615/978-954-452-084-7_043

| Language | Sample Text | English Translation | Label |
|---|---|---|---|
| **Bulgarian** | Искам да ви попитам един важен въпрос който ме мъчи но ако може да е на лично | I want to ask you one important question that bothers me but if it can be done personally | **Not-Hope** |
| **English** | And might not be in a position to come out safely | And might not be in a position to come out safely | **Hope** |
| **Hindi** | ye koi bimary nahi hai natural state hai apni apni sabko choice honi chahiye apni marzi se jeeene ki | This is not a disease, it is a natural state, everyone should have their own choice to live according to their wish | **Hope** |
| **Spanish** | Ser lgtb y zurdo al mismo tiempo es ser un reverendo imbécil, basta con ver como viven estas comunidades en los países zurdos y ver como viven en los países capitalistas para darse cuenta que el capitalismo es el verdadero camino | If you are LGBT and you are an imbecile at the same time, you just have to see how these communities live in poor countries and how they live in capitalist countries to see that capitalism is the true way | **Not-Hope** |

Table 1: Sample comments from Hope Speech detection dataset along with the English translation

and workshops (Fake News Detection (Hegde and Shashirekha, 2021), Sentiment Analysis (Hegde et al., 2022a), Word Level Language Identification (Balouchzahi et al., 2022a), Machine Translation (Hegde et al., 2022b; Hegde and Lakshmaiah, 2022), Threatening Language Detection (Hegde and Shashirekha, 2022) and Offensive Language Identification (Hegde et al., 2021a)). Processing code-mixed texts is challenging due to mixing languages within the same utterance or text. These challenges include tokenization, language identification, linguistic variation, and unavailability of pretrained models trained to represent code-mixed text. To address these challenges, "Hope Speech Detection for Equality, Diversity, and Inclusion" shared task[1] at RANLP 2023[2] aims to classify comment/post in English and code-mixed texts in Spanish, Bulgarian, and Hindi, into one of the two predefined categories, namely: "Hope" or "Non hope". The sample comments/posts from the shared task dataset along with their English translations are shown in Table 1.

In this paper, we team MUCS, describe the two binary classification models: Hope_BERT and Hope_mBERT, submitted to "Hope Speech Detection for Equality, Diversity, and Inclusion" shared task (Kumaresan et al., 2023). While Hope_BERT uses a combination of TF-IDF of char_wb and BERT embeddings extracted from $\text{BERT}_{\text{base}}$ models, to train LinearSVC for hope speech detection in English, Hope_mBERT makes use of Multilingual BERT (mBERT) embeddings combined with TF-IDF of char_wb to train LinearSVC for hope speech detection in Bulgarian, Spanish, and Hindi code-mixed texts. The code to reproduce the proposed models is available in github[3].

The rest of paper is organized as follows: while Section 2 describes the recent literature on code-mixed text processing and hope speech detection, Section 3 focuses on the description of the proposed models submitted to the shared task followed by the experiments and results in Section 4. Conclusion and future works are included in Section 5.

## 2 Related Work

Hope is a positive state of mind that is based on an expectation of confident outcomes with respect to an occurrence of any event in one's life. Researchers have explored many algorithms to detect the hope speech in text and few of the relevant works are described below:

Balouchzahi et al. (2021a) describes the models to detect hope speech in English, Tamil-English and Malayalam-English code-mixed texts. The authors proposed three distinct models: i) CoHope-ML - ensemble of Machine Learning (ML) classifiers (eXtreme Gradient Boosting (XGB), and Logistic Regression (LR), and MultiLayer Perceptron (MLP)) with hard voting, ii) CoHope-NN - based on keras Neural Network (NN) and iii) CoHope-TL - Bidirectional Long Short Term Memory (BiLSTM) with 1 Dimensional Convolutional Neural Network (1DCNN) trained with BERT embeddings. Both, CoHope-ML and CoHope-NN models are

[1]https://codalab.lisn.upsaclay.fr/competitions/11076
[2]http://ranlp.org/ranlp2023/
[3]https://github.com/hegdekasha/Hope_speech

trained with character n-grams in the range (3, 6) and syntactic n-grams in the range (2, 3). CoHope-ML model outperformed the other models and obtained weighted F1 scores of 0.85, 0.92, and 0.59 for Malayalam-English, English and Tamil-English texts respectively. Balouchzahi et al. (2023) created a dataset to identify hope content in code-mixed Spanish-English tweets and implemented several baselines based on ML, Deep Learning (DL), and Transfer Learning (TL) approaches to benchmark their dataset. Their work consists of two subtasks: subtask 1 - a binary classification and subtask 2 - a multiclass classification. TF-IDF of word uni-grams are used to train ML models (Support Vector Machine (SVM), Decision Tree (DT), Random Forest (RF), LR, XGB, MLP, Categorical Boosting (CB)), Global Vectors for Word Representation (GloVe) and fastText embeddings are used to train the DL models (Long Short Term Memory (LSTM), Bidirectional LSTM, and Convolutional Neural Network (CNN)) and TL based models are trained using BERT, Robustly Optimized BERT Approach (RoBERTA), mBERT, and MLNet features. Among all the learning models, LR and CB classifiers outperformed the other models obtaining macro F1 scores of 0.80 and 0.79 for binary and 0.64 and 0.54 for multiclass classifications respectively. The learning models submitted by Gowda et al. (2022) aims to classify the given comments in English into 'Hope' or 'Not-Hope' using 1DCNN with LSTM model trained with keras embeddings features. Using Synthetic Minority Oversampling Technique (SMOTE) to handle data imbalance in the dataset, they obtained macro F1 score of 0.55 and weighted F1 score of 0.860. Balouchzahi et al. (2022b) presents the ensemble model (two DT classifiers and one Random Forest (RF) classifier) with soft voting to select the best word and character n-grams to train keras NN for hope speech detection. Their models obtained weighted F1 scores of 0.870 and 0.790 for English and Spanish texts respectively. Vijayakumar et al. (2022) presented fine-tuning of A Lite BERT (ALBERT) - a transformer-based model to detect hope speech in code-mixed Dravidian languages (Malayalam and Kannada) and English. During fine-tuning ALBERT model, they used Adam optimizer and obtained weighted average F1 scores of 0.880, 0.740, and 0.750 for English, Malayalam, and Kannada languages respectively. Hande et al. (2021) created the hope speech dataset with 6,176 user-generated comments in code-mixed Kannada language scraped from YouTube and manually annotated them as 'Hope' or 'Not-hope' to detect hope speech. They benchmarked their dataset with ML (LR, k-Nearest Neighbors (k-NN), DT, RF, and Naive Bayes), DL (LSTM, BiLSTM, and CNN), and TL (BERT, mBERT, RoBERTa, RoBERTa-mBERT, Cross Lingual Language Model RoBERTa, and Dual-Channel BERT (DC-BERT4HOPE)) based approaches. Among all the models, RF and DC-BERT4HOPE with RoBERTa-mBERT models outperformed other models with weighted F1 scores of 0.706 and 0.752 respectively.

From the above literature, it is clear that hope speech detection task is not even explored for high-resource languages. It also indicates that there is enough space for developing models and tools for detecting hope speech content in code-mixed low-resource languages.

## 3 Methodology

The framework of the proposed methodology visualized in Figure 1 includes the following steps:

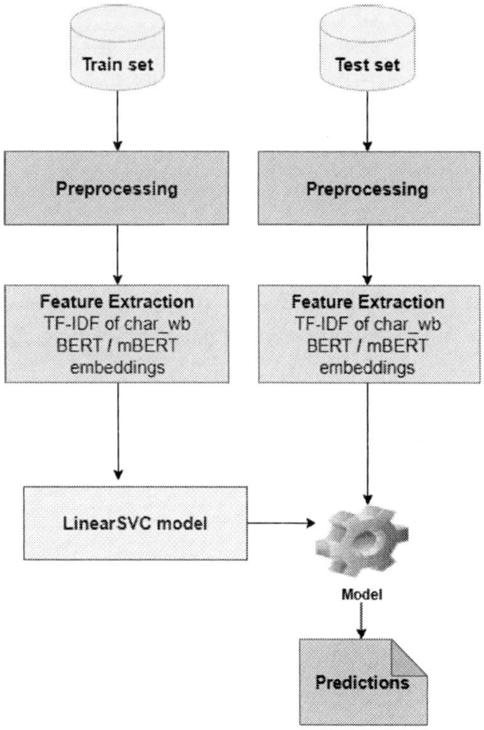


Figure 1: The framework of the proposed methodology

| Configuration | Values |
|---|---|
| WordPiece Vocab size (BERT) | 30,522 |
| WordPiece Vocab size (mBERT) | 1,19,547 |
| attention heads | 12 |
| layers | 6 |
| dimension | 768 |
| max_length | 100 |

Table 2: Configurations and their values used in BERT and mBERT models

### 3.1 Preprocessing

Preprocessing steps involve converting emojis to their corresponding text, eliminating punctuation, digits, and unwanted characters (such as !()-[];:'" ¡¿./?$=%+@* ', etc.) and lowercasing the text. Further, Bulgarian, Hindi, and Spanish stopwords list available at github[4] and English stopwords available at Natural Language Tool Kit[5] are used as references to remove stopwords. These steps help to reduce the irrelevant textual content and improve the performance of the learning models.

### 3.2 Feature Extraction

Feature extraction is a crucial step which helps to extract features in the given data and the distinguishing features helps to improve the performance of the learning models (Hegde et al., 2022d). A fusion of TF-IDF of char_wb, and BERT/mBERT embeddings (BERT embeddings for English text and mBERT embeddings for Spanish, Bulgarian, and Hindi texts) are used as features to train Hope_BERT/Hope_mBERT models in the proposed approach.

- **TF-IDF of char_wb** - character sequences of length 1 to 3 are extracted using char_wb[6] n-grams and represented as TF-IDF vectors.
- **BERT and mBERT embeddings** - are pretrained models trained on huge unlabeled text data for word representations. BERT is trained on Toronto Book Corpus and Wikipedia and exclusively used for tasks involving English texts, whereas mBERT is trained on wikipedia data and blogs that belong to more than 104 languages and exclusively used for tasks that includes multiple languages. These pretrained models provide tokenizers and for each token/word they provide embeddings which encode the semantic information.

[4]https://github.com/stopwords-iso/

[5]https://pythonspot.com/nltk-stop-words/

[6]https://scikit-learn.org/stable/modules/generated/sklearn.feature_extraction.text.TfidfVectorizer.html

| Hyperparameters | Values |
|---|---|
| penalty | 12 |
| C | 1.0 |
| class_weight | balanced |
| max_iter | max_iter |
| random_state | 100 |
| loss | squared_hinge |

Table 3: Hyperparameters and their values used in LinearSVC model

| Language | Train set | | Development set | |
|---|---|---|---|---|
| | Hope | Not-Hope | Hope | Not-Hope |
| **Bulgarian** | 223 | 4,448 | 75 | 514 |
| **English** | 1,562 | 16,630 | 400 | 4,148 |
| **Hindi** | 343 | 2,219 | 45 | 275 |
| **Spanish** | 691 | 621 | 100 | 200 |

Table 4: Statistics of the Train and Development sets

### 3.3 Model Description

Language Model (LM) analyzes large collections of text data to gain insights into the relationships between words and generate accurate predictions based on the context of the input text. Inspired by the LM, the framework described by Balouchzahi et al. (2021a) is adopted for the proposed models.

#### 3.3.1 Hope_BERT

This model makes use of pretrained BertTokenizer[7] and TFBertModel[8] modules for tokenization and loading the BERT LM respectively for English text. BertTokenizer is a pretrained tokenizer trained on a large amount of English text. It tokenizes the words based on WordPiece[9] tokenizer. Further, 'TFBertModel' is a class in the huggingface transformers library that loads the pretrained BERT LM for English text. This LM can predict the next word in a sentence by considering both the left and right context of the input text. The steps involved in designing Hope_BERT model are described below:

- Tokenization - BertTokenizer is loaded and fine-tuned on the English text provided by the shared task organizers
- Creating features - a pre-trained BERT LM is loaded with a WordPiece vocabulary of

[7]https://huggingface.co/docs/transformers/main_classes/tokenizer

[8]https://huggingface.co/docs/transformers/model_doc/bert

[9]https://huggingface.co/learn/nlp/course/chapter6/6?fw=pt

| Language | Development set | | Test set | |
|---|---|---|---|---|
| | With imbalanced data | With balanced data | With imbalanced data | With balanced data |
| **Hope_mBERT** | | | | |
| **Spanish** | 0.76 | 0.79 | 0.6 | **0.61** |
| **Bulgarian** | 0.80 | 0.81 | 0.73 | **0.75** |
| **Hindi** | 0.70 | 0.73 | 0.65 | **0.67** |
| **Hope_BERT** | | | | |
| **English** | 0.65 | 0.67 | 0.42 | 0.44 |

Table 5: Results of the proposed models

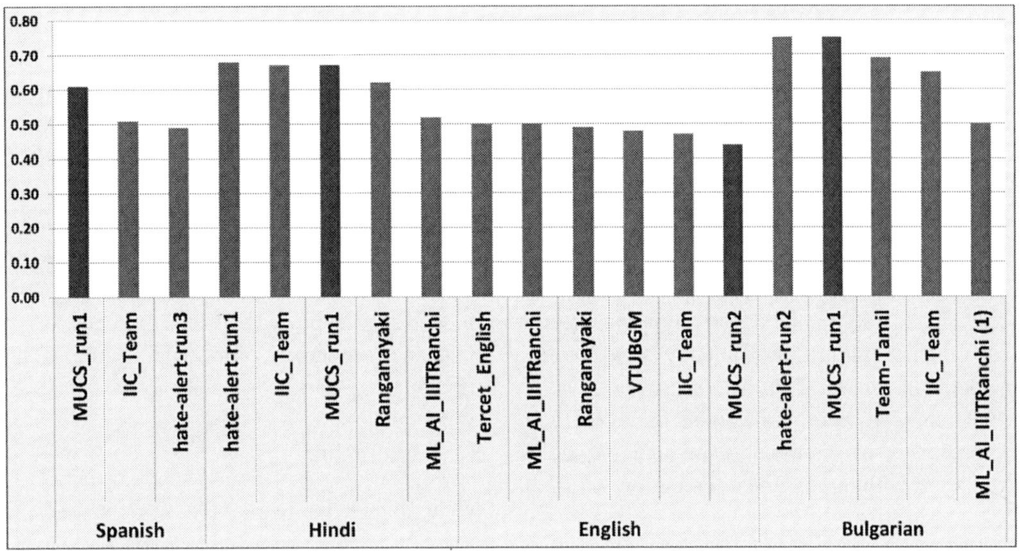


Figure 2: Comparison of macro F1 scores of the participating teams in the shared task

size 30,522 and fine-tuned on the English dataset provided by the organizers, allowing the model to generate feature vectors. These vectors are then used to train the LinearSVC model

The configuration and their values used in constructing Hope_BERT model are shown in Table 2.

#### 3.3.2 Hope_mBERT

Hope_mBERT model utilizes pretrained multilingual BertTokenizer (mBERT tokenizer) and multilingual TFBertModel[10] (mBERT LM) modules to load the pretrained multilingual tokenizer and mBERT LM respectively for the multilingual texts. The steps, configurations and the corresponding values to build Hope_mBERT model are the same as used in constructing the Hope_BERT model. The resulting multilingual word embeddings contains WordPiece vocabulary of size 1,19,547. Hope_mBERT LM is fine-tuned on Spanish/ Bulgarian/ Hindi languages, to build the models for the respective languages. This fine-tuning enables the model to create feature vectors, which are subsequently employed to train the LinearSVC models.

#### 3.3.3 Classifier Construction

LinearSVC is a supervised ML algorithm typically used for classification tasks. It works by mapping data points to a high-dimensional space and then finding the optimal hyperplane that divides the data into consequent classes (Fung and Mangasarian, 2001). This algorithm aims to maximize the margin between the classes, allowing for better generalization of unseen data. Hyperparameters and their values used to train LinearSVC model are shown in Table 3. The hyperparameters which are not mentioned in Table 3 are used with their default values. As the dataset provided by the organizers is imbal-

[10]https://huggingface.co/bert-base-multilingual-cased

| Language | Comments | Actual Label | Predicted Label | Remarks |
|---|---|---|---|---|
| English | I dont respect LGBT community.. and because of this video I unsubscribe your channel | Not-Hope | Hope | Removing the stopwords (I, don't, and, because, of, this, you) results in the content words (respect, LGBT, community, video, unsubscribe, channel). Among these content words, the word 'respect' speaks about hope and hence the comment is classified as 'Hope'. |
| | excelent and comprehensive video for understand the LGBTQ topic... | Not-Hope | Hope | The content words 'excellent' and 'comprehensive' speaks about hope. This indicates the incorrect annotation of the comment. |
| Hindi | @LIMITED GAMER usne glt kya kha. Ye to mujhe bhi odd lga. But doesn't mean ki main culture tabahh kr rhi hu. | Hope | Not-Hope | The words 'glt', 'odd', and 'tabah' used in the comments are associated with 'Not-Hope' class and hence, the comment is classified as 'Not-Hope'. |
| | ग़ज़ब खबरे okkk but Mene Bola apko Bura to nhi लगा न अगर लगा हो तो sorry pr Boone Ka hak to sbko मिलना चाहिए | Not-Hope | Hope | The content words 'ग़ज़ब', 'खबरे', 'sorry', 'Boone' and 'Bura' are seen in Train set with 'Hope' class and because of this, the comment is classified as 'Hope'. |

Table 6: Sample misclassified comments along with the probable reasons

anced, class_weight ='balanced' hyperparameter is used during training the LinearSVC to handle the data imbalance. This hyperparameter value automatically adjusts class weights based on their frequencies, resolving the data imbalance issue to some extent without manual intervention.

## 4 Experiments and Results

Statistics of the datasets provided by the organizers of the shared task is shown in Table 4 (Chakravarthi, 2020). Hope_BERT and Hope_mBERT models are evaluated using the Test sets and the predictions are submitted to the organizers for evaluation in terms of macro F1 score. The performance of the proposed models are shown in Table 5. Hope_BERT model exhibited a macro F1 score of 0.44 securing 5$^{th}$ rank in the shared task for English text and Hope_mBERT models exhibited macro F1 scores of 0.61, 0.75, and 0.67 securing 1$^{st}$, 1$^{st}$, and 2$^{nd}$ ranks for Spanish, Bulgarian, and Hindi code-mixed texts respectively. The low macro F1 score for English may be due to severe class imbalance in the English train set. Few misclassified comments along with the actual and predicted labels (obtained from Hope_BERT and Hope_mBERT models evaluating on the English and Hindi Test sets respectively), and the probable reasons for misclassification are shown in Table 6. From Table 6, it is clear that, removing stopwords and incorrect annotations have shown the impact in deciding the polarity of the comments. Figure 2 gives the comparison of macro F1 scores of all the participating teams for the shared task.

## 5 Conclusion

In this paper, we team MUCS, presented the description of the proposed models for the "Hope Speech Detection for Equality, Diversity, and Inclusion-LT-EDI" shared task at RANLP-2023. The proposed models: Hope_BERT - trained with a combination of TF-IDF of char_wb and BERT embeddings for English texts exhibited a macro F1 score of 0.44 securing 5$^{th}$ rank and Hope_mBERT trained with a combination of TF-IDF of char_wb and mBERT embeddings for code-mixed Spanish, Bulgarian, and Hindi texts, exhibited macro F1 scores of 0.61, 0.75, and 0.67 securing 1$^{st}$, 1$^{st}$, and 2$^{nd}$ ranks for Spanish, Bulgarian, and Hindi respectively. Suitable features that could efficiently capture the contextual information from the code-mixed text will be explored further.

## References


Fazlourrahman Balouchzahi, BK Aparna, and HL Shashirekha. 2021a. MUCS@ LT-EDI-EACL2021: CoHope-Hope Speech Detection for Equality, Diversity, and Inclusion in Code-Mixed Texts. In *Proceedings of the First Workshop on Language Technology for Equality, Diversity and Inclusion*, pages 180–187.

Fazlourrahman Balouchzahi, Sabur Butt, A Hegde, Noman Ashraf, HL Shashirekha, Grigori Sidorov, and Alexander Gelbukh. 2022a. Overview of CoLI-Kanglish: Word Level Language Identification in Code-mixed Kannada-English Texts at ICON 2022. In *Proceedings of the 19th International Conference on Natural Language Processing (ICON): Shared Task on Word Level Language Identification in Code-mixed Kannada-English Texts*, pages 38–45.

Fazlourrahman Balouchzahi, Sabur Butt, Grigori Sidorov, and Alexander Gelbukh. 2022b. CIC@LT-EDI-ACL2022: Are Transformers the only Hope? Hope Speech Detection for Spanish and English Comments. In *Proceedings of the Second Workshop on Language Technology for Equality, Diversity and Inclusion*, pages 206–211, Dublin, Ireland. Association for Computational Linguistics.

Fazlourrahman Balouchzahi, Hosahalli Lakshmaiah Shashirekha, and Grigori Sidorov. 2021b. HSSD: Hate Speech Spreader Detection using N-grams and Voting Classifier. In *CLEF (Working Notes)*, pages 1829–1836.

Fazlourrahman Balouchzahi, Grigori Sidorov, and Alexander Gelbukh. 2023. PolyHope: Two-level Hope Speech Detection from Tweets. In *Expert Systems with Applications*, page 120078. Elsevier.

Bharathi Raja Chakravarthi. 2020. HopeEDI: A Multilingual Hope Speech Detection Dataset for Equality, Diversity, and Inclusion. In *Proceedings of the Third Workshop on Computational Modeling of People's Opinions, Personality, and Emotion's in Social Media*, pages 41–53, Barcelona, Spain (Online). Association for Computational Linguistics.

Bharathi Raja Chakravarthi and Vigneshwaran Muralidaran. 2021. Findings of the Shared Task on Hope Speech Detection for Equality, Diversity, and Inclusion. In *Proceedings of the first workshop on language technology for equality, diversity and inclusion*, pages 61–72.

Bharathi Raja Chakravarthi, Vigneshwaran Muralidaran, Ruba Priyadharshini, Subalalitha Cn, John McCrae, Miguel Ángel García, Salud María Jiménez-Zafra, Rafael Valencia-García, Prasanna Kumaresan, Rahul Ponnusamy, Daniel García-Baena, and José García-Díaz. 2022. Overview of the Shared Task on Hope Speech Detection for Equality, Diversity, and Inclusion. In *Proceedings of the Second Workshop on Language Technology for Equality, Diversity and Inclusion*, pages 378–388, Dublin, Ireland. Association for Computational Linguistics.

Glenn Fung and Olvi L Mangasarian. 2001. Proximal Support Vector Machine Classifiers. In *Proceedings of the seventh ACM SIGKDD international conference on Knowledge discovery and data mining*, pages 77–86.

Nikhil Ghanghor, Rahul Ponnusamy, Prasanna Kumar Kumaresan, Ruba Priyadharshini, Sajeetha Thavareesan, and Bharathi Raja Chakravarthi. 2021. IIITK@ LT-EDI-EACL2021: Hope Speech Detection for Equality, Diversity, and Inclusion in Tamil, Malayalam and English. In *Proceedings of the First Workshop on Language Technology for Equality, Diversity and Inclusion*, pages 197–203.

Anusha Gowda, Fazlourrahman Balouchzahi, Hosahalli Shashirekha, and Grigori Sidorov. 2022. MUCIC@LT-EDI-ACL2022: Hope Speech Detection using Data Re-Sampling and 1D Conv-LSTM. In *Proceedings of the Second Workshop on Language Technology for Equality, Diversity and Inclusion*, pages 161–166, Dublin, Ireland. Association for Computational Linguistics.

Adeep Hande, Ruba Priyadharshini, Anbukkarasi Sampath, Kingston Pal Thamburaj, Prabakaran Chandran, and Bharathi Raja Chakravarthi. 2021. Hope Speech Detection in Under-Resourced Kannada Language. In *arXiv preprint arXiv:2108.04616*.

Asha Hegde, Mudoor Devadas Anusha, Sharal Coelho, and Hosahalli Lakshmaiah Shashirekha. 2021a. MUM at ComMA@ICON: Multilingual Gender Biased and Communal Language Identification Using Supervised Learning Approaches. In *Proceedings of the 18th International Conference on Natural Language Processing: Shared Task on Multilingual Gender Biased and Communal Language Identification*, pages 64–69, NIT Silchar. NLP Association of India (NLPAI).

Asha Hegde, Mudoor Devadas Anusha, Sharal Coelho, Hosahalli Lakshmaiah Shashirekha, and Bharathi Raja Chakravarthi. 2022a. Corpus Creation for Sentiment Analysis in Code-Mixed Tulu Text. In *Proceedings of the 1st Annual Meeting of the ELRA/ISCA Special Interest Group on Under-Resourced Languages*, pages 33–40.

Asha Hegde, Mudoor Devadas Anusha, and Hosahalli Lakshmaiah Shashirekha. 2021b. Ensemble Based Machine Learning Models for Hate Speech and Offensive Content Identification. In *Forum for Information Retrieval Evaluation (Working Notes)(FIRE), CEUR-WS. org*.

Asha Hegde, Shubhanker Banerjee, Bharathi Raja Chakravarthi, Ruba Priyadharshini, Hosahalli Shashirekha, John Philip McCrae, et al. 2022b. Overview of the Shared Task on Machine Translation in Dravidian Languages. In *Proceedings of the Second Workshop on Speech and Language Technologies for Dravidian Languages*, pages 271–278.

Asha Hegde, Sharal Coelho, Ahmad Elyas Dashti, and Hosahalli Shashirekha. 2022c. MUCS@ Text-LT-EDI@ ACL 2022: Detecting Sign of Depression from Social Media Text using Supervised Learning Approach. In *Proceedings of the Second Workshop on Language Technology for Equality, Diversity and Inclusion*, pages 312–316.

Asha Hegde, Sharal Coelho, and Hosahalli Shashirekha. 2022d. MUCS@DravidianLangTech@ACL2022:

Ensemble of Logistic Regression Penalties to Identify Emotions in Tamil text. In *Proceedings of the Second Workshop on Speech and Language Technologies for Dravidian Languages*, pages 145–150, Dublin, Ireland. Association for Computational Linguistics.

Asha Hegde and Shashirekha Lakshmaiah. 2022. Mucs@ mixmt: Indictrans-based Machine Translation for Hinglish Text. In *Proceedings of the Seventh Conference on Machine Translation (WMT)*, pages 1131–1135.

Asha Hegde and Hosahalli Lakshmaiah Shashirekha. 2021. Urdu Fake News Detection Using Ensemble of Machine Learning Models.

Asha Hegde and Hosahalli Lakshmaiah Shashirekha. 2022. Leveraging Dynamic Meta Embedding for Sentiment Analysis and Detection of Homophobic/Transphobic Content in Code-mixed Dravidian Languages.

Prasanna Kumar Kumaresan, Bharathi Raja Chakravarthi, Subalalitha Chinnaudayar Navaneethakrishnan, Miguel Ángel García-Cumbreras, Salud María Jiménez-Zafra, José Antonio García-Díaz, Rafael Valencia-García, Momchil Hardalov, Ivan Koychev, Preslav Nakov, Daniel García-Baena, and Kishore Kumar Ponnusamy. 2023. Overview of the Third Shared Task on Hope Speech Detection for Equality, Diversity, and Inclusion. In *Proceedings of the Third Workshop on Speech and Language Technologies for Dravidian Languages*, Varna, Bulgaria. Recent Advances in Natural Language Processing.

Praveenkumar Vijayakumar, Prathyush S, Aravind P, Angel S, Rajalakshmi Sivanaiah, Sakaya Milton Rajendram, and Mirnalinee T T. 2022. SSN_ARMM@ LT-EDI -ACL2022: Hope Speech Detection for Equality, Diversity, and Inclusion Using ALBERT Model. In *Proceedings of the Second Workshop on Language Technology for Equality, Diversity and Inclusion*, pages 172–176, Dublin, Ireland. Association for Computational Linguistics.

# MUCS@LT-EDI2023: Homophobic/Transphobic Content Detection in Social Media Text using mBERT

**Asha Hegde[a], Kavya G[b], Sharal Coelho[c], Hosahalli Lakshmaiah Shashirekha[d]**
Department of Computer Science, Mangalore University, Mangalore, India
{[a]hegdekasha, [b]kavyamujk, [c]sharalmucs}@gmail.com
[e]hlsrekha@mangaloreuniversity.ac.in

## Abstract

Homophobic/Transphobic (H/T) content includes hate speech, discrimination text, and abusive comments against Lesbian, Gay, Bisexual, Transgender, and Queer (LGBTQ) individuals. With the increase in user generated text in social media, there has been an increase in H/T content also. Further, most of the text data on social media is code-mixed and this poses challenges for efficient analysis and detection of H/T content on social media. The complex nature of code-mixed text necessitates the development of advanced tools and techniques to effectively tackle this issue on social media platforms. Hence, in this paper, we - team MUCS, describe the transformer based models submitted to "Homophobia/Transphobia Detection in social media comments" shared task in Language Technology for Equality, Diversity and Inclusion (LT-EDI) at Recent Advances in Natural Language Processing (RANLP)-2023. The proposed methodology makes use of oversampling technique to handle data imbalance in the given Train set and this oversampled data is used to fine-tune the Transfer Learning (TL) based Multilingual Bidirectional Encoder Representations from Transformers (mBERT) models. These models obtained weighted F1 scores of 0.91, 0.91, 0.95, 0.94, and 0.81 securing 11$^{th}$, 5$^{th}$, 3$^{rd}$, 3$^{rd}$, and 7$^{th}$ ranks for English, Tamil, Malayalam, Spanish, and Hindi languages respectively in Task A and weighted F1 scores of 0.14, 0.82, and 0.85 securing 8$^{th}$, 2$^{nd}$, and 2$^{nd}$ ranks for English, Tamil, and Malayalam languages respectively in Task B.

## 1 Introduction

Social media platforms provide a means for users to express their views, ideas, reviews, comments, opinions, and emotions, freely and instantaneously without any barriers of the language and content. This has given raise to the creation and sharing of useful content as well as unhealthy posts, such as offensive, abusive, and hatred content, targeting a person, a group, or a community (Hegde et al., 2021; Balouchzahi et al., 2021b). H/T content is one such content that expresses the hatredness towards LGBTQ community on their sexual orientation or gender identity (Chakravarthi et al., 2021). LGBTQ individuals face various forms of textual violence and discrimination such as, hate speech, cyberbullying, exculsion and isolation, online shaming, and misgendering in online environment or on social media platforms. They also become targets of threats and abuse, leading to significant mental health issues (Hegde et al., 2022b). Hence, identifying and removing H/T content on social media platforms is a crucial aspect in order to promote equality, diversity, and inclusion in the society. By implementing these measures, it is possible to create a safer online environment for the LGBTQ community and support their well-being and mental health (Mandl et al., 2020).

Identifying H/T content in social media text poses challenges due to the complex nature of code-mixed text prevalent on these platforms (Chakravarthi, 2023; Hegde and Shashirekha, 2022). Social media text often includes the mixing of local or regional languages such as Hindi, Malayalam, Tamil, etc., with English, at sub-word, word and sentence level leading to code-mixed content. (Jose et al., 2020; Hegde et al., 2022a; Balouchzahi et al., 2022). This code-mixing makes the identification and analysis of H/T content more difficult, as traditional language processing models may fail to accurately interpret and classify such mixed-language texts. To effectively address this challenge, Natural Language Processing (NLP) techniques need to be explored for code-mixed text, taking into consideration the linguistic nuances and variations in different languages. By developing robust algorithms and models to handle code-mixed H/T text, it is possible to identify and combat H/T



*LT-EDI 2023 – Third Workshop on Language Technology for Equality, Diversity and Inclusion*, pages 287–294, Varna, Bulgaria, Sep 7, 2023.
https://doi.org/10.26615/978-954-452-084-7_044

| Language | Sample Text | English Translations | Label |
|---|---|---|---|
| **English** | I too feel the same Her shyness is cute | I too feel the same Her shyness is cute | Non-anti-LGBT+ content |
| **Tamil** | நல்லா வந்துருண்டா மக்கள் தொகையை குரைக்கவா | Have you come here and bark at the population? | Homophobia |
| **Hindi** | सच मे सर आपकी पढ़ाने का तरीका देख के मन करता है हमेशा हम पढ़ते ही रहे | Really sir, I feel like seeing your way of teaching, we always keep on studying. | Non-anti-LGBT+ content |
| **Spanish** | Que yo soy lesbiana reprimida por decirles feos a los manes que se creen el putas, dice | That I am a repressed lesbian for calling ugly men who think they are whores, she says | Homophobia |
| **Malayalam** | ഇന്ന് ആൺകുട്ടികളും സുരക്ഷിതർ ഒന്നും അല്ലെടോ | Are the girls safe today? | Transphobia |

**Table 1:** Sample text and their English Translations for Task A

content in a better way ensuring a safer and more inclusive online environment for all users.

To address the challenges of H/T content identification in social media text, in this paper, we - team MUCS, describe the models submitted to "Homophobia/Transphobia Detection in Social media Comments" shared task[1] at RANLP-2023[2]. The shared task consists of two subtasks: i) Task A - a comment-level polarity classification task to identify H/T content in English, Tamil, Hindi, Malayalam, and Spanish languages, with 3 labels (Non-anti-LGBT+, Homophobia, and Transphobia) and ii) Task B - to identify H/T content in English, Tamil, and Malayalam texts, with 7 labels (None-of-the-above, Hope-speech, Counter-speech, Homophobic-derogation, Homophobic-Threatening, Transphobic-derogation, and Transphobic-derogation) (Chakravarthi et al., 2023). Sample comments from the datasets provided by the organizers of the shared task for Task A and Task B are shown in Table 1 and Table 2 respectively. As there are more than two classes in the dataset, the shared task is modeled as a multi-class text classification problem. The proposed methodology includes oversampling the Training set as the given data is imbalanced and fine-tuning the BERT models for both Task A and Task B.

The rest of the paper is structured as follows: Section 2 contains related works and Section 3 explains the methodology. Section 4 describes the experiments and results and the paper concludes in Section 5 with future work.

## 2 Related work

Several researchers have explored H/T content detection, offensive language identification and hate speech and offensive content detection in various languages and few of the relevant ones are described below:

Hegde and Shashirekha (2022) describe the learning models to perform Sentiment Analysis (SA) and H/T content detection in code-mixed Dravidian languages as Task A (Malayalam and Kannada) and Task B (Tamil and romanized Tamil (Tamil-English)) respectively. Using conventional preprocessing of converting emojis to text and removal of digits and stopwords, these models make use of Dynamic Meta Embedding (DME) to train Long Short Term Memory (LSTM) model for SA and H/T content identification in code-mixed Dravidian languages. These models obtained macro F1 scores of 0.61 and 0.44 for Malayalam and Kannada languages respectively in Task A and 0.58 and 0.74 for Tamil and Tamil-English texts respectively in Task B. Singh and Motlicek (2022) presented TL approach for fine-tuning Cross Lingual Language Models Robustly Optimized BERT (XLM ROBERTA) model in Zero-Shot learning framework for the detection of H/T contents in English and Tamil-English and obtained macro F1 scores of 0.89 and 0.85 for English and Tamil-English texts respectively.

Ashraf et al. (2022) proposed the Machine Learning (ML) models (Support Vector Machines (SVM), Random Forest (RF), Passive Aggressive

[1]https://codalab.lisn.upsaclay.fr/competitions/11077/

[2]http://ranlp.org/ranlp2023/

| Language | Sample Text | English Translation | Label |
| --- | --- | --- | --- |
| English | You are so pretty, you really look like a girl | You are so pretty, you really look like a girl | None |
| | Pro please Boxing prank part2 | Pro please Boxing prank part2 | Hope-Speech |
| | Best movie and people not understand relationship feeling I miss my life | Best movie and people not understand relationship feeling I miss my life | Hope-Speech |
| Tamil | இந்திய ஒன்றியம் நூறு வருஷத்துக்கு பின் தங்கியுள்ளோம் இது இயற்கை அனைத்தது உயிரினங்களிடம் உள்ளது | Union of India is behind a hundred years and it is all about nature | Counter-speech |
| | இன விருத்தி எப்படி செய்வது என்பதையும் அந்த நீதிபதி சொல்லியருக்க வேண்டும் | That judge should also have told how to do ethnic development | Homophobic-derogation |
| Malayalam | കണ്ടൻ polayadi മക്കൾ അണ്ടി ചെത്തി കളയണം | Kundan polayadi children should be undressed | Homophobic-Threatening |
| | ഒന്ന് പോടാ ശിഖണ്ഡി ഒമ്പതുകളെ ത്ഫൂ | Shikhandi tfoo nines if not one | Transphobic-Threatening |
| | പിടിച്ച് കല്ലെറിഞ്ഞു കൊല്ലലാണ് ഇസ്ലാം മതം ഇവർക്ക് വിധിച്ചിട്ടുള്ളത് | Islam has condemned them to be caught and stoned to death | Transphobic-Threatening |

**Table 2:** Sample texts and their English Translations for Task B

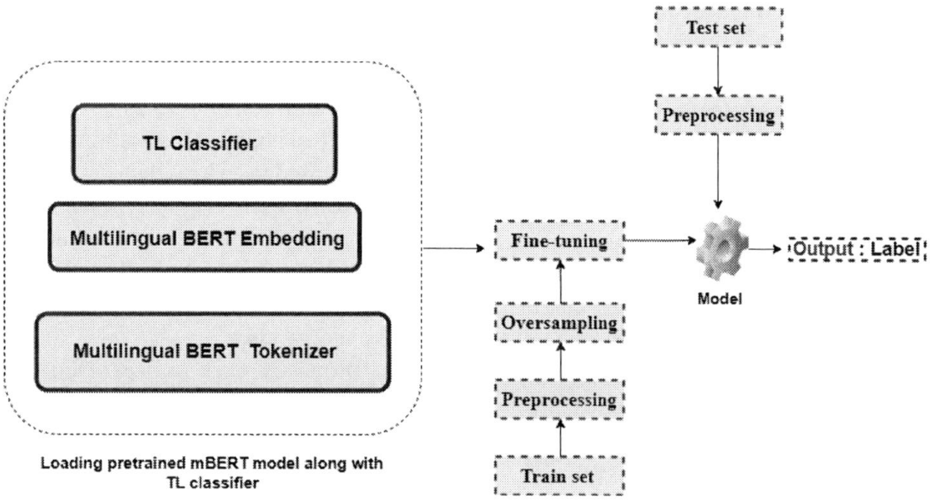


**Figure 1:** The framework of the proposed model

Classifier (PA), Gaussian Naive Bayes (GNB), Multi-Layer Perceptron (MLP)) to detect H/T content in three languages (English, Tamil and Tamil-English) trained with Term Frequency-Inverse Document Frequency (TF-IDF) of word bigrams. Among these models, SVM outperformed all other classifiers with weighted F1 scores of 0.91, 0.92, 0.88 for English, Tamil and Tamil-English languages respectively.

Two distinct models: COOLI-Ensemble - a Voting Classifier with three estimators (Multi Layer Perceptron (MLP), eXtreme Gradient Boosting (XGB) and Logistic Regression (LR)) and COOLI-Keras - a Keras dense neural network architecture model, described by Balouchzahi et al. (2021a) aims to classify code-mixed texts in Kannada-English, Malayalam-English, and Tamil-English language pairs into six predefined categories and Malayalam-English language pair into five categories for identifying offensive content. Character and word sequences extracted are vectorized using CountVectorizer[3] and the relevant fea-

[3]https://scikit-learn.org/stable/modules/generated/sklearn.feature_extraction.text.CountVectorizer.html

| Language | Train set | | | Development set | | |
|---|---|---|---|---|---|---|
| | Non-anti-LGBT+content | Homophobia | Transphobia | Non-anti-LGBT+content | Homophobia | Transphobia |
| **English** | 2,978 | 179 | 7 | 748 | 42 | 2 |
| **Tamil** | 2,064 | 453 | 145 | 507 | 118 | 41 |
| **Hindi** | 2,423 | 45 | 92 | 305 | 2 | 13 |
| **Malayalam** | 2,468 | 476 | 170 | 937 | 197 | 79 |
| **Spanish** | 450 | 200 | 200 | 150 | 43 | 43 |

**Table 3:** : Classwise distribution of labels in the dataset for Task A

tures are selected using feature selection algorithms (Chi-Square test, Mutual Information (MI), and F test). COOLI-Ensemble model performed better and obtained weighted F1 scores of 0.97, 0.75, and 0.69 for Malayalam-English, Tamil-English and Kannada-English language pairs respectively. Balouchzahi and Shashirekha (2020) proposed three distinct models: ensemble of ML classifiers (Random Forest Classifier, LR, and Support Vector Classifier (SVC)) with hard voting, TL classifier using Universal Language Model Fine-tuning (ULMFiT) model, and ML-TL - an ensemble of ML and TL models with hard voting, to detect hate speech and offensive content in English, German and Hindi languages. Among all the models, ensemble of ML models exhibited better macro F1 score of 0.5044 for German language and ML-TL model obtained better macro F1 score of 0.5182 for Hindi language.

From the literature review, it is clear that identification of H/T content in low-resource languages like, Tamil, Malayalam, and Hindi are rarely explored. Hence, there is lot of scope in this direction for further research.

## 3 Methodology

The proposed methodology includes preprocessing, resampling, and classifiers construction using mBERT models to address the challenges of Task A and Task B of the shared task. The framework of the proposed methodology is visualized in Figure 1 and the steps involved in the methodology are given below:

### 3.1 Preprocessing

Preprocessing plays a crucial role in preparing text for further processing. Using a preprocessing pipeline, URLs, punctuation, digits, unrelated characters, and stopwords (English, Tamil, Hindi and Spanish languages) are removed as these elements do not contribute to the classification task. Additionally, as emojis - a visual representation of emotions, objects, and symbols carry valuable information, they are converted into corresponding English text allowing their content to be utilized along with the textual data.

### 3.2 Resampling

Data imbalance refers to the situation where the number of instances belonging to different classes vary significantly (Srinivasan and Subalalitha, 2021). Because of this, learning models become biased towards majority class exhibiting poor performance for minority class. This biased training could be resolved to some extent using resampling techniques. Resampling is a technique commonly used to address data imbalance in classification tasks. There are two types of resampling: i) Oversampling - duplicates samples in the minority class and adds them to the Train set until it get balanced and ii) Undersampling - deletes the samples in the majority class.

The proposed work utilizes oversampling the Train set for both Task A and Task B and the description of the parameters used in oversampling is given below:

- replace = True - indicates whether sampling should be done with replacement. When set to True, it allows the same sample to be selected more than once
- n_samples = n_samples - specifies the number of samples in the majority class for the resampling process
- random_state = None - determines the random seed used for sampling. If set to None, the random seed is not fixed and will vary for each resampling

This technique creates a balanced dataset which is further used for training purposes, ensuring that the model receives an equal representation of both

| Label | Train set | | | Development set | | |
|---|---|---|---|---|---|---|
| | English | Tamil | Malayalam | English | Tamil | Malayalam |
| None-of-the -above | 2,240 | 1,634 | 2,247 | 553 | 395 | 848 |
| Hope-Speech | 436 | 218 | 69 | 111 | 52 | 29 |
| Counter-Speech | 302 | 212 | 152 | 84 | 60 | 60 |
| Homophobic-derogation | 162 | 416 | 419 | 41 | 107 | 181 |
| Homophobic-Threatening | 12 | 37 | 57 | 1 | 11 | 16 |
| Transphobic-derogation | 6 | 111 | 163 | 2 | 31 | 75 |
| Transphobic-Threatening | 1 | 34 | 7 | - | 10 | 4 |

**Table 4:** : Classwise distribution of labels in the dataset for Task B

| Hyperparameters | Values |
|---|---|
| Layers | 6 |
| Dimension | 768 |
| Attention heads | 12 |
| Learning Rate | 2e-5 |
| Batch Size | 32 |
| Maximum Sequence Length | 128 |
| Dropout | 0.3 |

**Table 5:** Hyperparameters and their values used in mDistilBERT model

the classes potentially addressing issues related to class imbalance.

### 3.3 Model construction

TL involves training a model on one task and utilizing the learned knowledge to improve the performance on a similar task. Instead of creating a model from the scratch, the pre-trained knowledge obtained from the source task is transferred to accelerate learning and enhance the performance of the target task. This approach leverages the generalizable features and representations learned from a large dataset in the source task, allowing for efficient adaptation to the target task even for potentially less amount of labeled data (Fazlourrahman et al., 2022; Hegde and Lakshmaiah, 2022). mBERT is a variant of the BERT model that has been trained on multilingual data using the pretraining strategy similar to that used for pretraining BERT, viz. Masked Language Modeling (MLM) and Next Sentence Prediction (NSP) (Pires et al., 2019). This model leverages the power of transformer architecture to learn contextualized representation of words in multiple languages.

mBERT model works in two stages: pretraining and fine-tuning. During pretraining, the model is trained on a large corpus of text from different languages. It learns to predict the next word in the sentences using the MLM objective. Further, it learns to predict if two sentences are consecutive in a document using the Next Sentence Prediction (NSP) objective. This process enables the model to capture both word-level and sentence-level contextual information (Yasaswini et al., 2021). After pretraining, the model is fine-tuned for specific downstream tasks, such as SA, hate speech detection, offensive language detection, and opinion mining. This involves training the model on task-specific labeled data, for tasks such as sentiment analysis, hate speech detection, or named entity recognition. During both pretraining and fine-tuning, the model utilizes attention mechanisms to process the input text. It considers the context of each word by attending to its surrounding words, capturing long-range dependencies effectively. Thus, mBERT model is designed to provide a powerful and flexible framework for multilingual NLP tasks such as SA, text categorization, named entity recognition, and language identification, leveraging its pretrained knowledge and ability to handle code-mixed text effectively with the multilingual support (Chen and Kong, 2021).

## 4 Experiments and Results

Statistics of the dataset provided by the organizers of the shared task for the identification of H/T content in social media text for Task A and Task B are shown in Tables 3 and 4 respectively (Chakravarthi et al., 2022). From the tables, it is clear that the datasets provided by the organizers are highly imbalanced. To overcome this, oversampling is carried out for both the tasks using oversampling methods provided by the sklearn library[4].

bert-base-multilingual-cased[5] - a mBERT model from the huggingface repository is used to extract

[4]https://scikit-learn.org/stable/modules/generated/sklearn.utils.resample.html

[5]https://huggingface.co/bert-base-multilingual-cased

| Language | Development set | | Test set | |
|---|---|---|---|---|
| | **Before Oversampling** | **After Oversampling** | **Before Oversampling** | **After Oversampling** |
| **Task A** | | | | |
| **English** | 0.82 | 0.93 | 0.81 | **0.91** |
| **Tamil** | 0.69 | 0.85 | 0.69 | **0.91** |
| **Malayalam** | 0.79 | 0.95 | 0.76 | **0.95** |
| **Hindi** | 0.81 | 0.93 | 0.81 | **0.94** |
| **Spanish** | 0.83 | 0.84 | 0.80 | **0.81** |
| **Task B** | | | | |
| **English** | 0.15 | 0.15 | 0.13 | 0.14 |
| **Tamil** | 0.68 | 0.83 | 0.67 | **0.82** |
| **Malayalam** | 0.66 | 0.85 | 0.60 | **0.85** |

**Table 6:** Performance of the proposed models before and after oversampling for both Task A and Task B on Development and Test set

| Language | Comments | Actual Label | Predicted Label | Remarks |
|---|---|---|---|---|
| English | Stefanie Suhashini This is much worse than male commenters who talk cheap and call them prostitutes and insult them. Women are not helping them at all. This needs to change. | None | Homophobia | After removing stopwords (This, is, much, than, etc.) the content words, 'worse', 'cheap', 'prostitutes' 'insult' are associated with homophobia class and hence, the model has classified this comment as 'Homophobia'. |
| | I accept that you are a lesbian. but the body language and the way you given answers to the question is like a rowdi. Change your attitude it might help you in future. | None | Transphobia | The content words 'lesbian' and 'body language' are associated with Transphobia class and hence the model has labeled this comment as 'Transphobia' as it fails to capture the rest of the information that indicates the class 'None'. |
| Hindi | Kya gay. | None | Homophobia | The word 'gay' speaks about homophobia and hence this comment is classified as 'Homophobia'. |
| | मोन्त्री रोय कि तो बात अलग ह | | None | Transphobia | The word 'मोन्त्री' is present in the comments belonging to 'Transphobia' class during training and hence the model has predicted the label of this comment as 'Transphobia'. |

**Table 7:** Samples of misclassification in Task A for English and Hindi language datasets

the feature vectors. After loading the pretrained mBERT model with its default parameter values, the model is frozen to prevent further updates to its weights. ClassificationModel[6] - a transformer-based classifier is employed to make predictions and the hyperparameters and their values used in the model are shown in Table 5. The hyperparameters which are not mentioned in Table 5 are used with their default values.

The models are evaluated based on weighted F1 scores by incorporating class weights. Performance of the proposed models before and after oversampling for both Task A and Task B on Development and Test sets are reported in Table 6. The proposed models obtained weighted F1 scores of 0.91, 0.91, 0.95, 0.94, and 0.81 securing 11th, 5th, 3rd, 3rd, and 7th ranks for English, Tamil, Malayalam, Hindi, and Spanish languages respectively in Task A and weighted F1 scores of 0.14, 0.82, and 0.85 securing 8th, 2nd, and 2nd ranks for English, Tamil, and Malayalam languages respectively in Task B. From the table, it is clear that the mBERT models with oversampling has exhibited comparatively better weighted F1 scores over the mBERT models without oversampling. Though oversampling technique is used to resolve the data imbalance issues, the proposed methodology has still exhibited low weighted F1 score for English text. As the oversampling technique increases the number of instances in the minority classes by duplicating the samples

[6]10https://simpletransformers.ai/docs/classificationmodels/

| Comments | Actual Label | Predicted Label | Remarks |
|---|---|---|---|
| I wish I could give her hug such a swt soul. | None | Counter -speech | In both the comments, the content words 'hug', 'swt soul' and 'kindful' are annotated with the class 'Counter-speech' during training and hence the model has classified this sample as 'Counter-speech'. |
| She is so kindful. | None | Counter -speech | |
| World health organization is controlled by rich people, if they support this shit, it could be a conspiracy. | None | Homophobic -Threatening | The content words 'shit' and 'conspiracy' speaks about threatening, whereas none of the other content words explicitly indicate 'None'. Hence, the model has predicted the comment as 'Homophobic-Threatening'. |
| Plz all should share and respect ever Transgender equal in our society. | Counter-speech | Hope -Speech | After removing the stopwords (all, should, and, ever, in, and our), the content words (share, respect, Transgender, equal, and society) speaks about hope, though the comment is labelled as counter speech. Hence, the classifier has classified this comment as 'Hope-Speech'. |

**Table 8:** Samples of misclassification in Task B for English language dataset

in the minority classes, the model becomes too specialized on the minority class and fails to generalize well to unseen data resulting in over-fitting.

Table 7 shows the sample text from English and Hindi labeled Test sets, the actual and predicted labels (obtained for the Test sets after evaluating mBERT models fine-tuned with oversampled Train sets) along with the remarks for Task A and Table 8 shows the sample text from English labeled Test set, the actual and predicted labels along with the remarks for Task B. It can be observed that most of the wrong classifications are due to lack of context. The data presented in Tables 7 and 8 highlights a noticeable inconsistency in the usage of content words within the classes of the Train set. This inconsistency could potentially be responsible for erroneous classifications, as the lack of uniformity in the content word usage might be leading the misclassification model.

## 5 Conclusion and Future work

This paper describes the models submitted by our team - MUCS, to the shared task "Homophobia/-Transphobia Detection in social media comments" at RANLP 2023 for the identification of H/T content in social media text. TL model with mBERT are proposed for both Tasks A and B along with oversampling. These models secured 11$^{th}$, 5$^{th}$, 3$^{rd}$, 3$^{rd}$, and 7$^{th}$ ranks for English, Tamil, Malayalam, Spanish, and Hindi respectively in Task A and 8$^{th}$, 2$^{nd}$, and 2$^{nd}$ ranks for English, Tamil, and Malayalam respectively in Task B. Data augmentation techniques for handling imbalanced classes with effective feature extraction techniques will be explored in future.

## References


Nsrin Ashraf, Mohamed Taha, Ahmed Abd Elfattah, and Hamada Nayel. 2022. Nayel@ lt-edi-acl2022: Homophobia/Transphobia Detection for Equality, Diversity, and Inclusion using SVM. In *Proceedings of the Second Workshop on Language Technology for Equality, Diversity and Inclusion*, pages 287–290.

Fazlourrahman Balouchzahi, Aparna B K, and H L Shashirekha. 2021a. MUCS@DravidianLangTech-EACL2021:COOLI-Code-Mixing Offensive Language Identification. In *Proceedings of the First Workshop on Speech and Language Technologies for Dravidian Languages*, pages 323–329, Kyiv. Association for Computational Linguistics.

Fazlourrahman Balouchzahi and H. Shashirekha. 2020. LAs for HASOC-Learning Approaches for Hate Speech and Offensive Content Identification. pages 145–151.

Fazlourrahman Balouchzahi, Hosahalli Lakshmaiah Shashirekha, and Grigori Sidorov. 2021b. HSSD: Hate Speech Spreader Detection using N-grams and Voting Classifier. In *CLEF (Working Notes)*, pages 1829–1836.

Fazlourrahman Balouchzahi, Hosahalli Lakshmaiah Shashirekha, Grigori Sidorov, and Alexander Gelbukh. 2022. A Comparative Study of Syllables and Character Level N-grams for Dravidian Multi-Script and Code-Mixed Offensive Language Identification.

In *Journal of Intelligent & Fuzzy Systems*, pages 1–11. IOS Press.

Bharathi Raja Chakravarthi. 2023. Detection of Homophobia and Transphobia in YouTube Comments. *International Journal of Data Science and Analytics*, pages 1–20.

Bharathi Raja Chakravarthi, Adeep Hande, Rahul Ponnusamy, Prasanna Kumar Kumaresan, and Ruba Priyadharshini. 2022. How can we Detect Homophobia and Transphobia? Experiments in a Multilingual Code-mixed setting for Social Media Governance. *International Journal of Information Management Data Insights*, pages 100–119.

Bharathi Raja Chakravarthi, Rahul Ponnusamy, Malliga Subramanian, Paul Buitelaar, Miguel Ángel García-Cumbreras, Salud María Jiménez-Zafra, José Antonio García-Díaz, Rafael Valencia-García, and Nitesh Jindal. 2023. Overview of Second Shared Task on Homophobia and Transphobia Detection in English, Spanish, Hindi, Tamil, and Malayalam. In *Proceedings of the Third Workshop on Language Technology for Equality, Diversity and Inclusion*, Varna, Bulgaria. Recent Advances in Natural Language Processing.

Bharathi Raja Chakravarthi, Ruba Priyadharshini, Rahul Ponnusamy, Prasanna Kumar Kumaresan, Kayalvizhi Sampath, Durairaj Thenmozhi, Sathiyaraj Thangasamy, Rajendran Nallathambi, and John Phillip McCrae. 2021. Dataset for Identification of Homophobia and Transophobia in Multilingual YouTube Comments. In *arXiv preprint arXiv:2109.00227*.

Shi Chen and Bing Kong. 2021. cs@ DravidianLangTech-EACL2021: Offensive Language Identification based on Multilingual BERT Model. In *Proceedings of the First Workshop on Speech and Language Technologies for Dravidian Languages*, pages 230–235.

B Fazlourrahman, BK Aparna, and HL Shashirekha. 2022. CoFFiTT-COVID-19 Fake News Detection Using Fine-Tuned Transfer Learning Approaches. In *Congress on Intelligent Systems: Proceedings of CIS 2021, Volume 2*, pages 879–890. Springer.

Asha Hegde, Mudoor Devadas Anusha, Sharal Coelho, Hosahalli Lakshmaiah Shashirekha, and Bharathi Raja Chakravarthi. 2022a. Corpus Creation for Sentiment Analysis in Code-Mixed Tulu Text. In *Proceedings of the 1st Annual Meeting of the ELRA/ISCA Special Interest Group on Under-Resourced Languages*, pages 33–40.

Asha Hegde, Mudoor Devadas Anusha, and Hosahalli Lakshmaiah Shashirekha. 2021. Ensemble Based Machine Learning Models for Hate Speech and Offensive Content Identification. In *Forum for Information Retrieval Evaluation (Working Notes)(FIRE), CEUR-WS. org*.

Asha Hegde, Sharal Coelho, Ahmad Elyas Dashti, and Hosahalli Shashirekha. 2022b. MUCS@ Text-LT-EDI@ ACL 2022: Detecting Sign of Depression from Social Media Text using Supervised Learning Approach. In *Proceedings of the Second Workshop on Language Technology for Equality, Diversity and Inclusion*, pages 312–316.

Asha Hegde and Shashirekha Lakshmaiah. 2022. Mucs@ mixmt: Indictrans-based Machine Translation for Hinglish Text. In *Proceedings of the Seventh Conference on Machine Translation (WMT)*, pages 1131–1135.

Asha Hegde and Hosahalli Lakshmaiah Shashirekha. 2022. Leveraging Dynamic Meta Embedding for Sentiment Analysis and Detection of Homophobic/-Transphobic Content in Code-mixed Dravidian Languages.

Navya Jose, Bharathi Raja Chakravarthi, Shardul Suryawanshi, Elizabeth Sherly, and John P McCrae. 2020. A survey of Current Datasets for Code-Switching Research. In *2020 6th international conference on advanced computing and communication systems (ICACCS)*, pages 136–141. IEEE.

Thomas Mandl, Sandip Modha, Anand Kumar M, and Bharathi Raja Chakravarthi. 2020. Overview of the hasoc Track at Fire 2020: Hate Speech and Offensive Language Identification in Tamil, Malayalam, Hindi, English and German. In *Forum for information retrieval evaluation*, pages 29–32.

Telmo Pires, Eva Schlinger, and Dan Garrette. 2019. How Multilingual is Multilingual BERT? In *arXiv preprint arXiv:1906.01502*.

Muskaan Singh and Petr Motlicek. 2022. IDIAP Submission@ LT-EDI-ACL2022: Homophobia/Transphobia Detection in Social Media Comments. In *Proceedings of the Second Workshop on Language Technology for Equality, Diversity and Inclusion*, pages 356–361.

R Srinivasan and CN Subalalitha. 2021. Sentimental Analysis from Imbalanced Code-mixed Data using Machine Learning Approaches. In *arXiv preprint arXiv:1906.01502*.

Konthala Yasaswini, Karthik Puranik, Adeep Hande, Ruba Priyadharshini, Sajeetha Thavareesan, and Bharathi Raja Chakravarthi. 2021. IIITT@ DravidianLangTech-EACL2021: Transfer Learning for Offensive Language Detection in Dravidian Languages. In *Proceedings of the First Workshop on Speech and Language Technologies for Dravidian Languages*, pages 187–194.

# MUCS@LT-EDI2023: Detecting Signs of Depression in Social Media Text

**Sharal Coelho**[a], **Asha Hegde**[b],
**Kavya G**[c], **Hosahalli Lakshmaiah Shashirekha**[d]
Department of Computer Science, Mangalore University, Mangalore, India
{[a]sharalmucs, [b]hegdekasha, [c]kavyamujk}@gmail.com,
[d]hlsrekha@mangaloreuniversity.ac.in

## Abstract

Depression is a term used to characterize mental health disorders and it can worsen over time if left untreated, leading to more severe mental health problems and a lowered quality of life. Regardless of age, gender, or social background, anyone can be a victim of depression. Social media platforms are open to anyone including users suffering from depression, to write opinions on anything, post photos, videos etc., seek online help and so on. As depression can lead to significant changes in the individuals' posts on social media, analysing social media posts can provide insights into their mental health and reveal the signs of depression. However, manually analyzing the growing volume of social media text to detect signs of depression is time-consuming. To address the challenges of identifying signs of depression in social media content, in this paper, we - team MUCS, describe Transfer Learning (TL) and Machine Learning (ML) approaches, submitted to "Detecting Signs of Depression from Social Media Text" shared task, organised by LT-EDI@RANLP-2023. The objective of the shared task is to identify the signs of depression from social media posts in English and classify them into one of three categories: "not depressed", "moderately depressed", and "severely depressed". The TL model with fine-tuning Bidirectional Encoder Representations from Transformers (BERT) and ML models (Logistic Regression (LR) and Multinomial Naive Bayes (MNB)) trained with Term Frequency-Inverse Document Frequency (TF-IDF) of word n-grams in the range (1, 3) are submitted to the shared task. Among the two proposed models, the TL model performed better with a macro averaged F1-score of 0.361 for the Test set.

## 1 Introduction

Depression is a mental health condition resulting in feelings like sorrow, emptiness, loss of interest or distress and these feelings vary from individual to individual (Salas-Zárate et al., 2022). In severe conditions, depression may cause thoughts of suicide or death.

The user-friendly social media platforms allow users to share their posts or seek help from the online community (Hegde et al., 2022b). Depressed people might feel more ease in sharing their feelings, difficulties, and experiences, via posts on social media. Further, some people find it therapeutic to talk about their problems with others to get guidance, mental support, and sympathy from their online community. According to research, it might be possible to predict the signs of depression an online user is facing by reading the content of such users' posts on social media sites (Chiong et al., 2021). As depression can lead to significant changes in the individuals' posts on social media, analysing such posts can help in identifying the signs of depression in users. Once identified, any help or support can be extended to the users suffering from depression.

The increase in the number of social media users is increasing the user-generated text drastically (Kayalvizhi and Thenmozhi, 2022). Such user-generated text consists of hashtags, emojis, alphanumeric characters, slangs, short forms, etc. in addition to the actual content. Processing and analyzing this complex social media text using conventional text analysis techniques to get valuable insights into the data is challenging. This necessitates the need for automated tools/approaches to process social media text.

The automated approaches can identify depressive symptoms by systematically examining signs of depression in social media texts, providing a possibility for timely intervention and support for depressed individuals (Saqib et al., 2021). Though researchers have explored several techniques to detect signs of depression in social media text, it still remains a challenge because of the complexities of



*LT-EDI 2023 – Third Workshop on Language Technology for Equality, Diversity and Inclusion*, pages 295–299, Varna, Bulgaria, Sep 7, 2023.
https://doi.org/10.26615/978-954-452-084-7_045

social media text.

To address the challenges of identifying signs of depression in social media text, in this paper, we - team MUCS, describe the models submitted to "Detecting Signs of Depression from Social Media Text" shared task, organised by DepSign-LT-EDI@RANLP-2023[1] (Sampath et al., 2023). The goal of this task is to detect the signs of depression from social media posts and classify them into one of three categories: "not depressed", "moderately depressed", and "severely depressed". The shared task is modeled as a multi-class text classification problem and two approaches: i) TL model with fine-tuning BERT and ii) ML classifiers (LR and MNB) trained on TF-IDF word n-grams, are proposed for the task.

The rest of the paper is as follows: related work is contained in Section 2 followed by the methodology in Section 3. Experiments with their results are explained in Section 4 and the paper concludes with future work in Section 5.

## 2 Related Work

Researchers have experimented many techniques to recognise signs of depression in social media content, and the description of some of the most useful studies are given below:

To address the early sign of depression in Reddit social media posts, Tadesse et al. (2020) developed ML models (Support Vector Machine (SVM), Naive Bayes (NB), Random Forest (RF), Extreme Gradient Boosting) trained with TF-IDF and statistical features and Deep Learning (DL) models (combination of Long Short Term Memory and Convolutional Neural Network (LSTM+CNN) model) trained with Word2Vec embeddings. Among the proposed models, LSTM+CNN model obtained an accuracy of 93.8%. To identify the signs of depression in social media posts, Hegde et al. (2022a) used two learning models: i) TL model with fine-tuning BERT and ii) Ensemble (RF, Multilayer Perceptron, MNB, and Gradient Boosting (GB)) model with soft voting. As the dataset is imbalanced resampling technique (i.e. randomoversampling) is used to balance the dataset. Among the two models, the TL model performed better with a macro-average F1-score of 0.479.

Aswathy et al. (2019) utilized Word2Vec for generating word embeddings to train LSTM+CNN and SVM models to identify the signs of depression from the tweets. Their models obtained the weighted average F1-scores of 0.97 and 0.85 for the LSTM+CNN and SVM models respectively. Mowery et al. (2016), developed ML (Decision Tree, Linear Perceptron, RF, LR, SVM, and NB) models for determining whether a tweet represents evidence of depression or not and experimented on "Depressive Symptoms and Psychosocial Stressors Associated with Depression (SAD)" dataset which contains 9,300 tweets. To train their models, they used features including unigrams, emoticons, age, gender, linguistic inquiry word counts, etc. and obtained 0.52 average F1-score for SVM classifier. Janatdoust et al. (2022) proposed an ensemble of fine-tuned BERT models (A Lite BERT (ALBERT), DistilBERT, Robustly optimized BERT (RoBERTa), and BERT base model) with majority voting and experimented on social media comments in English (Kayalvizhi et al., 2022) and obtained a macro F1 score of 0.54.

To summarize, different learning approaches including ML, DL, and TL models are explored for detecting signs of depression in social media text. Though several techniques are experimented to detect the signs of depression in social media text in English, not all models have performed well. Further, the dynamic nature of user-generated content on social media makes the task more challenging. This emphasises the need for developing models to enhance the performance of identifying depressive symptoms from social media text.

## 3 Methodology

To detect the signs of depression in social media texts, the proposed methodology comprises of two learning models: i) TL model with fine-tuning BERT and ii) ML model trained with TF-IDF n-grams. Description of the two models are given below:

### 3.1 Pre-processing

User-generated social media texts consist of noise that includes non-ASCII characters, digits, hashtags, user mentions, URLs, and emojis. The given English text is converted to lowercase, contractions are expanded, and the URLs, digits, non-ASCII characters, punctuation, and extra spaces, are removed from the text as they do not contribute to the classification task. Pre-processing step remains the same for both the approaches.

[1]https://codalab.lisn.upsaclay.fr/competitions/11075

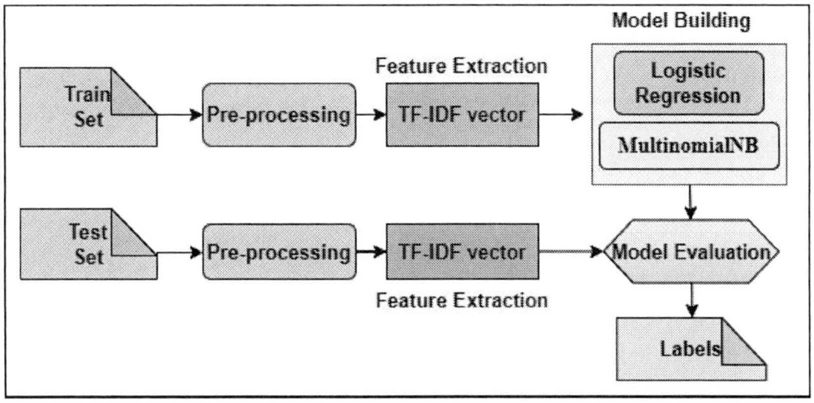


Figure 1: The proposed framework of Machine Learning classifiers

| Dataset | Classes | | |
|---|---|---|---|
| | Moderate | Not Depression | Severe |
| **Train set** | 3,678 | 2,755 | 768 |
| **Development set** | 2,169 | 848 | 228 |

Table 1: Class-wise distribution of the dataset

### 3.2 Model Construction

Methodology of the proposed TL model and ML models, to detect signs of depression in social media texts are given below:

**TL Model** - consists of training a model for source task and then applying the knowledge acquired from that task to the target task (Hegde and Shashirekha, 2022). It enables the model to start learning from a partially trained state, saving time and resources. BERT[2] is a Language Model (LM), pre-trained on 800 million English words from the Huggingface Book Corpus and 2,500 million English words from the Wikipedia corpus (Devlin et al., 2018). Using the concept of masked language model, it learns to predict the next words in the sentence. Further, it captures the context of words within a given sentence considering the nearby words on both the left and right sides and generates contextualized representations for words.

For the proposed TL model, the bert-base-uncased[3] - a BERT variant is used to represent text. From the huggingface library[4], BERT LM is loaded and fine-tuned with the Train set. A transformer based classifier - ClassificationModel is used to make the predictions.

[2]https://huggingface.co/docs/transformers/model_doc/bert
[3]https://huggingface.co/bert-base-uncased
[4]https://huggingface.co/docs/hub/models-libraries

| Text | Label |
|---|---|
| My life is objectively very easy but my depression makes it all feel like a struggle | Moderate |
| I'm so tired and I hate everything. | Severe |
| i like being alone but i hate being alone anyone else | Not Depression |

Table 2: Sample texts of 'Signs of Depression' from the dataset

| Classifier | Development set | Test set |
|---|---|---|
| LR | 0.457 | 0.346 |
| MNB | 0.313 | 0.236 |
| **TL model with BERT** | **0.557** | **0.361** |

Table 3: Performances of the proposed models in terms of macro-averaged F1-score

**Machine Learning models** - consists of Feature Extraction and Classifier Construction. The framework of the ML model is shown in Figure 1. The significance of a word in a document relative to its frequency across all the documents in a corpus is captured by TF-IDF (Hegde et al., 2021). The proposed work utilizes TF-IDF of word n-grams in the range (1, 3), obtained using TfidfVectorizer[5]. 51,505 word n-grams are obtained from the Train set to train the classifiers.

Two classifiers: i) LR and ii) MNB are employed to predict the class labels for the input text. The regularization techniques in LR classifier helps to control the complexity of the model and discourage it from fitting noise in the data, making them effective tools for preventing overfitting in high-dimensional environments. The MNB classifier is

[5]https://scikit-learn.org/stable/modules/generated/sklearn.feature_extraction.text.TfidfVectorizer.html

| Text | Actual label | Predicted label | Remarks |
|---|---|---|---|
| It's the closest thing to dying. This life sucks. | Severe | Moderate | The words "thing", "sucks" and "life" are frequently employed with samples of "Moderate" class in the Train set. Hence, the model has classified this sample as "Moderate". |
| I miss when I was happy and life wasn't pointless. | Moderate | Not Depression | None of the words represent the signs of depression. Hence, this sample is classified as "Not Depression". |
| I wonder how much longer I can continue like this | Moderate | Not Depression | The words "wonder", "like", and "much" indicate the absence of depression. Hence, the model has classified as "Not Depression". |

Table 4: Few misclassified samples from the Test set obtained by TL model

the probabilistic model (Harjule et al., 2020) which computes the prior probabilities of given classes and the dependent probabilities of words given the class. The class with the highest probability is selected as the predicted class for the given input text.

## 4 Experiments and Results

The proposed models aim to detect the signs of depression from the social media posts and classify them into one of levels of the signs of depression: "not depressed", "moderately depressed", and "severely depressed".

The statistics of the dataset provided by the shared task organizers (S et al., 2022) is shown in Table 1. The given dataset consists of social media posts in English and few samples from the dataset are shown in Table 2.

Predictions obtained from the proposed TL model and ML models are evaluated by the shared task organizers based on macro-averaged F1-score. The performances of the proposed models on Development and Test sets are shown in Table 3. Among the two proposed approaches, the TL model obtained a macro-averaged F1-score of 0.361 for the Test set.

The performances of the proposed models are influenced by issues like: the imbalanced dataset, an incorrect spelling of words, and limited vocabulary in the dataset. Further, the given Train set consists of very less number of samples for 'severe' class compared to the other classes. As a result, the proposed model failed to understand the features and patterns associated with the 'severe' class during the training process. Few misclassified samples in the Test set along with the actual and predicted labels and remarks are shown in Table 4.

## 5 Conclusion and Future work

In this paper, we describe two models: TL model with fine-tuning BERT and ML models (LR and MNB), for detecting signs of depression in social media text and classify them into one of three categories: "not depressed", "moderately depressed", and "severely depressed". These models are submitted to the "Detecting Signs of Depression from Social Media Text" shared task at LT-EDI@RANLP2023. Among proposed models, the TL model outperformed the ML models with a macro-averaged F1-score of 0.361. Efficient techniques will be explored to handle the imbalanced dataset and improve the performance of the proposed models.

## References

KS Aswathy, PC Rafeeque, and Reena Murali. 2019. Deep Learning Approach for the Detection of Depression in Twitter. In *Proceedings of the International Conference on Systems, Energy Environment (ICSEE)*.

Raymond Chiong, Gregorius Satia Budhi, Sandeep Dhakal, and Fabian Chiong. 2021. A Textual-based Featuring Approach for Depression Detection using Machine Learning Classifiers and Social Media Texts. volume 135, page 104499. Elsevier.

Jacob Devlin, Ming-Wei Chang, Kenton Lee, and Kristina Toutanova. 2018. BERT: Pre-training of Deep Bidirectional Transformers for Language Understanding. *arXiv preprint arXiv:1810.04805*.

Priyanka Harjule, Astha Gurjar, Harshita Seth, and Priya Thakur. 2020. Text Classification on Twitter Data. In *2020 3rd International Conference on Emerging Technologies in Computer Engineering: Machine Learning and Internet of Things (ICETCE)*, pages 160–164.

Asha Hegde, Mudoor Devadas Anusha, and Hosahalli Lakshmaiah Shashirekha. 2021. Ensemble Based Machine Learning Models for Hate

Speech and Offensive Content Identification. In *Forum for Information Retrieval Evaluation (Working Notes)(FIRE), CEUR-WS. org*.

Asha Hegde, Sharal Coelho, Ahmad Elyas Dashti, and Hosahalli Shashirekha. 2022a. MUCS@ Text-LT-EDI@ ACL 2022: Detecting Sign of Depression from Social Media Text using Supervised Learning Approach. In *Proceedings of the Second Workshop on Language Technology for Equality, Diversity and Inclusion*, pages 312–316.

Asha Hegde, Sharal Coelho, and Hosahalli Shashirekha. 2022b. MUCS@ DravidianLangTech@ ACL2022: Ensemble of Logistic Regression Penalties to Identify Emotions in Tamil Text. In *Proceedings of the Second Workshop on Speech and Language Technologies for Dravidian Languages*, pages 145–150.

Asha Hegde and Hosahalli Lakshmaiah Shashirekha. 2022. Learning Models for Emotion Analysis and Threatening Language Detection in Urdu Tweets.

Morteza Janatdoust, Fatemeh Ehsani-Besheli, and Hossein Zeinali. 2022. KADO@ LT-EDI-ACL2022: BERT-based Ensembles for Detecting Signs of Depression from Social Media Text. In *Proceedings of the Second Workshop on Language Technology for Equality, Diversity and Inclusion*, pages 265–269.

S Kayalvizhi, Thenmozhi Durairaj, Bharathi Raja Chakravarthi, et al. 2022. Findings of the Shared Task on Detecting Signs of Depression from Social Media. In *Proceedings of the Second Workshop on Language Technology for Equality, Diversity and Inclusion*, pages 331–338.

S Kayalvizhi and D Thenmozhi. 2022. Data Set Creation and Empirical Analysis for Detecting Signs of Depression from Social Media Postings. *arXiv preprint arXiv:2202.03047*.

Danielle L Mowery, Y Albert Park, Craig Bryan, and Mike Conway. 2016. Towards Automatically Classifying Depressive Symptoms from Twitter Data for Population Health. In *Proceedings of the workshop on computational modeling of people's opinions, personality, and emotions in social media (PEOPLES)*, pages 182–191.

Kayalvizhi S, Thenmozhi Durairaj, Bharathi Raja Chakravarthi, and Jerin Mahibha C. 2022. Findings of the Shared Task on Detecting Signs of Depression from Social Media. In *Proceedings of the Second Workshop on Language Technology for Equality, Diversity and Inclusion*, pages 331–338, Dublin, Ireland. Association for Computational Linguistics.

Rafael Salas-Zárate, Giner Alor-Hernández, María del Pilar Salas-Zárate, Mario Andrés Paredes-Valverde, Maritza Bustos-López, and José Luis Sánchez-Cervantes. 2022. Detecting Depression Signs on Social Media: A Systematic Literature Review. In *Healthcare*, volume 10, page 291. MDPI.

Kayalvizhi Sampath, Thenmozhi Durairaj, Bharathi Raja Chakravarthi, Jerin Mahibha C, Kogilavani Shanmugavadivel, and Pratik Anil Rahood. 2023. Overview of the second shared task on detecting signs of depression from social media text. In *Proceedings of the Third Workshop on Language Technology for Equality, Diversity and Inclusion*, Varna, Bulgaria. Recent Advances in Natural Language Processing.

Kiran Saqib, Amber Fozia Khan, and Zahid Ahmad Butt. 2021. Machine Learning Methods for Predicting Postpartum Depression: Scoping Review. *JMIR mental health*, 8(11):e29838.

Michael Mesfin Tadesse, Hongfei Lin, Bo Xu, and Liang Yang. 2020. Detection of Suicide Ideation in Social Media Forums Using Deep Learning. volume 13, page 7. Multidisciplinary Digital Publishing Institute.

# KEC_AI_NLP_DEP @ LT-EDI : Detecting Signs of Depression From Social Media Texts

**Kogilavani Shanmugavadivel**[1], **Malliga Subramanian**[1], **Vasantharan K**[1], **Prethish GA**[1], **Sankar S**[2], **Sabari S**[3]

[123]Department of AI, Kongu Engineering College, Perundurai, Erode.
[1]Department of CSE, Kongu Engineering College, Perundurai, Erode.
{kogilavani.sv, mallinishanth72}@gmail.com
{vasantharank.21aid, prethishga.21aid}@kongu.edu
{sankars.21aid, sabaris.21aid}@kongu.edu

## Abstract

The goal of this study is to use machine learning approaches to detect depression indications in social media articles. Data gathering, pre-processing, feature extraction, model training, and performance evaluation are all aspects of the research. The collection consists of social media messages classified into three categories: not depressed, somewhat depressed, and severely depressed. The study contributes to the growing field of social media data-driven mental health analysis by stressing the use of feature extraction algorithms for obtaining relevant information from text data. The use of social media communications to detect depression has the potential to increase early intervention and help for people at risk. Several feature extraction approaches, such as TF-IDF, Count Vectorizer, and Hashing Vectorizer, are used to quantitatively represent textual data. These features are used to train and evaluate a wide range of machine learning models, including Logistic Regression, Random Forest, Decision Tree, Gaussian Naive Bayes, and Multinomial Naive Bayes. To assess the performance of the models, metrics such as accuracy, precision, recall, F1 score, and the confusion matrix are utilized. The Random Forest model with Count Vectorizer had the greatest accuracy on the development dataset, coming in at 92.99 percent. And with a macro F1-score of 0.362, we came in 19th position in the shared task. The findings show that machine learning is effective in detecting depression markers in social media articles.

## 1 Introduction

Millions of individuals throughout the world suffer from depression, a widespread mental health illness that causes personal and social problems. Early detection and response are critical for effective aid and therapy. The rise of social media platforms has offered new options for detecting depression symptoms by monitoring people's online expressions, which might be used for early diagnosis. However, appropriately interpreting these hints from social media postings may be difficult. Due to the massive volume of data and the inherent problems of text analysis, a robust strategy is required. To address this issue, we developed a method in this paper that integrates data pre-processing, feature extraction, and machine learning models to identify depressed symptoms in social media articles. The initial step in our methodology is data preparation, which involves cleaning and preparing the social media posts for analysis. We employ resampling techniques to get over problems with class imbalance and provide a representative dataset. We can lessen biases that may arise from data collection and sampling procedures thanks to this strategy. In the next part, the emphasis changes to feature extraction using popular techniques including Term Frequency-Inverse Document Frequency (TF-IDF), Count Vectorizer, and Hashing Vectorizer. By identifying the text's unique language patterns and word frequencies, these tools allow us to pinpoint relevant qualities for depression diagnosis. To assess the success of our plan, we employ a range of machine learning models, such as Logistic Regression, Random Forest, Decision Tree, Gaussian Naive Bayes, and Multinomial Naive Bayes.

These models are created using the obtained attributes, and they are evaluated for their accuracy in identifying depression or not in social media message classification. According to our findings, the Random Forest model with Count Vectorizer feature extraction had the highest level of accuracy out of all the models we studied. The use of this combination may enable the identification and distinction of language patterns associated with depression, enabling accurate prediction and detection. Everywhere there is an increase in concern over the prevalence of mental health issues, notably depression. Early detection and intervention are



*LT-EDI 2023 – Third Workshop on Language Technology for Equality, Diversity and Inclusion*, pages 300–306, Varna, Bulgaria, Sep 7, 2023.
https://doi.org/10.26615/978-954-452-084-7_046

crucial for effective treatment and support. This gives a potential technique to identify depressed symptoms since more individuals are expressing their thoughts, feelings, and experiences online as a result of the rise of social media platforms. Despite the fact that many tactics have been studied in previous research, there are still several limitations, including the lack of a consistent approach, the significance of context in text interpretation, and the need for automated and scalable solutions. Ethical concerns including privacy and authorization pose questions regarding the use of personal data for mental health detection. It is necessary to create a trustworthy system that can recognize signs of sadness from social media texts while taking contextual factors, privacy difficulties, and ethical considerations into account. A technique like this would help identify people who are at risk early, enabling immediate treatment and assistance to decrease the effects of depression. The pivotal work in (Sampath et al., 2023) not only provided us with valuable guidance to successfully complete the shared task but also empowered us to construct a high-accuracy model.

## 2 Literature Review

A literature review is a critical and rigorous analysis of academic articles, research papers, and published books that are relevant to a certain subject or area of study. It comprises evaluating, synthesizing, and summarizing prior research and information in order to uncover gaps, contradictions, and trends in the field. A literature review aims to provide a comprehensive account of the existing body of knowledge on a particular topic. It helps researchers find pertinent concepts, theories, and practices, as well as shape their own study design and objectives. It also helps researchers gain a more thorough understanding of the current research environment.

(Hegde et al., 2022) aims to develop automated tools using ensemble machine learning models and transfer learning with BERT to detect signs of depression in social media text. The goal is to improve identification and support for individuals exhibiting depressive behavior. (Victor et al., 2019) discusses about accurately identifying clinical depression using machine learning and automated data collection procedures. The proposed framework combines advanced machine learning techniques with automated data collection to reduce subjective biases and provide a more objective analysis of depression symptoms. In (Islam et al., 2018), the authors discusses about to design a system or model that can accurately identify and classify individuals likely to be experiencing depression based on their social network data. It explores the potential of using machine learning techniques to detect depression symptoms or individuals at risk of depression based on their social network data. In (Liu et al., 2022), the authors suggests directions for future research on using machine learning methods to detect depressive symptoms using text data from social media. Machine learning approaches applied to social media text data can effectively detect depression symptoms, serving as complementary tools in public mental health practice. The research done in (Dinkel et al., 2019) focuses on text-based depression detection in sparse clinical conversations using a multi-task Bidirectional Gated Recurrent Unit (BGRU) network with pre-trained word embeddings. The proposed system models patients' responses during clinical interviews to detect depression severity and binary health state. (Dinkel et al., 2019) addresses about the need for effective depression detection using text-based models and understanding the model's decision-making process. The proposed system is a text-based multitask Bidirectional Long Short-Term Memory (BLSTM) model with pre-trained word embeddings for depression detection and severity prediction. It achieves state-of-the-art performance and provides insights into the words and sentences contributing to predictions. The authors in (Tsugawa et al., 2015) aims to develop an efficient approach using LSTM-based Recurrent Neural Networks (RNN) to identify and predict texts describing self-perceived symptoms of depression. The proposed system utilizes symptom-based feature extraction and outperforms traditional word frequency-based approaches. (Ernala et al., 2019) discusses the lack of reliable and effective emotion detection systems for analyzing and extracting emotions from text data. It surveys approaches, proposals, datasets, strengths, weaknesses, and open issues in text-based emotion detection. The focus is on designing and developing a text-based emotion detection system. (De Choudhury et al., 2014) discuss to develops a metric-based depression detection system using text analysis. It aims to design a metric to describe the level of depression based on text analysis and classify participants accordingly. The proposed system focuses on participant replies for generalized results, but limitations of text-based depression measurement are discussed. The authors in (Guntuku et al., 2017) analyses existing research on detecting depression signs from social media. It focuses on computing tools, linguistic feature extraction methods, statistical analysis techniques, and machine learning algorithms used in the field. The goal is to provide comprehensive information on research papers related to depression sign detection from social media.

## 3 Methodology

The purpose of this study is to offer a practical method for spotting depressed symptoms in posts from social media. Our dataset is divided into three categories, "not depression," "moderate," and "severe," which represent varying levels of depression severity. Our approach includes feature extraction with TF-IDF, Count Vectorizer, and Hashing Vectorizer as well as the usage of several machine learning models, including Logistic Regression, Random Forest, Decision Tree, Gaussian Naive Bayes, and Multinomial Naive Bayes. We also deal with class disparity by employing resampling methods. The first step in our methodology is data preparation. We clean and prepare the social media messages to make sure they are ready for inspection. This process involves removing unnecessary information, such as URLs, special characters, and numbers. We also employ techniques like lowercasing and stop-word removal to reduce noise and enhance the text data quality. To address the issue of class imbalance in the dataset, we employ resampling techniques. A class imbalance exists when one or more classes are excessively underrepresented in relation to others. Models that are skewed in favor of the dominant class may be the outcome of this discrepancy. To address this, we employ resampling methods like oversampling (like SMOTE) or undersampling (like random undersampling) to balance the classes and give a representative dataset.

Feature extraction, which requires reducing a big collection of characteristics into a smaller, more manageable set, is a crucial stage in machine learning and data analysis. In the field of text analysis, the process of converting textual data into numerical representations that may be used as inputs for machine learning algorithms is referred to as feature extraction. Feature extraction seeks to extract the relevant information from the raw data by eliminating excess or unneeded information. The extraction of key features reduces the complexity of the data, enabling rapid and precise analysis. Feature extraction is essential when unstructured text data is the source for text analysis activities. By utilizing feature extraction techniques, textual data from documents, phrases, or words is converted into numerical representations that algorithms may analyze in text analysis.

Machine learning (ML) models are computer algorithms that extrapolate patterns and predict outcomes from data, as opposed to traditional programming. These models are frequently used in applications such as speech recognition, image recognition, natural language processing, and predictive analytics. ML models have the ability to analyze complex data, identify trends, and make inferences based on the patterns and correlations found in the data. Numerous sectors, including social media analysis, marketing, healthcare, and finance, use ML models extensively. They are able to handle challenging datasets, uncover buried patterns, and provide intelligent predictions and advice. The two primary types of machine learning models are regression models and classification models, each of which focuses on a particular class of problems and has a unique purpose. Regression models are used when the aim variable or result is continuous or numerical.

We evaluate how effective different machine learning algorithms are in identifying depression symptoms. Gaussian Naive Bayes, Multinomial Naive Bayes, Random Forest, Decision Tree, and Logistic Regression are some of the models we employ. These models are trained using the retrieved features and associated class labels. They investigate the best way to divide social media posts into the three categories of "not depression," "moderate," and "severe." We examine the performance of each model using pertinent assessment criteria including accuracy, precision, recall, and F1-score. These metrics reveal how well the models categorize instances into different classes. To make sure that our models are trustworthy and generalizable, we may also employ techniques like cross-validation. After the models have been assessed, we compare their results using the chosen assessment metrics. We identify the model that is most effective at identifying depressive signs. We find that the Random Forest model with Count Vectorizer

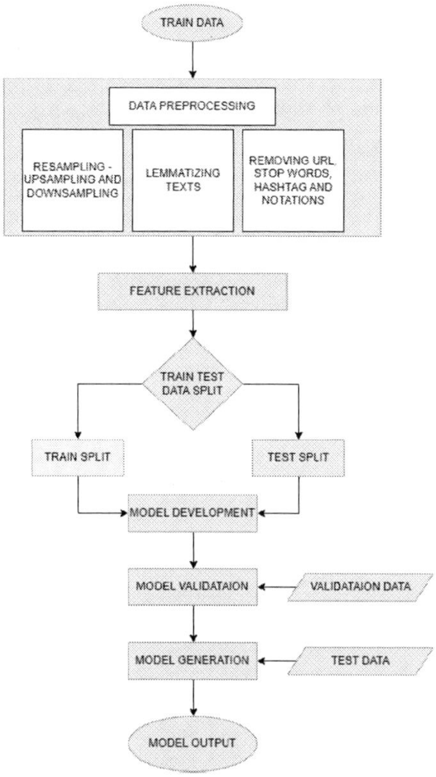


Figure 1: Proposed Model Workflow

feature extraction has the highest accuracy among the models tested in this study. Our research combines data pre-treatment methods, resampling techniques, feature extraction, and machine learning models to effectively identify depression signals from social media articles. The selected Random Forest model offers accurate predictions and helps in the early identification of people who are at risk for getting depression. It employs Count Vectorizer as the feature extraction approach. The general workflow of the system for recognizing indicators of depression is shown in Figure 1.

### 3.1 Logistic Regression

The logistic regression classification method simulates the relationship between the independent variables and the probability of a certain outcome. It is often used for binary classification problems and may be extended to accommodate multi-class classification tasks. The log-odds of the target variable and the input features are assumed to be linearly connected in logistic regression. The parameters are estimated using maximum likelihood estimation, and the logistic function is used to predict the likelihood of each class. In the context of detecting depressive symptoms based on the characteristics that were gathered from social media texts, the severity of depression may be predicted using logistic regression.

### 3.2 Gaussian Naive Bayes

The Bayes theorem and the feature independence presumption serve as the foundation for the Naive Bayes classifier, which employs probabilistic classification. A variation of Naive Bayes called Gaussian Naive Bayes assumes that the traits have a Gaussian distribution. The Bayes theorem is used to calculate the posterior probability of each class, and the likelihood of each feature value given the class is then calculated. High-dimensional data can be successfully handled using the computationally effective approach known as Gaussian Naive Bayes. It works well for issues where the independence assumption is partially violated. Gaussian Naive Bayes may be used in the context of this study to categorize social media postings into various degrees of depression severity based on the identified features.

### 3.3 Random Forest

Many decision trees are used in the Random Forest ensemble learning approach to provide predictions. This versatile and effective strategy may be used to solve classification and regression challenges. Random Forest generates several decision trees by bootstrapping the data and employing random feature groups. The forecasts of all decision trees, each of which was trained on a different sample of the data, are combined to create the final forecast. Random Forest delivers perceptions of feature value, is resistant to overfitting, and excels at processing high-dimensional data. In the context of this study, Random Forest may be used to classify social media messages into different levels of depression severity.

### 3.4 Decision Tree

Decision Tree, a non-parametric supervised learning system that consists of a hierarchical structure of if-else rules, is trained using data. Each internal node is represented as a feature, each branch as a rule for making decisions, and each leaf node as the result, resulting in a model that resembles a tree. Decision trees can handle both categorical and numerical data and are simple to grasp. To improve the homogeneity of the target variable within each group, they iteratively divided the data based on the most crucial characteristics. Overfitting may occur in decision trees, but it may be prevented by using strategies like pruning, setting a maximum depth, or agreeing on the minimum number of samples per leaf. Decision trees may be used in the context of this study to categorize social media posts into different degrees of depression intensity.

### 3.5 Multinomial Naive Bayes

Another Naive Bayes variation appropriate for discrete feature variables is multinomial Naive Bayes. It is believed that the features have a multinomial distribution, which is frequently utilized for text classification issues. Using the training data, Multinomial Naive Bayes models each feature value's likelihood given the class, and Bayes' theorem is then applied to get the posterior probability of each class. It is frequently used for text classification tasks including subject classification and sentiment analysis. Multinomial Naive Bayes may be used in the context of this study to categorize social media postings into different degrees of depression severity based on the collected data.

## 4 Performance Evaluation

The evaluation of model performance is a crucial step in establishing the effectiveness and reliability of machine learning models. To evaluate different aspects of model performance, numerous metrics are utilized. Some examples of regularly employed measures are accuracy, precision, recall, F1 score, and the confusion matrix. These measures are essential for evaluating how well our study's algorithms work at spotting depression symptoms in social media messages. In our work, we trained many models and then used the development dataset to measure their performance. With a score of 92.99%, Random Forest with Count Vectorizer feature extraction was the most accurate model.

This shows that the algorithm correctly predicted the class labels for a large portion of the social media messages in the development dataset. The patterns and characteristics indicative of melancholy in social media communications appear to have been successfully recognized by the Random Forest model with Count Vectorizer feature extraction due to its high accuracy. It is essential to look at additional performance metrics including accuracy, recall, F1 score, and the confusion matrix to get a whole view of the model's performance. By examining accuracy, recall, and F1 score, we can assess the model's capacity to correctly classify texts with indications of melancholy while minimizing false positives. The confusion matrix also provides detailed information on the distribution of the expected and actual class labels, which enables us to identify problem regions and potential misclassification sources. Overall, the development dataset demonstrated the Random Forest model's use of Count Vectorizer feature extraction to achieve the highest accuracy (92.11%). In the tables 1, 2 and 3 below, the accuracy, precision and F1-score are used to compare the performance of various models.

## 5 Conclusion

To detect signs of sorrow in social media postings, this investigation also used machine learning techniques. The study included the gathering of data, pre-processing, feature extraction, training of the model, and performance assessment. Many models were trained and evaluated using a variety of feature extraction techniques, including Logistic Regression, Random Forest, Decision Tree, Gaus-

| Models Used | TF-IDF | Count Vectorizer | Hashing Vectorizer |
|---|---|---|---|
| Logistic Regression | 81.93% | 86.38% | 42.86% |
| Multinomial Naive Bayes | 76.4% | 81.82% | 41.83% |
| Random Forest | 92.11% | 92.99% | 91.4% |
| Gaussian Naive Bayes | 74.96% | 72.3% | 43.68% |
| Decision Tree | 77.57% | 79.52% | 77.01% |

Table 1: Accuracy of Model with Dev Data

| Models Used | TF-IDF | Count Vectorizer | Hashing Vectorizer |
|---|---|---|---|
| Logistic Regression | 81.9% | 86.3% | 42.8% |
| Multinomial Naive Bayes | 76.4% | 81.8% | 41.8% |
| Random Forest | 92.1% | 92.9% | 91.3% |
| Gaussian Naive Bayes | 74.9% | 72.2% | 60.8% |
| Decision Tree | 77.5% | 79.5% | 71.7% |

Table 2: Precision of Model with Dev Data

| Models Used | TF-IDF | Count Vectorizer | Hashing Vectorizer |
|---|---|---|---|
| Logistic Regression | 0.81 | 0.86 | 0.41 |
| Multinomial Naive Bayes | 0.76 | 0.81 | 0.42 |
| Random Forest | 0.92 | 0.93 | 0.91 |
| Gaussian Naive Bayes | 0.74 | 0.72 | 0.42 |
| Decision Tree | 0.75 | 0.78 | 0.74 |

Table 3: Macro F1-Score of Model with Dev Data

sian Naive Bayes, and Multinomial Naive Bayes. After thorough examination and analysis, the Random Forest model with Count Vectorizer feature extraction achieved the highest accuracy of 92.99% on the development dataset. This shows that the model successfully identified the recurring themes and personality factors linked to depression in social media posts. The study demonstrated how machine learning models can identify depression-related signs in social media data, which can help with early identification and intervention for people who are at risk. Using natural language processing and classification approaches, the models were able to analyse text data and provide insights on the presence and severity of depression symptoms. The results highlight the value of feature extraction techniques like Count Vectorizer in sifting out important data from text input. Additionally, a complete evaluation of the models' effectiveness was provided through the measurement of performance metrics including accuracy, recall, F1 score, and confusion matrix. While the Random Forest model with the Count Vectorizer shown better accuracy, future research should explore novel feature extraction techniques, model architectures, and data sources to enhance the diagnosis of sorrow from social media postings. Overall, this study contributes to the growing body of research on utilizing machine learning for mental health analysis and lays the framework for developing scalable and efficient methods for leveraging social media data to identify and treat depression cases early on.

## References


Munmun De Choudhury, Scott Counts, Eric J Horvitz, and Aaron Hoff. 2014. Characterizing and predicting postpartum depression from shared facebook data. In *Proceedings of the 17th ACM conference on Computer supported cooperative work & social computing*, pages 626–638.

Heinrich Dinkel, Mengyue Wu, and Kai Yu. 2019. Text-based depression detection on sparse data. *arXiv preprint arXiv:1904.05154*.

Sindhu Kiranmai Ernala, Michael L Birnbaum, Kristin A Candan, Asra F Rizvi, William A Sterling, John M Kane, and Munmun De Choudhury. 2019. Methodological gaps in predicting mental health states from social media: Triangulating diagnostic signals. In *Proceedings of the 2019 chi conference on human factors in computing systems*, pages 1–16.

Sharath Chandra Guntuku, David B Yaden, Margaret L Kern, Lyle H Ungar, and Johannes C Eichstaedt. 2017. Detecting depression and mental illness on social media: an integrative review. *Current Opinion in Behavioral Sciences*, 18:43–49.

Asha Hegde, Sharal Coelho, Ahmad Elyas Dashti, and Hosahalli Shashirekha. 2022. Mucs@ text-lt-edi@ acl 2022: Detecting sign of depression from social media text using supervised learning approach. In *Proceedings of the Second Workshop on Language Technology for Equality, Diversity and Inclusion*, pages 312–316.

Md Rafiqul Islam, Muhammad Ashad Kabir, Ashir Ahmed, Abu Raihan M Kamal, Hua Wang, and Anwaar Ulhaq. 2018. Depression detection from social network data using machine learning techniques. *Health information science and systems*, 6:1–12.

Danxia Liu, Xing Lin Feng, Farooq Ahmed, Muhammad Shahid, Jing Guo, et al. 2022. Detecting and measuring depression on social media using a machine learning approach: systematic review. *JMIR Mental Health*, 9(3):e27244.

Kayalvizhi Sampath, Thenmozhi Durairaj, Bharathi Raja Chakravarthi, Jerin Mahibha C, Kogilavani Shanmugavadivel, and Pratik Anil Rahood. 2023. Overview of the second shared task on detecting signs of depression from social media text. In *Proceedings of the Third Workshop on Language Technology for Equality, Diversity and Inclusion*, Varna, Bulgaria. Recent Advances in Natural Language Processing.

S. Tsugawa, Y. Kikuchi, F. Kishino, and T. Takahashi. 2015. Monitoring depression via social media: Preliminary results. In *Proceedings of the 2015 IEEE International Conference on Healthcare Informatics*. IEEE.

Ezekiel Victor, Zahra M Aghajan, Amy R Sewart, and Ray Christian. 2019. Detecting depression using a framework combining deep multimodal neural networks with a purpose-built automated evaluation. *Psychological assessment*, 31(8):1019.

# Flamingos_python@LT-EDI: An Ensemble Model to Detect Severity of Depression

**Abirami P S, Amritha S, Pavithra M, C.Jerin Mahiba**
Meenakshi Sundararajan Engineering College, Chennai
{abiabhi2712, pavithrameganathan15, amrithasenthil2001, jerinmahibha}@gmail.com

## Abstract

The prevalence of depression is increasing globally, and there is a need for effective screening and detection tools. Social media platforms offer a rich source of data for mental health research. The paper aims to detect the signs of depression of a person from their social media postings wherein people share their feelings and emotions. The task is to create a system that, given social media posts in English, should classify the level of depression as 'not depressed', 'moderately depressed' or 'severely depressed'. The paper presents the solution for the Shared Task on Detecting Signs of Depression from Social Media Text at LT-EDI@RANLP 2023. The proposed system aims to develop a machine learning model using machine learning algorithms like SVM, Random forest and Naive Bayes to detect signs of depression from social media text. The model is trained on a dataset of social media posts to detect the level of depression of the individuals as 'not depressed', 'moderately depressed' or 'severely depressed'. The dataset is pre-processed to remove duplicates and irrelevant features, and then, feature engineering techniques is used to extract meaningful features from the text data. The model is trained on these features to classify the text into the three categories. The performance of the model is evaluated using metrics such as accuracy, precision, recall, and F1-score. The ensemble model is used to combine these algorithms which gives accuracy of 47.7% and the F1 score is 0.262. The results of the proposed approach could potentially aid in the early detection and prevention of depression for individuals who may be at risk.

## 1 Introduction

Depression is a mood disorder that causes a persistent feeling of sadness and loss of interest. It is also called major depressive disorder or clinical depression, it affects how one feel, think and behave and can lead to a variety of emotional and physical problems. Detecting depression is important since it has to be observed and treated at an early stage to avoid severe consequences. It aims to detect the signs of depression of a person from their social media postings wherein people share their feelings and emotions. Social media platforms have emerged as a valuable source of data for mental health research. They provide an opportunity to study the language and behaviour patterns of individuals, which may reveal early signs of depression. Given social media postings in English, the system should classify the signs of depression into three labels namely "not depressed", "moderately depressed", and "severely depressed". This project aims to develop a machine learning model using Support Vector Machine (SVM), Random forest and Naive Bayes algorithm to detect signs of depression from social media text.

## 2 Related Works

A depression recognition method for college students [3] proposed by Yan Ding et al., had used a deep integrated support vector machine (DISVM) algorithm to classify the input data, and finally realize the recognition of depression. Wolohan et al., (2018) created a dataset based on Reddit posts in which users were assigned to one group: depressed or control. A transformers approach to detect depression in social media [6] by Malviya et al., had analyzed the posts using the linguistic inquiry and word count tool (LIWC). Findings of the Shared Task on Detecting Signs of Depression from Social Media [7] had used a variety of technologies from traditional machine learning algorithms to deep learning models. ScubeMSEC@LT-EDI-ACL2022: Detection of Depression using Transformer Models [8] by S, Sivamanikandan et al., used different transformer models like DistilBERT, RoBERTa and ALBERT to detect depression which had achieved a Macro F1 score of 0.337, 0.457 and



*LT-EDI 2023 – Third Workshop on Language Technology for Equality, Diversity and Inclusion*, pages 307–311, Varna, Bulgaria, Sep 7, 2023.
https://doi.org/10.26615/978-954-452-084-7_047

| Text Data | Label |
|---|---|
| Like no matter how much sleep I get always fatigued. | not depression |
| All I wanna do right now is crawl out of myself. Does that make sense? | moderate |
| A few anxiety attacks and I'm ready to go | severe |

Table 1: Example Instances

0.387 respectively. Early Detection of Depression from Social Media Data Using Machine Learning Algorithms [4] by G. Geetha et al., had used machine learning algorithms like Support Vector Machine (svm), Logistic Regression, Random Forest, Bayes Theorem for the early detection of depression. A machine learning based depression analysis and suicidal ideation detection system using questionnaires and Twitter [5] by Jain et al., had proposed a system for predicting the suicidal acts based on the level of depression using XGBoost classifier. Depression detection by analyzing social media posts of user [2] by Nafiz Al Asad, et al., had presented a structural model that identified users' depression level from their social media posts. This system had used SVM classifier and Naïve Bayes classifier. A machine learning approach to detect depression and anxiety using supervised learning [1] by A. Ahmed et al., had aimed to apply natural language processing on Twitter feeds for conducting emotion analysis focusing on depression. Detection of depression related posts in Reddit social media forum [12] by Tadesse et al. had implemented class prediction using support vector machine and Naive-Bayes classifier. Sentiment analysis from depression related user generated contents in social media texts by Ananna Saha etal. [9] had found the usage and effectiveness of the five different types of AI algorithms: Convolutional Neural Network, Support Vector Machine, Linear Discriminant Analysis, K Nearest Neighbor Classifier and Linear Regression on two datasets of anxiety and depression. Detection of major depressive disorder using signal processing and machine learning approaches [10] had used classification algorithms such as Logistic Regression, Support Vector Machine, and Naive-Bayes classifier for the process of classification. To check the accuracy and precision, ten-fold cross validation had been performed. [11] All the related works helps to know the research works carried out to detect depression from social media texts using different machine learning algorithms.

## 3 Dataset

The dataset used by the proposed approach consists of social media text posts that have been annotated with labels indicating the presence or absence of signs of depression. Specifically, the labels are 'not depressed', 'moderately depressed' or 'severely depressed'. The dataset has been collected from a variety of social media platforms and contains text data in English. Example texts with labels from the dataset are presented in Table 1. The dataset is divided into three parts: train data, development data, and test data. Train data and Development data consists of three columns namely PID, Text_Data and Label. Each label column in the train data and development data consists of three different values namely 'not depressed', 'moderately depressed' or 'severely depressed' according to the text data which consists of the social media comments of an individual. There are about 7202 entries in the training dataset and 3246 entries in the development dataset. After removing the duplicates there are about 7202 entries in the training dataset and 3246 entries in the development dataset.

## 4 Solution

### 4.1 Ensemble model to combine Random Forest Classifier, Naïve Bayes Classifier, and SVM

Ensemble learning helps to improve machine learning results by combining several models. This approach allows the production of better predictive performance compared to a single model. The main challenge is not to obtain highly accurate base models, but rather to obtain base models which make different kinds of errors. For example, if ensembles are used for classification, high accuracies can be accomplished if different base models misclassify different training examples, even if the base classifier accuracy is low.

The training set is fitted to the SVM classifier. To create the SVM classifier, we import SVC class from Sklearn.svm library.

```
classifier=SVC(kernel='linear', random_state=0)
classifier.fit(x_train, y_train)
```

### 4.2 Methods for Independently Constructing Ensembles

The different methods for constructing ensemble models are:
• Majority Vote
• Bagging and Random Forest
• Randomness Injection
• Feature-Selection Ensembles
• Error-Correcting Output Coding

**Majority Vote:** A voting ensemble involves summing the predictions made by classification models or averaging the predictions made by regression models. How voting ensembles work, when to use voting ensembles, and the limitations of the approach. How to implement a hard voting ensemble and soft voting ensemble for classification predictive modeling.
**Bagging and Random Forest:** Bagging is an ensemble algorithm that fits multiple models on different subsets of a training dataset, then combines the predictions from all models.

Random forest is an extension of bagging that also randomly selects subsets of features used in each data sample. Both bagging and random forests have proven effective on a wide range of different predictive modeling problems.
**Randomness Injection:** Random values in machine learning are derived by random number generators. To create random values, the generator is first initialized with a seed, a number that represents the starting point for the random number generation. The generator then creates random values from that starting point with a specific algorithm.
**Feature-Selection Ensembles:** The idea behind ensemble feature selection is to combine multiple different feature selection methods, taking into account their strengths, and create an optimal best subset. In general, it makes a better feature space and reduces the risk of choosing an unstable subset.
**Error-Correcting Output Coding:** The Error-Correcting Output Coding method is a technique that allows a multi-class classification problem to be reframed as multiple binary classification problems, allowing the use of native binary classification models to be used directly.

### 4.3 Types of Ensemble models

**Bagging:** Bagging (Bootstrap Aggregation) is used to reduce the variance of a decision tree. Suppose a set D of d tuples, at each iteration i, a training set Di of d tuples is sampled with replacement from D. Then a classifier model Mi is learned for each training set D < i. Each classifier Mi returns its class prediction. The bagged classifier M* counts the votes and assigns the class with the most votes to X (unknown sample).
**Stacking:** There are many ways to ensemble models in machine learning, such as Bagging, Boosting, and stacking. Stacking is one of the most popular ensemble machine learning techniques used to predict multiple nodes to build a new model and improve model performance. Stacking enables us to train multiple models to solve similar problems, and based on their combined output, it builds a new model with improved performance.
**Boosting:** Boosting is an ensemble method that enables each member to learn from the preceding member's mistakes and make better predictions for the future. Unlike the bagging method, in boosting, all base learners (weak) are arranged in a sequential format so that they can learn from the mistakes of their preceding learner.
Hence, in this way, all weak learners get turned into strong learners and make a better predictive model with significantly improved performance.

### 4.4 Creating the confusion matrix

To create the confusion matrix, we need to import the confusion_matrix function of the sklearn library. After importing the function, we will call it using a new variable cm. The function takes two parameters, mainly y_true (the actual values) and y_pred (the targeted value return by the classifier).

```
cm= confusion_matrix(y_test, y_pred)
```

## 5 Results and Discussions

### 5.1 Metrics

The metrics used during the experiments are accuracy, macro-averaged precision, macro-averaged recall and macro-averaged F1-score across all the classes. The macro-averaged F1-score was the main measure when evaluating solutions.

| Model | Accuracy | Precision | Recall | F1- score |
|---|---|---|---|---|
| Random Forest Classifier | 0.599 | 0.62 | 0.60 | 0.56 |
| Naive Bayes Classifier | 0.523 | 0.58 | 0.52 | 0.40 |
| SVM Classifier | 0.636 | 0.63 | 0.61 | 0.63 |
| Ensemble Model | 0.902 | 0.91 | 0.89 | 0.91 |

Table 2: Results of model on the development dataset

### 5.2 Performance

Table 2 shows the result of each model on the training dataset. Among the machine learning language models as shown in the Table 2 Ensemble model was the best in terms of accuracy (0.90) and F1-score (0.89). Sklearn SVC is the implementation of SVC provided by the popular machine learning library Scikit-learn. There are three datasets namely training dataset, development dataset and test dataset. The training dataset is pre-processed and is used to train the SVM model. Flask server is used to display the depression detection website. In the website the user will be prompted to enter a comment. The SVM classifier is used to detect depression and classify them as 'not depressed', 'moderately depressed' or 'severely depressed'. The result is displayed on the next webpage. Confusion matrix is plotted to determine the performance of the classification models for a given set of test data. Figure 1 to 4 shows the confusion matrix for the three machine learning models used: Random Forest Classifier, Naive Bayes Classifier and SVM Classifier.

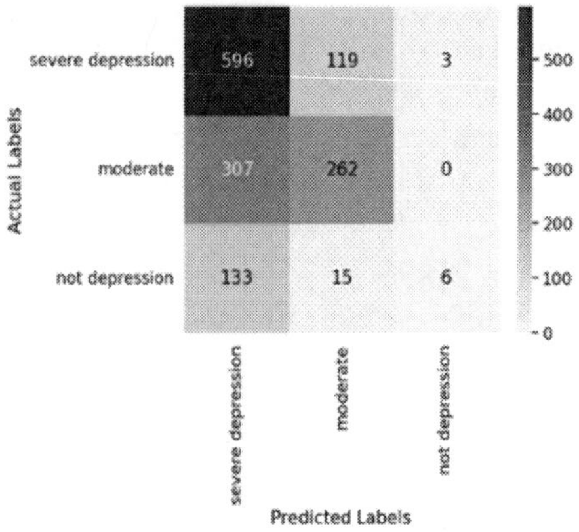


Figure 1: Random Forest

## 6 Conclusion

The proposed system aim to detect severity of depression from social media text using machine

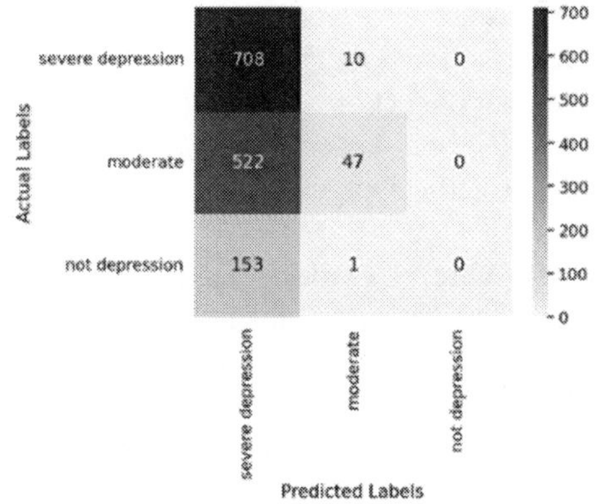


Figure 2: Naive Bayes

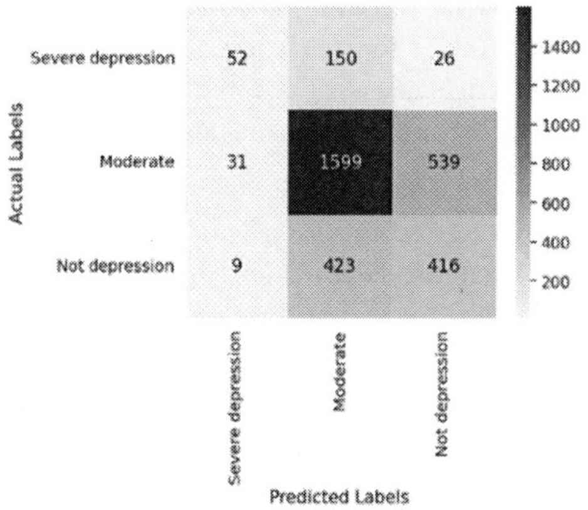


Figure 3: SVM

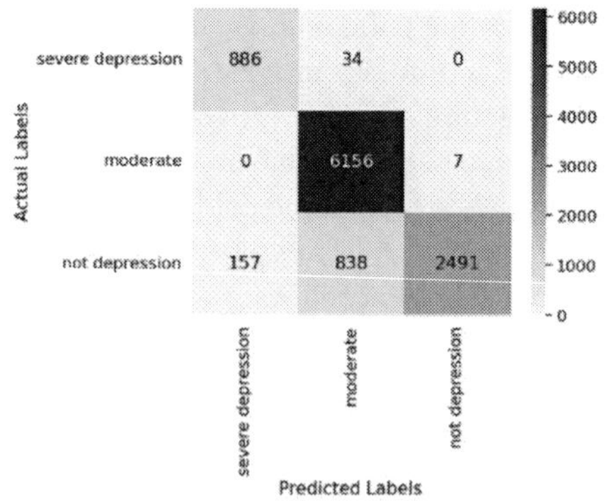


Figure 4: Ensemble model

learning techniques. The given data is pre-processed by cleaning, tokenizing, and removing stop words. Then, feature engineering techniques like TF-IDF are applied to represent the text data. Experimentation was conducted using three machine learning algorithms, namely SVM, Random Forest and Naive Bayes, and evaluated their performance using various metrics like accuracy, precision, recall, and F1-score. By using ensemble model the accuracy obtained is 47.7% and the F1 score is 0.262. Overall, the proposed system demonstrate the potential of machine learning techniques to detect severity of depression from social media text, which can aid in early detection and intervention of depression.

## References


[1] Anamika Ahmed, Raihan Sultana, Md Tahmidur Rahman Ullas, Mariyam Begom, Md. Muzahidul Islam Rahi, and Md. Ashraful Alam. A machine learning approach to detect depression and anxiety using supervised learning. In *2020 IEEE Asia-Pacific Conference on Computer Science and Data Engineering (CSDE)*, pages 1–6, 2020.

[2] Nafiz Al Asad, Md. Appel Mahmud Pranto, Sadia Afreen, and Md. Maynul Islam. Depression detection by analyzing social media posts of user. In *2019 IEEE International Conference on Signal Processing, Information, Communication Systems (SPICSCON)*, pages 13–17, 2019.

[3] Yan Ding, Xuemei Chen, Qiming Fu, and Shan Zhong. A depression recognition method for college students using deep integrated support vector algorithm. *IEEE Access*, 8:75616–75629, 2020.

[4] G. Geetha, G. Saranya, K. Chakrapani, J. Godwin Ponsam, M. Safa, and S. Karpagaselvi. Early detection of depression from social media data using machine learning algorithms. In *2020 International Conference on Power, Energy, Control and Transmission Systems (ICPECTS)*, pages 1–6, 2020.

[5] Swati Jain, Suraj Prakash Narayan, Rupesh Kumar Dewang, Utkarsh Bhartiya, Nalini Meena, and Varun Kumar. A machine learning based depression analysis and suicidal ideation detection system using questionnaires and twitter. In *2019 IEEE Students Conference on Engineering and Systems (SCES)*, pages 1–6, 2019.

[6] Keshu Malviya, Bholanath Roy, and SK Saritha. A transformers approach to detect depression in social media. In *2021 International Conference on Artificial Intelligence and Smart Systems (ICAIS)*, pages 718–723, 2021.

[7] Kayalvizhi S, Thenmozhi Durairaj, Bharathi Raja Chakravarthi, and Jerin Mahibha C. Findings of the shared task on detecting signs of depression from social media. In *Proceedings of the Second Workshop on Language Technology for Equality, Diversity and Inclusion*, pages 331–338, Dublin, Ireland, May 2022. Association for Computational Linguistics.

[8] Sivamanikandan S, Santhosh V, Sanjaykumar N, Jerin Mahibha C, and Thenmozhi Durairaj. scubeMSEC@LT-EDI-ACL2022: Detection of depression using transformer models. In *Proceedings of the Second Workshop on Language Technology for Equality, Diversity and Inclusion*, pages 212–217, Dublin, Ireland, May 2022. Association for Computational Linguistics.

[9] Ananna Saha, Ahmed Al Marouf, and Rafayet Hossain. Sentiment analysis from depression-related user-generated contents from social media. In *2021 8th International Conference on Computer and Communication Engineering (ICCCE)*, pages 259–264, 2021.

[10] Shahriar Saleque, Gul-A-Zannat Spriha, Rasheeq Ishraq Kamal, Rafia Tabassum Khan, Amitabha Chakrabarty, and Mohammad Zavid Parvez. Detection of major depressive disorder using signal processing and machine learning approaches. In *2020 15th IEEE Conference on Industrial Electronics and Applications (ICIEA)*, pages 1032–1037, 2020.

[11] Kayalvizhi Sampath, Thenmozhi Durairaj, Bharathi Raja Chakravarthi, Jerin Mahibha C, Kogilavani Shanmugavadivel, and Pratik Anil booktitle = Rahood. Overview of the second shared task on detecting signs of depression from social media text.

[12] Michael M. Tadesse, Hongfei Lin, Bo Xu, and Liang Yang. Detection of depression-related posts in reddit social media forum. *IEEE Access*, 7:44883–44893, 2019.

# Author Index